AHA Hospital Statistics™

2019 Edition

AHA Institutional Members $240.00
Nonmembers $310.00
AHA Catalog NUMBER 082010
Telephone: ORDERS 1-800-AHA-2626

ISSN 0090-6662
ISBN-13: 978-0-87258-988-9

AHA Institutional Members $240.00
Nonmembers $310.00
AHA Catalog NUMBER 082019
Telephone ORDERS 1-800-AHA-2626

ISSN 0090-6662
ISBN-13: 978-0-87258-988-9

Contents

Acknowledgments
& Advisements

Acknowledgments

The 2019 edition of *AHA Hospital Statistics* is published by Health Forum, an affiliate of the American Hospital Association, Rick Pollack, President and CEO.

Advisements

The data published here should be used with the following advisements: The data are based on replies to an annual survey that seeks a variety of information, not all of which is published in this book. The information gathered by the survey includes specific services, but not all of each hospital's services. Therefore, the data do not reflect an exhaustive list of all services offered by all hospitals. For information on the availability of additional data, please contact Health Forum, (800) 821-2039.

Health Forum does not assume responsibility for the accuracy of information voluntarily reported by the individual institutions surveyed. The purpose of this publication is to provide basic data reflecting the delivery of health care in the United States and associated areas, and is not to serve an official and all-inclusive list of services offered by individual hospitals.

Caring for Rural Communities: Trends and Challenges Facing Rural Hospitals

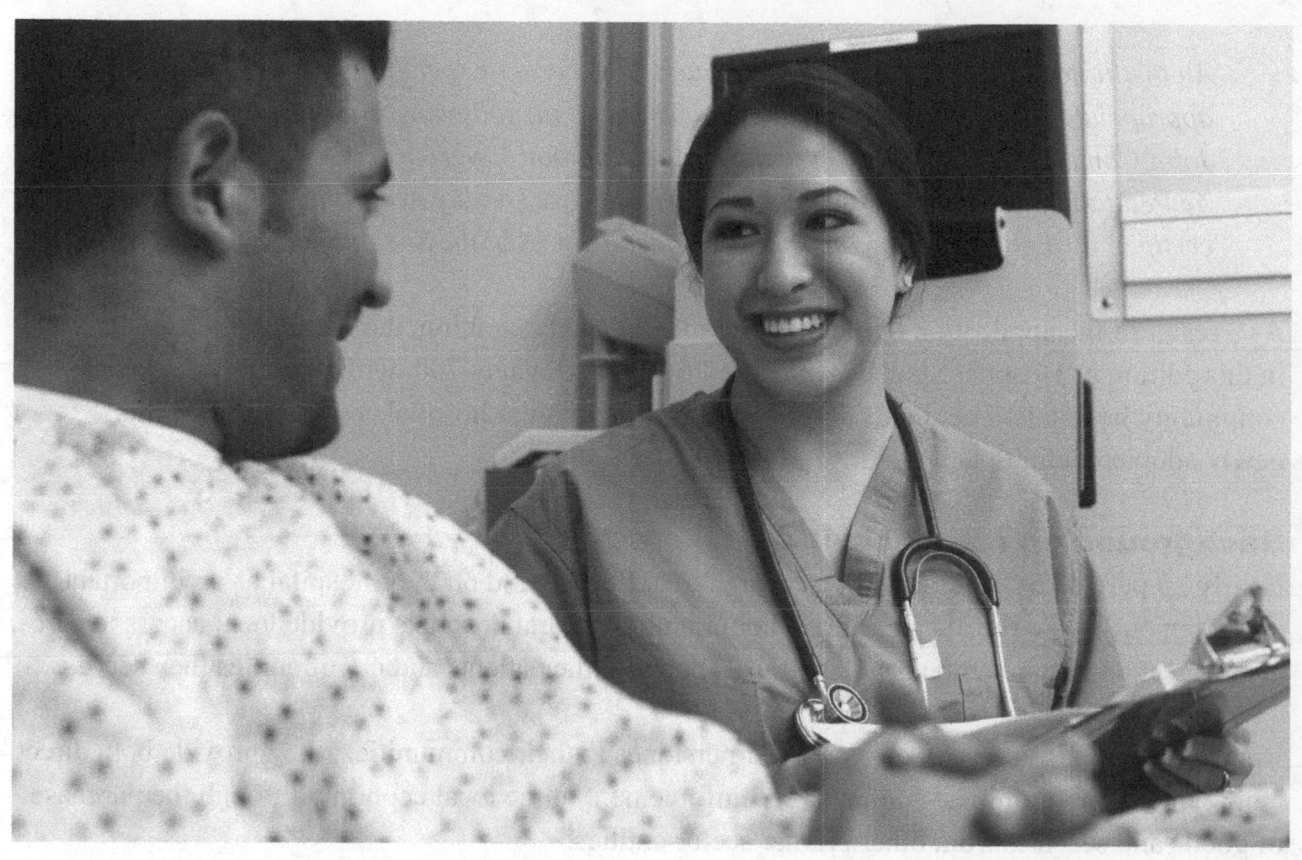

Introduction

America's rural hospitals are committed to serving their communities and ensuring local access to high-quality, affordable health care. Below, we highlight data from the AHA Annual Survey that illustrate trends and challenges that rural hospitals face. Included are new data from the survey on behavioral health.

These data are based on a new methodology for defining hospitals, which the AHA will use starting with the 2019 edition of Hospital Statistics. The AHA has previously employed its own methodology to classify hospitals as "registered." Going forward, the AHA will use the more generally known and accepted definition:

> *An institution is a hospital if it is licensed as a general or specialty hospital by the appropriate state agency and accredited by one of the following organizations: the Joint Commission Healthcare Facilities Accreditation Program (HFAP), DNV Health Accreditation, Center for Improvement in Healthcare Quality Accreditation, or Medicare certified as a provider of acute services under Title 18 of the Social Security Act.*

As a result of the application of the new, broader hospital definition, the number of hospitals in this edition of Hospital Statistics increased by approximately 700, with 400 of those being community hospitals. The trends described in this section use hospital counts based on this newly adopted definition.

Background on rural hospitals

Nearly 20 percent of Americans live in rural areas and depend on their hospital as an important – and often only – source of care in their communities.[1] Rural hospitals provide local access to care and protect and improve the health and well-being of the patients and communities they serve.

Rural hospitals also serve as economic cornerstones in their communities; they provide both direct employment opportunities[2] and indirect reinforcement of the local economy through the purchase of goods and services from other private-sector entities.[3]

---

[1] United States Census Bureau. (2016 December 8). New Census Data Show Differences between Urban and Rural Populations. Release Number: CB16-210. Retrieved from: https://www.census.gov/newsroom/press-releases/2016/cb16-210.html; (2010). Urban and Rural. Retrieved from: https://www.census.gov/geo/reference/urban-rural.html

[2] Doekson, G.A., St. Clair, C.F., Eilrich, F.C. (2016 October). Economic Impact of a Critical Access Hospital on a Rural Community. National Center for Rural Health Works. Retrieved from: http://ruralhealthworks.org/wp-content/files/CAH-Study-FINAL-101116.pdf

[3] America Hospital Association. (2018 March 29). Hospitals are Economic Anchors in their Communities. Retrieved from: https://www.aha.org/statistics/2018-03-29-hospitals-are-economic-anchors-their-communities

---

Although rural hospitals endeavor to meet the health care needs in their communities, many still struggle to address the persistent challenges of providing health care in rural America, such as low patient volumes and geographic isolation. They also must work to manage other recent and emergent challenges, including economic fluctuations, increased regulatory burden, and the opioid epidemic. In response to these difficulties, some hospitals have elected to merge with larger health systems, engage in other types of affiliations or partnerships, or modify their service offerings in order to stay viable and protect health care access for their communities.

While some hospitals are continuing to thrive, others find that the mounting burden of persistent, recent and emerging challenges threaten their ability to maintain access to services. The North Carolina Rural Health Research Program reports that, as of October 2018, 89 rural hospitals have closed since 2010. These closures stem from numerous factors, including failure to recover from the recession, population demographic trends, ongoing financial struggles and decreased demand for inpatient services.[4]

The AHA annual survey shows consistent decreases in the total number of rural hospitals in recent years (Figure 1). However, not all the decreases in the number of rural hospitals are attributable to closures; some changes in the number of rural hospitals include conversion to other types of health care facilities (e.g., urgent care centers) or reclassification from rural to urban. For example, from 2013 to 2014, there was a sudden drop in the number of rural hospitals, mostly attributable to reclassifications of hospitals from rural to urban based on the 2010 Census. As a result, several of the charts in this section focus on the period from 2014 to 2017 only (Figures 7-9), as the abnormal change from 2013 to 2014 may skew the longitudinal results over this period.

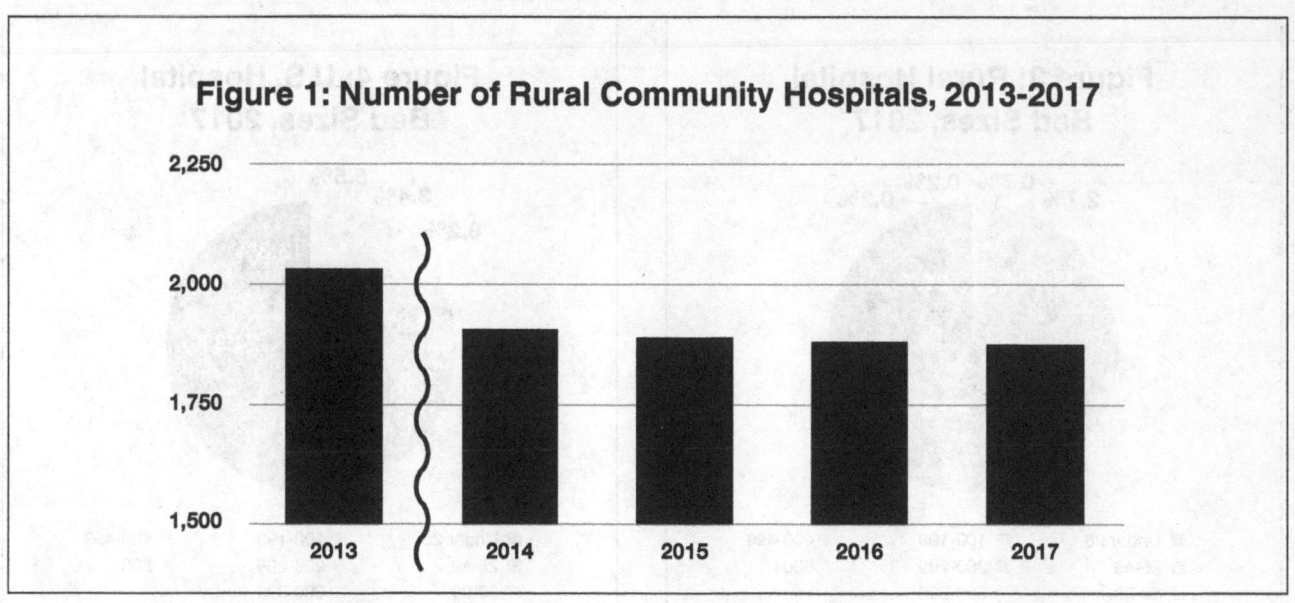

Figure 1: Number of Rural Community Hospitals, 2013-2017

---

4   The Cecil G. Sheps Center for Health Services Research. (2018 January). 87 Rural Hospital Closures: January 2010-Present. Retrieved from: http://www.shepscenter.unc.edu/programs-projects/rural-health/rural-hospital-closures/

In addition to decreases in the number of rural hospitals, there are ongoing changes in the characteristics of these hospitals. Over the last several years, there have been steady decreases in the number of beds at rural hospitals, dropping 8 percent from 2013 to 2017 (Figure 2).

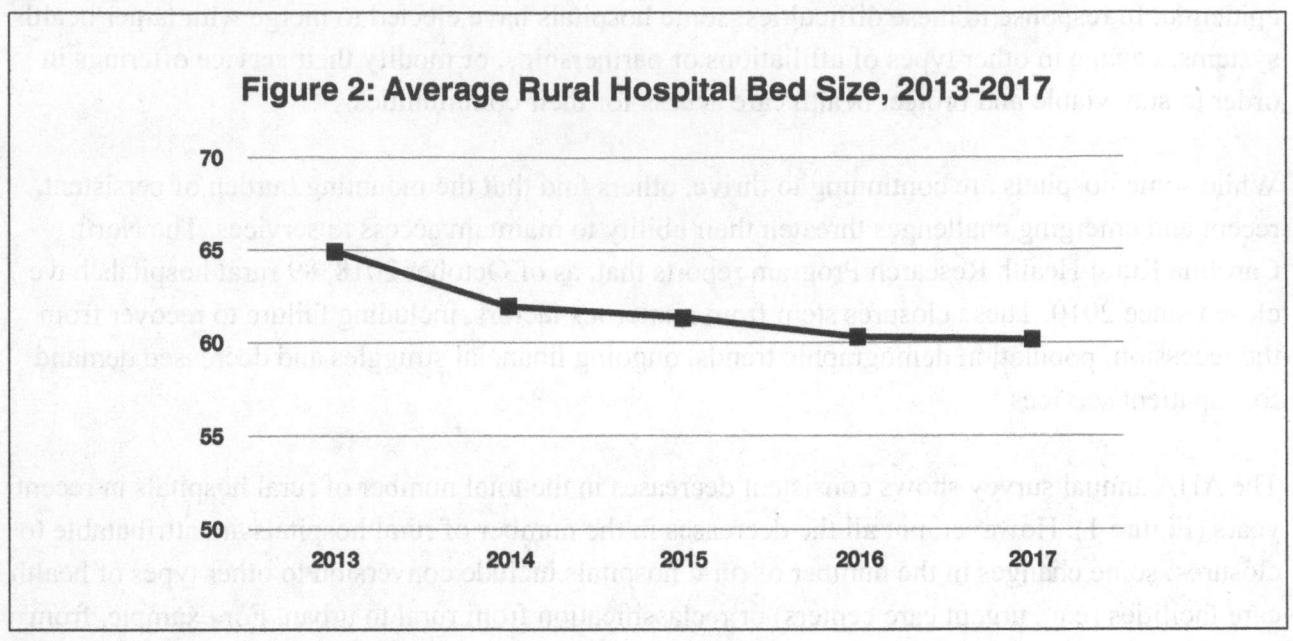

Figure 2: Average Rural Hospital Bed Size, 2013-2017

Generally, rural hospitals have fewer beds than U.S. hospitals overall. In 2017, 62 percent of rural hospitals had fewer than 50 beds (Figure 3) compared to 38 percent of all U.S. hospitals (Figure 4).

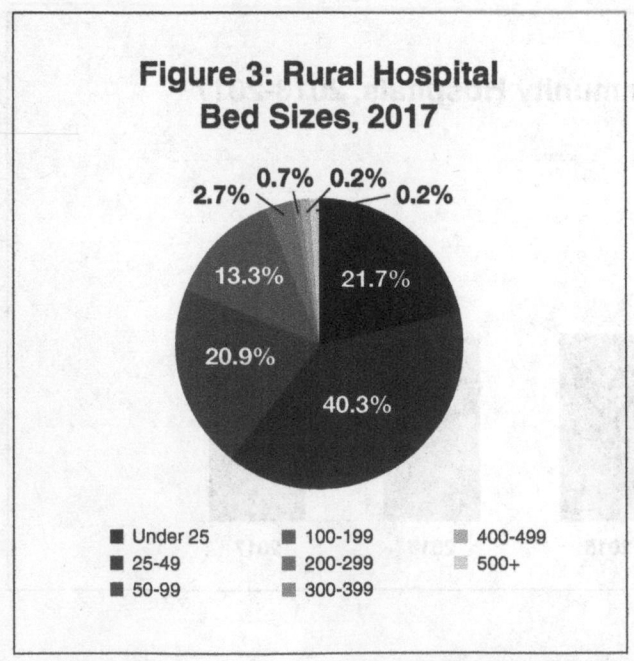

Figure 3: Rural Hospital Bed Sizes, 2017

Under 25	100-199	400-499
25-49	200-299	500+
50-99	300-399	

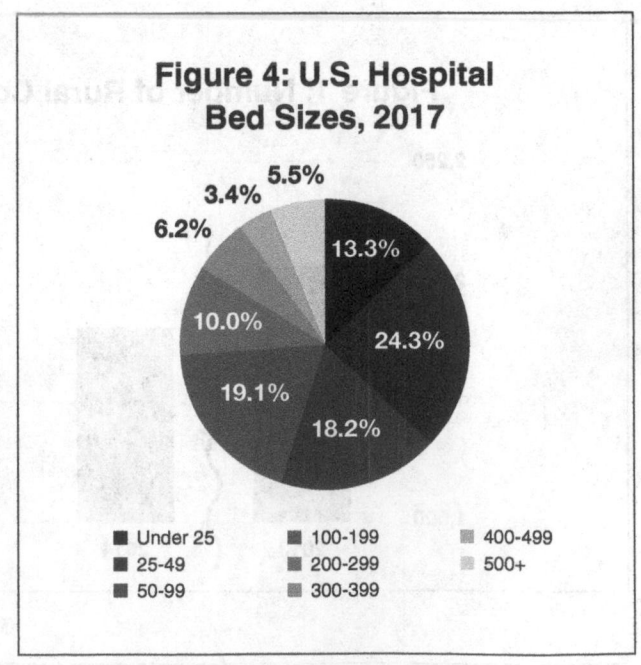

Figure 4: U.S. Hospital Bed Sizes, 2017

Under 25	100-199	400-499
25-49	200-299	500+
50-99	300-399	

Trends among rural hospitals

Rural hospitals have always faced a unique set of circumstances, including a challenging payer and patient mix and geographic isolation. Below we discuss trends among rural hospitals in several key areas: payer mix, utilization, workforce, behavioral health and telehealth.

Payer mix

Medicare and Medicaid each pay 87 cents for every dollar spent caring for patients, according to the 2017 AHA Annual Survey. Medicare underpayment was unchanged from 2016, but this represents a decrease for Medicaid from 2016 when hospitals were paid 88 cents for every dollar spent on care. Rural hospitals are especially dependent on Medicare and Medicaid. In 2017, Medicare and Medicaid made up 56 percent of rural hospitals' net revenue (Figure 5). For all U.S. hospitals, Medicare and Medicaid made up 52 percent of net revenue (Figure 6).

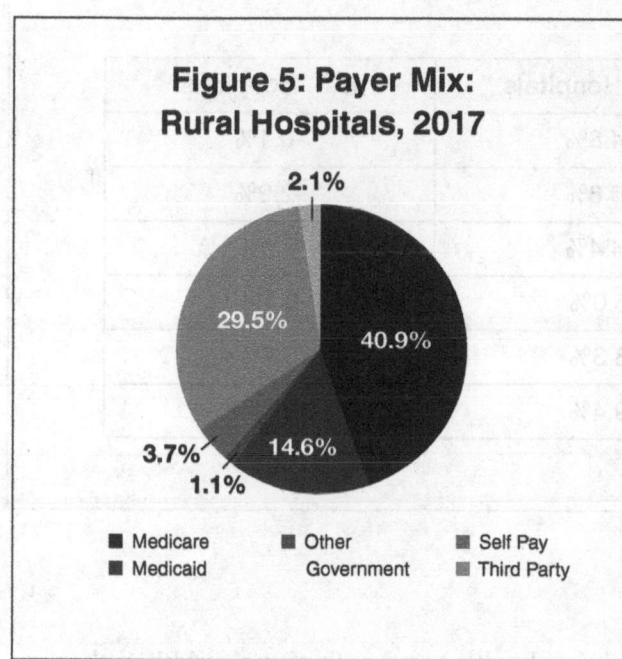

Figure 5: Payer Mix: Rural Hospitals, 2017

2.1%
29.5%
40.9%
3.7%
1.1%
14.6%

■ Medicare ■ Other ■ Self Pay
■ Medicaid Government ■ Third Party

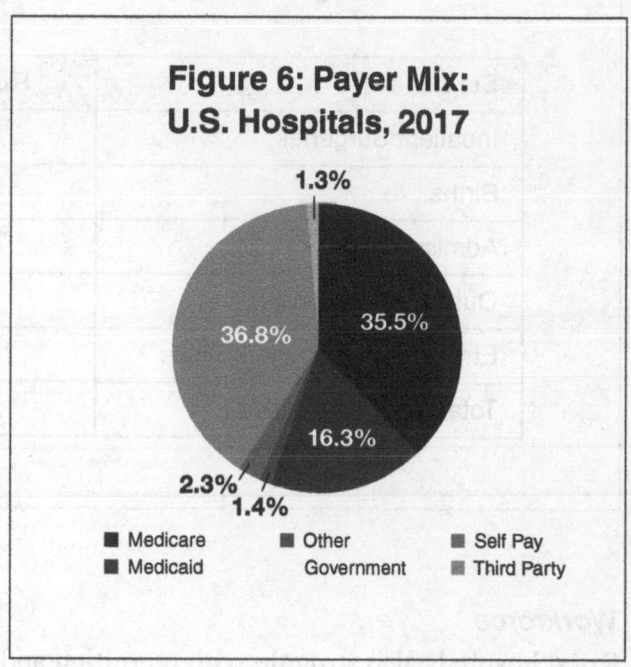

Figure 6: Payer Mix: U.S. Hospitals, 2017

1.3%
36.8%
35.5%
2.3%
1.4%
16.3%

■ Medicare ■ Other ■ Self Pay
■ Medicaid Government ■ Third Party

Utilization

Rural hospitals' ability to serve their communities also has been affected by changing utilization patterns. Lower population density in rural areas means hospitals often lack scale to cover high-fixed operating costs. Rural hospitals have seen decreases in inpatient utilization in recent years: total admissions decreased 4 percent from 2014 to 2017; inpatient surgeries decreased 5 percent; births decreased 7 percent; and total inpatient days decreased 5 percent. These rural inpatient decreases are slightly greater than those seen in inpatient utilization nationally, which have been somewhat offset by increases in outpatient utilization (Figure 7). In the rural setting, outpatient utilization has not increased as steadily. From 2014 to 2017, total outpatient visits in rural hospitals increased 9 percent, emergency outpatient visits increased 3 percent and outpatient surgeries increased 5 percent.

Figure 7: Percent Change in Utilization, 2014-2017

Services	Rural Hospitals	U.S. Hospitals
Inpatient Surgeries	-4.8%	-0.1%
Births	-6.8%	-2.9%
Admissions	-4.4%	2.4%
Outpatient Surgeries	5.0%	6.1%
Emergency Outpatient Visits	3.3%	5.1%
Total Outpatient Visits	9.4%	9.4%

Workforce

Rural hospitals also struggle with recruiting and retaining health care professionals. Although 20 percent of the U.S. population lives in rural areas, less than 10 percent of physicians practice in these communities.[5] Health care professional shortages can have serious effects on access to care. As of November 2018, two-thirds of the nation's 6,941 primary care Health Professional Shortage Areas (HPSAs) were in rural or partially rural areas.[6] Data from the AHA Annual Survey show that, as overall staffing (i.e., clinical and non-clinical staff) at U.S. hospitals increased by 8 percent from 2014 to 2017 (Figure 8), staffing at rural hospitals increased at half that rate (Figure 9).

---

[5] Johnt E. K., Nguyen N., Samson W. L., Snyder E. J. (2016 October 19). Rural Hospital Participation and Performance in Value-Based Purchasing and Other Delivery System Reform Initiatives. ASPE Office of Health Policy Retrieved from: https://aspe.hhs.gov/system/files/pdf/211061/RuralHospitalsDSR.pdf

[6] Health Resource & Services Administration. (2018). Data Warehouse. Retrieved from: https://data.hrsa.gov/hdw/Topics/shortageareas.aspx

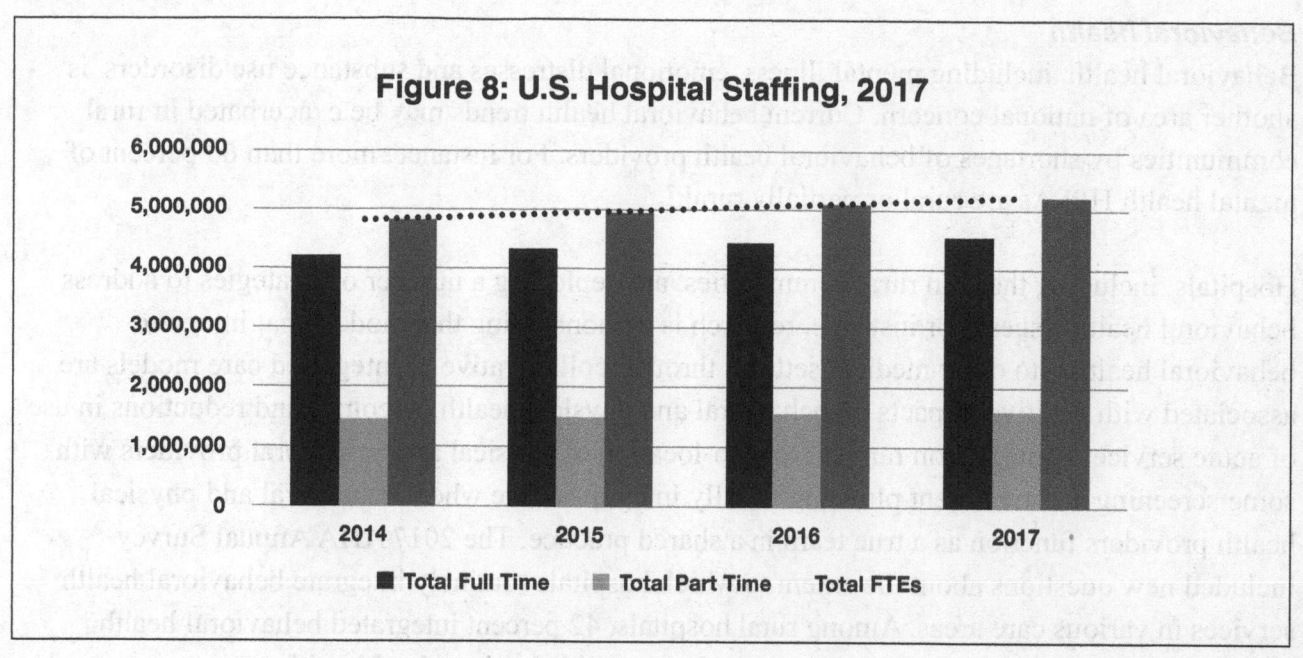

Figure 8: U.S. Hospital Staffing, 2017

Legend: ■ Total Full Time ■ Total Part Time Total FTEs

Figure 9: Rural Hospital Staffing, 2017

Legend: ■ Total Full Time ■ Total Part Time Total FTEs

Behavioral health

Behavioral health, including mental illness, emotional distresses and substance use disorders, is another area of national concern. Current behavioral health trends may be exacerbated in rural communities by shortages of behavioral health providers. For instance, more than 60 percent of mental health HPSAs are rural or partially rural.[7]

Hospitals, including those in rural communities, are deploying a number of strategies to address behavioral health issues. For instance, research is demonstrating that models that integrate behavioral health into other medical settings through collaborative or integrated care models are associated with positive impacts on behavioral and physical health outcomes and reductions in use of acute services.[8] Integration ranges from co-location of physical and behavioral providers with some screening and treatment planning to fully integrated care where behavioral and physical health providers function as a true team in a shared practice. The 2017 AHA Annual Survey included new questions about the extent to which hospitals routinely integrate behavioral health services in various care areas. Among rural hospitals, 42 percent integrated behavioral health services with emergency services, 31 percent integrated behavioral health with primary care, and 30 percent integrated behavioral health with acute inpatient care (Figure 10).

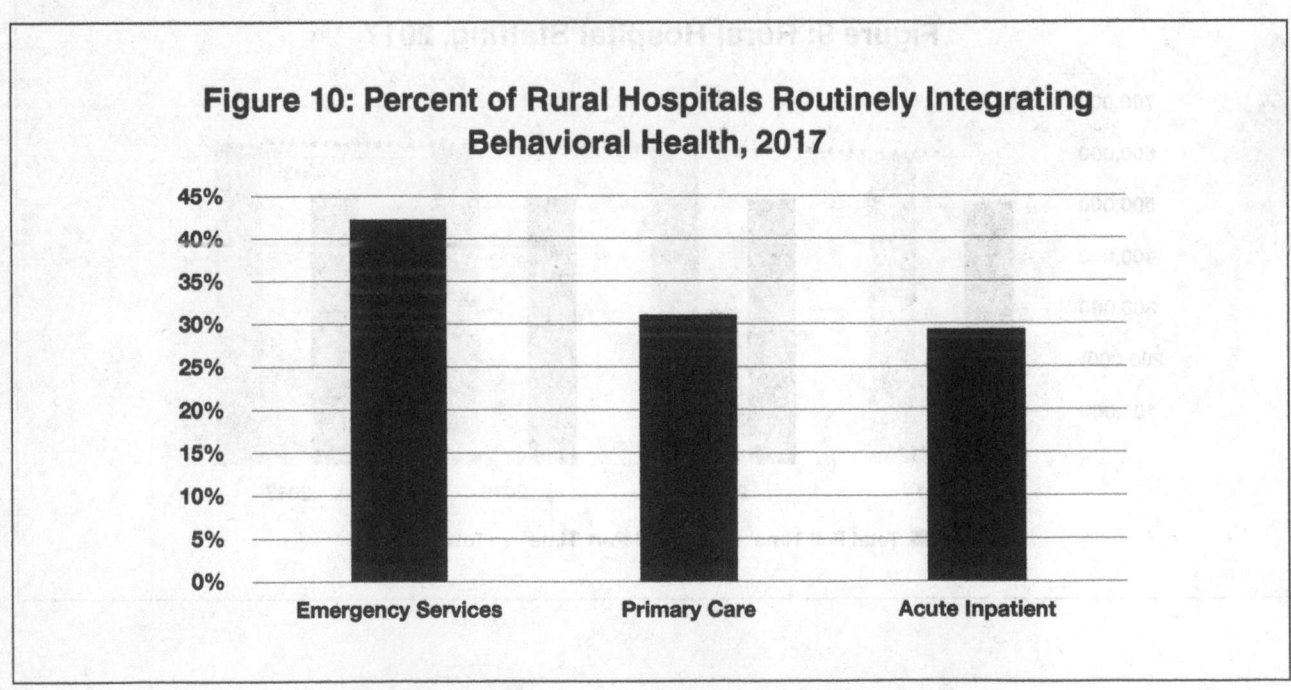

Figure 10: Percent of Rural Hospitals Routinely Integrating Behavioral Health, 2017

---

7 Centers for Disease Control and Prevention. (2018 March 22). Suicide Policy Brief: Preventing Suicide in Rural America. Retrieved from: https://www.cdc.gov/ruralhealth/suicide/policybrief.html

8 American Hospital Association (AHA). (2014). Integrating behavioral health across the continuum of care. Health Research & Educational Trust. http://www.hpoe.org/Reports-HPOE/Behavioral%20health%20FINAL.pdf

---

Telehealth

Telehealth expands access to services which may not otherwise be sustained locally due to provider recruitment/retention difficulties, low patient volume, or inadequate local resources. As technology has improved and people are increasingly comfortable with the delivery of care through virtual connections, the utilization of telehealth services has dramatically increased. Data from the AHA Annual Survey Information Technology Supplement show that the percent of rural hospitals that implemented telehealth fully or in at least one unit increased from 50 percent in 2013 to 74 percent in 2017. (Figure 11).

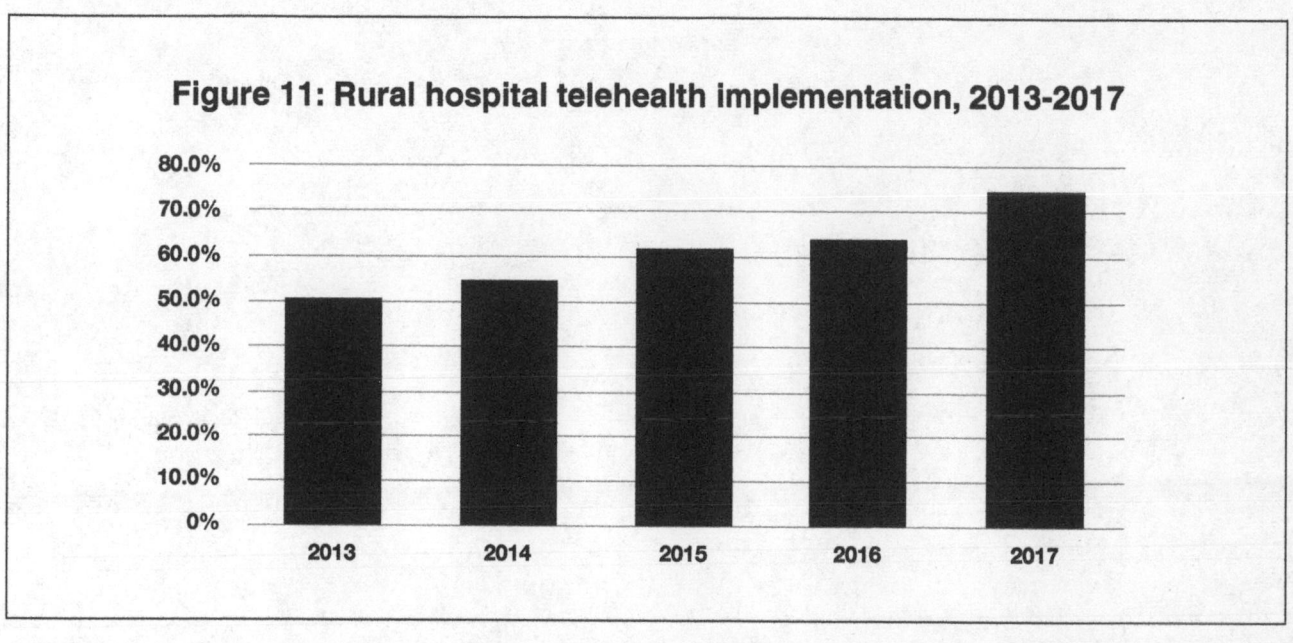

Figure 11: Rural hospital telehealth implementation, 2013-2017

Data correction

This section of the 2018 edition of Hospital Statistics examined hospital activities to address community needs, including the extent to which hospitals enter into community partnerships. The percent of hospitals that participated in at least one community partnership was inadvertently understated. Based on the prior definition of AHA registered hospitals, the percent of hospitals with at least one community partnership in 2016 was 91 percent. Using the more broad definition of hospitals described previously in this section, the rate was 90 percent in 2016 and 91 percent in 2017.

How to Use this Book

For more than seven decades, *AHA Hospital Statistics*™ has reported aggregate hospital data derived from the AHA Annual Survey and is the definitive source when doing trend analysis with data by bed size category, U.S. Census Divisions, States, and Metropolitan Statistical Areas (MSAs). As the health care delivery system changes, so have the data tracked by the survey and presented in this report.

Discontinuation of AHA's Registration Program Resulting in an Increase in the Number of Hospitals

Starting with the 2019 edition of Hospital Statistics, the AHA will no longer employ its own methodology to classify hospitals as registered. We will use the following definition, which is more generally known and accepted: An institution is a hospital if it is licensed as a general or specialty hospital by the appropriate state agency and accredited by one of the following organizations: The Joint Commission Healthcare Facilities Accreditation Program (HFAP), DNV Health Accreditation, Center for Improvement in Healthcare Quality Accreditation, or Medicare certified as a provider of acute services under Title 18 of the Social Security Act. As a result of the application of the new, broader hospital definition, the number of hospitals in this edition of Hospital Statistics increased by approximately 700 with 400 of those being community hospitals.

For consistency purposes, Tables 1, 3, 4, 5, and 6 in this Edition have been recreated, going back to 2013, to include all hospitals that meet the new definition; hence, this year's release will not agree with previous editions of Hospital Statistics during the affected time span.

Other recent additions include:

- **Community health indicators** that offer readers a connection to the community for their analysis and planning: the data are broken down into beds, admissions, inpatient days, ER outpatient visits, and other indicators per 1000 population, as well as expense per capita.

- **Utilization, personnel and finance** by all MSAs in the United States.

- **Five-year trend data** on physician models, insurance products, and managed care contracts enable you to identify changes in relationships between hospitals and other health care systems and providers.

- **Tables 3 through 6 have been organized** to show breakdowns between inpatient and outpatient care to better reflect market shifts toward outpatient-centered care. Additional clarity is gained by the breakdown between total facility data (which includes nursing home type units under the control of the hospital) and hospital units (which exclude the nursing home data).

TABLE 6	Sample State

U.S. Community Hospitals
(Nonfederal, short-term general and other special hospitals)

Overview 2013-2017

	2017	2016	2015	2014	2013
Physician Models					
Independent Practice Association	14	17	17	17	14
Group Practice without Walls	4	5	5	8	4
Open Physician-Hospital Organization	20	21	24	23	18
Closed Physician-Hospital Organization	21	17	18	17	11
Management Service Organization	14	18	20	14	9
Integrated Salary Model	35	29	30	26	24
Equity Model	4	3	4	6	3
Foundation	9	8	23	21	19

Example of five-year trend data

- **Facilities and Services information** on more than 100 categories of hospital facilities and services in Table 7. At a glance, you can determine the number and percentage of hospitals offering a specific service such as Oncology, Palliative Care Program, Complementary Medicine, Women's Health Services and Tobacco Cessation.

- **Plus, System and Network involvement along with Group Purchasing Organizations** that demonstrate ways in which organizations are linked.

The survey instrument and the glossary

A good place to begin your analysis is the AHA Annual Survey instrument. Found on page 217, it includes the instructions, questions, and terms that were used to gather the data for fiscal year 2017. This can be extremely valuable for a clearer understanding of the data we collect and the tables presented in *AHA Hospital Statistics*.

Please also review the glossary in the back of the book. The glossary contains complete definitions for specific terms used in the tables and text of *AHA Hospital Statistics*. These definitions will clarify how terminology is being used.

As mentioned above, it is important to note that the primary focus of the most detailed data contained in *AHA Hospital Statistics* is community hospitals. As defined, community hospitals are all non-federal, short-term general and special hospitals whose facilities and services are available to the public. If the majority of a hospital's patients are admitted to units where the average length of stay is 30 days or less, a hospital may still be classified as short-term even if it includes a nursing- home-type unit. (For a more complete definition of community hospitals, please see the glossary definition, located on page 203.)

Getting the most out of *AHA Hospital Statistics*
This section of the book provides an introduction for getting the most out of your *AHA Hospital Statistics* 2019 edition. Here, you'll find a guide to the book, with insights into each table.

Equity model: An arrangement that allows established practitioners to become shareholders in a professional corporation in exchange for tangible and intangible assets of their existing practices.

Expenses: Includes all expenses for the reporting period including payroll, non-payroll, and all nonoperating expenses. *Payroll expenses* include all salaries and wages. *Non-payroll expenses* are all professional fees and those salary expenditures excluded from payroll. *Labor related expenses* are defined as payroll expenses plus employee benefits. *Non-labor related expenses* are all other non-payroll expenses. *Bad debt* has been reclassified from a "reduction in revenue" to an expense in accordance with the revised AICPA Audit Guide. However, for purposes of historical consistency, the expense total that appears throughout *AHA Hospital Statistics does not include "bad debt" as an expense item*. Note: Financial data may not add due to rounding.

Extracorporeal shock wave lithotripter (ESWL): A medical device used for treating stones in the kidney or urethra. The device disintegrates kidney stones noninvasively through the transmission of acoustic shock waves directed at the stones.

Fitness center: Provides exercise, testing, or evaluation programs and fitness activities to the community and hospital employees.

Example of Glossary definitions.

CLASSIFICATION	YEAR	HOSPITALS	BEDS (in thousands)	ADMISSIONS (in thousands)	AVERAGE DAILY CENSUS (in thousands)	ADJUSTED AVERAGE DAILY CENSUS (in thousands)
Total United States	1946	6,125	1,436	15,675	1,142	—
	1950	6,788	1,456	18,483	1,253	—
	1955	6,956	1,604	21,073	1,363	—
	1960	6,876	1,658	25,027	1,402	—
	1965	7,123	1,704	28,812	1,403	—
	1970	7,123	1,616	31,759	1,298	—
	1971	7,097	1,556	32,664	1,237	—
	1972	7,061	1,550	33,265	1,209	—
	1973	7,123	1,535	34,352	1,189	—
	1974	7,174	1,513	35,506	1,167	—
	1975	7,156	1,466	36,157	1,125	—
	1976	7,082	1,434	36,776	1,090	—
	1977	7,099	1,407	37,060	1,066	—
	1978	7,015	1,381	37,243	1,042	—
	1979	6,988	1,372	37,802	1,043	—
	1980	6,965	1,365	38,892	1,060	—
	1981	6,933	1,362	39,169	1,061	—
	1982	6,915	1,360	39,095	1,053	—
	1983	6,888	1,350	38,887	1,028	—
	1984	6,872	1,339	37,938	970	—
	1985	6,872	1,318	36,304	910	—
	1986	6,841	1,290	35,219	883	—
	1987	6,821	1,267	34,439	873	—
	1988	6,780	1,248	34,107	863	—
	1989	6,720	1,226	33,742	853	—
	1990	6,649	1,213	33,774	844	—
	1991	6,634	1,202	33,567	827	—
	1992	6,539	1,178	33,536	807	—
	1993	6,467	1,163	33,201	783	—
	1994	6,374	1,128	33,125	745	—
	1995	6,291	1,081	33,282	710	—
	1996	6,201	1,062	33,307	685	—
	1997	6,097	1,035	33,624	673	—
	1998	6,021	1,013	33,766	662	—
	1999	5,890	994	34,181	657	—
	2000	5,810	984	34,891	650	—
	2001	5,801	987	35,644	658	—
	2002	5,794	976	36,326	662	—
	2003	5,764	965	36,611	657	—
	2004	5,759	956	36,942	658	—
	2005	5,756	947	37,006	656	—

Example of Table 1

Table 1 — Historical Trends in Utilization, Personnel and Finances for Selected Years from 1946 through 2017

Table 1 at a Glance

This table is used to evaluate historical data and allows you to examine long-term trends in health care with data dating back more than sixty years. Table 1 reports on all hospitals in the United States. One important note: Hospitals included in this table include AHA-member and non-member hospitals. A hospital does not need to be an AHA member to be included.

This table segments the data into various organizational structure categories. Here's a brief look at these different classifications:

- Total United States Hospitals
- Total Non-Federal Short-term and other special hospitals
- Community hospitals
- Non-government not-for-profit community hospitals
- Investor-owned (for-profit) community hospitals
- State and local government community hospitals

Table 1 also provides input on nationwide utilization, personnel and finance trends. You'll find answers to questions such as: *Over the past 25 years, what trends do I see comparing the average length of stay at government and non-government not-for-profit community hospitals and investor-owned for-profit community hospitals? or What has been the trend in outpatient visits?*

Table 2 — 2017 U.S. Hospitals: Utilization, Personnel and Finances

Table 2 at a Glance

This table takes a closer look at U.S. Hospitals for 2017. It offers a snapshot of utilization, personnel and finance statistics, and breaks down this information for specialty hospitals. In addition, this is the only table that outlines data on federal hospitals. You'll be able to use this table to better understand the number of beds set-up and staffed, how many personnel and trainees are on the payroll, and what the financial implications of these may be.

TABLE 3

TOTAL UNITED STATES

U.S. Community Hospitals
(Nonfederal, short-term general and other special hospitals)

Utilization, Personnel, Revenue and Expenses, Community Health Indicators 2013–2017

	2017	2016	2015	2014	2013
TOTAL FACILITY (Includes Hospital and Nursing Home Units)					
Utilization - Inpatient					
Beds	798,921	799,444	800,828	802,088	811,154
Admissions	34,305,620	34,031,587	33,817,285	33,516,951	34,062,869
Inpatient Days	186,198,977	186,089,454	185,171,082	183,342,577	185,325,318
Average Length of Stay	5.5	5.5	5.5	5.5	5.4
Inpatient Surgeries	9,146,015	9,163,230	9,090,300	9,156,859	9,279,901
Births	3,656,809	3,769,965	3,792,223	3,766,328	3,728,411
Utilization - Outpatient					
Emergency Outpatient Visits	144,814,804	144,842,743	143,472,685	137,807,901	134,869,015
Other Outpatient Visits	621,261,320	611,955,033	587,316,680	562,424,090	549,358,304
Total Outpatient Visits	766,076,124	756,797,776	730,789,365	700,231,991	684,227,319
Outpatient Surgeries	19,075,759	18,987,342	18,255,921	17,974,397	17,978,474
Personnel					
Full Time RNs	1,286,055	1,243,105	1,209,663	1,170,228	1,137,567
Full Time LPNs	65,258	65,671	65,168	64,001	68,296
Part Time RNs	543,927	530,458	511,318	502,481	500,762
Part Time LPNs	22,550	22,602	22,800	22,805	25,027
Total Full Time	4,536,326	4,428,178	4,316,593	4,211,435	4,183,224
Total Part Time	1,615,066	1,562,816	1,498,135	1,471,483	1,479,747
Revenue - Inpatient					
Gross Inpatient Revenue	$1,828,199,494,787	$1,724,871,915,665	$1,626,668,095,308	$1,514,448,739,994	$1,442,275,606,491
Revenue - Outpatient					
Gross Outpatient Revenue	$1,735,481,161,564	$1,595,298,023,801	$1,449,622,014,476	$1,308,063,724,756	$1,191,794,532,181

Total U.S.

Example of Table 3. Helps contrast acute and long-term care

Table 3 — Total United States

Table 3 at a Glance

This table provides a look at all U.S. Community Hospitals, in terms of general overview with utilization by inpatient and outpatient, personnel, revenue, expenses and community health indicators. It provides a snapshot of the past five years, allowing you to track emerging trends.

This national information can be compared to local or regional trends, for benchmarking:

- Both inpatient and outpatient information is included, for better evaluation of data.

- Reporting by total facility *Includes hospital and Nursing Home Units* and hospital unit only *Excludes Separate Nursing Home Units* helps contrast acute and long-term care.

- Community health indicators can help uncover trends and help determine future facility needs.

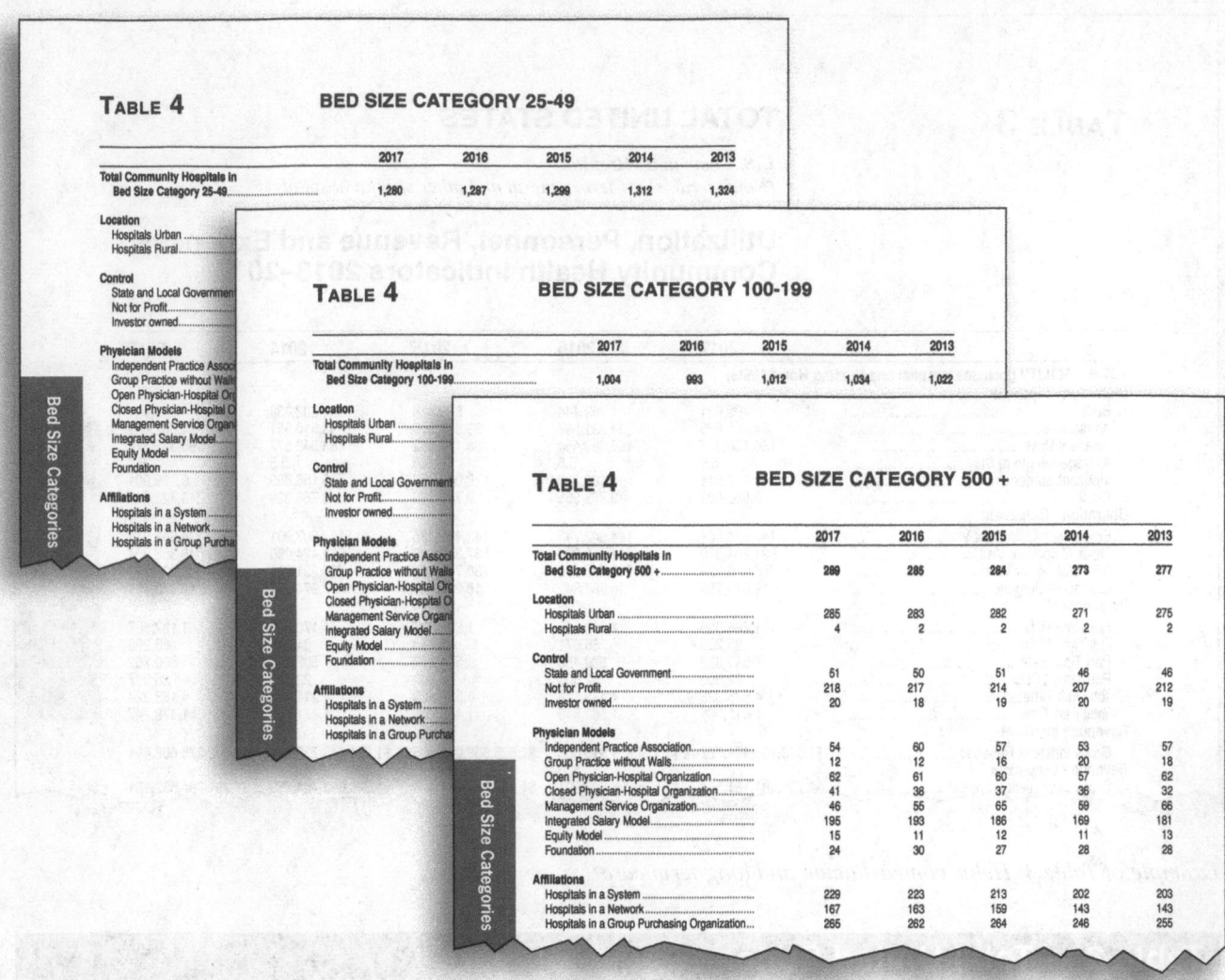

Example of Table 4. Compares facilities with peers.

Table 4 — Bed Size Categories

Table 4 at a Glance

This table provides a look at all U.S. Community Hospitals, broken down by bed size. The table includes general overview, utilization, personnel, and revenue and expense information. These categories of bed sizes were developed by the AHA, and have become an industry standard. By categorizing each facility into a peer group, this table provides a snapshot of the past five years allowing you to compare facilities with their peers.

TABLE 5

U.S. CENSUS DIVISION 2: MIDDLE ATLANTIC

U.S. Community Hospitals
(Nonfederal, short-term general and other special hospitals)

Utilization, Personnel, Revenue and Expenses, Community Health Indicators 2013-2017

	2017	2016	2015	2014	2013
COMMUNITY HEALTH INDICATORS PER 1000 POPULATION					
Total Population (in thousands)....	38,292	38,216	38,184	38,147	38,108
Inpatient					
Beds	3.6	3.8	3.9	4.0	4.1
Admissions	135.8	136.7	136.2	138.3	137.4
Inpatient Days..................	963.5	988.8	1,019.0	1,093.8	1,145.0
Inpatient Surgeries	42.2	41.4	41.2	42.7	43.6
Births..........................	13.0	13.2	13.6	13.7	14.3
Outpatient					
Emergency Outpatient Visits......	367.7	362.0	363.4	379.5	360.1
Other Outpatient Visits..........	1,970.9	1,802.3	1,767.7	1,680.3	1,573.9
Total Outpatient Visits	2,338.6	2,164.3	2,131.1	2,059.8	1,934.0
Outpatient Surgeries............	67.8	62.4	59.9	55.4	53.5
Expense per Capita (per person)....	$1,494.9	$1,462.7	$1,428.6	$1,429.8	$1,369.2

Example of Table 5. Uncovers trends to determine future facility needs.

Table 5 — U.S. Census Divisions

Table 5 at a Glance

This table provides a look at all U.S. Community Hospitals, broken down by Census Division. The table includes general overview, utilization, personnel, and expenses, and community health indicator information. It provides a snapshot of the past five years, allowing you to track trends on a regional level. In addition, this allows you to compare this data to other population based health indicators, offering a more comprehensive look than the survey data alone. Community health indicators can help uncover trends and help determine future facility needs.

Table 6 — States

Table 6 at a Glance

This table provides a look at all U.S. Community Hospitals, broken down by State. The table includes general overview, utilization, personnel, revenue and expenses, and community health indicator information. It provides a snapshot of the past five years, allowing you to track trends on a state level.

Note:

You can use the information in tables 3, 4, 5 and 6 to make accurate comparisons across Total U.S., Bed Size Category, Census Division and State.

Table 7 — 2017 Facilities and Services in the U.S. Census Divisions and States

Table 7 at a Glance

This table examines facilities and services by both Census Division and State. A comprehensive alphabetical guide helps make each facility or service easy to find. This table will allow you to better understand what service lines are emerging and how many facilities offer a particular service in a discrete state or region.

This collection of facilities and services information data is unique to *AHA Hospital Statistics* and the list is continually growing. Recent additions include:

- Alcoholism-chemical dependency partial hospitalization services
- Psychiatric intensive outpatient services
- Telehealth

These new categories reflect the trends as hospitals expand their service lines to mirror the needs of their patients. For example, services such as acupuncture or massage therapy are now accounted for in the Complementary Medicine service item.

This table can answer questions such as: *What percentage of hospitals in the United States offer complementary medicine or wound management? or How are these new services distributed by state?*

Table 7 (Continued)

CLASSIFICATION	HOSPITALS REPORTING	CHILDREN'S WELLNESS PROGRAM Number	Percent	CHIROPRACTIC SERVICES Number	Percent	COMMUNITY OUTREACH Number	Percent	COMPLEMENTARY AND ALTERNATIVE MEDICINE SERVI. Number	Perce
UNITED STATES	4,590	894	19.5	131	2.9	3,221	70.2	950	20.
COMMUNITY HOSPITALS	3,865	864	22.4	100	2.6	2,970	76.8	867	22
CENSUS DIVISION 1, NEW ENGLAND	172	62	36.0	9	5.2	145	84.3	82	47.7
Connecticut	30	9	30.0	0	0.0	26	86.7	19	63.3
Maine	32	12	37.5	2	6.3	27	84.4	13	40.6
Massachusetts	64	25	39.1	3	4.7	52	81.3	27	42.2
New Hampshire	25	12	48.0	2	8.0	21	84.0	14	56.0
Rhode Island	10	1	10.0	1	10.0	9	90.0	3	30.0
Vermont	11	3	27.3	1	9.1	10	90.9	6	54.5
CENSUS DIVISION 2, MIDDLE ATLANTIC	404	131	32.4	20	5.0	322	79.7	140	34.7
New Jersey	62	33	53.2	2	3.2	53	85.5	31	50.0
New York	142	58	40.8	11	7.7	125	88.0	56	39.
Pennsylvania	200	40	20.0	7	3.5	144	72.0	53	
CENSUS DIVISION 3, SOUTH ATLANTIC	671	115	17.1	10	1.5	499	74.4	131	
Delaware	10	6	60.0	0	0.0	9	90.0	3	
District of Columbia	11	5	45.5	0	0.0	9	81.8	8	54.5
Florida	180	21	11.7	4	2.2	125	69.4	31	17.2
Georgia	100	9	9.0	2	2.0	70	70.0	17	17.0
Maryland	44	15	34.1	0	0.0	38	86.4	22	50.0
North Carolina	108	18	16.7	1	0.9	90	83.3	17	15.7
South Carolina	79	14	17.7	0	0.0	57	72.2	5	6.3
Virginia	84	13	15.5	2	2.4	66	78.6	26	31.
West Virginia	55	14	25.5	1	1.8	38	69.1	4	
CENSUS DIVISION 4, EAST NORTH CENTRAL	706	184	26.1	31	4.4	560	79.3	226	
Illinois	165	55	33.3	8	4.8	137	83.0	40	24.
Indiana	122	25	20.5	5	4.1	100	82.0	29	23.
Michigan	130	45	34.6	5	3.8	113	86.9	46	35.4
Ohio	144	29	20.1	10	6.9	123	85.4	52	36.
Wisconsin	145	30	20.7	3	2.1	87	60.0	53	36.
CENSUS DIVISION 5, EAST SOUTH CENTRAL	367	49	13.4	4	1.1	230	62.7	23	6.3
Alabama	102	9	8.8	2	2.0	55	53.9	0	0.0
Kentucky	88	14	15.9	1	1.1	64	72.7	12	13.6
Mississippi	104	17	16.3	1	1.0	64	61.5	4	3.
Tennessee	73	9	12.3	0	0.0	47	64.4	7	
CENSUS DIVISION 6, WEST NORTH CENTRAL	637	111	17.4	26	4.1	421	66.1	109	17.
Iowa	124	25	20.2	4	3.2	96	77.4	29	23.
Kansas	143	10	7.0	1	0.7	64	44.8	8	5.6
Minnesota	105	24	22.9	8	7.6	81	77.1	31	29.5
Missouri	143	28	19.6	5	4.2	96	66.4	24	16.8
Nebraska	54	11	20.4	0	0.0	44	81.5	7	13.0
North Dakota	26	6	23.1	6	23.1	16	61.5	6	23.
South Dakota	42	7	16.7	1	2.4	25	59.5	4	
CENSUS DIVISION 7, WEST SOUTH CENTRAL	991	9	10.5	5	0	471	52.9	48	
Arkansas	88	8	9.1	0	0.0	50	56.8	5	
Louisiana	96	20	21.1	1	1.1	52	54.7	5	
Oklahoma	116	9	7.8	0	0.0	60	51.7	5	
Texas	592	57	9.6	5	0.8	309	52.2	30	5
CENSUS DIVISION 8, MOUNTAIN	319	71	22.3	13	4.1	235	73.7	83	25.
Arizona	48	13	27.1	3	6.3	35	72.9	19	
Colorado	72	16	22.2	4	5.5	58	80.6	33	
Idaho	32	9	28.1	2	6.3	26	81.3	6	
Montana	57	11	19.3	2	3.5	37	64.9	10	
Nevada	26	4	15.4	2	7.7	16	61.5	3	
New Mexico	29	9	31.0	0	0.0	22	75.9	3	
Utah	35	7	20.0	0	0.0	24	68.6	3	
Wyoming	20	2	10.0	0	0.0	17	85.0	3	
CENSUS DIVISION 9, PACIFIC	423	77	18.2	12	2.8	338	79.9	108	
Alaska	15	4	26.7	1	6.7	9	53.3	2	
California	248	38	15.3	6	2.4	197	79.4	65	
Hawaii	17	6	35.3	1	5.9	14	82.4	5	
Oregon	62	12	19.4	2	3.2	56	90.3	18	
Washington	81	17	21.0	2	2.5	63	77.8	16	

Example of Table 7.

Table 8 — Utilization, Personnel and Finances in Community Hospitals by MSAs for 2017

Table 8 at a Glance

This table provides a look at all U.S. Community Hospitals, broken down by Metropolitan Statistical Area (MSA). The table includes general overview, utilization, personnel, and finance information. It provides a snapshot of the past year.

Additional Resources

Again, in the back of the book you will find the comprehensive glossary and the 2017 annual survey questionnaire. The survey itself can be a valuable resource to understanding what was asked in order to gather the data in the book. This survey is also used to produce the *AHA Guide*® and AHA Annual Survey Database™.

Hospital Requirements

An institution is considered a hospital by the American Hospital Association if it is licensed as general or specialty hospital by the appropriate state agency, and accredited as a hospital by one of the following organizations: The Joint Commission; Healthcare Facilities Accreditation Program (HFAP); DNV Healthcare accreditation; Center for Improvement in Healthcare Quality accreditation; or Medicare certified as a provider of acute service under Title 18 of the Social Security Act.

Types of Hospitals

Hospitals are categorized as one of four types of hospitals: general, special, rehabilitation and chronic disease, or psychiatric.

General

The primary function of the institution is to provide patient services, diagnostic and therapeutic, for a variety of medical conditions. A general hospital also shall provide:

- diagnostic x-ray services with facilities and staff for a variety of procedures
- clinical laboratory service with facilities and staff for a variety of procedures and with anatomical pathology services regularly and conveniently available
- operating room service with facilities and staff.

Special

The primary function of the institution is to provide diagnostic and treatment services for patients who have specified medical conditions, both surgical and nonsurgical. A special hospital also shall provide:

- such diagnostic and treatment services as may be determined by the Executive Committee of the Board of Trustees of the American Hospital Association to be appropriate for the specified medical conditions for which medical services are provided shall be maintained in the institution with suitable facilities and staff. If such conditions do not normally require diagnostic x-ray service, laboratory service, or operating room service, and if any such services are therefore not maintained in the institution, there shall be written arrangements to make them available to patients requiring them.
- clinical laboratory services capable of providing tissue diagnosis when offering pregnancy termination services.

Rehabilitation and Chronic Disease

The primary function of the institution is to provide diagnostic and treatment services to handicapped or disabled individuals requiring restorative and adjustive services. A rehabilitation and chronic disease hospital also shall provide:

- arrangements for diagnostic x-ray services, as required, on a regular and conveniently available basis
- arrangements for clinical laboratory service, as required on a regular and conveniently available basis
- arrangements for operating room service, as required, on a regular and conveniently available basis
- a physical therapy service with suitable facilities and staff in the institution
- an occupational therapy service with suitable facilities and staff in the institution
- arrangements for psychological and social work services on a regular and conveniently available basis

- arrangements for educational and vocational services on a regular and conveniently available basis
- written arrangements with a general hospital for the transfer of patients who require medical, obstetrical, or surgical services not available in the institution.

Psychiatric

The primary function of the institution is to provide diagnostic and treatment services for patients who have psychiatric-related illnesses. A psychiatric hospital also shall provide:

- arrangements for clinical laboratory service, as required, on a regular and conveniently available basis
- arrangements for diagnostic x-ray services, as required on a regular and conveniently available basis
- psychiatric, psychological, and social work service with facilities and staff in the institution
- arrangements for electroencephalograph services, as required, on a regular and conveniently available basis.
- written arrangements with a general hospital for the transfer of patients who require medical, obstetrical, or surgical services not available in the institution.

Data Comparability

The economic climate, demographic characteristics, personnel issues, and health care financing and payment policies differ by region, state, and city across the country. *Differences in these factors must be taken into account when using the data.* In addition, the profiles of hospitals across comparison groups vary. For example, states will differ in terms of the number and percentage of hospitals by size, ownership, services provided, types of patients treated, and so forth. *Differences in these variables also must be taken into consideration when doing a comparative analysis.*

Notes on the Survey

The 2019 edition of *AHA Hospital Statistics*™ draws its data from the 2017 AHA Annual Survey of Hospitals. It is the statistical complement to the 2019 edition of the *AHA Guide*®, which contains selected data about individual hospitals.

The AHA Survey was mailed to all hospitals, in the U.S. and its associated areas: American Samoa, Guam, the Marshall Islands, Puerto Rico, and the Virgin Islands. U.S. government hospitals located outside the U.S. were not included. Overall, the average response rate over the past five years has been approximately 83 percent.

Reporting Period
In completing the survey, hospitals were requested to report data for a full year, in accord with their fiscal year, ending in 2017. The statistical table present data reported or estimated for a 12-month period, except for data on personnel, which represent situations as they existed at the end of the reporting period.

Respondents
Data for Tables 1 and 2 include 6,210 hospitals in the U.S. Data on community hospitals (nonfederal, short-term general and other special hospitals) only are presented in Tables 3-6, and Table 8.

It is important to note that the hospitals included in *AHA Hospital Statistics* are not necessarily identical to those included in *AHA Guide*. The institutions listed in the 2019 edition of *AHA Guide* include all of those institutions CMS certified, or Joint Commission accredited as of September 2018. Tables 1-6 in *AHA Hospital Statistics* present data for hospitals that were in operation during the 12-month reporting period ending 2017.

Estimates
Estimates were made of data for nonreporting hospitals and for reporting hospitals that submitted incomplete AHA Annual Survey questionnaires. Estimates were not made for beds, bassinets and facilities and services. Data for beds and bassinets of nonreporting hospitals were based on the most recent information from those hospitals. (Note that in all statistical tables, whenever bed-size categories are listed, all eight categories appear, whether or not there are hospitals in every category.)

Missing revenue, expenses, admissions, births, inpatient days, surgical operations, outpatient visits, and full-time-equivalent personnel values are estimates from regression models. For all other variables the estimates were based on ratios such as per bed averages derived from data reported by hospitals similar in size, control, major service provided, length of stay, and geographical characteristics to the hospitals that did not report this information.

Table		Page

Table

1

Historical Trends in Utilization, Personnel, and Finances for Selected Years from 1946 through 2017

Data are for all hospitals in the United States. Data are estimated for nonreporting hospitals with the exception of newborn and outpatient data before 1972. Personnel data exclude residents, interns, and students from 1952 on; personnel data include full-time personnel and full-time equivalents for part-time personnel from 1954 on. As a result of the AHA Annual Survey validation process, the New York state expense data from 1976 were revised after the 1977 edition was published. The revised figures are included below. In order to provide trend data on a consistent basis, the 1970 and 1971 psychiatric and long-term data have been slightly modified. The 1982 FTE figures have updated to provide the most accurate data possible. The data for 2013–2016 have been recalculated for the 2019 Edition to reflect all hospitals, not just AHA-registered hospitals. For more information, please see the Discontinuation of AHA's Registration Program section on page xv.

CLASSIFICATION: Total United States

YEAR	HOSPITALS	BEDS (in thousands)	ADMISSIONS (in thousands)	AVERAGE DAILY CENSUS (in thousands)	ADJUSTED AVERAGE DAILY CENSUS (in thousands)	AVERAGE STAY (days)	OUTPATIENT VISITS (in thousands)	NEWBORNS		FTE PERSONNEL		TOTAL EXPENSES		
								Bassinets	Births	Number (in thousands)	Per 100 Adjusted Census	Amount (in Millions of dollars)	Adjusted per Inpatient Stay (dollars)	Adjusted per Inpatient Day (dollars)
1946	6,125	1,436	15,675	1,142	—	—	—	85,585	2,135,327	830	—	$1,963	—	—
1950	6,788	1,456	18,483	1,253	—	—	—	90,101	2,742,780	1,058	—	$3,651	—	—
1955	6,956	1,604	21,073	1,363	—	—	—	98,823	3,476,753	1,301	—	$5,594	—	—
1960	6,876	1,658	25,027	1,402	—	—	—	102,764	3,835,735	1,598	—	$8,421	—	—
1965	7,123	1,704	28,812	1,403	—	—	125,793	101,287	3,565,344	1,952	—	$12,948	—	—
1970	7,123	1,616	31,759	1,298	—	—	181,370	97,128	3,537,000	2,537	—	$25,556	—	—
1971	7,097	1,556	32,664	1,237	—	—	199,725	94,344	3,464,513	2,589	—	$28,812	—	—
1972	7,061	1,550	33,265	1,209	—	—	219,182	92,960	3,231,875	2,671	—	$32,667	—	—
1973	7,123	1,535	34,352	1,189	—	—	233,555	90,071	3,087,210	2,769	—	$36,290	—	—
1974	7,174	1,513	35,506	1,167	—	—	250,481	88,269	3,043,386	2,919	—	$41,406	—	—
1975	7,156	1,466	36,157	1,125	—	—	254,844	86,875	3,091,629	3,023	—	$48,706	—	—
1976	7,082	1,434	36,776	1,090	—	—	270,951	85,284	3,067,063	3,108	—	$56,005	—	—
1977	7,099	1,407	37,060	1,066	—	—	263,775	83,193	3,223,699	3,213	—	$63,630	—	—
1978	7,015	1,381	37,243	1,042	—	—	263,606	80,650	3,250,373	3,280	—	$70,927	—	—
1979	6,988	1,372	37,802	1,043	—	—	262,009	79,720	3,376,467	3,382	—	$79,796	—	—
1980	6,965	1,365	38,892	1,060	—	—	262,951	79,842	3,500,043	3,492	—	$91,886	—	—
1981	6,933	1,362	39,169	1,061	—	—	265,332	78,823	3,558,274	3,661	—	$107,146	—	—
1982	6,915	1,360	39,095	1,053	—	—	313,667	77,998	3,615,751	3,746	—	$123,219	—	—
1983	6,888	1,350	38,887	1,028	—	—	273,168	77,837	3,596,146	3,707	—	$136,315	—	—
1984	6,872	1,339	37,938	970	—	—	276,566	77,845	3,563,106	3,630	—	$144,114	—	—
1985	6,872	1,318	36,304	910	—	—	282,140	77,202	3,630,961	3,625	—	$153,327	—	—
1986	6,841	1,290	35,219	883	—	—	294,634	76,002	3,680,178	3,647	—	$165,194	—	—
1987	6,821	1,267	34,439	873	—	—	310,707	74,770	3,698,294	3,742	—	$178,662	—	—
1988	6,780	1,248	34,107	863	—	—	336,208	72,568	3,794,369	3,839	—	$196,704	—	—
1989	6,720	1,226	33,742	853	—	—	352,248	71,491	3,920,384	3,937	—	$214,886	—	—
1990	6,649	1,213	33,774	844	—	—	368,184	70,539	4,046,704	4,063	—	$234,870	—	—
1991	6,634	1,202	33,567	827	—	—	387,675	69,464	4,047,504	4,165	—	$258,508	—	—
1992	6,539	1,178	33,536	807	—	—	417,874	69,052	4,007,179	4,236	—	$282,531	—	—
1993	6,467	1,163	33,201	783	—	—	435,619	67,911	3,949,788	4,289	—	$301,538	—	—
1994	6,374	1,128	33,125	745	—	—	453,584	67,311	3,886,667	4,270	—	$310,834	—	—
1995	6,291	1,081	33,282	710	—	—	483,195	66,256	3,833,132	4,273	—	$320,252	—	—
1996	6,201	1,062	33,307	685	—	—	505,455	65,138	3,790,678	4,276	—	$330,531	—	—
1997	6,097	1,035	33,624	673	—	—	520,600	64,649	3,811,522	4,333	—	$342,334	—	—
1998	6,021	1,013	33,766	662	—	—	545,481	63,485	3,795,212	4,407	—	$355,450	—	—
1999	5,890	994	34,181	657	—	—	573,461	62,714	3,829,881	4,369	—	$372,933	—	—
2000	5,810	984	34,891	650	—	—	592,673	61,915	3,940,017	4,454	—	$395,391	—	—
2001	5,801	987	35,644	658	—	—	612,276	61,527	3,929,733	4,535	—	$426,849	—	—
2002	5,794	976	36,326	662	—	—	640,515	62,151	3,934,421	4,610	—	$462,222	—	—
2003	5,764	965	36,611	657	—	—	648,560	60,699	3,976,886	4,651	—	$498,104	—	—
2004	5,759	956	36,942	658	—	—	662,131	59,660	3,965,906	4,696	—	$533,853	—	—
2005	5,756	947	37,006	656	—	—	673,689	59,073	4,048,442	4,791	—	$570,534	—	—
2006	5,747	947	37,189	653	—	—	690,425	58,670	4,126,598	4,907	—	$607,355	—	—
2007	5,708	945	37,120	645	—	—	693,510	58,429	4,128,796	5,024	—	$641,124	—	—
2008	5,815	951	37,529	649	—	—	709,960	58,133	4,109,081	5,116	—	$690,074	—	—
2009	5,795	944	37,480	641	—	—	741,551	58,078	4,001,748	5,178	—	$726,671	—	—
2010	5,754	942	36,915	627	—	—	750,408	57,396	3,871,751	5,184	—	$750,602	—	—
2011	5,724	924	36,565	615	—	—	754,454	57,022	3,767,697	5,196	—	$773,547	—	—
2012	5,723	921	36,156	600	—	—	777,961	56,693	3,754,085	5,258	—	$829,665	—	—
2013	6,230	940	36,095	607	—	—	795,759	57,539	3,778,696	5,456	—	$873,841	—	—
2014	6,174	928	35,562	600	—	—	811,975	56,951	3,818,308	5,413	—	$907,755	—	—
2015	6,180	930	35,899	608	—	—	844,487	56,606	3,826,138	5,522	—	$955,976	—	—
2016	6,168	928	36,110	610	—	—	877,137	56,449	3,804,132	5,698	—	$1,012,752	—	—
2017	6,210		36,510	614	—	—	890,451	55,901	3,693,124	5,841	—	$1,060,933	—	—

Table 1 (Continued)

Total nonfederal short-term general and other special

YEAR	HOSPITALS	BEDS (in thousands)	ADMISSIONS (in thousands)	AVERAGE DAILY CENSUS (in thousands)	ADJUSTED AVERAGE DAILY CENSUS (in thousands)	AVERAGE STAY (days)	OUTPATIENT VISITS (in thousands)	NEWBORNS Bassinets	NEWBORNS Births	FTE PERSONNEL Number (in thousands)	FTE PERSONNEL Per 100 Adjusted Census	TOTAL EXPENSES Amount (In Millions of dollars)	TOTAL EXPENSES per Inpatient Stay (dollars)	TOTAL EXPENSES Adjusted per Inpatient Day (dollars)
1946	4,444	473	13,655	341	—	9.1	—	80,987	2,087,503	505	—	$1,169	—	—
1950	5,031	505	16,663	372	—	8.1	—	86,019	2,660,982	662	—	$2,120	—	—
1955	5,237	568	19,100	407	—	7.8	—	93,868	3,304,451	826	—	$3,434	—	—
1960	5,407	639	22,970	477	—	7.6	—	98,127	3,678,051	1,080	—	$5,617	—	—
1965	5,736	741	26,463	563	620	7.8	92,631	96,782	3,413,370	1,386	224	$9,147	$316.37	$40.56
1970	5,859	848	29,252	662	727	8.2	133,545	93,079	3,403,064	1,929	265	$19,560	$604.59	$73.73
1971	5,865	867	30,142	665	736	8.0	148,423	90,444	3,337,605	1,999	272	$22,400	$667.44	$83.43
1972	5,843	884	30,777	664	739	7.9	166,983	89,315	3,119,446	2,056	278	$25,549	$747.42	$94.61
1973	5,891	903	31,761	681	768	7.8	178,939	86,851	2,987,089	2,149	280	$28,496	$793.88	$101.78
1974	5,977	931	32,943	701	793	7.8	194,838	85,208	2,947,342	2,289	289	$32,751	$883.04	$113.21
1975	5,979	947	33,519	708	806	7.7	196,311	83,834	2,998,590	2,399	298	$39,110	$1,024.72	$133.08
1976	5,956	961	34,068	715	816	7.7	207,725	82,307	2,962,305	2,483	304	$45,402	$1,172.25	$152.24
1977	5,973	974	34,353	717	820	7.6	204,238	80,228	3,117,756	2,581	315	$51,832	$1,316.70	$173.25
1978	5,935	980	34,575	720	841	7.6	204,461	78,090	3,156,570	2,662	323	$58,348	$1,470.13	$193.81
1979	5,923	988	35,160	729	841	7.6	203,873	77,277	3,287,157	2,762	328	$66,184	$1,631.16	$215.75
1980	5,904	992	36,198	748	861	7.6	206,752	77,539	3,408,699	2,879	334	$76,970	$1,844.19	$244.44
1981	5,879	1,007	36,494	764	876	7.6	206,729	76,567	3,465,683	3,039	347	$90,739	$2,167.70	$283.94
1982	5,863	1,015	36,429	763	882	7.6	250,888	75,739	3,514,761	3,110	353	$105,094	$2,493.09	$326.68
1983	5,843	1,021	36,201	750	869	7.6	213,995	75,471	3,490,629	3,102	357	$116,632	$2,775.55	$368.01
1984	5,814	1,020	35,202	703	824	7.3	216,474	75,587	3,456,467	3,023	367	$123,550	$2,984.00	$409.85
1985	5,784	1,003	33,501	650	780	7.1	222,773	74,899	3,521,296	3,003	385	$130,700	$3,238.94	$459.57
1986	5,728	982	32,410	631	774	7.1	234,270	73,688	3,584,530	3,032	392	$140,907	$3,529.60	$499.19
1987	5,659	961	31,633	624	780	7.2	247,704	72,516	3,602,416	3,120	400	$152,909	$3,848.79	$536.96
1988	5,579	949	31,480	622	795	7.2	271,436	70,361	3,706,748	3,209	404	$168,941	$4,194.39	$581.08
1989	5,497	936	31,141	619	805	7.3	287,909	69,436	3,831,051	3,307	411	$185,204	$4,572.23	$630.59
1990	5,420	929	31,203	620	820	7.3	302,691	68,443	3,958,646	3,423	417	$203,927	$4,929.93	$681.52
1991	5,370	926	31,084	612	828	7.2	323,202	67,440	3,965,489	3,539	427	$225,230	$5,345.63	$745.37
1992	5,321	923	31,053	606	832	7.1	349,397	67,095	3,925,024	3,624	436	$248,318	$5,788.52	$815.99
1993	5,289	921	30,770	593	834	7.0	368,358	66,060	3,870,392	3,681	441	$266,382	$6,120.94	$874.98
1994	5,256	904	30,739	569	814	6.8	384,880	65,728	3,809,367	3,697	454	$276,148	$6,230.33	$929.65
1995	5,220	874	30,966	549	800	6.5	415,710	64,742	3,764,756	3,718	458	$276,073	$6,220.54	$966.79
1996	5,160	864	31,116	531	813	6.2	440,845	63,646	3,723,907	3,728	466	$293,920	$6,225.95	$1,005.45
1997	5,082	855	31,595	529	821	6.1	450,907	63,247	3,742,240	3,794	467	$306,088	$6,266.24	$1,031.68
1998	5,039	842	31,830	527	835	6.0	474,366	62,162	3,726,234	3,835	467	$319,035	$6,387.53	$1,064.93
1999	4,977	831	32,377	527	850	5.9	495,850	61,534	3,760,295	3,840	460	$335,405	$6,512.44	$1,101.47
2000	4,934	825	33,102	534	866	5.8	522,970	60,845	3,880,166	3,916	461	$356,757	$6,650.68	$1,147.99
2001	4,927	828	33,834	541	887	5.8	539,316	60,454	3,873,395	3,990	459	$383,911	$6,979.29	$1,216.04
2002	4,949	823	34,501	540	895	5.7	557,336	59,974	3,870,191	4,072	459	$416,791	$7,353.17	$1,288.63
2003	4,918	815	34,800	542	910	5.7	563,804	59,662	3,915,842	4,112	456	$450,403	$7,798.19	$1,378.78
2004	4,942	810	35,098	542	930	5.6	573,126	58,710	3,931,508	4,151	458	$481,517	$8,168.06	$1,449.90
2005	4,956	804	35,265	540	940	5.6	587,296	58,195	3,987,766	4,260	462	$516,172	$8,538.30	$1,521.58
2006	4,947	805	35,403	535	944	5.6	599,597	57,832	4,075,193	4,347	473	$552,276	$8,972.85	$1,610.76
2007	4,915	803	35,370	538	963	5.5	603,411	57,546	4,077,962	4,468	472	$583,550	$9,377.82	$1,694.38
2008	5,026	810	35,776	529	973	5.5	624,185	57,301	4,073,724	4,552	456	$626,823	$9,789.69	$1,780.45
2009	5,023	807	35,603	520	974	5.6	643,420	57,302	3,960,432	4,594	458	$657,242	$10,042.56	$1,851.44
2010	4,995	806	35,160	514	983	5.4	651,617	56,610	3,818,399	4,603	458	$678,254	$10,316.07	$1,908.59
2011	4,983	799	34,852	508	992	5.4	657,071	56,290	3,730,342	4,654	462	$702,822	$10,542.09	$1,959.69
2012	5,010	802	34,438	509	977	5.4	675,223	55,987	3,715,479	4,732	473	$757,213	$11,222.23	$2,089.07
2013	5,372	813	34,079	504	1,018	5.4	684,488	56,844	3,728,411	4,829	473	$794,245	$11,663.39	$2,157.53
2014	5,330	804	33,545	508	1,046	5.4	700,472	56,294	3,766,328	4,874	472	$821,766	$12,019.23	$2,213.34
2015	5,293	802	33,861	511	1,077	5.5	731,067	55,953	3,792,223	4,948	473	$867,108	$12,356.58	$2,271.71
2016	5,278	801	34,052	511	1,093	5.5	757,095	55,824	3,769,965	5,088	473	$920,188	$12,756.07	$2,337.15
2017	5,274	800	34,351	511	1,093	5.4	766,368	55,181	3,656,809	5,217	477	$966,492	$13,121.85	$2,423.23

Table 1 (Continued)

Total community hospitals

YEAR	HOSPITALS	BEDS (in thousands)	ADMISSIONS (in thousands)	AVERAGE DAILY CENSUS (in thousands)	ADJUSTED AVERAGE DAILY CENSUS (in thousands)	AVERAGE STAY (days)	OUTPATIENT VISITS (in thousands)	NEWBORNS Bassinets	NEWBORNS Births	FTE PERSONNEL Number (in thousands)	FTE PERSONNEL Per 100 Adjusted Census	TOTAL EXPENSES Amount (in Millions of dollars)	TOTAL EXPENSES Adjusted per Inpatient Stay (dollars)	TOTAL EXPENSES Adjusted per Inpatient Day (dollars)
1975	5,875	942	33,435	706	798	7.7	190,672	83,829	2,998,552	2,392	300	$38,962	$1,030.34	$133.81
1976	5,857	956	33,979	713	810	7.7	201,247	82,296	2,962,216	2,475	306	$45,240	$1,176.25	$152.76
1979	5,842	984	35,099	727	833	7.6	198,778	77,266	3,287,012	2,756	331	$66,004	$1,641.67	$217.34
1980	5,830	988	36,143	747	857	7.6	202,310	77,522	3,408,482	2,873	335	$76,851	$1,851.04	$245.12
1981	5,813	1,003	36,438	763	873	7.6	202,768	76,561	3,465,401	3,033	347	$90,572	$2,171.20	$284.33
1982	5,801	1,012	36,379	762	878	7.6	248,124	75,733	3,514,457	3,103	353	$104,876	$2,500.52	$327.37
1983	5,783	1,018	36,152	749	864	7.6	210,044	75,465	3,490,254	3,096	358	$116,438	$2,789.18	$369.49
1984	5,759	1,017	35,155	702	820	7.3	211,961	75,581	3,456,308	3,017	368	$123,336	$2,995.38	$411.10
1985	5,732	1,001	33,449	649	777	7.1	218,716	74,893	3,521,135	2,997	386	$130,499	$3,244.74	$460.19
1986	5,678	978	32,379	629	770	7.1	231,912	73,682	3,584,408	3,025	393	$140,654	$3,532.51	$500.81
1987	5,611	958	31,601	622	776	7.2	245,524	72,510	3,602,296	3,114	401	$152,585	$3,850.16	$538.96
1988	5,533	947	31,453	620	787	7.2	269,129	70,325	3,706,402	3,205	407	$168,722	$4,206.73	$586.33
1989	5,455	933	31,116	618	796	7.2	285,712	69,405	3,830,615	3,303	415	$184,898	$4,587.87	$636.96
1990	5,384	927	31,181	619	813	7.2	301,329	68,412	3,958,263	3,420	421	$203,693	$4,946.68	$686.83
1991	5,342	924	31,064	611	820	7.2	322,048	67,434	3,965,396	3,535	431	$225,023	$5,359.56	$752.10
1992	5,292	921	31,034	604	827	7.1	348,522	67,089	3,924,944	3,620	437	$248,095	$5,794.43	$819.83
1993	5,261	919	30,748	592	828	7.0	366,885	66,054	3,870,376	3,677	444	$266,089	$6,132.06	$880.52
1994	5,229	902	30,718	568	812	6.7	382,924	65,722	3,809,367	3,692	455	$275,779	$6,229.83	$930.71
1995	5,194	873	30,945	548	809	6.5	414,345	64,736	3,764,698	3,714	459	$285,588	$6,215.51	$967.69
1996	5,134	862	31,099	531	799	6.2	439,863	63,640	3,723,871	3,725	466	$293,755	$6,224.94	$1,006.14
1997	5,057	853	31,577	528	811	6.1	450,140	63,241	3,742,191	3,790	467	$305,763	$6,261.93	$1,032.70
1998	5,015	840	31,812	525	819	6.0	474,193	62,156	3,726,233	3,831	468	$318,834	$6,385.99	$1,066.96
1999	4,956	830	32,359	526	833	5.9	495,346	61,528	3,760,295	3,838	461	$335,246	$6,511.72	$1,102.61
2000	4,915	824	33,089	526	849	5.8	521,404	60,839	3,880,166	3,911	461	$356,564	$6,648.82	$1,149.40
2001	4,908	826	33,814	533	865	5.7	538,480	60,448	3,873,395	3,987	461	$383,735	$6,979.53	$1,217.27
2002	4,927	821	34,478	540	886	5.7	556,404	59,974	3,870,191	4,069	459	$416,591	$7,354.60	$1,289.87
2003	4,895	813	34,783	539	894	5.7	563,186	59,662	3,915,842	4,109	460	$450,124	$7,796.41	$1,379.48
2004	4,919	808	35,086	541	909	5.6	571,569	58,710	3,931,508	4,148	456	$481,247	$8,165.55	$1,450.35
2005	4,936	802	35,239	540	929	5.6	584,429	58,195	3,987,766	4,257	458	$515,740	$8,534.90	$1,522.42
2006	4,927	803	35,378	538	939	5.6	599,553	57,832	4,075,193	4,343	463	$551,835	$8,970.31	$1,612.23
2007	4,897	801	35,346	533	943	5.5	603,300	57,546	4,077,962	4,465	474	$583,252	$9,377.17	$1,696.10
2008	5,010	808	35,761	536	962	5.5	624,098	57,301	4,073,724	4,550	473	$626,577	$9,788.25	$1,782.28
2009	5,008	806	35,527	528	970	5.4	641,953	57,282	3,959,605	4,585	472	$656,156	$10,045.15	$1,852.59
2010	4,985	805	35,149	520	973	5.4	651,424	56,610	3,818,399	4,600	473	$677,968	$10,313.44	$1,909.64
2011	4,973	797	34,843	513	982	5.4	656,079	56,290	3,730,342	4,650	473	$702,091	$10,532.52	$1,959.58
2012	4,999	801	34,422	507	991	5.4	674,971	55,987	3,715,479	4,731	477	$756,917	$11,220.70	$2,090.01
2013	5,359	811	34,063	509	976	5.4	684,227	56,844	3,728,411	4,872	499	$793,919	$11,661.64	$2,158.83
2014	5,280	802	33,517	503	1,017	5.5	700,233	56,294	3,766,328	4,826	475	$821,224	$12,017.28	$2,214.84
2015	5,280	801	33,818	507	1,045	5.5	730,789	55,953	3,792,223	4,947	473	$866,817	$12,360.16	$2,272.58
2016	5,267	799	34,032	510	1,076	5.5	756,798	55,824	3,769,965	5,087	473	$919,821	$12,755.62	$2,338.07
2017	5,262	798	34,306	510	1,092	5.4	766,077	55,181	3,656,809	5,215	478	$966,204	$13,126.02	$2,424.17

Table 1 (Continued)

CLASSIFICATION / YEAR	HOSPITALS	BEDS (in thousands)	ADMISSIONS (in thousands)	AVERAGE DAILY CENSUS (in thousands)	ADJUSTED AVERAGE DAILY CENSUS (in thousands)	AVERAGE STAY (days)	OUTPATIENT VISITS (in thousands)	NEWBORNS Bassinets	NEWBORNS Births	FTE PERSONNEL Number (in thousands)	FTE PERSONNEL Per 100 Adjusted Census	TOTAL EXPENSES Amount (in Millions of dollars)	TOTAL EXPENSES Adjusted per Inpatient Stay (dollars)	TOTAL EXPENSES Adjusted per Inpatient Day (dollars)
Nongovernment not-for-profit community hospitals														
1975	3,339	658	23,722	510	574	7.8	131,435	57,496	2,131,057	1,712	298	$27,938	$1,040.21	$133.36
1976	3,345	670	24,082	517	586	7.9	140,914	56,442	2,100,917	1,791	306	$32,764	$1,208.23	$152.94
1979	3,330	690	24,874	528	603	7.7	139,565	52,859	2,308,548	1,999	332	$47,937	$1,684.40	$218.06
1980	3,322	692	25,566	542	621	7.7	142,156	52,659	2,389,478	2,086	336	$55,780	$1,901.64	$245.74
1981	3,340	706	25,945	555	636	7.8	143,380	52,302	2,455,033	2,213	348	$66,267	$2,225.17	$285.64
1982	3,338	712	25,898	553	637	7.8	176,245	51,566	2,483,345	2,265	355	$76,806	$2,572.93	$330.41
1983	3,347	718	25,827	544	629	7.7	150,839	51,649	2,465,604	2,270	362	$85,637	$2,868.80	$373.78
1984	3,351	716	25,236	512	598	7.4	153,281	51,491	2,446,540	2,222	372	$90,814	$3,072.51	$415.04
1985	3,349	707	24,179	476	569	7.2	158,953	51,424	2,507,288	2,216	389	$96,150	$3,307.41	$462.69
1986	3,323	689	23,483	460	563	7.2	167,633	50,885	2,547,170	2,241	398	$103,524	$3,589.64	$503.64
1987	3,274	673	22,937	455	566	7.2	177,413	50,133	2,557,294	2,298	406	$112,325	$3,914.23	$543.67
1988	3,242	668	22,939	456	577	7.3	195,363	48,828	2,653,794	2,373	412	$124,703	$4,272.95	$591.13
1989	3,220	661	22,792	455	584	7.3	209,191	48,305	2,751,426	2,454	420	$136,889	$4,649.22	$642.45
1990	3,191	657	22,878	455	596	7.3	221,073	47,441	2,833,204	2,533	424	$150,673	$5,001.24	$692.36
1991	3,175	656	22,964	451	603	7.2	238,204	47,229	2,845,995	2,624	435	$166,806	$5,393.30	$758.21
1992	3,173	656	23,056	445	606	7.1	257,887	47,185	2,846,386	2,692	443	$183,793	$5,808.80	$828.44
1993	3,154	651	22,749	432	602	6.9	270,138	46,214	2,802,164	2,711	451	$197,187	$6,177.69	$897.70
1994	3,139	637	22,704	413	589	6.6	282,653	46,381	2,792,116	2,719	462	$204,219	$6,256.72	$950.31
1995	3,092	610	22,557	393	578	6.4	303,851	45,198	2,725,641	2,702	468	$209,614	$6,279.17	$994.39
1996	3,045	598	22,542	379	567	6.1	320,746	44,650	2,683,750	2,711	478	$215,950	$6,344.05	$1,042.04
1997	3,000	591	22,905	376	575	6.0	330,215	44,484	2,698,086	2,765	481	$225,287	$6,392.74	$1,074.26
1998	3,026	588	23,282	377	587	5.9	352,114	44,087	2,715,958	2,834	483	$237,978	$6,525.68	$1,110.50
1999	3,012	587	23,871	381	605	5.8	370,784	44,172	2,746,453	2,862	473	$251,534	$6,607.51	$1,139.89
2000	3,003	583	24,452	382	618	5.7	393,168	43,655	2,833,615	2,919	472	$267,051	$6,717.48	$1,182.32
2001	2,998	585	24,983	385	628	5.6	404,901	43,640	2,829,691	2,971	473	$287,250	$7,051.76	$1,255.25
2002	3,025	582	25,425	391	646	5.6	416,910	43,241	2,820,591	3,039	471	$312,726	$7,457.84	$1,328.81
2003	2,984	575	25,668	389	647	5.5	424,215	42,965	2,854,764	3,059	473	$337,696	$7,904.93	$1,429.62
2004	2,967	568	25,757	388	655	5.5	430,262	41,968	2,844,617	3,077	470	$359,414	$8,266.64	$1,501.09
2005	2,958	561	25,881	388	667	5.5	441,653	41,585	2,876,677	3,155	473	$385,993	$8,670.83	$1,585.34
2006	2,919	559	25,798	385	671	5.4	453,501	40,888	2,905,275	3,207	478	$412,868	$9,189.58	$1,685.62
2007	2,913	554	25,752	380	673	5.4	455,825	40,681	2,907,002	3,286	488	$436,319	$9,592.93	$1,776.06
2008	2,923	557	25,899	380	683	5.4	469,804	40,567	2,901,854	3,340	489	$468,080	$10,080.50	$1,875.78
2009	2,918	556	25,783	375	690	5.3	485,935	40,467	2,822,527	3,369	488	$492,853	$10,379.09	$1,956.71
2010	2,904	556	25,532	368	691	5.3	494,178	39,946	2,750,163	3,388	490	$510,744	$10,651.81	$2,025.05
2011	2,903	548	25,185	362	694	5.2	496,643	39,651	2,692,577	3,427	494	$528,303	$10,932.55	$2,088.05
2012	2,894	545	24,751	354	697	5.2	512,237	39,778	2,684,600	3,477	499	$563,960	$11,563.17	$2,214.26
2013	2,975	548	24,470	354	687	5.3	518,438	40,498	2,706,635	3,523	513	$589,184	$12,002.72	$2,288.81
2014	2,943	539	23,895	347	709	5.3	528,258	39,768	2,728,345	3,513	496	$606,297	$12,375.64	$2,344.81
2015	2,932	537	24,115	350	729	5.3	551,762	39,510	2,744,467	3,593	493	$641,799	$12,745.02	$2,412.96
2016	2,943	540	24,356	353	751	5.3	574,044	39,641	2,750,958	3,716	494	$683,326	$13,157.14	$2,486.48
2017	2,968	545	24,789	357	768	5.3	581,848	39,744	2,710,049	3,841	500	$721,391	$13,503.97	$2,573.64

Table 1 (Continued)

CLASSIFICATION: Investor-owned (for-profit) community hospitals

YEAR	HOSPITALS	BEDS (in thousands)	ADMISSIONS (in thousands)	AVERAGE DAILY CENSUS (in thousands)	ADJUSTED AVERAGE DAILY CENSUS (in thousands)	AVERAGE STAY (days)	OUTPATIENT VISITS (in thousands)	NEWBORNS Bassinets	NEWBORNS Births	FTE PERSONNEL Number (in thousands)	FTE PERSONNEL Per 100 Adjusted Census	TOTAL EXPENSES Amount (In Millions of dollars)	TOTAL EXPENSES Adjusted per Inpatient Stay (dollars)	TOTAL EXPENSES Adjusted per Inpatient Day (dollars)
1975	775	73	2,646	48	53	6.6	7,713	4,062	141,392	139	263	$2,561	$876.48	$132.80
1976	752	76	2,734	50	54	6.6	8,048	4,044	144,751	147	272	$3,085	$1,031.91	$156.35
1979	727	83	2,963	53	59	6.6	9,289	4,110	174,843	174	300	$4,820	$1,476.42	$225.87
1980	730	87	3,165	57	62	6.5	9,696	4,439	199,722	189	304	$5,847	$1,675.85	$257.12
1981	729	88	3,239	58	63	6.5	9,961	4,523	207,405	203	322	$6,856	$1,952.56	$299.02
1982	748	91	3,316	60	66	6.6	13,193	4,736	219,675	212	320	$8,177	$2,224.75	$340.03
1983	757	94	3,299	59	66	6.5	10,389	5,039	228,883	213	323	$9,208	$2,517.53	$385.42
1984	786	100	3,314	57	64	6.3	11,090	5,807	242,088	214	335	$10,251	$2,748.51	$438.30
1985	805	104	3,242	54	63	6.1	12,378	6,117	266,839	221	350	$11,486	$3,033.06	$500.48
1986	834	107	3,231	54	65	6.1	14,896	6,305	291,112	229	354	$12,987	$3,341.19	$552.40
1987	828	106	3,157	54	66	6.2	16,566	6,391	306,492	242	367	$14,067	$3,617.19	$585.01
1988	790	104	3,090	53	66	6.2	17,926	6,254	308,828	249	379	$15,545	$4,022.77	$649.33
1989	769	102	3,071	53	67	6.3	19,341	6,261	325,711	261	390	$17,240	$4,406.20	$707.90
1990	749	101	3,066	54	69	6.4	20,110	6,358	340,555	273	396	$18,822	$4,727.27	$751.55
1991	738	100	3,016	52	69	6.3	21,174	6,519	359,115	281	409	$20,516	$5,133.53	$820.19
1992	723	99	2,969	51	69	6.3	22,900	6,395	357,776	285	412	$22,496	$5,548.24	$888.73
1993	717	99	2,946	51	69	6.2	24,936	6,329	363,358	289	417	$23,077	$5,643.21	$914.39
1994	719	101	3,035	50	70	6.1	26,443	7,164	354,477	302	434	$23,445	$5,528.91	$923.90
1995	752	106	3,428	55	77	5.8	31,940	7,441	408,339	343	443	$26,653	$5,425.20	$946.99
1996	759	109	3,684	56	82	5.6	37,347	8,026	444,697	359	437	$28,385	$5,207.44	$945.49
1997	797	115	3,953	60	89	5.5	40,919	7,895	465,919	385	433	$31,179	$5,218.69	$961.96
1998	771	113	3,971	60	90	5.5	42,072	7,486	466,025	383	425	$31,732	$5,262.44	$968.00
1999	747	107	3,905	58	86	5.5	39,896	7,792	467,585	362	422	$31,179	$5,350.07	$999.03
2000	749	110	4,141	61	90	5.4	43,378	7,413	503,497	378	418	$34,969	$5,642.18	$1,057.32
2001	754	109	4,197	63	92	5.4	44,706	7,467	494,669	379	413	$37,348	$5,971.81	$1,121.31
2002	766	108	4,365	64	93	5.3	45,215	7,491	496,988	380	407	$40,082	$6,161.44	$1,180.83
2003	790	110	4,481	65	95	5.3	44,246	7,763	515,693	391	411	$43,953	$6,589.91	$1,264.50
2004	835	113	4,599	68	100	5.4	44,962	7,714	534,503	406	406	$48,971	$7,139.13	$1,362.42
2005	868	114	4,618	68	101	5.3	46,016	8,012	546,307	421	418	$51,833	$7,351.96	$1,412.74
2006	890	115	4,735	68	103	5.2	44,237	7,760	574,113	423	413	$55,030	$7,422.08	$1,471.53
2007	873	116	4,626	66	101	5.2	43,943	7,791	555,670	432	429	$56,405	$7,823.44	$1,535.98
2008	982	121	4,839	70	109	5.3	44,897	7,965	562,711	450	414	$61,762	$7,984.62	$1,555.55
2009	998	122	4,887	70	112	5.3	47,281	7,965	553,233	464	414	$64,367	$8,037.18	$1,573.64
2010	1,013	125	4,925	71	113	5.3	48,201	7,965	525,427	474	420	$67,168	$8,336.16	$1,628.90
2011	1,025	128	5,060	73	119	5.3	50,013	8,137	508,330	485	409	$70,340	$8,262.74	$1,627.65
2012	1,068	135	5,224	77	124	5.3	53,854	8,192	530,941	515	414	$79,114	$8,860.94	$1,746.85
2013	1,351	145	5,346	81	126	5.5	56,935	8,400	532,235	613	487	$89,444	$9,519.01	$1,839.53
2014	1,341	146	5,407	82	139	5.5	60,277	8,665	547,008	572	411	$93,780	$9,649.97	$1,849.54
2015	1,345	146	5,506	83	143	5.5	62,567	8,863	560,964	588	410	$97,949	$9,758.88	$1,876.67
2016	1,350	146	5,625	84	148	5.5	65,542	8,876	550,448	609	413	$104,138	$9,903.56	$1,929.73
2017	1,322	142	5,433	81	144	5.5	63,203	8,319	487,406	591	412	$104,704	$10,273.14	$1,996.11

Table 1 (Continued)

CLASSIFICATION	YEAR	HOSPITALS	BEDS (in thousands)	ADMISSIONS (in thousands)	AVERAGE DAILY CENSUS (in thousands)	ADJUSTED AVERAGE DAILY CENSUS (in thousands)	AVERAGE STAY (days)	OUTPATIENT VISITS (in thousands)	NEWBORNS		FTE PERSONNEL		TOTAL EXPENSES		
									Bassinets	Births	Number (in thousands)	Per 100 Adjusted Census	Amount (In Millions of dollars)	Adjusted per Inpatient Stay (dollars)	Adjusted per Inpatient Day (dollars)
State and local government community hospitals	1975	1,761	210	7,067	148	171	7.6	51,525	22,271	726,103	540	316	$8,463	$1,030.86	$135.64
	1976	1,760	210	7,163	146	170	7.5	52,286	21,810	716,548	537	315	$9,391	$1,132.50	$151.00
	1979	1,785	211	7,262	146	171	7.4	49,924	20,297	803,621	583	341	$13,247	$1,561.04	$211.89
	1980	1,778	209	7,413	149	174	7.3	50,459	20,424	819,282	598	343	$15,204	$1,750.13	$238.63
	1981	1,744	210	7,255	150	174	7.6	49,427	19,736	802,963	618	354	$17,449	$2,071.57	$274.25
	1982	1,715	210	7,165	149	175	7.6	58,685	19,431	811,437	627	320	$19,893	$2,364.09	$311.56
	1983	1,679	207	7,025	145	170	7.6	48,816	18,777	795,767	613	360	$21,593	$2,621.28	$347.56
	1984	1,622	201	6,606	133	158	7.3	47,590	18,283	767,680	581	368	$22,271	$2,823.13	$385.17
	1985	1,578	189	6,028	119	145	7.2	47,386	17,352	747,008	561	387	$22,863	$3,106.14	$432.84
	1986	1,521	182	5,665	114	142	7.4	49,383	16,492	746,126	555	391	$24,143	$3,404.69	$466.17
	1987	1,509	180	5,507	113	144	7.5	51,544	15,986	738,510	573	399	$26,192	$3,717.77	$499.33
	1988	1,501	175	5,424	112	145	7.6	55,840	15,243	743,780	583	403	$28,474	$4,033.67	$538.63
	1989	1,466	170	5,253	110	145	7.7	57,179	14,746	753,478	589	406	$30,769	$4,430.12	$582.15
	1990	1,444	169	5,236	111	148	7.7	60,146	14,710	784,504	614	415	$34,198	$4,837.76	$634.45
	1991	1,429	168	5,084	108	148	7.8	62,670	13,847	760,286	630	424	$37,701	$5,339.75	$695.89
	1992	1,396	166	5,008	108	152	7.9	67,734	13,385	720,782	643	424	$41,806	$5,870.76	$753.92
	1993	1,390	169	5,054	109	157	7.8	71,811	13,445	704,854	676	430	$45,825	$6,205.52	$799.73
	1994	1,371	164	4,979	104	154	7.6	73,828	13,012	662,774	672	438	$48,115	$6,513.39	$858.62
	1995	1,350	157	4,961	100	154	7.4	78,554	12,374	630,718	670	435	$49,322	$6,445.18	$877.85
	1996	1,330	155	4,873	96	150	7.2	81,770	11,549	595,424	654	437	$49,420	$6,418.65	$903.41
	1997	1,260	148	4,720	92	148	7.1	79,007	10,731	578,186	640	433	$49,298	$6,475.07	$913.62
	1998	1,218	139	4,559	87	142	7.0	80,008	10,174	544,250	614	433	$49,123	$6,612.23	$949.36
	1999	1,197	136	4,583	86	143	6.9	84,667	9,870	546,257	614	430	$52,534	$6,923.35	$1,006.91
	2000	1,163	131	4,496	83	140	6.7	84,858	9,392	543,054	614	438	$54,544	$7,106.05	$1,063.75
	2001	1,156	132	4,634	85	145	6.7	88,873	9,395	549,035	637	438	$59,137	$7,400.01	$1,113.79
	2002	1,136	130	4,688	84	147	6.6	94,280	9,266	553,044	651	442	$63,783	$7,772.93	$1,188.12
	2003	1,121	129	4,634	84	152	6.6	94,725	9,206	545,385	658	434	$68,475	$8,205.10	$1,237.64
	2004	1,117	128	4,730	85	154	6.5	96,345	8,979	552,388	666	431	$72,861	$8,473.18	$1,291.06
	2005	1,110	128	4,740	85	161	6.5	96,760	8,896	564,782	681	424	$77,914	$8,793.26	$1,329.64
	2006	1,119	128	4,848	86	165	6.5	101,845	8,932	595,805	713	433	$83,974	$9,147.40	$1,400.09
	2007	1,111	131	4,967	87	169	6.4	103,532	9,105	615,290	747	443	$90,528	$9,523.22	$1,472.26
	2008	1,105	131	5,023	86	170	6.3	109,398	8,943	609,159	760	446	$96,735	$9,826.94	$1,552.32
	2009	1,092	127	4,857	83	168	6.2	108,738	8,850	583,845	751	447	$98,937	$10,067.96	$1,611.31
	2010	1,068	125	4,693	80	169	6.2	109,045	8,699	542,809	738	437	$100,056	$10,283.35	$1,624.93
	2011	1,045	121	4,598	78	170	6.2	109,423	8,502	529,435	738	434	$103,448	$10,531.65	$1,666.96
	2012	1,037	120	4,447	77	170	6.3	108,880	8,017	499,938	739	435	$113,843	$11,668.15	$1,831.00
	2013	1,033	118	4,247	74	163	6.3	108,854	7,946	489,541	796	451	$115,291	$12,014.95	$1,868.24
	2014	1,024	117	4,215	74	169	6.4	111,698	7,861	490,975	741	440	$121,147	$12,583.26	$1,969.61
	2015	1,003	118	4,197	74	173	6.4	116,460	7,580	486,792	766	442	$127,069	$13,051.3	$2,008.96
	2016	974	113	4,051	73	177	6.5	117,212	7,307	468,559	762	431	$132,357	$13,701.45	$2,047.97
	2017	972	111	4,084	72	180	6.4	121,026	7,118	459,354	783	434	$140,109	$14,014.85	$2,128.78

Table 2

2017 U.S. Hospitals: Utilization, Personnel, and Finances

Excludes U.S.-Associated Areas and Puerto Rico hospitals.

CLASSIFICATION	HOSPITALS	BEDS	ADMISSIONS	INPATIENT DAYS	ADJUSTED INPATIENT DAYS	AVERAGE DAILY CENSUS	ADJUSTED AVERAGE DAILY CENSUS	AVERAGE STAY (DAYS)	SURGICAL OPERATIONS	OUTPATIENT VISITS Emergency	OUTPATIENT VISITS Total	NEWBORNS Bassinets	NEWBORNS Births
UNITED STATES	6,210	931,203	36,510,207	224,035,179	—	613,775	—	—	28,996,129	150,158,619	880,451,166	55,801	3,693,124
6-24 Beds	818	13,412	340,146	1,769,146	—	4,853	—	—	797,169	3,057,466	21,154,222	612	21,026
25-49	1,424	46,722	1,264,750	7,787,647	—	21,332	—	—	1,746,685	10,149,909	61,452,575	3,075	115,203
50-99	1,205	85,570	2,483,492	17,901,127	—	49,038	—	—	2,287,318	12,872,027	80,749,576	4,932	213,096
100-199	1,247	177,398	6,533,123	40,380,391	—	110,620	—	—	5,055,795	31,520,607	164,784,463	11,554	628,592
200-299	629	153,591	6,292,136	36,467,237	—	99,905	—	—	4,641,677	25,884,532	137,917,244	9,890	652,444
300-399	370	128,121	5,603,701	31,491,969	—	86,276	—	—	3,750,738	21,446,186	101,797,163	8,343	607,994
400-499	195	86,646	3,775,493	22,020,079	—	60,333	—	—	2,830,883	13,269,915	84,719,550	5,204	411,062
500 or more	322	239,743	10,217,366	66,217,583	—	181,418	—	—	7,885,864	31,957,977	227,876,373	12,191	1,043,707
Psychiatric	631	85,220	1,219,155	25,736,688	—	70,509	—	—	9,121	142,923	12,109,350	0	0
Hospitals	624	82,489	1,218,695	24,874,275	—	68,147	—	—	9,121	142,923	12,109,350	0	0
Inst. for Intellectual Disabilities	7	2,731	460	862,413	—	2,362	—	—	0	0	0	0	0
General	4,680	788,056	34,174,612	184,719,653	—	506,068	—	—	27,903,170	148,958,570	846,669,112	55,099	3,629,993
Hospitals	4,665	786,861	34,127,971	184,441,640	—	505,308	—	—	27,885,134	148,800,052	845,935,981	55,099	3,629,993
Hospital units of institutions	15	1,195	46,641	278,013	—	760	—	—	18,036	158,518	733,131	0	0
TB and other respiratory diseases	2	107	97	11,307	—	31	—	—	0	0	114,167	0	0
Obstetrics and gynecology	9	1,621	77,906	367,546	—	1,007	—	—	57,353	160,181	1,282,250	542	49,874
Eye, ear, nose and throat	4	137	1,674	6,117	—	17	—	—	65,554	47,550	904,582	0	0
Rehabilitation	292	21,319	386,297	5,321,772	—	14,582	—	—	17,347	1	6,974,526	40	304
Orthopedic	45	1,646	81,462	229,873	—	630	—	—	238,415	93,059	1,723,541	0	0
Chronic Disease	5	296	1,223	50,221	—	137	—	—	32	5,143	61,612	0	0
Surgical	86	1,816	77,759	199,968	—	550	—	—	313,324	179,028	1,361,864	26	2,398
Cancer	18	2,592	108,250	769,856	—	2,110	—	—	114,289	29,735	6,029,317	0	0
Heart	17	1,071	52,562	213,767	—	587	—	—	49,915	75,344	703,099	0	0
Acute long-term care hospital	396	25,571	280,813	5,929,763	—	16,237	—	—	178,731	322,810	1,656,294	0	0
All other	25	1,751	48,397	478,648	—	1,310	—	—	48,878	144,275	861,452	94	10,555
Federal	208	38,184	883,685	9,645,769	—	26,427	—	—	732,335	4,868,001	103,998,134	615	36,081
Psychiatric	11	2,964	19,663	711,528	—	1,948	—	—	3,810	14,549	3,776,016	0	0
General and other special	197	35,220	864,022	8,934,241	—	24,479	—	—	728,525	4,853,452	100,222,118	615	36,081
Nonfederal	6,002	893,019	35,626,522	214,389,410	—	587,348	—	—	28,263,794	145,290,618	776,453,032	55,186	3,657,043
Psychiatric	620	82,256	1,199,492	25,025,160	—	68,561	—	—	5,311	128,374	8,333,334	0	0
Hospitals	613	79,525	1,199,032	24,162,747	—	66,199	—	—	5,311	128,374	8,333,334	0	0
Inst. for Intellectual Disabilities	7	2,731	460	862,413	—	2,362	—	—	0	0	0	0	0
TB and other respiratory diseases	2	107	97	11,307	13,989	31	39	116.6	0	0	114,167	—	0
Long-term general and other special	106	10,585	76,020	2,879,735	3,418,686	7,883	9,362	37.9	21,228	214,746	1,637,483	5	234
Short-term general and other special	5,274	800,071	34,350,913	186,473,208	398,845,189	510,873	1,092,883	5.4	28,237,255	144,947,498	766,368,048	55,181	3,656,809
Hospital units of institutions	12	1,150	45,293	274,231	274,231	750	750	6.1	15,481	132,694	291,924	0	0
Community Hospitals	5,262	798,921	34,305,620	186,198,977	398,570,958	510,123	1,092,133	5.4	28,221,774	144,814,804	766,076,124	55,181	3,656,809
6-24 Beds	702	11,420	286,420	1,311,383	6,846,711	3,600	18,761	4.6	774,323	2,826,451	16,731,987	547	16,930
25-49	1,280	41,577	1,152,958	6,524,153	23,850,533	17,874	65,391	5.7	1,709,387	9,597,498	57,703,781	2,937	111,036
50-99	958	67,626	2,009,164	13,205,034	37,425,559	36,178	102,553	6.6	2,156,594	11,821,744	61,918,852	4,731	206,130
100-199	1,004	144,449	5,832,423	31,065,823	74,221,522	85,093	203,455	5.3	4,912,898	30,807,241	143,457,653	11,465	618,215
200-299	525	128,567	5,901,380	29,357,896	60,712,002	80,428	166,330	5	4,461,640	24,991,925	115,243,059	9,763	641,735
300-399	326	112,745	5,423,160	27,202,964	51,610,599	74,526	141,398	5	3,641,000	20,167,290	89,244,372	8,343	607,994
400-499	178	78,819	3,702,602	19,681,221	37,639,464	53,926	103,123	5.3	2,783,841	13,024,540	77,067,953	5,204	411,062
500 or more	289	213,718	9,997,513	57,850,503	106,264,568	158,498	291,122	5.8	7,782,091	31,578,115	204,708,467	12,191	1,043,707
Nongovernment not-for-profit	2,968	545,129	24,788,938	130,397,929	280,300,460	357,258	768,081	5.3	20,416,355	103,251,806	581,847,862	39,744	2,710,049
Investor-owned (for profit)	1,322	142,386	5,432,727	29,696,387	52,453,921	81,349	143,726	5.5	4,325,617	21,738,320	63,202,739	8,319	487,406
State and Local Government	972	111,406	4,083,955	26,104,661	65,816,577	71,516	180,326	6.4	3,479,802	19,824,678	121,025,523	7,118	459,354

Table 2 (Continued)

CLASSIFICATION	FULL-TIME EQUIVALENT PERSONNEL					FULL-TIME EQUIVALENT TRAINEES			LABOR		EXPENSES			TOTAL	
	Physicians and Dentists	Registered Nurses	Licensed Practical Nurses	Other Salaried Personnel	Total Personnel	Medical and Dental Residents	Other Trainees	Total Trainees	Payroll (in thousands)	Employee Benefits (in thousands)	Total (in thousands)	Percent of Total	Amount (in thousands)	Adjusted Per Admission	Adjusted Per Inpatient Day
UNITED STATES	180,091	1,679,260	104,646	3,877,068	5,841,065	123,653	17,292	140,945	$407,411,845	$110,658,428	$518,070,272	48.8	$1,060,933,249	—	—
6-24 Beds	3,200	24,859	4,023	76,314	108,396	135	129	264	$6,441,177	$1,750,510	$8,191,687	45.7	$17,925,263	—	—
25-49	7,831	72,810	11,787	214,842	307,270	332	729	1,061	$18,546,357	$4,830,895	$23,377,252	48.8	$47,925,240	—	—
50-99	12,314	113,866	13,597	311,222	450,999	1,336	267	1,603	$28,628,323	$7,510,234	$36,138,557	50.5	$71,629,503	—	—
100-199	24,935	271,467	20,106	645,655	962,163	6,460	1,124	7,584	$64,874,806	$17,149,309	$82,024,115	49.1	$165,919,622	—	—
200-299	26,055	258,658	16,984	611,006	912,703	11,857	2,580	14,437	$62,750,295	$17,279,854	$80,030,149	49.4	$163,082,464	—	—
300-399	19,961	234,783	10,081	476,718	741,543	9,492	1,174	10,666	$53,427,353	$14,085,615	$67,512,968	47.4	$142,316,461	—	—
400-499	17,968	172,006	6,986	383,969	580,929	17,719	1,285	19,004	$44,519,953	$12,505,689	$57,025,642	49.0	$116,343,399	—	—
500 or more	67,827	530,811	21,082	1,157,342	1,777,062	76,322	10,004	86,326	$128,223,581	$35,546,321	$163,769,902	48.8	$335,791,298	—	—
Psychiatric	5,220	36,374	7,655	178,851	228,100	599	400	999	$12,299,069	$4,206,385	$16,505,453	68.0	$24,288,510	—	—
Hospitals	5,163	36,056	7,346	172,412	220,977	599	400	999	$12,063,963	$4,100,029	$16,163,992	67.7	$23,893,473	—	—
Inst. for Intellectual Disabilities	57	318	309	6,439	7,123	0	0	0	$235,106	$106,356	$341,462	86.4	$395,037	—	—
General	168,120	1,571,046	89,644	3,502,191	5,331,001	121,572	15,404	136,976	$376,076,928	$101,730,328	$477,807,256	48.4	$986,779,095	—	—
Hospitals	167,822	1,570,758	89,472	3,500,315	5,328,367	121,558	15,390	136,948	$375,876,320	$101,664,269	$477,540,588	48.4	$986,252,011	—	—
Hospital units of institutions	298	288	172	1,876	2,634	14	14	28	$200,608	$66,059	$266,668	50.6	$527,085	—	—
TB and other respiratory diseases	155	138	27	1,451	1,771	0	14	14	$134,467	$18,894	$153,361	57.5	$266,485	—	—
Obstetrics and gynecology	101	3,572	33	5,146	8,852	72	1	73	$683,910	$170,733	$854,643	39.9	$2,144,204	—	—
Eye, ear, nose and throat	181	469	10	2,850	3,510	115	47	162	$169,290	$54,904	$224,194	38.6	$580,581	—	—
Rehabilitation	867	18,223	1,888	56,710	77,688	396	32	428	$4,334,342	$1,036,472	$5,370,814	54.6	$9,836,831	—	—
Orthopedic	605	3,746	200	10,814	15,365	62	10	72	$1,289,058	$344,851	$1,633,909	46.5	$3,510,190	—	—
Chronic Disease	13	177	20	828	1,038	0	0	0	$62,509	$22,172	$84,681	63.8	$132,737	—	—
Surgical	74	4,331	190	8,071	12,666	0	0	0	$807,754	$180,454	$988,209	31.6	$3,126,903	—	—
Cancer	4,118	13,342	203	47,501	65,164	798	1,374	2,172	$5,496,209	$1,544,024	$7,040,233	45.2	$15,586,297	—	—
Heart	81	2,743	99	4,898	7,821	15	6	21	$545,908	$132,727	$678,635	40.2	$1,688,810	—	—
Acute long-term care hospital	266	21,876	4,505	50,226	76,873	4	3	7	$4,678,827	$971,301	$5,650,128	51.8	$10,915,646	—	—
All other	290	3,223	172	7,531	11,216	20	1	21	$833,573	$245,183	$1,078,755	51.9	$2,076,960	—	—
Federal	28,665	81,053	20,060	252,034	381,812	4,995	7,586	12,581	$30,071,826	$9,513,173	$39,584,999	58.5	$67,635,586	—	—
Psychiatric	779	2,665	814	11,677	15,935	61	150	211	$807,519	$259,943	$1,067,462	61.6	$1,734,280	—	—
General and other special	27,886	78,388	19,246	240,357	365,877	4,934	7,436	12,370	$29,264,307	$9,253,230	$38,517,538	58.4	$65,901,305	—	—
Nonfederal	151,426	1,598,207	84,586	3,625,034	5,459,253	118,658	9,706	128,364	$377,340,018	$101,145,255	$478,485,273	48.2	$993,297,663	—	—
Psychiatric	4,441	33,709	6,841	167,174	212,165	538	250	788	$11,491,550	$3,946,442	$15,437,992	68.4	$22,554,230	—	—
Hospitals	4,384	33,391	6,532	160,735	205,042	538	250	788	$11,256,444	$3,840,086	$15,096,530	68.1	$22,159,193	—	—
Inst. for Intellectual Disabilities	57	318	309	6,439	7,123	0	14	14	$235,106	$106,356	$341,462	86.4	$395,037	—	—
TB and other respiratory diseases	155	138	27	1,451	1,771	0	14	14	$134,467	$18,894	$153,361	57.5	$266,485	$206,257.54	$19,049.59
Long-term general and other special	323	6,207	1,069	20,406	28,005	45	2	47	$1,812,025	$473,467	$2,285,492	57.3	$3,985,210	$41,232.99	$1,165.71
Short-term general and other special	146,507	1,558,153	76,649	3,436,003	5,217,312	118,075	9,440	127,515	$363,901,977	$96,706,451	$460,608,428	47.7	$966,491,739	$13,121.85	$2,423.23
Hospital units of institutions	126	115	115	608	964	0	0	0	$95,833	$19,167	$115,000	40.0	$287,500	$6,347.56	$1,048.39
Community Hospitals	146,381	1,558,038	76,534	3,435,395	5,216,348	118,075	9,440	127,515	$363,806,143	$96,687,284	$460,493,428	47.7	$966,204,238	$13,126.02	$2,424.17
6-24 Beds	1,789	22,385	3,391	61,699	89,264	25	20	45	$5,293,310	$1,296,261	$6,589,571	43.0	$15,339,423	$9,618.64	$2,240.41
25-49	6,645	67,538	10,027	193,469	277,679	300	726	1,026	$16,865,654	$4,365,171	$21,230,826	48.4	$43,902,826	$9,395.26	$1,840.75
50-99	7,335	94,778	9,063	244,066	355,242	880	110	990	$22,402,119	$5,562,266	$27,964,385	49.0	$57,027,149	$9,592.06	$1,523.75
100-199	18,267	241,238	14,849	548,763	823,117	5,981	461	6,442	$54,558,154	$13,994,009	$68,552,163	47.9	$143,208,395	$10,521.74	$1,929.47
200-299	18,447	234,920	10,241	513,992	777,600	9,186	905	10,091	$54,547,779	$14,356,091	$68,903,871	47.7	$144,573,168	$11,929.55	$2,381.29
300-399	14,955	221,511	7,273	428,026	671,765	9,064	807	9,871	$48,255,132	$12,411,430	$60,666,561	46.5	$130,558,478	$12,750.73	$2,529.68
400-499	16,133	165,928	5,817	358,366	546,244	17,620	1,132	18,752	$41,441,946	$11,831,466	$53,273,412	48.4	$110,015,554	$15,579.24	$2,922.88
500 or more	62,810	509,740	15,873	1,087,014	1,675,437	75,019	5,279	80,298	$120,442,047	$32,870,591	$153,312,638	47.7	$321,579,245	$17,509.14	$3,026.21
Nongovernment not-for-profit	120,106	1,139,560	46,553	2,535,240	3,841,459	84,852	7,203	92,055	$271,277,861	$70,763,139	$342,041,000	47.4	$721,391,380	$13,503.97	$2,573.64
Investor-owned (for profit)	4,850	205,593	12,826	368,206	591,475	6,425	149	6,574	$38,044,740	$8,461,672	$46,506,412	44.4	$104,703,539	$10,273.14	$1,996.11
State and Local Government	21,425	212,885	17,155	531,949	783,414	26,798	2,088	28,886	$54,483,542	$17,462,473	$71,946,015	51.3	$140,109,320	$14,014.85	$2,128.78

Tables 3–6

Total U.S.

TABLE **3**

TOTAL UNITED STATES

U.S. Community Hospitals
(Nonfederal, short-term general and other special hospitals)

Overview 2013–2017

	2017	2016	2015	2014	2013
TOTAL U.S. Community Hospitals	5,262	5,267	5,280	5,308	5,359
Bed Size Category					
6-24	702	679	661	642	633
25-49	1,280	1,287	1,299	1,312	1,324
50-99	958	984	981	992	1,012
100-199	1,004	993	1,012	1,034	1,022
200-299	525	536	540	537	572
300-399	326	326	326	330	336
400-499	178	177	177	188	183
500 + ...	289	285	284	273	277
Location					
Hospitals Urban	3,387	3,385	3,393	3,402	3,326
Hospitals Rural....................................	1,875	1,882	1,887	1,906	2,033
Control					
State and Local Government	972	974	1,003	1,024	1,033
Not for Profit.......................................	2,968	2,943	2,932	2,943	2,975
Investor owned	1,322	1,350	1,345	1,341	1,351
Physician Models					
Independent Practice Association......................	531	534	532	504	493
Group Practice without Walls	137	162	161	203	192
Open Physician-Hospital Organization	601	590	574	592	612
Closed Physician-Hospital Organization..............	259	239	239	232	237
Management Service Organization	365	399	438	406	431
Integrated Salary Model.....................................	1,890	1,959	1,978	1,933	1,921
Equity Model	110	111	102	106	112
Foundation	287	306	300	292	309
Affiliations					
Hospitals in a System	3,494	3,467	3,418	3,376	3,322
Hospitals in a Network.......................................	1,749	1,750	1,728	1,664	1,624
Hospitals in a Group Purchasing Organization....	3,583	3,726	3,753	3,686	3,776

TABLE 3

TOTAL UNITED STATES

U.S. Community Hospitals
(Nonfederal, short-term general and other special hospitals)

Utilization, Personnel, Revenue and Expenses, Community Health Indicators 2013–2017

	2017	2016	2015	2014	2013
TOTAL FACILITY (Includes Hospital and Nursing Home Units)					
Utilization - Inpatient					
Beds	798,921	799,444	800,828	802,088	811,154
Admissions	34,305,620	34,031,587	33,817,285	33,516,951	34,062,869
Inpatient Days	186,198,977	186,089,454	185,171,082	183,342,577	185,325,318
Average Length of Stay	5.5	5.5	5.5	5.5	5.4
Inpatient Surgeries	9,146,015	9,163,230	9,090,300	9,156,859	9,279,901
Births	3,656,809	3,769,965	3,792,223	3,766,328	3,728,411
Utilization - Outpatient					
Emergency Outpatient Visits	144,814,804	144,842,743	143,472,685	137,807,901	134,869,015
Other Outpatient Visits	621,261,320	611,955,033	587,316,680	562,424,090	549,358,304
Total Outpatient Visits	766,076,124	756,797,776	730,789,365	700,231,991	684,227,319
Outpatient Surgeries	19,075,759	18,987,342	18,255,921	17,974,397	17,978,474
Personnel					
Full Time RNs	1,286,055	1,243,105	1,209,663	1,170,228	1,137,567
Full Time LPNs	65,258	65,671	65,168	64,001	68,296
Part Time RNs	543,927	530,458	511,318	502,481	500,762
Part Time LPNs	22,550	22,602	22,800	22,805	25,027
Total Full Time	4,536,326	4,428,178	4,316,593	4,211,435	4,183,224
Total Part Time	1,615,066	1,562,816	1,498,135	1,471,483	1,479,747
Revenue - Inpatient					
Gross Inpatient Revenue	$1,828,199,494,787	$1,724,871,915,665	$1,626,668,095,308	$1,514,448,739,994	$1,442,275,606,491
Revenue - Outpatient					
Gross Outpatient Revenue	$1,735,481,161,564	$1,595,298,023,801	$1,449,622,014,476	$1,308,063,724,756	$1,191,794,532,181
Revenue and Expenses - Totals					
(Includes Inpatient and Outpatient)*					
Total Gross Revenue	$3,563,680,656,351	$3,320,169,939,466	$3,076,290,109,784	$2,822,512,464,646	$2,634,070,124,255
Deductions from Revenue	2,593,749,705,025	2,390,464,007,070	2,193,434,642,349	1,995,060,443,704	1,841,289,570,089
Net Patient Revenue	969,930,951,326	929,705,932,396	882,855,467,435	827,452,020,942	792,780,554,166
Other Operating Revenue	62,161,422,278	56,838,224,377	53,572,386,431	51,424,932,121	50,437,309,016
Other Nonoperating Revenue	22,129,124,318	11,530,927,436	5,666,404,837	17,816,927,843	19,851,115,645
Total Net Revenue	1,054,221,497,922	998,075,084,209	942,094,258,703	896,693,880,906	863,068,978,827
Total Expenses	966,204,238,616	919,821,623,351	866,817,436,729	821,223,657,409	793,918,148,756
HOSPITAL UNIT (Excludes Separate Nursing Home Units)					
Utilization - Inpatient					
Beds	762,082	757,845	756,638	759,226	763,974
Admissions	34,177,056	33,879,304	33,658,444	33,348,036	33,873,069
Inpatient Days	174,595,676	172,927,585	171,607,055	169,893,546	170,456,884
Average Length of Stay	5.1	5.1	5.1	5.1	5
Personnel					
Total Full Time	4,510,522	4,401,015	4,288,501	4,177,566	4,149,830
Total Part Time	1,601,249	1,548,166	1,482,541	1,453,956	1,461,440
Revenue and Expenses - Totals					
(Includes Inpatient and Outpatient)					
Total Net Revenue	$1,050,729,351,406	$994,186,728,374	$937,897,597,460	$892,817,617,572	$858,937,579,004
Total Expenses	963,274,967,298	916,791,175,275	863,389,336,253	817,935,787,390	790,283,788,053
COMMUNITY HEALTH INDICATORS PER 1000 POPULATION					
Total Population (in thousands)	325,719	323,128	321,419	318,857	316,129
Inpatient					
Beds	2.5	2.5	2.5	2.5	2.6
Admissions	105.3	105.3	105.2	105.1	107.7
Inpatient Days	571.7	575.9	576.1	575.0	586.2
Inpatient Surgeries	28.1	28.4	28.3	28.7	29.4
Births	11.2	11.7	11.8	11.8	11.8
Outpatient					
Emergency Outpatient Visits	444.6	448.3	446.4	432.2	426.6
Other Outpatient Visits	1,907.4	1,893.8	1,827.3	1,763.9	1,737.8
Total Outpatient Visits	2,352	2,342.1	2,273.6	2,196.1	2,164.4
Outpatient Surgeries	58.6	58.8	56.8	56.4	56.9
Expense per Capita (per person)	$2,966.4	$2,846.6	$2,696.8	$2,575.5	$2,511.4

*Calculating the total margin using an aggregate average for all U.S. hospitals based on total revenue and expenses can be misleading and should be avoided. Individual hospital margins vary widely and are driven by a range of factors, including facility or system size and type; local payer mix; geographic location; patient demographics; services provided, both clinical and non-medical; and relationships and affiliations with other entities in the community.

TABLE 4

BED SIZE CATEGORY 6-24

U.S. Community Hospitals
(Nonfederal, short-term general and other special hospitals)

Overview 2013–2017

	2017	2016	2015	2014	2013
Total Community Hospitals in					
Bed Size Category 6-24................................	702	679	661	642	633
Location					
Hospitals Urban	296	280	271	267	248
Hospitals Rural	406	399	390	375	385
Control					
State and Local Government	207	200	189	183	182
Not for Profit...	305	290	284	278	263
Investor owned	190	189	188	181	188
Physician Models					
Independent Practice Association......................	58	57	48	46	46
Group Practice without Walls	12	16	14	16	15
Open Physician-Hospital Organization	50	40	32	37	36
Closed Physician-Hospital Organization............	18	17	19	10	7
Management Service Organization	17	19	19	17	16
Integrated Salary Model....................................	207	214	208	198	175
Equity Model	12	15	9	7	14
Foundation	15	18	12	19	18
Affiliations					
Hospitals in a System	315	299	288	275	255
Hospitals in a Network......................................	178	179	172	160	156
Hospitals in a Group Purchasing Organization...	426	438	415	405	408

TABLE 4

BED SIZE CATEGORY 6-24

U.S. Community Hospitals
(Nonfederal, short-term general and other special hospitals)

Utilization, Personnel, Revenue and Expenses, Community Health Indicators 2013–2017

	2017	2016	2015	2014	2013
TOTAL FACILITY (Includes Hospital and Nursing Home Units)					
Utilization - Inpatient					
Beds	11,420	11,113	10,774	10,422	10,346
Admissions	286,420	274,695	269,510	253,997	263,323
Inpatient Days	1,311,383	1,276,782	1,249,593	1,208,035	1,199,688
Average Length of Stay	4.6	4.6	4.6	4.8	4.6
Inpatient Surgeries	96,791	93,894	85,293	80,228	77,141
Births	16,930	17,632	16,291	15,491	16,520
Utilization - Outpatient					
Emergency Outpatient Visits	2,826,451	2,518,497	2,417,585	2,248,899	2,213,365
Other Outpatient Visits	13,905,536	12,632,030	11,522,438	10,993,777	10,403,231
Total Outpatient Visits	16,731,987	15,150,527	13,940,023	13,242,676	12,616,596
Outpatient Surgeries	677,532	741,276	717,094	635,126	609,901
Personnel					
Full Time RNs	16,675	15,747	15,235	14,696	13,871
Full Time LPNs	2,742	2,708	2,678	2,530	2,625
Part Time RNs	11,384	10,194	9,731	8,820	8,440
Part Time LPNs	1,283	1,110	1,175	1,040	1,139
Total Full Time	71,027	67,929	64,546	61,960	59,558
Total Part Time	36,550	33,843	31,925	30,598	28,870
Revenue - Inpatient					
Gross Inpatient Revenue	$9,778,688,709	$9,142,081,581	$9,088,328,423	$7,550,604,454	$7,167,411,594
Revenue - Outpatient					
Gross Outpatient Revenue	$29,547,336,214	$26,198,110,530	$23,331,509,886	$20,159,171,842	$17,987,227,910
Revenue and Expenses - Totals **(Includes Inpatient and Outpatient)**					
Total Gross Revenue	$39,326,024,923	$35,340,192,111	$32,419,838,309	$27,709,776,296	$25,154,639,504
Deductions from Revenue	24,219,961,379	21,589,046,761	19,509,123,127	16,237,003,376	14,410,870,764
Net Patient Revenue	15,106,063,544	13,751,145,350	12,910,715,182	11,472,772,920	10,743,768,740
Other Operating Revenue	1,173,202,312	1,065,907,619	1,006,317,298	948,174,729	830,863,019
Other Nonoperating Revenue	264,323,188	156,929,101	125,822,443	193,242,895	170,243,555
Total Net Revenue	16,543,589,044	14,973,982,070	14,042,854,923	12,614,190,544	11,744,875,314
Total Expenses	15,339,422,895	13,691,403,067	12,655,032,137	11,526,687,099	10,683,441,660
HOSPITAL UNIT (Excludes Separate Nursing Home Units)					
Utilization - Inpatient					
Beds	11,388	11,099	10,736	10,398	10,296
Admissions	286,401	274,656	269,488	253,835	263,292
Inpatient Days	1,299,954	1,264,707	1,235,131	1,182,983	1,184,018
Average Length of Stay	4.5	4.6	4.6	4.7	4.5
Personnel					
Total Full Time	70,900	67,875	64,420	61,832	59,180
Total Part Time	36,502	33,814	31,820	30,507	28,418
Revenue and Expenses - Totals **(Includes Inpatient and Outpatient)**					
Total Net Revenue	$16,534,305,204	$14,970,628,566	$14,029,507,210	$12,607,354,684	$11,739,011,631
Total Expenses	15,330,350,410	13,689,670,442	12,647,866,538	11,521,146,459	10,680,414,248

Bed Size Categories

TABLE 4

BED SIZE CATEGORY 25-49

U.S. Community Hospitals
(Nonfederal, short-term general and other special hospitals)

Overview 2013–2017

	2017	2016	2015	2014	2013
Total Community Hospitals in					
Bed Size Category 25-49..............................	1,280	1,287	1,299	1,312	1,324
Location					
Hospitals Urban	525	534	549	541	532
Hospitals Rural..	755	753	750	771	792
Control					
State and Local Government	345	348	358	371	372
Not for Profit..	599	602	598	596	602
Investor owned..	336	337	343	345	350
Physician Models					
Independent Practice Association......................	90	109	103	99	96
Group Practice without Walls	27	31	28	38	32
Open Physician-Hospital Organization	88	84	74	77	76
Closed Physician-Hospital Organization	40	38	36	37	38
Management Service Organization	47	55	60	56	53
Integrated Salary Model.................................	391	400	415	410	393
Equity Model	12	14	12	14	15
Foundation	42	47	43	46	50
Affiliations					
Hospitals in a System	744	735	722	727	716
Hospitals in a Network	347	359	347	349	342
Hospitals in a Group Purchasing Organization...	825	856	864	850	861

TABLE 4

BED SIZE CATEGORY 25-49

U.S. Community Hospitals
(Nonfederal, short-term general and other special hospitals)

Utilization, Personnel, Revenue and Expenses, Community Health Indicators 2013–2017

	2017	2016	2015	2014	2013
TOTAL FACILITY (Includes Hospital and Nursing Home Units)					
Utilization - Inpatient					
Beds	41,577	41,873	42,432	42,686	42,957
Admissions	1,152,958	1,158,573	1,174,221	1,156,278	1,194,154
Inpatient Days	6,524,153	6,664,309	6,843,482	6,828,346	6,930,308
Average Length of Stay	5.7	5.8	5.8	5.9	5.8
Inpatient Surgeries	277,388	274,982	265,572	247,463	260,201
Births	111,036	117,092	117,682	118,277	118,810
Utilization - Outpatient					
Emergency Outpatient Visits	9,597,498	9,627,150	9,588,377	9,066,831	8,791,008
Other Outpatient Visits	48,106,283	45,989,021	43,712,954	40,340,090	40,104,504
Total Outpatient Visits	57,703,781	55,616,171	53,301,331	49,406,921	48,895,512
Outpatient Surgeries	1,431,999	1,438,892	1,315,512	1,289,034	1,259,432
Personnel					
Full Time RNs	52,041	51,219	50,240	48,560	48,496
Full Time LPNs	8,226	8,386	8,590	8,717	8,954
Part Time RNs	30,989	29,900	29,568	28,801	27,498
Part Time LPNs	3,615	3,603	3,603	3,522	3,445
Total Full Time	224,884	224,394	220,934	214,920	216,340
Total Part Time	107,614	104,414	101,989	98,542	95,570
Revenue - Inpatient					
Gross Inpatient Revenue	$42,200,271,489	$40,859,498,214	$36,665,977,457	$35,129,544,487	$33,430,103,295
Revenue - Outpatient					
Gross Outpatient Revenue	$80,927,112,832	$73,479,316,580	$65,092,119,761	$59,269,188,314	$54,720,061,978
Revenue and Expenses - Totals					
(Includes Inpatient and Outpatient)					
Total Gross Revenue	$123,127,384,321	$114,338,814,794	$101,758,097,218	$94,398,732,801	$88,150,165,273
Deductions from Revenue	79,919,021,230	72,521,186,543	62,405,035,622	57,500,768,989	52,646,333,190
Net Patient Revenue	43,208,363,091	41,817,628,251	39,353,061,596	36,897,963,812	35,503,832,083
Other Operating Revenue	3,437,207,504	3,165,988,389	3,381,277,188	2,943,457,002	2,881,577,946
Other Nonoperating Revenue	800,579,184	453,216,555	290,603,836	642,301,035	643,312,279
Total Net Revenue	47,446,149,779	45,436,833,195	43,024,942,620	40,483,721,849	39,028,722,308
Total Expenses	43,902,826,128	41,990,899,330	39,447,143,677	37,227,195,822	36,064,356,682
HOSPITAL UNIT (Excludes Separate Nursing Home Units)					
Utilization - Inpatient					
Beds	40,507	40,782	41,006	41,169	41,514
Admissions	1,151,645	1,156,428	1,170,796	1,152,940	1,191,437
Inpatient Days	6,205,300	6,327,160	6,405,967	6,379,318	6,456,827
Average Length of Stay	5.4	5.5	5.5	5.5	5.4
Personnel					
Total Full Time	224,119	223,573	219,983	213,860	215,350
Total Part Time	107,091	103,857	101,417	97,843	94,781
Revenue and Expenses - Totals					
(Includes Inpatient and Outpatient)					
Total Net Revenue	$47,361,509,525	$45,355,140,097	$42,931,418,685	$40,372,108,900	$38,920,471,642
Total Expenses	43,844,827,581	41,929,469,606	39,367,348,971	37,134,760,357	35,963,875,665

TABLE 4

BED SIZE CATEGORY 50-99

U.S. Community Hospitals
(Nonfederal, short-term general and other special hospitals)

Overview 2013–2017

	2017	2016	2015	2014	2013
Total Community Hospitals in					
Bed Size Category 50-99..................................	958	984	981	992	1,012
Location					
Hospitals Urban	566	579	567	579	551
Hospitals Rural...	392	405	414	413	461
Control					
State and Local Government.............................	152	157	170	177	185
Not for Profit...	472	471	474	478	486
Investor owned..	334	356	337	337	341
Physician Models					
Independent Practice Association......................	51	58	55	55	58
Group Practice without Walls	15	19	18	25	20
Open Physician-Hospital Organization	83	88	89	92	100
Closed Physician-Hospital Organization.............	27	25	29	30	31
Management Service Organization	43	46	57	49	47
Integrated Salary Model..................................	275	300	301	303	305
Equity Model	11	13	11	14	11
Foundation	34	39	39	34	37
Affiliations					
Hospitals in a System......................................	649	667	656	655	652
Hospitals in a Network.....................................	240	243	251	257	267
Hospitals in a Group Purchasing Organization...	591	651	656	645	677

TABLE 4

BED SIZE CATEGORY 50-99

U.S. Community Hospitals
(Nonfederal, short-term general and other special hospitals)

Utilization, Personnel, Revenue and Expenses, Community Health Indicators 2013–2017

	2017	2016	2015	2014	2013
TOTAL FACILITY (Includes Hospital and Nursing Home Units)					
Utilization - Inpatient					
Beds	67,626	69,353	69,428	69,940	71,375
Admissions	2,009,164	2,051,600	2,068,108	2,041,086	2,126,223
Inpatient Days	13,205,034	13,757,454	13,944,884	13,896,288	14,322,449
Average Length of Stay	6.6	6.7	6.7	6.8	6.7
Inpatient Surgeries	463,475	477,900	475,783	475,272	492,410
Births	206,130	217,012	223,851	229,940	232,423
Utilization - Outpatient					
Emergency Outpatient Visits	11,821,744	12,325,400	12,300,312	12,042,749	12,049,524
Other Outpatient Visits	50,097,108	49,763,388	50,061,523	49,068,125	47,283,810
Total Outpatient Visits	61,918,852	62,088,788	62,361,835	61,110,874	59,333,334
Outpatient Surgeries	1,693,119	1,677,328	1,627,896	1,630,144	1,604,814
Personnel					
Full Time RNs	73,880	73,248	70,989	70,260	69,176
Full Time LPNs	7,493	7,875	7,521	7,490	8,274
Part Time RNs	41,802	40,239	38,553	38,102	37,730
Part Time LPNs	3,130	3,228	3,296	3,203	3,662
Total Full Time	288,891	288,209	282,937	279,261	279,717
Total Part Time	134,689	133,104	129,805	128,255	129,565
Revenue - Inpatient					
Gross Inpatient Revenue	$75,850,968,886	$78,004,363,998	$72,496,665,325	$66,708,782,076	$64,842,041,025
Revenue - Outpatient					
Gross Outpatient Revenue	$116,294,503,085	$108,608,744,641	$99,303,107,157	$89,334,829,686	$82,092,199,118
Revenue and Expenses - Totals					
(Includes Inpatient and Outpatient)					
Total Gross Revenue	$192,145,471,971	$186,613,108,639	$171,799,772,482	$156,043,611,658	$146,934,240,143
Deductions from Revenue	133,443,528,400	129,271,400,259	116,619,928,734	104,101,681,042	96,421,159,273
Net Patient Revenue	58,701,943,571	57,341,708,380	55,179,843,748	51,941,930,616	50,513,080,870
Other Operating Revenue	2,841,250,532	2,407,584,609	2,297,948,097	2,600,860,596	2,538,519,387
Other Nonoperating Revenue	976,628,990	1,010,087,635	474,657,665	1,357,991,688	777,836,918
Total Net Revenue	62,519,823,093	60,759,380,624	57,952,449,510	55,900,782,900	53,829,437,175
Total Expenses	57,027,149,040	55,024,483,921	52,625,115,630	50,447,690,484	48,767,737,565
HOSPITAL UNIT (Excludes Separate Nursing Home Units)					
Utilization - Inpatient					
Beds	60,921	61,412	61,225	61,813	62,785
Admissions	1,997,189	2,035,369	2,052,732	2,024,730	2,109,537
Inpatient Days	11,110,149	11,301,269	11,443,238	11,406,836	11,654,751
Average Length of Stay	5.6	5.6	5.6	5.6	5.5
Personnel					
Total Full Time	284,814	283,403	278,170	273,985	274,776
Total Part Time	131,682	129,831	126,385	124,265	125,789
Revenue and Expenses - Totals					
(Includes Inpatient and Outpatient)					
Total Net Revenue	$61,992,352,547	$60,176,787,492	$57,370,883,476	$55,299,163,607	$53,253,633,149
Total Expenses	56,620,413,956	54,587,299,929	52,175,749,266	49,987,503,221	48,305,792,827

Bed Size Categories

TABLE **4**

BED SIZE CATEGORY 100-199

U.S. Community Hospitals
(Nonfederal, short-term general and other special hospitals)

Overview 2013–2017

	2017	2016	2015	2014	2013
Total Community Hospitals in					
Bed Size Category 100-199	1,004	993	1,012	1,034	1,022
Location					
Hospitals Urban	754	741	759	774	736
Hospitals Rural	250	252	253	260	286
Control					
State and Local Government	112	120	128	129	124
Not for Profit	630	614	615	637	635
Investor owned	262	259	269	268	263
Physician Models					
Independent Practice Association	109	89	115	103	94
Group Practice without Walls	30	30	32	42	39
Open Physician-Hospital Organization	130	130	128	147	141
Closed Physician-Hospital Organization	56	48	46	48	46
Management Service Organization	85	83	94	89	92
Integrated Salary Model	363	370	386	373	360
Equity Model	27	25	25	25	26
Foundation	70	62	66	64	72
Affiliations					
Hospitals in a System	769	751	755	742	711
Hospitals in a Network	343	339	345	327	299
Hospitals in a Group Purchasing Organization	688	696	722	722	723

TABLE 4

BED SIZE CATEGORY 100-199

U.S. Community Hospitals
(Nonfederal, short-term general and other special hospitals)

Utilization, Personnel, Revenue and Expenses, Community Health Indicators 2013–2017

	2017	2016	2015	2014	2013
TOTAL FACILITY (Includes Hospital and Nursing Home Units)					
Utilization - Inpatient					
Beds	144,449	143,276	146,402	150,085	147,371
Admissions	5,832,423	5,792,440	5,874,950	5,971,095	5,888,439
Inpatient Days	31,065,823	30,839,169	31,197,826	31,568,902	30,923,784
Average Length of Stay	5.3	5.3	5.3	5.3	5.3
Inpatient Surgeries	1,393,776	1,410,645	1,432,005	1,523,740	1,498,569
Births	618,215	661,966	685,860	694,581	664,081
Utilization - Outpatient					
Emergency Outpatient Visits	30,807,241	30,347,648	30,524,600	29,135,894	27,677,866
Other Outpatient Visits	112,650,412	108,921,984	105,452,877	106,205,824	97,452,463
Total Outpatient Visits	143,457,653	139,269,632	135,977,477	135,341,718	125,130,329
Outpatient Surgeries	3,519,122	3,468,590	3,428,174	3,516,221	3,475,743
Personnel					
Full Time RNs	195,418	188,253	186,608	182,583	172,844
Full Time LPNs	12,714	12,961	12,986	12,606	13,223
Part Time RNs	91,651	89,108	89,124	90,603	87,201
Part Time LPNs	4,284	4,490	4,785	4,750	5,333
Total Full Time	685,798	664,767	657,239	664,264	632,097
Total Part Time	287,514	272,582	268,823	275,384	267,420
Revenue - Inpatient					
Gross Inpatient Revenue	$261,616,656,494	$244,638,343,616	$242,773,915,327	$229,824,114,767	$213,123,944,557
Revenue - Outpatient					
Gross Outpatient Revenue	$308,226,085,579	$283,794,182,313	$263,510,107,907	$242,900,266,854	$212,986,777,931
Revenue and Expenses - Totals					
(Includes Inpatient and Outpatient)					
Total Gross Revenue	$569,842,742,073	$528,432,525,929	$506,284,023,234	$472,724,381,621	$426,110,708,071
Deductions from Revenue	421,195,235,299	385,763,913,509	369,351,494,568	339,282,028,755	302,830,859,572
Net Patient Revenue	148,647,506,774	142,668,612,420	136,932,528,666	133,442,352,866	123,279,848,499
Other Operating Revenue	6,069,573,210	5,538,614,499	5,297,327,380	5,984,263,286	5,601,755,244
Other Nonoperating Revenue	2,384,719,238	1,588,767,597	1,087,873,784	2,299,712,733	2,611,346,431
Total Net Revenue	157,101,799,222	149,795,994,516	143,317,729,830	141,726,328,885	131,492,950,174
Total Expenses	143,208,395,246	137,745,139,413	131,156,836,622	129,764,786,126	120,335,727,093
HOSPITAL UNIT (Excludes Separate Nursing Home Units)					
Utilization - Inpatient					
Beds	133,173	131,565	133,813	138,256	135,334
Admissions	5,798,467	5,754,004	5,833,603	5,934,151	5,847,451
Inpatient Days	27,530,031	27,043,414	27,180,189	27,921,054	27,188,731
Average Length of Stay	4.7	4.7	4.7	4.7	4.6
Personnel					
Total Full Time	678,751	657,840	649,799	656,721	624,373
Total Part Time	283,425	268,422	264,301	270,732	262,484
Revenue and Expenses - Totals					
(Includes Inpatient and Outpatient)					
Total Net Revenue	$156,120,327,656	$148,749,917,312	$142,258,138,929	$140,866,893,057	$130,637,155,151
Total Expenses	142,388,712,781	136,974,942,673	130,325,913,440	129,041,881,269	119,585,803,344

TABLE 4

BED SIZE CATEGORY 200-299

U.S. Community Hospitals
(Nonfederal, short-term general and other special hospitals)

Overview 2013–2017

	2017	2016	2015	2014	2013
Total Community Hospitals In					
Bed Size Category 200-299..............................	525	536	540	537	572
Location					
Hospitals Urban	474	483	480	468	487
Hospitals Rural.......................................	51	53	60	69	85
Control					
State and Local Government	56	47	49	58	57
Not for Profit...	362	376	377	365	399
Investor owned	107	113	114	114	116
Physician Models					
Independent Practice Association.......................	71	72	70	63	65
Group Practice without Walls	17	23	26	26	28
Open Physician-Hospital Organization	93	92	93	83	91
Closed Physician-Hospital Organization............	32	34	32	26	38
Management Service Organization	57	74	70	63	73
Integrated Salary Model................................	218	234	229	221	247
Equity Model	16	13	15	14	20
Foundation	41	47	47	40	46
Affiliations					
Hospitals in a System	398	408	401	393	411
Hospitals in a Network................................	222	220	212	190	197
Hospitals in a Group Purchasing Organization...	379	410	413	378	418

TABLE 4

BED SIZE CATEGORY 200-299

U.S. Community Hospitals
(Nonfederal, short-term general and other special hospitals)

Utilization, Personnel, Revenue and Expenses, Community Health Indicators 2013–2017

	2017	2016	2015	2014	2013
TOTAL FACILITY (Includes Hospital and Nursing Home Units)					
Utilization - Inpatient					
Beds	128,567	130,944	132,511	131,746	140,333
Admissions	5,901,380	5,899,749	5,961,613	5,760,717	6,157,637
Inpatient Days	29,357,896	29,685,052	30,185,830	29,569,980	31,480,295
Average Length of Stay	5.0	5.0	5.1	5.1	5.1
Inpatient Surgeries	1,477,047	1,543,196	1,556,491	1,523,670	1,623,431
Births	641,735	669,548	681,351	658,373	668,891
Utilization - Outpatient					
Emergency Outpatient Visits	24,991,925	25,357,995	25,394,219	24,481,880	24,975,730
Other Outpatient Visits	90,251,134	92,626,063	88,712,242	81,281,903	87,945,698
Total Outpatient Visits	115,243,059	117,984,058	114,106,461	105,763,783	112,921,428
Outpatient Surgeries	2,984,593	3,037,046	2,973,379	2,839,857	2,999,674
Personnel					
Full Time RNs	191,481	188,761	185,992	178,794	181,500
Full Time LPNs	8,848	8,731	8,965	8,810	10,052
Part Time RNs	86,857	87,628	85,457	80,271	87,944
Part Time LPNs	2,781	3,002	3,190	3,309	3,698
Total Full Time	663,746	658,090	646,286	613,480	647,864
Total Part Time	247,905	250,868	247,434	230,920	254,173
Revenue - Inpatient					
Gross Inpatient Revenue	$293,205,465,736	$288,233,540,105	$275,115,799,389	$248,360,114,982	$244,036,474,221
Revenue - Outpatient					
Gross Outpatient Revenue	$274,681,515,373	$260,731,807,994	$239,981,662,067	$211,653,531,352	$200,235,561,475
Revenue and Expenses - Totals					
(Includes Inpatient and Outpatient)					
Total Gross Revenue	$567,886,981,109	$548,965,348,099	$515,097,461,456	$460,013,646,334	$444,272,035,696
Deductions from Revenue	422,295,188,737	406,609,958,906	377,088,997,065	335,189,138,859	316,428,605,580
Net Patient Revenue	145,591,792,372	142,355,389,193	138,008,464,391	124,824,507,475	127,843,430,116
Other Operating Revenue	8,558,847,012	7,590,883,742	7,089,406,292	6,649,234,119	6,482,580,894
Other Nonoperating Revenue	2,997,312,305	1,121,754,713	661,460,068	3,014,665,295	2,877,558,570
Total Net Revenue	157,147,951,689	151,068,027,648	145,759,330,751	134,488,406,889	137,203,569,580
Total Expenses	144,573,168,126	139,577,553,074	133,990,565,452	122,901,646,818	127,021,878,096
HOSPITAL UNIT (Excludes Separate Nursing Home Units)					
Utilization - Inpatient					
Beds	123,225	124,879	125,940	124,662	132,659
Admissions	5,879,090	5,870,263	5,929,111	5,723,625	6,115,888
Inpatient Days	27,713,594	27,774,329	28,108,010	27,380,991	29,093,808
Average Length of Stay	4.7	4.7	4.7	4.8	4.8
Personnel					
Total Full Time	659,895	653,525	641,497	607,125	642,238
Total Part Time	246,062	248,463	244,907	227,762	251,572
Revenue and Expenses - Totals					
(Includes Inpatient and Outpatient)					
Total Net Revenue	$156,626,396,116	$150,481,613,192	$145,108,108,511	$133,856,813,403	$136,514,839,660
Total Expenses	144,165,193,240	139,115,462,086	133,426,533,719	122,377,385,375	126,423,473,062

TABLE 4

BED SIZE CATEGORY 300-399

U.S. Community Hospitals
(Nonfederal, short-term general and other special hospitals)

Overview 2013–2017

	2017	2016	2015	2014	2013
Total Community Hospitals in Bed Size Category 300-399............................	326	326	326	330	336
Location					
Hospitals Urban	313	311	311	317	318
Hospitals Rural..	13	15	15	13	18
Control					
State and Local Government.....................	24	28	31	29	37
Not for Profit...	251	241	239	244	243
Investor owned	51	57	56	57	56
Physician Models					
Independent Practice Association......................	53	45	44	51	47
Group Practice without Walls	8	13	13	21	24
Open Physician-Hospital Organization	65	66	69	66	70
Closed Physician-Hospital Organization.............	31	23	18	25	25
Management Service Organization	40	39	39	39	49
Integrated Salary Model..................................	152	152	161	156	162
Equity Model	9	13	12	14	6
Foundation	38	34	39	37	31
Affiliations					
Hospitals in a System	257	252	251	241	239
Hospitals in a Network..................................	153	149	152	153	135
Hospitals in a Group Purchasing Organization...	259	258	267	278	280

TABLE **4**

BED SIZE CATEGORY 300-399

U.S. Community Hospitals
(Nonfederal, short-term general and other special hospitals)

Utilization, Personnel, Revenue and Expenses, Community Health Indicators 2013–2017

	2017	2016	2015	2014	2013
TOTAL FACILITY (Includes Hospital and Nursing Home Units)					
Utilization - Inpatient					
Beds	112,745	112,577	112,455	113,594	116,247
Admissions	5,423,160	5,331,203	5,262,176	5,222,120	5,376,310
Inpatient Days	27,202,964	27,121,803	26,795,261	26,731,664	27,507,501
Average Length of Stay	5.0	5.1	5.1	5.1	5.1
Inpatient Surgeries	1,344,675	1,359,326	1,357,395	1,416,580	1,428,854
Births	607,994	613,760	615,418	605,018	616,591
Utilization - Outpatient					
Emergency Outpatient Visits	20,167,290	20,499,067	20,225,688	19,584,356	18,996,072
Other Outpatient Visits	69,077,082	65,722,792	67,637,921	66,311,908	71,077,740
Total Outpatient Visits	89,244,372	86,221,859	87,863,609	85,896,264	90,073,812
Outpatient Surgeries	2,296,325	2,286,604	2,241,108	2,230,790	2,322,791
Personnel					
Full Time RNs	186,324	179,329	172,767	167,838	166,507
Full Time LPNs	6,370	6,889	6,586	6,962	7,595
Part Time RNs	70,363	69,248	67,627	71,722	69,494
Part Time LPNs	1,810	1,890	1,874	2,110	2,230
Total Full Time	583,150	576,077	562,350	561,480	575,147
Total Part Time	196,975	194,564	186,034	196,327	192,304
Revenue - Inpatient					
Gross Inpatient Revenue	$304,818,908,631	$280,597,556,752	$265,645,362,957	$251,553,353,566	$242,304,761,782
Revenue - Outpatient					
Gross Outpatient Revenue	$244,167,243,699	$222,604,869,777	$207,236,507,753	$188,549,199,403	$176,107,438,163
Revenue and Expenses - Totals					
(Includes Inpatient and Outpatient)					
Total Gross Revenue	$548,986,152,330	$503,202,426,529	$472,881,870,710	$440,102,552,969	$418,412,199,945
Deductions from Revenue	416,336,037,183	375,800,264,832	350,115,114,752	321,837,704,800	302,186,344,683
Net Patient Revenue	132,650,115,147	127,402,161,697	122,766,755,958	118,264,848,169	116,225,855,262
Other Operating Revenue	6,345,361,823	6,462,417,145	5,932,273,631	6,040,541,269	6,940,998,130
Other Nonoperating Revenue	2,808,947,575	1,440,869,063	579,235,644	2,212,710,308	3,467,770,541
Total Net Revenue	141,804,424,545	135,305,447,905	129,278,265,233	126,518,099,746	126,634,623,933
Total Expenses	130,558,477,866	125,675,146,111	119,036,254,837	114,827,947,507	115,067,903,393
HOSPITAL UNIT (Excludes Separate Nursing Home Units)					
Utilization - Inpatient					
Beds	109,507	109,709	108,969	109,589	111,341
Admissions	5,403,146	5,311,011	5,240,771	5,193,815	5,343,977
Inpatient Days	26,229,602	26,253,272	25,845,364	25,519,588	26,060,336
Average Length of Stay	4.9	4.9	4.9	4.9	4.9
Personnel					
Total Full Time	580,848	574,021	559,783	557,207	571,113
Total Part Time	195,980	193,655	184,990	194,945	190,612
Revenue and Expenses - Totals					
(Includes Inpatient and Outpatient)					
Total Net Revenue	$141,392,172,422	$134,954,919,007	$128,804,888,548	$125,896,983,847	$126,052,364,907
Total Expenses	130,265,500,477	125,428,359,609	118,779,535,305	114,356,635,114	114,596,811,356

TABLE 4

BED SIZE CATEGORY 400-499

U.S. Community Hospitals
(Nonfederal, short-term general and other special hospitals)

Overview 2013–2017

	2017	2016	2015	2014	2013
Total Community Hospitals in					
Bed Size Category 400-499............................	178	177	177	188	183
Location					
Hospitals Urban	174	174	174	185	179
Hospitals Rural..	4	3	3	3	4
Control					
State and Local Government	25	24	27	31	30
Not for Profit...	131	132	131	138	135
Investor owned	22	21	19	19	18
Physician Models					
Independent Practice Association......................	45	44	40	34	30
Group Practice without Walls	16	18	14	15	16
Open Physician-Hospital Organization	30	29	29	33	36
Closed Physician-Hospital Organization............	14	16	22	20	20
Management Service Organization	30	28	34	34	35
Integrated Salary Model....................................	89	96	92	103	98
Equity Model	8	7	6	7	7
Foundation	23	29	27	24	27
Affiliations					
Hospitals in a System	133	132	132	141	135
Hospitals in a Network.......................................	99	98	90	85	85
Hospitals in a Group Purchasing Organization...	150	155	152	162	154

TABLE 4

BED SIZE CATEGORY 400-499

U.S. Community Hospitals
(Nonfederal, short-term general and other special hospitals)

Utilization, Personnel, Revenue and Expenses, Community Health Indicators 2013–2017

	2017	2016	2015	2014	2013
TOTAL FACILITY (Includes Hospital and Nursing Home Units)					
Utilization - Inpatient					
Beds	78,819	78,381	78,276	83,285	81,148
Admissions	3,702,602	3,635,759	3,623,728	3,899,412	3,750,238
Inpatient Days	19,681,221	19,526,076	19,473,188	20,633,887	20,029,447
Average Length of Stay	5.3	5.4	5.4	5.3	5.3
Inpatient Surgeries	1,068,403	1,023,758	1,010,724	1,084,572	1,038,085
Births	411,062	423,939	411,527	461,565	417,270
Utilization - Outpatient					
Emergency Outpatient Visits	13,024,540	13,365,313	12,899,493	13,464,443	12,285,620
Other Outpatient Visits	64,043,413	63,490,384	60,672,737	64,482,715	59,073,331
Total Outpatient Visits	77,067,953	76,855,697	73,572,230	77,947,158	71,358,951
Outpatient Surgeries	1,715,438	1,731,964	1,657,487	1,748,750	1,607,610
Personnel					
Full Time RNs	133,957	130,381	130,384	136,099	125,451
Full Time LPNs	4,922	4,685	5,331	5,063	5,246
Part Time RNs	63,947	62,368	55,114	56,071	54,284
Part Time LPNs	1,791	1,637	1,672	1,612	1,992
Total Full Time	475,228	459,454	455,341	468,458	440,221
Total Part Time	179,541	168,874	148,821	153,436	152,826
Revenue - Inpatient					
Gross Inpatient Revenue	$210,182,049,797	$195,381,045,588	$180,553,181,341	$178,999,206,730	$165,377,218,755
Revenue - Outpatient					
Gross Outpatient Revenue	$179,560,208,114	$165,777,551,470	$147,175,644,365	$143,088,198,726	$125,422,311,131
Revenue and Expenses - Totals					
(Includes Inpatient and Outpatient)					
Total Gross Revenue	$389,742,257,911	$361,158,597,058	$327,728,825,706	$322,087,405,456	$290,799,529,886
Deductions from Revenue	281,916,354,523	259,825,436,261	232,365,473,589	227,067,664,476	204,455,874,952
Net Patient Revenue	107,825,903,388	101,333,160,797	95,363,352,117	95,019,740,980	86,343,654,934
Other Operating Revenue	8,282,744,699	7,037,077,408	6,844,706,592	6,360,621,218	5,485,613,820
Other Nonoperating Revenue	2,974,682,811	1,510,800,476	629,938,259	2,149,108,579	2,567,834,662
Total Net Revenue	119,083,330,898	109,881,038,681	102,837,996,968	103,529,470,777	94,397,103,416
Total Expenses	110,015,554,300	101,971,588,975	95,428,252,524	96,135,582,660	87,818,900,913
HOSPITAL UNIT (Excludes Separate Nursing Home Units)					
Utilization - Inpatient					
Beds	76,442	75,456	75,634	80,282	77,123
Admissions	3,692,145	3,623,636	3,612,535	3,886,098	3,734,868
Inpatient Days	18,918,935	18,582,706	18,592,108	19,618,360	18,697,496
Average Length of Stay	5.1	5.1	5.1	5.0	5.0
Personnel					
Total Full Time	473,219	456,875	453,504	466,094	436,927
Total Part Time	178,390	167,786	147,860	152,150	151,242
Revenue and Expenses - Totals					
(Includes Inpatient and Outpatient)					
Total Net Revenue	$118,815,857,506	$109,423,042,300	$102,416,396,046	$103,193,608,338	$93,975,576,086
Total Expenses	109,780,991,366	101,678,240,509	95,075,355,257	95,830,792,663	87,456,206,840

TABLE **4**

BED SIZE CATEGORY 500 +

U.S. Community Hospitals
(Nonfederal, short-term general and other special hospitals)

Overview 2013–2017

	2017	2016	2015	2014	2013
Total Community Hospitals in					
Bed Size Category 500 + ...	289	285	284	273	277
Location					
Hospitals Urban	285	283	282	271	275
Hospitals Rural	4	2	2	2	2
Control					
State and Local Government	51	50	51	46	46
Not for Profit	218	217	214	207	212
Investor owned	20	18	19	20	19
Physician Models					
Independent Practice Association......................	54	60	57	53	57
Group Practice without Walls	12	12	16	20	18
Open Physician-Hospital Organization	62	61	60	57	62
Closed Physician-Hospital Organization............	41	38	37	36	32
Management Service Organization	46	55	65	59	66
Integrated Salary Model................................	195	193	186	169	181
Equity Model	15	11	12	11	13
Foundation	24	30	27	28	28
Affiliations					
Hospitals in a System	229	223	213	202	203
Hospitals in a Network...............................	167	163	159	143	143
Hospitals in a Group Purchasing Organization...	265	262	264	246	255

TABLE 4

BED SIZE CATEGORY 500 +

U.S. Community Hospitals
(Nonfederal, short-term general and other special hospitals)

Utilization, Personnel, Revenue and Expenses, Community Health Indicators 2013–2017

	2017	2016	2015	2014	2013
TOTAL FACILITY (Includes Hospital and Nursing Home Units)					
Utilization - Inpatient					
Beds	213,718	211,927	208,550	200,330	201,377
Admissions	9,997,513	9,887,568	9,582,979	9,212,246	9,306,545
Inpatient Days	57,850,503	57,218,809	55,481,018	52,905,475	52,931,846
Average Length of Stay	5.8	5.8	5.8	5.7	5.7
Inpatient Surgeries	3,024,460	2,979,529	2,907,037	2,805,334	2,861,210
Births	1,043,707	1,049,016	1,040,243	983,083	993,825
Utilization - Outpatient					
Emergency Outpatient Visits	31,578,115	30,801,673	30,122,411	27,782,849	27,879,830
Other Outpatient Visits	173,130,352	172,809,371	159,543,988	143,739,748	136,017,527
Total Outpatient Visits	204,708,467	203,611,044	189,666,399	171,522,597	163,897,357
Outpatient Surgeries	4,757,631	4,605,642	4,295,271	4,084,475	4,098,509
Personnel					
Full Time RNs	436,279	416,167	397,448	371,398	359,722
Full Time LPNs	13,943	13,436	12,511	11,823	12,327
Part Time RNs	146,934	141,773	136,144	128,091	128,171
Part Time LPNs	3,856	3,642	3,205	3,259	3,528
Total Full Time	1,543,602	1,489,258	1,426,960	1,347,612	1,332,280
Total Part Time	424,278	404,567	383,304	358,021	359,019
Revenue - Inpatient					
Gross Inpatient Revenue	$630,546,485,045	$588,015,485,811	$544,328,865,089	$496,323,018,932	$471,993,651,262
Revenue - Outpatient					
Gross Outpatient Revenue	$502,077,156,668	$454,103,440,496	$403,991,355,580	$353,109,338,579	$322,242,954,475
Revenue and Expenses - Totals **(Includes Inpatient and Outpatient)**					
Total Gross Revenue	$1,132,623,641,713	$1,042,118,926,307	$948,320,220,669	$849,432,357,511	$794,236,605,737
Deductions from Revenue	814,424,378,274	739,082,799,999	665,979,474,892	593,844,453,407	551,909,522,075
Net Patient Revenue	318,199,263,439	303,036,126,308	282,340,745,777	255,587,904,104	242,327,083,662
Other Operating Revenue	25,453,235,186	23,569,750,966	21,723,129,953	19,897,779,902	19,675,400,576
Other Nonoperating Revenue	8,921,931,027	4,248,502,296	1,816,813,138	5,947,195,310	6,735,212,689
Total Net Revenue	352,574,429,652	330,854,379,570	305,880,688,868	281,432,879,316	268,737,696,927
Total Expenses	321,579,245,015	304,145,409,460	282,478,235,850	258,392,120,893	248,158,203,354
HOSPITAL UNIT (Excludes Separate Nursing Home Units)					
Utilization - Inpatient					
Beds	206,919	202,943	199,315	193,057	192,922
Admissions	9,968,973	9,853,937	9,549,408	9,178,842	9,266,619
Inpatient Days	55,588,111	54,380,728	52,797,048	50,484,416	50,120,917
Average Length of Stay	5.6	5.5	5.5	5.5	5.4
Personnel					
Total Full Time	1,537,976	1,483,903	1,421,345	1,340,742	1,325,873
Total Part Time	422,117	402,338	380,861	355,752	356,542
Revenue and Expenses - Totals **(Includes Inpatient and Outpatient)**					
Total Net Revenue	$351,886,430,430	$330,074,680,408	$304,978,256,055	$280,724,691,736	$267,844,526,778
Total Expenses	320,878,977,487	303,387,730,421	281,591,033,757	257,685,682,932	247,271,410,711

Bed Size Categories

Census Divisions

Census Division 1

New England
Connecticut, Maine, Massachusetts, New Hampshire, Rhode Island, Vermont

Census Division 2

Middle Atlantic
New Jersey, New York, Pennsylvania

Census Division 3

South Atlantic
Delaware, District of Columbia, Florida, Georgia, Maryland, North Carolina, South Carolina, Virginia, West Virginia

Census Division 4

East North Central
Illinois, Indiana, Michigan, Ohio, Wisconsin

Census Division 5

East South Central
Alabama, Kentucky, Mississippi, Tennessee

Census Division 6

West North Central
Iowa, Kansas, Minnesota, Missouri, Nebraska, North Dakota, South Dakota

Census Division 7

West South Central
Arkansas, Louisiana, Oklahoma, Texas

Census Division 8

Mountain
Arizona, Colorado, Idaho, Montana, Nevada, New Mexico, Utah, Wyoming

Census Division 9

Pacific
Alaska, California, Hawaii, Oregon, Washington

U.S. Census Divisions

TABLE **5**

U.S. CENSUS DIVISION 1: NEW ENGLAND

U.S. Community Hospitals
(Nonfederal, short-term general and other special hospitals)

Overview 2013–2017

	2017	2016	2015	2014	2013
Total Community Hospitals in Census Division 1, New England..............	194	197	198	201	205
Bed Size Category					
6-24	7	8	9	8	7
25-49	45	44	43	44	45
50-99	44	45	46	46	46
100-199	49	50	50	54	55
200-299	20	20	19	19	23
300-399	13	13	13	14	13
400-499	6	6	7	5	5
500 + ...	10	11	11	11	11
Location					
Hospitals Urban	139	142	143	146	148
Hospitals Rural	55	55	55	55	57
Control					
State and Local Government	6	6	7	7	6
Not for Profit.................................	165	165	165	167	170
Investor owned	23	26	26	27	29
Physician Models					
Independent Practice Association......	25	34	34	32	34
Group Practice without Walls	5	9	6	6	8
Open Physician-Hospital Organization	39	37	40	44	41
Closed Physician-Hospital Organization.............	7	7	8	9	10
Management Service Organization	13	19	16	16	17
Integrated Salary Model..................	88	90	87	87	93
Equity Model	8	6	5	5	5
Foundation	19	18	15	14	12
Affiliations					
Hospitals in a System	116	114	111	107	107
Hospitals in a Network	76	79	78	79	77
Hospitals in a Group Purchasing Organization...	136	144	143	141	147

TABLE 5

U.S. CENSUS DIVISION 1: NEW ENGLAND

U.S. Community Hospitals
(Nonfederal, short-term general and other special hospitals)

Utilization, Personnel, Revenue and Expenses, Community Health Indicators 2013–2017

	2017	2016	2015	2014	2013
TOTAL FACILITY (Includes Hospital and Nursing Home Units)					
Utilization - Inpatient					
Beds	32,381	32,798	32,982	33,645	34,142
Admissions	1,575,699	1,572,638	1,564,096	1,544,388	1,600,890
Inpatient Days	8,500,057	8,389,746	8,414,349	8,470,206	8,630,440
Average Length of Stay	5.4	5.3	5.4	5.5	5.4
Inpatient Surgeries	409,253	421,285	403,646	407,432	409,361
Births	142,432	145,980	146,737	147,729	146,765
Utilization - Outpatient					
Emergency Outpatient Visits	7,169,939	7,203,699	7,432,227	7,027,573	7,168,129
Other Outpatient Visits	41,935,936	41,650,761	42,528,908	41,362,713	41,568,927
Total Outpatient Visits	49,105,875	48,854,460	49,961,135	48,390,286	48,737,056
Outpatient Surgeries	945,843	955,559	933,953	951,420	950,265
Personnel					
Full Time RNs	52,855	51,635	49,718	48,777	47,144
Full Time LPNs	1,819	1,906	1,876	1,801	1,829
Part Time RNs	42,823	42,561	42,203	41,452	41,003
Part Time LPNs	989	1,022	1,065	1,074	1,226
Total Full Time	245,661	241,784	232,406	230,928	230,516
Total Part Time	130,616	129,384	124,979	125,071	122,994
Revenue - Inpatient					
Gross Inpatient Revenue	$65,351,524,702	$61,830,211,505	$59,894,209,408	$58,289,349,460	$56,228,499,083
Revenue - Outpatient					
Gross Outpatient Revenue	$85,502,734,369	$79,400,285,127	$73,575,255,239	$68,139,408,959	$64,867,560,035
Revenue and Expenses - Totals					
(Includes Inpatient and Outpatient)					
Total Gross Revenue	$150,854,259,071	$141,230,496,632	$133,469,464,647	$126,428,758,419	$121,096,059,118
Deductions from Revenue	97,672,640,734	89,734,448,326	84,542,326,724	79,573,673,825	75,371,477,015
Net Patient Revenue	53,181,618,337	51,496,048,306	48,927,137,923	46,855,084,594	45,724,582,103
Other Operating Revenue	6,403,861,165	5,852,308,514	5,443,226,980	5,202,912,728	5,171,943,672
Other Nonoperating Revenue	1,349,590,545	435,024,537	1,610,536	594,702,559	1,095,439,810
Total Net Revenue	60,935,070,047	57,783,381,357	54,371,975,439	52,652,699,881	51,991,965,585
Total Expenses	58,229,116,358	55,722,351,201	52,320,879,636	49,930,915,708	48,936,923,033
HOSPITAL UNIT (Excludes Separate Nursing Home Units)					
Utilization - Inpatient					
Beds	31,545	31,971	32,099	32,746	33,249
Admissions	1,573,483	1,568,033	1,560,023	1,541,222	1,597,909
Inpatient Days	8,229,699	8,111,694	8,190,451	8,171,200	8,320,726
Average Length of Stay	5.2	5.2	5.3	5.3	5.2
Personnel					
Total Full Time	244,828	240,793	231,833	230,092	229,670
Total Part Time	129,934	128,662	124,482	124,262	122,447
Revenue and Expenses - Totals					
(Includes Inpatient and Outpatient)					
Total Net Revenue	$60,842,803,483	$57,713,090,473	$54,306,839,201	$52,568,842,181	$51,896,428,782
Total Expenses	58,146,580,760	55,650,107,626	52,258,626,830	49,843,257,614	48,854,810,812
COMMUNITY HEALTH INDICATORS PER 1000 POPULATION					
Total Population (in thousands)	14,810	14,736	14,728	14,681	14,619
Inpatient					
Beds	2.2	2.2	2.2	2.3	2.3
Admissions	106.4	106.7	106.2	105.2	109.5
Inpatient Days	573.9	569.4	571.3	577.0	590.4
Inpatient Surgeries	27.6	28.6	27.4	27.8	28
Births	9.6	9.9	10.0	10.1	10.0
Outpatient					
Emergency Outpatient Visits	484.1	488.9	504.6	478.7	490.3
Other Outpatient Visits	2,831.6	2,826.6	2,887.7	2,817.5	2,843.5
Total Outpatient Visits	3,315.7	3,315.4	3,392.4	3,296.2	3,333.9
Outpatient Surgeries	63.9	64.8	63.4	64.8	65.0
Expense per Capita (per person)	$3,931.7	$3,781.5	$3,552.6	$3,401.1	$3,347.5

TABLE 5

U.S. CENSUS DIVISION 2: MIDDLE ATLANTIC

U.S. Community Hospitals
(Nonfederal, short-term general and other special hospitals)

Overview 2013–2017

	2017	2016	2015	2014	2013
Total Community Hospitals					
in Census Division 2, Middle Atlantic............	451	447	450	451	462
Bed Size Category					
6-24	19	17	17	17	18
25-49	49	45	45	40	41
50-99	71	68	69	67	66
100-199	120	114	110	111	109
200-299	68	79	81	80	90
300-399	46	43	50	52	53
400-499	23	25	21	28	27
500 + ...	55	56	57	56	58
Location					
Hospitals Urban	378	373	376	376	376
Hospitals Rural...	73	74	74	75	86
Control					
State and Local Government	24	25	26	27	31
Not for Profit..	357	348	349	355	359
Investor owned..	70	74	75	69	72
Physician Models					
Independent Practice Association......................	86	73	69	64	63
Group Practice without Walls	10	18	16	16	16
Open Physician-Hospital Organization	43	47	44	40	42
Closed Physician-Hospital Organization	19	16	19	17	16
Management Service Organization	45	47	57	52	49
Integrated Salary Model...................................	211	204	195	190	197
Equity Model	13	11	10	9	9
Foundation	22	12	14	17	17
Affiliations					
Hospitals in a System	313	309	297	283	284
Hospitals in a Network	205	202	192	176	171
Hospitals in a Group Purchasing Organization...	310	320	318	307	341

TABLE 5

U.S. CENSUS DIVISION 2: MIDDLE ATLANTIC

U.S. Community Hospitals
(Nonfederal, short-term general and other special hospitals)

Utilization, Personnel, Revenue and Expenses, Community Health Indicators 2013–2017

	2017	2016	2015	2014	2013
TOTAL FACILITY (Includes Hospital and Nursing Home Units)					
Utilization - Inpatient					
Beds	110,228	111,576	111,933	114,793	117,463
Admissions	4,952,686	4,881,134	4,801,155	4,866,768	5,010,484
Inpatient Days	28,747,702	28,914,190	28,945,442	29,591,465	30,437,282
Average Length of Stay	5.8	5.9	6.0	6.1	6.1
Inpatient Surgeries	1,260,590	1,291,183	1,278,886	1,305,303	1,335,941
Births	453,226	458,856	456,132	463,141	461,910
Utilization - Outpatient					
Emergency Outpatient Visits	19,015,614	19,270,939	18,800,932	18,583,767	18,590,122
Other Outpatient Visits	95,492,856	94,082,875	94,685,833	93,012,400	92,292,418
Total Outpatient Visits	114,508,470	113,353,814	113,486,765	111,596,167	110,882,540
Outpatient Surgeries	2,755,513	2,791,357	2,638,686	2,640,799	2,678,766
Personnel					
Full Time RNs	187,285	181,017	172,602	170,386	167,599
Full Time LPNs	8,050	7,631	7,756	7,956	8,550
Part Time RNs	62,635	63,572	62,891	62,650	62,217
Part Time LPNs	2,356	2,083	2,345	2,392	2,722
Total Full Time	709,056	686,863	664,024	659,961	670,848
Total Part Time	207,512	204,785	200,419	197,064	200,017
Revenue - Inpatient					
Gross Inpatient Revenue	$290,627,007,329	$273,728,219,303	$259,514,194,359	$246,995,739,244	$239,423,323,953
Revenue - Outpatient					
Gross Outpatient Revenue	$244,410,827,628	$223,895,470,604	$199,070,271,649	$182,772,095,331	$171,316,545,257
Revenue and Expenses - Totals (Includes Inpatient and Outpatient)					
Total Gross Revenue	$535,037,834,957	$497,623,689,907	$458,584,466,008	$429,767,834,575	$410,739,869,210
Deductions from Revenue	392,884,763,242	360,654,188,619	330,264,595,845	306,882,577,009	292,605,650,995
Net Patient Revenue	142,153,071,715	136,969,501,288	128,319,870,163	122,885,257,566	118,134,218,215
Other Operating Revenue	10,485,737,315	10,075,295,538	8,788,492,843	8,892,690,146	8,789,549,804
Other Nonoperating Revenue	3,092,173,756	1,766,195,709	822,319,089	2,065,051,755	2,944,279,238
Total Net Revenue	155,730,982,786	148,810,992,535	137,930,682,095	133,842,999,467	129,868,047,257
Total Expenses	147,584,661,438	141,061,102,926	132,115,490,562	127,749,896,339	124,110,621,867
HOSPITAL UNIT (Excludes Separate Nursing Home Units)					
Utilization - Inpatient					
Beds	103,972	105,327	105,383	107,604	109,013
Admissions	4,927,855	4,855,503	4,773,917	4,835,467	4,971,959
Inpatient Days	26,587,023	26,813,342	26,714,754	27,163,078	27,601,686
Average Length of Stay	5.4	5.5	5.6	5.6	5.6
Personnel					
Total Full Time	704,448	682,044	659,101	653,930	664,248
Total Part Time	204,986	202,194	197,710	194,178	196,734
Revenue and Expenses - Totals (Includes Inpatient and Outpatient)					
Total Net Revenue	$155,067,991,642	$148,100,904,512	$137,158,329,913	$132,976,258,121	$128,956,904,442
Total Expenses	146,977,890,632	140,507,459,911	131,381,363,604	126,946,407,650	123,246,946,768
COMMUNITY HEALTH INDICATORS PER 1000 POPULATION					
Total Population (in thousands)	41,661	41,474	41,556	41,472	41,324
Inpatient					
Beds	2.6	2.7	2.7	2.8	2.8
Admissions	118.9	117.7	115.5	117.4	121.2
Inpatient Days	690.0	697.2	696.5	713.5	736.5
Inpatient Surgeries	30.3	31.1	30.8	31.5	32.3
Births	10.9	11.1	11.0	11.2	11.2
Outpatient					
Emergency Outpatient Visits	456.4	464.7	452.4	448.1	449.9
Other Outpatient Visits	2,292.2	2,268.5	2,278.5	2,242.8	2,233.4
Total Outpatient Visits	2,748.6	2,733.1	2,730.9	2,690.9	2,683.2
Outpatient Surgeries	66.1	67.3	63.5	63.7	64.8
Expense per Capita (per person)	$3,542.5	$3,401.2	$3,179.2	$3,080.4	$3,003.3

TABLE 5

U.S. CENSUS DIVISION 3: SOUTH ATLANTIC

U.S. Community Hospitals
(Nonfederal, short-term general and other special hospitals)

Overview 2013–2017

	2017	2016	2015	2014	2013
Total Community Hospitals					
in Census Division 3, South Atlantic............	772	777	776	780	781
Bed Size Category					
6-24	37	35	33	33	26
25-49	136	141	146	153	154
50-99	155	159	150	144	145
100-199	179	180	185	182	179
200-299	106	97	100	104	110
300-399	57	63	58	60	64
400-499	38	39	43	41	36
500 + ...	64	63	61	63	67
Location					
Hospitals Urban	577	576	575	577	542
Hospitals Rural...................................	195	201	201	203	239
Control					
State and Local Government................	117	120	130	132	132
Not for Profit......................................	431	426	416	413	420
Investor owned	224	231	230	235	229
Physician Models					
Independent Practice Association.......................	49	49	59	51	49
Group Practice without Walls	20	27	27	28	32
Open Physician-Hospital Organization	59	65	65	67	71
Closed Physician-Hospital Organization	53	49	48	48	47
Management Service Organization	43	55	68	55	73
Integrated Salary Model.....................................	273	300	309	288	297
Equity Model	22	20	17	17	18
Foundation	18	20	19	18	18
Affiliations					
Hospitals in a System	616	609	603	589	578
Hospitals in a Network.......................................	226	245	257	238	233
Hospitals in a Group Purchasing Organization...	472	518	531	525	537

TABLE 5

U.S. CENSUS DIVISION 3: SOUTH ATLANTIC

U.S. Community Hospitals
(Nonfederal, short-term general and other special hospitals)

Utilization, Personnel, Revenue and Expenses, Community Health Indicators 2013–2017

	2017	2016	2015	2014	2013
TOTAL FACILITY (Includes Hospital and Nursing Home Units)					
Utilization - Inpatient					
Beds	156,661	156,005	155,048	156,169	157,556
Admissions	6,984,783	6,964,479	6,928,987	6,821,922	6,809,898
Inpatient Days	38,275,242	38,040,494	37,744,998	37,534,388	37,583,414
Average Length of Stay	5.5	5.5	5.4	5.5	5.5
Inpatient Surgeries	1,853,499	1,858,852	1,848,627	1,844,970	1,891,468
Births	692,369	718,961	713,380	690,802	688,979
Utilization - Outpatient					
Emergency Outpatient Visits	29,427,572	30,111,854	29,291,065	28,358,669	27,326,880
Other Outpatient Visits	89,486,998	89,269,211	81,308,444	77,846,121	76,326,351
Total Outpatient Visits	118,914,570	119,381,065	110,599,509	106,204,790	103,653,231
Outpatient Surgeries	3,549,269	3,571,128	3,461,813	3,383,773	3,421,181
Personnel					
Full Time RNs	254,336	248,715	245,634	238,426	230,453
Full Time LPNs	11,281	11,657	11,226	10,869	11,610
Part Time RNs	84,437	80,780	79,807	75,208	74,235
Part Time LPNs	3,180	2,992	3,019	2,862	3,297
Total Full Time	842,087	828,955	819,601	794,757	781,871
Total Part Time	244,142	230,625	230,190	215,150	212,358
Revenue - Inpatient					
Gross Inpatient Revenue	$337,071,905,359	$323,223,182,426	$303,627,447,165	$279,983,142,817	$264,207,829,450
Revenue - Outpatient					
Gross Outpatient Revenue	$308,366,745,577	$289,502,664,972	$263,543,811,931	$234,304,758,731	$212,342,301,367
Revenue and Expenses - Totals					
(Includes Inpatient and Outpatient)					
Total Gross Revenue	$645,438,650,936	$612,725,847,398	$567,171,259,096	$514,287,901,548	$476,550,130,817
Deductions from Revenue	472,523,824,118	446,974,466,650	410,233,958,738	367,103,074,355	336,337,842,566
Net Patient Revenue	172,914,826,818	165,751,380,748	156,937,300,358	147,184,827,193	140,212,288,251
Other Operating Revenue	7,423,653,408	7,222,778,667	7,124,386,646	6,519,532,361	6,406,140,892
Other Nonoperating Revenue	3,641,262,398	1,624,905,284	847,067,335	3,177,383,776	3,309,761,466
Total Net Revenue	183,979,742,624	174,599,064,699	164,908,754,339	156,881,743,330	149,928,190,609
Total Expenses	163,845,481,573	157,287,329,689	149,736,371,726	141,543,572,578	136,637,586,736
HOSPITAL UNIT (Excludes Separate Nursing Home Units)					
Utilization - Inpatient					
Beds	148,474	147,494	146,512	147,232	147,687
Admissions	6,954,431	6,930,946	6,895,436	6,785,886	6,768,745
Inpatient Days	35,667,474	35,317,674	34,938,376	34,657,950	34,463,947
Average Length of Stay	5.1	5.1	5.1	5.1	5.1
Personnel					
Total Full Time	835,911	822,891	813,376	787,985	774,815
Total Part Time	241,984	228,612	227,914	212,965	209,852
Revenue and Expenses - Totals					
(Includes Inpatient and Outpatient)					
Total Net Revenue	$183,305,444,355	$173,929,226,809	$164,194,813,402	$156,095,696,877	$149,123,388,591
Total Expenses	163,233,180,906	156,691,799,119	149,094,286,196	140,832,388,019	135,902,907,070
COMMUNITY HEALTH INDICATORS PER 1000 POPULATION					
Total Population (in thousands)	64,706	63,923	63,277	62,515	61,784
Inpatient					
Beds	2.4	2.4	2.5	2.5	2.6
Admissions	107.9	109	109.5	109.1	110.2
Inpatient Days	591.5	595.1	596.5	600.4	608.3
Inpatient Surgeries	28.6	29.1	29.2	29.5	30.6
Births	10.7	11.2	11.3	11.1	11.2
Outpatient					
Emergency Outpatient Visits	454.8	471.1	462.9	453.6	442.3
Other Outpatient Visits	1,383.0	1,396.5	1,285.0	1,245.2	1,235.4
Total Outpatient Visits	1,837.8	1,867.6	1,747.9	1,698.9	1,677.7
Outpatient Surgeries	54.9	55.9	54.7	54.1	55.4
Expense per Capita (per person)	$2,532.2	$2,460.6	$2,366.4	$2,264.2	$2,211.5

TABLE 5

U.S. CENSUS DIVISION 4: EAST NORTH CENTRAL

U.S. Community Hospitals
(Nonfederal, short-term general and other special hospitals)

Overview 2013–2017

	2017	2016	2015	2014	2013
Total Community Hospitals					
in Census Division 4, East North Central	798	800	799	804	813
Bed Size Category					
6-24	86	85	82	78	75
25-49	215	209	211	212	219
50-99	130	140	141	141	150
100-199	162	158	160	173	164
200-299	87	93	90	85	91
300-399	48	48	48	46	43
400-499	29	26	25	30	30
500 + ...	41	41	42	39	41
Location					
Hospitals Urban	527	529	525	529	535
Hospitals Rural	271	271	274	275	278
Control					
State and Local Government	74	77	82	86	87
Not for Profit	594	592	589	591	599
Investor owned	130	131	128	127	127
Physician Models					
Independent Practice Association	57	60	71	72	68
Group Practice without Walls	29	29	35	41	43
Open Physician-Hospital Organization	180	177	169	166	179
Closed Physician-Hospital Organization	64	67	57	61	58
Management Service Organization	67	72	68	69	75
Integrated Salary Model	332	348	347	363	357
Equity Model	31	36	33	35	39
Foundation	36	46	42	48	54
Affiliations					
Hospitals in a System	565	557	548	537	521
Hospitals in a Network	322	328	311	297	288
Hospitals in a Group Purchasing Organization...	616	614	613	627	629

TABLE 5

U.S. CENSUS DIVISION 4: EAST NORTH CENTRAL

U.S. Community Hospitals
(Nonfederal, short-term general and other special hospitals)

Utilization, Personnel, Revenue and Expenses, Community Health Indicators 2013–2017

	2017	2016	2015	2014	2013
TOTAL FACILITY (Includes Hospital and Nursing Home Units)					
Utilization - Inpatient					
Beds	120,736	121,229	121,622	121,024	121,809
Admissions	5,214,548	5,228,579	5,242,877	5,226,620	5,364,064
Inpatient Days	26,260,795	26,365,860	26,505,511	26,350,601	26,652,725
Average Length of Stay	5.0	5.0	5.1	5.0	5.0
Inpatient Surgeries	1,380,263	1,398,408	1,389,830	1,408,604	1,432,751
Births	516,804	526,761	529,316	528,252	527,581
Utilization - Outpatient					
Emergency Outpatient Visits	23,897,233	23,605,718	23,449,181	22,413,291	22,064,528
Other Outpatient Visits	136,706,994	133,694,756	128,207,598	121,656,758	116,623,008
Total Outpatient Visits	160,604,227	157,300,474	151,656,779	144,070,049	138,687,536
Outpatient Surgeries	3,315,630	3,338,721	3,237,099	3,173,926	3,169,565
Personnel					
Full Time RNs	203,759	198,727	192,693	185,253	180,061
Full Time LPNs	7,467	7,483	7,320	7,298	8,070
Part Time RNs	100,528	100,456	96,641	99,934	97,703
Part Time LPNs	3,575	3,697	3,888	3,883	4,386
Total Full Time	727,272	720,352	699,819	683,209	676,373
Total Part Time	324,355	311,429	298,257	306,468	300,205
Revenue - Inpatient					
Gross Inpatient Revenue	$243,538,573,096	$230,746,665,771	$219,502,768,303	$206,644,795,843	$195,877,897,950
Revenue - Outpatient					
Gross Outpatient Revenue	$284,277,236,033	$262,668,327,994	$242,488,289,719	$222,857,495,271	$202,812,771,392
Revenue and Expenses - Totals					
(Includes Inpatient and Outpatient)					
Total Gross Revenue	$527,815,809,129	$493,414,993,765	$461,991,058,022	$429,502,291,114	$398,690,669,342
Deductions from Revenue	368,675,734,372	339,703,465,116	314,575,493,329	289,461,157,173	266,134,331,112
Net Patient Revenue	159,140,074,757	153,711,528,649	147,415,564,693	140,041,133,941	132,556,338,230
Other Operating Revenue	10,409,900,979	9,302,273,067	8,952,183,723	8,905,856,353	8,409,323,634
Other Nonoperating Revenue	4,992,318,253	3,135,831,056	152,534,827	3,752,324,602	3,977,533,146
Total Net Revenue	174,542,293,989	166,149,632,772	156,520,283,243	152,699,314,896	144,943,195,010
Total Expenses	157,010,029,843	150,771,194,405	143,004,245,304	136,910,665,676	131,765,166,722
HOSPITAL UNIT (Excludes Separate Nursing Home Units)					
Utilization - Inpatient					
Beds	116,999	117,012	116,923	116,360	117,329
Admissions	5,195,053	5,203,892	5,217,258	5,198,132	5,335,679
Inpatient Days	25,162,892	25,104,084	25,122,980	24,950,775	25,316,823
Average Length of Stay	4.8	4.8	4.8	4.8	4.7
Personnel					
Total Full Time	724,883	717,812	697,066	680,684	673,882
Total Part Time	322,818	309,605	296,145	304,241	297,895
Revenue and Expenses - Totals					
(Includes Inpatient and Outpatient)					
Total Net Revenue	$174,197,294,404	$165,629,888,462	$156,016,367,637	$152,314,526,551	$144,559,884,258
Total Expenses	156,743,956,191	150,459,681,796	142,675,288,534	136,582,109,988	131,432,751,274
COMMUNITY HEALTH INDICATORS PER 1000 POPULATION					
Total Population (in thousands)	46,885	46,756	46,787	46,739	46,662
Inpatient					
Beds	2.6	2.6	2.6	2.6	2.6
Admissions	111.2	111.8	112.1	111.8	115
Inpatient Days	560.1	563.9	566.5	563.8	571.2
Inpatient Surgeries	29.4	29.9	29.7	30.1	30.7
Births	11.0	11.3	11.3	11.3	11.3
Outpatient					
Emergency Outpatient Visits	509.7	504.9	501.2	479.5	472.9
Other Outpatient Visits	2,915.8	2,859.4	2,740.2	2,602.9	2,499.3
Total Outpatient Visits	3,425.5	3,364.3	3,241.4	3,082.4	2,972.2
Outpatient Surgeries	70.7	71.4	69.2	67.9	67.9
Expense per Capita (per person)	$3,348.8	$3,224.6	$3,056.5	$2,929.3	$2,823.8

U.S. Census Divisions

TABLE 5

U.S. CENSUS DIVISION 5: EAST SOUTH CENTRAL

U.S. Community Hospitals
(Nonfederal, short-term general and other special hospitals)

Overview 2013–2017

	2017	2016	2015	2014	2013
Total Community Hospitals in Census Division 5, East South Central.....	433	436	438	443	454
Bed Size Category					
6-24	21	22	21	21	24
25-49	134	130	137	134	138
50-99	98	104	93	97	99
100-199	87	89	92	96	98
200-299	35	37	39	41	42
300-399	25	24	26	25	24
400-499	10	10	9	8	9
500 +	23	20	21	21	20
Location					
Hospitals Urban	210	213	213	216	214
Hospitals Rural	223	223	225	227	240
Control					
State and Local Government	107	106	109	111	115
Not for Profit	189	186	183	185	189
Investor owned	137	144	146	147	150
Physician Models					
Independent Practice Association	30	25	26	27	24
Group Practice without Walls	6	6	9	8	7
Open Physician-Hospital Organization	35	40	46	49	44
Closed Physician-Hospital Organization	27	18	13	9	8
Management Service Organization	41	47	46	35	32
Integrated Salary Model	92	98	111	114	113
Equity Model	3	3	4	4	4
Foundation	22	24	23	16	20
Affiliations					
Hospitals in a System	307	311	310	312	313
Hospitals in a Network	108	106	98	104	102
Hospitals in a Group Purchasing Organization...	250	255	255	173	179

TABLE 5

U.S. CENSUS DIVISION 5: EAST SOUTH CENTRAL

U.S. Community Hospitals
(Nonfederal, short-term general and other special hospitals)

Utilization, Personnel, Revenue and Expenses, Community Health Indicators 2013–2017

	2017	2016	2015	2014	2013
TOTAL FACILITY (Includes Hospital and Nursing Home Units)					
Utilization - Inpatient					
Beds	61,933	61,566	61,840	62,266	63,057
Admissions	2,408,935	2,410,333	2,375,117	2,393,434	2,429,499
Inpatient Days	13,763,525	13,776,156	13,730,078	13,426,108	13,605,620
Average Length of Stay	5.7	5.7	5.8	5.6	5.6
Inpatient Surgeries	660,467	674,940	654,679	670,748	678,773
Births	205,116	216,788	218,837	215,390	215,234
Utilization - Outpatient					
Emergency Outpatient Visits	10,175,145	10,208,107	10,291,598	9,934,924	9,765,149
Other Outpatient Visits	33,910,566	31,805,510	29,436,831	26,451,618	26,004,184
Total Outpatient Visits	44,085,711	42,013,617	39,728,429	36,386,542	35,769,333
Outpatient Surgeries	1,411,863	1,415,800	1,342,713	1,339,784	1,357,354
Personnel					
Full Time RNs	89,214	84,698	81,184	79,908	78,397
Full Time LPNs	5,186	5,431	5,756	5,556	6,146
Part Time RNs	28,285	29,775	26,724	23,815	24,965
Part Time LPNs	1,353	1,430	1,384	1,398	1,573
Total Full Time	295,100	277,141	272,012	272,150	269,523
Total Part Time	75,873	81,603	72,314	66,300	68,951
Revenue - Inpatient					
Gross Inpatient Revenue	$110,850,380,099	$103,537,591,698	$97,423,609,419	$90,606,482,024	$86,623,832,585
Revenue - Outpatient					
Gross Outpatient Revenue	$112,324,249,572	$102,216,851,815	$94,635,629,536	$85,895,097,985	$77,052,657,187
Revenue and Expenses - Totals					
(Includes Inpatient and Outpatient)					
Total Gross Revenue	$223,174,629,671	$205,754,443,513	$192,059,238,955	$176,501,580,009	$163,676,489,772
Deductions from Revenue	170,613,750,920	155,562,498,971	143,924,680,071	130,854,742,695	119,309,380,401
Net Patient Revenue	52,560,878,751	50,191,944,542	48,134,558,884	45,646,837,314	44,367,109,371
Other Operating Revenue	2,530,319,162	2,122,408,528	2,026,642,821	2,058,294,557	1,946,905,986
Other Nonoperating Revenue	862,457,322	432,014,508	270,564,942	720,899,460	764,477,625
Total Net Revenue	55,953,655,235	52,746,367,578	50,431,766,647	48,426,031,331	47,078,492,982
Total Expenses	52,142,988,014	48,065,025,107	45,792,700,335	44,811,208,786	43,106,610,349
HOSPITAL UNIT (Excludes Separate Nursing Home Units)					
Utilization - Inpatient					
Beds	58,702	58,249	57,974	58,749	58,821
Admissions	2,399,564	2,399,500	2,360,408	2,381,797	2,413,752
Inpatient Days	12,734,582	12,708,944	12,522,541	12,318,994	12,250,428
Average Length of Stay	5.3	5.3	5.3	5.2	5.1
Personnel					
Total Full Time	293,169	274,875	269,548	269,093	265,803
Total Part Time	75,224	80,928	71,587	65,466	67,591
Revenue and Expenses - Totals					
(Includes Inpatient and Outpatient)					
Total Net Revenue	$55,689,546,150	$52,426,793,648	$50,104,387,026	$48,222,111,895	$46,795,875,739
Total Expenses	51,949,397,807	47,828,983,049	45,538,459,158	44,640,838,676	42,870,626,624
COMMUNITY HEALTH INDICATORS PER 1000 POPULATION					
Total Population (in thousands)	19,029	18,940	18,877	18,806	18,716
Inpatient					
Beds	3.3	3.3	3.3	3.3	3.4
Admissions	126.6	127.3	125.8	127.3	129.8
Inpatient Days	723.3	727.4	727.4	713.9	726.9
Inpatient Surgeries	34.7	35.6	34.7	35.7	36.3
Births	10.8	11.4	11.6	11.5	11.5
Outpatient					
Emergency Outpatient Visits	534.7	539	545.2	528.3	521.7
Other Outpatient Visits	1,782.0	1,679.3	1,559.4	1,406.5	1,389.4
Total Outpatient Visits	2,316.8	2,218.2	2,104.6	1,934.8	1,911.1
Outpatient Surgeries	74.2	74.8	71.1	71.2	72.5
Expense per Capita (per person)	$2,740.2	$2,537.7	$2,425.9	$2,382.8	$2,303.2

U.S. Census Divisions

TABLE 5

U.S. CENSUS DIVISION 6: WEST NORTH CENTRAL

U.S. Community Hospitals
(Nonfederal, short-term general and other special hospitals)

Overview 2013–2017

	2017	2016	2015	2014	2013
Total Community Hospitals					
in Census Division 6, West North Central	707	707	711	712	708
Bed Size Category					
6-24	175	166	160	152	151
25-49	215	221	224	226	219
50-99	143	144	149	151	157
100-199	84	87	90	95	90
200-299	33	33	34	35	37
300-399	23	22	22	22	24
400-499	13	12	13	13	14
500 + ...	21	22	19	18	16
Location					
Hospitals Urban	255	255	259	258	238
Hospitals Rural	452	452	452	454	470
Control					
State and Local Government	223	223	225	229	230
Not for Profit	406	407	409	406	404
Investor owned	78	77	77	77	74
Physician Models					
Independent Practice Association	53	46	50	57	57
Group Practice without Walls	9	10	7	10	12
Open Physician-Hospital Organization	69	69	64	63	68
Closed Physician-Hospital Organization	24	23	20	21	23
Management Service Organization	11	12	13	13	13
Integrated Salary Model	343	358	353	365	344
Equity Model	7	5	7	7	7
Foundation	10	13	13	16	19
Affiliations					
Hospitals in a System	387	380	377	382	373
Hospitals in a Network	299	308	305	299	294
Hospitals in a Group Purchasing Organization...	545	566	559	570	567

TABLE 5

U.S. CENSUS DIVISION 6: WEST NORTH CENTRAL

U.S. Community Hospitals
(Nonfederal, short-term general and other special hospitals)

Utilization, Personnel, Revenue and Expenses, Community Health Indicators 2013–2017

	2017	2016	2015	2014	2013
TOTAL FACILITY (Includes Hospital and Nursing Home Units)					
Utilization - Inpatient					
Beds	66,538	66,863	67,175	67,410	67,891
Admissions	2,364,074	2,342,091	2,362,168	2,348,661	2,372,275
Inpatient Days	14,368,825	14,407,021	14,500,523	14,235,081	14,365,970
Average Length of Stay	6.1	6.2	6.1	6.1	6.1
Inpatient Surgeries	640,065	640,714	637,649	649,950	659,665
Births	263,309	268,409	269,450	270,587	267,736
Utilization - Outpatient					
Emergency Outpatient Visits	9,279,951	9,333,691	9,086,629	8,801,787	8,702,585
Other Outpatient Visits	59,949,830	58,815,832	54,821,386	53,859,087	52,138,160
Total Outpatient Visits	69,229,781	68,149,523	63,908,015	62,660,874	60,840,745
Outpatient Surgeries	1,513,858	1,474,098	1,441,415	1,406,475	1,392,662
Personnel					
Full Time RNs	90,570	86,845	85,648	83,084	82,487
Full Time LPNs	7,851	7,872	7,295	7,190	7,210
Part Time RNs	62,180	59,993	57,486	55,057	53,531
Part Time LPNs	3,840	4,089	3,998	3,980	3,976
Total Full Time	363,788	350,055	341,426	332,836	338,486
Total Part Time	182,796	178,375	169,794	162,652	161,960
Revenue - Inpatient					
Gross Inpatient Revenue	$101,222,231,765	$96,350,276,173	$91,076,952,927	$85,848,791,659	$81,309,001,608
Revenue - Outpatient					
Gross Outpatient Revenue	$119,625,573,925	$110,840,488,972	$100,766,113,874	$90,824,219,153	$81,929,119,494
Revenue and Expenses - Totals					
(Includes Inpatient and Outpatient)					
Total Gross Revenue	$220,847,805,690	$207,190,765,145	$191,843,066,801	$176,673,010,812	$163,238,121,102
Deductions from Revenue	147,648,643,930	136,875,950,492	125,564,533,862	114,080,872,198	103,554,645,332
Net Patient Revenue	73,199,161,760	70,314,814,653	66,278,532,939	62,592,138,614	59,683,475,770
Other Operating Revenue	4,453,925,579	4,080,125,886	3,945,267,080	3,697,825,131	3,521,010,890
Other Nonoperating Revenue	1,776,845,712	690,644,022	519,461,226	1,398,130,530	1,695,912,700
Total Net Revenue	79,429,933,051	75,085,584,561	70,743,261,245	67,688,094,275	64,900,399,360
Total Expenses	74,332,887,649	70,756,761,886	65,575,921,394	62,832,166,380	59,997,136,994
HOSPITAL UNIT (Excludes Separate Nursing Home Units)					
Utilization - Inpatient					
Beds	58,591	58,456	58,629	58,583	58,929
Admissions	2,349,441	2,326,725	2,345,773	2,328,104	2,353,255
Inpatient Days	11,881,917	11,693,107	11,793,242	11,480,718	11,564,130
Average Length of Stay	5.1	5.0	5.0	4.9	4.9
Personnel					
Total Full Time	359,134	345,419	336,821	327,351	333,097
Total Part Time	178,757	174,221	165,607	157,878	157,594
Revenue and Expenses - Totals					
(Includes Inpatient and Outpatient)					
Total Net Revenue	$78,851,249,035	$74,484,223,614	$70,145,580,361	$67,077,555,657	$64,330,425,374
Total Expenses	73,790,388,076	70,244,857,066	65,062,430,876	62,307,313,606	59,457,521,879
COMMUNITY HEALTH INDICATORS PER 1000 POPULATION					
Total Population (in thousands)	21,294	21,185	21,120	21,006	20,886
Inpatient					
Beds	3.1	3.2	3.2	3.2	3.3
Admissions	111	110.6	111.8	111.8	113.6
Inpatient Days	674.8	680.0	686.6	677.7	687.8
Inpatient Surgeries	30.1	30.2	30.2	30.9	31.6
Births	12.4	12.7	12.8	12.9	12.8
Outpatient					
Emergency Outpatient Visits	435.8	440.6	430.2	419.0	416.7
Other Outpatient Visits	2,815.3	2,776.2	2,595.7	2,564.0	2,496.4
Total Outpatient Visits	3,251.1	3,216.8	3,025.9	2,983.0	2,913.0
Outpatient Surgeries	71.1	69.6	68.2	67.0	66.7
Expense per Capita (per person)	$3,490.8	$3,339.9	$3,104.9	$2,991.1	$2,872.6

TABLE 5

U.S. CENSUS DIVISION 7: WEST SOUTH CENTRAL

U.S. Community Hospitals
(Nonfederal, short-term general and other special hospitals)

Overview 2013–2017

	2017	2016	2015	2014	2013
Total Community Hospitals					
In Census Division 7, West South Central	908	915	919	926	937
Bed Size Category					
6-24	214	209	203	201	205
25-49	273	282	279	286	286
50-99	153	167	173	178	184
100-199	116	104	113	110	107
200-299	59	61	61	59	62
300-399	41	40	34	37	39
400-499	14	15	18	20	19
500 + ...	38	37	38	35	35
Location					
Hospitals Urban	612	617	620	619	604
Hospitals Rural	296	298	299	307	333
Control					
State and Local Government	196	195	198	203	205
Not for Profit	289	291	289	292	295
Investor owned	423	429	432	431	437
Physician Models					
Independent Practice Association	91	94	89	93	91
Group Practice without Walls	31	32	30	54	37
Open Physician-Hospital Organization	102	109	105	112	120
Closed Physician-Hospital Organization	22	27	29	39	43
Management Service Organization	81	84	85	84	84
Integrated Salary Model	272	260	267	237	244
Equity Model	16	17	14	16	20
Foundation	51	47	47	45	54
Affiliations					
Hospitals in a System	542	547	535	542	536
Hospitals in a Network	234	228	222	223	218
Hospitals in a Group Purchasing Organization...	711	735	731	743	760

TABLE 5

U.S. CENSUS DIVISION 7: WEST SOUTH CENTRAL

U.S. Community Hospitals
(Nonfederal, short-term general and other special hospitals)

Utilization, Personnel, Revenue and Expenses, Community Health Indicators 2013–2017

	2017	2016	2015	2014	2013
TOTAL FACILITY (Includes Hospital and Nursing Home Units)					
Utilization - Inpatient					
Beds	103,632	104,550	105,504	103,714	104,630
Admissions	4,140,484	4,083,773	4,061,793	3,994,813	4,030,542
Inpatient Days	22,004,809	22,428,019	22,152,153	21,526,766	21,522,414
Average Length of Stay	5.3	5.5	5.5	5.4	5.3
Inpatient Surgeries	1,160,291	1,141,313	1,143,331	1,122,970	1,123,492
Births	526,266	546,527	557,494	556,928	537,179
Utilization - Outpatient					
Emergency Outpatient Visits	18,272,095	17,776,792	17,407,271	16,973,006	16,725,027
Other Outpatient Visits	53,945,843	52,700,393	51,593,031	48,629,604	47,054,783
Total Outpatient Visits	72,217,938	70,477,185	69,000,302	65,602,610	63,779,810
Outpatient Surgeries	2,238,829	2,233,905	2,167,878	2,107,418	2,030,410
Personnel					
Full Time RNs	156,517	147,458	146,482	142,067	138,050
Full Time LPNs	12,803	12,946	13,342	13,244	14,163
Part Time RNs	46,578	42,998	41,328	40,468	41,435
Part Time LPNs	3,169	3,371	3,244	3,305	3,525
Total Full Time	497,635	491,716	483,728	472,636	464,382
Total Part Time	130,105	123,953	120,056	115,652	120,982
Revenue - Inpatient					
Gross Inpatient Revenue	$234,136,883,451	$219,217,167,814	$203,967,767,145	$187,109,685,287	$175,276,719,653
Revenue - Outpatient					
Gross Outpatient Revenue	$210,883,979,867	$191,661,353,361	$172,325,001,033	$153,944,559,050	$139,186,029,010
Revenue and Expenses - Totals					
(Includes Inpatient and Outpatient)					
Total Gross Revenue	$445,020,863,318	$410,878,521,175	$376,292,768,178	$341,054,244,233	$314,462,748,663
Deductions from Revenue	342,825,712,608	312,294,718,576	281,570,972,294	252,722,866,918	230,960,087,441
Net Patient Revenue	102,195,150,710	98,583,802,599	94,721,795,884	88,331,377,315	83,502,661,222
Other Operating Revenue	8,076,640,558	7,359,754,157	6,884,471,468	6,628,281,026	6,686,806,453
Other Nonoperating Revenue	1,985,706,768	1,376,270,607	961,453,633	2,130,976,225	1,462,782,117
Total Net Revenue	112,257,498,036	107,319,827,363	102,567,720,985	97,090,634,566	91,652,249,792
Total Expenses	102,290,621,099	97,186,117,632	91,348,374,898	86,031,405,070	82,781,914,979
HOSPITAL UNIT (Excludes Separate Nursing Home Units)					
Utilization - Inpatient					
Beds	101,976	101,124	102,029	102,084	102,478
Admissions	4,132,590	4,070,222	4,051,052	3,984,646	4,017,728
Inpatient Days	21,542,774	21,471,621	21,552,026	21,077,513	20,933,050
Average Length of Stay	5.2	5.3	5.3	5.3	5.2
Personnel					
Total Full Time	496,385	490,236	482,456	469,611	462,745
Total Part Time	129,850	123,578	119,709	114,491	120,471
Revenue and Expenses - Totals					
(Includes Inpatient and Outpatient)					
Total Net Revenue	$112,145,199,486	$107,140,343,993	$102,353,166,397	$96,968,911,560	$91,485,520,567
Total Expenses	102,185,229,938	97,023,654,812	91,159,380,304	85,930,440,282	82,648,566,862
COMMUNITY HEALTH INDICATORS PER 1000 POPULATION					
Total Population (in thousands)	39,924	39,456	39,029	38,451	37,884
Inpatient					
Beds	2.6	2.6	2.7	2.7	2.8
Admissions	103.7	103.5	104.1	103.9	106.4
Inpatient Days	551.2	568.4	567.6	559.8	568.1
Inpatient Surgeries	29.1	28.9	29.3	29.2	29.7
Births	13.2	13.9	14.3	14.5	14.2
Outpatient					
Emergency Outpatient Visits	457.7	450.5	446	441.4	441.5
Other Outpatient Visits	1,351.2	1,335.7	1,321.9	1,264.7	1,242.1
Total Outpatient Visits	1,808.9	1,786.2	1,767.9	1,706.1	1,683.6
Outpatient Surgeries	56.1	56.6	55.5	54.8	53.6
Expense per Capita (per person)	$2,562.1	$2,463.1	$2,340.5	$2,237.4	$2,185.2

U.S. Census Divisions

TABLE 5

U.S. CENSUS DIVISION 8: MOUNTAIN

U.S. Community Hospitals
(Nonfederal, short-term general and other special hospitals)

Overview 2013–2017

	2017	2016	2015	2014	2013
Total Community Hospitals					
in Census Division 8, Mountain	440	431	431	433	436
Bed Size Category					
6-24	94	87	86	83	78
25-49	117	116	113	114	119
50-99	84	82	87	92	89
100-199	66	66	65	66	72
200-299	34	34	34	33	33
300-399	17	18	19	19	20
400-499	11	11	11	14	13
500 + ...	17	17	16	12	12
Location					
Hospitals Urban	239	232	232	234	229
Hospitals Rural	201	199	199	199	207
Control					
State and Local Government	95	93	94	95	95
Not for Profit	208	203	206	208	208
Investor owned	137	135	131	130	133
Physician Models					
Independent Practice Association	40	46	46	30	35
Group Practice without Walls	10	11	9	12	14
Open Physician-Hospital Organization	47	30	29	37	34
Closed Physician-Hospital Organization	12	22	30	15	14
Management Service Organization	17	18	17	20	22
Integrated Salary Model	137	158	165	159	152
Equity Model	3	5	3	4	4
Foundation	10	15	11	14	13
Affiliations					
Hospitals in a System	268	264	264	262	260
Hospitals in a Network	108	108	113	109	111
Hospitals in a Group Purchasing Organization...	243	243	259	262	279

TABLE 5

U.S. CENSUS DIVISION 8: MOUNTAIN

U.S. Community Hospitals
(Nonfederal, short-term general and other special hospitals)

Utilization, Personnel, Revenue and Expenses, Community Health Indicators 2013–2017

	2017	2016	2015	2014	2013
TOTAL FACILITY (Includes Hospital and Nursing Home Units)					
Utilization - Inpatient					
Beds	49,910	49,691	49,745	49,143	49,489
Admissions	2,088,118	2,064,230	2,047,337	2,014,135	2,025,216
Inpatient Days	10,849,687	10,860,416	10,701,261	10,338,303	10,392,125
Average Length of Stay	5.2	5.3	5.2	5.1	5.1
Inpatient Surgeries	571,857	545,833	547,910	554,753	567,455
Births	256,103	270,077	276,794	270,311	270,260
Utilization - Outpatient					
Emergency Outpatient Visits	8,741,450	8,540,234	8,857,912	8,294,489	7,936,104
Other Outpatient Visits	39,392,323	38,753,142	37,101,728	35,383,057	33,352,434
Total Outpatient Visits	48,133,773	47,293,376	45,959,640	43,677,546	41,288,538
Outpatient Surgeries	1,188,246	1,144,071	1,090,393	1,074,473	1,065,799
Personnel					
Full Time RNs	81,652	79,537	77,678	75,249	72,149
Full Time LPNs	3,060	3,112	3,148	3,237	3,316
Part Time RNs	30,664	29,098	25,732	25,831	27,372
Part Time LPNs	1,109	1,099	1,042	1,067	1,206
Total Full Time	278,710	274,117	264,643	255,549	248,726
Total Part Time	90,331	86,903	76,673	77,447	83,111
Revenue - Inpatient					
Gross Inpatient Revenue	$127,065,584,270	$114,320,337,601	$107,570,651,520	$97,843,801,353	$90,397,885,554
Revenue - Outpatient					
Gross Outpatient Revenue	$118,381,642,743	$105,495,701,593	$96,561,960,931	$84,928,300,550	$75,327,470,145
Revenue and Expenses - Totals **(Includes Inpatient and Outpatient)**					
Total Gross Revenue	$245,447,227,013	$219,816,039,194	$204,132,612,451	$182,772,101,903	$165,725,355,699
Deductions from Revenue	181,193,923,278	160,309,936,042	148,266,285,800	130,882,161,233	117,054,136,942
Net Patient Revenue	64,253,303,735	59,506,103,152	55,866,326,651	51,889,940,670	48,671,218,757
Other Operating Revenue	2,431,647,680	2,249,148,855	2,142,968,711	2,110,850,159	2,228,366,607
Other Nonoperating Revenue	984,257,937	406,012,596	375,435,111	911,492,275	699,926,152
Total Net Revenue	67,669,209,352	62,161,264,603	58,384,730,473	54,912,283,104	51,599,511,516
Total Expenses	59,207,230,262	55,285,409,890	52,063,591,337	48,521,374,786	46,273,343,338
HOSPITAL UNIT (Excludes Separate Nursing Home Units)					
Utilization - Inpatient					
Beds	47,489	46,882	46,678	46,113	46,253
Admissions	2,082,167	2,057,743	2,039,745	2,007,194	2,017,351
Inpatient Days	10,138,723	10,026,784	9,786,684	9,480,082	9,420,431
Average Length of Stay	4.9	4.9	4.8	4.7	4.7
Personnel					
Total Full Time	277,141	272,318	262,908	253,752	246,352
Total Part Time	89,378	85,867	75,665	76,353	81,497
Revenue and Expenses - Totals **(Includes Inpatient and Outpatient)**					
Total Net Revenue	$67,427,260,242	$61,940,126,738	$58,168,286,532	$54,704,559,672	$51,363,433,720
Total Expenses	59,022,094,359	55,116,798,098	51,891,279,458	48,349,914,738	46,084,487,963
COMMUNITY HEALTH INDICATORS PER 1000 POPULATION					
Total Population (in thousands)	24,158	23,855	23,530	23,197	22,881
Inpatient					
Beds	2.1	2.1	2.1	2.1	2.2
Admissions	86.4	86.5	87	86.8	88.5
Inpatient Days	449.1	455.3	454.8	445.7	454.2
Inpatient Surgeries	23.7	22.9	23.3	23.9	24.8
Births	10.6	11.3	11.8	11.7	11.8
Outpatient					
Emergency Outpatient Visits	361.8	358	376.4	357.6	346.8
Other Outpatient Visits	1,630.6	1,624.5	1,576.8	1,525.3	1,457.6
Total Outpatient Visits	1,992.4	1,982.5	1,953.2	1,882.9	1,804.5
Outpatient Surgeries	49.2	48.0	46.3	46.3	46.6
Expense per Capita (per person)	$2,450.8	$2,317.6	$2,212.6	$2,091.7	$2,022.3

TABLE 5

U.S. CENSUS DIVISION 9: PACIFIC

U.S. Community Hospitals
(Nonfederal, short-term general and other special hospitals)

Overview 2013–2017

	2017	2016	2015	2014	2013
Total Community Hospitals					
in Census Division 9, Pacific	559	557	558	558	563
Bed Size Category					
6-24	49	50	50	49	49
25-49	96	99	101	103	103
50-99	80	75	73	76	76
100-199	141	145	147	147	148
200-299	83	82	82	81	84
300-399	56	55	56	55	56
400-499	34	33	30	29	30
500 +	20	18	19	18	17
Location					
Hospitals Urban	450	448	450	447	440
Hospitals Rural	109	109	108	111	123
Control					
State and Local Government	130	129	132	134	132
Not for Profit	329	325	326	326	331
Investor owned	100	103	100	98	100
Physician Models					
Independent Practice Association	100	107	88	78	72
Group Practice without Walls	17	20	22	28	23
Open Physician-Hospital Organization	27	16	12	14	13
Closed Physician-Hospital Organization	31	10	15	13	18
Management Service Organization	47	45	68	62	66
Integrated Salary Model	142	143	144	130	124
Equity Model	7	8	9	9	6
Foundation	99	111	116	104	102
Affiliations					
Hospitals in a System	380	376	373	362	350
Hospitals in a Network	171	146	152	139	130
Hospitals in a Group Purchasing Organization	300	331	344	338	337

TABLE 5

U.S. CENSUS DIVISION 9: PACIFIC

U.S. Community Hospitals
(Nonfederal, short-term general and other special hospitals)

Utilization, Personnel, Revenue and Expenses, Community Health Indicators 2013–2017

	2017	2016	2015	2014	2013
TOTAL FACILITY (Includes Hospital and Nursing Home Units)					
Utilization - Inpatient					
Beds	96,902	95,166	94,979	93,924	95,117
Admissions	4,576,293	4,484,330	4,433,755	4,306,210	4,420,001
Inpatient Days	23,428,335	22,907,552	22,476,767	21,869,659	22,135,328
Average Length of Stay	5.1	5.1	5.1	5.1	5.0
Inpatient Surgeries	1,209,730	1,190,702	1,185,742	1,192,129	1,180,995
Births	601,184	617,606	624,083	623,188	612,767
Utilization - Outpatient					
Emergency Outpatient Visits	18,835,805	18,791,709	18,855,870	17,420,395	16,590,491
Other Outpatient Visits	70,439,974	71,182,553	67,632,921	64,222,732	63,998,039
Total Outpatient Visits	89,275,779	89,974,262	86,488,791	81,643,127	80,588,530
Outpatient Surgeries	2,156,708	2,062,703	1,941,971	1,896,329	1,912,472
Personnel					
Full Time RNs	169,867	164,473	158,024	147,078	141,227
Full Time LPNs	7,741	7,633	7,449	6,850	7,402
Part Time RNs	85,797	81,225	78,506	78,066	78,301
Part Time LPNs	2,979	2,819	2,815	2,844	3,116
Total Full Time	577,017	557,195	538,934	509,409	502,499
Total Part Time	229,336	215,759	205,453	205,679	209,169
Revenue - Inpatient					
Gross Inpatient Revenue	$318,335,404,716	$301,918,263,374	$284,090,495,062	$261,126,952,307	$252,930,616,655
Revenue - Outpatient					
Gross Outpatient Revenue	$251,708,171,850	$229,616,879,363	$206,655,680,564	$184,397,789,726	$166,960,078,294
Revenue and Expenses - Totals					
(Includes Inpatient and Outpatient)					
Total Gross Revenue	$570,043,576,566	$531,535,142,737	$490,746,175,626	$445,524,742,033	$419,890,680,532
Deductions from Revenue	419,710,711,823	388,354,334,278	354,491,795,686	323,499,318,298	299,962,018,285
Net Patient Revenue	150,332,864,743	143,180,808,459	136,254,379,940	122,025,423,735	119,928,662,247
Other Operating Revenue	9,945,736,432	8,574,131,165	8,264,746,159	7,408,689,660	7,277,261,078
Other Nonoperating Revenue	3,444,511,627	1,664,029,117	1,715,958,138	3,065,966,661	3,901,003,391
Total Net Revenue	163,723,112,802	153,418,968,741	146,235,084,237	132,500,080,056	131,106,926,716
Total Expenses	151,561,222,380	143,686,330,615	134,859,861,537	122,892,452,086	120,308,844,738
HOSPITAL UNIT (Excludes Separate Nursing Home Units)					
Utilization - Inpatient					
Beds	94,334	91,330	90,411	89,755	90,215
Admissions	4,562,472	4,466,740	4,414,832	4,285,588	4,396,691
Inpatient Days	22,650,592	21,680,335	20,986,001	20,593,236	20,585,663
Average Length of Stay	5.0	4.9	4.8	4.8	4.7
Personnel					
Total Full Time	574,623	554,627	535,392	505,068	499,218
Total Part Time	228,318	214,499	203,722	204,122	207,359
Revenue and Expenses - Totals					
(Includes Inpatient and Outpatient)					
Total Net Revenue	$163,202,562,609	$152,822,130,125	$145,449,826,991	$131,889,155,058	$130,425,717,531
Total Expenses	151,226,248,629	143,267,833,798	134,328,221,293	122,503,116,817	119,785,168,801
COMMUNITY HEALTH INDICATORS PER 1000 POPULATION					
Total Population (in thousands)	53,253	52,802	52,514	51,991	51,373
Inpatient					
Beds	1.8	1.8	1.8	1.8	1.9
Admissions	85.9	84.9	84.4	82.8	86.0
Inpatient Days	439.9	433.8	428.0	420.6	430.9
Inpatient Surgeries	22.7	22.6	22.6	22.9	23.0
Births	11.3	11.7	11.9	12.0	11.9
Outpatient					
Emergency Outpatient Visits	353.7	355.9	359.1	335.1	322.9
Other Outpatient Visits	1,322.8	1,348.1	1,287.9	1,235.3	1,245.7
Total Outpatient Visits	1,676.5	1,704.0	1,647.0	1,570.3	1,568.7
Outpatient Surgeries	40.5	39.1	37.0	36.5	37.2
Expense per Capita (per person)	$2,846.1	$2,721.2	$2,568.1	$2,363.7	$2,341.9

TABLE 6

ALABAMA

U.S. Community Hospitals
(Nonfederal, short-term general and other special hospitals)

Overview 2013–2017

	2017	2016	2015	2014	2013
Total Community Hospitals in Alabama............	102	103	103	104	105
Bed Size Category					
6-24	4	5	6	5	5
25-49	30	29	32	29	31
50-99	25	26	20	23	22
100-199	21	21	23	26	25
200-299	8	8	9	8	9
300-399	7	7	6	6	6
400-499	1	2	2	2	2
500 + ...	6	5	5	5	5
Location					
Hospitals Urban	62	62	62	63	60
Hospitals Rural	40	41	41	41	45
Control					
State and Local Government	38	39	38	40	39
Not for Profit	27	26	26	29	30
Investor owned	37	38	39	35	36
Physician Models					
Independent Practice Association.......	5	4	4	2	2
Group Practice without Walls	0	0	0	0	0
Open Physician-Hospital Organization ...	0	0	5	6	6
Closed Physician-Hospital Organization ...	6	5	1	0	0
Management Service Organization	4	5	6	3	3
Integrated Salary Model......................	9	9	9	8	9
Equity Model	0	0	0	0	0
Foundation	4	6	6	4	4
Affiliations					
Hospitals in a System	69	68	67	67	68
Hospitals in a Network.........................	10	12	7	9	7
Hospitals in a Group Purchasing Organization...	35	37	39	38	39

TABLE 6

ALABAMA

U.S. Community Hospitals
(Nonfederal, short-term general and other special hospitals)

Utilization, Personnel, Revenue and Expenses, Community Health Indicators 2013–2017

	2017	2016	2015	2014	2013
TOTAL FACILITY (Includes Hospital and Nursing Home Units)					
Utilization - Inpatient					
Beds	15,216	15,426	14,946	15,268	15,437
Admissions	628,563	635,617	621,258	636,939	646,146
Inpatient Days	3,596,377	3,611,737	3,470,865	3,391,201	3,428,219
Average Length of Stay	5.7	5.7	5.6	5.3	5.3
Inpatient Surgeries	186,128	188,602	179,423	182,044	190,779
Births	55,178	58,959	59,221	57,863	57,811
Utilization - Outpatient					
Emergency Outpatient Visits	2,327,525	2,219,724	2,483,878	2,365,295	2,299,583
Other Outpatient Visits	6,932,284	6,578,133	6,254,117	6,179,508	6,043,912
Total Outpatient Visits	9,259,809	8,797,857	8,737,995	8,544,803	8,343,495
Outpatient Surgeries	412,077	397,205	369,010	361,342	381,522
Personnel					
Full Time RNs	23,991	22,476	22,006	21,667	20,690
Full Time LPNs	1,055	1,156	1,157	1,166	1,262
Part Time RNs	7,995	8,554	8,115	5,997	6,468
Part Time LPNs	343	347	331	305	392
Total Full Time	71,611	70,463	70,142	69,763	68,409
Total Part Time	21,313	22,352	20,777	16,483	17,317
Revenue - Inpatient					
Gross Inpatient Revenue	$28,875,634,627	$27,037,976,778	$25,293,057,844	$22,987,546,186	$22,223,301,104
Revenue - Outpatient					
Gross Outpatient Revenue	$26,213,584,324	$24,614,811,000	$23,422,875,009	$21,005,094,227	$19,260,488,004
Revenue and Expenses - Totals					
(Includes Inpatient and Outpatient)					
Total Gross Revenue	$55,089,218,951	$51,652,787,778	$48,715,932,853	$43,992,640,413	$41,483,789,108
Deductions from Revenue	43,466,133,232	40,225,680,622	37,858,963,918	33,661,600,274	31,208,902,907
Net Patient Revenue	11,623,085,719	11,427,107,156	10,856,968,935	10,331,040,139	10,274,886,201
Other Operating Revenue	675,713,884	670,890,505	628,727,907	615,822,225	576,890,316
Other Nonoperating Revenue	268,557,069	170,649,053	34,680,595	222,131,131	240,972,875
Total Net Revenue	12,567,356,672	12,268,646,714	11,520,377,437	11,168,993,495	11,092,749,392
Total Expenses	11,596,934,569	10,943,795,352	10,424,031,054	9,994,535,612	9,803,241,648
HOSPITAL UNIT (Excludes Separate Nursing Home Units)					
Utilization - Inpatient					
Beds	14,579	14,793	14,416	14,902	15,003
Admissions	627,790	634,134	619,945	636,000	644,936
Inpatient Days	3,393,391	3,398,467	3,303,436	3,274,483	3,289,639
Average Length of Stay	5.4	5.4	5.3	5.1	5.1
Personnel					
Total Full Time	71,259	69,892	69,711	69,292	67,763
Total Part Time	21,241	22,189	20,642	16,405	16,896
Revenue and Expenses - Totals					
(Includes Inpatient and Outpatient)					
Total Net Revenue	$12,539,717,204	$12,211,589,964	$11,491,426,915	$11,149,841,334	$11,067,575,588
Total Expenses	11,582,886,825	10,902,476,926	10,387,274,180	9,979,511,941	9,779,993,645
COMMUNITY HEALTH INDICATORS PER 1000 POPULATION					
Total Population (in thousands)	4,875	4,863	4,859	4,849	4,834
Inpatient					
Beds	3.1	3.2	3.1	3.1	3.2
Admissions	128.9	130.7	127.9	131.3	133.7
Inpatient Days	737.8	742.7	714.3	699.3	709.2
Inpatient Surgeries	38.2	38.8	36.9	37.5	39.5
Births	11.3	12.1	12.2	11.9	12.0
Outpatient					
Emergency Outpatient Visits	477.5	456.4	511.2	487.8	475.7
Other Outpatient Visits	1,422.1	1,352.6	1,287.1	1,274.3	1,250.4
Total Outpatient Visits	1,899.5	1,809	1,798.3	1,762	1,726.1
Outpatient Surgeries	84.5	81.7	75.9	74.5	78.9
Expense per Capita (per person)	$2,379.0	$2,250.3	$2,145.3	$2,061.0	$2,028.1

TABLE 6

ALASKA

U.S. Community Hospitals
(Nonfederal, short-term general and other special hospitals)

Overview 2013–2017

	2017	2016	2015	2014	2013
Total Community Hospitals in Alaska	21	21	21	22	22
Bed Size Category					
6-24	5	4	4	5	5
25-49	6	7	7	7	9
50-99	5	5	5	5	3
100-199	3	3	3	3	3
200-299	1	1	1	1	1
300-399	0	0	0	0	1
400-499	1	1	1	1	0
500 +	0	0	0	0	0
Location					
Hospitals Urban	6	6	6	6	6
Hospitals Rural	15	15	15	16	16
Control					
State and Local Government	8	7	7	7	7
Not for Profit	10	11	11	13	13
Investor owned	3	3	3	2	2
Physician Models					
Independent Practice Association	1	2	2	1	1
Group Practice without Walls	0	1	1	0	0
Open Physician-Hospital Organization	0	1	1	1	1
Closed Physician-Hospital Organization	0	1	1	0	1
Management Service Organization	1	0	0	0	0
Integrated Salary Model	7	7	7	5	4
Equity Model	0	0	0	0	0
Foundation	1	2	2	0	1
Affiliations					
Hospitals in a System	7	7	8	8	8
Hospitals in a Network	1	2	2	2	1
Hospitals in a Group Purchasing Organization	8	9	10	8	9

TABLE 6

ALASKA

U.S. Community Hospitals
(Nonfederal, short-term general and other special hospitals)

Utilization, Personnel, Revenue and Expenses, Community Health Indicators 2013–2017

	2017	2016	2015	2014	2013
TOTAL FACILITY (Includes Hospital and Nursing Home Units)					
Utilization - Inpatient					
Beds	1,630	1,647	1,634	1,633	1,560
Admissions	52,418	51,022	52,637	53,386	57,621
Inpatient Days	381,239	384,938	378,062	376,135	376,393
Average Length of Stay	7.3	7.5	7.2	7.0	6.5
Inpatient Surgeries	20,079	18,924	13,138	14,712	13,001
Births	8,465	9,687	9,721	8,985	7,372
Utilization - Outpatient					
Emergency Outpatient Visits	381,678	342,017	324,973	303,956	257,285
Other Outpatient Visits	1,839,755	1,717,104	1,635,792	1,474,745	1,110,025
Total Outpatient Visits	2,221,433	2,059,121	1,960,765	1,778,701	1,367,310
Outpatient Surgeries	44,729	51,311	33,963	37,675	39,216
Personnel					
Full Time RNs	2,821	2,597	2,338	2,492	2,095
Full Time LPNs	133	120	86	129	150
Part Time RNs	1,088	1,165	822	862	823
Part Time LPNs	34	49	22	34	45
Total Full Time	10,328	10,134	8,453	9,228	8,364
Total Part Time	2,982	3,196	2,251	2,357	2,726
Revenue - Inpatient					
Gross Inpatlent Revenue	$4,545,321,364	$3,953,723,400	$3,489,110,219	$3,131,261,783	$2,857,156,569
Revenue - Outpatient					
Gross Outpatient Revenue	$5,069,155,066	$4,330,578,373	$3,360,897,973	$3,067,062,814	$2,965,846,524
Revenue and Expenses - Totals					
(Includes Inpatient and Outpatient)					
Total Gross Revenue	$9,614,476,430	$8,284,301,773	$6,850,008,192	$6,198,324,597	$5,823,003,093
Deductions from Revenue	6,987,397,369	5,740,953,226	4,496,841,752	3,994,064,697	3,746,662,160
Net Patient Revenue	2,627,079,061	2,543,348,547	2,353,166,440	2,204,259,900	2,076,340,933
Other Operating Revenue	365,717,138	255,918,888	284,505,976	170,454,937	100,248,551
Other Nonoperating Revenue	82,054,896	44,074,181	7,386,912	31,062,392	42,606,280
Total Net Revenue	3,074,851,095	2,843,341,616	2,645,059,328	2,405,777,229	2,219,195,764
Total Expenses	2,642,628,585	2,291,293,712	1,963,422,824	1,932,865,572	1,824,096,637
HOSPITAL UNIT (Excludes Separate Nursing Home Units)					
Utilization - Inpatient					
Beds	1,491	1,424	1,379	1,387	1,273
Admissions	52,209	50,600	52,272	53,166	57,215
Inpatient Days	348,206	312,802	296,315	298,489	282,965
Average Length of Stay	6.7	6.2	5.7	5.6	4.9
Personnel					
Total Full Time	10,142	9,871	8,119	8,949	8,116
Total Part Time	2,917	3,042	2,108	2,259	2,596
Revenue and Expenses - Totals					
(Includes Inpatient and Outpatient)					
Total Net Revenue	$3,040,547,422	$2,790,416,270	$2,596,163,699	$2,362,196,823	$2,171,602,536
Total Expenses	2,617,428,807	2,251,240,758	1,923,795,139	1,898,027,765	1,783,712,793
COMMUNITY HEALTH INDICATORS PER 1000 POPULATION					
Total Population (in thousands)	740	742	738	737	735
Inpatient					
Beds	2.2	2.2	2.2	2.2	2.1
Admissions	70.9	68.8	71.3	72.5	78.4
Inpatient Days	515.3	518.9	512.0	510.5	512.0
Inpatient Surgeries	27.1	25.5	17.8	20.0	17.7
Births	11.4	13.1	13.2	12.2	10.0
Outpatient					
Emergency Outpatient Visits	515.9	461.0	440.1	412.6	350.0
Other Outpatient Visits	2,486.8	2,314.5	2,215.2	2,001.7	1,510.0
Total Outpatient Visits	3,002.8	2,775.5	2,655.3	2,414.3	1,860.0
Outpatient Surgeries	60.5	69.2	46.0	51.1	53.3
Expense per Capita (per person)	$3,572.1	$3,088.4	$2,658.9	$2,623.6	$2,481.3

States

TABLE 6

ARIZONA

U.S. Community Hospitals
(Nonfederal, short-term general and other special hospitals)

Overview 2013–2017

	2017	2016	2015	2014	2013
Total Community Hospitals in Arizona...............	83	84	84	84	86
Bed Size Category					
6-24	15	14	12	12	12
25-49	13	14	15	15	16
50-99	16	15	15	17	15
100-199	11	14	16	13	16
200-299	11	10	9	11	11
300-399	6	6	6	6	5
400-499	6	6	6	5	6
500 + ...	5	5	5	5	5
Location					
Hospitals Urban	74	75	75	75	72
Hospitals Rural..	9	9	9	9	14
Control					
State and Local Government	5	4	5	4	4
Not for Profit	42	43	46	47	48
Investor owned..	36	37	33	33	34
Physician Models					
Independent Practice Association.....................	14	19	19	8	6
Group Practice without Walls	2	3	1	3	2
Open Physician-Hospital Organization	1	2	0	5	4
Closed Physician-Hospital Organization............	5	10	16	6	4
Management Service Organization	3	5	2	5	5
Integrated Salary Model...................................	14	29	29	19	16
Equity Model	0	0	0	0	0
Foundation	1	1	1	1	1
Affiliations					
Hospitals in a System	59	60	60	60	58
Hospitals in a Network	25	25	25	21	19
Hospitals in a Group Purchasing Organization...	41	36	44	42	45

TABLE 6

ARIZONA

U.S. Community Hospitals
(Nonfederal, short-term general and other special hospitals)

Utilization, Personnel, Revenue and Expenses, Community Health Indicators 2013–2017

	2017	2016	2015	2014	2013
TOTAL FACILITY (Includes Hospital and Nursing Home Units)					
Utilization - Inpatient					
Beds	13,918	13,903	14,012	13,777	14,063
Admissions	651,064	638,265	636,419	638,906	655,536
Inpatient Days	3,079,118	3,069,875	3,006,541	2,935,332	3,002,739
Average Length of Stay	4.7	4.8	4.7	4.6	4.6
Inpatient Surgeries	172,616	166,231	166,370	181,939	190,770
Births	73,229	76,051	78,101	74,465	75,480
Utilization - Outpatient					
Emergency Outpatient Visits	2,173,898	2,128,481	2,328,632	2,122,297	2,112,455
Other Outpatient Visits	6,385,894	6,351,899	6,631,501	6,496,908	6,808,592
Total Outpatient Visits	8,559,792	8,480,380	8,960,133	8,619,205	8,921,047
Outpatient Surgeries	316,655	293,483	268,525	280,148	294,940
Personnel					
Full Time RNs	24,648	25,095	23,946	23,948	22,643
Full Time LPNs	520	639	569	545	651
Part Time RNs	7,121	6,693	5,150	4,999	6,095
Part Time LPNs	136	145	97	92	141
Total Full Time	73,874	74,820	71,818	72,321	69,094
Total Part Time	17,375	17,416	13,238	13,062	15,583
Revenue - Inpatient					
Gross Inpatient Revenue	$38,592,599,767	$35,349,524,715	$32,283,089,602	$30,393,537,927	$28,892,179,697
Revenue - Outpatient					
Gross Outpatient Revenue	$33,132,876,010	$30,494,034,624	$27,543,122,602	$24,525,273,926	$21,926,726,698
Revenue and Expenses - Totals					
(Includes Inpatient and Outpatient)					
Total Gross Revenue	$71,725,475,777	$65,843,559,339	$59,826,212,204	$54,918,811,853	$50,818,906,395
Deductions from Revenue	55,530,228,554	50,768,979,353	45,392,282,623	41,078,307,387	37,839,582,378
Net Patient Revenue	16,195,247,223	15,074,579,986	14,433,929,581	13,840,504,466	12,979,324,017
Other Operating Revenue	701,646,183	554,015,620	545,903,135	540,869,143	610,329,498
Other Nonoperating Revenue	215,957,431	77,391,425	51,879,312	192,398,672	143,491,197
Total Net Revenue	17,112,850,837	15,705,987,031	15,031,712,028	14,573,772,281	13,733,144,712
Total Expenses	15,492,616,879	14,499,241,249	14,098,268,721	13,325,589,531	12,735,970,681
HOSPITAL UNIT (Excludes Separate Nursing Home Units)					
Utilization - Inpatient					
Beds	13,840	13,825	13,910	13,675	13,968
Admissions	649,629	636,819	634,650	637,038	653,814
Inpatient Days	3,058,136	3,049,581	2,983,884	2,911,570	2,975,157
Average Length of Stay	4.7	4.8	4.7	4.6	4.6
Personnel					
Total Full Time	73,811	74,762	71,747	72,244	69,019
Total Part Time	17,362	17,404	13,222	13,046	15,567
Revenue and Expenses - Totals					
(Includes Inpatient and Outpatient)					
Total Net Revenue	$17,066,085,299	$15,670,525,036	$14,997,280,215	$14,543,654,897	$13,702,601,747
Total Expenses	15,480,970,646	14,487,932,710	14,089,184,781	13,313,129,779	12,723,236,533
COMMUNITY HEALTH INDICATORS PER 1000 POPULATION					
Total Population (in thousands)	7,016	6,931	6,828	6,731	6,627
Inpatient					
Beds	2.0	2.0	2.1	2.0	2.1
Admissions	92.8	92.1	93.2	94.9	98.9
Inpatient Days	438.9	442.9	440.3	436.1	453.1
Inpatient Surgeries	24.6	24.0	24.4	27.0	28.8
Births	10.4	11.0	11.4	11.1	11.4
Outpatient					
Emergency Outpatient Visits	309.8	307.1	341.0	315.3	318.8
Other Outpatient Visits	910.2	916.4	971.2	965.2	1,027.5
Total Outpatient Visits	1,220.0	1,223.5	1,312.3	1,280.4	1,346.2
Outpatient Surgeries	45.1	42.3	39.3	41.6	44.5
Expense per Capita (per person)	$2,208.1	$2,091.9	$2,064.8	$1,979.6	$1,921.9

States

TABLE 6

ARKANSAS

U.S. Community Hospitals
(Nonfederal, short-term general and other special hospitals)

Overview 2013–2017

	2017	2016	2015	2014	2013
Total Community Hospitals in Arkansas	88	88	87	87	90
Bed Size Category					
6-24	7	7	7	8	8
25-49	37	38	35	31	34
50-99	13	14	15	19	17
100-199	14	11	13	13	15
200-299	7	8	9	8	7
300-399	7	7	5	5	6
400-499	1	1	2	2	2
500 +	2	2	1	1	1
Location					
Hospitals Urban	39	39	38	38	40
Hospitals Rural	49	49	49	49	50
Control					
State and Local Government	10	10	10	10	11
Not for Profit	48	52	51	50	51
Investor owned	30	26	26	27	28
Physician Models					
Independent Practice Association	8	7	8	5	6
Group Practice without Walls	5	4	4	3	5
Open Physician-Hospital Organization	21	21	22	23	24
Closed Physician-Hospital Organization	3	2	4	5	7
Management Service Organization	9	10	12	12	12
Integrated Salary Model	33	29	29	28	30
Equity Model	1	2	2	2	2
Foundation	6	6	7	6	6
Affiliations					
Hospitals in a System	48	48	47	45	47
Hospitals in a Network	32	30	28	28	28
Hospitals in a Group Purchasing Organization	73	73	74	71	81

TABLE 6

ARKANSAS

U.S. Community Hospitals
(Nonfederal, short-term general and other special hospitals)

Utilization, Personnel, Revenue and Expenses, Community Health Indicators 2013–2017

	2017	2016	2015	2014	2013
TOTAL FACILITY (Includes Hospital and Nursing Home Units)					
Utilization - Inpatient					
Beds	9,664	9,634	9,569	9,449	9,617
Admissions	363,070	359,359	357,286	350,431	358,359
Inpatient Days	1,861,122	1,846,634	1,859,244	1,795,753	1,842,902
Average Length of Stay	5.1	5.1	5.2	5.1	5.1
Inpatient Surgeries	95,013	94,627	94,607	96,353	100,360
Births	35,517	35,864	36,206	35,407	36,313
Utilization - Outpatient					
Emergency Outpatient Visits	1,519,156	1,515,989	1,492,359	1,359,029	1,446,183
Other Outpatient Visits	4,629,383	4,570,177	4,184,351	3,790,058	3,728,501
Total Outpatient Visits	6,148,539	6,086,166	5,676,710	5,149,087	5,174,684
Outpatient Surgeries	203,105	200,832	195,650	180,684	181,402
Personnel					
Full Time RNs	12,629	12,661	12,720	12,158	12,069
Full Time LPNs	1,446	1,472	1,474	1,556	1,606
Part Time RNs	5,093	3,699	3,663	3,578	3,398
Part Time LPNs	370	380	361	427	392
Total Full Time	42,385	42,533	41,865	40,372	39,764
Total Part Time	15,207	10,725	10,694	11,161	9,651
Revenue - Inpatient					
Gross Inpatient Revenue	$13,396,489,708	$12,460,694,916	$11,700,149,701	$11,007,915,107	$10,605,082,886
Revenue - Outpatient					
Gross Outpatient Revenue	$14,212,477,805	$12,952,790,887	$11,967,218,307	$10,568,638,798	$9,645,405,883
Revenue and Expenses - Totals					
(Includes Inpatient and Outpatient)					
Total Gross Revenue	$27,608,967,513	$25,413,485,803	$23,667,368,008	$21,576,553,905	$20,250,488,769
Deductions from Revenue	20,249,177,829	18,458,098,464	17,048,393,940	15,544,835,789	14,359,922,959
Net Patient Revenue	7,359,789,684	6,955,387,339	6,618,974,068	6,031,718,116	5,890,565,810
Other Operating Revenue	381,973,773	307,097,211	250,191,038	310,383,539	271,018,970
Other Nonoperating Revenue	118,736,986	82,544,865	42,144,248	98,655,117	88,171,599
Total Net Revenue	7,860,500,443	7,345,029,415	6,911,309,354	6,440,756,772	6,249,756,379
Total Expenses	7,372,516,174	6,803,364,553	6,428,954,340	6,090,855,820	6,020,388,342
HOSPITAL UNIT (Excludes Separate Nursing Home Units)					
Utilization - Inpatient					
Beds	9,311	9,326	9,201	9,081	9,341
Admissions	362,439	358,734	356,680	349,874	357,944
Inpatient Days	1,762,734	1,756,049	1,758,250	1,694,087	1,764,188
Average Length of Stay	4.9	4.9	4.9	4.8	4.9
Personnel					
Total Full Time	42,099	42,354	41,654	40,144	39,613
Total Part Time	15,172	10,699	10,636	11,110	9,621
Revenue and Expenses - Totals					
(Includes Inpatient and Outpatient)					
Total Net Revenue	$7,841,622,879	$7,325,492,355	$6,890,484,637	$6,420,088,618	$6,235,770,392
Total Expenses	7,356,700,895	6,789,080,213	6,412,183,234	6,077,423,193	6,010,319,727
COMMUNITY HEALTH INDICATORS PER 1000 POPULATION					
Total Population (in thousands)	3,004	2,988	2,978	2,966	2,959
Inpatient					
Beds	3.2	3.2	3.2	3.2	3.2
Admissions	120.9	120.3	120.0	118.1	121.1
Inpatient Days	619.5	618.0	624.3	605.4	622.7
Inpatient Surgeries	31.6	31.7	31.8	32.5	33.9
Births	11.8	12.0	12.2	11.9	12.3
Outpatient					
Emergency Outpatient Visits	505.7	507.3	501.1	458.1	488.7
Other Outpatient Visits	1,540.9	1,529.4	1,405.0	1,277.7	1,259.9
Total Outpatient Visits	2,046.6	2,036.7	1,906.1	1,735.8	1,748.6
Outpatient Surgeries	67.6	67.2	65.7	60.9	61.3
Expense per Capita (per person)	$2,454.0	$2,276.7	$2,158.7	$2,053.3	$2,034.3

States

TABLE 6

CALIFORNIA

U.S. Community Hospitals
(Nonfederal, short-term general and other special hospitals)

Overview 2013–2017

	2017	2016	2015	2014	2013
Total Community Hospitals in California	362	360	360	358	363
Bed Size Category					
6-24	15	15	16	17	18
25-49	40	41	42	42	44
50-99	49	45	43	44	42
100-199	103	110	110	112	112
200-299	68	65	66	61	64
300-399	47	46	46	48	48
400-499	26	25	24	22	22
500 +	14	13	13	12	13
Location					
Hospitals Urban	332	330	330	327	332
Hospitals Rural	30	30	30	31	31
Control					
State and Local Government	65	63	64	64	63
Not for Profit	208	208	210	209	212
Investor owned	89	89	86	85	88
Physician Models					
Independent Practice Association	89	93	73	66	59
Group Practice without Walls	13	14	13	19	14
Open Physician-Hospital Organization	18	6	4	6	6
Closed Physician-Hospital Organization	27	3	7	7	9
Management Service Organization	36	32	54	50	54
Integrated Salary Model	37	32	29	22	22
Equity Model	7	8	9	8	3
Foundation	96	107	112	100	94
Affiliations					
Hospitals in a System	261	258	253	245	237
Hospitals in a Network	103	71	79	69	71
Hospitals in a Group Purchasing Organization	170	199	213	203	205

TABLE 6

CALIFORNIA

U.S. Community Hospitals
(Nonfederal, short-term general and other special hospitals)

Utilization, Personnel, Revenue and Expenses, Community Health Indicators 2013–2017

	2017	2016	2015	2014	2013
TOTAL FACILITY (Includes Hospital and Nursing Home Units)					
Utilization - Inpatient					
Beds	73,195	72,004	71,715	70,474	71,554
Admissions	3,452,477	3,384,619	3,324,507	3,226,168	3,309,244
Inpatient Days	17,744,125	17,375,662	17,019,301	16,552,067	16,754,461
Average Length of Stay	5.1	5.1	5.1	5.1	5.1
Inpatient Surgeries	857,163	841,709	847,174	852,003	845,655
Births	446,852	461,287	469,747	479,040	474,364
Utilization - Outpatient					
Emergency Outpatient Visits	13,460,106	13,688,436	13,792,047	12,768,341	12,176,137
Other Outpatient Visits	43,696,913	45,898,449	43,798,963	41,661,959	41,972,108
Total Outpatient Visits	57,157,019	59,586,885	57,591,010	54,430,300	54,148,245
Outpatient Surgeries	1,479,725	1,376,228	1,342,559	1,288,139	1,329,879
Personnel					
Full Time RNs	128,579	121,266	117,086	110,213	105,534
Full Time LPNs	6,418	6,033	5,974	5,645	6,018
Part Time RNs	62,556	60,798	57,468	56,120	54,970
Part Time LPNs	2,347	2,206	2,186	2,249	2,385
Total Full Time	426,573	399,525	389,414	368,515	364,412
Total Part Time	164,147	156,905	148,916	144,535	143,097
Revenue - Inpatient					
Gross Inpatient Revenue	$259,909,932,608	$247,487,254,287	$232,570,927,093	$214,559,475,989	$208,055,903,554
Revenue - Outpatient					
Gross Outpatient Revenue	$191,470,747,704	$174,838,843,059	$156,754,034,665	$139,467,948,617	$125,306,167,664
Revenue and Expenses - Totals					
(Includes Inpatient and Outpatient)					
Total Gross Revenue	$451,380,680,312	$422,326,097,346	$389,324,961,758	$354,027,424,606	$333,362,056,801
Deductions from Revenue	340,809,314,083	317,209,061,450	289,551,701,992	265,060,977,456	245,304,638,314
Net Patient Revenue	110,571,366,229	105,117,035,896	99,773,259,766	88,966,447,150	88,057,418,487
Other Operating Revenue	7,373,673,021	6,237,432,451	5,915,855,092	5,458,055,984	5,450,019,421
Other Nonoperating Revenue	2,678,576,375	1,263,341,664	1,336,798,281	2,579,981,389	3,355,491,073
Total Net Revenue	120,623,615,625	112,617,810,011	107,025,913,139	97,004,484,523	96,862,928,981
Total Expenses	110,902,410,525	105,192,746,282	98,800,359,182	89,778,835,703	88,101,857,134
HOSPITAL UNIT (Excludes Separate Nursing Home Units)					
Utilization - Inpatient					
Beds	70,915	68,777	68,059	67,027	67,584
Admissions	3,439,379	3,369,165	3,308,119	3,207,781	3,288,481
Inpatient Days	17,042,357	16,335,596	15,833,308	15,492,434	15,517,450
Average Length of Stay	5.0	4.8	4.8	4.8	4.7
Personnel					
Total Full Time	424,523	397,558	386,762	364,845	361,779
Total Part Time	163,260	156,032	147,625	143,310	141,637
Revenue and Expenses - Totals					
(Includes Inpatient and Outpatient)					
Total Net Revenue	$120,157,794,110	$112,141,226,910	$106,372,486,411	$96,497,642,708	$96,286,964,774
Total Expenses	110,613,699,579	104,868,183,144	98,382,552,632	89,478,250,563	87,677,995,439
COMMUNITY HEALTH INDICATORS PER 1000 POPULATION					
Total Population (in thousands)	39,537	39,250	39,145	38,803	38,333
Inpatient					
Beds	1.9	1.8	1.8	1.8	1.9
Admissions	87.3	86.2	84.9	83.1	86.3
Inpatient Days	448.8	442.7	434.8	426.6	437.1
Inpatient Surgeries	21.7	21.4	21.6	22.0	22.1
Births	11.3	11.8	12.0	12.3	12.4
Outpatient					
Emergency Outpatient Visits	340.4	348.7	352.3	329.1	317.6
Other Outpatient Visits	1,105.2	1,169.4	1,118.9	1,073.7	1,094.9
Total Outpatient Visits	1,445.7	1,518.1	1,471.2	1,402.8	1,412.6
Outpatient Surgeries	37.4	35.1	34.3	33.2	34.7
Expense per Capita (per person)	$2,805.1	$2,680.1	$2,524.0	$2,313.7	$2,298.4

States

TABLE 6

COLORADO

U.S. Community Hospitals
(Nonfederal, short-term general and other special hospitals)

Overview 2013–2017

	2017	2016	2015	2014	2013
Total Community Hospitals in Colorado	89	86	88	87	86
Bed Size Category					
6-24	20	16	18	15	14
25-49	22	23	24	22	22
50-99	18	17	17	19	19
100-199	11	10	10	12	13
200-299	6	8	7	7	6
300-399	5	5	5	5	7
400-499	4	4	4	6	4
500 + ...	3	3	3	1	1
Location					
Hospitals Urban	49	46	48	47	46
Hospitals Rural	40	40	40	40	40
Control					
State and Local Government	26	24	25	25	25
Not for Profit	43	43	42	42	41
Investor owned	20	19	21	20	20
Physician Models					
Independent Practice Association	13	14	13	10	11
Group Practice without Walls	5	2	2	2	3
Open Physician-Hospital Organization	6	8	8	12	11
Closed Physician-Hospital Organization	3	5	5	2	3
Management Service Organization	4	4	4	4	4
Integrated Salary Model	32	40	43	42	40
Equity Model	2	1	1	1	1
Foundation	3	4	2	2	3
Affiliations					
Hospitals in a System	56	52	55	51	50
Hospitals in a Network	20	18	18	18	20
Hospitals in a Group Purchasing Organization...	56	60	60	61	61

Table 6

COLORADO

U.S. Community Hospitals
(Nonfederal, short-term general and other special hospitals)

Utilization, Personnel, Revenue and Expenses, Community Health Indicators 2013–2017

	2017	2016	2015	2014	2013
TOTAL FACILITY (Includes Hospital and Nursing Home Units)					
Utilization - Inpatient					
Beds	10,793	10,874	10,646	10,660	10,392
Admissions	445,190	429,370	428,378	416,407	408,566
Inpatient Days	2,225,569	2,222,898	2,189,200	2,160,542	2,160,998
Average Length of Stay	5.0	5.2	5.1	5.2	5.3
Inpatient Surgeries	142,249	132,068	127,395	125,118	122,888
Births	59,221	61,795	62,844	61,277	56,439
Utilization - Outpatient					
Emergency Outpatient Visits	2,000,092	2,038,472	2,084,609	1,927,010	1,879,118
Other Outpatient Visits	7,398,577	7,074,702	6,783,043	6,615,845	6,919,299
Total Outpatient Visits	9,398,669	9,113,174	8,867,652	8,542,855	8,798,417
Outpatient Surgeries	251,802	254,491	249,948	243,332	239,951
Personnel					
Full Time RNs	18,007	17,694	17,035	16,765	15,530
Full Time LPNs	574	502	554	571	487
Part Time RNs	7,777	7,595	6,735	6,612	6,785
Part Time LPNs	234	226	206	184	191
Total Full Time	61,837	59,978	57,797	56,820	55,010
Total Part Time	24,313	22,728	19,225	19,017	20,590
Revenue - Inpatient					
Gross Inpatient Revenue	$33,700,836,075	$30,693,433,843	$28,980,827,929	$26,045,445,521	$23,206,992,718
Revenue - Outpatient					
Gross Outpatient Revenue	$31,433,059,267	$27,169,644,489	$25,845,024,764	$22,634,021,371	$20,123,709,011
Revenue and Expenses - Totals					
(Includes Inpatient and Outpatient)					
Total Gross Revenue	$65,133,895,342	$57,863,078,332	$54,825,852,693	$48,679,466,892	$43,330,701,729
Deductions from Revenue	49,382,913,078	43,179,452,597	40,732,139,747	35,595,438,625	31,111,384,528
Net Patient Revenue	15,750,982,264	14,683,625,735	14,093,712,946	13,084,028,267	12,219,317,201
Other Operating Revenue	660,542,442	624,912,473	555,943,564	577,927,126	602,479,404
Other Nonoperating Revenue	419,008,905	143,935,558	140,814,200	316,648,685	289,746,598
Total Net Revenue	16,830,533,611	15,452,473,766	14,790,470,710	13,978,604,078	13,111,543,203
Total Expenses	14,271,275,490	13,425,728,556	12,842,090,285	12,197,042,680	11,510,680,305
HOSPITAL UNIT (Excludes Separate Nursing Home Units)					
Utilization - Inpatient					
Beds	10,290	10,279	10,052	10,062	9,652
Admissions	444,220	428,006	426,663	414,875	406,774
Inpatient Days	2,090,680	2,043,296	2,012,216	2,000,692	1,937,457
Average Length of Stay	4.7	4.8	4.7	4.8	4.8
Personnel					
Total Full Time	61,608	59,594	57,438	56,481	54,365
Total Part Time	24,197	22,578	19,082	18,842	20,088
Revenue and Expenses - Totals					
(Includes Inpatient and Outpatient)					
Total Net Revenue	$16,801,588,272	$15,407,441,587	$14,748,533,542	$13,947,809,243	$13,063,875,078
Total Expenses	14,235,109,577	13,384,654,709	12,800,429,586	12,167,624,048	11,458,012,277
COMMUNITY HEALTH INDICATORS PER 1000 POPULATION					
Total Population (in thousands)	5,607	5,541	5,457	5,356	5,268
Inpatient					
Beds	1.9	2.0	2.0	2.0	2.0
Admissions	79.4	77.5	78.5	77.7	77.6
Inpatient Days	396.9	401.2	401.2	403.4	410.2
Inpatient Surgeries	25.4	23.8	23.3	23.4	23.3
Births	10.6	11.2	11.5	11.4	10.7
Outpatient					
Emergency Outpatient Visits	356.7	367.9	382.0	359.8	356.7
Other Outpatient Visits	1,319.5	1,276.9	1,243.1	1,235.3	1,313.4
Total Outpatient Visits	1,676.2	1,644.8	1,625.1	1,595.0	1,670.0
Outpatient Surgeries	44.9	45.9	45.8	45.4	45.5
Expense per Capita (per person)	$2,545.2	$2,423.2	$2,353.5	$2,277.3	$2,184.9

States

TABLE 6

CONNECTICUT

U.S. Community Hospitals
(Nonfederal, short-term general and other special hospitals)

Overview 2013–2017

	2017	2016	2015	2014	2013
Total Community Hospitals in Connecticut........	32	32	32	32	33
Bed Size Category					
6-24	0	0	0	0	0
25-49	3	3	3	3	3
50-99	8	8	8	8	8
100-199	12	12	11	11	12
200-299	3	2	2	2	2
300-399	3	3	3	4	4
400-499	1	1	2	1	1
500 + ...	2	3	3	3	3
Location					
Hospitals Urban	30	30	30	30	28
Hospitals Rural..	2	2	2	2	5
Control					
State and Local Government	1	1	1	1	1
Not for Profit..	31	30	30	30	31
Investor owned	0	1	1	1	1
Physician Models					
Independent Practice Association....................	5	6	5	5	8
Group Practice without Walls	0	1	0	0	2
Open Physician-Hospital Organization	7	6	6	7	6
Closed Physician-Hospital Organization.............	0	0	1	1	3
Management Service Organization	0	4	3	3	3
Integrated Salary Model................................	15	14	12	13	16
Equity Model	4	4	4	4	4
Foundation	14	13	11	10	8
Affiliations					
Hospitals in a System	21	20	19	16	17
Hospitals in a Network	18	18	14	17	16
Hospitals in a Group Purchasing Organization...	24	25	24	24	26

TABLE 6

CONNECTICUT

U.S. Community Hospitals
(Nonfederal, short-term general and other special hospitals)

Utilization, Personnel, Revenue and Expenses, Community Health Indicators 2013–2017

	2017	2016	2015	2014	2013
TOTAL FACILITY (Includes Hospital and Nursing Home Units)					
Utilization - Inpatient					
Beds	7,086	7,278	7,531	7,806	7,811
Admissions	371,009	375,154	377,150	376,644	391,394
Inpatient Days	1,993,586	1,951,522	2,008,771	2,091,854	2,144,945
Average Length of Stay	5.4	5.2	5.3	5.6	5.5
Inpatient Surgeries	104,658	111,590	102,747	103,981	105,579
Births	35,626	36,478	36,680	36,730	36,851
Utilization - Outpatient					
Emergency Outpatient Visits	1,698,661	1,671,516	1,663,519	1,587,150	1,626,044
Other Outpatient Visits	7,634,946	7,644,309	7,239,266	6,900,412	7,648,981
Total Outpatient Visits	9,333,607	9,315,825	8,902,785	8,487,562	9,275,025
Outpatient Surgeries	216,877	220,046	209,981	214,675	217,602
Personnel					
Full Time RNs	11,858	11,502	11,070	10,250	10,664
Full Time LPNs	240	224	225	239	240
Part Time RNs	7,858	8,256	7,884	7,420	6,924
Part Time LPNs	150	142	148	166	190
Total Full Time	45,784	45,080	43,638	43,917	44,827
Total Part Time	24,670	25,222	22,897	22,315	20,843
Revenue - Inpatient					
Gross Inpatient Revenue	$16,681,363,756	$16,384,469,099	$16,472,383,493	$16,003,371,951	$15,912,651,412
Revenue - Outpatient					
Gross Outpatient Revenue	$19,187,823,394	$18,392,571,010	$17,231,977,464	$16,409,353,871	$15,494,331,680
Revenue and Expenses - Totals					
(Includes Inpatient and Outpatient)					
Total Gross Revenue	$35,869,187,150	$34,777,040,109	$33,704,360,957	$32,412,725,822	$31,406,983,092
Deductions from Revenue	24,591,177,189	23,650,482,376	22,907,056,578	21,993,137,480	21,131,372,170
Net Patient Revenue	11,278,009,961	11,126,557,733	10,797,304,379	10,419,588,342	10,275,610,922
Other Operating Revenue	681,684,437	620,331,081	507,484,212	485,957,179	567,209,554
Other Nonoperating Revenue	365,707,447	219,500,367	-14,004,628	168,117,622	234,905,027
Total Net Revenue	12,325,401,845	11,966,389,181	11,290,783,963	11,073,663,143	11,077,725,503
Total Expenses	11,649,294,414	11,386,587,495	10,833,514,095	10,341,323,608	10,399,557,016
HOSPITAL UNIT (Excludes Separate Nursing Home Units)					
Utilization - Inpatient					
Beds	6,982	7,174	7,427	7,588	7,599
Admissions	370,645	374,812	376,759	375,481	390,412
Inpatient Days	1,956,827	1,914,811	1,972,229	2,017,478	2,069,739
Average Length of Stay	5.3	5.1	5.2	5.4	5.3
Personnel					
Total Full Time	45,734	45,012	43,557	43,765	44,665
Total Part Time	24,618	25,152	22,803	22,239	20,672
Revenue and Expenses - Totals					
(Includes Inpatient and Outpatient)					
Total Net Revenue	$12,312,136,145	$11,953,471,349	$11,277,901,563	$11,049,447,956	$11,043,626,112
Total Expenses	11,640,088,731	11,377,360,293	10,824,084,611	10,314,425,719	10,376,600,813
COMMUNITY HEALTH INDICATORS PER 1000 POPULATION					
Total Population (in thousands)	3,588	3,576	3,591	3,597	3,596
Inpatient					
Beds	2.0	2.0	2.1	2.2	2.2
Admissions	103.4	104.9	105	104.7	108.8
Inpatient Days	555.6	545.7	559.4	581.6	596.5
Inpatient Surgeries	29.2	31.2	28.6	28.9	29.4
Births	9.9	10.2	10.2	10.2	10.2
Outpatient					
Emergency Outpatient Visits	473.4	467.4	463.3	441.3	452.2
Other Outpatient Visits	2,127.8	2,137.4	2,016.0	1,918.6	2,127.0
Total Outpatient Visits	2,601.2	2,604.8	2,479.3	2,359.8	2,579.2
Outpatient Surgeries	60.4	61.5	58.5	59.7	60.5
Expense per Capita (per person)	$3,246.6	$3,183.8	$3,016.9	$2,875.2	$2,891.9

States

TABLE 6

DELAWARE

U.S. Community Hospitals
(Nonfederal, short-term general and other special hospitals)

Overview 2013–2017

	2017	2016	2015	2014	2013
Total Community Hospitals in Delaware	8	7	7	7	7
Bed Size Category					
6-24	0	0	0	0	0
25-49	2	1	1	1	1
50-99	1	1	1	1	1
100-199	2	2	2	2	2
200-299	1	1	1	1	1
300-399	1	1	1	1	1
400-499	0	0	0	0	0
500 + ...	1	1	1	1	1
Location					
Hospitals Urban	8	7	7	7	5
Hospitals Rural	0	0	0	0	2
Control					
State and Local Government	0	0	0	0	0
Not for Profit	6	6	6	6	6
Investor owned	2	1	1	1	1
Physician Models					
Independent Practice Association	0	0	0	1	0
Group Practice without Walls	1	1	1	1	1
Open Physician-Hospital Organization	0	0	0	0	0
Closed Physician-Hospital Organization	0	0	0	0	0
Management Service Organization	0	0	0	0	0
Integrated Salary Model	2	3	2	2	1
Equity Model	0	0	0	0	0
Foundation	2	1	1	1	1
Affiliations					
Hospitals in a System	5	4	4	4	4
Hospitals in a Network	0	1	0	0	0
Hospitals in a Group Purchasing Organization...	7	6	6	6	5

TABLE 6

DELAWARE

U.S. Community Hospitals
(Nonfederal, short-term general and other special hospitals)

Utilization, Personnel, Revenue and Expenses, Community Health Indicators 2013–2017

	2017	2016	2015	2014	2013
TOTAL FACILITY (Includes Hospital and Nursing Home Units)					
Utilization - Inpatient					
Beds	2,111	2,059	2,106	2,053	2,034
Admissions	103,162	100,716	106,139	105,109	104,769
Inpatient Days	555,629	519,070	567,289	557,672	538,590
Average Length of Stay	5.4	5.2	5.3	5.3	5.1
Inpatient Surgeries	29,675	29,481	32,640	33,278	31,227
Births	10,972	11,430	11,269	11,201	11,037
Utilization - Outpatient					
Emergency Outpatient Visits	470,429	469,403	463,845	451,296	441,756
Other Outpatient Visits	1,618,485	1,710,846	1,787,677	1,656,267	1,648,654
Total Outpatient Visits	2,088,914	2,180,249	2,251,522	2,107,563	2,090,410
Outpatient Surgeries	62,312	60,646	64,599	62,667	63,281
Personnel					
Full Time RNs	4,535	4,443	4,424	4,258	4,156
Full Time LPNs	136	118	119	131	134
Part Time RNs	2,056	2,118	2,229	2,076	2,082
Part Time LPNs	100	38	43	136	123
Total Full Time	17,127	16,675	16,428	15,712	15,155
Total Part Time	6,257	5,952	6,177	5,971	5,682
Revenue - Inpatient					
Gross Inpatient Revenue	$4,224,418,870	$3,947,910,339	$3,785,257,174	$3,558,726,356	$3,299,554,275
Revenue - Outpatient					
Gross Outpatient Revenue	$4,140,812,973	$3,856,305,152	$3,578,655,796	$3,223,470,034	$2,900,967,707
Revenue and Expenses - Totals					
(Includes Inpatient and Outpatient)					
Total Gross Revenue	$8,365,231,843	$7,804,215,491	$7,363,912,970	$6,782,196,390	$6,200,521,982
Deductions from Revenue	4,783,774,142	4,386,738,942	4,088,740,893	3,736,411,693	3,349,882,012
Net Patient Revenue	3,581,457,701	3,417,476,549	3,275,172,077	3,045,784,697	2,850,639,970
Other Operating Revenue	113,064,550	121,878,449	112,919,384	126,674,850	110,674,336
Other Nonoperating Revenue	177,838,022	-23,074,370	48,098,253	185,293,240	136,656,471
Total Net Revenue	3,872,360,273	3,516,280,628	3,436,189,714	3,357,752,787	3,097,970,777
Total Expenses	3,350,000,939	3,246,810,925	3,130,591,165	2,946,252,827	2,744,800,158
HOSPITAL UNIT (Excludes Separate Nursing Home Units)					
Utilization - Inpatient					
Beds	2,111	2,059	2,106	2,053	2,034
Admissions	103,162	100,716	106,139	105,109	104,769
Inpatient Days	555,629	519,070	567,289	557,672	538,590
Average Length of Stay	5.4	5.2	5.3	5.3	5.1
Personnel					
Total Full Time	17,127	16,675	16,428	15,712	15,155
Total Part Time	6,257	5,952	6,177	5,971	5,682
Revenue and Expenses - Totals					
(Includes Inpatient and Outpatient)					
Total Net Revenue	$3,872,360,273	$3,516,280,628	$3,436,189,714	$3,357,752,787	$3,097,970,777
Total Expenses	3,350,000,939	3,246,810,925	3,130,591,165	2,946,252,827	2,744,800,158
COMMUNITY HEALTH INDICATORS PER 1000 POPULATION					
Total Population (in thousands)	962	952	946	936	926
Inpatient					
Beds	2.2	2.2	2.2	2.2	2.2
Admissions	107.2	105.8	112.2	112.3	113.2
Inpatient Days	577.6	545.2	599.7	596	581.8
Inpatient Surgeries	30.8	31.0	34.5	35.6	33.7
Births	11.4	12.0	11.9	12.0	11.9
Outpatient					
Emergency Outpatient Visits	489.0	493.0	490.4	482.4	477.2
Other Outpatient Visits	1,682.5	1,797.0	1,889.9	1,770.2	1,780.9
Total Outpatient Visits	2,171.6	2,290.0	2,380.2	2,252.6	2,258.1
Outpatient Surgeries	64.8	63.7	68.3	67.0	68.4
Expense per Capita (per person)	$3,482.6	$3,410.3	$3,309.5	$3,149.0	$2,965.0

States

TABLE 6

DISTRICT OF COLUMBIA

U.S. Community Hospitals
(Nonfederal, short-term general and other special hospitals)

Overview 2013–2017

	2017	2016	2015	2014	2013
Total Community Hospitals in District of Columbia	11	11	11	11	11
Bed Size Category					
6-24	0	0	0	0	0
25-49	0	0	0	0	0
50-99	1	1	1	1	1
100-199	2	3	2	2	2
200-299	2	1	2	2	2
300-399	3	3	3	4	4
400-499	2	2	2	1	0
500 +	1	1	1	1	2
Location					
Hospitals Urban	11	11	11	11	11
Hospitals Rural	0	0	0	0	0
Control					
State and Local Government	0	0	0	0	1
Not for Profit	8	8	8	8	7
Investor owned	3	3	3	3	3
Physician Models					
Independent Practice Association	1	1	1	0	1
Group Practice without Walls	1	1	2	1	2
Open Physician-Hospital Organization	1	1	1	0	0
Closed Physician-Hospital Organization	3	2	2	2	2
Management Service Organization	1	3	3	0	1
Integrated Salary Model	5	6	6	4	4
Equity Model	0	0	0	0	0
Foundation	0	0	0	0	1
Affiliations					
Hospitals in a System	8	8	8	8	8
Hospitals in a Network	0	0	0	1	2
Hospitals in a Group Purchasing Organization	6	5	6	7	9

TABLE 6

DISTRICT OF COLUMBIA

U.S. Community Hospitals
(Nonfederal, short-term general and other special hospitals)

Utilization, Personnel, Revenue and Expenses, Community Health Indicators 2013–2017

	2017	2016	2015	2014	2013
TOTAL FACILITY (Includes Hospital and Nursing Home Units)					
Utilization - Inpatient					
Beds	3,542	3,449	3,590	3,542	3,609
Admissions	127,666	126,578	129,047	127,293	132,633
Inpatient Days	938,804	948,524	950,661	924,407	946,679
Average Length of Stay	7.4	7.5	7.4	7.3	7.1
Inpatient Surgeries	39,004	37,194	37,098	40,866	43,045
Births	14,592	14,725	13,139	13,689	13,718
Utilization - Outpatient					
Emergency Outpatient Visits	474,464	476,259	496,827	497,658	482,319
Other Outpatient Visits	2,087,625	2,129,340	2,251,154	2,155,117	2,095,979
Total Outpatient Visits	2,562,089	2,605,599	2,747,981	2,652,775	2,578,298
Outpatient Surgeries	70,512	65,550	63,068	66,333	72,560
Personnel					
Full Time RNs	6,331	6,278	6,294	6,097	5,930
Full Time LPNs	178	172	200	236	190
Part Time RNs	2,303	1,672	1,453	1,416	1,544
Part Time LPNs	39	33	36	57	27
Total Full Time	24,689	23,369	23,215	22,603	23,125
Total Part Time	6,162	4,553	4,481	4,350	3,984
Revenue - Inpatient					
Gross Inpatient Revenue	$9,758,645,187	$8,407,719,505	$8,076,303,894	$7,521,916,741	$7,091,366,429
Revenue - Outpatient					
Gross Outpatient Revenue	$6,539,182,922	$5,626,000,810	$5,437,986,154	$4,731,589,184	$4,311,322,460
Revenue and Expenses - Totals					
(Includes Inpatient and Outpatient)					
Total Gross Revenue	$16,297,828,109	$14,033,720,315	$13,514,290,048	$12,253,505,925	$11,402,688,889
Deductions from Revenue	11,568,354,654	9,464,321,731	9,162,113,899	8,288,747,229	7,509,944,561
Net Patient Revenue	4,729,473,455	4,569,398,584	4,352,176,149	3,964,758,696	3,892,744,328
Other Operating Revenue	327,835,003	288,482,386	298,773,643	267,439,583	300,528,852
Other Nonoperating Revenue	99,186,000	-1,681,270	30,835,705	124,213,686	118,719,257
Total Net Revenue	5,156,494,458	4,856,199,700	4,681,785,497	4,356,411,965	4,311,992,437
Total Expenses	4,692,276,685	4,503,224,661	4,252,693,489	4,112,356,988	3,946,217,682
HOSPITAL UNIT (Excludes Separate Nursing Home Units)					
Utilization - Inpatient					
Beds	3,245	3,161	3,218	3,125	3,192
Admissions	126,215	125,103	128,394	125,602	130,885
Inpatient Days	839,619	846,819	823,863	782,484	802,846
Average Length of Stay	6.7	6.8	6.4	6.2	6.1
Personnel					
Total Full Time	24,620	23,308	23,079	22,285	23,026
Total Part Time	6,123	4,528	4,438	4,205	3,968
Revenue and Expenses - Totals					
(Includes Inpatient and Outpatient)					
Total Net Revenue	$5,120,843,109	$4,820,039,291	$4,642,415,151	$4,306,684,083	$4,286,006,742
Total Expenses	4,657,103,082	4,493,486,091	4,220,791,003	4,072,559,344	3,922,587,203
COMMUNITY HEALTH INDICATORS PER 1000 POPULATION					
Total Population (in thousands)	694	681	672	659	646
Inpatient					
Beds	5.1	5.1	5.3	5.4	5.6
Admissions	184	185.8	192	193.2	205.2
Inpatient Days	1352.8	1392.5	1414.2	1403	1464.4
Inpatient Surgeries	56.2	54.6	55.2	62.0	66.6
Births	21.0	21.6	19.5	20.8	21.2
Outpatient					
Emergency Outpatient Visits	683.7	699.2	739.1	755.3	746.1
Other Outpatient Visits	3,008.2	3,126.0	3,348.8	3,270.8	3,242.3
Total Outpatient Visits	3,691.9	3,825.2	4,087.9	4,026.1	3,988.4
Outpatient Surgeries	101.6	96.2	93.8	100.7	112.2
Expense per Capita (per person)	$6,761.5	$6,611.0	$6,326.3	$6,241.3	$6,104.5

States

TABLE 6

FLORIDA

U.S. Community Hospitals
(Nonfederal, short-term general and other special hospitals)

Overview 2013–2017

	2017	2016	2015	2014	2013
Total Community Hospitals in Florida...............	220	222	222	221	221
Bed Size Category					
6-24...	7	7	5	4	3
25-49...	20	22	27	28	29
50-99...	47	48	45	42	42
100-199...	51	50	51	52	52
200-299...	37	37	38	36	37
300-399...	24	25	23	24	24
400-499...	12	13	14	13	11
500 +...	22	20	19	22	23
Location					
Hospitals Urban	200	200	200	199	191
Hospitals Rural...	20	22	22	22	30
Control					
State and Local Government	23	25	24	23	24
Not for Profit..	84	84	85	85	85
Investor owned..	113	113	113	113	112
Physician Models					
Independent Practice Association....................	5	7	7	4	4
Group Practice without Walls	2	5	5	6	8
Open Physician-Hospital Organization	15	20	17	16	17
Closed Physician-Hospital Organization	8	6	5	5	5
Management Service Organization	4	9	14	13	25
Integrated Salary Model..................................	57	70	69	65	74
Equity Model	2	2	1	1	1
Foundation	2	3	2	3	3
Affiliations					
Hospitals in a System	188	187	185	181	181
Hospitals in a Network....................................	53	59	63	55	54
Hospitals in a Group Purchasing Organization...	100	120	119	122	117

TABLE 6

FLORIDA

U.S. Community Hospitals
(Nonfederal, short-term general and other special hospitals)

Utilization, Personnel, Revenue and Expenses, Community Health Indicators 2013–2017

	2017	2016	2015	2014	2013
TOTAL FACILITY (Includes Hospital and Nursing Home Units)					
Utilization - Inpatient					
Beds	55,111	54,487	53,712	54,073	53,766
Admissions	2,569,757	2,571,170	2,538,567	2,498,384	2,428,752
Inpatient Days	13,018,789	12,936,721	12,704,463	12,450,378	12,186,513
Average Length of Stay	5.1	5.0	5.0	5.0	5.0
Inpatient Surgeries	616,561	623,555	609,507	596,286	606,065
Births	203,121	217,888	210,929	196,786	198,685
Utilization - Outpatient					
Emergency Outpatient Visits	9,198,458	9,537,747	9,169,808	9,161,595	8,505,487
Other Outpatient Visits	17,107,814	17,065,686	17,253,783	16,649,704	15,668,921
Total Outpatient Visits	26,306,272	26,603,433	26,423,591	25,811,299	24,174,408
Outpatient Surgeries	883,477	893,911	862,005	844,325	844,499
Personnel					
Full Time RNs	83,588	81,690	80,086	76,027	72,778
Full Time LPNs	2,642	2,910	2,875	2,819	3,077
Part Time RNs	24,569	21,953	22,425	20,232	20,730
Part Time LPNs	957	828	844	752	849
Total Full Time	256,360	252,336	248,245	236,554	230,851
Total Part Time	71,582	61,943	64,415	58,546	58,882
Revenue - Inpatient					
Gross Inpatient Revenue	$146,699,233,586	$146,637,782,412	$135,105,433,289	$121,775,307,264	$114,178,396,085
Revenue - Outpatient					
Gross Outpatient Revenue	$113,576,911,399	$108,684,986,260	$97,418,931,615	$86,001,621,141	$77,636,660,851
Revenue and Expenses - Totals					
(Includes Inpatient and Outpatient)					
Total Gross Revenue	$260,276,144,985	$255,322,768,672	$232,524,364,904	$207,776,928,405	$191,815,056,936
Deductions from Revenue	206,697,621,079	203,817,838,489	183,886,903,596	162,060,958,731	148,957,742,279
Net Patient Revenue	53,578,523,906	51,504,930,183	48,637,461,308	45,715,969,674	42,857,314,657
Other Operating Revenue	2,331,832,452	2,426,902,454	2,496,569,643	2,272,889,766	2,238,142,567
Other Nonoperating Revenue	871,232,021	774,706,694	388,322,871	715,739,234	682,481,520
Total Net Revenue	56,781,588,379	54,706,539,331	51,522,353,822	48,704,598,674	45,777,938,744
Total Expenses	49,114,873,588	47,496,444,148	45,968,770,839	43,175,864,827	41,319,283,007
HOSPITAL UNIT (Excludes Separate Nursing Home Units)					
Utilization - Inpatient					
Beds	54,258	53,602	52,709	53,080	52,772
Admissions	2,565,679	2,566,404	2,533,255	2,492,987	2,423,418
Inpatient Days	12,735,121	12,655,416	12,384,395	12,121,486	11,861,162
Average Length of Stay	5.0	4.9	4.9	4.9	4.9
Personnel					
Total Full Time	255,378	251,343	247,239	235,193	229,916
Total Part Time	71,274	61,662	64,086	58,255	58,586
Revenue and Expenses - Totals					
(Includes Inpatient and Outpatient)					
Total Net Revenue	$56,699,990,364	$54,619,316,402	$51,396,606,880	$48,598,773,589	$45,672,877,710
Total Expenses	49,025,979,384	47,394,790,722	45,837,729,168	43,058,782,468	41,212,274,064
COMMUNITY HEALTH INDICATORS PER 1000 POPULATION					
Total Population (in thousands)	20,984	20,612	20,271	19,893	19,553
Inpatient					
Beds	2.6	2.6	2.6	2.7	2.7
Admissions	122.5	124.7	125.2	125.6	124.2
Inpatient Days	620.4	627.6	626.7	625.9	623.3
Inpatient Surgeries	29.4	30.3	30.1	30.0	31.0
Births	9.7	10.6	10.4	9.9	10.2
Outpatient					
Emergency Outpatient Visits	438.3	462.7	452.4	460.5	435.0
Other Outpatient Visits	815.3	827.9	851.1	837.0	801.4
Total Outpatient Visits	1,253.6	1,290.6	1,303.5	1,297.5	1,236.4
Outpatient Surgeries	42.1	43.4	42.5	42.4	43.2
Expense per Capita (per person)	$2,340.5	$2,304.3	$2,267.7	$2,170.4	$2,113.2

States

TABLE 6

GEORGIA

U.S. Community Hospitals
(Nonfederal, short-term general and other special hospitals)

Overview 2013–2017

	2017	2016	2015	2014	2013
Total Community Hospitals in Georgia	147	150	149	146	147
Bed Size Category					
6-24	6	7	7	4	5
25-49	39	40	39	42	41
50-99	25	27	26	24	25
100-199	36	36	37	35	34
200-299	13	12	12	14	15
300-399	10	10	9	9	8
400-499	6	6	7	7	9
500 + ...	12	12	12	11	10
Location					
Hospitals Urban	91	93	92	89	87
Hospitals Rural......................................	56	57	57	57	60
Control					
State and Local Government	37	40	48	48	47
Not for Profit	83	79	70	65	68
Investor owned.......................................	27	31	31	33	32
Physician Models					
Independent Practice Association.......................	13	8	12	10	8
Group Practice without Walls	1	1	2	3	0
Open Physician-Hospital Organization	13	8	8	9	12
Closed Physician-Hospital Organization............	19	17	19	19	19
Management Service Organization	4	3	3	3	5
Integrated Salary Model............................	43	41	44	36	34
Equity Model	2	2	2	2	2
Foundation	2	2	2	3	5
Affiliations					
Hospitals in a System	98	95	92	87	83
Hospitals in a Network............................	36	39	44	38	38
Hospitals in a Group Purchasing Organization...	80	79	80	81	84

Table 6

GEORGIA

U.S. Community Hospitals
(Nonfederal, short-term general and other special hospitals)

Utilization, Personnel, Revenue and Expenses, Community Health Indicators 2013–2017

	2017	2016	2015	2014	2013
TOTAL FACILITY (Includes Hospital and Nursing Home Units)					
Utilization - Inpatient					
Beds	25,244	25,214	24,913	24,671	24,891
Admissions	1,003,595	994,538	980,203	947,817	953,300
Inpatient Days	6,348,851	6,307,933	6,216,226	6,181,453	6,074,696
Average Length of Stay	6.3	6.3	6.3	6.5	6.4
Inpatient Surgeries	262,586	260,874	257,763	256,968	260,270
Births	123,813	123,918	125,173	121,828	119,564
Utilization - Outpatient					
Emergency Outpatient Visits	4,740,490	4,658,874	4,470,800	4,174,361	4,280,535
Other Outpatient Visits	14,678,150	14,470,559	12,497,612	11,453,001	11,840,639
Total Outpatient Visits	19,418,640	19,129,433	16,968,412	15,627,362	16,121,174
Outpatient Surgeries	499,283	490,011	474,256	462,343	470,268
Personnel					
Full Time RNs	36,664	35,727	35,635	34,451	32,861
Full Time LPNs	2,430	2,554	2,408	2,338	2,364
Part Time RNs	11,577	11,611	10,979	10,322	9,424
Part Time LPNs	597	684	652	562	629
Total Full Time	125,979	126,754	123,015	118,874	115,517
Total Part Time	34,087	34,153	32,506	29,901	27,756
Revenue - Inpatient					
Gross Inpatient Revenue	$47,337,447,155	$44,291,642,662	$42,401,157,349	$38,893,162,660	$36,307,834,758
Revenue - Outpatient					
Gross Outpatient Revenue	$45,623,717,681	$41,884,620,409	$39,002,432,686	$34,801,692,795	$31,350,898,944
Revenue and Expenses - Totals					
(Includes Inpatient and Outpatient)					
Total Gross Revenue	$92,961,164,836	$86,176,263,071	$81,403,590,035	$73,694,855,455	$67,658,733,702
Deductions from Revenue	67,897,462,826	62,179,729,640	58,650,136,866	52,858,507,430	47,841,756,094
Net Patient Revenue	25,063,702,010	23,996,533,431	22,753,453,169	20,836,348,025	19,816,977,608
Other Operating Revenue	1,318,216,089	1,164,429,971	1,048,482,786	937,449,830	940,706,867
Other Nonoperating Revenue	501,200,885	14,527,578	155,650,000	492,436,111	591,690,404
Total Net Revenue	26,883,118,984	25,175,490,980	23,957,585,955	22,266,233,966	21,349,374,879
Total Expenses	24,699,064,139	23,351,736,425	21,785,219,076	20,109,973,293	19,625,417,570
HOSPITAL UNIT (Excludes Separate Nursing Home Units)					
Utilization - Inpatient					
Beds	22,196	22,223	21,990	21,815	21,970
Admissions	996,519	987,575	973,576	942,095	945,877
Inpatient Days	5,356,502	5,318,927	5,203,277	5,244,421	5,184,839
Average Length of Stay	5.4	5.4	5.3	5.6	5.5
Personnel					
Total Full Time	123,958	124,849	120,868	117,003	113,673
Total Part Time	33,703	33,763	31,931	29,574	27,440
Revenue and Expenses - Totals					
(Includes Inpatient and Outpatient)					
Total Net Revenue	$26,684,779,204	$25,005,658,757	$23,769,377,707	$22,098,154,572	$21,172,335,402
Total Expenses	24,532,894,862	23,196,248,891	21,618,044,952	19,966,912,465	19,471,610,976
COMMUNITY HEALTH INDICATORS PER 1000 POPULATION					
Total Population (in thousands)	10,429	10,310	10,215	10,097	9,992
Inpatient					
Beds	2.4	2.4	2.4	2.4	2.5
Admissions	96.2	96.5	96	93.9	95.4
Inpatient Days	608.7	611.8	608.5	612.2	607.9
Inpatient Surgeries	25.2	25.3	25.2	25.4	26.0
Births	11.9	12.0	12.3	12.1	12.0
Outpatient					
Emergency Outpatient Visits	454.5	451.9	437.7	413.4	428.4
Other Outpatient Visits	1,407.4	1,403.5	1,223.5	1,134.3	1,185.0
Total Outpatient Visits	1,861.9	1,855.4	1,661.1	1,547.7	1,613.4
Outpatient Surgeries	47.9	47.5	46.4	45.8	47.1
Expense per Capita (per person)	$2,368.2	$2,264.9	$2,132.7	$1,991.6	$1,964.1

TABLE 6

HAWAII

U.S. Community Hospitals
(Nonfederal, short-term general and other special hospitals)

Overview 2013–2017

	2017	2016	2015	2014	2013
Total Community Hospitals in Hawaii	23	23	24	25	25
Bed Size Category					
6-24	6	6	6	6	6
25-49	3	3	3	3	3
50-99	4	5	5	6	6
100-199	7	6	7	5	5
200-299	2	2	2	4	4
300-399	0	0	0	0	0
400-499	0	0	0	0	1
500 +	1	1	1	1	0
Location					
Hospitals Urban	15	15	16	16	12
Hospitals Rural	8	8	8	9	13
Control					
State and Local Government	5	6	9	10	9
Not for Profit	18	17	15	15	16
Investor owned	0	0	0	0	0
Physician Models					
Independent Practice Association	1	2	2	1	2
Group Practice without Walls	0	0	0	0	0
Open Physician-Hospital Organization	4	4	2	3	2
Closed Physician-Hospital Organization	1	2	2	2	2
Management Service Organization	0	0	0	0	0
Integrated Salary Model	3	6	7	7	6
Equity Model	0	0	0	0	0
Foundation	1	1	0	0	0
Affiliations					
Hospitals in a System	19	19	20	21	20
Hospitals in a Network	6	7	6	8	4
Hospitals in a Group Purchasing Organization	8	13	16	14	13

TABLE 6

HAWAII

U.S. Community Hospitals
(Nonfederal, short-term general and other special hospitals)

Utilization, Personnel, Revenue and Expenses, Community Health Indicators 2013–2017

	2017	2016	2015	2014	2013
TOTAL FACILITY (Includes Hospital and Nursing Home Units)					
Utilization - Inpatient					
Beds	2,594	2,488	2,645	2,861	2,817
Admissions	111,293	110,104	110,061	109,311	110,374
Inpatient Days	706,540	703,010	717,607	749,201	760,960
Average Length of Stay	6.3	6.4	6.5	6.9	6.9
Inpatient Surgeries	25,051	29,232	30,138	26,095	26,137
Births	19,322	18,495	17,140	10,626	10,229
Utilization - Outpatient					
Emergency Outpatient Visits	452,405	468,601	487,500	432,641	401,191
Other Outpatient Visits	2,215,832	2,107,180	1,962,647	1,858,155	1,752,696
Total Outpatient Visits	2,668,237	2,575,781	2,450,147	2,290,796	2,153,887
Outpatient Surgeries	60,366	58,636	56,872	51,497	47,416
Personnel					
Full Time RNs	3,910	4,510	4,331	4,331	4,045
Full Time LPNs	170	170	198	196	221
Part Time RNs	1,296	1,413	1,487	1,362	963
Part Time LPNs	55	48	43	47	37
Total Full Time	14,532	15,310	15,195	15,011	14,561
Total Part Time	3,989	3,973	4,007	3,762	2,660
Revenue - Inpatient					
Gross Inpatient Revenue	$5,064,700,177	$4,781,623,649	$4,577,583,888	$4,181,164,838	$4,009,282,994
Revenue - Outpatient					
Gross Outpatient Revenue	$5,252,961,749	$4,718,970,176	$4,190,277,597	$3,730,384,969	$3,536,452,224
Revenue and Expenses - Totals					
(Includes Inpatient and Outpatient)					
Total Gross Revenue	$10,317,661,926	$9,500,593,825	$8,767,861,485	$7,911,549,807	$7,545,735,218
Deductions from Revenue	6,795,830,332	6,134,403,356	5,555,573,283	5,025,528,223	4,709,531,039
Net Patient Revenue	3,521,831,594	3,366,190,469	3,212,288,202	2,886,021,584	2,836,204,179
Other Operating Revenue	225,694,184	217,984,188	233,450,364	208,715,461	208,314,941
Other Nonoperating Revenue	127,041,497	30,217,539	54,891,387	63,534,103	132,431,586
Total Net Revenue	3,874,567,275	3,614,392,196	3,500,629,953	3,158,271,148	3,176,950,706
Total Expenses	3,738,396,611	3,556,186,542	3,350,489,890	3,148,443,424	2,917,345,070
HOSPITAL UNIT (Excludes Separate Nursing Home Units)					
Utilization - Inpatient					
Beds	2,594	2,360	2,320	2,630	2,523
Admissions	111,275	109,558	108,928	108,182	108,687
Inpatient Days	706,319	671,095	610,787	680,962	660,686
Average Length of Stay	6.3	6.1	5.6	6.3	6.1
Personnel					
Total Full Time	14,517	15,265	14,918	14,838	14,355
Total Part Time	3,989	3,953	3,953	3,729	2,623
Revenue and Expenses - Totals					
(Includes Inpatient and Outpatient)					
Total Net Revenue	$3,874,567,275	$3,596,598,513	$3,450,094,108	$3,125,503,974	$3,149,956,310
Total Expenses	3,738,396,611	3,543,403,181	3,306,636,383	3,120,902,400	2,886,933,350
COMMUNITY HEALTH INDICATORS PER 1000 POPULATION					
Total Population (in thousands)	1,428	1,429	1,432	1,420	1,404
Inpatient					
Beds	1.8	1.7	1.8	2.0	2.0
Admissions	78.0	77.1	76.9	77.0	78.6
Inpatient Days	494.9	492.1	501.3	527.8	542.0
Inpatient Surgeries	17.5	20.5	21.1	18.4	18.6
Births	13.5	12.9	12.0	7.5	7.3
Outpatient					
Emergency Outpatient Visits	316.9	328.0	340.5	304.8	285.7
Other Outpatient Visits	1,552.2	1,475.0	1,370.9	1,309.0	1,248.3
Total Outpatient Visits	1,869.1	1,803.1	1,711.5	1,613.7	1,534.0
Outpatient Surgeries	42.3	41.0	39.7	36.3	33.8
Expense per Capita (per person)	$2,618.8	$2,489.4	$2,340.4	$2,217.9	$2,077.8

States

TABLE 6

IDAHO

U.S. Community Hospitals
(Nonfederal, short-term general and other special hospitals)

Overview 2013–2017

	2017	2016	2015	2014	2013
Total Community Hospitals in Idaho	46	44	44	45	45
Bed Size Category					
6-24	16	17	15	14	14
25-49	12	11	12	14	13
50-99	9	8	9	9	9
100-199	4	3	3	3	4
200-299	3	3	2	2	2
300-399	1	1	2	2	2
400-499	0	0	0	0	0
500 +	1	1	1	1	1
Location					
Hospitals Urban	19	17	17	18	18
Hospitals Rural	27	27	27	27	27
Control					
State and Local Government	18	18	18	19	18
Not for Profit	18	17	17	16	17
Investor owned	10	9	9	10	10
Physician Models					
Independent Practice Association	1	1	1	1	1
Group Practice without Walls	0	0	0	0	0
Open Physician-Hospital Organization	7	6	5	6	6
Closed Physician-Hospital Organization	1	1	2	3	1
Management Service Organization	1	0	1	0	0
Integrated Salary Model	11	13	13	14	14
Equity Model	1	1	1	1	1
Foundation	1	1	2	2	1
Affiliations					
Hospitals in a System	24	23	23	24	23
Hospitals in a Network	14	12	13	10	9
Hospitals in a Group Purchasing Organization	26	27	25	23	25

TABLE 6

IDAHO

U.S. Community Hospitals
(Nonfederal, short-term general and other special hospitals)

Utilization, Personnel, Revenue and Expenses, Community Health Indicators 2013–2017

	2017	2016	2015	2014	2013
TOTAL FACILITY (Includes Hospital and Nursing Home Units)					
Utilization - Inpatient					
Beds	3,531	3,388	3,425	3,455	3,499
Admissions	142,843	133,215	131,581	125,417	130,067
Inpatient Days	722,719	674,515	643,867	614,820	631,986
Average Length of Stay	5.1	5.1	4.9	4.9	4.9
Inpatient Surgeries	38,797	36,562	36,100	36,322	36,898
Births	19,347	19,484	20,474	20,225	19,676
Utilization - Outpatient					
Emergency Outpatient Visits	697,045	675,761	682,440	637,143	599,544
Other Outpatient Visits	5,138,377	4,904,213	5,206,241	4,649,936	4,255,960
Total Outpatient Visits	5,835,422	5,579,974	5,888,681	5,287,079	4,855,504
Outpatient Surgeries	98,424	94,377	91,487	90,957	79,761
Personnel					
Full Time RNs	6,013	5,599	5,686	5,291	5,085
Full Time LPNs	507	491	478	473	483
Part Time RNs	2,652	2,361	2,520	2,704	2,793
Part Time LPNs	175	174	172	202	213
Total Full Time	25,974	26,608	25,769	24,097	22,844
Total Part Time	8,419	7,961	8,414	9,214	9,135
Revenue - Inpatient					
Gross Inpatient Revenue	$7,312,478,673	$5,922,043,662	$5,320,925,720	$4,905,497,397	$4,445,689,550
Revenue - Outpatient					
Gross Outpatient Revenue	$7,706,151,712	$6,956,049,447	$6,220,752,093	$5,607,993,070	$4,883,754,985
Revenue and Expenses - Totals					
(Includes Inpatient and Outpatient)					
Total Gross Revenue	$15,018,630,385	$12,878,093,109	$11,541,677,813	$10,513,490,467	$9,329,444,535
Deductions from Revenue	9,461,988,644	8,051,698,061	7,086,862,605	6,344,144,192	5,505,866,102
Net Patient Revenue	5,556,641,741	4,826,395,048	4,454,815,208	4,169,346,275	3,823,578,433
Other Operating Revenue	183,596,412	144,054,151	136,171,360	126,844,834	151,293,138
Other Nonoperating Revenue	64,784,568	29,924,550	15,031,098	57,176,980	38,841,704
Total Net Revenue	5,805,022,721	5,000,373,749	4,606,017,666	4,353,368,089	4,013,713,275
Total Expenses	5,339,960,660	4,563,697,020	4,195,690,588	3,934,206,961	3,679,797,471
HOSPITAL UNIT (Excludes Separate Nursing Home Units)					
Utilization - Inpatient					
Beds	3,295	3,183	3,180	3,280	3,231
Admissions	142,393	132,815	131,113	125,156	129,120
Inpatient Days	655,819	615,828	579,403	565,024	558,785
Average Length of Stay	4.6	4.6	4.4	4.5	4.3
Personnel					
Total Full Time	25,789	26,485	25,619	23,968	22,613
Total Part Time	8,305	7,889	8,296	9,114	9,011
Revenue and Expenses - Totals					
(Includes Inpatient and Outpatient)					
Total Net Revenue	$5,785,009,783	$4,981,847,536	$4,588,407,928	$4,341,048,819	$3,986,223,243
Total Expenses	5,323,613,091	4,551,852,106	4,183,033,932	3,921,130,787	3,660,688,633
COMMUNITY HEALTH INDICATORS PER 1000 POPULATION					
Total Population (in thousands)	1,717	1,683	1,655	1,634	1,612
Inpatient					
Beds	2.1	2.0	2.1	2.1	2.2
Admissions	83.2	79.1	79.5	76.7	80.7
Inpatient Days	420.9	400.7	389.1	376.2	392.0
Inpatient Surgeries	22.6	21.7	21.8	22.2	22.9
Births	11.3	11.6	12.4	12.4	12.2
Outpatient					
Emergency Outpatient Visits	406.0	401.5	412.4	389.8	371.9
Other Outpatient Visits	2,992.7	2,913.7	3,145.9	2,844.9	2,640.0
Total Outpatient Visits	3,398.7	3,315.2	3,558.3	3,234.7	3,011.8
Outpatient Surgeries	57.3	56.1	55.3	55.6	49.5
Expense per Capita (per person)	$3,110.2	$2,711.4	$2,535.3	$2,407.0	$2,282.6

States

TABLE 6

ILLINOIS

U.S. Community Hospitals
(Nonfederal, short-term general and other special hospitals)

Overview 2013–2017

	2017	2016	2015	2014	2013
Total Community Hospitals in Illinois	189	189	188	189	189
Bed Size Category					
6-24	14	14	16	14	13
25-49	37	35	35	36	37
50-99	28	32	29	29	29
100-199	54	49	49	55	54
200-299	24	29	29	25	25
300-399	17	15	16	16	17
400-499	7	7	6	6	6
500 + ...	8	8	8	8	8
Location					
Hospitals Urban	131	131	130	130	125
Hospitals Rural	58	58	58	59	64
Control					
State and Local Government	23	23	24	24	23
Not for Profit	146	145	143	144	146
Investor owned	20	21	21	21	20
Physician Models					
Independent Practice Association	20	23	31	26	24
Group Practice without Walls	7	4	10	10	12
Open Physician-Hospital Organization	60	54	53	53	56
Closed Physician-Hospital Organization	15	12	10	10	11
Management Service Organization	26	21	17	19	19
Integrated Salary Model	68	70	72	74	71
Equity Model	3	4	4	4	5
Foundation	6	8	8	9	10
Affiliations					
Hospitals in a System	128	126	125	120	118
Hospitals in a Network	80	76	70	67	58
Hospitals in a Group Purchasing Organization...	144	144	149	151	149

TABLE 6

ILLINOIS

U.S. Community Hospitals
(Nonfederal, short-term general and other special hospitals)

Utilization, Personnel, Revenue and Expenses, Community Health Indicators 2013–2017

	2017	2016	2015	2014	2013
TOTAL FACILITY (Includes Hospital and Nursing Home Units)					
Utilization - Inpatient					
Beds	31,996	31,873	31,823	31,573	31,745
Admissions	1,364,376	1,377,652	1,385,953	1,380,085	1,426,848
Inpatient Days	6,882,225	6,898,909	6,827,990	6,841,826	6,865,573
Average Length of Stay	5.0	5.0	4.9	5.0	4.8
Inpatient Surgeries	330,136	347,888	354,815	360,213	368,428
Births	141,539	147,094	148,744	147,464	146,392
Utilization - Outpatient					
Emergency Outpatient Visits	5,630,049	5,533,962	5,556,422	5,273,213	5,252,340
Other Outpatient Visits	31,945,388	32,555,203	32,014,417	28,160,509	27,556,186
Total Outpatient Visits	37,575,437	38,089,165	37,570,839	33,433,722	32,808,526
Outpatient Surgeries	717,855	740,446	755,329	736,891	743,687
Personnel					
Full Time RNs	51,577	50,475	49,064	47,039	46,160
Full Time LPNs	1,458	1,432	1,448	1,468	1,679
Part Time RNs	24,693	21,840	23,064	23,887	21,818
Part Time LPNs	597	512	529	558	633
Total Full Time	176,871	176,838	173,895	170,080	168,524
Total Part Time	91,256	70,056	72,077	75,417	70,370
Revenue - Inpatient					
Gross Inpatient Revenue	$68,234,158,866	$65,264,725,254	$61,802,651,499	$59,479,867,913	$55,496,665,893
Revenue - Outpatient					
Gross Outpatient Revenue	$79,158,726,167	$72,424,068,382	$67,143,188,040	$62,657,072,479	$55,220,592,255
Revenue and Expenses - Totals					
(Includes Inpatient and Outpatient)					
Total Gross Revenue	$147,392,885,033	$137,688,793,636	$128,945,839,539	$122,136,940,392	$110,717,258,148
Deductions from Revenue	107,849,899,103	99,650,575,691	92,652,197,929	86,861,936,578	78,196,471,517
Net Patient Revenue	39,542,985,930	38,038,217,945	36,293,641,610	35,275,003,814	32,520,786,631
Other Operating Revenue	2,270,985,342	1,830,045,808	2,137,345,481	2,092,681,737	2,131,938,656
Other Nonoperating Revenue	1,357,513,730	1,723,122,194	163,550,113	1,406,842,660	1,098,662,582
Total Net Revenue	43,171,485,002	41,591,385,947	38,594,537,204	38,774,528,211	35,751,387,869
Total Expenses	39,236,137,639	37,077,167,759	35,872,183,416	35,123,918,794	32,752,851,815
HOSPITAL UNIT (Excludes Separate Nursing Home Units)					
Utilization - Inpatient					
Beds	31,227	30,868	30,729	30,374	30,716
Admissions	1,358,521	1,369,118	1,377,209	1,369,430	1,417,171
Inpatient Days	6,697,835	6,628,569	6,549,361	6,547,258	6,623,180
Average Length of Stay	4.9	4.8	4.8	4.8	4.7
Personnel					
Total Full Time	176,460	176,384	173,327	169,603	167,903
Total Part Time	90,959	69,741	71,658	75,033	69,892
Revenue and Expenses - Totals					
(Includes Inpatient and Outpatient)					
Total Net Revenue	$43,111,397,814	$41,380,305,019	$38,393,201,864	$38,682,715,068	$35,673,229,824
Total Expenses	39,187,355,431	36,982,904,648	35,779,914,464	35,048,528,192	32,686,336,226
COMMUNITY HEALTH INDICATORS PER 1000 POPULATION					
Total Population (in thousands)	12,802	12,802	12,860	12,881	12,882
Inpatient					
Beds	2.5	2.5	2.5	2.5	2.5
Admissions	106.6	107.6	107.8	107.1	110.8
Inpatient Days	537.6	538.9	530.9	531.2	533.0
Inpatient Surgeries	25.8	27.2	27.6	28.0	28.6
Births	11.1	11.5	11.6	11.4	11.4
Outpatient					
Emergency Outpatient Visits	439.8	432.3	432.1	409.4	407.7
Other Outpatient Visits	2,495.3	2,543.1	2,489.5	2,186.3	2,139.1
Total Outpatient Visits	2,935.1	2,975.4	2,921.5	2,595.7	2,546.8
Outpatient Surgeries	56.1	57.8	58.7	57.2	57.7
Expense per Capita (per person)	$3,064.8	$2,896.3	$2,789.4	$2,726.9	$2,542.5

States

TABLE 6

INDIANA

U.S. Community Hospitals
(Nonfederal, short-term general and other special hospitals)

Overview 2013–2017

	2017	2016	2015	2014	2013
Total Community Hospitals in Indiana	132	134	136	138	142
Bed Size Category					
6-24	14	14	14	15	14
25-49	43	45	47	47	49
50-99	23	22	22	23	27
100-199	24	25	25	28	25
200-299	12	13	12	9	12
300-399	5	5	5	5	4
400-499	6	5	5	6	6
500 + ...	5	5	6	5	5
Location					
Hospitals Urban	91	93	93	95	101
Hospitals Rural	41	41	43	43	41
Control					
State and Local Government	26	26	27	30	30
Not for Profit	72	72	72	71	73
Investor owned	34	36	37	37	39
Physician Models					
Independent Practice Association	6	9	7	7	6
Group Practice without Walls	4	5	6	4	4
Open Physician-Hospital Organization	16	21	19	21	27
Closed Physician-Hospital Organization	6	4	4	6	6
Management Service Organization	3	6	7	9	10
Integrated Salary Model	59	61	63	64	63
Equity Model	1	2	2	4	4
Foundation	5	5	4	6	6
Affiliations					
Hospitals in a System	93	95	97	98	97
Hospitals in a Network	39	47	46	51	50
Hospitals in a Group Purchasing Organization...	99	102	96	101	103

TABLE 6

INDIANA

U.S. Community Hospitals
(Nonfederal, short-term general and other special hospitals)

Utilization, Personnel, Revenue and Expenses, Community Health Indicators 2013–2017

	2017	2016	2015	2014	2013
TOTAL FACILITY (Includes Hospital and Nursing Home Units)					
Utilization - Inpatient					
Beds	17,821	17,936	18,306	18,209	18,389
Admissions	715,442	715,146	715,653	724,440	744,073
Inpatient Days	3,686,520	3,713,338	3,789,207	3,774,854	3,857,311
Average Length of Stay	5.2	5.2	5.3	5.2	5.2
Inpatient Surgeries	190,373	199,452	188,854	193,851	200,604
Births	77,809	79,396	78,764	79,089	78,396
Utilization - Outpatient					
Emergency Outpatient Visits	3,526,829	3,480,695	3,546,717	3,420,667	3,267,116
Other Outpatient Visits	17,385,991	17,861,240	16,829,211	16,623,596	15,803,498
Total Outpatient Visits	20,912,820	21,341,935	20,375,928	20,044,263	19,070,614
Outpatient Surgeries	455,449	502,004	446,076	426,610	446,013
Personnel					
Full Time RNs	25,221	24,338	23,989	24,126	24,379
Full Time LPNs	1,246	1,158	1,261	1,386	1,578
Part Time RNs	15,419	16,000	14,442	14,684	15,658
Part Time LPNs	613	592	613	676	805
Total Full Time	92,299	92,372	91,030	90,978	90,868
Total Part Time	46,153	44,992	41,644	43,488	44,212
Revenue - Inpatient					
Gross Inpatient Revenue	$36,994,949,495	$34,460,007,043	$32,553,063,266	$30,248,020,933	$28,381,389,137
Revenue - Outpatient					
Gross Outpatient Revenue	$41,931,420,629	$38,998,210,596	$35,372,605,251	$32,090,339,147	$29,636,588,206
Revenue and Expenses - Totals					
(Includes Inpatient and Outpatient)					
Total Gross Revenue	$78,926,370,124	$73,458,217,639	$67,925,668,517	$62,338,360,080	$58,017,977,343
Deductions from Revenue	55,420,080,141	50,940,632,393	46,270,658,365	41,383,337,776	38,223,549,051
Net Patient Revenue	23,506,289,983	22,517,585,246	21,655,010,152	20,955,022,304	19,794,428,292
Other Operating Revenue	1,674,318,897	1,824,366,987	1,535,969,523	1,335,638,535	1,095,154,276
Other Nonoperating Revenue	996,835,885	449,845,276	-68,660,470	499,556,235	618,415,209
Total Net Revenue	26,177,444,765	24,791,797,509	23,122,319,205	22,790,217,074	21,507,997,777
Total Expenses	22,215,113,382	21,662,042,795	19,780,623,659	19,018,943,947	18,897,842,439
HOSPITAL UNIT (Excludes Separate Nursing Home Units)					
Utilization - Inpatient					
Beds	17,126	17,186	17,267	17,461	17,677
Admissions	713,575	712,265	712,566	721,520	740,677
Inpatient Days	3,507,737	3,514,723	3,514,053	3,558,617	3,645,966
Average Length of Stay	4.9	4.9	4.9	4.9	4.9
Personnel					
Total Full Time	91,885	92,015	90,323	90,480	90,401
Total Part Time	45,845	44,634	41,167	43,052	43,822
Revenue and Expenses - Totals					
(Includes Inpatient and Outpatient)					
Total Net Revenue	$26,125,262,164	$24,729,147,061	$23,033,995,206	$22,723,456,981	$21,444,609,503
Total Expenses	22,176,512,621	21,622,019,579	19,713,185,720	18,964,668,171	18,846,045,334
COMMUNITY HEALTH INDICATORS PER 1000 POPULATION					
Total Population (in thousands)	6,667	6,633	6,620	6,597	6,571
Inpatient					
Beds	2.7	2.7	2.8	2.8	2.8
Admissions	107.3	107.8	108.1	109.8	113.2
Inpatient Days	553.0	559.8	572.4	572.2	587.0
Inpatient Surgeries	28.6	30.1	28.5	29.4	30.5
Births	11.7	12.0	11.9	12.0	11.9
Outpatient					
Emergency Outpatient Visits	529.0	524.8	535.8	518.5	497.2
Other Outpatient Visits	2,607.8	2,692.8	2,542.3	2,519.9	2,405.1
Total Outpatient Visits	3,136.9	3,217.5	3,078.1	3,038.5	2,902.3
Outpatient Surgeries	68.3	75.7	67.4	64.7	67.9
Expense per Capita (per person)	$3,332.2	$3,265.8	$2,988.2	$2,883.0	$2,876.0

States

TABLE 6

IOWA

U.S. Community Hospitals
(Nonfederal, short-term general and other special hospitals)

Overview 2013–2017

	2017	2016	2015	2014	2013
Total Community Hospitals in Iowa..................	117	118	119	119	119
Bed Size Category					
6-24	25	25	22	22	21
25-49	48	48	51	50	49
50-99	20	20	22	23	26
100-199	10	11	10	10	9
200-299	7	7	7	7	6
300-399	4	4	4	4	5
400-499	0	0	0	0	1
500 + ...	3	3	3	3	2
Location					
Hospitals Urban	34	35	36	36	35
Hospitals Rural	83	83	83	83	84
Control					
State and Local Government	58	58	59	59	59
Not for Profit	57	58	58	58	58
Investor owned	2	2	2	2	2
Physician Models					
Independent Practice Association	8	8	10	13	13
Group Practice without Walls	2	2	2	3	5
Open Physician-Hospital Organization ...	17	17	17	18	20
Closed Physician-Hospital Organization ...	12	11	10	10	11
Management Service Organization	5	6	7	7	8
Integrated Salary Model	75	77	77	76	77
Equity Model	1	1	1	1	1
Foundation	3	4	4	4	5
Affiliations					
Hospitals in a System	78	77	74	74	71
Hospitals in a Network	81	82	81	79	80
Hospitals in a Group Purchasing Organization...	113	117	119	118	118

TABLE 6

IOWA

U.S. Community Hospitals
(Nonfederal, short-term general and other special hospitals)

Utilization, Personnel, Revenue and Expenses, Community Health Indicators 2013–2017

	2017	2016	2015	2014	2013
TOTAL FACILITY (Includes Hospital and Nursing Home Units)					
Utilization - Inpatient					
Beds	9,365	9,552	9,608	9,756	9,855
Admissions	315,667	315,146	325,123	319,169	326,762
Inpatient Days	1,937,198	1,930,469	1,977,340	1,963,387	2,006,117
Average Length of Stay	6.1	6.1	6.1	6.2	6.1
Inpatient Surgeries	81,261	82,456	79,852	79,279	80,936
Births	38,237	39,034	39,100	39,101	38,344
Utilization - Outpatient					
Emergency Outpatient Visits	1,348,809	1,369,607	1,363,799	1,290,755	1,292,810
Other Outpatient Visits	10,222,405	10,066,760	9,692,797	9,501,854	9,316,036
Total Outpatient Visits	11,571,214	11,436,367	11,056,596	10,792,609	10,608,846
Outpatient Surgeries	253,467	254,174	255,548	250,088	247,077
Personnel					
Full Time RNs	12,716	12,860	12,402	11,998	11,675
Full Time LPNs	814	759	742	738	702
Part Time RNs	6,892	6,777	6,449	6,518	6,743
Part Time LPNs	403	518	519	505	497
Total Full Time	48,393	47,907	46,747	45,773	45,547
Total Part Time	23,108	22,932	21,640	22,114	22,583
Revenue - Inpatient					
Gross Inpatient Revenue	$10,516,870,326	$10,204,775,701	$9,783,286,716	$9,152,636,474	$8,824,658,665
Revenue - Outpatient					
Gross Outpatient Revenue	$14,972,359,965	$14,161,466,846	$12,979,201,679	$11,904,002,918	$10,917,710,660
Revenue and Expenses - Totals					
(Includes Inpatient and Outpatient)					
Total Gross Revenue	$25,489,230,291	$24,366,242,547	$22,762,488,395	$21,056,639,392	$19,742,369,325
Deductions from Revenue	16,656,693,131	15,643,117,079	14,413,539,150	13,235,236,955	12,205,232,504
Net Patient Revenue	8,832,537,160	8,723,125,468	8,348,949,245	7,821,402,437	7,537,136,821
Other Operating Revenue	739,484,280	712,536,434	667,629,369	642,997,787	620,141,780
Other Nonoperating Revenue	327,631,324	146,959,168	140,063,075	306,092,900	292,293,006
Total Net Revenue	9,899,652,764	9,582,621,070	9,156,641,689	8,770,493,124	8,449,571,607
Total Expenses	9,376,783,236	8,998,959,972	8,472,369,408	8,137,351,819	7,840,111,892
HOSPITAL UNIT (Excludes Separate Nursing Home Units)					
Utilization - Inpatient					
Beds	7,824	7,986	8,030	8,139	8,169
Admissions	313,180	312,326	322,071	315,986	323,882
Inpatient Days	1,449,722	1,436,856	1,478,571	1,450,366	1,487,169
Average Length of Stay	4.6	4.6	4.6	4.6	4.6
Personnel					
Total Full Time	47,656	47,185	46,025	44,960	44,754
Total Part Time	22,288	22,151	20,871	21,335	21,804
Revenue and Expenses - Totals					
(Includes Inpatient and Outpatient)					
Total Net Revenue	$9,800,591,168	$9,492,100,853	$9,070,795,149	$8,681,515,659	$8,356,833,139
Total Expenses	9,295,878,507	8,924,734,007	8,399,843,682	8,063,229,802	7,763,195,162
COMMUNITY HEALTH INDICATORS PER 1000 POPULATION					
Total Population (in thousands)	3,146	3,135	3,124	3,107	3,090
Inpatient					
Beds	3.0	3.0	3.1	3.1	3.2
Admissions	100.3	100.5	104.1	102.7	105.7
Inpatient Days	615.8	615.8	633.0	631.9	649.1
Inpatient Surgeries	25.8	26.3	25.6	25.5	26.2
Births	12.2	12.5	12.5	12.6	12.4
Outpatient					
Emergency Outpatient Visits	428.8	436.9	436.6	415.4	418.3
Other Outpatient Visits	3,249.6	3,211.4	3,102.8	3,058.1	3,014.5
Total Outpatient Visits	3,678.4	3,648.3	3,539.4	3,473.5	3,432.8
Outpatient Surgeries	80.6	81.1	81.8	80.5	79.9
Expense per Capita (per person)	$2,980.8	$2,870.8	$2,712.1	$2,618.9	$2,536.9

States

TABLE 6

KANSAS

U.S. Community Hospitals
(Nonfederal, short-term general and other special hospitals)

Overview 2013–2017

	2017	2016	2015	2014	2013
Total Community Hospitals in Kansas	144	143	143	143	140
Bed Size Category					
6-24	33	33	31	27	27
25-49	59	57	57	57	52
50-99	30	30	31	33	36
100-199	12	13	14	16	16
200-299	5	5	5	5	4
300-399	2	1	2	1	2
400-499	0	1	0	1	0
500 +	3	3	3	3	3
Location					
Hospitals Urban	45	44	44	44	40
Hospitals Rural	99	99	99	99	100
Control					
State and Local Government	62	62	65	65	62
Not for Profit	52	52	51	51	51
Investor owned	30	29	27	27	27
Physician Models					
Independent Practice Association	9	10	11	11	12
Group Practice without Walls	3	3	3	3	3
Open Physician-Hospital Organization	7	8	9	8	11
Closed Physician-Hospital Organization	0	0	0	0	1
Management Service Organization	2	1	1	1	2
Integrated Salary Model	80	87	85	86	79
Equity Model	3	2	2	2	2
Foundation	2	4	3	3	4
Affiliations					
Hospitals in a System	58	54	53	52	53
Hospitals in a Network	64	75	79	81	81
Hospitals in a Group Purchasing Organization	115	131	137	139	139

TABLE 6

KANSAS

U.S. Community Hospitals
(Nonfederal, short-term general and other special hospitals)

Utilization, Personnel, Revenue and Expenses, Community Health Indicators 2013–2017

	2017	2016	2015	2014	2013
TOTAL FACILITY (Includes Hospital and Nursing Home Units)					
Utilization - Inpatient					
Beds	9,899	9,913	10,079	10,253	10,225
Admissions	316,472	312,254	308,536	306,183	299,701
Inpatient Days	1,910,634	1,952,068	1,939,567	1,919,564	1,928,108
Average Length of Stay	6.0	6.3	6.3	6.3	6.4
Inpatient Surgeries	75,280	77,376	76,009	77,566	79,002
Births	36,477	38,049	38,418	38,500	37,640
Utilization - Outpatient					
Emergency Outpatient Visits	1,195,636	1,233,808	1,237,301	1,189,246	1,142,328
Other Outpatient Visits	7,088,959	6,647,463	6,244,996	6,094,175	6,065,744
Total Outpatient Visits	8,284,595	7,881,271	7,482,297	7,283,421	7,208,072
Outpatient Surgeries	194,337	195,575	191,715	186,189	181,225
Personnel					
Full Time RNs	13,293	13,410	12,432	12,304	12,502
Full Time LPNs	1,241	1,207	1,030	1,027	1,057
Part Time RNs	5,447	5,387	5,226	4,839	4,991
Part Time LPNs	373	355	392	360	395
Total Full Time	46,833	45,167	42,298	41,907	41,892
Total Part Time	17,645	17,419	15,564	14,405	14,998
Revenue - Inpatient					
Gross Inpatient Revenue	$14,825,538,265	$13,754,805,803	$12,829,556,393	$12,000,981,558	$10,999,211,131
Revenue - Outpatient					
Gross Outpatient Revenue	$17,380,326,815	$15,547,913,194	$13,858,975,826	$12,328,780,962	$10,851,031,626
Revenue and Expenses - Totals					
(Includes Inpatient and Outpatient)					
Total Gross Revenue	$32,205,865,080	$29,302,718,997	$26,688,532,219	$24,329,762,520	$21,850,242,757
Deductions from Revenue	23,420,655,882	20,983,340,008	18,936,223,597	17,085,780,814	14,985,625,109
Net Patient Revenue	8,785,209,198	8,319,378,989	7,752,308,622	7,243,981,706	6,864,617,648
Other Operating Revenue	404,599,928	420,295,497	415,203,315	350,212,230	293,110,117
Other Nonoperating Revenue	203,067,179	71,735,083	2,201,599	163,558,997	171,584,497
Total Net Revenue	9,392,876,305	8,811,409,569	8,169,713,536	7,757,752,933	7,329,312,262
Total Expenses	8,717,686,849	8,089,610,415	7,543,430,309	7,132,611,158	6,787,638,044
HOSPITAL UNIT (Excludes Separate Nursing Home Units)					
Utilization - Inpatient					
Beds	8,766	8,625	8,678	8,730	8,667
Admissions	314,640	310,634	306,569	303,938	297,254
Inpatient Days	1,569,660	1,501,114	1,516,264	1,463,880	1,454,497
Average Length of Stay	5.0	4.8	4.9	4.8	4.9
Personnel					
Total Full Time	46,060	44,242	41,368	40,842	40,877
Total Part Time	17,236	16,943	15,055	13,917	14,513
Revenue and Expenses - Totals					
(Includes Inpatient and Outpatient)					
Total Net Revenue	$9,313,318,330	$8,738,217,315	$8,090,610,426	$7,675,923,547	$7,246,318,978
Total Expenses	8,634,099,185	8,030,136,721	7,476,082,228	7,060,201,250	6,719,163,015
COMMUNITY HEALTH INDICATORS PER 1000 POPULATION					
Total Population (in thousands)	2,913	2,907	2,912	2,904	2,894
Inpatient					
Beds	3.4	3.4	3.5	3.5	3.5
Admissions	108.6	107.4	106.0	105.4	103.6
Inpatient Days	655.9	671.4	666.1	661.0	666.3
Inpatient Surgeries	25.8	26.6	26.1	26.7	27.3
Births	12.5	13.1	13.2	13.3	13.0
Outpatient					
Emergency Outpatient Visits	410.4	424.4	424.9	409.5	394.7
Other Outpatient Visits	2,433.5	2,286.5	2,144.8	2,098.5	2,096.0
Total Outpatient Visits	2,843.9	2,710.9	2,569.8	2,508.0	2,490.7
Outpatient Surgeries	66.7	67.3	65.8	64.1	62.6
Expense per Capita (per person)	$2,992.6	$2,782.5	$2,590.8	$2,456.1	$2,345.5

TABLE 6

KENTUCKY

U.S. Community Hospitals
(Nonfederal, short-term general and other special hospitals)

Overview 2013–2017

	2017	2016	2015	2014	2013
Total Community Hospitals in Kentucky............	109	110	108	110	112
Bed Size Category					
6-24	5	4	3	4	5
25-49	40	38	37	37	38
50-99	16	20	20	21	19
100-199	24	24	24	24	27
200-299	11	11	9	11	10
300-399	9	9	11	9	9
400-499	1	1	1	3	2
500 + ...	3	3	3	1	2
Location					
Hospitals Urban	43	44	44	45	46
Hospitals Rural	66	66	64	65	66
Control					
State and Local Government	11	10	12	12	12
Not for Profit	76	77	76	75	78
Investor owned	22	23	20	23	22
Physician Models					
Independent Practice Association	4	3	3	4	3
Group Practice without Walls	1	1	1	1	1
Open Physician-Hospital Organization	5	6	6	5	5
Closed Physician-Hospital Organization	5	4	4	0	1
Management Service Organization	12	12	12	9	9
Integrated Salary Model	37	38	43	43	40
Equity Model	0	0	0	0	0
Foundation	5	5	5	1	2
Affiliations					
Hospitals in a System	87	88	87	86	83
Hospitals in a Network	32	35	32	33	30
Hospitals in a Group Purchasing Organization...	67	73	75	74	72

TABLE 6

KENTUCKY

U.S. Community Hospitals
(Nonfederal, short-term general and other special hospitals)

Utilization, Personnel, Revenue and Expenses, Community Health Indicators 2013–2017

	2017	2016	2015	2014	2013
TOTAL FACILITY (Includes Hospital and Nursing Home Units)					
Utilization - Inpatient					
Beds	14,115	14,314	14,372	14,282	14,309
Admissions	560,311	563,240	558,979	561,267	581,918
Inpatient Days	3,109,708	3,131,068	3,124,169	3,049,897	3,115,000
Average Length of Stay	5.5	5.6	5.6	5.4	5.4
Inpatient Surgeries	157,202	161,015	149,677	159,668	159,809
Births	51,034	55,003	53,551	52,786	54,263
Utilization - Outpatient					
Emergency Outpatient Visits	2,551,891	2,607,126	2,512,293	2,342,082	2,290,074
Other Outpatient Visits	11,861,846	11,277,451	10,530,286	8,464,748	8,261,868
Total Outpatient Visits	14,413,737	13,884,577	13,042,579	10,806,830	10,551,942
Outpatient Surgeries	375,896	381,540	371,144	363,996	371,426
Personnel					
Full Time RNs	21,673	20,687	19,312	18,664	18,701
Full Time LPNs	932	1,114	1,423	1,155	1,279
Part Time RNs	7,077	7,117	7,018	6,869	6,664
Part Time LPNs	248	239	289	257	271
Total Full Time	68,966	67,323	66,318	62,462	63,218
Total Part Time	18,818	19,595	19,962	18,891	19,163
Revenue - Inpatient					
Gross Inpatient Revenue	$25,439,271,058	$23,957,337,034	$21,689,736,794	$20,203,306,441	$18,556,563,500
Revenue - Outpatient					
Gross Outpatient Revenue	$28,181,172,622	$26,219,689,105	$24,030,691,691	$22,453,768,847	$18,558,312,692
Revenue and Expenses - Totals					
(Includes Inpatient and Outpatient)					
Total Gross Revenue	$53,620,443,680	$50,177,026,139	$45,720,428,485	$42,657,075,288	$37,114,876,192
Deductions from Revenue	39,974,240,869	36,989,058,278	33,221,412,847	30,662,102,306	25,911,884,950
Net Patient Revenue	13,646,202,811	13,187,967,861	12,499,015,638	11,994,972,982	11,202,991,242
Other Operating Revenue	460,278,980	527,907,529	493,337,445	542,647,182	415,245,951
Other Nonoperating Revenue	262,751,428	73,557,949	29,244,430	171,069,138	240,130,013
Total Net Revenue	14,369,233,219	13,789,433,339	13,021,597,513	12,708,689,302	11,858,367,206
Total Expenses	13,526,306,127	12,870,942,144	11,871,401,511	12,000,294,485	11,083,913,262
HOSPITAL UNIT (Excludes Separate Nursing Home Units)					
Utilization - Inpatient					
Beds	13,623	13,779	13,651	13,720	13,497
Admissions	556,142	558,270	552,288	556,450	575,680
Inpatient Days	2,964,296	2,978,210	2,911,955	2,891,608	2,854,816
Average Length of Stay	5.3	5.3	5.3	5.2	5.0
Personnel					
Total Full Time	68,623	66,896	65,683	61,958	62,441
Total Part Time	18,657	19,475	19,797	18,744	18,925
Revenue and Expenses - Totals					
(Includes Inpatient and Outpatient)					
Total Net Revenue	$14,300,441,899	$13,704,097,399	$12,926,276,245	$12,651,405,675	$11,795,309,916
Total Expenses	13,480,070,188	12,812,542,345	11,806,227,301	11,952,399,318	11,011,285,804
COMMUNITY HEALTH INDICATORS PER 1000 POPULATION					
Total Population (in thousands)	4,454	4,437	4,425	4,413	4,395
Inpatient					
Beds	3.2	3.2	3.2	3.2	3.3
Admissions	125.8	126.9	126.3	127.2	132.4
Inpatient Days	698.2	705.7	706.0	691.0	708.7
Inpatient Surgeries	35.3	36.3	33.8	36.2	36.4
Births	11.5	12.4	12.1	12.0	12.3
Outpatient					
Emergency Outpatient Visits	572.9	587.6	567.7	530.7	521.0
Other Outpatient Visits	2,663.1	2,541.7	2,379.7	1,917.9	1,879.7
Total Outpatient Visits	3,236.0	3,129.3	2,947.4	2,448.6	2,400.7
Outpatient Surgeries	84.4	86.0	83.9	82.5	84.5
Expense per Capita (per person)	$3,036.8	$2,900.8	$2,682.7	$2,719.0	$2,521.8

States

TABLE 6

LOUISIANA

U.S. Community Hospitals
(Nonfederal, short-term general and other special hospitals)

Overview 2013–2017

	2017	2016	2015	2014	2013
Total Community Hospitals in Louisiana	163	164	168	172	176
Bed Size Category					
6-24	46	46	46	46	51
25-49	53	51	53	56	53
50-99	23	25	26	24	28
100-199	20	20	21	22	20
200-299	10	12	12	12	10
300-399	5	5	4	6	7
400-499	2	2	2	3	4
500 + ...	4	3	4	3	3
Location					
Hospitals Urban	118	119	123	127	113
Hospitals Rural	45	45	45	45	63
Control					
State and Local Government	44	45	47	50	49
Not for Profit	47	48	46	44	44
Investor owned	72	71	75	78	83
Physician Models					
Independent Practice Association	6	9	8	10	8
Group Practice without Walls	3	4	3	5	4
Open Physician-Hospital Organization	9	11	8	8	8
Closed Physician-Hospital Organization ...	3	3	4	4	6
Management Service Organization	7	7	9	8	7
Integrated Salary Model	36	34	37	34	26
Equity Model	1	1	1	0	2
Foundation	3	3	3	2	5
Affiliations					
Hospitals in a System	82	84	86	86	80
Hospitals in a Network	28	27	29	22	20
Hospitals in a Group Purchasing Organization...	65	67	70	65	68

States

TABLE 6

LOUISIANA

U.S. Community Hospitals
(Nonfederal, short-term general and other special hospitals)

Utilization, Personnel, Revenue and Expenses, Community Health Indicators 2013–2017

	2017	2016	2015	2014	2013
TOTAL FACILITY (Includes Hospital and Nursing Home Units)					
Utilization - Inpatient					
Beds	15,649	15,484	15,730	16,495	17,028
Admissions	582,708	580,466	587,438	591,817	596,167
Inpatient Days	3,269,781	3,280,472	3,348,738	3,336,692	3,341,947
Average Length of Stay	5.6	5.7	5.7	5.6	5.6
Inpatient Surgeries	161,723	164,445	156,035	151,961	143,582
Births	61,233	64,144	69,229	70,969	64,083
Utilization - Outpatient					
Emergency Outpatient Visits	2,884,237	2,924,310	2,757,044	2,786,063	2,614,013
Other Outpatient Visits	10,147,792	8,999,058	9,743,346	8,252,515	7,320,180
Total Outpatient Visits	13,032,029	11,923,368	12,500,390	11,038,578	9,934,193
Outpatient Surgeries	328,365	342,743	322,376	321,654	305,668
Personnel					
Full Time RNs	21,328	21,346	21,647	21,435	20,312
Full Time LPNs	3,009	2,877	3,021	2,887	2,967
Part Time RNs	9,009	8,612	8,593	8,081	7,761
Part Time LPNs	912	831	861	1,022	1,056
Total Full Time	73,574	76,674	76,359	77,919	76,027
Total Part Time	25,330	24,820	25,037	24,003	23,969
Revenue - Inpatient					
Gross Inpatient Revenue	$26,353,243,868	$25,367,115,795	$23,636,202,281	$22,455,411,702	$21,083,346,948
Revenue - Outpatient					
Gross Outpatient Revenue	$27,895,243,945	$25,105,248,635	$23,069,411,270	$20,615,210,768	$18,635,460,584
Revenue and Expenses - Totals					
(Includes Inpatient and Outpatient)					
Total Gross Revenue	$54,248,487,813	$50,472,364,430	$46,705,613,551	$43,070,622,470	$39,718,807,532
Deductions from Revenue	40,544,198,814	37,258,510,377	33,788,626,465	31,084,242,734	28,319,893,596
Net Patient Revenue	13,704,288,999	13,213,854,053	12,916,987,086	11,986,379,736	11,398,913,936
Other Operating Revenue	1,159,947,074	1,042,706,509	815,860,125	711,272,219	702,809,835
Other Nonoperating Revenue	160,894,753	83,899,016	45,037,057	266,171,019	174,118,732
Total Net Revenue	15,025,130,826	14,340,459,578	13,777,884,268	12,963,822,974	12,275,842,503
Total Expenses	14,288,866,792	13,455,133,714	12,672,224,525	12,146,185,498	11,603,451,647
HOSPITAL UNIT (Excludes Separate Nursing Home Units)					
Utilization - Inpatient					
Beds	14,996	14,957	15,217	15,934	16,313
Admissions	580,815	578,071	585,053	589,923	593,946
Inpatient Days	3,081,441	3,087,996	3,203,314	3,174,576	3,159,620
Average Length of Stay	5.3	5.3	5.5	5.4	5.3
Personnel					
Total Full Time	73,117	76,399	75,960	76,216	75,550
Total Part Time	25,165	24,693	24,908	23,172	23,721
Revenue and Expenses - Totals					
(Includes Inpatient and Outpatient)					
Total Net Revenue	$14,992,270,856	$14,306,399,774	$13,746,355,871	$12,936,892,171	$12,229,294,000
Total Expenses	14,255,029,380	13,426,836,407	12,645,746,776	12,123,832,593	11,559,561,051
COMMUNITY HEALTH INDICATORS PER 1000 POPULATION					
Total Population (in thousands)	4,684	4,682	4,671	4,650	4,625
Inpatient					
Beds	3.3	3.3	3.4	3.5	3.7
Admissions	124.4	124.0	125.8	127.3	128.9
Inpatient Days	698.0	700.7	717.0	717.6	722.5
Inpatient Surgeries	34.5	35.1	33.4	32.7	31.0
Births	13.1	13.7	14.8	15.3	13.9
Outpatient					
Emergency Outpatient Visits	615.7	624.6	590.3	599.2	565.1
Other Outpatient Visits	2,166.3	1,922.2	2,086.0	1,774.9	1,582.6
Total Outpatient Visits	2,782.0	2,546.8	2,676.3	2,374.1	2,147.7
Outpatient Surgeries	70.1	73.2	69.0	69.2	66.1
Expense per Capita (per person)	$3,050.4	$2,874.0	$2,713.1	$2,612.3	$2,508.6

States

TABLE 6

MAINE

U.S. Community Hospitals
(Nonfederal, short-term general and other special hospitals)

Overview 2013–2017

	2017	2016	2015	2014	2013
Total Community Hospitals in Maine...............	34	34	34	35	35
Bed Size Category					
6-24	3	3	3	2	1
25-49	14	14	15	16	17
50-99	8	8	7	8	7
100-199	6	5	5	6	6
200-299	0	1	1	0	2
300-399	2	2	2	1	1
400-499	0	0	0	0	0
500 + ...	1	1	1	1	1
Location					
Hospitals Urban	13	13	13	14	14
Hospitals Rural...	21	21	21	21	21
Control					
State and Local Government	2	2	3	2	2
Not for Profit...	31	31	30	32	32
Investor owned	1	1	1	1	1
Physician Models					
Independent Practice Association......................	0	3	3	0	0
Group Practice without Walls	0	2	1	0	1
Open Physician-Hospital Organization	6	7	7	9	8
Closed Physician-Hospital Organization............	2	3	3	3	2
Management Service Organization	2	3	2	2	2
Integrated Salary Model...................................	16	14	13	13	17
Equity Model	0	0	0	0	0
Foundation	0	0	0	0	0
Affiliations					
Hospitals in a System	21	22	22	18	18
Hospitals in a Network......................................	11	12	15	16	17
Hospitals in a Group Purchasing Organization...	26	28	29	26	28

TABLE 6

MAINE

U.S. Community Hospitals
(Nonfederal, short-term general and other special hospitals)

Utilization, Personnel, Revenue and Expenses, Community Health Indicators 2013–2017

	2017	2016	2015	2014	2013
TOTAL FACILITY (Includes Hospital and Nursing Home Units)					
Utilization - Inpatient					
Beds	3,410	3,397	3,478	3,379	3,474
Admissions	132,963	135,281	137,950	135,001	139,976
Inpatient Days	860,280	851,357	816,880	772,923	782,150
Average Length of Stay	6.5	6.3	5.9	5.7	5.6
Inpatient Surgeries	40,716	40,697	39,339	39,374	40,786
Births	12,260	12,524	11,798	11,495	11,687
Utilization - Outpatient					
Emergency Outpatient Visits	682,348	678,948	964,240	771,696	795,374
Other Outpatient Visits	5,648,238	5,271,196	6,239,268	7,063,404	6,358,880
Total Outpatient Visits	6,330,586	5,950,144	7,203,508	7,835,100	7,154,254
Outpatient Surgeries	107,700	108,801	105,713	112,626	103,239
Personnel					
Full Time RNs	6,083	5,762	6,119	5,779	5,509
Full Time LPNs	280	269	335	255	242
Part Time RNs	3,317	2,945	3,511	3,944	3,503
Part Time LPNs	107	106	141	121	118
Total Full Time	28,471	27,178	26,456	25,520	24,591
Total Part Time	11,996	10,927	11,607	12,346	11,034
Revenue - Inpatient					
Gross Inpatient Revenue	$5,049,483,409	$4,429,901,617	$4,571,897,264	$4,059,334,894	$3,801,387,888
Revenue - Outpatient					
Gross Outpatient Revenue	$7,228,971,325	$6,500,678,123	$6,083,795,956	$5,658,735,515	$5,272,970,618
Revenue and Expenses - Totals					
(Includes Inpatient and Outpatient)					
Total Gross Revenue	$12,278,454,734	$10,930,579,740	$10,655,693,220	$9,718,070,409	$9,074,358,506
Deductions from Revenue	7,023,784,148	5,972,381,386	5,991,204,223	5,323,172,816	4,805,408,453
Net Patient Revenue	5,254,670,586	4,958,198,354	4,664,488,997	4,394,897,593	4,268,950,053
Other Operating Revenue	444,432,749	409,506,843	344,974,562	322,528,528	307,982,903
Other Nonoperating Revenue	106,196,522	39,795,272	16,792,277	107,159,154	85,107,098
Total Net Revenue	5,805,299,857	5,407,500,469	5,026,255,836	4,824,585,275	4,662,040,054
Total Expenses	5,561,474,952	5,281,349,738	4,912,530,828	4,635,468,221	4,501,336,652
HOSPITAL UNIT (Excludes Separate Nursing Home Units)					
Utilization - Inpatient					
Beds	2,876	2,901	2,984	2,983	3,078
Admissions	131,517	131,949	135,289	134,085	139,093
Inpatient Days	687,357	677,182	714,550	638,945	646,155
Average Length of Stay	5.2	5.1	5.3	4.8	4.6
Personnel					
Total Full Time	27,832	26,427	26,139	24,953	24,087
Total Part Time	11,479	10,396	11,351	11,679	10,755
Revenue and Expenses - Totals					
(Includes Inpatient and Outpatient)					
Total Net Revenue	$5,746,316,576	$5,372,226,471	$4,998,768,917	$4,791,979,724	$4,629,095,790
Total Expenses	5,509,149,337	5,243,064,736	4,886,600,125	4,601,902,809	4,470,359,564
COMMUNITY HEALTH INDICATORS PER 1000 POPULATION					
Total Population (in thousands)	1,336	1,331	1,329	1,330	1,328
Inpatient					
Beds	2.6	2.6	2.6	2.5	2.6
Admissions	99.5	101.6	103.8	101.5	105.4
Inpatient Days	644.0	639.4	614.5	581.1	588.8
Inpatient Surgeries	30.5	30.6	29.6	29.6	30.7
Births	9.2	9.4	8.9	8.6	8.8
Outpatient					
Emergency Outpatient Visits	510.8	509.9	725.4	580.2	598.8
Other Outpatient Visits	4,228.0	3,958.9	4,693.6	5,310.5	4,787.2
Total Outpatient Visits	4,738.8	4,468.8	5,418.9	5,890.7	5,386.0
Outpatient Surgeries	80.6	81.7	79.5	84.7	77.7
Expense per Capita (per person)	$4,163.1	$3,966.5	$3,695.5	$3,485.1	$3,388.8

States

TABLE 6

MARYLAND

U.S. Community Hospitals
(Nonfederal, short-term general and other special hospitals)

Overview 2013–2017

	2017	2016	2015	2014	2013
Total Community Hospitals in Maryland	51	51	51	50	50
Bed Size Category					
6-24	0	0	0	0	0
25-49	3	4	4	3	3
50-99	9	8	7	9	9
100-199	14	15	15	12	9
200-299	12	9	10	12	14
300-399	6	8	7	6	8
400-499	5	5	6	6	4
500 +	2	2	2	2	3
Location					
Hospitals Urban	47	47	47	46	44
Hospitals Rural	4	4	4	4	6
Control					
State and Local Government	0	0	0	0	0
Not for Profit	50	50	50	49	49
Investor owned	1	1	1	1	1
Physician Models					
Independent Practice Association	3	3	7	6	9
Group Practice without Walls	3	4	4	3	6
Open Physician-Hospital Organization	7	7	6	6	5
Closed Physician-Hospital Organization	8	7	7	9	9
Management Service Organization	5	7	10	5	10
Integrated Salary Model	28	28	31	30	31
Equity Model	2	2	1	2	3
Foundation	2	3	6	6	5
Affiliations					
Hospitals in a System	37	37	36	35	35
Hospitals in a Network	14	13	18	14	16
Hospitals in a Group Purchasing Organization	38	37	43	36	41

TABLE 6

MARYLAND

U.S. Community Hospitals
(Nonfederal, short-term general and other special hospitals)

Utilization, Personnel, Revenue and Expenses, Community Health Indicators 2013–2017

	2017	2016	2015	2014	2013
TOTAL FACILITY (Includes Hospital and Nursing Home Units)					
Utilization - Inpatient					
Beds	11,607	11,648	11,879	12,027	12,392
Admissions	581,640	589,392	596,516	609,185	628,485
Inpatient Days	2,991,695	3,027,850	3,052,607	3,067,846	3,165,089
Average Length of Stay	5.1	5.1	5.1	5.0	5.0
Inpatient Surgeries	165,197	168,882	171,451	176,580	182,075
Births	64,273	67,010	67,711	65,730	66,699
Utilization - Outpatient					
Emergency Outpatient Visits	2,403,879	2,517,321	2,488,461	2,341,061	2,542,407
Other Outpatient Visits	6,900,993	10,323,775	6,940,745	6,671,728	6,879,374
Total Outpatient Visits	9,304,872	12,841,096	9,429,206	9,012,789	9,421,781
Outpatient Surgeries	348,568	363,303	350,235	352,010	355,688
Personnel					
Full Time RNs	21,875	21,287	20,865	21,205	19,966
Full Time LPNs	354	389	414	420	434
Part Time RNs	9,985	9,087	8,309	8,779	8,383
Part Time LPNs	133	155	157	160	212
Total Full Time	75,552	75,818	74,949	78,634	75,810
Total Part Time	29,554	28,763	27,279	27,551	25,681
Revenue - Inpatient					
Gross Inpatient Revenue	$12,811,275,178	$12,263,125,916	$12,932,959,279	$11,825,919,787	$10,661,965,230
Revenue - Outpatient					
Gross Outpatient Revenue	$11,259,051,688	$10,786,754,638	$11,342,366,816	$9,739,331,110	$8,799,199,791
Revenue and Expenses - Totals					
(Includes Inpatient and Outpatient)					
Total Gross Revenue	$24,070,326,866	$23,049,880,554	$24,275,326,095	$21,565,250,897	$19,461,165,021
Deductions from Revenue	8,369,790,182	7,827,604,972	9,592,824,701	7,462,716,486	5,848,369,205
Net Patient Revenue	15,700,536,684	15,222,275,582	14,682,501,394	14,102,534,411	13,612,795,816
Other Operating Revenue	956,698,682	892,444,891	790,914,902	745,533,295	720,549,006
Other Nonoperating Revenue	319,979,452	-114,814,750	-19,539,599	432,996,623	258,822,436
Total Net Revenue	16,977,214,818	15,999,905,723	15,453,876,697	15,281,064,329	14,592,167,258
Total Expenses	15,928,893,444	15,670,406,755	14,840,392,246	14,187,741,189	13,836,110,822
HOSPITAL UNIT (Excludes Separate Nursing Home Units)					
Utilization - Inpatient					
Beds	11,394	11,417	11,554	11,725	11,614
Admissions	579,880	586,857	593,348	605,304	621,936
Inpatient Days	2,942,114	2,966,565	2,957,249	2,976,468	2,926,235
Average Length of Stay	5.1	5.1	5.0	4.9	4.7
Personnel					
Total Full Time	75,379	75,658	74,679	78,206	75,010
Total Part Time	29,388	28,629	27,132	27,297	25,282
Revenue and Expenses - Totals					
(Includes Inpatient and Outpatient)					
Total Net Revenue	$16,958,186,929	$15,974,822,998	$15,418,373,557	$15,213,654,834	$14,477,831,557
Total Expenses	15,907,000,858	15,646,829,355	14,805,360,651	14,129,417,337	13,728,619,619
COMMUNITY HEALTH INDICATORS PER 1000 POPULATION					
Total Population (in thousands)	6,052	6,016	6,006	5,976	5,929
Inpatient					
Beds	1.9	1.9	2.0	2.0	2.1
Admissions	96.1	98.0	99.3	101.9	106.0
Inpatient Days	494.3	503.3	508.2	513.3	533.8
Inpatient Surgeries	27.3	28.1	28.5	29.5	30.7
Births	10.6	11.1	11.3	11.0	11.2
Outpatient					
Emergency Outpatient Visits	397.2	418.4	414.3	391.7	428.8
Other Outpatient Visits	1,140.2	1,715.9	1,155.6	1,116.3	1,160.3
Total Outpatient Visits	1,537.4	2,134.3	1,569.9	1,508.1	1,589.2
Outpatient Surgeries	57.6	60.4	58.3	58.9	60.0
Expense per Capita (per person)	$2,631.9	$2,604.6	$2,470.8	$2,374.0	$2,333.7

States

TABLE **6**

MASSACHUSETTS

U.S. Community Hospitals
(Nonfederal, short-term general and other special hospitals)

Overview 2013–2017

	2017	2016	2015	2014	2013
Total Community Hospitals in Massachusetts ...	75	77	78	80	83
Bed Size Category					
6-24	3	3	4	4	4
25-49	8	8	8	7	7
50-99	15	17	18	18	19
100-199	22	22	22	25	25
200-299	11	11	10	10	13
300-399	7	7	7	8	6
400-499	3	3	3	2	3
500 +	6	6	6	6	6
Location					
Hospitals Urban	72	74	75	77	81
Hospitals Rural	3	3	3	3	2
Control					
State and Local Government	3	3	3	4	3
Not for Profit	56	56	57	57	59
Investor owned	16	18	18	19	21
Physician Models					
Independent Practice Association	14	18	19	19	19
Group Practice without Walls	2	3	2	2	1
Open Physician-Hospital Organization	22	19	18	17	17
Closed Physician-Hospital Organization	5	4	4	5	5
Management Service Organization	8	8	9	9	9
Integrated Salary Model	28	32	33	32	30
Equity Model	1	1	1	1	1
Foundation	1	1	2	2	2
Affiliations					
Hospitals in a System	51	52	51	54	53
Hospitals in a Network	27	29	30	26	24
Hospitals in a Group Purchasing Organization ...	47	52	51	52	50

TABLE 6

MASSACHUSETTS

U.S. Community Hospitals
(Nonfederal, short-term general and other special hospitals)

Utilization, Personnel, Revenue and Expenses, Community Health Indicators 2013–2017

	2017	2016	2015	2014	2013
TOTAL FACILITY (Includes Hospital and Nursing Home Units)					
Utilization - Inpatient					
Beds	15,650	15,783	15,609	16,134	16,557
Admissions	780,695	769,189	764,216	757,572	789,701
Inpatient Days	4,139,660	4,070,997	4,066,706	4,131,272	4,195,540
Average Length of Stay	5.3	5.3	5.3	5.5	5.3
Inpatient Surgeries	186,558	192,700	188,021	190,086	188,191
Births	65,673	67,394	67,950	69,068	68,965
Utilization - Outpatient					
Emergency Outpatient Visits	3,323,247	3,333,951	3,259,551	3,186,679	3,221,445
Other Outpatient Visits	19,552,119	19,725,735	19,708,626	18,787,637	18,896,896
Total Outpatient Visits	22,875,366	23,059,686	22,968,177	21,974,316	22,118,341
Outpatient Surgeries	430,006	435,484	430,891	426,604	427,620
Personnel					
Full Time RNs	24,399	23,987	22,258	22,773	21,946
Full Time LPNs	763	848	798	819	856
Part Time RNs	23,829	23,611	23,415	22,550	23,094
Part Time LPNs	487	533	520	543	656
Total Full Time	121,875	120,773	114,981	115,131	116,013
Total Part Time	69,931	69,656	67,367	67,465	67,740
Revenue - Inpatient					
Gross Inpatient Revenue	$32,419,915,790	$30,265,082,301	$28,369,343,026	$27,754,064,927	$26,336,182,059
Revenue - Outpatient					
Gross Outpatient Revenue	$40,032,642,495	$36,706,063,615	$33,805,120,905	$30,746,618,755	$29,751,580,199
Revenue and Expenses - Totals					
(Includes Inpatient and Outpatient)					
Total Gross Revenue	$72,452,558,285	$66,971,145,916	$62,174,463,931	$58,500,683,682	$56,087,762,258
Deductions from Revenue	46,657,933,670	42,104,612,780	38,645,096,775	35,969,379,132	34,139,796,532
Net Patient Revenue	25,794,624,615	24,866,533,136	23,529,367,156	22,531,304,550	21,947,965,726
Other Operating Revenue	4,512,682,152	4,149,885,652	3,950,093,994	3,805,639,607	3,773,155,828
Other Nonoperating Revenue	638,968,323	151,858,972	13,933,523	157,514,304	600,619,645
Total Net Revenue	30,946,275,090	29,168,277,760	27,493,394,673	26,494,458,461	26,321,741,199
Total Expenses	29,941,210,139	28,367,505,871	26,502,594,673	25,405,408,634	24,723,675,782
HOSPITAL UNIT (Excludes Separate Nursing Home Units)					
Utilization - Inpatient					
Beds	15,650	15,754	15,580	16,105	16,528
Admissions	780,695	768,592	763,589	756,939	789,013
Inpatient Days	4,139,660	4,062,940	4,058,460	4,122,726	4,186,838
Average Length of Stay	5.3	5.3	5.3	5.4	5.3
Personnel					
Total Full Time	121,875	120,764	114,974	115,125	116,007
Total Part Time	69,931	69,642	67,350	67,450	67,721
Revenue and Expenses - Totals					
(Includes Inpatient and Outpatient)					
Total Net Revenue	$30,946,275,090	$29,164,160,915	$27,489,025,820	$26,489,878,640	$26,317,066,788
Total Expenses	29,941,210,139	28,362,196,974	26,497,267,680	25,400,413,437	24,718,326,052
COMMUNITY HEALTH INDICATORS PER 1000 POPULATION					
Total Population (in thousands)	6,860	6,812	6,794	6,745	6,693
Inpatient					
Beds	2.3	2.3	2.3	2.4	2.5
Admissions	113.8	112.9	112.5	112.3	118.0
Inpatient Days	603.5	597.6	598.5	612.5	626.9
Inpatient Surgeries	27.2	28.3	27.7	28.2	28.1
Births	9.6	9.9	10.0	10.2	10.3
Outpatient					
Emergency Outpatient Visits	484.5	489.4	479.7	472.4	481.3
Other Outpatient Visits	2,850.2	2,895.8	2,900.7	2,785.2	2,823.5
Total Outpatient Visits	3,334.7	3,385.3	3,380.4	3,257.7	3,304.8
Outpatient Surgeries	62.7	63.9	63.4	63.2	63.9
Expense per Capita (per person)	$4,364.7	$4,164.5	$3,900.6	$3,766.3	$3,694.1

TABLE 6

MICHIGAN

U.S. Community Hospitals
(Nonfederal, short-term general and other special hospitals)

Overview 2013–2017

	2017	2016	2015	2014	2013
Total Community Hospitals in Michigan	145	147	148	149	152
Bed Size Category					
6-24	14	14	13	12	13
25-49	46	43	44	42	44
50-99	22	27	30	32	32
100-199	21	21	19	21	19
200-299	10	10	12	13	16
300-399	11	13	12	11	10
400-499	10	8	8	8	6
500 + ...	11	11	10	10	12
Location					
Hospitals Urban	91	93	93	94	94
Hospitals Rural.......................................	54	54	55	55	58
Control					
State and Local Government	7	10	12	12	14
Not for Profit..	112	110	111	111	114
Investor owned	26	27	25	26	24
Physician Models					
Independent Practice Association...............	5	3	8	11	12
Group Practice without Walls	3	3	7	8	8
Open Physician-Hospital Organization	48	47	39	42	40
Closed Physician-Hospital Organization......	21	21	19	15	16
Management Service Organization	6	6	8	9	13
Integrated Salary Model...........................	84	89	85	89	88
Equity Model	1	2	1	1	1
Foundation	3	6	7	6	6
Affiliations					
Hospitals in a System	114	111	110	107	101
Hospitals in a Network.............................	66	65	60	63	58
Hospitals in a Group Purchasing Organization...	116	112	108	116	116

TABLE 6

MICHIGAN

U.S. Community Hospitals
(Nonfederal, short-term general and other special hospitals)

Utilization, Personnel, Revenue and Expenses, Community Health Indicators 2013–2017

	2017	2016	2015	2014	2013
TOTAL FACILITY (Includes Hospital and Nursing Home Units)					
Utilization - Inpatient					
Beds	24,987	25,144	24,943	24,618	25,279
Admissions	1,148,126	1,160,797	1,168,830	1,126,291	1,159,952
Inpatient Days	5,774,074	5,824,152	5,889,759	5,747,174	5,926,448
Average Length of Stay	5.0	5.0	5.0	5.1	5.1
Inpatient Surgeries	310,832	309,796	306,288	310,581	315,259
Births	106,026	106,510	107,136	106,127	107,429
Utilization - Outpatient					
Emergency Outpatient Visits	5,088,160	5,157,734	5,007,114	4,814,596	4,875,899
Other Outpatient Visits	33,130,754	32,275,038	30,689,235	29,132,991	27,692,598
Total Outpatient Visits	38,218,914	37,432,772	35,696,349	33,947,587	32,568,497
Outpatient Surgeries	666,907	681,704	658,070	681,337	675,239
Personnel					
Full Time RNs	45,037	43,621	42,217	41,448	38,836
Full Time LPNs	1,310	1,534	1,321	1,271	1,349
Part Time RNs	17,927	18,824	18,513	19,103	18,762
Part Time LPNs	503	719	690	714	805
Total Full Time	158,816	160,077	153,910	150,033	144,417
Total Part Time	59,077	62,924	59,354	61,760	61,866
Revenue - Inpatient					
Gross Inpatient Revenue	$43,389,473,979	$41,494,261,701	$39,351,728,038	$36,347,546,528	$35,224,566,507
Revenue - Outpatient					
Gross Outpatient Revenue	$48,760,756,193	$45,930,141,227	$42,357,655,090	$38,770,523,187	$36,804,042,573
Revenue and Expenses - Totals					
(Includes Inpatient and Outpatient)					
Total Gross Revenue	$92,150,230,172	$87,424,402,928	$81,709,383,128	$75,118,069,715	$72,028,609,080
Deductions from Revenue	60,241,364,080	56,422,123,195	52,481,922,913	47,779,458,269	45,293,666,435
Net Patient Revenue	31,908,866,092	31,002,279,733	29,227,460,215	27,338,611,446	26,734,942,645
Other Operating Revenue	1,497,587,151	1,418,608,721	1,345,964,491	1,388,706,026	1,525,863,654
Other Nonoperating Revenue	668,174,494	228,345,738	55,142,541	715,584,333	551,358,421
Total Net Revenue	34,074,627,737	32,649,234,192	30,628,567,247	29,442,901,805	28,812,164,720
Total Expenses	31,762,862,798	30,678,766,927	29,000,739,583	27,729,695,403	27,291,208,963
HOSPITAL UNIT (Excludes Separate Nursing Home Units)					
Utilization - Inpatient					
Beds	24,116	24,252	24,050	23,671	24,341
Admissions	1,144,691	1,157,039	1,164,723	1,122,174	1,155,748
Inpatient Days	5,490,437	5,536,643	5,590,264	5,427,727	5,619,744
Average Length of Stay	4.8	4.8	4.8	4.8	4.9
Personnel					
Total Full Time	158,107	159,297	153,145	149,408	143,837
Total Part Time	58,582	62,531	58,780	61,107	61,312
Revenue and Expenses - Totals					
(Includes Inpatient and Outpatient)					
Total Net Revenue	$33,987,039,192	$32,556,335,061	$30,535,532,440	$29,344,452,822	$28,717,965,168
Total Expenses	31,702,143,480	30,619,374,769	28,933,640,822	27,647,892,067	27,219,819,405
COMMUNITY HEALTH INDICATORS PER 1000 POPULATION					
Total Population (in thousands)	9,962	9,928	9,923	9,910	9,896
Inpatient					
Beds	2.5	2.5	2.5	2.5	2.6
Admissions	115.2	116.9	117.8	113.7	117.2
Inpatient Days	579.6	586.6	593.6	579.9	598.9
Inpatient Surgeries	31.2	31.2	30.9	31.3	31.9
Births	10.6	10.7	10.8	10.7	10.9
Outpatient					
Emergency Outpatient Visits	510.7	519.5	504.6	485.8	492.7
Other Outpatient Visits	3,325.6	3,250.8	3,092.9	2,939.8	2,798.5
Total Outpatient Visits	3,836.4	3,770.3	3,597.5	3,425.6	3,291.2
Outpatient Surgeries	66.9	68.7	66.3	68.8	68.2
Expense per Capita (per person)	$3,188.3	$3,090.0	$2,922.7	$2,798.2	$2,757.9

States

TABLE 6

MINNESOTA

U.S. Community Hospitals
(Nonfederal, short-term general and other special hospitals)

Overview 2013–2017

	2017	2016	2015	2014	2013
Total Community Hospitals in Minnesota	129	129	130	131	131
Bed Size Category					
6-24	32	27	24	21	21
25-49	31	33	33	35	34
50-99	29	30	33	34	35
100-199	22	24	25	26	25
200-299	2	2	3	3	4
300-399	4	4	4	5	6
400-499	6	6	5	4	3
500 +	3	3	3	3	3
Location					
Hospitals Urban	53	53	54	55	49
Hospitals Rural	76	76	76	76	82
Control					
State and Local Government	32	32	31	33	36
Not for Profit	97	97	99	98	95
Investor owned	0	0	0	0	0
Physician Models					
Independent Practice Association	16	9	10	10	11
Group Practice without Walls	1	1	1	1	2
Open Physician-Hospital Organization	8	6	6	7	9
Closed Physician-Hospital Organization	5	2	2	2	2
Management Service Organization	1	1	2	2	1
Integrated Salary Model	55	59	61	62	61
Equity Model	0	0	1	1	1
Foundation	1	0	0	1	1
Affiliations					
Hospitals in a System	85	83	84	85	81
Hospitals in a Network	30	31	29	29	31
Hospitals in a Group Purchasing Organization	90	92	91	94	92

TABLE 6

MINNESOTA

U.S. Community Hospitals
(Nonfederal, short-term general and other special hospitals)

Utilization, Personnel, Revenue and Expenses, Community Health Indicators 2013–2017

	2017	2016	2015	2014	2013
TOTAL FACILITY (Includes Hospital and Nursing Home Units)					
Utilization - Inpatient					
Beds	13,992	14,277	14,393	14,562	14,781
Admissions	557,820	546,613	547,399	548,360	562,035
Inpatient Days	3,310,521	3,319,384	3,357,517	3,346,653	3,395,406
Average Length of Stay	5.9	6.1	6.1	6.1	6.0
Inpatient Surgeries	177,900	174,253	173,157	175,793	181,758
Births	66,404	67,449	67,081	66,960	67,898
Utilization - Outpatient					
Emergency Outpatient Visits	2,092,544	2,019,387	1,961,075	1,946,061	1,933,651
Other Outpatient Visits	11,751,668	11,499,803	10,278,747	10,023,292	9,732,473
Total Outpatient Visits	13,844,212	13,519,190	12,239,822	11,969,353	11,666,124
Outpatient Surgeries	381,553	335,648	335,562	322,191	322,895
Personnel					
Full Time RNs	13,762	12,678	13,120	12,942	12,220
Full Time LPNs	1,465	1,579	1,554	1,492	1,559
Part Time RNs	27,944	27,073	25,092	23,902	22,010
Part Time LPNs	1,619	1,679	1,615	1,681	1,666
Total Full Time	86,026	83,523	83,073	80,627	83,940
Total Part Time	72,011	71,017	66,846	64,045	61,875
Revenue - Inpatient					
Gross Inpatient Revenue	$24,252,197,440	$23,766,111,231	$22,441,151,417	$21,280,123,954	$20,263,141,343
Revenue - Outpatient					
Gross Outpatient Revenue	$25,746,965,622	$24,607,182,442	$22,431,972,337	$20,107,877,258	$18,010,747,799
Revenue and Expenses - Totals					
(Includes Inpatient and Outpatient)					
Total Gross Revenue	$49,999,163,062	$48,373,293,673	$44,873,123,754	$41,388,001,212	$38,273,889,142
Deductions from Revenue	30,772,082,886	29,987,533,574	27,385,010,912	24,738,287,806	22,240,528,284
Net Patient Revenue	19,227,080,176	18,385,760,099	17,488,112,842	16,649,713,406	16,033,360,858
Other Operating Revenue	1,119,105,564	974,290,684	879,946,693	857,887,159	797,395,199
Other Nonoperating Revenue	479,293,091	60,420,818	85,927,538	285,082,518	285,377,987
Total Net Revenue	20,825,478,831	19,420,471,601	18,453,987,073	17,792,683,083	17,116,134,044
Total Expenses	19,400,142,385	18,651,840,870	17,156,049,679	16,528,924,367	15,886,275,897
HOSPITAL UNIT (Excludes Separate Nursing Home Units)					
Utilization - Inpatient					
Beds	12,017	12,144	12,098	12,428	12,773
Admissions	554,420	542,848	543,432	544,181	558,324
Inpatient Days	2,677,440	2,622,349	2,602,118	2,631,904	2,749,985
Average Length of Stay	4.8	4.8	4.8	4.8	4.9
Personnel					
Total Full Time	85,179	82,582	82,103	79,565	82,892
Total Part Time	70,607	69,419	65,186	62,199	60,139
Revenue and Expenses - Totals					
(Includes Inpatient and Outpatient)					
Total Net Revenue	$20,664,678,838	$19,238,547,023	$18,281,872,718	$17,618,940,851	$16,969,593,334
Total Expenses	19,244,214,744	18,485,511,994	16,999,260,248	16,384,436,397	15,749,642,682
COMMUNITY HEALTH INDICATORS PER 1000 POPULATION					
Total Population (in thousands)	5,577	5,520	5,490	5,457	5,420
Inpatient					
Beds	2.5	2.6	2.6	2.7	2.7
Admissions	100.0	99.0	99.7	100.5	103.7
Inpatient Days	593.6	601.3	611.6	613.3	626.4
Inpatient Surgeries	31.9	31.6	31.5	32.2	33.5
Births	11.9	12.2	12.2	12.3	12.5
Outpatient					
Emergency Outpatient Visits	375.2	365.8	357.2	356.6	356.7
Other Outpatient Visits	2,107.3	2,083.3	1,872.4	1,836.7	1,795.5
Total Outpatient Visits	2,482.6	2,449.1	2,229.6	2,193.3	2,152.3
Outpatient Surgeries	68.4	60.8	61.1	59.0	59.6
Expense per Capita (per person)	$3,478.8	$3,379.0	$3,125.2	$3,028.8	$2,930.8

States

TABLE 6

MISSISSIPPI

U.S. Community Hospitals
(Nonfederal, short-term general and other special hospitals)

Overview 2013–2017

	2017	2016	2015	2014	2013
Total Community Hospitals in Mississippi	100	99	101	103	106
Bed Size Category					
6-24	5	6	5	4	5
25-49	36	33	35	37	36
50-99	22	24	23	22	25
100-199	20	20	20	21	22
200-299	6	6	8	10	10
300-399	4	3	3	2	1
400-499	3	3	3	2	3
500 + ...	4	4	4	5	4
Location					
Hospitals Urban	29	28	28	29	31
Hospitals Rural	71	71	73	74	75
Control					
State and Local Government	39	39	40	40	42
Not for Profit	35	32	30	30	31
Investor owned	26	28	31	33	33
Physician Models					
Independent Practice Association	7	6	6	6	5
Group Practice without Walls	2	2	2	2	2
Open Physician-Hospital Organization	16	17	17	21	16
Closed Physician-Hospital Organization	4	3	4	4	4
Management Service Organization	13	13	11	8	8
Integrated Salary Model	23	22	25	26	30
Equity Model	0	0	1	2	1
Foundation	6	5	4	7	8
Affiliations					
Hospitals in a System	51	52	54	56	54
Hospitals in a Network	31	29	29	27	28
Hospitals in a Group Purchasing Organization...	91	91	86	1	2

TABLE 6

MISSISSIPPI

U.S. Community Hospitals
(Nonfederal, short-term general and other special hospitals)

Utilization, Personnel, Revenue and Expenses, Community Health Indicators 2013–2017

	2017	2016	2015	2014	2013
TOTAL FACILITY (Includes Hospital and Nursing Home Units)					
Utilization - Inpatient					
Beds	12,328	12,243	12,451	12,649	13,016
Admissions	378,375	381,882	361,998	376,396	381,863
Inpatient Days	2,481,030	2,477,062	2,516,647	2,544,822	2,525,484
Average Length of Stay	6.6	6.5	7.0	6.8	6.6
Inpatient Surgeries	87,969	94,477	96,762	97,407	100,900
Births	35,445	36,114	37,441	37,728	36,911
Utilization - Outpatient					
Emergency Outpatient Visits	1,805,514	1,834,612	1,790,278	1,822,226	1,797,333
Other Outpatient Visits	4,942,015	4,326,306	3,820,752	3,299,180	3,164,304
Total Outpatient Visits	6,747,529	6,160,918	5,611,030	5,121,406	4,961,637
Outpatient Surgeries	188,279	186,674	176,609	181,266	174,122
Personnel					
Full Time RNs	13,274	12,968	13,049	12,459	12,429
Full Time LPNs	1,217	1,232	1,284	1,261	1,457
Part Time RNs	4,839	4,855	4,408	4,181	4,204
Part Time LPNs	339	290	321	385	391
Total Full Time	46,427	47,296	47,977	46,798	47,187
Total Part Time	12,963	13,233	12,361	12,271	12,180
Revenue - Inpatient					
Gross Inpatient Revenue	$15,641,056,256	$15,123,310,237	$14,372,764,006	$14,277,275,412	$14,033,521,301
Revenue - Outpatient					
Gross Outpatient Revenue	$16,875,769,849	$16,009,248,352	$14,145,489,387	$13,081,154,515	$12,333,845,643
Revenue and Expenses - Totals					
(Includes Inpatient and Outpatient)					
Total Gross Revenue	$32,516,826,105	$31,132,558,589	$28,518,253,393	$27,358,429,927	$26,367,366,944
Deductions from Revenue	24,746,105,041	23,391,369,766	21,015,239,533	20,102,674,790	19,132,249,484
Net Patient Revenue	7,770,721,064	7,741,188,823	7,503,013,860	7,255,755,137	7,235,117,460
Other Operating Revenue	270,227,976	319,121,912	301,727,802	326,751,793	322,991,911
Other Nonoperating Revenue	84,966,831	72,583,587	82,928,542	111,080,545	123,827,757
Total Net Revenue	8,125,915,871	8,132,894,322	7,887,670,204	7,693,587,475	7,681,937,128
Total Expenses	7,806,529,535	7,291,741,978	7,313,556,349	7,278,099,635	7,201,486,600
HOSPITAL UNIT (Excludes Separate Nursing Home Units)					
Utilization - Inpatient					
Beds	10,709	10,658	10,925	11,036	11,227
Admissions	377,360	380,987	361,013	375,361	380,772
Inpatient Days	1,949,699	1,932,996	1,992,552	1,999,578	1,923,311
Average Length of Stay	5.2	5.1	5.5	5.3	5.1
Personnel					
Total Full Time	45,600	46,522	47,284	45,535	45,751
Total Part Time	12,599	12,899	12,057	11,808	11,687
Revenue and Expenses - Totals					
(Includes Inpatient and Outpatient)					
Total Net Revenue	$8,002,112,719	$8,003,374,011	$7,764,801,938	$7,630,500,343	$7,578,414,018
Total Expenses	7,713,801,855	7,198,296,105	7,234,720,309	7,229,820,515	7,140,355,902
COMMUNITY HEALTH INDICATORS PER 1000 POPULATION					
Total Population (in thousands)	2,984	2,989	2,992	2,994	2,991
Inpatient					
Beds	4.1	4.1	4.2	4.2	4.4
Admissions	126.8	127.8	121.0	125.7	127.7
Inpatient Days	831.4	828.8	841.0	850.0	844.3
Inpatient Surgeries	29.5	31.6	32.3	32.5	33.7
Births	11.9	12.1	12.5	12.6	12.3
Outpatient					
Emergency Outpatient Visits	605.0	613.8	598.3	608.6	600.9
Other Outpatient Visits	1,656.1	1,447.5	1,276.8	1,101.9	1,057.9
Total Outpatient Visits	2,261.2	2,061.4	1,875.1	1,710.5	1,658.7
Outpatient Surgeries	63.1	62.5	59.0	60.5	58.2
Expense per Capita (per person)	$2,616.0	$2,439.7	$2,444.1	$2,430.8	$2,407.6

States

TABLE 6

MISSOURI

U.S. Community Hospitals
(Nonfederal, short-term general and other special hospitals)

Overview 2013–2017

	2017	2016	2015	2014	2013
Total Community Hospitals in Missouri	126	126	128	130	130
Bed Size Category					
6-24	16	15	15	14	15
25-49	35	37	38	41	41
50-99	21	22	22	20	19
100-199	22	21	24	26	25
200-299	12	12	10	10	11
300-399	8	7	7	7	7
400-499	4	3	5	6	6
500 + ...	8	9	7	6	6
Location					
Hospitals Urban	73	73	75	75	72
Hospitals Rural	53	53	53	55	58
Control					
State and Local Government	31	31	31	32	33
Not for Profit	66	66	66	67	67
Investor owned	29	29	31	31	30
Physician Models					
Independent Practice Association	12	12	10	11	8
Group Practice without Walls	0	0	0	0	0
Open Physician-Hospital Organization	14	15	14	14	15
Closed Physician-Hospital Organization	5	5	4	5	6
Management Service Organization	0	0	0	0	0
Integrated Salary Model	75	77	72	77	72
Equity Model	2	1	1	1	1
Foundation	2	2	1	3	4
Affiliations					
Hospitals in a System	79	79	79	83	82
Hospitals in a Network	58	56	54	48	40
Hospitals in a Group Purchasing Organization...	122	125	121	125	126

TABLE 6

MISSOURI

U.S. Community Hospitals
(Nonfederal, short-term general and other special hospitals)

Utilization, Personnel, Revenue and Expenses, Community Health Indicators 2013–2017

	2017	2016	2015	2014	2013
TOTAL FACILITY (Includes Hospital and Nursing Home Units)					
Utilization - Inpatient					
Beds	18,930	18,771	18,810	18,816	19,042
Admissions	773,308	774,128	787,250	782,099	783,023
Inpatient Days	4,141,096	4,134,271	4,153,017	4,096,640	4,094,055
Average Length of Stay	5.4	5.3	5.3	5.2	5.2
Inpatient Surgeries	190,597	192,909	194,981	196,360	199,770
Births	71,671	73,188	73,498	74,548	74,688
Utilization - Outpatient					
Emergency Outpatient Visits	3,090,141	3,151,743	3,124,931	2,993,001	3,004,949
Other Outpatient Visits	21,759,933	21,272,728	20,059,461	19,096,289	18,894,370
Total Outpatient Visits	24,850,074	24,424,471	23,184,392	22,089,290	21,899,319
Outpatient Surgeries	396,669	398,758	388,076	383,155	386,032
Personnel					
Full Time RNs	31,537	30,877	30,507	29,923	29,078
Full Time LPNs	2,375	2,463	2,425	2,476	2,410
Part Time RNs	11,536	11,034	11,454	11,068	11,286
Part Time LPNs	523	549	552	551	575
Total Full Time	112,366	110,257	107,121	105,350	104,681
Total Part Time	35,268	34,155	34,443	33,289	33,734
Revenue - Inpatient					
Gross Inpatient Revenue	$34,196,874,205	$32,682,788,508	$31,179,811,756	$29,720,051,870	$28,116,653,277
Revenue - Outpatient					
Gross Outpatient Revenue	$39,777,826,054	$36,651,885,244	$33,124,620,409	$30,145,914,497	$27,976,290,685
Revenue and Expenses - Totals					
(Includes Inpatient and Outpatient)					
Total Gross Revenue	$73,974,700,259	$69,334,673,752	$64,304,432,165	$59,865,966,367	$56,092,943,962
Deductions from Revenue	51,954,522,721	48,294,313,912	44,364,341,627	40,973,356,391	37,862,510,635
Net Patient Revenue	22,020,177,538	21,040,359,840	19,940,090,538	18,892,609,976	18,230,433,327
Other Operating Revenue	1,375,671,345	1,236,609,926	1,252,755,683	1,105,918,918	1,156,010,180
Other Nonoperating Revenue	518,082,536	292,279,236	237,769,792	383,177,440	666,504,456
Total Net Revenue	23,913,931,419	22,569,249,002	21,430,616,013	20,381,706,334	20,052,947,963
Total Expenses	22,608,623,983	21,452,674,937	20,253,175,567	19,465,855,103	18,822,862,591
HOSPITAL UNIT (Excludes Separate Nursing Home Units)					
Utilization - Inpatient					
Beds	18,029	17,841	17,841	17,853	18,047
Admissions	769,280	769,871	782,515	774,826	777,321
Inpatient Days	3,901,459	3,890,237	3,891,041	3,808,554	3,801,191
Average Length of Stay	5.1	5.1	5.0	4.9	4.9
Personnel					
Total Full Time	111,686	109,568	106,342	104,546	103,832
Total Part Time	34,957	33,836	34,114	32,839	33,318
Revenue and Expenses - Totals					
(Includes Inpatient and Outpatient)					
Total Net Revenue	$23,852,254,053	$22,500,329,976	$21,346,760,255	$20,292,656,797	$19,981,665,027
Total Expenses	22,550,816,214	21,391,192,093	20,178,157,068	19,402,907,409	18,748,105,995
COMMUNITY HEALTH INDICATORS PER 1000 POPULATION					
Total Population (in thousands)	6,114	6,093	6,084	6,064	6,044
Inpatient					
Beds	3.1	3.1	3.1	3.1	3.2
Admissions	126.5	127.1	129.4	129.0	129.6
Inpatient Days	677.4	678.5	682.6	675.6	677.4
Inpatient Surgeries	31.2	31.7	32.0	32.4	33.1
Births	11.7	12.0	12.1	12.3	12.4
Outpatient					
Emergency Outpatient Visits	505.5	517.3	513.7	493.6	497.2
Other Outpatient Visits	3,559.3	3,491.3	3,297.3	3,149.3	3,126.0
Total Outpatient Visits	4,064.8	4,008.6	3,810.9	3,642.9	3,623.2
Outpatient Surgeries	64.9	65.4	63.8	63.2	63.9
Expense per Capita (per person)	$3,698.1	$3,520.9	$3,329.1	$3,210.3	$3,114.2

States

TABLE 6

MONTANA

U.S. Community Hospitals
(Nonfederal, short-term general and other special hospitals)

Overview 2013–2017

	2017	2016	2015	2014	2013
Total Community Hospitals in Montana	55	54	54	54	54
Bed Size Category					
6-24	13	12	12	13	11
25-49	22	20	17	16	18
50-99	11	13	16	16	16
100-199	6	5	5	6	6
200-299	1	2	2	1	1
300-399	0	0	1	1	1
400-499	1	1	0	1	1
500 + ...	1	1	1	0	0
Location					
Hospitals Urban	8	8	8	8	8
Hospitals Rural	47	46	46	46	46
Control					
State and Local Government	7	8	9	9	10
Not for Profit	43	40	40	42	41
Investor owned	5	6	5	3	3
Physician Models					
Independent Practice Association	1	2	1	2	5
Group Practice without Walls	2	2	2	2	5
Open Physician-Hospital Organization	4	2	5	4	4
Closed Physician-Hospital Organization	1	1	1	0	1
Management Service Organization	3	2	3	4	6
Integrated Salary Model	29	29	30	33	31
Equity Model	0	0	0	1	1
Foundation	3	5	3	6	6
Affiliations					
Hospitals in a System	12	13	13	12	12
Hospitals in a Network	22	24	24	24	24
Hospitals in a Group Purchasing Organization...	41	43	43	43	46

TABLE 6

MONTANA

U.S. Community Hospitals
(Nonfederal, short-term general and other special hospitals)

Utilization, Personnel, Revenue and Expenses, Community Health Indicators 2013–2017

	2017	2016	2015	2014	2013
TOTAL FACILITY (Includes Hospital and Nursing Home Units)					
Utilization - Inpatient					
Beds	3,622	3,757	3,914	3,800	3,837
Admissions	98,752	94,522	94,844	94,146	96,780
Inpatient Days	772,654	807,341	863,320	821,780	842,227
Average Length of Stay	7.8	8.5	9.1	8.7	8.7
Inpatient Surgeries	30,154	28,054	27,672	28,031	28,213
Births	11,091	10,933	11,561	10,613	10,245
Utilization - Outpatient					
Emergency Outpatient Visits	496,531	427,836	414,058	374,246	377,152
Other Outpatient Visits	3,887,431	3,619,140	3,249,436	3,122,584	3,402,422
Total Outpatient Visits	4,383,962	4,046,976	3,663,494	3,496,830	3,779,574
Outpatient Surgeries	75,718	63,216	58,591	56,001	53,929
Personnel					
Full Time RNs	4,084	3,642	3,646	3,443	3,372
Full Time LPNs	329	348	420	533	505
Part Time RNs	2,828	2,721	2,242	1,996	2,098
Part Time LPNs	198	218	216	225	245
Total Full Time	18,955	17,770	17,014	16,731	16,156
Total Part Time	10,173	9,914	7,993	7,823	8,362
Revenue - Inpatient					
Gross Inpatient Revenue	$3,501,728,307	$3,366,743,226	$3,022,578,540	$2,622,707,479	$2,551,017,463
Revenue - Outpatient					
Gross Outpatient Revenue	$4,998,732,851	$4,385,747,039	$3,937,326,560	$3,551,491,511	$3,426,425,170
Revenue and Expenses - Totals					
(Includes Inpatient and Outpatient)					
Total Gross Revenue	$8,500,461,158	$7,752,490,265	$6,959,905,100	$6,174,198,990	$5,977,442,633
Deductions from Revenue	4,690,985,631	4,317,474,812	3,705,665,159	3,191,800,766	3,097,829,766
Net Patient Revenue	3,809,475,527	3,435,015,453	3,254,239,941	2,982,398,224	2,879,612,867
Other Operating Revenue	204,620,060	177,120,640	136,136,733	143,828,977	156,724,704
Other Nonoperating Revenue	88,317,593	43,682,886	51,831,904	110,962,249	72,607,799
Total Net Revenue	4,102,413,180	3,655,818,979	3,442,208,578	3,237,189,450	3,108,945,370
Total Expenses	3,574,679,836	3,363,175,798	3,091,174,733	2,894,569,612	2,912,933,338
HOSPITAL UNIT (Excludes Separate Nursing Home Units)					
Utilization - Inpatient					
Beds	2,747	2,633	2,683	2,510	2,496
Admissions	97,211	92,823	93,137	92,397	94,712
Inpatient Days	515,745	491,147	491,442	451,159	435,497
Average Length of Stay	5.3	5.3	5.3	4.9	4.6
Personnel					
Total Full Time	18,362	17,041	16,331	15,969	15,401
Total Part Time	9,724	9,284	7,469	7,234	7,749
Revenue and Expenses - Totals					
(Includes Inpatient and Outpatient)					
Total Net Revenue	$4,028,828,782	$3,590,657,886	$3,371,448,104	$3,160,429,337	$3,029,668,482
Total Expenses	3,519,469,009	3,301,831,163	3,027,941,902	2,826,186,515	2,849,310,594
COMMUNITY HEALTH INDICATORS PER 1000 POPULATION					
Total Population (in thousands)	1,050	1,043	1,033	1,024	1,015
Inpatient					
Beds	3.4	3.6	3.8	3.7	3.8
Admissions	94.0	90.7	91.8	92.0	95.3
Inpatient Days	735.5	774.4	835.8	802.8	829.6
Inpatient Surgeries	28.7	26.9	26.8	27.4	27.8
Births	10.6	10.5	11.2	10.4	10.1
Outpatient					
Emergency Outpatient Visits	472.7	410.4	400.9	365.6	371.5
Other Outpatient Visits	3,700.6	3,471.5	3,145.8	3,050.7	3,351.6
Total Outpatient Visits	4,173.2	3,881.9	3,546.6	3,416.3	3,723.1
Outpatient Surgeries	72.1	60.6	56.7	54.7	53.1
Expense per Capita (per person)	$3,402.9	$3,226.0	$2,992.6	$2,827.9	$2,869.4

States

TABLE 6

NEBRASKA

U.S. Community Hospitals
(Nonfederal, short-term general and other special hospitals)

Overview 2013–2017

	2017	2016	2015	2014	2013
Total Community Hospitals in Nebraska.............	94	94	94	92	90
Bed Size Category					
6-24	36	33	32	30	29
25-49	20	24	24	23	21
50-99	19	18	19	20	21
100-199	10	10	9	9	7
200-299	3	3	4	5	7
300-399	3	4	4	4	4
400-499	1	0	0	0	0
500 + ...	2	2	2	1	1
Location					
Hospitals Urban	28	28	28	26	21
Hospitals Rural	66	66	66	66	69
Control					
State and Local Government	36	36	35	36	36
Not for Profit	51	51	52	49	49
Investor owned	7	7	7	7	5
Physician Models					
Independent Practice Association	4	4	5	5	4
Group Practice without Walls	0	0	0	1	1
Open Physician-Hospital Organization	19	20	14	12	11
Closed Physician-Hospital Organization	1	3	3	2	2
Management Service Organization	1	3	2	2	2
Integrated Salary Model	23	22	23	26	21
Equity Model	0	1	1	0	0
Foundation	0	0	1	2	2
Affiliations					
Hospitals in a System	29	29	29	30	28
Hospitals in a Network	35	34	32	31	30
Hospitals in a Group Purchasing Organization...	49	48	45	38	37

TABLE 6

NEBRASKA

U.S. Community Hospitals
(Nonfederal, short-term general and other special hospitals)

Utilization, Personnel, Revenue and Expenses, Community Health Indicators 2013–2017

	2017	2016	2015	2014	2013
TOTAL FACILITY (Includes Hospital and Nursing Home Units)					
Utilization - Inpatient					
Beds	6,975	6,946	7,031	6,724	6,834
Admissions	204,819	199,599	199,725	198,300	202,185
Inpatient Days	1,427,631	1,366,767	1,383,745	1,338,186	1,342,537
Average Length of Stay	7.0	6.8	6.9	6.7	6.6
Inpatient Surgeries	61,973	62,320	63,598	68,947	61,882
Births	24,334	25,223	26,263	26,037	25,323
Utilization - Outpatient					
Emergency Outpatient Visits	816,532	847,018	736,871	716,873	702,972
Other Outpatient Visits	4,804,344	4,505,795	4,114,418	3,931,785	4,128,606
Total Outpatient Visits	5,620,876	5,352,813	4,851,289	4,648,658	4,831,578
Outpatient Surgeries	144,538	148,823	133,347	133,548	128,452
Personnel					
Full Time RNs	9,367	8,369	8,611	7,973	8,444
Full Time LPNs	772	697	655	578	624
Part Time RNs	4,575	4,548	4,052	4,058	3,985
Part Time LPNs	304	350	285	277	298
Total Full Time	32,783	30,555	30,531	27,690	28,821
Total Part Time	15,107	15,576	13,951	12,935	12,697
Revenue - Inpatient					
Gross Inpatient Revenue	$8,882,408,899	$8,135,440,019	$7,825,388,016	$7,269,388,278	$6,783,311,530
Revenue - Outpatient					
Gross Outpatient Revenue	$9,851,318,080	$9,066,638,392	$8,139,489,940	$7,723,430,941	$6,810,972,619
Revenue and Expenses - Totals					
(Includes Inpatient and Outpatient)					
Total Gross Revenue	$18,733,726,979	$17,202,078,411	$15,964,877,956	$14,992,819,219	$13,594,284,149
Deductions from Revenue	11,922,150,052	10,718,822,128	10,052,446,972	9,227,364,086	8,234,186,449
Net Patient Revenue	6,811,576,927	6,483,256,283	5,912,430,984	5,765,455,133	5,360,097,700
Other Operating Revenue	382,243,135	333,314,914	339,525,035	319,581,277	314,734,449
Other Nonoperating Revenue	87,068,433	84,764,683	18,939,078	136,859,549	177,223,519
Total Net Revenue	7,280,888,495	6,901,335,880	6,270,895,097	6,221,895,959	5,852,055,668
Total Expenses	6,656,754,805	6,214,549,605	5,511,683,885	5,341,017,446	4,956,776,399
HOSPITAL UNIT (Excludes Separate Nursing Home Units)					
Utilization - Inpatient					
Beds	6,282	6,198	6,392	5,832	5,971
Admissions	203,913	198,698	198,978	196,472	200,065
Inpatient Days	1,216,341	1,139,416	1,185,617	1,101,724	1,081,210
Average Length of Stay	6.0	5.7	6.0	5.6	5.4
Personnel					
Total Full Time	32,331	30,126	30,141	27,201	28,282
Total Part Time	14,870	15,296	13,728	12,549	12,425
Revenue and Expenses - Totals					
(Includes Inpatient and Outpatient)					
Total Net Revenue	$7,239,685,510	$6,858,425,960	$6,233,927,758	$6,166,291,283	$5,790,253,935
Total Expenses	6,620,503,865	6,180,817,671	5,480,873,779	5,282,134,398	4,885,192,980
COMMUNITY HEALTH INDICATORS PER 1000 POPULATION					
Total Population (in thousands)	1,920	1,907	1,896	1,882	1,869
Inpatient					
Beds	3.6	3.6	3.7	3.6	3.7
Admissions	106.7	104.7	105.3	105.4	108.2
Inpatient Days	743.5	716.7	729.8	711.2	718.5
Inpatient Surgeries	32.3	32.7	33.5	36.6	33.1
Births	12.7	13.2	13.9	13.8	13.6
Outpatient					
Emergency Outpatient Visits	425.3	444.1	388.6	381.0	376.2
Other Outpatient Visits	2,502.2	2,362.6	2,169.8	2,089.7	2,209.6
Total Outpatient Visits	2,927.4	2,806.8	2,558.4	2,470.7	2,585.8
Outpatient Surgeries	75.3	78.0	70.3	71.0	68.7
Expense per Capita (per person)	$3,466.9	$3,258.6	$2,906.7	$2,838.7	$2,652.8

TABLE 6

NEVADA

U.S. Community Hospitals
(Nonfederal, short-term general and other special hospitals)

Overview 2013–2017

	2017	2016	2015	2014	2013
Total Community Hospitals in Nevada	44	42	41	43	44
Bed Size Category					
6-24	5	7	8	9	8
25-49	7	6	5	6	7
50-99	11	10	9	9	10
100-199	11	9	9	10	10
200-299	4	3	4	3	3
300-399	3	4	3	3	3
400-499	0	0	0	0	0
500 + ...	3	3	3	3	3
Location					
Hospitals Urban	33	31	30	32	32
Hospitals Rural..	11	11	11	11	12
Control					
State and Local Government	7	6	5	6	6
Not for Profit..	14	14	14	13	13
Investor owned	23	22	22	24	25
Physician Models					
Independent Practice Association....................	4	1	2	1	2
Group Practice without Walls	0	0	1	1	1
Open Physician-Hospital Organization	3	2	2	2	3
Closed Physician-Hospital Organization	1	1	1	1	2
Management Service Organization	5	4	4	2	2
Integrated Salary Model...............................	11	11	9	9	8
Equity Model	0	0	0	0	0
Foundation	1	0	0	1	1
Affiliations					
Hospitals in a System	31	30	30	31	30
Hospitals in a Network................................	6	5	6	4	6
Hospitals in a Group Purchasing Organization...	16	14	17	18	23

TABLE 6

NEVADA

U.S. Community Hospitals
(Nonfederal, short-term general and other special hospitals)

Utilization, Personnel, Revenue and Expenses, Community Health Indicators 2013–2017

	2017	2016	2015	2014	2013
TOTAL FACILITY (Includes Hospital and Nursing Home Units)					
Utilization - Inpatient					
Beds	6,475	6,187	6,028	6,060	6,166
Admissions	287,029	297,845	289,024	284,124	281,761
Inpatient Days	1,622,253	1,684,508	1,632,124	1,527,382	1,514,385
Average Length of Stay	5.7	5.7	5.6	5.4	5.4
Inpatient Surgeries	58,219	52,272	60,831	58,697	64,329
Births	22,228	25,666	26,424	25,298	30,175
Utilization - Outpatient					
Emergency Outpatient Visits	987,106	950,434	1,003,568	953,861	964,213
Other Outpatient Visits	2,286,818	2,497,214	2,172,449	2,201,129	1,818,123
Total Outpatient Visits	3,273,924	3,447,648	3,176,017	3,154,990	2,782,336
Outpatient Surgeries	99,109	101,909	101,016	98,338	94,447
Personnel					
Full Time RNs	9,202	8,393	8,675	8,327	8,454
Full Time LPNs	355	338	299	329	368
Part Time RNs	2,226	2,020	2,191	1,998	2,015
Part Time LPNs	69	64	76	66	80
Total Full Time	28,401	25,520	25,688	24,716	24,823
Total Part Time	6,421	5,774	6,418	5,686	5,614
Revenue - Inpatient					
Gross Inpatient Revenue	$19,013,184,691	$16,359,057,382	$16,806,038,705	$15,063,102,856	$14,489,354,387
Revenue - Outpatient					
Gross Outpatient Revenue	$14,249,772,510	$12,492,666,320	$11,440,956,313	$10,029,889,425	$8,779,953,772
Revenue and Expenses - Totals					
(Includes Inpatient and Outpatient)					
Total Gross Revenue	$33,262,957,201	$28,851,723,702	$28,246,995,018	$25,092,992,281	$23,269,308,159
Deductions from Revenue	26,902,721,416	23,020,302,981	22,719,000,011	19,957,835,728	18,380,212,764
Net Patient Revenue	6,360,235,785	5,831,420,721	5,527,995,007	5,135,156,553	4,889,095,395
Other Operating Revenue	110,436,759	180,827,619	176,174,838	159,953,297	156,566,899
Other Nonoperating Revenue	49,781,829	36,685,552	35,548,963	54,129,336	33,481,549
Total Net Revenue	6,520,454,373	6,048,933,892	5,739,718,808	5,349,239,186	5,079,143,843
Total Expenses	5,832,395,986	5,649,355,966	5,232,106,601	4,837,976,226	4,695,530,866
HOSPITAL UNIT (Excludes Separate Nursing Home Units)					
Utilization - Inpatient					
Beds	6,404	6,071	5,965	6,060	6,166
Admissions	286,936	297,744	289,004	284,124	281,761
Inpatient Days	1,601,399	1,652,758	1,612,344	1,527,382	1,514,385
Average Length of Stay	5.6	5.6	5.6	5.4	5.4
Personnel					
Total Full Time	28,375	25,461	25,665	24,716	24,823
Total Part Time	6,395	5,747	6,406	5,686	5,614
Revenue and Expenses - Totals					
(Includes Inpatient and Outpatient)					
Total Net Revenue	$6,515,344,842	$6,041,928,217	$5,737,786,585	$5,349,239,186	$5,079,143,843
Total Expenses	5,828,112,631	5,644,534,936	5,230,109,375	4,837,976,226	4,695,530,866
COMMUNITY HEALTH INDICATORS PER 1000 POPULATION					
Total Population (in thousands)	2,998	2,940	2,891	2,839	2,790
Inpatient					
Beds	2.2	2.1	2.1	2.1	2.2
Admissions	95.7	101.3	100.0	100.1	101.0
Inpatient Days	541.1	573	564.6	538.0	542.8
Inpatient Surgeries	19.4	17.8	21.0	20.7	23.1
Births	7.4	8.7	9.1	8.9	10.8
Outpatient					
Emergency Outpatient Visits	329.3	323.3	347.2	336.0	345.6
Other Outpatient Visits	762.8	849.4	751.5	775.3	651.6
Total Outpatient Visits	1,092.0	1,172.6	1,098.6	1,111.3	997.2
Outpatient Surgeries	33.1	34.7	34.9	34.6	33.9
Expense per Capita (per person)	$1,945.4	$1,921.5	$1,809.9	$1,704.1	$1,682.9

States

TABLE 6

NEW HAMPSHIRE

U.S. Community Hospitals
(Nonfederal, short-term general and other special hospitals)

Overview 2013–2017

	2017	2016	2015	2014	2013
Total Community Hospitals in New Hampshire..	28	28	28	28	28
Bed Size Category					
6-24	1	1	1	1	1
25-49	11	11	10	10	10
50-99	7	6	7	7	7
100-199	5	6	6	6	6
200-299	3	3	3	3	3
300-399	0	0	0	0	1
400-499	1	1	1	1	0
500 +	0	0	0	0	0
Location					
Hospitals Urban	11	11	11	11	11
Hospitals Rural	17	17	17	17	17
Control					
State and Local Government	0	0	0	0	0
Not for Profit	24	24	24	24	24
Investor owned	4	4	4	4	4
Physician Models					
Independent Practice Association	1	2	2	2	2
Group Practice without Walls	2	2	2	2	2
Open Physician-Hospital Organization	3	4	4	4	4
Closed Physician-Hospital Organization	0	0	0	0	0
Management Service Organization	0	0	0	0	0
Integrated Salary Model	20	20	20	18	19
Equity Model	0	0	0	0	0
Foundation	0	0	0	0	0
Affiliations					
Hospitals in a System	12	8	7	7	7
Hospitals in a Network	11	12	12	13	11
Hospitals in a Group Purchasing Organization...	24	24	23	22	24

TABLE 6

NEW HAMPSHIRE

U.S. Community Hospitals
(Nonfederal, short-term general and other special hospitals)

Utilization, Personnel, Revenue and Expenses, Community Health Indicators 2013–2017

	2017	2016	2015	2014	2013
TOTAL FACILITY (Includes Hospital and Nursing Home Units)					
Utilization - Inpatient					
Beds	2,784	2,792	2,819	2,839	2,809
Admissions	125,925	124,840	120,080	117,327	119,566
Inpatient Days	650,448	654,451	651,556	630,685	628,043
Average Length of Stay	5.2	5.2	5.4	5.4	5.3
Inpatient Surgeries	35,712	34,031	33,616	34,546	32,881
Births	12,671	13,017	13,485	13,516	12,664
Utilization - Outpatient					
Emergency Outpatient Visits	653,750	653,672	670,738	644,075	700,141
Other Outpatient Visits	4,733,688	4,589,175	4,732,025	4,265,408	4,346,816
Total Outpatient Visits	5,387,438	5,242,847	5,402,763	4,909,483	5,046,957
Outpatient Surgeries	88,265	86,929	85,009	85,589	89,108
Personnel					
Full Time RNs	5,318	5,247	5,164	4,982	4,648
Full Time LPNs	295	310	265	254	283
Part Time RNs	3,129	2,747	2,666	2,926	2,889
Part Time LPNs	98	79	81	96	111
Total Full Time	24,837	24,027	23,186	22,877	21,980
Total Part Time	10,159	9,049	9,131	9,680	10,181
Revenue - Inpatient					
Gross Inpatient Revenue	$5,198,315,247	$4,868,308,563	$4,681,725,519	$4,989,417,217	$4,696,146,268
Revenue - Outpatient					
Gross Outpatient Revenue	$9,575,854,906	$8,756,510,168	$7,960,187,285	$7,220,073,530	$6,733,412,770
Revenue and Expenses - Totals					
(Includes Inpatient and Outpatient)					
Total Gross Revenue	$14,774,170,153	$13,624,818,731	$12,641,912,804	$12,209,490,747	$11,429,559,038
Deductions from Revenue	9,538,315,281	8,668,511,254	8,085,622,586	7,808,011,257	7,139,588,921
Net Patient Revenue	5,235,854,872	4,956,307,477	4,556,290,218	4,401,479,490	4,289,970,117
Other Operating Revenue	276,634,876	240,104,568	210,402,508	197,582,231	165,027,209
Other Nonoperating Revenue	112,456,780	6,673,937	3,370,504	123,495,316	87,925,169
Total Net Revenue	5,624,946,528	5,203,085,982	4,770,063,230	4,722,557,037	4,542,922,495
Total Expenses	5,127,353,481	4,814,609,303	4,465,458,316	4,250,644,036	4,089,847,120
HOSPITAL UNIT (Excludes Separate Nursing Home Units)					
Utilization - Inpatient					
Beds	2,739	2,747	2,716	2,736	2,706
Admissions	125,898	124,825	119,988	117,253	119,473
Inpatient Days	634,407	638,304	618,237	595,536	592,762
Average Length of Stay	5.0	5.1	5.2	5.1	5.0
Personnel					
Total Full Time	24,822	24,003	23,135	22,817	21,933
Total Part Time	10,150	9,034	9,104	9,646	10,159
Revenue and Expenses - Totals					
(Includes Inpatient and Outpatient)					
Total Net Revenue	$5,621,471,313	$5,199,781,022	$4,763,300,694	$4,715,825,712	$4,535,848,627
Total Expenses	5,125,234,911	4,812,487,558	4,459,583,467	4,244,135,217	4,083,503,383
COMMUNITY HEALTH INDICATORS PER 1000 POPULATION					
Total Population (in thousands)	1,343	1,335	1,331	1,327	1,323
Inpatient					
Beds	2.1	2.1	2.1	2.1	2.1
Admissions	93.8	93.5	90.2	88.4	90.3
Inpatient Days	484.4	490.3	489.7	475.3	474.5
Inpatient Surgeries	26.6	25.5	25.3	26.0	24.8
Births	9.4	9.8	10.1	10.2	9.6
Outpatient					
Emergency Outpatient Visits	486.9	489.7	504.1	485.4	529.0
Other Outpatient Visits	3,525.2	3,438.1	3,556.3	3,214.8	3,284.4
Total Outpatient Visits	4,012.1	3,927.8	4,060.4	3,700.2	3,813.5
Outpatient Surgeries	65.7	65.1	63.9	64.5	67.3
Expense per Capita (per person)	$3,818.4	$3,607.0	$3,356.0	$3,203.6	$3,090.3

States

TABLE 6

NEW JERSEY

U.S. Community Hospitals
(Nonfederal, short-term general and other special hospitals)

Overview 2013–2017

	2017	2016	2015	2014	2013
Total Community Hospitals in New Jersey	82	81	81	80	81
Bed Size Category					
6-24	1	1	1	1	1
25-49	6	5	4	4	3
50-99	11	11	11	10	11
100-199	23	21	21	23	19
200-299	11	12	13	11	16
300-399	16	16	17	16	15
400-499	4	5	4	6	7
500 +	10	10	10	9	9
Location					
Hospitals Urban	82	81	81	80	81
Hospitals Rural	0	0	0	0	0
Control					
State and Local Government	0	1	1	2	4
Not for Profit	62	60	61	60	60
Investor owned	20	20	19	18	17
Physician Models					
Independent Practice Association	23	14	12	11	12
Group Practice without Walls	2	10	5	4	4
Open Physician-Hospital Organization	6	10	10	6	6
Closed Physician-Hospital Organization	8	5	6	6	5
Management Service Organization	16	16	19	18	15
Integrated Salary Model	46	36	37	39	38
Equity Model	7	5	3	3	3
Foundation	19	9	10	10	8
Affiliations					
Hospitals in a System	61	59	58	54	55
Hospitals in a Network	42	38	35	32	32
Hospitals in a Group Purchasing Organization	58	53	56	58	60

TABLE 6

NEW JERSEY

U.S. Community Hospitals
(Nonfederal, short-term general and other special hospitals)

Utilization, Personnel, Revenue and Expenses, Community Health Indicators 2013–2017

	2017	2016	2015	2014	2013
TOTAL FACILITY (Includes Hospital and Nursing Home Units)					
Utilization - Inpatient					
Beds	21,201	21,201	21,045	20,722	21,513
Admissions	1,076,863	1,007,338	980,822	975,417	1,008,901
Inpatient Days	5,085,634	4,962,663	5,075,803	5,066,063	5,210,741
Average Length of Stay	4.7	4.9	5.2	5.2	5.2
Inpatient Surgeries	221,055	230,250	235,740	231,455	237,839
Births	97,326	97,658	99,344	99,550	99,416
Utilization - Outpatient					
Emergency Outpatient Visits	3,785,951	3,751,369	3,543,837	3,613,702	3,584,950
Other Outpatient Visits	11,641,301	10,896,969	12,700,484	11,919,605	12,054,942
Total Outpatient Visits	15,427,252	14,648,338	16,244,321	15,533,307	15,639,892
Outpatient Surgeries	352,422	357,762	370,753	359,239	363,649
Personnel					
Full Time RNs	31,376	31,573	29,758	27,395	27,821
Full Time LPNs	646	721	666	635	722
Part Time RNs	13,700	13,627	13,996	13,661	13,251
Part Time LPNs	251	256	242	260	258
Total Full Time	108,578	108,882	104,655	100,154	101,068
Total Part Time	45,793	44,695	43,019	42,924	41,167
Revenue - Inpatient					
Gross Inpatient Revenue	$65,967,060,435	$62,344,355,839	$60,854,355,384	$59,759,980,012	$60,040,746,471
Revenue - Outpatient					
Gross Outpatient Revenue	$46,792,506,732	$42,302,262,480	$39,698,016,898	$36,670,956,612	$34,194,887,592
Revenue and Expenses - Totals					
(Includes Inpatient and Outpatient)					
Total Gross Revenue	$112,759,567,167	$104,646,618,319	$100,552,372,282	$96,430,936,624	$94,235,634,063
Deductions from Revenue	89,304,707,257	81,712,559,502	78,676,009,040	75,931,125,638	74,595,552,675
Net Patient Revenue	23,454,859,910	22,934,058,817	21,876,363,242	20,499,810,986	19,640,081,388
Other Operating Revenue	1,413,452,650	1,561,631,361	1,438,561,075	1,395,672,680	1,401,015,821
Other Nonoperating Revenue	518,351,086	434,767,553	-10,775,588	231,958,671	561,690,746
Total Net Revenue	25,386,663,646	24,930,457,731	23,304,148,729	22,127,442,337	21,602,787,955
Total Expenses	23,641,356,793	22,900,963,558	21,902,851,599	20,790,881,638	20,264,640,379
HOSPITAL UNIT (Excludes Separate Nursing Home Units)					
Utilization - Inpatient					
Beds	20,620	20,810	20,801	20,338	21,094
Admissions	1,072,428	1,004,285	977,681	972,010	1,005,130
Inpatient Days	4,897,361	4,833,242	4,995,981	4,942,202	5,074,051
Average Length of Stay	4.6	4.8	5.1	5.1	5.0
Personnel					
Total Full Time	108,255	108,414	104,456	99,841	100,754
Total Part Time	45,602	44,474	42,925	42,703	41,016
Revenue and Expenses - Totals					
(Includes Inpatient and Outpatient)					
Total Net Revenue	$25,314,988,333	$24,877,478,184	$23,265,863,043	$22,082,356,855	$21,550,259,292
Total Expenses	23,585,081,884	22,863,182,639	21,878,470,259	20,757,013,242	20,225,089,646
COMMUNITY HEALTH INDICATORS PER 1000 POPULATION					
Total Population (in thousands)	9,006	8,944	8,958	8,938	8,899
Inpatient					
Beds	2.4	2.4	2.3	2.3	2.4
Admissions	119.6	112.6	109.5	109.1	113.4
Inpatient Days	564.7	554.8	566.6	566.8	585.5
Inpatient Surgeries	24.5	25.7	26.3	25.9	26.7
Births	10.8	10.9	11.1	11.1	11.2
Outpatient					
Emergency Outpatient Visits	420.4	419.4	395.6	404.3	402.8
Other Outpatient Visits	1,292.7	1,218.3	1,417.8	1,333.6	1,354.6
Total Outpatient Visits	1,713.1	1,637.7	1,813.4	1,737.9	1,757.4
Outpatient Surgeries	39.1	40.0	41.4	40.2	40.9
Expense per Capita (per person)	$2,625.2	$2,560.3	$2,445.1	$2,326.1	$2,277.1

States

TABLE 6

NEW MEXICO

U.S. Community Hospitals
(Nonfederal, short-term general and other special hospitals)

Overview 2013–2017

	2017	2016	2015	2014	2013
Total Community Hospitals in New Mexico	41	41	41	42	42
Bed Size Category					
6-24..........................	7	6	7	7	7
25-49..........................	14	14	12	12	12
50-99..........................	10	10	12	13	11
100-199..........................	6	7	5	5	6
200-299..........................	2	2	3	3	4
300-399..........................	0	0	0	0	0
400-499..........................	0	0	0	1	1
500 +..........................	2	2	2	1	1
Location					
Hospitals Urban	16	16	16	17	17
Hospitals Rural................................	25	25	25	25	25
Control					
State and Local Government	8	8	8	8	8
Not for Profit	15	15	15	16	16
Investor owned	18	18	18	18	18
Physician Models					
Independent Practice Association......................	2	3	3	4	4
Group Practice without Walls	0	0	0	0	0
Open Physician-Hospital Organization	5	5	5	4	2
Closed Physician-Hospital Organization.............	0	0	0	0	0
Management Service Organization	0	0	1	1	1
Integrated Salary Model........................	9	9	10	12	16
Equity Model	0	0	0	0	0
Foundation	0	0	0	0	0
Affiliations					
Hospitals in a System	31	30	28	30	32
Hospitals in a Network........................	10	10	13	13	13
Hospitals in a Group Purchasing Organization...	17	19	22	25	26

TABLE 6

NEW MEXICO

U.S. Community Hospitals
(Nonfederal, short-term general and other special hospitals)

Utilization, Personnel, Revenue and Expenses, Community Health Indicators 2013–2017

	2017	2016	2015	2014	2013
TOTAL FACILITY (Includes Hospital and Nursing Home Units)					
Utilization - Inpatient					
Beds	3,876	3,966	4,106	3,939	3,988
Admissions	179,750	183,887	182,030	179,236	173,917
Inpatient Days	903,657	884,294	887,182	845,290	806,155
Average Length of Stay	5.0	4.8	4.9	4.7	4.6
Inpatient Surgeries	47,063	46,533	45,804	41,220	44,627
Births	18,730	20,200	22,899	23,004	23,847
Utilization - Outpatient					
Emergency Outpatient Visits	1,035,170	1,068,994	1,055,068	986,520	872,650
Other Outpatient Visits	5,333,029	5,756,551	5,126,614	4,826,847	3,753,369
Total Outpatient Visits	6,368,199	6,825,545	6,181,682	5,813,367	4,626,019
Outpatient Surgeries	125,413	111,577	107,261	85,346	96,409
Personnel					
Full Time RNs	6,926	7,265	7,241	6,627	6,596
Full Time LPNs	372	309	345	335	355
Part Time RNs	2,583	2,561	2,310	2,523	2,340
Part Time LPNs	133	122	111	118	122
Total Full Time	25,320	25,300	25,753	22,413	22,702
Total Part Time	7,530	7,591	7,106	7,093	7,121
Revenue - Inpatient					
Gross Inpatient Revenue	$9,443,175,880	$8,425,914,812	$8,197,233,564	$7,031,803,165	$6,449,851,854
Revenue - Outpatient					
Gross Outpatient Revenue	$11,548,841,298	$10,143,015,763	$9,099,714,998	$7,419,935,409	$6,807,923,602
Revenue and Expenses - Totals					
(Includes Inpatient and Outpatient)					
Total Gross Revenue	$20,992,017,178	$18,568,930,575	$17,296,948,562	$14,451,738,574	$13,257,775,456
Deductions from Revenue	14,828,970,155	12,673,373,255	12,016,779,875	10,081,225,168	9,018,465,253
Net Patient Revenue	6,163,047,023	5,895,557,320	5,280,168,687	4,370,513,406	4,239,310,203
Other Operating Revenue	275,482,731	261,439,767	272,553,422	260,931,128	233,278,767
Other Nonoperating Revenue	78,147,688	38,114,532	49,880,430	88,021,125	56,453,773
Total Net Revenue	6,516,677,442	6,195,111,619	5,602,602,539	4,719,465,659	4,529,042,743
Total Expenses	5,744,621,613	5,467,066,379	4,914,551,926	4,217,747,598	3,980,303,441
HOSPITAL UNIT (Excludes Separate Nursing Home Units)					
Utilization - Inpatient					
Beds	3,861	3,966	4,106	3,887	3,988
Admissions	179,611	183,887	182,030	179,213	173,917
Inpatient Days	901,360	884,294	887,182	835,720	806,155
Average Length of Stay	5.0	4.8	4.9	4.7	4.6
Personnel					
Total Full Time	25,301	25,300	25,753	22,386	22,514
Total Part Time	7,529	7,591	7,106	7,092	7,010
Revenue and Expenses - Totals					
(Includes Inpatient and Outpatient)					
Total Net Revenue	$6,505,219,925	$6,195,111,619	$5,602,602,539	$4,714,319,746	$4,529,042,743
Total Expenses	5,740,295,527	5,467,066,379	4,914,551,926	4,214,435,675	3,980,303,441
COMMUNITY HEALTH INDICATORS PER 1000 POPULATION					
Total Population (in thousands)	2,088	2,081	2,085	2,086	2,085
Inpatient					
Beds	1.9	1.9	2.0	1.9	1.9
Admissions	86.1	88.4	87.3	85.9	83.4
Inpatient Days	432.8	424.9	425.5	405.3	386.6
Inpatient Surgeries	22.5	22.4	22.0	19.8	21.4
Births	9.0	9.7	11.0	11.0	11.4
Outpatient					
Emergency Outpatient Visits	495.8	513.7	506.0	473.0	418.5
Other Outpatient Visits	2,554.0	2,766.2	2,458.7	2,314.4	1,799.9
Total Outpatient Visits	3,049.8	3,279.9	2,964.7	2,787.4	2,218.4
Outpatient Surgeries	60.1	53.6	51.4	40.9	46.2
Expense per Capita (per person)	$2,751.2	$2,627.1	$2,357.0	$2,022.3	$1,908.8

States

TABLE 6

NEW YORK

U.S. Community Hospitals
(Nonfederal, short-term general and other special hospitals)

Overview 2013–2017

	2017	2016	2015	2014	2013
Total Community Hospitals in New York	168	170	171	175	178
Bed Size Category					
6-24	9	8	8	7	7
25-49	11	11	11	9	8
50-99	16	17	17	19	17
100-199	45	42	40	40	40
200-299	29	36	38	36	40
300-399	15	12	13	18	20
400-499	14	14	12	13	12
500 + ...	29	30	32	33	34
Location					
Hospitals Urban	133	134	135	138	139
Hospitals Rural	35	36	36	37	39
Control					
State and Local Government	23	23	24	24	25
Not for Profit	145	147	147	151	153
Investor owned	0	0	0	0	0
Physician Models					
Independent Practice Association	53	46	47	42	39
Group Practice without Walls	6	4	7	7	6
Open Physician-Hospital Organization	14	14	14	12	12
Closed Physician-Hospital Organization	5	5	7	5	7
Management Service Organization	13	14	22	18	13
Integrated Salary Model	92	86	80	77	83
Equity Model	1	1	1	1	1
Foundation	2	1	2	4	5
Affiliations					
Hospitals in a System	105	105	97	96	95
Hospitals in a Network	97	91	90	81	78
Hospitals in a Group Purchasing Organization...	126	126	129	127	129

TABLE 6

NEW YORK

U.S. Community Hospitals
(Nonfederal, short-term general and other special hospitals)

Utilization, Personnel, Revenue and Expenses, Community Health Indicators 2013–2017

	2017	2016	2015	2014	2013
TOTAL FACILITY (Includes Hospital and Nursing Home Units)					
Utilization - Inpatient					
Beds	51,808	52,575	52,854	55,331	56,295
Admissions	2,272,583	2,275,661	2,215,822	2,278,580	2,333,362
Inpatient Days	14,972,556	15,243,808	15,084,390	15,679,619	15,941,867
Average Length of Stay	6.6	6.7	6.8	6.9	6.8
Inpatient Surgeries	580,655	586,743	569,541	595,238	599,984
Births	221,466	226,884	225,215	231,715	232,325
Utilization - Outpatient					
Emergency Outpatient Visits	8,632,643	9,056,617	8,631,910	8,610,050	8,637,188
Other Outpatient Visits	48,967,490	48,626,937	48,846,990	48,503,051	47,781,622
Total Outpatient Visits	57,600,133	57,683,554	57,478,900	57,113,101	56,418,810
Outpatient Surgeries	1,460,200	1,465,369	1,314,186	1,371,672	1,375,851
Personnel					
Full Time RNs	93,135	90,016	84,767	85,909	82,830
Full Time LPNs	5,021	4,602	4,859	5,010	5,144
Part Time RNs	24,994	25,457	23,789	23,491	23,315
Part Time LPNs	1,296	1,043	1,240	1,179	1,361
Total Full Time	378,431	365,018	348,489	349,448	358,706
Total Part Time	90,199	89,026	85,558	81,209	84,460
Revenue - Inpatient					
Gross Inpatient Revenue	$124,932,631,504	$116,374,216,764	$106,728,200,045	$102,330,754,611	$93,802,476,117
Revenue - Outpatient					
Gross Outpatient Revenue	$98,626,535,779	$90,435,926,427	$78,090,536,716	$73,815,219,199	$68,925,351,416
Revenue and Expenses - Totals					
(Includes Inpatient and Outpatient)					
Total Gross Revenue	$223,559,167,283	$206,810,143,191	$184,818,736,761	$176,145,973,810	$162,727,827,533
Deductions from Revenue	150,611,189,817	136,436,439,702	120,123,763,642	113,403,738,444	103,114,241,131
Net Patient Revenue	72,947,977,466	70,373,703,489	64,694,973,119	62,742,235,366	59,613,586,402
Other Operating Revenue	6,472,538,104	6,253,412,226	5,122,999,466	5,426,290,946	5,367,874,578
Other Nonoperating Revenue	1,867,219,220	1,239,270,779	506,419,429	964,440,761	1,789,769,287
Total Net Revenue	81,287,734,790	77,866,386,494	70,324,392,014	69,132,967,073	66,771,230,267
Total Expenses	78,606,242,354	75,137,848,371	68,887,871,710	67,416,478,834	64,954,987,698
HOSPITAL UNIT (Excludes Separate Nursing Home Units)					
Utilization - Inpatient					
Beds	47,306	48,027	47,650	49,759	50,209
Admissions	2,261,181	2,264,800	2,203,015	2,263,945	2,316,201
Inpatient Days	13,374,285	13,680,222	13,278,628	13,757,670	13,839,854
Average Length of Stay	5.9	6.0	6.0	6.1	6.0
Personnel					
Total Full Time	374,813	361,427	344,453	344,637	353,485
Total Part Time	88,197	87,075	83,320	79,056	81,988
Revenue and Expenses - Totals					
(Includes Inpatient and Outpatient)					
Total Net Revenue	$80,821,129,744	$77,339,027,537	$69,717,914,289	$68,445,919,920	$66,130,539,718
Total Expenses	78,156,794,479	74,714,804,194	68,311,960,203	66,758,957,946	64,314,974,603
COMMUNITY HEALTH INDICATORS PER 1000 POPULATION					
Total Population (in thousands)	19,849	19,745	19,796	19,746	19,651
Inpatient					
Beds	2.6	2.7	2.7	2.8	2.9
Admissions	114.5	115.3	111.9	115.4	118.7
Inpatient Days	754.3	772.0	762.0	794.1	811.2
Inpatient Surgeries	29.3	29.7	28.8	30.1	30.5
Births	11.2	11.5	11.4	11.7	11.8
Outpatient					
Emergency Outpatient Visits	434.9	458.7	436.0	436.0	439.5
Other Outpatient Visits	2,467.0	2,462.7	2,467.5	2,456.3	2,431.5
Total Outpatient Visits	2,901.9	2,921.4	2,903.6	2,892.4	2,871.0
Outpatient Surgeries	73.6	74.2	66.4	69.5	70.0
Expense per Capita (per person)	$3,960.1	$3,805.4	$3,479.9	$3,414.1	$3,305.4

States

TABLE 6

NORTH CAROLINA

U.S. Community Hospitals
(Nonfederal, short-term general and other special hospitals)

Overview 2013–2017

	2017	2016	2015	2014	2013
Total Community Hospitals in North Carolina	114	115	115	118	119
Bed Size Category					
6-24	7	6	6	8	6
25-49	24	24	24	24	25
50-99	23	27	26	25	24
100-199	32	29	30	30	30
200-299	11	10	10	11	12
300-399	2	4	4	5	7
400-499	3	3	3	3	2
500 +	12	12	12	12	13
Location					
Hospitals Urban	67	66	66	69	62
Hospitals Rural	47	49	49	49	57
Control					
State and Local Government	30	28	27	28	28
Not for Profit	69	67	68	69	73
Investor owned	15	20	20	21	18
Physician Models					
Independent Practice Association	5	5	9	8	8
Group Practice without Walls	3	5	4	3	3
Open Physician-Hospital Organization	4	7	8	7	9
Closed Physician-Hospital Organization	4	5	5	5	5
Management Service Organization	9	15	16	16	15
Integrated Salary Model	51	58	60	61	61
Equity Model	1	0	0	0	1
Foundation	2	2	2	1	1
Affiliations					
Hospitals in a System	101	101	104	102	101
Hospitals in a Network	44	50	49	47	45
Hospitals in a Group Purchasing Organization	76	91	95	97	97

TABLE 6

NORTH CAROLINA

U.S. Community Hospitals
(Nonfederal, short-term general and other special hospitals)

Utilization, Personnel, Revenue and Expenses, Community Health Indicators 2013–2017

	2017	2016	2015	2014	2013
TOTAL FACILITY (Includes Hospital and Nursing Home Units)					
Utilization - Inpatient					
Beds	21,841	21,878	21,632	22,118	22,701
Admissions	1,018,888	1,009,284	1,007,043	997,832	1,013,279
Inpatient Days	5,545,924	5,485,726	5,467,511	5,519,572	5,736,834
Average Length of Stay	5.4	5.4	5.4	5.5	5.7
Inpatient Surgeries	294,024	281,805	281,589	278,907	279,715
Births	113,203	115,681	116,273	114,799	112,844
Utilization - Outpatient					
Emergency Outpatient Visits	4,960,946	4,952,316	4,817,883	4,661,360	4,689,431
Other Outpatient Visits	18,613,003	15,815,321	15,082,446	15,015,881	15,093,918
Total Outpatient Visits	23,573,949	20,767,637	19,900,329	19,677,241	19,783,349
Outpatient Surgeries	586,833	595,644	569,849	556,720	563,004
Personnel					
Full Time RNs	41,514	41,297	40,565	40,394	40,456
Full Time LPNs	1,588	1,382	1,371	1,384	1,579
Part Time RNs	13,413	13,171	14,362	13,925	13,227
Part Time LPNs	372	313	329	329	393
Total Full Time	142,583	138,790	140,686	139,345	139,167
Total Part Time	36,444	36,178	37,615	37,718	36,384
Revenue - Inpatient					
Gross Inpatient Revenue	$43,354,278,672	$40,033,087,884	$38,149,057,513	$35,869,119,478	$34,543,529,229
Revenue - Outpatient					
Gross Outpatient Revenue	$51,441,079,747	$47,263,405,140	$42,434,511,142	$38,173,062,370	$34,530,648,765
Revenue and Expenses - Totals					
(Includes Inpatient and Outpatient)					
Total Gross Revenue	$94,795,358,419	$87,296,493,024	$80,583,568,655	$74,042,181,848	$69,074,177,994
Deductions from Revenue	65,614,306,443	59,671,446,299	54,619,685,081	50,300,258,882	45,991,119,274
Net Patient Revenue	29,181,051,976	27,625,046,725	25,963,883,574	23,741,922,966	23,083,058,720
Other Operating Revenue	1,055,549,303	909,206,892	875,711,323	845,972,436	859,859,557
Other Nonoperating Revenue	568,086,844	489,754,286	70,175,039	493,237,081	551,721,706
Total Net Revenue	30,804,688,123	29,024,007,903	26,909,769,936	25,081,132,483	24,494,639,983
Total Expenses	27,043,562,604	25,578,336,019	24,472,546,863	23,275,581,624	22,596,531,907
HOSPITAL UNIT (Excludes Separate Nursing Home Units)					
Utilization - Inpatient					
Beds	20,877	20,592	20,570	20,675	21,176
Admissions	1,013,765	1,003,299	1,001,513	991,680	1,006,940
Inpatient Days	5,243,844	5,093,710	5,132,545	5,066,538	5,250,516
Average Length of Stay	5.2	5.1	5.1	5.1	5.2
Personnel					
Total Full Time	142,003	138,040	139,894	138,435	138,139
Total Part Time	36,235	35,830	37,225	37,303	35,896
Revenue and Expenses - Totals					
(Includes Inpatient and Outpatient)					
Total Net Revenue	$30,728,667,407	$28,939,245,077	$26,830,202,110	$24,978,832,069	$24,387,254,322
Total Expenses	26,975,139,476	25,495,396,508	24,405,142,483	23,178,130,160	22,489,874,259
COMMUNITY HEALTH INDICATORS PER 1000 POPULATION					
Total Population (in thousands)	10,273	10,147	10,043	9,944	9,848
Inpatient					
Beds	2.1	2.2	2.2	2.2	2.3
Admissions	99.2	99.5	100.3	100.3	102.9
Inpatient Days	539.8	540.6	544.4	555.1	582.5
Inpatient Surgeries	28.6	27.8	28.0	28.0	28.4
Births	11.0	11.4	11.6	11.5	11.5
Outpatient					
Emergency Outpatient Visits	482.9	488.1	479.7	468.8	476.2
Other Outpatient Visits	1,811.8	1,558.7	1,501.8	1,510.0	1,532.7
Total Outpatient Visits	2,294.7	2,046.7	1,981.6	1,978.8	2,008.9
Outpatient Surgeries	57.1	58.7	56.7	56.0	57.2
Expense per Capita (per person)	$2,632.4	$2,520.8	$2,436.8	$2,340.7	$2,294.5

TABLE 6

NORTH DAKOTA

U.S. Community Hospitals
(Nonfederal, short-term general and other special hospitals)

Overview 2013–2017

	2017	2016	2015	2014	2013
Total Community Hospitals in North Dakota	40	40	40	40	40
Bed Size Category					
6-24	12	12	14	16	15
25-49	10	10	10	9	10
50-99	11	11	9	8	9
100-199	2	2	2	2	1
200-299	2	2	3	3	3
300-399	1	1	0	0	0
400-499	1	1	1	1	2
500 +	1	1	1	1	0
Location					
Hospitals Urban	8	8	8	8	8
Hospitals Rural	32	32	32	32	32
Control					
State and Local Government	0	0	0	0	0
Not for Profit	38	38	38	38	38
Investor owned	2	2	2	2	2
Physician Models					
Independent Practice Association	1	0	1	1	2
Group Practice without Walls	0	1	0	0	0
Open Physician-Hospital Organization	1	1	2	2	1
Closed Physician-Hospital Organization	0	0	0	0	0
Management Service Organization	1	0	0	0	0
Integrated Salary Model	9	11	10	11	10
Equity Model	0	0	0	0	0
Foundation	1	2	2	1	1
Affiliations					
Hospitals in a System	19	19	19	19	19
Hospitals in a Network	7	8	8	9	9
Hospitals in a Group Purchasing Organization	18	19	17	21	19

TABLE 6

NORTH DAKOTA

U.S. Community Hospitals
(Nonfederal, short-term general and other special hospitals)

Utilization, Personnel, Revenue and Expenses, Community Health Indicators 2013–2017

	2017	2016	2015	2014	2013
TOTAL FACILITY (Includes Hospital and Nursing Home Units)					
Utilization - Inpatient					
Beds	3,210	3,260	3,183	3,144	2,924
Admissions	88,600	90,877	92,352	92,692	94,743
Inpatient Days	683,497	701,386	666,539	644,992	658,748
Average Length of Stay	7.7	7.7	7.2	7.0	7.0
Inpatient Surgeries	25,922	25,612	26,043	27,107	27,930
Births	13,254	13,137	13,109	12,561	11,061
Utilization - Outpatient					
Emergency Outpatient Visits	408,172	371,089	385,322	360,374	328,299
Other Outpatient Visits	1,866,620	2,273,123	2,267,225	2,159,913	2,007,191
Total Outpatient Visits	2,274,792	2,644,212	2,652,547	2,520,287	2,335,490
Outpatient Surgeries	74,643	78,048	76,448	76,723	73,072
Personnel					
Full Time RNs	4,603	4,100	3,715	3,320	3,701
Full Time LPNs	629	795	540	558	509
Part Time RNs	2,889	2,634	2,736	2,562	2,579
Part Time LPNs	367	444	456	462	413
Total Full Time	17,219	15,967	14,792	15,290	16,391
Total Part Time	9,446	8,946	8,934	8,980	8,850
Revenue - Inpatient					
Gross Inpatient Revenue	$3,782,933,634	$3,533,156,153	$2,756,294,460	$2,706,066,510	$2,807,963,590
Revenue - Outpatient					
Gross Outpatient Revenue	$5,655,386,851	$5,218,580,430	$4,961,154,801	$4,252,502,194	$3,905,959,216
Revenue and Expenses - Totals					
(Includes Inpatient and Outpatient)					
Total Gross Revenue	$9,438,320,485	$8,751,736,583	$7,717,449,261	$6,958,568,704	$6,713,922,806
Deductions from Revenue	5,747,888,702	5,001,324,621	4,281,622,247	3,822,990,720	3,821,510,799
Net Patient Revenue	3,690,431,783	3,750,411,962	3,435,827,014	3,135,577,984	2,892,412,007
Other Operating Revenue	188,898,228	184,634,957	195,835,576	231,190,503	161,549,912
Other Nonoperating Revenue	39,963,723	22,168,901	16,523,124	26,912,185	28,978,906
Total Net Revenue	3,919,293,734	3,957,215,820	3,648,185,714	3,393,680,672	3,082,940,825
Total Expenses	3,747,438,919	3,764,650,593	3,394,209,261	3,186,530,035	2,966,838,008
HOSPITAL UNIT (Excludes Separate Nursing Home Units)					
Utilization - Inpatient					
Beds	2,696	2,755	2,682	2,674	2,422
Admissions	87,732	90,062	91,487	91,882	93,845
Inpatient Days	512,269	531,621	504,193	494,750	495,592
Average Length of Stay	5.8	5.9	5.5	5.4	5.3
Personnel					
Total Full Time	16,762	15,722	14,550	14,779	16,134
Total Part Time	9,235	8,821	8,729	8,693	8,700
Revenue and Expenses - Totals					
(Includes Inpatient and Outpatient)					
Total Net Revenue	$3,869,365,865	$3,904,906,417	$3,595,128,392	$3,355,550,091	$3,051,733,992
Total Expenses	3,700,930,403	3,726,681,439	3,355,476,243	3,147,793,319	2,925,639,027
COMMUNITY HEALTH INDICATORS PER 1000 POPULATION					
Total Population (in thousands)	755	758	757	739	723
Inpatient					
Beds	4.2	4.3	4.2	4.3	4.0
Admissions	117.3	119.9	122.0	125.3	131.0
Inpatient Days	904.8	925.4	880.6	872.2	910.6
Inpatient Surgeries	34.3	33.8	34.4	36.7	38.6
Births	17.5	17.3	17.3	17.0	15.3
Outpatient					
Emergency Outpatient Visits	540.3	489.6	509.1	487.3	453.8
Other Outpatient Visits	2,471.1	2,999.0	2,995.3	2,920.8	2,774.7
Total Outpatient Visits	3,011.4	3,488.6	3,504.4	3,408.2	3,228.5
Outpatient Surgeries	98.8	103.0	101.0	103.8	101.0
Expense per Capita (per person)	$4,960.9	$4,966.9	$4,484.2	$4,309.1	$4,101.3

TABLE 6

OHIO

U.S. Community Hospitals
(Nonfederal, short-term general and other special hospitals)

Overview 2013–2017

	2017	2016	2015	2014	2013
Total Community Hospitals in Ohio	198	196	194	193	195
Bed Size Category					
6-24	14	12	12	11	8
25-49	53	54	51	51	55
50-99	30	29	29	26	30
100-199	39	40	44	45	44
200-299	30	30	25	28	26
300-399	12	11	12	10	8
400-499	6	6	6	9	11
500 +	14	14	15	13	13
Location					
Hospitals Urban	139	137	135	134	138
Hospitals Rural	59	59	59	59	57
Control					
State and Local Government	16	16	17	18	18
Not for Profit	142	143	141	141	142
Investor owned	40	37	36	34	35
Physician Models					
Independent Practice Association	20	18	18	21	18
Group Practice without Walls	14	17	12	18	18
Open Physician-Hospital Organization	48	48	51	43	47
Closed Physician-Hospital Organization	19	26	22	25	21
Management Service Organization	30	35	34	30	32
Integrated Salary Model	73	80	74	84	80
Equity Model	13	14	14	17	18
Foundation	18	24	21	25	30
Affiliations					
Hospitals in a System	137	136	132	128	125
Hospitals in a Network	80	83	80	73	76
Hospitals in a Group Purchasing Organization	128	127	130	128	131

TABLE 6

OHIO

U.S. Community Hospitals
(Nonfederal, short-term general and other special hospitals)

Utilization, Personnel, Revenue and Expenses, Community Health Indicators 2013–2017

	2017	2016	2015	2014	2013
TOTAL FACILITY (Includes Hospital and Nursing Home Units)					
Utilization - Inpatient					
Beds	33,621	33,876	33,954	33,849	33,522
Admissions	1,452,329	1,439,585	1,430,892	1,440,437	1,462,845
Inpatient Days	7,266,478	7,248,654	7,240,349	7,212,805	7,175,483
Average Length of Stay	5.0	5.0	5.1	5.0	4.9
Inpatient Surgeries	377,028	366,543	368,376	372,601	373,688
Births	128,419	129,375	129,950	130,969	130,639
Utilization - Outpatient					
Emergency Outpatient Visits	7,152,080	7,040,720	6,884,267	6,684,281	6,549,584
Other Outpatient Visits	37,061,651	34,565,927	33,209,434	32,463,555	30,997,230
Total Outpatient Visits	44,213,731	41,606,647	40,093,701	39,147,836	37,546,814
Outpatient Surgeries	958,009	911,579	887,852	851,819	830,386
Personnel					
Full Time RNs	61,993	61,290	60,411	56,526	54,988
Full Time LPNs	2,781	2,721	2,631	2,629	2,842
Part Time RNs	26,666	27,646	25,262	26,166	25,287
Part Time LPNs	1,225	1,278	1,409	1,341	1,447
Total Full Time	222,143	218,967	212,919	208,006	207,414
Total Part Time	79,065	83,407	78,358	77,353	73,824
Revenue - Inpatient					
Gross Inpatient Revenue	$72,689,711,162	$68,662,538,596	$65,574,002,406	$61,591,934,939	$58,694,210,746
Revenue - Outpatient					
Gross Outpatient Revenue	$81,246,806,136	$74,452,340,262	$69,352,958,894	$64,254,687,118	$58,570,947,201
Revenue and Expenses - Totals					
(Includes Inpatient and Outpatient)					
Total Gross Revenue	$153,936,517,298	$143,114,878,858	$134,926,961,300	$125,846,622,057	$117,265,157,947
Deductions from Revenue	109,458,420,234	100,414,765,582	93,603,143,993	86,709,633,758	80,140,840,752
Net Patient Revenue	44,478,097,064	42,700,113,276	41,323,817,307	39,136,988,299	37,124,317,195
Other Operating Revenue	3,538,489,750	3,181,814,697	3,083,802,721	3,112,885,965	2,935,130,917
Other Nonoperating Revenue	1,540,654,457	571,420,327	-128,364,418	685,194,556	1,253,032,526
Total Net Revenue	49,557,241,271	46,453,348,300	44,279,255,610	42,935,068,820	41,312,480,638
Total Expenses	44,155,244,109	42,637,034,035	40,491,640,251	38,561,690,970	37,265,233,810
HOSPITAL UNIT (Excludes Separate Nursing Home Units)					
Utilization - Inpatient					
Beds	33,079	33,238	33,303	33,179	32,870
Admissions	1,445,941	1,432,175	1,423,344	1,432,059	1,454,129
Inpatient Days	7,079,649	7,037,483	7,026,457	6,992,591	6,958,305
Average Length of Stay	4.9	4.9	4.9	4.9	4.8
Personnel					
Total Full Time	221,672	218,436	212,481	207,531	206,937
Total Part Time	78,825	83,025	78,077	77,038	73,481
Revenue and Expenses - Totals					
(Includes Inpatient and Outpatient)					
Total Net Revenue	$49,491,045,840	$46,380,721,370	$44,217,058,327	$42,874,988,355	$41,245,285,601
Total Expenses	44,100,481,881	42,577,842,814	40,434,174,525	38,506,704,351	37,202,156,741
COMMUNITY HEALTH INDICATORS PER 1000 POPULATION					
Total Population (in thousands)	11,659	11,614	11,613	11,594	11,571
Inpatient					
Beds	2.9	2.9	2.9	2.9	2.9
Admissions	124.6	123.9	123.2	124.2	126.4
Inpatient Days	623.3	624.1	623.4	622.1	620.1
Inpatient Surgeries	32.3	31.6	31.7	32.1	32.3
Births	11.0	11.1	11.2	11.3	11.3
Outpatient					
Emergency Outpatient Visits	613.5	606.2	592.8	576.5	566
Other Outpatient Visits	3,178.9	2,976.1	2,859.6	2,800.0	2,678.9
Total Outpatient Visits	3,792.4	3,582.3	3,452.4	3,376.5	3,245.0
Outpatient Surgeries	82.2	78.5	76.5	73.5	71.8
Expense per Capita (per person)	$3,787.4	$3,671.1	$3,486.6	$3,326.0	$3,220.6

States

TABLE 6

OKLAHOMA

U.S. Community Hospitals
(Nonfederal, short-term general and other special hospitals)

Overview 2013–2017

	2017	2016	2015	2014	2013
Total Community Hospitals in Oklahoma	129	128	128	133	135
Bed Size Category					
6-24	36	34	34	31	29
25-49	44	47	47	50	55
50-99	23	22	22	27	25
100-199	14	13	12	11	12
200-299	3	2	3	4	4
300-399	3	4	4	4	4
400-499	0	0	0	0	0
500 + ...	6	6	6	6	6
Location					
Hospitals Urban	65	65	65	63	65
Hospitals Rural	64	63	63	70	70
Control					
State and Local Government	39	39	40	40	40
Not for Profit	41	37	36	39	40
Investor owned	49	52	52	54	55
Physician Models					
Independent Practice Association	10	15	13	15	15
Group Practice without Walls	5	6	6	8	6
Open Physician-Hospital Organization	8	7	9	10	11
Closed Physician-Hospital Organization	5	4	5	5	3
Management Service Organization	10	9	11	9	9
Integrated Salary Model	54	53	59	57	56
Equity Model	4	4	2	3	4
Foundation	4	4	3	1	2
Affiliations					
Hospitals in a System	70	72	68	69	69
Hospitals in a Network	45	41	41	41	39
Hospitals in a Group Purchasing Organization...	87	89	90	98	104

TABLE 6

OKLAHOMA

U.S. Community Hospitals
(Nonfederal, short-term general and other special hospitals)

Utilization, Personnel, Revenue and Expenses, Community Health Indicators 2013–2017

	2017	2016	2015	2014	2013
TOTAL FACILITY (Includes Hospital and Nursing Home Units)					
Utilization - Inpatient					
Beds	11,475	11,733	11,681	11,851	11,937
Admissions	420,377	423,192	417,874	419,674	439,551
Inpatient Days	2,278,209	2,322,517	2,274,841	2,295,401	2,345,604
Average Length of Stay	5.4	5.5	5.4	5.5	5.3
Inpatient Surgeries	111,298	114,257	110,626	111,607	114,878
Births	48,385	52,663	48,485	51,509	52,910
Utilization - Outpatient					
Emergency Outpatient Visits	1,915,881	1,872,023	1,918,470	1,905,800	1,919,232
Other Outpatient Visits	5,931,786	5,400,094	4,877,209	5,125,640	5,396,542
Total Outpatient Visits	7,847,667	7,272,117	6,795,679	7,031,440	7,315,774
Outpatient Surgeries	298,062	308,705	286,478	283,644	272,548
Personnel					
Full Time RNs	14,367	14,320	13,911	13,991	13,989
Full Time LPNs	1,418	1,520	1,571	1,621	1,761
Part Time RNs	4,772	4,537	4,406	4,751	3,916
Part Time LPNs	344	395	378	374	411
Total Full Time	48,031	48,944	48,288	48,936	50,092
Total Part Time	14,185	13,754	13,670	13,767	12,345
Revenue - Inpatient					
Gross Inpatient Revenue	$20,802,461,884	$20,644,933,881	$18,297,261,931	$16,495,302,167	$15,591,272,658
Revenue - Outpatient					
Gross Outpatient Revenue	$21,114,422,128	$19,789,096,790	$17,705,595,827	$15,942,357,277	$14,436,629,683
Revenue and Expenses - Totals					
(Includes Inpatient and Outpatient)					
Total Gross Revenue	$41,916,884,012	$40,434,030,671	$36,002,857,758	$32,437,659,444	$30,027,902,341
Deductions from Revenue	31,692,210,283	30,536,433,222	26,410,602,517	23,356,331,727	21,391,617,860
Net Patient Revenue	10,224,673,729	9,897,597,449	9,592,255,241	9,081,327,717	8,636,284,481
Other Operating Revenue	343,746,238	313,647,471	308,129,033	340,467,251	307,089,738
Other Nonoperating Revenue	221,877,932	38,443,530	83,638,733	200,499,798	246,282,521
Total Net Revenue	10,790,297,899	10,249,688,450	9,984,023,007	9,622,294,766	9,189,656,740
Total Expenses	9,667,546,273	9,370,788,599	9,066,246,642	8,620,820,854	8,381,615,310
HOSPITAL UNIT (Excludes Separate Nursing Home Units)					
Utilization - Inpatient					
Beds	11,254	11,442	11,468	11,608	11,667
Admissions	419,826	422,324	417,402	419,325	438,729
Inpatient Days	2,209,530	2,231,521	2,212,654	2,222,942	2,267,449
Average Length of Stay	5.3	5.3	5.3	5.3	5.2
Personnel					
Total Full Time	47,882	48,692	48,059	48,707	49,806
Total Part Time	14,163	13,710	13,612	13,689	12,281
Revenue and Expenses - Totals					
(Includes Inpatient and Outpatient)					
Total Net Revenue	$10,778,365,699	$10,234,060,884	$9,973,680,613	$9,611,613,887	$9,177,377,353
Total Expenses	9,653,400,032	9,354,497,305	9,057,450,178	8,612,711,892	8,370,382,175
COMMUNITY HEALTH INDICATORS PER 1000 POPULATION					
Total Population (in thousands)	3,931	3,924	3,911	3,878	3,851
Inpatient					
Beds	2.9	3.0	3.0	3.1	3.1
Admissions	106.9	107.9	106.8	108.2	114.2
Inpatient Days	579.6	591.9	581.6	591.9	609.2
Inpatient Surgeries	28.3	29.1	28.3	28.8	29.8
Births	12.3	13.4	12.4	13.3	13.7
Outpatient					
Emergency Outpatient Visits	487.4	477.1	490.5	491.4	498.4
Other Outpatient Visits	1,509.0	1,376.3	1,246.9	1,321.7	1,401.5
Total Outpatient Visits	1,996.4	1,853.4	1,737.4	1,813.1	1,899.9
Outpatient Surgeries	75.8	78.7	73.2	73.1	70.8
Expense per Capita (per person)	$2,459.4	$2,388.3	$2,317.9	$2,223.0	$2,176.7

States

TABLE 6

OREGON

U.S. Community Hospitals
(Nonfederal, short-term general and other special hospitals)

Overview 2013–2017

	2017	2016	2015	2014	2013
Total Community Hospitals in Oregon	61	61	61	61	61
Bed Size Category					
6-24	12	13	12	9	9
25-49	20	20	21	23	20
50-99	6	5	5	6	9
100-199	13	12	12	12	12
200-299	2	3	3	4	4
300-399	3	3	3	2	2
400-499	3	4	3	3	3
500 + ...	2	1	2	2	2
Location					
Hospitals Urban	35	35	35	35	32
Hospitals Rural	26	26	26	26	29
Control					
State and Local Government	11	11	11	12	12
Not for Profit	47	47	47	46	46
Investor owned	3	3	3	3	3
Physician Models					
Independent Practice Association	8	9	9	9	9
Group Practice without Walls	3	3	5	6	7
Open Physician-Hospital Organization	3	3	3	2	2
Closed Physician-Hospital Organization	1	2	4	3	6
Management Service Organization	10	11	12	11	10
Integrated Salary Model	55	54	56	55	56
Equity Model	0	0	0	0	0
Foundation	1	1	2	2	1
Affiliations					
Hospitals in a System	44	44	43	43	43
Hospitals in a Network	28	30	30	31	30
Hospitals in a Group Purchasing Organization...	59	59	59	59	59

TABLE 6

OREGON

U.S. Community Hospitals
(Nonfederal, short-term general and other special hospitals)

Utilization, Personnel, Revenue and Expenses, Community Health Indicators 2013–2017

	2017	2016	2015	2014	2013
TOTAL FACILITY (Includes Hospital and Nursing Home Units)					
Utilization - Inpatient					
Beds	6,906	6,863	6,950	6,930	6,968
Admissions	348,059	346,517	352,347	339,573	341,056
Inpatient Days	1,572,311	1,543,944	1,541,696	1,475,935	1,474,572
Average Length of Stay	4.5	4.5	4.4	4.3	4.3
Inpatient Surgeries	124,481	125,700	123,098	123,528	125,270
Births	43,286	44,145	44,304	44,108	42,898
Utilization - Outpatient					
Emergency Outpatient Visits	1,584,195	1,597,435	1,569,323	1,465,627	1,407,732
Other Outpatient Visits	10,447,396	9,899,003	9,324,868	9,374,958	8,989,956
Total Outpatient Visits	12,031,591	11,496,438	10,894,191	10,840,585	10,397,688
Outpatient Surgeries	210,270	209,719	202,767	193,810	193,652
Personnel					
Full Time RNs	13,350	12,904	12,229	11,456	11,242
Full Time LPNs	156	154	155	160	171
Part Time RNs	8,219	7,921	7,274	7,738	7,322
Part Time LPNs	76	89	78	85	92
Total Full Time	45,821	45,134	43,567	42,098	40,632
Total Part Time	22,300	21,149	18,971	19,981	19,324
Revenue - Inpatient					
Gross Inpatient Revenue	$13,743,363,797	$12,943,793,855	$12,109,866,304	$11,274,393,559	$10,525,989,984
Revenue - Outpatient					
Gross Outpatient Revenue	$14,719,541,782	$13,597,783,846	$12,189,067,679	$10,874,007,584	$9,884,329,597
Revenue and Expenses - Totals					
(Includes Inpatient and Outpatient)					
Total Gross Revenue	$28,462,905,579	$26,541,577,701	$24,298,933,983	$22,148,401,143	$20,410,319,581
Deductions from Revenue	16,481,954,247	15,139,777,925	13,504,391,340	12,255,147,682	11,156,730,387
Net Patient Revenue	11,980,951,332	11,401,799,776	10,794,542,643	9,893,253,461	9,253,589,194
Other Operating Revenue	698,321,177	714,136,123	691,731,339	557,165,415	493,445,387
Other Nonoperating Revenue	266,061,673	102,198,075	253,652,658	147,920,814	118,881,562
Total Net Revenue	12,945,334,182	12,218,133,974	11,739,926,640	10,598,339,690	9,865,916,143
Total Expenses	12,089,476,807	11,595,877,741	10,848,340,732	10,128,420,502	9,479,206,311
HOSPITAL UNIT (Excludes Separate Nursing Home Units)					
Utilization - Inpatient					
Beds	6,866	6,834	6,899	6,849	6,800
Admissions	348,040	346,504	352,317	339,459	340,923
Inpatient Days	1,565,993	1,536,570	1,526,203	1,452,558	1,432,840
Average Length of Stay	4.5	4.4	4.3	4.3	4.2
Personnel					
Total Full Time	45,793	45,110	43,530	42,053	40,567
Total Part Time	22,295	21,137	18,937	19,941	19,270
Revenue and Expenses - Totals					
(Includes Inpatient and Outpatient)					
Total Net Revenue	$12,943,459,087	$12,216,694,195	$11,737,220,370	$10,592,505,785	$9,855,960,379
Total Expenses	12,087,627,674	11,593,720,376	10,845,467,436	10,123,355,238	9,479,638,775
COMMUNITY HEALTH INDICATORS PER 1000 POPULATION					
Total Population (in thousands)	4,143	4,093	4,029	3,970	3,930
Inpatient					
Beds	1.7	1.7	1.7	1.7	1.8
Admissions	84.0	84.7	87.5	85.5	86.8
Inpatient Days	379.5	377.2	382.7	371.7	375.2
Inpatient Surgeries	30.0	30.7	30.6	31.1	31.9
Births	10.4	10.8	11.0	11.1	10.9
Outpatient					
Emergency Outpatient Visits	382.4	390.2	389.5	369.2	358.2
Other Outpatient Visits	2,521.8	2,418.2	2,314.5	2,361.3	2,287.5
Total Outpatient Visits	2,904.2	2,808.5	2,704.0	2,730.5	2,645.7
Outpatient Surgeries	50.8	51.2	50.3	48.8	49.3
Expense per Capita (per person)	$2,918.2	$2,832.8	$2,692.6	$2,551.1	$2,414.3

TABLE 6

PENNSYLVANIA

U.S. Community Hospitals
(Nonfederal, short-term general and other special hospitals)

Overview 2013–2017

	2017	2016	2015	2014	2013
Total Community Hospitals in Pennsylvania	201	196	198	196	203
Bed Size Category					
6-24	9	8	8	9	10
25-49	32	29	30	27	30
50-99	44	40	41	38	38
100-199	52	51	49	48	50
200-299	28	31	30	33	34
300-399	15	15	20	18	18
400-499	5	6	5	9	8
500 + ...	16	16	15	14	15
Location					
Hospitals Urban	163	158	160	158	156
Hospitals Rural	38	38	38	38	47
Control					
State and Local Government	1	1	1	1	2
Not for Profit	150	141	141	144	146
Investor owned	50	54	56	51	55
Physician Models					
Independent Practice Association	10	13	10	11	12
Group Practice without Walls	2	4	4	5	6
Open Physician-Hospital Organization	23	23	20	22	24
Closed Physician-Hospital Organization	6	6	6	6	4
Management Service Organization	16	17	16	16	21
Integrated Salary Model	73	82	78	74	76
Equity Model	5	5	6	5	5
Foundation	1	2	2	3	4
Affiliations					
Hospitals in a System	147	145	142	133	134
Hospitals in a Network	66	73	67	63	61
Hospitals in a Group Purchasing Organization...	126	141	133	122	152

TABLE 6

PENNSYLVANIA

U.S. Community Hospitals
(Nonfederal, short-term general and other special hospitals)

Utilization, Personnel, Revenue and Expenses, Community Health Indicators 2013–2017

	2017	2016	2015	2014	2013
TOTAL FACILITY (Includes Hospital and Nursing Home Units)					
Utilization - Inpatient					
Beds	37,219	37,800	38,034	38,740	39,655
Admissions	1,603,240	1,598,135	1,604,511	1,612,771	1,668,221
Inpatient Days	8,689,512	8,707,719	8,785,249	8,845,783	9,284,674
Average Length of Stay	5.4	5.4	5.5	5.5	5.6
Inpatient Surgeries	458,880	474,190	473,605	478,610	498,118
Births	134,434	134,314	131,573	131,876	130,169
Utilization - Outpatient					
Emergency Outpatient Visits	6,597,020	6,462,953	6,625,185	6,360,015	6,367,984
Other Outpatient Visits	34,884,065	34,558,969	33,138,359	32,589,744	32,455,854
Total Outpatient Visits	41,481,085	41,021,922	39,763,544	38,949,759	38,823,838
Outpatient Surgeries	942,891	968,226	953,747	909,888	939,266
Personnel					
Full Time RNs	62,774	59,428	58,077	57,082	56,948
Full Time LPNs	2,383	2,308	2,231	2,311	2,684
Part Time RNs	23,941	24,488	25,106	25,498	25,651
Part Time LPNs	809	784	863	953	1,103
Total Full Time	222,047	212,963	210,880	210,359	211,074
Total Part Time	71,520	71,064	71,842	72,931	74,390
Revenue - Inpatient					
Gross Inpatient Revenue	$99,727,315,390	$95,009,646,700	$91,931,638,930	$84,905,004,621	$85,580,101,365
Revenue - Outpatient					
Gross Outpatient Revenue	$98,991,785,117	$91,157,281,697	$81,281,718,035	$72,285,919,520	$68,196,306,249
Revenue and Expenses - Totals					
(Includes Inpatient and Outpatient)					
Total Gross Revenue	$198,719,100,507	$186,166,928,397	$173,213,356,965	$157,190,924,141	$153,776,407,614
Deductions from Revenue	152,968,866,168	142,505,189,415	131,464,823,163	117,547,712,927	114,895,857,189
Net Patient Revenue	45,750,234,339	43,661,738,982	41,748,533,802	39,643,211,214	38,880,550,425
Other Operating Revenue	2,599,746,561	2,260,251,951	2,226,932,302	2,070,726,520	2,020,659,405
Other Nonoperating Revenue	706,603,450	92,157,377	326,675,248	868,652,323	592,819,205
Total Net Revenue	49,056,584,350	46,014,148,310	44,302,141,352	42,582,590,057	41,494,029,035
Total Expenses	45,337,062,291	43,022,290,997	41,324,767,253	39,542,535,867	38,890,993,790
HOSPITAL UNIT (Excludes Separate Nursing Home Units)					
Utilization - Inpatient					
Beds	36,046	36,490	36,932	37,507	37,710
Admissions	1,594,246	1,586,418	1,593,221	1,599,512	1,650,628
Inpatient Days	8,315,377	8,299,878	8,440,145	8,463,206	8,687,781
Average Length of Stay	5.2	5.2	5.3	5.3	5.3
Personnel					
Total Full Time	221,380	212,203	210,192	209,452	210,009
Total Part Time	71,187	70,645	71,465	72,419	73,730
Revenue and Expenses - Totals					
(Includes Inpatient and Outpatient)					
Total Net Revenue	$48,931,873,565	$45,884,398,791	$44,174,552,581	$42,447,981,346	$41,276,105,432
Total Expenses	45,236,014,269	42,929,473,078	41,190,933,142	39,430,436,462	38,706,882,519
COMMUNITY HEALTH INDICATORS PER 1000 POPULATION					
Total Population (in thousands)	12,806	12,784	12,803	12,787	12,774
Inpatient					
Beds	2.9	3.0	3.0	3.0	3.1
Admissions	125.2	125	125.3	126.1	130.6
Inpatient Days	678.6	681.1	686.2	691.8	726.9
Inpatient Surgeries	35.8	37.1	37.0	37.4	39.0
Births	10.5	10.5	10.3	10.3	10.2
Outpatient					
Emergency Outpatient Visits	515.2	505.5	517.5	497.4	498.5
Other Outpatient Visits	2,724.1	2,703.3	2,588.4	2,548.6	2,540.8
Total Outpatient Visits	3,239.3	3,208.8	3,105.9	3,046.0	3,039.3
Outpatient Surgeries	73.6	75.7	74.5	71.2	73.5
Expense per Capita (per person)	$3,540.4	$3,365.3	$3,227.9	$3,092.4	$3,044.6

States

TABLE 6

RHODE ISLAND

U.S. Community Hospitals
(Nonfederal, short-term general and other special hospitals)

Overview 2013–2017

	2017	2016	2015	2014	2013
Total Community Hospitals in Rhode Island	11	12	12	12	12
Bed Size Category					
6-24	0	0	0	0	0
25-49	1	1	0	1	1
50-99	3	3	3	2	2
100-199	3	4	5	5	5
200-299	2	2	2	2	2
300-399	1	1	1	1	1
400-499	0	0	0	0	0
500 + ...	1	1	1	1	1
Location					
Hospitals Urban	11	12	12	12	12
Hospitals Rural	0	0	0	0	0
Control					
State and Local Government	0	0	0	0	0
Not for Profit...	9	10	10	10	10
Investor owned	2	2	2	2	2
Physician Models					
Independent Practice Association.......................	5	5	5	5	5
Group Practice without Walls	0	0	0	1	1
Open Physician-Hospital Organization	0	0	4	5	5
Closed Physician-Hospital Organization............	0	0	0	0	0
Management Service Organization	3	4	2	2	3
Integrated Salary Model....................................	6	6	5	6	6
Equity Model	3	1	0	0	0
Foundation	4	4	2	2	2
Affiliations					
Hospitals in a System	10	11	11	11	11
Hospitals in a Network	5	5	4	4	5
Hospitals in a Group Purchasing Organization...	7	7	7	7	8

TABLE 6

RHODE ISLAND

U.S. Community Hospitals
(Nonfederal, short-term general and other special hospitals)

Utilization, Personnel, Revenue and Expenses, Community Health Indicators 2013–2017

	2017	2016	2015	2014	2013
TOTAL FACILITY (Includes Hospital and Nursing Home Units)					
Utilization - Inpatient					
Beds	2,156	2,307	2,339	2,287	2,290
Admissions	115,669	118,327	117,005	111,880	111,789
Inpatient Days	554,246	564,857	577,681	554,970	576,207
Average Length of Stay	4.8	4.8	4.9	5.0	5.2
Inpatient Surgeries	27,405	29,475	27,987	27,265	29,139
Births	10,853	11,283	11,349	11,363	11,352
Utilization - Outpatient					
Emergency Outpatient Visits	500,399	547,657	546,113	510,907	522,861
Other Outpatient Visits	1,589,171	1,835,025	1,776,845	1,528,406	1,537,747
Total Outpatient Visits	2,089,570	2,382,682	2,322,958	2,039,313	2,060,608
Outpatient Surgeries	62,985	65,860	64,721	66,310	66,445
Personnel					
Full Time RNs	2,907	2,906	2,911	2,774	2,371
Full Time LPNs	57	71	66	61	58
Part Time RNs	2,895	3,258	2,946	3,005	2,947
Part Time LPNs	37	52	51	51	60
Total Full Time	12,645	12,794	12,792	12,457	12,731
Total Part Time	8,533	9,440	8,628	8,580	8,539
Revenue - Inpatient					
Gross Inpatient Revenue	$4,297,561,050	$4,311,146,280	$4,289,888,054	$4,108,544,543	$4,046,192,501
Revenue - Outpatient					
Gross Outpatient Revenue	$5,527,295,528	$5,266,236,508	$4,864,838,086	$4,659,908,388	$4,417,636,992
Revenue and Expenses - Totals					
(Includes Inpatient and Outpatient)					
Total Gross Revenue	$9,824,856,578	$9,577,382,788	$9,154,726,140	$8,768,452,931	$8,463,829,493
Deductions from Revenue	6,587,087,008	6,287,937,110	5,991,680,759	5,769,020,611	5,589,986,970
Net Patient Revenue	3,237,769,570	3,289,445,678	3,163,045,381	2,999,432,320	2,873,842,523
Other Operating Revenue	299,961,004	271,331,562	268,801,154	251,337,196	256,461,048
Other Nonoperating Revenue	24,652,681	-16,102,465	-1,554,971	10,846,132	18,169,267
Total Net Revenue	3,562,383,255	3,544,674,775	3,430,291,564	3,261,615,648	3,148,472,838
Total Expenses	3,510,873,781	3,557,534,952	3,404,037,616	3,196,921,483	3,179,903,981
HOSPITAL UNIT (Excludes Separate Nursing Home Units)					
Utilization - Inpatient					
Beds	2,156	2,307	2,339	2,287	2,290
Admissions	115,669	118,327	117,005	111,880	111,789
Inpatient Days	554,246	564,857	577,681	554,970	576,207
Average Length of Stay	4.8	4.8	4.9	5.0	5.2
Personnel					
Total Full Time	12,645	12,794	12,792	12,457	12,731
Total Part Time	8,533	9,440	8,628	8,580	8,539
Revenue and Expenses - Totals					
(Includes Inpatient and Outpatient)					
Total Net Revenue	$3,562,383,255	$3,544,674,775	$3,430,291,564	$3,261,615,648	$3,148,472,838
Total Expenses	3,510,873,781	3,557,534,952	3,404,037,616	3,196,921,483	3,179,903,981
COMMUNITY HEALTH INDICATORS PER 1000 POPULATION					
Total Population (in thousands)	1,060	1,056	1,056	1,055	1,052
Inpatient					
Beds	2.0	2.2	2.2	2.2	2.2
Admissions	109.2	112.0	110.8	106.0	106.3
Inpatient Days	523.1	534.7	546.9	526.0	548.0
Inpatient Surgeries	25.9	27.9	26.5	25.8	27.7
Births	10.2	10.7	10.7	10.8	10.8
Outpatient					
Emergency Outpatient Visits	472.2	518.4	517.0	484.2	497.2
Other Outpatient Visits	1,499.7	1,737.0	1,682.1	1,448.5	1,462.4
Total Outpatient Visits	1,972.0	2,255.4	2,199.2	1,932.7	1,959.7
Outpatient Surgeries	59.4	62.3	61.3	62.8	63.2
Expense per Capita (per person)	$3,313.3	$3,367.5	$3,222.6	$3,029.8	$3,024.1

TABLE 6

SOUTH CAROLINA

U.S. Community Hospitals
(Nonfederal, short-term general and other special hospitals)

Overview 2013–2017

	2017	2016	2015	2014	2013
Total Community Hospitals in South Carolina ...	70	70	70	72	71
Bed Size Category					
6-24	2	1	2	5	2
25-49	16	17	17	17	17
50-99	17	17	16	15	14
100-199	12	13	13	13	14
200-299	10	8	9	8	9
300-399	4	4	3	4	5
400-499	5	5	6	6	5
500 + ...	4	5	4	4	5
Location					
Hospitals Urban	55	55	55	55	46
Hospitals Rural	15	15	15	17	25
Control					
State and Local Government	15	15	19	19	18
Not for Profit	31	30	28	28	29
Investor owned	24	25	23	25	24
Physician Models					
Independent Practice Association	3	8	8	6	6
Group Practice without Walls	0	0	0	0	1
Open Physician-Hospital Organization	4	3	3	3	3
Closed Physician-Hospital Organization	4	5	5	3	3
Management Service Organization	2	0	0	0	1
Integrated Salary Model	19	17	16	19	19
Equity Model	6	5	4	2	2
Foundation	4	6	5	1	0
Affiliations					
Hospitals in a System	58	58	58	55	52
Hospitals in a Network	24	24	22	20	13
Hospitals in a Group Purchasing Organization...	62	65	63	62	63

TABLE **6**

SOUTH CAROLINA

U.S. Community Hospitals
(Nonfederal, short-term general and other special hospitals)

Utilization, Personnel, Revenue and Expenses, Community Health Indicators 2013–2017

	2017	2016	2015	2014	2013
TOTAL FACILITY (Includes Hospital and Nursing Home Units)					
Utilization - Inpatient					
Beds	12,357	12,388	12,347	12,312	12,847
Admissions	525,641	525,029	523,730	499,931	499,697
Inpatient Days	2,822,503	2,820,750	2,829,685	2,805,236	2,885,898
Average Length of Stay	5.4	5.4	5.4	5.6	5.8
Inpatient Surgeries	169,712	179,421	183,355	177,731	194,834
Births	52,509	53,735	54,587	53,437	52,388
Utilization - Outpatient					
Emergency Outpatient Visits	2,471,755	2,543,747	2,470,621	2,217,906	1,575,728
Other Outpatient Visits	6,958,171	6,887,043	5,790,738	5,317,946	5,134,748
Total Outpatient Visits	9,429,926	9,430,790	8,261,359	7,535,852	6,710,476
Outpatient Surgeries	338,299	327,895	314,828	308,359	317,318
Personnel					
Full Time RNs	20,582	20,504	20,365	19,650	18,745
Full Time LPNs	684	725	593	656	722
Part Time RNs	5,960	5,878	5,190	4,906	4,641
Part Time LPNs	184	197	142	163	174
Total Full Time	65,350	66,130	64,131	61,698	60,509
Total Part Time	17,085	15,767	14,551	13,665	13,327
Revenue - Inpatient					
Gross Inpatient Revenue	$25,527,354,490	$24,390,196,272	$23,100,092,850	$22,024,960,289	$21,632,957,588
Revenue - Outpatient					
Gross Outpatient Revenue	$25,206,112,553	$24,185,225,044	$21,189,443,623	$18,535,766,559	$17,627,241,118
Revenue and Expenses - Totals					
(Includes Inpatient and Outpatient)					
Total Gross Revenue	$50,733,467,043	$48,575,421,316	$44,289,536,473	$40,560,726,848	$39,260,198,706
Deductions from Revenue	38,012,804,829	36,235,963,574	32,878,860,388	29,303,397,887	28,514,962,719
Net Patient Revenue	12,720,662,214	12,339,457,742	11,410,676,085	11,257,328,961	10,745,235,987
Other Operating Revenue	372,224,361	333,129,054	491,319,749	379,440,192	321,644,648
Other Nonoperating Revenue	297,293,199	225,878,085	122,029,853	249,320,467	293,480,599
Total Net Revenue	13,390,179,774	12,898,464,881	12,024,025,687	11,886,089,620	11,360,361,234
Total Expenses	12,103,968,251	11,514,797,706	10,634,789,126	10,325,602,432	10,056,055,292
HOSPITAL UNIT (Excludes Separate Nursing Home Units)					
Utilization - Inpatient					
Beds	11,907	11,968	11,935	11,773	12,104
Admissions	523,105	521,968	520,952	496,115	496,333
Inpatient Days	2,686,062	2,694,138	2,697,309	2,645,492	2,671,433
Average Length of Stay	5.1	5.2	5.2	5.3	5.4
Personnel					
Total Full Time	64,759	65,647	63,793	61,260	59,797
Total Part Time	16,807	15,603	14,419	13,520	13,133
Revenue and Expenses - Totals					
(Includes Inpatient and Outpatient)					
Total Net Revenue	$13,323,998,593	$12,831,443,432	$11,985,271,771	$11,785,475,201	$11,294,414,487
Total Expenses	12,043,658,997	11,458,089,086	10,591,085,495	10,240,938,190	9,996,996,651
COMMUNITY HEALTH INDICATORS PER 1000 POPULATION					
Total Population (in thousands)	5,024	4,961	4,896	4,832	4,775
Inpatient					
Beds	2.5	2.5	2.5	2.5	2.7
Admissions	104.6	105.8	107.0	103.5	104.7
Inpatient Days	561.8	568.6	577.9	580.5	604.4
Inpatient Surgeries	33.8	36.2	37.4	36.8	40.8
Births	10.5	10.8	11.1	11.1	11.0
Outpatient					
Emergency Outpatient Visits	492.0	512.7	504.6	459.0	330.0
Other Outpatient Visits	1,384.9	1,388.2	1,182.7	1,100.5	1,075.4
Total Outpatient Visits	1,876.8	1,900.9	1,687.3	1,559.4	1,405.4
Outpatient Surgeries	67.3	66.1	64.3	63.8	66.5
Expense per Capita (per person)	$2,409.1	$2,321.0	$2,172.1	$2,136.7	$2,106.1

States

TABLE 6

SOUTH DAKOTA

U.S. Community Hospitals
(Nonfederal, short-term general and other special hospitals)

Overview 2013–2017

	2017	2016	2015	2014	2013
Total Community Hospitals in South Dakota......	57	57	57	57	58
Bed Size Category					
6-24	21	21	22	22	23
25-49	12	12	11	11	12
50-99	13	13	13	13	11
100-199	6	6	6	6	7
200-299	2	2	2	2	2
300-399	1	1	1	1	0
400-499	1	1	2	1	2
500 + ...	1	1	0	1	1
Location					
Hospitals Urban	14	14	14	14	13
Hospitals Rural...	43	43	43	43	45
Control					
State and Local Government	4	4	4	4	4
Not for Profit..	45	45	45	45	46
Investor owned..	8	8	8	8	8
Physician Models					
Independent Practice Association...............	3	3	3	6	7
Group Practice without Walls	3	3	1	2	1
Open Physician-Hospital Organization	3	2	2	2	1
Closed Physician-Hospital Organization	1	2	1	2	1
Management Service Organization	1	1	1	1	0
Integrated Salary Model.............................	26	25	25	27	24
Equity Model	1	0	1	2	2
Foundation	1	1	2	2	2
Affiliations					
Hospitals in a System	39	39	39	39	39
Hospitals in a Network................................	24	22	22	22	23
Hospitals in a Group Purchasing Organization...	38	34	29	35	36

TABLE 6

SOUTH DAKOTA

U.S. Community Hospitals
(Nonfederal, short-term general and other special hospitals)

Utilization, Personnel, Revenue and Expenses, Community Health Indicators 2013–2017

	2017	2016	2015	2014	2013
TOTAL FACILITY (Includes Hospital and Nursing Home Units)					
Utilization - Inpatient					
Beds	4,167	4,144	4,071	4,155	4,230
Admissions	107,388	103,474	101,783	101,858	103,826
Inpatient Days	958,248	1,002,676	1,022,798	925,659	940,999
Average Length of Stay	8.9	9.7	10.0	9.1	9.1
Inpatient Surgeries	27,132	25,788	24,009	24,898	28,387
Births	12,932	12,329	11,981	12,880	12,782
Utilization - Outpatient					
Emergency Outpatient Visits	328,117	341,039	277,330	305,477	297,576
Other Outpatient Visits	2,455,901	2,550,160	2,163,742	3,051,779	1,993,740
Total Outpatient Visits	2,784,018	2,891,199	2,441,072	3,357,256	2,291,316
Outpatient Surgeries	68,651	63,072	60,719	54,581	53,909
Personnel					
Full Time RNs	5,292	4,551	4,861	4,624	4,867
Full Time LPNs	555	372	349	321	349
Part Time RNs	2,897	2,540	2,477	2,110	1,937
Part Time LPNs	251	194	179	144	132
Total Full Time	20,168	16,679	16,864	16,199	17,214
Total Part Time	10,211	8,330	8,416	6,884	7,223
Revenue - Inpatient					
Gross Inpatient Revenue	$4,765,408,996	$4,273,198,758	$4,261,464,169	$3,719,543,015	$3,514,062,072
Revenue - Outpatient					
Gross Outpatient Revenue	$6,241,390,538	$5,586,822,424	$5,270,698,882	$4,361,710,383	$3,456,406,889
Revenue and Expenses - Totals					
(Includes Inpatient and Outpatient)					
Total Gross Revenue	$11,006,799,534	$9,860,021,182	$9,532,163,051	$8,081,253,398	$6,970,468,961
Deductions from Revenue	7,174,650,556	6,247,499,170	6,131,349,357	4,997,855,426	4,205,051,552
Net Patient Revenue	3,832,148,978	3,612,522,012	3,400,813,694	3,083,397,972	2,765,417,409
Other Operating Revenue	243,923,099	218,443,474	194,371,409	190,037,257	178,069,253
Other Nonoperating Revenue	121,739,426	12,316,133	18,037,020	96,446,941	73,950,329
Total Net Revenue	4,197,811,503	3,843,281,619	3,613,222,123	3,369,882,170	3,017,436,991
Total Expenses	3,825,457,472	3,584,475,494	3,245,003,285	3,039,876,452	2,736,634,163
HOSPITAL UNIT (Excludes Separate Nursing Home Units)					
Utilization - Inpatient					
Beds	2,977	2,907	2,908	2,927	2,880
Admissions	106,276	102,286	100,721	100,819	102,564
Inpatient Days	555,026	571,514	615,438	529,540	494,486
Average Length of Stay	5.2	5.6	6.1	5.3	4.8
Personnel					
Total Full Time	19,460	15,994	16,292	15,458	16,326
Total Part Time	9,564	7,755	7,924	6,346	6,695
Revenue and Expenses - Totals					
(Includes Inpatient and Outpatient)					
Total Net Revenue	$4,111,355,271	$3,751,696,070	$3,526,485,663	$3,286,677,429	$2,934,026,969
Total Expenses	3,743,945,158	3,505,783,141	3,172,737,628	2,966,611,031	2,666,583,018
COMMUNITY HEALTH INDICATORS PER 1000 POPULATION					
Total Population (in thousands)	870	865	858	853	845
Inpatient					
Beds	4.8	4.8	4.7	4.9	5.0
Admissions	123.5	119.6	118.6	119.4	122.9
Inpatient Days	1,101.9	1,158.6	1,191.4	1,085.0	1,113.8
Inpatient Surgeries	31.2	29.8	28.0	29.2	33.6
Births	14.9	14.2	14.0	15.1	15.1
Outpatient					
Emergency Outpatient Visits	377.3	394.1	323.1	358.0	352.2
Other Outpatient Visits	2,824.0	2,946.6	2,520.5	3,577.0	2,359.8
Total Outpatient Visits	3,201.2	3,340.7	2,843.5	3,935.0	2,712.0
Outpatient Surgeries	78.9	72.9	70.7	64.0	63.8
Expense per Capita (per person)	$4,398.8	$4,141.7	$3,780.0	$3,563.0	$3,239.1

States

TABLE 6

TENNESSEE

U.S. Community Hospitals
(Nonfederal, short-term general and other special hospitals)

Overview 2013–2017

	2017	2016	2015	2014	2013
Total Community Hospitals in Tennessee..........	122	124	126	126	131
Bed Size Category					
6-24	7	7	7	8	9
25-49	28	30	33	31	33
50-99	35	34	30	31	33
100-199	22	24	25	25	24
200-299	10	12	13	12	13
300-399	5	5	6	8	8
400-499	5	4	3	1	2
500 + ...	10	8	9	10	9
Location					
Hospitals Urban	76	79	79	79	77
Hospitals Rural	46	45	47	47	54
Control					
State and Local Government	19	18	19	19	22
Not for Profit	51	51	51	51	50
Investor owned	52	55	56	56	59
Physician Models					
Independent Practice Association	14	12	13	15	14
Group Practice without Walls	3	3	6	5	4
Open Physician-Hospital Organization	14	17	18	17	17
Closed Physician-Hospital Organization	12	6	4	5	3
Management Service Organization	12	17	17	15	12
Integrated Salary Model	23	29	34	37	34
Equity Model	3	3	3	2	3
Foundation	7	8	8	4	6
Affiliations					
Hospitals in a System	100	103	102	103	108
Hospitals in a Network	35	30	30	35	37
Hospitals in a Group Purchasing Organization...	57	54	55	60	66

TABLE 6

TENNESSEE

U.S. Community Hospitals
(Nonfederal, short-term general and other special hospitals)

Utilization, Personnel, Revenue and Expenses, Community Health Indicators 2013–2017

	2017	2016	2015	2014	2013
TOTAL FACILITY (Includes Hospital and Nursing Home Units)					
Utilization - Inpatient					
Beds	20,274	19,583	20,071	20,067	20,295
Admissions	841,686	829,594	832,882	818,832	819,572
Inpatient Days	4,576,410	4,556,289	4,618,397	4,440,188	4,536,917
Average Length of Stay	5.4	5.5	5.5	5.4	5.5
Inpatient Surgeries	229,168	230,846	228,817	231,629	227,285
Births	63,459	66,712	68,624	67,013	66,249
Utilization - Outpatient					
Emergency Outpatient Visits	3,490,215	3,546,645	3,505,149	3,405,321	3,378,159
Other Outpatient Visits	10,174,421	9,623,620	8,831,676	8,508,182	8,534,100
Total Outpatient Visits	13,664,636	13,170,265	12,336,825	11,913,503	11,912,259
Outpatient Surgeries	435,611	450,381	425,950	433,180	430,284
Personnel					
Full Time RNs	30,276	28,567	26,817	27,118	26,577
Full Time LPNs	1,982	1,929	1,892	1,974	2,148
Part Time RNs	8,374	9,249	7,183	6,768	7,629
Part Time LPNs	423	554	443	451	519
Total Full Time	108,096	92,059	87,575	93,127	90,709
Total Part Time	22,779	26,423	19,214	18,655	20,291
Revenue - Inpatient					
Gross Inpatient Revenue	$40,894,418,158	$37,418,967,649	$36,068,050,775	$33,138,353,985	$31,810,446,680
Revenue - Outpatient					
Gross Outpatient Revenue	$41,053,722,777	$35,373,103,358	$33,036,573,449	$29,355,080,396	$26,900,010,848
Revenue and Expenses - Totals					
(Includes Inpatient and Outpatient)					
Total Gross Revenue	$81,948,140,935	$72,792,071,007	$69,104,624,224	$62,493,434,381	$58,710,457,528
Deductions from Revenue	62,427,271,778	54,956,390,305	51,829,063,773	46,428,365,325	43,056,343,060
Net Patient Revenue	19,520,869,157	17,835,680,702	17,275,560,451	16,065,069,056	15,654,114,468
Other Operating Revenue	1,124,098,322	604,488,582	602,849,667	573,073,357	631,777,808
Other Nonoperating Revenue	246,181,994	115,223,919	123,711,375	216,618,646	159,546,980
Total Net Revenue	20,891,149,473	18,555,393,203	18,002,121,493	16,854,761,059	16,445,439,256
Total Expenses	19,213,217,783	16,958,545,633	16,183,711,421	15,538,279,054	15,017,968,839
HOSPITAL UNIT (Excludes Separate Nursing Home Units)					
Utilization - Inpatient					
Beds	19,791	19,019	18,982	19,091	19,094
Admissions	838,272	826,109	827,162	813,986	812,364
Inpatient Days	4,427,196	4,399,271	4,314,598	4,153,325	4,182,662
Average Length of Stay	5.3	5.3	5.2	5.1	5.1
Personnel					
Total Full Time	107,687	91,565	86,870	92,308	89,848
Total Part Time	22,727	26,365	19,091	18,509	20,083
Revenue and Expenses - Totals					
(Includes Inpatient and Outpatient)					
Total Net Revenue	$20,847,274,328	$18,507,732,274	$17,921,881,928	$16,790,364,543	$16,354,576,217
Total Expenses	19,172,638,939	16,915,667,673	16,110,237,368	15,479,106,902	14,938,991,273
COMMUNITY HEALTH INDICATORS PER 1000 POPULATION					
Total Population (in thousands)	6,716	6,651	6,600	6,549	6,496
Inpatient					
Beds	3.0	2.9	3.0	3.1	3.1
Admissions	125.3	124.7	126.2	125.0	126.2
Inpatient Days	681.4	685	699.7	678.0	698.4
Inpatient Surgeries	34.1	34.7	34.7	35.4	35.0
Births	9.4	10.0	10.4	10.2	10.2
Outpatient					
Emergency Outpatient Visits	519.7	533.2	531.1	519.9	520.0
Other Outpatient Visits	1,515.0	1,446.9	1,338.1	1,299.1	1,313.8
Total Outpatient Visits	2,034.6	1,980.1	1,869.1	1,819.0	1,833.8
Outpatient Surgeries	64.9	67.7	64.5	66.1	66.2
Expense per Capita (per person)	$2,860.8	$2,549.7	$2,452.0	$2,372.5	$2,311.9

States

TABLE 6

TEXAS

U.S. Community Hospitals
(Nonfederal, short-term general and other special hospitals)

Overview 2013–2017

	2017	2016	2015	2014	2013
Total Community Hospitals in Texas	528	535	536	534	536
Bed Size Category					
6-24	125	122	116	116	117
25-49	139	146	144	149	144
50-99	94	106	110	108	114
100-199	68	60	67	64	60
200-299	39	39	37	35	41
300-399	26	24	21	22	22
400-499	11	12	14	15	13
500 + ...	26	26	27	25	25
Location					
Hospitals Urban	390	394	394	391	386
Hospitals Rural	138	141	142	143	150
Control					
State and Local Government	103	101	101	103	105
Not for Profit	153	154	156	159	160
Investor owned	272	280	279	272	271
Physician Models					
Independent Practice Association	67	63	60	63	62
Group Practice without Walls	18	18	17	38	22
Open Physician-Hospital Organization	64	70	66	71	77
Closed Physician-Hospital Organization	11	18	16	25	27
Management Service Organization	55	58	53	55	56
Integrated Salary Model	149	144	142	118	132
Equity Model	10	10	9	11	12
Foundation	38	34	34	36	41
Affiliations					
Hospitals in a System	342	343	334	342	340
Hospitals in a Network	129	130	124	132	131
Hospitals in a Group Purchasing Organization...	486	506	497	509	507

TABLE 6

TEXAS

U.S. Community Hospitals
(Nonfederal, short-term general and other special hospitals)

Utilization, Personnel, Revenue and Expenses, Community Health Indicators 2013–2017

	2017	2016	2015	2014	2013
TOTAL FACILITY (Includes Hospital and Nursing Home Units)					
Utilization - Inpatient					
Beds	66,844	67,699	68,524	65,919	66,048
Admissions	2,774,329	2,720,756	2,699,195	2,632,891	2,636,465
Inpatient Days	14,595,697	14,978,396	14,669,330	14,098,920	13,991,961
Average Length of Stay	5.3	5.5	5.4	5.4	5.3
Inpatient Surgeries	792,257	767,984	782,063	763,049	764,672
Births	381,131	393,856	403,574	399,043	383,873
Utilization - Outpatient					
Emergency Outpatient Visits	11,952,821	11,464,470	11,239,398	10,922,114	10,745,599
Other Outpatient Visits	33,236,882	33,731,064	32,788,125	31,461,391	30,609,560
Total Outpatient Visits	45,189,703	45,195,534	44,027,523	42,383,505	41,355,159
Outpatient Surgeries	1,409,297	1,381,625	1,363,374	1,321,436	1,270,792
Personnel					
Full Time RNs	108,193	99,131	98,204	94,483	91,680
Full Time LPNs	6,930	7,077	7,276	7,180	7,829
Part Time RNs	27,704	26,150	24,666	24,058	26,360
Part Time LPNs	1,543	1,765	1,644	1,482	1,666
Total Full Time	333,645	323,565	317,216	305,409	298,499
Total Part Time	75,383	74,654	70,655	66,721	75,017
Revenue - Inpatient					
Gross Inpatient Revenue	$173,584,687,991	$160,744,423,222	$150,334,153,232	$137,151,056,311	$127,997,017,161
Revenue - Outpatient					
Gross Outpatient Revenue	$147,661,835,989	$133,814,217,049	$119,582,775,629	$106,818,352,207	$96,468,532,860
Revenue and Expenses - Totals					
(Includes Inpatient and Outpatient)					
Total Gross Revenue	$321,246,523,980	$294,558,640,271	$269,916,928,861	$243,969,408,414	$224,465,550,021
Deductions from Revenue	250,340,125,682	226,041,676,513	204,323,349,372	182,737,456,668	166,888,653,026
Net Patient Revenue	70,906,398,298	68,516,963,758	65,593,579,489	61,231,951,746	57,576,896,995
Other Operating Revenue	6,190,973,473	5,696,302,966	5,510,291,272	5,266,158,017	5,405,887,910
Other Nonoperating Revenue	1,484,197,097	1,171,383,196	790,633,595	1,565,650,291	954,209,265
Total Net Revenue	78,581,568,868	75,384,649,920	71,894,504,356	68,063,760,054	63,936,994,170
Total Expenses	70,961,691,860	67,556,830,766	63,180,949,391	59,173,542,898	56,776,459,680
HOSPITAL UNIT (Excludes Separate Nursing Home Units)					
Utilization - Inpatient					
Beds	66,415	65,399	66,143	65,461	65,157
Admissions	2,769,510	2,711,093	2,691,917	2,625,524	2,627,109
Inpatient Days	14,489,069	14,396,055	14,377,808	13,985,908	13,741,793
Average Length of Stay	5.2	5.3	5.3	5.3	5.2
Personnel					
Total Full Time	333,287	322,791	316,783	304,544	297,776
Total Part Time	75,350	74,476	70,553	66,520	74,848
Revenue and Expenses - Totals					
(Includes Inpatient and Outpatient)					
Total Net Revenue	$78,532,940,052	$75,274,390,980	$71,742,645,276	$68,000,316,884	$63,843,078,822
Total Expenses	70,920,099,631	67,453,240,887	63,044,000,116	59,116,472,604	56,708,303,909
COMMUNITY HEALTH INDICATORS PER 1000 POPULATION					
Total Population (in thousands)	28,305	27,863	27,469	26,957	26,448
Inpatient					
Beds	2.4	2.4	2.5	2.4	2.5
Admissions	98.0	97.6	98.3	97.7	99.7
Inpatient Days	515.7	537.6	534.0	523.0	529.0
Inpatient Surgeries	28.0	27.6	28.5	28.3	28.9
Births	13.5	14.1	14.7	14.8	14.5
Outpatient					
Emergency Outpatient Visits	422.3	411.5	409.2	405.2	406.3
Other Outpatient Visits	1,174.3	1,210.6	1,193.6	1,167.1	1,157.3
Total Outpatient Visits	1,596.6	1,622.1	1,602.8	1,572.3	1,563.6
Outpatient Surgeries	49.8	49.6	49.6	49.0	48.0
Expense per Capita (per person)	$2,507.1	$2,424.6	$2,300.1	$2,195.1	$2,146.7

States

TABLE **6**

UTAH

U.S. Community Hospitals
(Nonfederal, short-term general and other special hospitals)

Overview 2013–2017

	2017	2016	2015	2014	2013
Total Community Hospitals in Utah....................	53	53	52	51	51
Bed Size Category					
6-24	11	10	9	10	10
25-49	18	19	19	18	18
50-99	3	3	3	3	3
100-199	12	12	12	11	11
200-299	5	5	5	5	5
300-399	2	2	2	2	2
400-499	0	0	1	1	1
500 + ...	2	2	1	1	1
Location					
Hospitals Urban	35	35	34	33	32
Hospitals Rural	18	18	18	18	19
Control					
State and Local Government	7	6	6	6	6
Not for Profit	27	27	27	27	27
Investor owned	19	20	19	18	18
Physician Models					
Independent Practice Association	2	4	4	3	3
Group Practice without Walls	1	4	2	2	2
Open Physician-Hospital Organization	21	4	3	2	2
Closed Physician-Hospital Organization	1	3	2	2	2
Management Service Organization	0	2	1	2	2
Integrated Salary Model	22	18	21	18	16
Equity Model	0	2	1	1	1
Foundation	1	3	2	1	1
Affiliations					
Hospitals in a System	43	43	42	41	41
Hospitals in a Network	7	10	10	15	16
Hospitals in a Group Purchasing Organization...	28	27	28	28	30

TABLE 6   **UTAH**

U.S. Community Hospitals
(Nonfederal, short-term general and other special hospitals)

Utilization, Personnel, Revenue and Expenses, Community Health Indicators 2013–2017

	2017	2016	2015	2014	2013
TOTAL FACILITY (Includes Hospital and Nursing Home Units)					
Utilization - Inpatient					
Beds	5,712	5,770	5,650	5,487	5,494
Admissions	240,934	243,709	240,052	232,726	232,207
Inpatient Days	1,139,575	1,129,420	1,103,164	1,049,912	1,038,223
Average Length of Stay	4.7	4.6	4.6	4.5	4.5
Inpatient Surgeries	70,404	72,448	72,696	72,058	68,219
Births	46,271	49,503	47,766	48,922	47,993
Utilization - Outpatient					
Emergency Outpatient Visits	1,112,859	1,007,531	1,041,543	1,057,085	892,850
Other Outpatient Visits	7,871,063	7,533,256	6,834,890	6,415,208	5,329,292
Total Outpatient Visits	8,983,922	8,540,787	7,876,433	7,472,293	6,222,142
Outpatient Surgeries	186,746	195,998	188,361	194,321	179,400
Personnel					
Full Time RNs	10,572	9,789	9,430	8,813	8,514
Full Time LPNs	276	333	359	318	350
Part Time RNs	4,850	4,632	4,025	4,382	4,605
Part Time LPNs	117	114	126	136	167
Total Full Time	35,302	34,989	32,298	30,113	29,913
Total Part Time	14,147	13,745	12,371	13,477	14,377
Revenue - Inpatient					
Gross Inpatient Revenue	$13,982,831,428	$12,735,004,491	$11,611,854,744	$10,575,144,343	$9,144,800,613
Revenue - Outpatient					
Gross Outpatient Revenue	$12,871,647,711	$11,723,900,325	$10,589,950,273	$9,485,685,679	$7,819,337,697
Revenue and Expenses - Totals					
(Includes Inpatient and Outpatient)					
Total Gross Revenue	$26,854,479,139	$24,458,904,816	$22,201,805,017	$20,060,830,022	$16,964,138,310
Deductions from Revenue	18,149,378,070	16,273,841,433	14,878,061,933	13,122,137,417	10,663,648,529
Net Patient Revenue	8,705,101,069	8,185,063,383	7,323,743,084	6,938,692,605	6,300,489,781
Other Operating Revenue	213,917,239	211,784,431	224,656,811	206,302,634	231,295,745
Other Nonoperating Revenue	8,770,044	15,002,583	16,639,658	31,510,703	26,301,071
Total Net Revenue	8,927,788,352	8,411,850,397	7,565,039,553	7,176,505,942	6,558,086,597
Total Expenses	7,255,419,720	6,744,726,492	6,217,782,791	5,737,696,572	5,463,281,903
HOSPITAL UNIT (Excludes Separate Nursing Home Units)					
Utilization - Inpatient					
Beds	5,525	5,564	5,438	5,359	5,367
Admissions	240,232	242,718	239,116	231,953	231,647
Inpatient Days	1,075,150	1,067,385	1,036,992	1,015,853	1,004,460
Average Length of Stay	4.5	4.4	4.3	4.4	4.3
Personnel					
Total Full Time	35,179	34,903	32,234	30,060	29,842
Total Part Time	14,039	13,708	12,325	13,440	14,328
Revenue and Expenses - Totals					
(Includes Inpatient and Outpatient)					
Total Net Revenue	$8,910,560,200	$8,396,910,741	$7,551,752,171	$7,168,670,901	$6,550,920,181
Total Expenses	7,239,413,429	6,731,514,820	6,207,466,257	5,732,683,301	5,459,375,368
COMMUNITY HEALTH INDICATORS PER 1000 POPULATION					
Total Population (in thousands)	3,102	3,051	2,996	2,943	2,901
Inpatient					
Beds	1.8	1.9	1.9	1.9	1.9
Admissions	77.7	79.9	80.1	79.1	80.0
Inpatient Days	367.4	370.2	368.2	356.8	357.9
Inpatient Surgeries	22.7	23.7	24.3	24.5	23.5
Births	14.9	16.2	15.9	16.6	16.5
Outpatient					
Emergency Outpatient Visits	358.8	330.2	347.7	359.2	307.8
Other Outpatient Visits	2,537.6	2,468.9	2,281.4	2,179.9	1,837.1
Total Outpatient Visits	2,896.3	2,799.1	2,629.1	2,539.1	2,144.9
Outpatient Surgeries	60.2	64.2	62.9	66.0	61.8
Expense per Capita (per person)	$2,339.1	$2,210.5	$2,075.4	$1,949.7	$1,883.3

States

TABLE 6

VERMONT

U.S. Community Hospitals
(Nonfederal, short-term general and other special hospitals)

Overview 2013–2017

	2017	2016	2015	2014	2013
Total Community Hospitals in Vermont...............	14	14	14	14	14
Bed Size Category					
6-24	0	1	1	1	1
25-49	8	7	7	7	7
50-99	3	3	3	3	3
100-199	1	1	1	1	1
200-299	1	1	1	1	1
300-399	0	0	0	0	0
400-499	1	1	1	1	1
500 + ...	0	0	0	0	0
Location					
Hospitals Urban	2	2	2	2	2
Hospitals Rural	12	12	12	12	12
Control					
State and Local Government	0	0	0	0	0
Not for Profit..	14	14	14	14	14
Investor owned	0	0	0	0	0
Physician Models					
Independent Practice Association......................	0	0	0	0	0
Group Practice without Walls	1	1	1	1	1
Open Physician-Hospital Organization	1	1	1	2	1
Closed Physician-Hospital Organization............	0	0	0	0	0
Management Service Organization	0	0	0	0	0
Integrated Salary Model....................................	3	4	4	5	5
Equity Model	0	0	0	0	0
Foundation	0	0	0	0	0
Affiliations					
Hospitals in a System	1	1	1	1	1
Hospitals in a Network	4	3	3	3	4
Hospitals in a Group Purchasing Organization...	8	8	9	10	11

TABLE 6

VERMONT

U.S. Community Hospitals
(Nonfederal, short-term general and other special hospitals)

Utilization, Personnel, Revenue and Expenses, Community Health Indicators 2013–2017

	2017	2016	2015	2014	2013
TOTAL FACILITY (Includes Hospital and Nursing Home Units)					
Utilization - Inpatient					
Beds	1,295	1,241	1,206	1,200	1,201
Admissions	49,438	49,847	47,695	45,964	48,464
Inpatient Days	301,837	296,562	292,755	288,502	303,555
Average Length of Stay	6.1	5.9	6.1	6.3	6.3
Inpatient Surgeries	14,204	12,792	11,936	12,180	12,785
Births	5,349	5,284	5,475	5,557	5,246
Utilization - Outpatient					
Emergency Outpatient Visits	311,534	317,955	328,066	327,066	302,264
Other Outpatient Visits	2,777,774	2,585,321	2,832,878	2,817,446	2,779,607
Total Outpatient Visits	3,089,308	2,903,276	3,160,944	3,144,512	3,081,871
Outpatient Surgeries	40,010	38,439	37,638	45,616	46,251
Personnel					
Full Time RNs	2,290	2,231	2,196	2,219	2,006
Full Time LPNs	184	184	187	173	150
Part Time RNs	1,795	1,744	1,781	1,607	1,646
Part Time LPNs	110	110	124	97	91
Total Full Time	12,049	11,932	11,353	11,026	10,374
Total Part Time	5,327	5,090	5,349	4,685	4,657
Revenue - Inpatient					
Gross Inpatient Revenue	$1,704,885,450	$1,571,303,645	$1,508,972,052	$1,374,615,928	$1,435,938,955
Revenue - Outpatient					
Gross Outpatient Revenue	$3,950,146,721	$3,778,225,703	$3,629,335,543	$3,444,718,900	$3,197,627,776
Revenue and Expenses - Totals					
(Includes Inpatient and Outpatient)					
Total Gross Revenue	$5,655,032,171	$5,349,529,348	$5,138,307,595	$4,819,334,828	$4,633,566,731
Deductions from Revenue	3,274,343,438	3,050,523,420	2,921,665,803	2,710,952,529	2,565,323,969
Net Patient Revenue	2,380,688,733	2,299,005,928	2,216,641,792	2,108,382,299	2,068,242,762
Other Operating Revenue	188,465,947	161,148,808	161,470,550	139,867,987	102,107,130
Other Nonoperating Revenue	101,608,792	33,298,454	-16,926,169	27,570,031	68,713,604
Total Net Revenue	2,670,763,472	2,493,453,190	2,361,186,173	2,275,820,317	2,239,063,496
Total Expenses	2,438,909,591	2,314,763,842	2,202,744,108	2,101,149,726	2,042,602,482
HOSPITAL UNIT (Excludes Separate Nursing Home Units)					
Utilization - Inpatient					
Beds	1,142	1,088	1,053	1,047	1,048
Admissions	49,059	49,528	47,393	45,584	48,129
Inpatient Days	257,202	253,600	249,294	241,545	249,025
Average Length of Stay	5.2	5.1	5.3	5.3	5.2
Personnel					
Total Full Time	11,920	11,793	11,236	10,975	10,247
Total Part Time	5,223	4,998	5,246	4,668	4,601
Revenue and Expenses - Totals					
(Includes Inpatient and Outpatient)					
Total Net Revenue	$2,654,221,104	$2,478,775,941	$2,347,550,643	$2,260,094,501	$2,222,318,627
Total Expenses	2,420,023,861	2,297,463,113	2,187,053,331	2,085,458,949	2,026,117,019
COMMUNITY HEALTH INDICATORS PER 1000 POPULATION					
Total Population (in thousands)	624	625	626	627	627
Inpatient					
Beds	2.1	2	1.9	1.9	1.9
Admissions	79.3	79.8	76.2	73.4	77.3
Inpatient Days	484.0	474.8	467.6	460.5	484.4
Inpatient Surgeries	22.8	20.5	19.1	19.4	20.4
Births	8.6	8.5	8.7	8.9	8.4
Outpatient					
Emergency Outpatient Visits	499.5	509.1	524.0	522.0	482.4
Other Outpatient Visits	4,454.0	4,139.2	4,525.1	4,496.7	4,435.8
Total Outpatient Visits	4,953.5	4,648.3	5,049.1	5,018.7	4,918.2
Outpatient Surgeries	64.2	61.5	60.1	72.8	73.8
Expense per Capita (per person)	$3,910.7	$3,706.0	$3,518.5	$3,353.5	$3,259.7

TABLE 6

VIRGINIA

U.S. Community Hospitals
(Nonfederal, short-term general and other special hospitals)

Overview 2013–2017

	2017	2016	2015	2014	2013
Total Community Hospitals in Virginia	95	95	95	99	98
Bed Size Category					
6-24	11	10	9	8	7
25-49	15	16	17	21	20
50-99	20	18	17	17	18
100-199	18	20	22	22	23
200-299	13	12	11	13	12
300-399	5	6	6	5	5
400-499	5	5	5	5	5
500 + ...	8	8	8	8	8
Location					
Hospitals Urban	69	68	68	72	69
Hospitals Rural	26	27	27	27	29
Control					
State and Local Government	4	4	4	6	6
Not for Profit	67	68	68	70	69
Investor owned	24	23	23	23	23
Physician Models					
Independent Practice Association	17	15	13	14	11
Group Practice without Walls	9	10	9	11	10
Open Physician-Hospital Organization	8	12	12	15	14
Closed Physician-Hospital Organization ...	4	3	4	4	3
Management Service Organization	18	17	20	16	15
Integrated Salary Model	45	51	54	44	45
Equity Model	9	9	9	10	9
Foundation	2	1	1	3	2
Affiliations					
Hospitals in a System	86	85	85	86	83
Hospitals in a Network	38	42	43	43	45
Hospitals in a Group Purchasing Organization...	59	67	66	61	67

TABLE 6

VIRGINIA

U.S. Community Hospitals
(Nonfederal, short-term general and other special hospitals)

Utilization, Personnel, Revenue and Expenses, Community Health Indicators 2013–2017

	2017	2016	2015	2014	2013
TOTAL FACILITY (Includes Hospital and Nursing Home Units)					
Utilization - Inpatient					
Beds	17,840	17,943	17,875	18,399	18,126
Admissions	797,032	794,741	791,388	778,708	782,607
Inpatient Days	4,513,293	4,494,671	4,423,932	4,470,709	4,472,564
Average Length of Stay	5.7	5.7	5.6	5.7	5.7
Inpatient Surgeries	205,163	204,056	200,330	206,566	213,555
Births	90,720	94,912	94,088	92,805	93,002
Utilization - Outpatient					
Emergency Outpatient Visits	3,522,286	3,776,039	3,718,523	3,663,903	3,634,219
Other Outpatient Visits	14,636,600	14,112,837	13,400,261	12,969,414	12,207,706
Total Outpatient Visits	18,158,886	17,888,876	17,118,784	16,633,317	15,841,925
Outpatient Surgeries	519,546	531,196	524,703	503,202	502,793
Personnel					
Full Time RNs	29,209	27,849	27,984	26,974	26,211
Full Time LPNs	2,096	2,235	2,038	1,782	1,959
Part Time RNs	11,516	12,212	11,792	10,571	10,828
Part Time LPNs	525	514	550	473	530
Total Full Time	96,042	92,350	92,784	86,007	86,046
Total Part Time	33,370	33,763	33,544	28,021	29,700
Revenue - Inpatient					
Gross Inpatient Revenue	$38,199,699,602	$35,433,087,260	$32,821,698,062	$31,585,779,334	$29,831,062,733
Revenue - Outpatient					
Gross Outpatient Revenue	$40,329,089,798	$37,920,140,697	$34,648,770,316	$31,504,154,797	$28,322,014,086
Revenue and Expenses - Totals					
(Includes Inpatient and Outpatient)					
Total Gross Revenue	$78,528,789,400	$73,353,227,957	$67,470,468,378	$63,089,934,131	$58,153,076,819
Deductions from Revenue	56,729,574,563	52,498,341,552	47,457,989,273	44,161,778,683	40,106,281,895
Net Patient Revenue	21,799,214,837	20,854,886,405	20,012,479,105	18,928,155,448	18,046,794,924
Other Operating Revenue	663,717,319	793,231,378	764,225,275	727,782,516	688,121,235
Other Nonoperating Revenue	604,010,698	206,319,395	70,943,172	395,829,268	484,820,925
Total Net Revenue	23,066,942,854	21,854,437,178	20,847,647,552	20,051,767,232	19,219,737,084
Total Expenses	20,280,704,720	19,705,571,358	18,796,506,872	17,857,798,102	17,101,883,999
HOSPITAL UNIT (Excludes Separate Nursing Home Units)					
Utilization - Inpatient					
Beds	16,176	16,259	16,234	16,751	16,478
Admissions	791,150	788,569	785,192	772,597	776,384
Inpatient Days	3,980,725	3,948,133	3,886,540	3,941,521	3,914,723
Average Length of Stay	5.0	5.0	4.9	5.1	5.0
Personnel					
Total Full Time	94,731	91,149	91,801	85,098	85,008
Total Part Time	32,752	33,240	33,074	27,635	29,313
Revenue and Expenses - Totals					
(Includes Inpatient and Outpatient)					
Total Net Revenue	$22,924,881,746	$21,712,032,835	$20,705,402,558	$19,919,435,060	$19,080,737,253
Total Expenses	20,140,841,542	19,572,253,756	18,667,568,401	17,731,900,106	16,972,379,291
COMMUNITY HEALTH INDICATORS PER 1000 POPULATION					
Total Population (in thousands)	8,470	8,412	8,383	8,326	8,260
Inpatient					
Beds	2.1	2.1	2.1	2.2	2.2
Admissions	94.1	94.5	94.4	93.5	94.7
Inpatient Days	532.9	534.3	527.7	536.9	541.4
Inpatient Surgeries	24.2	24.3	23.9	24.8	25.9
Births	10.7	11.3	11.2	11.1	11.3
Outpatient					
Emergency Outpatient Visits	415.9	448.9	443.6	440.0	440.0
Other Outpatient Visits	1,728.0	1,677.7	1,598.5	1,557.6	1,477.9
Total Outpatient Visits	2,143.9	2,126.6	2,042.1	1,997.7	1,917.8
Outpatient Surgeries	61.3	63.1	62.6	60.4	60.9
Expense per Capita (per person)	$2,394.4	$2,342.6	$2,242.2	$2,144.7	$2,070.3

States

TABLE 6

WASHINGTON

U.S. Community Hospitals
(Nonfederal, short-term general and other special hospitals)

Overview 2013–2017

	2017	2016	2015	2014	2013
Total Community Hospitals in Washington.........	92	92	92	92	92
Bed Size Category					
6-24.....................	11	12	12	12	11
25-49.....................	27	28	28	28	27
50-99.....................	16	15	15	15	16
100-199.....................	15	14	15	15	16
200-299.....................	10	11	10	11	11
300-399.....................	6	6	7	5	5
400-499.....................	4	3	2	3	4
500 +.....................	3	3	3	3	2
Location					
Hospitals Urban.....................	62	62	63	63	58
Hospitals Rural.....................	30	30	29	29	34
Control					
State and Local Government.....................	41	42	41	41	41
Not for Profit.....................	46	42	43	43	44
Investor owned.....................	5	8	8	8	7
Physician Models					
Independent Practice Association.....................	1	1	2	1	1
Group Practice without Walls.....................	1	2	3	3	2
Open Physician-Hospital Organization..............	2	2	2	2	2
Closed Physician-Hospital Organization............	2	2	1	1	0
Management Service Organization..................	0	2	2	1	2
Integrated Salary Model.....................	40	44	45	41	36
Equity Model.....................	0	0	0	1	3
Foundation.....................	0	0	0	0	6
Affiliations					
Hospitals in a System.....................	49	48	49	45	42
Hospitals in a Network.....................	33	36	35	29	24
Hospitals in a Group Purchasing Organization...	55	51	46	54	51

TABLE 6

WASHINGTON

U.S. Community Hospitals
(Nonfederal, short-term general and other special hospitals)

Utilization, Personnel, Revenue and Expenses, Community Health Indicators 2013–2017

	2017	2016	2015	2014	2013
TOTAL FACILITY (Includes Hospital and Nursing Home Units)					
Utilization - Inpatient					
Beds	12,577	12,164	12,035	12,026	12,218
Admissions	612,046	592,068	594,203	577,772	601,706
Inpatient Days	3,024,120	2,899,998	2,820,101	2,716,321	2,768,942
Average Length of Stay	4.9	4.9	4.7	4.7	4.6
Inpatient Surgeries	182,956	175,137	172,194	175,791	170,932
Births	83,259	83,992	83,171	80,429	77,904
Utilization - Outpatient					
Emergency Outpatient Visits	2,957,421	2,695,220	2,682,027	2,449,830	2,348,146
Other Outpatient Visits	12,240,078	11,560,817	10,910,651	9,852,915	10,173,254
Total Outpatient Visits	15,197,499	14,256,037	13,592,678	12,302,745	12,521,400
Outpatient Surgeries	361,618	366,809	305,810	325,208	302,309
Personnel					
Full Time RNs	21,207	23,196	22,040	18,586	18,311
Full Time LPNs	864	1,156	1,036	720	842
Part Time RNs	12,638	9,928	11,455	11,984	14,223
Part Time LPNs	467	427	486	429	557
Total Full Time	79,763	87,092	82,305	74,557	74,530
Total Part Time	35,918	30,536	31,308	35,044	41,362
Revenue - Inpatient					
Gross Inpatient Revenue	$35,072,086,770	$32,751,868,183	$31,343,007,558	$27,980,656,138	$27,482,283,554
Revenue - Outpatient					
Gross Outpatient Revenue	$35,195,765,549	$32,130,703,909	$30,161,402,650	$27,258,385,742	$25,267,282,285
Revenue and Expenses - Totals					
(Includes Inpatient and Outpatient)					
Total Gross Revenue	$70,267,852,319	$64,882,572,092	$61,504,410,208	$55,239,041,880	$52,749,565,839
Deductions from Revenue	48,636,215,792	44,130,138,321	41,383,287,319	37,163,600,240	35,044,456,385
Net Patient Revenue	21,631,636,527	20,752,433,771	20,121,122,889	18,075,441,640	17,705,109,454
Other Operating Revenue	1,282,330,912	1,148,659,515	1,139,203,388	1,014,297,863	1,025,232,778
Other Nonoperating Revenue	290,777,186	224,197,658	63,228,900	243,467,963	251,592,890
Total Net Revenue	23,204,744,625	22,125,290,944	21,323,555,177	19,333,207,466	18,981,935,122
Total Expenses	22,188,309,852	21,050,226,338	19,897,248,909	17,903,886,885	17,977,339,586
HOSPITAL UNIT (Excludes Separate Nursing Home Units)					
Utilization - Inpatient					
Beds	12,468	11,935	11,754	11,862	12,035
Admissions	611,569	590,913	593,196	577,000	601,385
Inpatient Days	2,987,717	2,824,272	2,719,388	2,668,793	2,691,722
Average Length of Stay	4.9	4.8	4.6	4.6	4.5
Personnel					
Total Full Time	79,648	86,823	82,063	74,383	74,401
Total Part Time	35,857	30,335	31,099	34,883	41,233
Revenue and Expenses - Totals					
(Includes Inpatient and Outpatient)					
Total Net Revenue	$23,186,194,715	$22,077,194,237	$21,293,862,403	$19,311,305,768	$18,961,233,532
Total Expenses	22,169,095,958	21,011,286,339	19,869,769,703	17,882,580,851	17,956,888,444
COMMUNITY HEALTH INDICATORS PER 1000 POPULATION					
Total Population (in thousands)	7,406	7,288	7,170	7,062	6,971
Inpatient					
Beds	1.7	1.7	1.7	1.7	1.8
Admissions	82.6	81.2	82.9	81.8	86.3
Inpatient Days	408.3	397.9	393.3	384.7	397.2
Inpatient Surgeries	24.7	24.0	24.0	24.9	24.5
Births	11.2	11.5	11.6	11.4	11.2
Outpatient					
Emergency Outpatient Visits	399.3	369.8	374.0	346.9	336.8
Other Outpatient Visits	1,652.8	1,586.3	1,521.6	1,395.3	1,459.3
Total Outpatient Visits	2,052.1	1,956.1	1,895.7	1,742.2	1,796.1
Outpatient Surgeries	48.8	50.3	42.6	46.1	43.4
Expense per Capita (per person)	$2,996.1	$2,888.3	$2,774.9	$2,535.4	$2,578.7

States

TABLE 6

WEST VIRGINIA

U.S. Community Hospitals
(Nonfederal, short-term general and other special hospitals)

Overview 2013–2017

	2017	2016	2015	2014	2013
Total Community Hospitals in West Virginia......	56	56	56	56	57
Bed Size Category					
6-24	4	4	4	4	3
25-49	17	17	17	17	18
50-99	12	12	11	10	11
100-199	12	12	13	14	13
200-299	7	7	7	7	8
300-399	2	2	2	2	2
400-499	0	0	0	0	0
500 + ...	2	2	2	2	2
Location					
Hospitals Urban	29	29	29	29	27
Hospitals Rural	27	27	27	27	30
Control					
State and Local Government	8	8	8	8	8
Not for Profit	33	34	33	33	34
Investor owned	15	14	15	15	15
Physician Models					
Independent Practice Association	2	2	2	2	2
Group Practice without Walls	0	0	0	0	1
Open Physician-Hospital Organization	7	7	10	11	11
Closed Physician-Hospital Organization	3	4	1	1	1
Management Service Organization	0	1	2	2	1
Integrated Salary Model	23	26	27	27	28
Equity Model	0	0	0	0	0
Foundation	2	2	0	0	0
Affiliations					
Hospitals in a System	35	34	31	31	31
Hospitals in a Network	17	17	18	20	20
Hospitals in a Group Purchasing Organization...	44	48	53	53	54

TABLE 6

WEST VIRGINIA

U.S. Community Hospitals
(Nonfederal, short-term general and other special hospitals)

Utilization, Personnel, Revenue and Expenses, Community Health Indicators 2013–2017

	2017	2016	2015	2014	2013
TOTAL FACILITY (Includes Hospital and Nursing Home Units)					
Utilization - Inpatient					
Beds	7,008	6,939	6,994	6,974	7,190
Admissions	257,402	253,031	256,354	257,663	266,376
Inpatient Days	1,539,754	1,499,249	1,532,624	1,557,115	1,576,551
Average Length of Stay	6.0	5.9	6.0	6.0	5.9
Inpatient Surgeries	71,577	73,584	74,894	77,788	80,682
Births	19,166	19,662	20,211	20,527	21,042
Utilization - Outpatient					
Emergency Outpatient Visits	1,184,865	1,180,148	1,194,297	1,189,529	1,174,998
Other Outpatient Visits	6,886,157	6,753,804	6,304,028	5,957,063	5,756,412
Total Outpatient Visits	8,071,022	7,933,952	7,498,325	7,146,592	6,931,410
Outpatient Surgeries	240,439	242,972	238,270	227,814	231,770
Personnel					
Full Time RNs	10,038	9,640	9,416	9,370	9,350
Full Time LPNs	1,173	1,172	1,208	1,103	1,151
Part Time RNs	3,058	3,078	3,068	2,981	3,376
Part Time LPNs	273	230	266	230	360
Total Full Time	38,405	36,733	36,148	35,330	35,691
Total Part Time	9,601	9,553	9,622	9,427	10,962
Revenue - Inpatient					
Gross Inpatient Revenue	$9,159,552,619	$7,818,630,176	$7,255,487,755	$6,928,250,908	$6,661,163,123
Revenue - Outpatient					
Gross Outpatient Revenue	$10,250,786,816	$9,295,226,822	$8,490,713,783	$7,594,070,741	$6,863,347,645
Revenue and Expenses - Totals					
(Includes Inpatient and Outpatient)					
Total Gross Revenue	$19,410,339,435	$17,113,856,998	$15,746,201,538	$14,522,321,649	$13,524,510,768
Deductions from Revenue	12,850,135,400	10,892,481,451	9,896,704,041	8,930,297,334	8,217,784,527
Net Patient Revenue	6,560,204,035	6,221,375,547	5,849,497,497	5,592,024,315	5,306,726,241
Other Operating Revenue	284,515,649	293,073,192	245,469,941	216,349,893	225,913,824
Other Nonoperating Revenue	202,435,277	53,289,636	-19,447,959	88,318,066	191,368,148
Total Net Revenue	7,047,154,961	6,567,738,375	6,075,519,479	5,896,692,274	5,724,008,213
Total Expenses	6,632,137,203	6,220,001,692	5,854,862,050	5,552,401,296	5,411,286,299
HOSPITAL UNIT (Excludes Separate Nursing Home Units)					
Utilization - Inpatient					
Beds	6,310	6,213	6,196	6,235	6,347
Admissions	254,956	250,455	253,067	254,397	262,203
Inpatient Days	1,327,858	1,274,896	1,285,909	1,321,868	1,313,603
Average Length of Stay	5.2	5.1	5.1	5.2	5.0
Personnel					
Total Full Time	37,956	36,222	35,595	34,793	35,091
Total Part Time	9,445	9,405	9,432	9,205	10,552
Revenue and Expenses - Totals					
(Includes Inpatient and Outpatient)					
Total Net Revenue	$6,991,736,730	$6,510,387,389	$6,010,973,954	$5,836,934,682	$5,653,960,341
Total Expenses	6,600,561,766	6,187,893,785	5,817,972,878	5,507,495,122	5,363,764,849
COMMUNITY HEALTH INDICATORS PER 1000 POPULATION					
Total Population (in thousands)	1,816	1,831	1,844	1,850	1,854
Inpatient					
Beds	3.9	3.8	3.8	3.8	3.9
Admissions	141.8	138.2	139	139.3	143.7
Inpatient Days	847.9	818.8	831.1	841.5	850.2
Inpatient Surgeries	39.4	40.2	40.6	42.0	43.5
Births	10.6	10.7	11	11.1	11.3
Outpatient					
Emergency Outpatient Visits	652.5	644.5	647.6	642.9	633.7
Other Outpatient Visits	3,792.2	3,688.4	3,418.4	3,219.5	3,104.4
Total Outpatient Visits	4,444.7	4,332.9	4,066.1	3,862.3	3,738.0
Outpatient Surgeries	132.4	132.7	129.2	123.1	125.0
Expense per Capita (per person)	$3,652.3	$3,396.9	$3,174.9	$3,000.8	$2,918.2

TABLE 6

WISCONSIN

U.S. Community Hospitals
(Nonfederal, short-term general and other special hospitals)

Overview 2013–2017

	2017	2016	2015	2014	2013
Total Community Hospitals in Wisconsin	134	134	133	135	135
Bed Size Category					
6-24	30	31	27	26	27
25-49	36	32	34	36	34
50-99	27	30	31	31	32
100-199	24	23	23	24	22
200-299	11	11	12	10	12
300-399	3	4	3	4	4
400-499	0	0	0	1	1
500 + ...	3	3	3	3	3
Location					
Hospitals Urban	75	75	74	76	77
Hospitals Rural	59	59	59	59	58
Control					
State and Local Government	2	2	2	2	2
Not for Profit	122	122	122	124	124
Investor owned	10	10	9	9	9
Physician Models					
Independent Practice Association	6	7	7	7	8
Group Practice without Walls	1	0	0	1	1
Open Physician-Hospital Organization	8	7	7	7	9
Closed Physician-Hospital Organization	3	4	2	5	4
Management Service Organization	2	4	2	2	1
Integrated Salary Model	48	48	53	52	55
Equity Model	13	14	12	9	11
Foundation	4	3	2	2	2
Affiliations					
Hospitals in a System	93	89	84	84	80
Hospitals in a Network	57	57	55	43	46
Hospitals in a Group Purchasing Organization...	129	129	130	131	130

TABLE 6

WISCONSIN

U.S. Community Hospitals
(Nonfederal, short-term general and other special hospitals)

Utilization, Personnel, Revenue and Expenses, Community Health Indicators 2013–2017

	2017	2016	2015	2014	2013
TOTAL FACILITY (Includes Hospital and Nursing Home Units)					
Utilization - Inpatient					
Beds	12,311	12,400	12,596	12,775	12,874
Admissions	534,275	535,399	541,549	555,367	570,346
Inpatient Days	2,651,498	2,680,807	2,758,206	2,773,942	2,827,910
Average Length of Stay	5.0	5.0	5.1	5.0	5.0
Inpatient Surgeries	171,894	174,729	171,497	171,358	174,772
Births	63,011	64,386	64,722	64,603	64,725
Utilization - Outpatient					
Emergency Outpatient Visits	2,500,115	2,392,607	2,454,661	2,220,534	2,119,589
Other Outpatient Visits	17,183,210	16,437,348	15,465,301	15,276,107	14,573,496
Total Outpatient Visits	19,683,325	18,829,955	17,919,962	17,496,641	16,693,085
Outpatient Surgeries	517,410	502,988	489,772	477,269	474,240
Personnel					
Full Time RNs	19,931	19,003	17,012	16,114	15,698
Full Time LPNs	672	638	659	544	622
Part Time RNs	15,823	16,146	15,360	16,094	16,178
Part Time LPNs	637	596	647	594	696
Total Full Time	77,143	72,098	68,065	64,112	65,150
Total Part Time	48,804	50,050	46,824	48,450	49,933
Revenue - Inpatient					
Gross Inpatient Revenue	$22,230,279,594	$20,865,133,177	$20,221,323,094	$18,977,425,530	$18,081,065,667
Revenue - Outpatient					
Gross Outpatient Revenue	$33,179,526,908	$30,863,567,527	$28,261,882,444	$25,084,873,340	$22,580,601,157
Revenue and Expenses - Totals					
(Includes Inpatient and Outpatient)					
Total Gross Revenue	$55,409,806,502	$51,728,700,704	$48,483,205,538	$44,062,298,870	$40,661,666,824
Deductions from Revenue	35,705,970,814	32,275,368,255	29,567,570,129	26,726,790,792	24,279,803,357
Net Patient Revenue	19,703,835,688	19,453,332,449	18,915,635,409	17,335,508,078	16,381,863,467
Other Operating Revenue	1,428,519,839	1,047,436,854	849,101,507	975,944,090	721,236,131
Other Nonoperating Revenue	429,139,687	163,097,521	130,867,061	445,146,818	456,064,408
Total Net Revenue	21,561,495,214	20,663,866,824	19,895,603,977	18,756,598,986	17,559,164,006
Total Expenses	19,640,671,915	18,716,182,889	17,859,058,395	16,476,416,562	15,558,029,695
HOSPITAL UNIT (Excludes Separate Nursing Home Units)					
Utilization - Inpatient					
Beds	11,451	11,468	11,574	11,675	11,725
Admissions	532,325	533,295	539,416	552,949	567,954
Inpatient Days	2,387,234	2,386,666	2,442,845	2,424,582	2,469,628
Average Length of Stay	4.5	4.5	4.5	4.4	4.3
Personnel					
Total Full Time	76,759	71,680	67,790	63,662	64,804
Total Part Time	48,607	49,674	46,463	48,011	49,388
Revenue and Expenses - Totals					
(Includes Inpatient and Outpatient)					
Total Net Revenue	$21,482,549,394	$20,583,379,951	$19,836,579,800	$18,688,913,325	$17,478,794,162
Total Expenses	19,577,462,778	18,657,539,986	17,814,373,003	16,414,317,207	15,478,393,568
COMMUNITY HEALTH INDICATORS PER 1000 POPULATION					
Total Population (in thousands)	5,795	5,779	5,771	5,758	5,743
Inpatient					
Beds	2.1	2.1	2.2	2.2	2.2
Admissions	92.2	92.7	93.8	96.5	99.3
Inpatient Days	457.5	463.9	477.9	481.8	492.4
Inpatient Surgeries	29.7	30.2	29.7	29.8	30.4
Births	10.9	11.1	11.2	11.2	11.3
Outpatient					
Emergency Outpatient Visits	431.4	414.0	425.3	385.7	369.1
Other Outpatient Visits	2,964.9	2,844.5	2,679.7	2,653.2	2,537.7
Total Outpatient Visits	3,396.3	3,258.5	3,105.0	3,038.9	2,906.8
Outpatient Surgeries	89.3	87.0	84.9	82.9	82.6
Expense per Capita (per person)	$3,389.0	$3,238.8	$3,094.4	$2,861.7	$2,709.2

TABLE 6

WYOMING

U.S. Community Hospitals
(Nonfederal, short-term general and other special hospitals)

Overview 2013–2017

	2017	2016	2015	2014	2013
Total Community Hospitals in Wyoming	29	27	27	27	28
Bed Size Category					
6-24	7	5	5	3	2
25-49	9	9	9	11	13
50-99	6	6	6	6	6
100-199	5	6	5	6	6
200-299	2	1	2	1	1
300-399	0	0	0	0	0
400-499	0	0	0	0	0
500 + ...	0	0	0	0	0
Location					
Hospitals Urban	5	4	4	4	4
Hospitals Rural	24	23	23	23	24
Control					
State and Local Government	17	19	18	18	18
Not for Profit	6	4	5	5	5
Investor owned	6	4	4	4	5
Physician Models					
Independent Practice Association	3	2	3	1	3
Group Practice without Walls	0	0	1	2	1
Open Physician-Hospital Organization	0	1	1	2	2
Closed Physician-Hospital Organization	0	1	3	1	1
Management Service Organization	1	1	1	2	2
Integrated Salary Model	9	9	10	12	11
Equity Model	0	1	0	0	0
Foundation	0	1	1	1	0
Affiliations					
Hospitals in a System	12	13	13	13	14
Hospitals in a Network	4	4	4	4	4
Hospitals in a Group Purchasing Organization...	18	17	20	22	23

TABLE 6

WYOMING

U.S. Community Hospitals
(Nonfederal, short-term general and other special hospitals)

Utilization, Personnel, Revenue and Expenses, Community Health Indicators 2013–2017

	2017	2016	2015	2014	2013
TOTAL FACILITY (Includes Hospital and Nursing Home Units)					
Utilization - Inpatient					
Beds	1,983	1,846	1,964	1,965	2,050
Admissions	42,556	43,417	45,009	43,173	46,382
Inpatient Days	384,142	387,565	375,863	383,245	395,412
Average Length of Stay	9.0	8.9	8.4	8.9	8.5
Inpatient Surgeries	12,355	11,665	11,042	11,368	11,511
Births	5,986	6,445	6,725	6,507	6,405
Utilization - Outpatient					
Emergency Outpatient Visits	238,749	242,725	247,994	236,327	238,122
Other Outpatient Visits	1,091,134	1,016,167	1,097,554	1,054,600	1,065,377
Total Outpatient Visits	1,329,883	1,258,892	1,345,548	1,290,927	1,303,499
Outpatient Surgeries	34,379	29,020	25,204	26,030	26,962
Personnel					
Full Time RNs	2,200	2,060	2,019	2,035	1,955
Full Time LPNs	127	152	124	133	117
Part Time RNs	627	515	559	617	641
Part Time LPNs	47	36	38	44	47
Total Full Time	9,047	9,132	8,506	8,338	8,184
Total Part Time	1,953	1,774	1,908	2,075	2,329
Revenue - Inpatient					
Gross Inpatient Revenue	$1,518,749,449	$1,468,615,470	$1,348,102,716	$1,206,562,665	$1,217,999,272
Revenue - Outpatient					
Gross Outpatient Revenue	$2,440,561,384	$2,130,643,586	$1,885,113,328	$1,674,010,159	$1,559,639,210
Revenue and Expenses - Totals					
(Includes Inpatient and Outpatient)					
Total Gross Revenue	$3,959,310,833	$3,599,259,056	$3,233,216,044	$2,880,572,824	$2,777,638,482
Deductions from Revenue	2,246,737,730	2,024,813,550	1,735,493,847	1,511,271,950	1,437,147,622
Net Patient Revenue	1,712,573,103	1,574,445,506	1,497,722,197	1,369,300,874	1,340,490,860
Other Operating Revenue	81,405,854	94,994,154	95,428,848	94,193,020	86,398,452
Other Nonoperating Revenue	59,489,879	21,275,510	13,809,546	60,644,525	39,002,461
Total Net Revenue	1,853,468,836	1,690,715,170	1,606,960,591	1,524,138,419	1,465,891,773
Total Expenses	1,696,260,078	1,572,418,430	1,471,925,692	1,376,545,606	1,294,845,333
HOSPITAL UNIT (Excludes Separate Nursing Home Units)					
Utilization - Inpatient					
Beds	1,527	1,361	1,344	1,280	1,385
Admissions	41,935	42,931	44,032	42,438	45,606
Inpatient Days	240,434	222,495	183,221	172,682	188,535
Average Length of Stay	5.7	5.2	4.2	4.1	4.1
Personnel					
Total Full Time	8,716	8,772	8,121	7,928	7,775
Total Part Time	1,827	1,666	1,759	1,899	2,130
Revenue and Expenses - Totals					
(Includes Inpatient and Outpatient)					
Total Net Revenue	$1,814,623,139	$1,655,704,116	$1,570,475,448	$1,479,387,543	$1,421,958,403
Total Expenses	1,655,110,449	1,547,411,275	1,438,561,699	1,336,748,407	1,258,030,251
COMMUNITY HEALTH INDICATORS PER 1000 POPULATION					
Total Population (in thousands)	579	586	586	584	583
Inpatient					
Beds	3.4	3.2	3.4	3.4	3.5
Admissions	73.5	74.2	76.8	73.9	79.6
Inpatient Days	663.1	661.9	641.3	656.1	678.6
Inpatient Surgeries	21.3	19.9	18.8	19.5	19.8
Births	10.3	11.0	11.5	11.1	11.0
Outpatient					
Emergency Outpatient Visits	412.1	414.6	423.1	404.6	408.7
Other Outpatient Visits	1,883.5	1,735.6	1,872.6	1,805.3	1,828.5
Total Outpatient Visits	2,295.6	2,150.1	2,295.7	2,209.9	2,237.2
Outpatient Surgeries	59.3	49.6	43.0	44.6	46.3
Expense per Capita (per person)	$2,928.0	$2,685.6	$2,511.4	$2,356.5	$2,222.3

States

Table 7

Table		Page

The facilities and services presented in Table 7 are listed below in alphabetical order by major heading (where applicable).

Table 7

2017 Facilities and Services in the U.S. Census Divisions and States

These data include only hospital-based facilities and services as reported by responding hospitals in Section C of the 2017 AHA Annual Survey, beginning on page 217. Census divisions represent all U.S. hospitals. Community hospitals are listed separately under United States. No estimates have been made for nonresponding hospitals. Definitions of facilities and services are listed in the Glossary, page 203.

CLASSIFICATION	HOSPITALS REPORTING	ADULT DAY CARE PROGRAM Number	Percent	AIRBORNE INFECTION ISOLATION ROOM Number	Percent	ALCOHOL/DRUG ABUSE OR DEPENDENCY INPATIENT CARE UNITS Number	Percent	ALCOHOL/DRUG ABUSE OR DEPENDENCY OUTPATIENT SERVICES Number	Percent	ALCOHOLISM-CHEMICAL DEPENDENCY PEDIATRIC SERVICES Number	Percent	ALCOHOLISM-CHEMICAL DEPENDENCY PARTIAL HOSPITALIZATION SERVICES Number	Percent	ALZHEIMER CENTER Number	Percent	AMBULANCE SERVICE Number	Percent	AMBULATORY SURGERY CENTER Number	Percent	ARTHRITIS TREATMENT CENTER Number	Percent
UNITED STATES	4,280	137	3.2	3,461	90.9	423	9.9	637	14.9	119	2.8	312	7.3	212	5.0	679	15.9	1,104	25.8	286	6.7
COMMUNITY HOSPITALS	3,877	124	3.2	3,350	86.4	293	7.6	495	12.8	77	2.0	217	5.6	199	5.1	662	17.1	1,069	27.6	272	7.0
CENSUS DIVISION 1, NEW ENGLAND	163	6	3.7	131	80.4	16	9.8	52	31.9	8	4.9	25	15.3	18	11.0	24	14.7	64	39.3	18	11.0
Connecticut	28	3	10.7	24	85.7	3	10.7	13	46.4	2	7.1	9	32.1	5	17.9	5	17.9	15	53.6	5	17.9
Maine	32	0	0.0	26	81.3	3	9.4	9	28.1	2	6.3	2	6.3	4	12.5	8	25.0	12	37.5	0	0.0
Massachusetts	56	2	3.6	42	75.0	6	10.7	16	28.6	3	5.4	10	17.9	6	10.7	6	10.7	21	37.5	0	0.0
New Hampshire	26	1	3.8	23	88.5	0	0.0	6	23.1	0	0.0	1	3.8	1	3.8	3	11.5	8	30.8	4	15.4
Rhode Island	9	0	0.0	8	88.9	1	11.1	3	33.3	0	0.0	1	11.1	1	11.1	1	11.1	5	55.6	0	0.0
Vermont	12	0	0.0	8	66.7	3	25.0	5	41.7	1	8.3	2	16.7	1	8.3	1	8.3	3	25.0	1	8.3
CENSUS DIVISION 2, MIDDLE ATLANTIC	373	28	7.5	319	85.5	68	18.2	109	29.2	14	3.8	39	10.5	31	8.3	84	22.5	168	45.0	53	14.2
New Jersey	73	7	9.6	57	78.1	9	12.3	22	30.1	1	1.4	8	11.0	5	6.8	26	35.6	28	38.4	13	17.8
New York	150	18	12.0	132	88.0	45	30.0	71	47.3	11	7.3	28	18.7	14	9.3	27	18.0	90	60.0	26	17.3
Pennsylvania	150	3	2.0	130	86.7	14	9.3	16	10.7	2	1.3	3	2.0	12	8.0	31	20.7	50	33.3	14	9.3
CENSUS DIVISION 3, SOUTH ATLANTIC	575	12	2.1	481	83.7	64	11.1	84	14.6	14	2.4	36	6.3	32	5.6	76	13.2	136	23.7	41	7.1
Delaware	9	1	11.1	6	66.7	0	0.0	2	22.2	0	0.0	0	0.0	1	11.1	1	11.1	3	33.3	0	0.0
District of Columbia	10	0	0.0	7	70.0	3	30.0	2	20.0	0	0.0	0	0.0	1	10.0	2	20.0	4	40.0	2	20.0
Florida	117	2	1.7	103	88.0	8	6.8	11	9.4	1	0.9	9	7.7	9	7.7	11	9.4	35	29.9	7	6.0
Georgia	103	3	2.9	79	76.7	7	6.8	13	12.6	4	3.9	8	7.8	4	3.9	16	15.5	18	17.5	3	2.9
Maryland	44	2	4.5	37	84.1	5	11.4	13	29.5	1	2.3	4	9.1	6	13.6	3	6.8	12	27.3	10	22.7
North Carolina	89	1	1.1	82	92.1	12	13.5	14	15.7	2	2.3	5	5.6	5	5.6	16	18.0	24	27.0	6	6.7
South Carolina	75	0	0.0	57	76.0	16	21.3	7	9.3	3	4.0	2	2.7	2	2.7	12	16.0	13	17.3	3	4.0
Virginia	76	3	3.9	69	90.8	8	10.5	18	23.7	0	0.0	6	7.9	3	3.9	8	10.5	20	26.3	6	7.9
West Virginia	52	0	0.0	41	78.8	4	7.7	4	7.7	1	1.9	2	3.8	1	1.9	7	13.5	7	13.5	4	7.7
CENSUS DIVISION 4, EAST NORTH CENTRAL	695	18	2.6	562	80.9	81	11.7	141	20.3	23	3.3	67	9.6	52	7.5	97	14.0	193	27.8	65	9.4
Illinois	162	7	4.3	140	86.4	20	12.3	37	22.8	6	3.7	22	13.6	8	4.9	17	10.5	35	21.6	15	9.3
Indiana	110	1	0.9	95	86.4	8	7.3	19	17.3	7	6.4	10	9.1	2	1.8	28	25.5	32	29.1	4	3.6
Michigan	135	3	2.2	116	85.9	16	11.9	21	15.6	3	2.2	6	4.4	9	6.7	16	11.9	40	29.6	12	8.9
Ohio	142	1	0.7	125	88.0	9	6.3	28	19.7	4	2.8	19	13.4	6	4.2	26	18.3	53	37.3	15	10.6
Wisconsin	146	6	4.1	86	58.9	28	19.2	36	24.7	3	2.1	10	6.8	27	18.5	10	6.8	33	22.6	19	13.0
CENSUS DIVISION 5, EAST SOUTH CENTRAL	308	5	1.6	229	74.4	32	10.4	30	9.7	9	2.9	19	6.2	14	4.5	50	16.2	55	17.9	19	6.2
Alabama	50	0	0.0	34	68.0	4	8.0	3	6.0	1	2.0	1	2.0	1	2.0	12	24.0	9	18.0	4	8.0
Kentucky	80	1	1.3	69	86.3	6	7.5	11	13.8	3	3.8	9	11.3	2	2.5	7	8.8	15	18.8	5	6.3
Mississippi	104	2	1.9	69	66.3	12	11.5	6	5.8	3	2.9	6	5.8	5	4.8	14	13.5	15	14.4	5	4.8
Tennessee	74	2	2.7	57	77.0	10	13.5	10	13.5	2	2.7	3	4.1	6	8.1	17	23.0	16	21.6	5	6.8
CENSUS DIVISION 6, WEST NORTH CENTRAL	614	32	5.2	478	77.9	56	9.1	63	10.3	11	1.8	28	4.6	26	4.2	155	25.2	115	18.7	27	4.4
Iowa	123	2	1.6	91	74.0	10	8.1	17	13.8	1	0.8	8	6.5	5	4.1	52	42.3	29	23.6	3	2.4
Kansas	127	8	6.3	96	75.6	4	3.1	4	3.1	2	1.6	2	1.6	3	2.4	19	15.0	9	9.4	3	2.4
Minnesota	97	10	10.3	83	85.6	8	8.2	14	14.4	4	4.1	6	6.2	7	7.2	32	33.0	25	25.8	4	4.1
Missouri	144	3	2.1	118	81.9	26	18.1	17	11.8	1	0.7	5	3.5	5	3.5	23	16.0	22	15.3	11	7.6
Nebraska	55	3	5.5	43	78.2	3	5.5	4	7.3	1	1.8	1	1.8	2	3.6	12	21.8	11	20.0	1	1.8
North Dakota	24	2	8.3	15	62.5	4	16.7	4	16.7	2	8.3	3	12.5	0	0.0	8	33.3	6	25.0	4	16.7
South Dakota	44	4	9.1	32	72.7	1	2.3	3	6.8	0	0.0	3	6.8	4	9.1	9	20.5	10	22.7	1	2.3
CENSUS DIVISION 7, WEST SOUTH CENTRAL	851	3	0.4	677	79.6	57	6.7	61	7.2	24	2.8	55	6.5	8	0.9	106	12.5	130	15.3	15	1.8
Arkansas	86	3	3.5	72	83.7	5	5.8	5	5.8	3	3.5	8	9.3	1	1.2	15	17.4	12	14.0	1	1.2
Louisiana	87	0	0.0	61	70.1	13	14.9	8	9.2	4	4.6	7	8.0	2	2.3	9	10.3	18	20.7	4	4.6
Oklahoma	113	0	0.0	90	79.6	8	7.1	8	7.1	3	2.7	5	4.4	3	2.7	15	13.3	18	15.9	1	0.9
Texas	565	2	0.4	454	80.4	31	5.5	38	6.7	14	2.5	35	6.2	2	0.4	67	11.9	82	14.5	9	1.6
CENSUS DIVISION 8, MOUNTAIN	324	18	5.6	243	75.0	23	7.1	50	15.4	10	3.1	21	6.5	13	4.0	59	18.2	88	27.2	19	5.9
Arizona	55	1	1.8	42	76.4	4	7.3	10	18.2	1	1.8	2	3.6	3	5.8	2	3.6	15	27.3	5	9.1
Colorado	69	3	4.3	59	85.5	6	8.7	11	15.9	3	4.3	4	5.8	4	5.8	19	27.5	17	24.6	4	5.8
Idaho	33	2	6.1	28	84.8	2	6.1	5	15.2	0	0.0	0	0.0	0	0.0	8	24.2	12	36.4	4	12.1
Montana	53	12	22.6	35	66.0	3	5.7	4	7.5	1	1.9	3	5.7	2	3.8	12	22.6	10	18.9	2	3.8
Nevada	27	0	0.0	16	59.3	2	7.4	5	18.5	1	3.7	3	11.1	0	0.0	2	7.4	10	37.0	2	7.4
New Mexico	27	0	0.0	19	70.4	2	7.4	5	18.5	0	0.0	2	7.4	0	0.0	5	17.2	10	37.0	2	7.4
Utah	38	0	0.0	27	71.1	3	7.9	7	18.4	3	7.9	4	10.5	2	5.3	4	10.5	8	21.1	0	0.0
Wyoming	20	0	0.0	17	85.0	1	5.0	3	15.0	1	5.0	3	15.0	2	10.0	7	35.0	6	30.0	0	0.0
CENSUS DIVISION 9, PACIFIC	377	15	4.0	341	90.5	22	5.8	50	13.3	6	1.6	22	5.8	18	4.8	28	7.4	155	41.1	29	7.7
Alaska	12	0	0.0	10	83.3	2	16.7	4	33.3	1	8.3	3	25.0	1	8.3	1	8.3	3	25.0	1	8.3
California	229	12	5.2	206	90.0	14	6.1	35	15.3	4	1.7	13	5.7	16	7.0	13	5.7	111	48.5	21	9.2
Hawaii	11	0	0.0	10	90.9	0	0.0	1	9.1	1	9.1	2	18.2	0	0.0	0	0.0	2	18.2	1	9.1
Oregon	60	1	1.7	59	98.3	2	3.3	4	6.7	0	0.0	0	0.0	1	1.7	9	15.0	12	20.0	2	3.3
Washington	65	2	3.1	56	86.2	4	6.2	6	9.2	0	0.0	4	6.2	0	0.0	5	7.7	27	41.5	4	6.2

Table 7 (Continued)

These data include only hospital-based facilities and services as reported by responding hospitals in Section C of the 2017 AHA Annual Survey, beginning on page 217. Census divisions represent all U.S. hospitals. Community hospitals are listed separately under United States. No estimates have been made for nonresponding hospitals. Definitions of facilities and services are listed in the Glossary, page 203.

CLASSIFICATION	HOSPITALS REPORTING	ASSISTED LIVING No.	ASSISTED LIVING %	AUXILIARY No.	AUXILIARY %	BARIATRIC/WEIGHT CONTROL No.	BARIATRIC/WEIGHT CONTROL %	BIRTHING/LDR/LDRP ROOM No.	BIRTHING/LDR/LDRP ROOM %	BLOOD DONOR CENTER No.	BLOOD DONOR CENTER %	BREAST CANCER SCREENING No.	BREAST CANCER SCREENING %	BURN CARE UNITS No.	BURN CARE UNITS %	CASE MANAGEMENT No.	CASE MANAGEMENT %	CHAPLAINCY/PASTORAL CARE No.	CHAPLAINCY/PASTORAL CARE %	CHEMOTHERAPY No.	CHEMOTHERAPY %
UNITED STATES	4,280	144	3.4	2,373	55.4	1,172	27.4	2,290	53.5	243	5.7	3,007	70.3	161	3.8	3,780	88.3	2,828	66.1	2,214	51.7
COMMUNITY HOSPITALS	3,877	135	3.5	2,338	60.3	1,134	29.2	2,280	58.8	237	6.1	2,971	76.6	160	4.1	3,555	91.7	2,665	68.7	2,164	55.8
CENSUS DIVISION 1, NEW ENGLAND	163	8	4.9	88	54.0	64	39.3	104	63.8	26	16.0	125	76.7	8	4.9	153	93.9	126	77.3	113	69.3
Connecticut	28	3	10.7	17	60.7	17	60.7	21	75.0	5	17.9	21	75.0	1	3.6	25	89.3	25	89.3	21	75.0
Maine	32	3	9.4	18	56.3	6	18.8	23	71.9	0	0.0	27	84.4	2	6.3	30	93.8	21	65.6	23	71.9
Massachusetts	56	0	0.0	25	44.6	29	51.8	33	58.9	17	30.4	41	73.2	4	7.1	53	94.6	46	82.1	35	62.5
New Hampshire	26	1	3.8	14	53.8	7	26.9	17	65.4	4	15.4	21	80.8	0	0.0	26	100.0	17	65.4	20	76.9
Rhode Island	9	0	0.0	7	77.8	3	33.3	3	33.3	0	0.0	7	77.8	1	11.1	8	88.9	8	88.9	7	77.8
Vermont	12	1	8.3	7	58.3	2	16.7	7	58.3	0	0.0	8	66.7	0	0.0	11	91.7	9	75.0	7	58.3
CENSUS DIVISION 2, MIDDLE ATLANTIC	373	6	1.6	239	64.1	166	44.5	216	57.9	50	13.4	305	81.8	18	4.8	347	93.0	311	83.4	262	70.2
New Jersey	73	2	2.7	47	64.4	42	57.5	40	54.8	8	11.0	54	74.0	4	5.5	64	87.7	64	87.7	52	71.2
New York	150	1	0.7	99	66.0	69	46.0	98	65.3	28	18.7	132	88.0	9	6.0	141	94.0	124	82.7	108	72.0
Pennsylvania	150	3	2.0	93	62.0	55	36.7	78	52.0	14	9.3	119	79.3	5	3.3	142	94.7	123	82.0	102	68.0
CENSUS DIVISION 3, SOUTH ATLANTIC	575	8	1.4	352	61.2	179	31.1	319	55.5	38	6.6	435	75.7	23	4.0	530	92.2	457	79.5	334	58.1
Delaware	10	1	10.0	4	40.0	7	70.0	6	60.0	1	10.0	5	50.0	0	0.0	9	90.0	9	90.0	8	80.0
District of Columbia	9	0	0.0	4	44.4	5	55.6	4	44.4	0	0.0	4	44.4	2	20.0	7	77.8	6	66.7	5	55.6
Florida	117	1	0.9	72	61.5	52	44.4	60	51.3	9	7.7	84	71.8	8	6.8	114	97.4	96	82.1	76	65.0
Georgia	103	2	1.9	69	67.0	28	27.2	56	54.4	3	2.9	83	80.6	2	1.9	94	91.3	76	73.8	53	51.5
Maryland	44	1	2.3	35	79.5	16	36.4	29	65.9	7	15.9	33	75.0	2	4.5	40	90.9	43	97.7	35	79.5
North Carolina	89	1	1.1	50	56.2	28	31.5	61	68.5	5	5.6	75	84.3	2	2.2	84	94.4	78	87.6	58	65.2
South Carolina	75	0	0.0	39	52.0	14	18.7	41	54.7	5	6.7	54	72.0	2	2.7	64	85.3	46	61.3	29	38.7
Virginia	76	1	1.3	49	64.5	21	27.6	39	51.3	8	10.5	59	77.6	4	5.3	73	96.1	65	85.5	48	63.2
West Virginia	52	1	1.9	30	57.7	8	15.4	23	44.2	0	0.0	38	73.1	1	1.9	44	84.6	38	73.1	22	42.3
CENSUS DIVISION 4, EAST NORTH CENTRAL	695	22	3.2	421	60.6	203	29.2	419	60.3	32	4.6	567	81.6	31	4.5	640	92.1	504	72.5	422	60.7
Illinois	162	2	1.2	107	66.0	55	34.0	97	59.9	10	6.2	138	85.2	7	4.3	150	92.6	130	80.2	110	67.9
Indiana	110	3	2.7	53	48.2	23	20.9	69	62.7	3	2.7	87	79.1	3	2.7	106	96.4	90	81.8	63	57.3
Michigan	135	4	3.0	91	67.4	50	37.0	73	54.1	7	5.2	112	83.0	7	5.2	116	85.9	98	72.6	91	67.4
Ohio	142	2	1.4	85	59.9	47	33.1	89	62.7	10	7.0	119	83.8	8	5.6	139	97.9	119	83.8	100	70.4
Wisconsin	146	11	7.5	85	58.2	28	19.2	91	62.3	2	1.4	111	76.0	6	4.1	129	88.4	67	45.9	58	39.7
CENSUS DIVISION 5, EAST SOUTH CENTRAL	308	4	1.3	146	47.4	68	22.1	136	44.2	6	1.9	206	66.9	8	2.6	266	86.4	192	62.3	115	37.3
Alabama	50	0	0.0	34	68.0	16	32.0	29	58.0	1	2.0	39	78.0	3	6.0	48	96.0	34	68.0	25	50.0
Kentucky	80	0	0.0	43	53.8	21	26.3	35	43.8	4	5.0	59	73.8	3	3.8	74	92.5	65	81.3	41	51.3
Mississippi	104	2	1.9	35	33.7	15	14.4	38	36.5	0	0.0	58	55.8	1	1.0	77	74.0	38	36.5	20	19.2
Tennessee	74	2	2.7	34	45.9	16	21.6	34	45.9	1	1.4	50	67.6	1	1.4	67	90.5	55	74.3	29	39.2
CENSUS DIVISION 6, WEST NORTH CENTRAL	614	53	8.6	384	62.5	129	21.0	324	52.8	19	3.1	459	74.8	25	4.1	480	78.2	320	52.1	330	53.7
Iowa	123	7	5.7	104	84.6	23	18.7	71	57.7	2	1.6	113	91.9	5	4.1	105	85.4	56	45.5	66	53.7
Kansas	127	7	5.5	68	53.5	18	14.2	61	48.0	0	0.0	72	56.7	5	3.9	83	65.4	57	44.9	44	34.6
Minnesota	97	14	14.4	62	63.9	27	27.8	70	72.2	4	4.1	86	88.7	3	3.1	80	82.5	59	60.8	65	67.0
Missouri	144	2	1.4	94	65.3	36	25.0	61	42.4	10	6.9	97	67.4	8	5.6	122	84.7	93	64.6	84	58.3
Nebraska	55	9	16.4	29	52.7	13	23.6	37	67.3	0	0.0	46	83.6	3	5.5	44	80.0	28	50.9	38	69.1
North Dakota	24	2	8.3	15	62.5	5	20.8	9	37.5	1	4.2	17	70.8	1	4.2	18	75.0	12	50.0	10	41.7
South Dakota	44	12	27.3	12	27.3	7	15.9	15	34.1	2	4.5	28	63.6	0	0.0	28	63.6	15	34.1	23	52.3
CENSUS DIVISION 7, WEST SOUTH CENTRAL	851	17	2.0	369	43.4	186	21.9	324	38.1	24	2.8	406	47.7	22	2.6	726	85.3	430	50.5	218	25.6
Arkansas	86	2	2.3	54	62.8	16	18.6	35	40.7	3	3.5	51	59.3	2	2.3	75	87.2	44	51.2	25	29.1
Louisiana	87	2	2.3	33	37.9	20	23.0	35	40.2	4	4.6	56	64.4	7	8.0	75	86.2	48	55.2	38	43.7
Oklahoma	113	3	2.7	56	49.6	15	13.3	43	38.1	4	3.5	60	53.1	5	4.4	98	86.7	65	57.5	23	20.4
Texas	565	10	1.8	226	40.0	135	23.9	211	37.3	13	2.3	239	42.3	8	1.4	478	84.6	273	48.3	132	23.4
CENSUS DIVISION 8, MOUNTAIN	324	17	5.2	158	48.8	62	19.1	194	59.9	16	4.9	221	68.2	10	3.1	277	85.5	179	55.2	167	51.5
Arizona	55	2	3.6	26	47.3	15	27.3	29	52.7	4	7.3	32	58.2	2	3.6	50	90.9	39	70.9	33	60.0
Colorado	69	4	5.8	38	55.1	17	24.6	46	66.7	9	13.0	57	82.6	2	2.9	63	91.3	45	65.2	46	66.7
Idaho	33	2	6.1	22	66.7	8	24.2	22	66.7	2	6.1	23	69.7	0	0.0	31	93.9	17	51.5	16	48.5
Montana	53	7	13.2	25	47.2	4	7.5	26	49.1	0	0.0	32	60.4	0	0.0	33	62.3	21	39.6	25	47.2
Nevada	27	1	3.7	8	29.6	4	14.8	10	37.0	0	0.0	14	51.9	2	7.4	24	88.9	14	51.9	14	51.9
New Mexico	29	0	0.0	18	62.1	4	13.8	21	72.4	1	3.4	21	72.4	3	10.3	27	93.1	21	72.4	10	34.5
Utah	38	0	0.0	8	21.1	7	18.4	26	68.4	0	0.0	27	71.1	1	2.6	33	86.8	13	34.2	13	34.2
Wyoming	20	1	5.0	13	65.0	3	15.0	14	70.0	0	0.0	15	75.0	0	0.0	16	80.0	9	45.0	10	50.0
CENSUS DIVISION 9, PACIFIC	377	9	2.4	216	57.3	115	30.5	254	67.4	32	8.5	283	75.1	16	4.2	361	95.8	309	82.0	253	67.1
Alaska	12	0	0.0	3	25.0	1	8.3	7	58.3	1	8.3	7	58.3	0	0.0	11	91.7	7	58.3	6	50.0
California	229	3	1.3	131	57.2	81	35.4	151	65.9	29	12.7	165	72.1	10	4.4	221	96.5	193	84.3	160	69.9
Hawaii	11	0	0.0	2	18.2	4	36.4	6	54.5	0	0.0	9	81.8	1	9.1	11	100.0	5	45.5	9	81.8
Oregon	60	4	6.7	44	73.3	12	20.0	49	81.7	0	0.0	54	90.0	3	5.0	58	96.7	48	80.0	40	66.7
Washington	65	2	3.1	36	55.4	17	26.2	41	63.1	2	3.1	47	72.3	1	1.5	60	92.3	56	86.2	38	58.5

Table 7 (Continued)

These data include only hospital-based facilities and services as reported by responding hospitals in Section C of the 2017 AHA Annual Survey, beginning on page 217. Census divisions represent all U.S. hospitals. Community hospitals are listed separately under United States. No estimates have been made for nonresponding hospitals. Definitions of facilities and services are listed in the Glossary, page 203.

CLASSIFICATION	HOSPITALS REPORTING	CHILDREN'S WELLNESS PROGRAM Number	Percent	CHIROPRACTIC SERVICES Number	Percent	COMMUNITY OUTREACH Number	Percent	COMPLEMENTARY AND ALTERNATIVE MEDICINE SERVICES Number	Percent	COMPUTER ASSISTED ORTHOPEDIC SURGERY (CAOS) Number	Percent	CRISIS PREVENTION Number	Percent	DENTAL SERVICES Number	Percent	ENABLING SERVICES Number	Percent	ENROLLMENT ASSISTANCE SERVICES Number	Percent	EXTRACORPOREAL SHOCK WAVE LITHOTRIPTER (ESWL) Number	Percent
UNITED STATES	4,280	842	19.7	140	3.3	3,053	71.3	932	21.8	754	17.6	1,078	25.2	875	20.4	1,323	30.9	2,615	61.1	1,266	29.6
COMMUNITY HOSPITALS	3,877	819	21.1	114	2.9	2,904	74.9	882	22.7	748	19.3	948	24.5	768	19.8	1,258	32.4	2,503	64.6	1,247	32.2
CENSUS DIVISION 1, NEW ENGLAND	163	59	36.2	10	6.1	135	82.8	78	47.9	42	25.8	63	38.7	42	25.8	77	47.2	137	84.0	81	49.7
Connecticut	28	9	32.1	0	0.0	23	82.1	18	64.3	9	32.1	18	64.3	12	42.9	15	53.6	25	89.3	19	67.9
Maine	32	11	34.4	1	3.1	25	78.1	12	37.5	3	9.4	6	18.8	4	12.5	13	40.6	23	71.9	13	40.6
Massachusetts	56	24	42.9	3	5.4	44	78.6	25	44.6	16	28.6	23	41.1	11	19.6	22	39.3	49	87.5	29	51.8
New Hampshire	26	12	46.2	4	15.4	24	92.3	16	61.5	8	30.8	11	42.3	9	34.6	14	53.8	23	88.5	11	42.3
Rhode Island	9	1	11.1	1	11.1	9	100.0	4	44.4	2	22.2	3	33.3	3	33.3	7	77.8	7	77.8	6	66.7
Vermont	12	2	16.7	1	8.3	10	83.3	3	25.0	4	33.3	2	16.7	3	25.0	6	50.0	10	83.3	3	25.0
CENSUS DIVISION 2, MIDDLE ATLANTIC	373	120	32.2	20	5.4	320	85.8	141	37.8	104	27.9	185	49.6	160	42.9	183	49.1	286	76.7	160	42.9
New Jersey	73	30	41.1	2	2.7	58	79.5	33	45.2	26	35.6	47	64.4	32	43.8	42	57.5	54	74.0	27	37.0
New York	150	57	38.0	12	8.0	136	90.7	61	40.7	44	29.3	83	55.3	73	48.7	64	42.7	123	82.0	72	48.0
Pennsylvania	150	33	22.0	6	4.0	126	84.0	47	31.3	34	22.7	55	36.7	55	36.7	77	51.3	109	72.7	61	40.7
CENSUS DIVISION 3, SOUTH ATLANTIC	575	107	18.6	16	2.8	438	76.2	121	21.0	128	22.3	147	25.6	136	23.7	209	36.3	375	65.2	202	35.1
Delaware	10	4	40.0	1	10.0	9	90.0	6	60.0	4	40.0	6	60.0	3	33.3	3	33.3	7	70.0	3	33.3
District of Columbia	10	5	55.6	0	0.0	4	44.4	2	22.2	3	33.3	2	22.2	7	70.0	7	70.0	7	70.0	4	40.0
Florida	117	22	18.8	3	2.6	86	73.5	26	22.2	45	38.5	26	22.2	20	17.1	39	33.3	81	69.2	51	43.6
Georgia	103	9	8.7	3	2.9	73	70.9	18	17.5	17	16.5	24	23.3	14	13.6	32	31.1	62	60.2	33	32.0
Maryland	44	15	34.1	0	0.0	38	86.4	21	47.7	13	29.5	21	47.7	21	47.7	30	68.2	38	86.4	27	61.4
North Carolina	89	14	15.7	1	1.1	73	82.0	16	18.0	13	14.6	20	22.5	27	30.3	31	34.8	54	60.7	19	21.3
South Carolina	75	13	17.3	0	0.0	55	73.3	5	6.7	10	13.3	8	10.7	21	28.0	12	16.0	36	48.0	23	30.7
Virginia	76	12	15.8	4	5.3	62	81.6	24	31.6	20	26.3	30	39.5	24	31.6	43	56.6	60	78.9	26	34.2
West Virginia	52	13	25.0	4	7.7	38	73.1	3	5.8	3	5.8	10	19.2	7	13.5	12	23.1	33	63.5	16	30.8
CENSUS DIVISION 4, EAST NORTH CENTRAL	695	177	25.5	31	4.5	534	76.8	230	33.1	130	18.7	223	32.1	131	18.8	280	40.3	463	66.6	232	33.4
Illinois	162	49	30.2	9	5.6	128	79.0	43	26.5	42	25.9	70	43.2	43	26.5	70	43.2	108	66.7	45	27.8
Indiana	110	26	23.6	3	2.7	95	86.4	29	26.4	11	10.0	25	22.7	16	14.5	31	28.2	79	71.8	34	30.9
Michigan	135	44	32.6	5	3.7	117	86.7	51	37.8	22	16.3	45	33.3	35	25.9	62	45.9	110	81.5	44	32.6
Ohio	142	28	19.7	9	6.3	124	87.3	55	38.7	34	23.9	50	35.2	36	25.4	67	47.2	106	74.6	67	47.2
Wisconsin	146	30	20.5	5	3.4	70	47.9	52	35.6	21	14.4	33	22.6	1	0.7	50	34.2	60	41.1	42	28.8
CENSUS DIVISION 5, EAST SOUTH CENTRAL	308	40	13.0	4	1.3	204	66.2	27	8.8	33	10.7	53	17.2	58	18.8	63	20.5	160	51.9	72	23.4
Alabama	50	3	6.0	2	4.0	33	66.0	2	4.0	8	16.0	11	22.0	4	8.0	7	14.0	33	66.0	15	30.0
Kentucky	80	13	16.3	0	0.0	59	73.8	15	18.8	10	12.5	11	13.8	17	21.3	11	13.8	54	67.5	25	31.3
Mississippi	104	15	14.4	1	1.0	62	59.6	2	1.9	6	5.8	12	11.5	24	23.1	24	23.1	31	29.8	10	9.6
Tennessee	74	9	12.2	1	1.4	50	67.6	8	10.8	9	12.2	19	25.7	13	17.6	13	17.6	42	56.8	22	29.7
CENSUS DIVISION 6, WEST NORTH CENTRAL	614	105	17.1	29	4.7	411	66.9	104	16.9	56	9.1	123	20.0	86	14.0	139	22.6	343	55.9	110	17.9
Iowa	123	24	19.5	4	3.3	96	78.0	28	22.8	16	13.0	31	25.2	18	14.6	35	28.5	96	78.0	15	12.2
Kansas	127	10	7.9	0	0.0	57	44.9	8	6.3	6	4.7	10	7.9	9	7.1	15	11.8	53	41.7	17	13.4
Minnesota	97	22	22.7	8	8.2	76	78.4	30	30.9	9	9.3	23	23.7	13	13.4	20	20.6	59	60.8	20	20.6
Missouri	144	27	18.8	8	5.6	96	66.7	22	15.3	12	8.3	36	25.0	34	23.6	51	35.4	81	56.3	38	26.4
Nebraska	55	11	20.0	1	1.8	43	78.2	8	14.5	8	14.5	10	18.2	4	7.3	9	16.4	30	54.5	12	21.8
North Dakota	24	6	25.0	6	25.0	17	70.8	4	16.7	2	8.3	6	25.0	5	20.8	5	20.8	12	50.0	3	12.5
South Dakota	44	5	11.4	2	4.5	26	59.1	4	9.1	3	6.8	7	15.9	4	9.1	4	9.1	12	27.3	5	11.4
CENSUS DIVISION 7, WEST SOUTH CENTRAL	851	86	10.1	6	0.7	461	54.2	44	5.2	111	13.0	94	11.0	113	13.3	129	15.2	366	43.0	171	20.1
Arkansas	86	8	9.3	0	0.0	52	60.5	4	4.7	4	4.7	11	12.8	11	12.8	9	10.5	41	47.7	12	14.0
Louisiana	87	20	23.0	1	1.1	53	60.9	7	8.0	16	18.4	21	24.1	15	17.2	20	23.0	53	60.9	20	23.0
Oklahoma	113	9	8.0	0	0.0	62	54.9	5	4.4	14	12.4	8	7.1	16	14.2	18	15.9	45	39.8	25	22.1
Texas	565	49	8.7	5	0.9	294	52.0	28	5.0	77	13.6	54	9.6	73	12.9	82	14.5	227	40.2	114	20.2
CENSUS DIVISION 8, MOUNTAIN	324	70	21.6	13	4.0	230	71.0	71	21.9	58	17.9	89	27.5	64	19.8	93	28.7	209	64.5	84	25.9
Arizona	55	14	25.5	2	3.6	37	67.3	14	25.5	13	23.6	15	27.3	10	18.2	15	27.3	36	65.5	25	45.5
Colorado	69	15	21.7	3	4.3	54	78.3	30	43.5	18	26.1	19	27.5	9	13.0	23	33.3	49	71.0	12	17.4
Idaho	33	10	30.3	3	9.1	28	84.8	7	21.2	5	15.2	5	15.2	10	30.3	8	24.2	19	57.6	5	15.2
Montana	53	12	22.6	3	5.7	32	60.4	10	18.9	5	9.4	11	20.8	4	7.5	6	11.3	32	60.4	7	13.2
Nevada	27	4	14.8	2	7.4	14	51.9	3	11.1	1	3.7	9	33.3	2	7.4	6	22.2	13	48.1	7	25.9
New Mexico	29	7	24.1	0	0.0	22	75.9	1	3.4	1	3.4	4	13.8	9	31.0	3	10.3	20	69.0	11	37.9
Utah	38	4	10.5	0	0.0	30	78.9	5	13.2	6	15.8	21	55.3	16	42.1	23	60.5	29	76.3	11	28.9
Wyoming	20	4	20.0	0	0.0	13	65.0	1	5.0	3	15.0	5	25.0	4	20.0	2	10.0	11	55.0	6	30.0
CENSUS DIVISION 9, PACIFIC	377	78	20.7	11	2.9	320	84.9	116	30.8	92	24.4	101	26.8	85	22.5	150	39.8	276	73.2	154	40.8
Alaska	12	2	16.7	1	8.3	9	75.0	4	33.3	0	0.0	6	50.0	5	41.7	2	16.7	7	58.3	3	25.0
California	229	45	19.7	6	2.6	193	84.3	72	31.4	55	24.0	52	22.7	62	27.1	91	39.7	173	75.5	107	46.7
Hawaii	11	5	45.5	0	0.0	10	90.9	4	36.4	3	27.3	3	27.3	2	18.2	8	72.7	8	72.7	8	72.7
Oregon	60	13	21.7	3	5.0	55	91.7	19	31.7	19	31.7	14	23.3	6	10.0	23	38.3	44	73.3	18	30.0
Washington	65	13	20.0	1	1.5	53	81.5	17	26.2	15	23.1	26	40.0	10	15.4	26	40.0	44	67.7	23	35.4

Facilities and Services

Table 7 (Continued)

These data include only hospital-based facilities and services as reported by responding hospitals in Section C of the 2017 AHA Annual Survey, beginning on page 217. Census divisions represent all U.S. hospitals. Community hospitals are listed separately under United States. No estimates have been made for nonresponding hospitals. Definitions of facilities and services are listed in the Glossary, page 203.

CLASSIFICATION	HOSPITALS REPORTING	FERTILITY CLINIC Number	Percent	FITNESS CENTER Number	Percent	FREESTANDING OUTPATIENT CARE CENTER Number	Percent	GENETIC TESTING/COUNSELING Number	Percent	GERIATRIC SERVICES Number	Percent	HEALTH FAIR Number	Percent	COMMUNITY HEALTH EDUCATION Number	Percent	HEALTH RESEARCH Number	Percent	HEALTH SCREENINGS Number	Percent	HEMODIALYSIS Number	Percent
UNITED STATES	4,280	217	5.1	1,315	30.7	1,466	34.3	823	19.2	1,701	39.7	3,109	72.6	3,378	78.9	1,175	27.5	3,277	76.6	1,331	31.1
COMMUNITY HOSPITALS	3,877	210	5.4	1,241	32.0	1,391	35.9	798	20.6	1,575	40.6	3,009	77.6	3,246	83.7	1,107	28.6	3,149	81.2	1,284	33.1
CENSUS DIVISION 1, NEW ENGLAND	163	25	15.3	53	32.5	91	55.8	61	37.4	86	52.8	127	77.9	140	85.9	75	46.0	142	87.1	50	30.7
Connecticut	32	6	21.4	15	53.6	22	78.6	14	50.0	17	60.7	21	75.0	25	89.3	18	64.3	26	92.9	10	35.7
Maine	28	2	6.3	9	28.1	16	50.0	7	21.9	16	50.0	27	84.4	28	87.5	6	18.8	28	87.5	3	9.4
Massachusetts	56	11	19.6	9	16.1	31	55.4	23	41.1	31	55.4	44	78.6	46	82.1	32	57.1	47	83.9	27	48.2
New Hampshire	26	4	15.4	10	38.5	13	50.0	10	38.5	13	50.0	21	80.8	23	88.5	11	42.3	24	92.3	2	7.7
Rhode Island	9	1	11.1	5	55.6	6	66.7	4	44.4	6	66.7	8	88.9	8	88.9	5	55.6	8	88.9	6	66.7
Vermont	12	1	8.3	5	41.7	3	25.0	3	25.0	3	25.0	6	50.0	10	83.3	3	25.0	9	75.0	2	16.7
CENSUS DIVISION 2, MIDDLE ATLANTIC	373	50	13.4	114	30.6	217	58.2	138	37.0	214	57.4	306	82.0	322	86.3	176	47.2	327	87.7	190	50.9
New Jersey	73	9	12.3	24	32.9	38	52.1	34	46.6	43	58.9	54	74.0	54	76.7	39	53.4	55	75.3	48	65.8
New York	150	28	18.7	48	32.0	103	68.7	60	40.0	92	61.3	130	86.7	141	94.0	78	52.0	139	92.7	91	60.7
Pennsylvania	150	13	8.7	42	28.0	76	50.7	44	29.3	79	52.7	122	81.3	125	83.3	59	39.3	133	88.7	51	34.0
CENSUS DIVISION 3, SOUTH ATLANTIC	575	23	4.0	197	34.3	231	40.2	147	25.6	225	39.1	441	76.7	461	80.2	198	34.4	472	82.1	245	42.6
Delaware	9	0	0.0	3	33.3	5	55.6	3	33.3	3	33.3	7	77.8	6	66.7	3	33.3	6	66.7	3	33.3
District of Columbia	10	0	0.0	4	40.0	9	90.0	6	60.0	7	70.0	7	70.0	9	90.0	9	90.0	9	90.0	7	70.0
Florida	117	3	2.6	45	38.5	49	41.9	39	33.3	43	36.8	90	76.9	100	85.5	52	44.4	92	78.6	60	51.3
Georgia	103	2	1.9	32	31.1	37	35.9	21	20.4	31	30.1	73	70.9	76	73.8	27	26.2	86	83.5	45	43.7
Maryland	44	3	6.8	15	34.1	20	45.5	20	45.5	30	68.2	38	86.4	35	79.5	29	61.4	38	86.4	32	72.7
North Carolina	89	6	6.7	30	33.7	39	43.8	20	22.5	37	41.6	70	78.7	77	86.5	29	32.6	76	85.4	30	33.7
South Carolina	75	2	2.7	23	30.7	19	25.3	5	6.7	29	38.7	53	70.7	55	73.3	13	17.3	55	73.3	25	33.3
Virginia	76	4	5.3	29	38.2	36	47.4	25	32.9	32	42.1	63	82.9	62	81.6	30	39.5	66	86.8	30	39.5
West Virginia	52	3	5.8	16	30.8	17	32.7	8	15.4	13	25.0	42	80.8	41	78.8	8	15.4	44	84.6	13	25.0
CENSUS DIVISION 4, EAST NORTH CENTRAL	695	34	4.9	266	38.3	308	44.3	147	21.2	332	47.8	538	77.4	604	86.9	214	30.8	561	80.7	221	31.8
Illinois	162	11	6.8	52	32.1	67	41.4	36	22.2	76	46.9	139	85.8	139	85.8	56	34.6	145	89.5	53	32.7
Indiana	110	2	1.8	34	30.9	45	40.9	22	20.0	40	36.4	88	80.0	90	81.8	29	26.4	88	80.0	22	20.0
Michigan	135	7	5.2	55	40.7	69	51.1	28	20.7	67	49.6	111	82.2	118	87.4	54	40.0	119	88.1	44	32.6
Ohio	142	8	5.6	62	43.7	78	54.9	38	26.8	58	40.8	123	86.6	129	90.8	57	40.1	128	90.1	65	45.8
Wisconsin	146	6	4.1	63	43.2	49	33.6	23	15.8	91	62.3	77	52.7	128	87.7	18	12.3	81	55.5	37	25.3
CENSUS DIVISION 5, EAST SOUTH CENTRAL	308	9	2.9	77	25.0	76	24.7	39	12.7	91	29.5	204	66.2	222	72.1	64	20.8	207	67.2	71	23.1
Alabama	50	2	4.0	15	30.0	13	26.0	5	10.0	17	34.0	35	70.0	40	80.0	14	28.0	40	80.0	17	34.0
Kentucky	80	2	2.5	16	20.0	23	28.8	12	15.0	25	31.3	60	75.0	64	80.0	20	25.0	59	73.8	20	25.0
Mississippi	104	1	1.0	28	26.9	17	16.3	9	8.7	23	22.1	53	51.0	63	60.6	13	12.5	56	53.8	13	12.5
Tennessee	74	4	5.4	18	24.3	23	31.1	13	17.6	26	35.1	56	75.7	60	81.1	17	23.0	52	70.3	21	28.4
CENSUS DIVISION 6, WEST NORTH CENTRAL	614	25	4.1	222	36.2	116	18.9	73	11.9	242	39.4	452	73.6	503	81.9	103	16.8	503	81.9	131	21.3
Iowa	123	3	2.4	49	39.8	20	16.3	12	9.8	57	46.3	108	87.8	115	93.5	16	13.0	118	95.9	18	14.6
Kansas	127	3	2.4	34	26.8	16	12.6	9	7.1	40	31.5	73	57.5	81	63.8	11	8.7	84	66.1	16	12.6
Minnesota	97	4	4.1	38	39.2	22	22.7	16	16.5	45	46.4	75	77.3	88	90.7	19	19.6	81	83.5	16	16.5
Missouri	144	11	7.6	53	36.8	41	28.5	17	11.8	54	37.5	103	71.5	115	79.9	34	23.6	113	78.5	51	35.4
Nebraska	55	1	1.8	22	40.0	7	12.7	11	20.0	20	36.4	42	76.4	47	85.5	12	21.8	47	85.5	13	23.6
North Dakota	24	2	8.3	8	33.3	4	16.7	4	16.7	13	54.2	17	70.8	18	75.0	5	20.8	19	79.2	7	29.2
South Dakota	44	1	2.3	18	40.9	6	13.6	4	9.1	13	29.5	34	77.3	39	88.6	6	13.6	41	93.2	10	22.7
CENSUS DIVISION 7, WEST SOUTH CENTRAL	851	15	1.8	195	22.9	185	21.7	69	8.1	232	27.3	521	61.2	536	63.0	120	14.1	516	60.6	183	21.5
Arkansas	86	1	1.2	20	23.3	9	10.5	3	3.5	29	33.7	60	69.8	57	66.3	11	12.8	62	72.1	15	17.4
Louisiana	87	4	4.6	22	25.3	31	35.6	17	19.5	30	34.5	59	67.8	65	74.7	23	26.4	57	65.5	24	27.6
Oklahoma	113	2	1.8	19	16.8	23	20.4	7	6.2	28	24.8	75	66.4	80	70.8	17	15.0	73	64.6	20	17.7
Texas	565	8	1.4	134	23.7	122	21.6	42	7.4	145	25.7	327	57.9	334	59.1	69	12.2	324	57.3	124	21.9
CENSUS DIVISION 8, MOUNTAIN	324	11	3.4	86	26.5	101	31.2	52	16.0	124	38.3	234	72.2	265	81.8	75	23.1	250	77.2	81	25.0
Arizona	55	1	1.8	14	25.5	18	32.7	10	18.2	17	30.9	37	67.3	44	80.0	22	40.0	40	72.7	25	45.5
Colorado	69	5	7.2	27	39.1	31	44.9	19	27.5	21	30.4	48	69.6	60	87.0	20	29.0	58	84.1	20	29.0
Idaho	33	1	3.0	6	18.2	11	33.3	4	12.1	16	48.5	28	84.8	29	87.9	7	21.2	26	78.8	7	21.2
Montana	53	2	3.8	11	20.8	10	18.9	9	17.0	29	54.7	42	79.2	44	83.0	10	18.9	48	90.6	4	7.5
Nevada	27	0	0.0	1	3.7	6	22.2	0	0.0	9	33.3	15	55.6	16	59.3	5	18.5	15	55.6	4	14.8
New Mexico	29	0	0.0	8	27.6	9	31.0	3	10.3	10	34.5	23	79.3	24	82.8	3	10.3	23	79.3	5	17.2
Utah	38	2	5.3	12	31.6	13	34.2	7	18.4	15	39.5	25	65.8	35	92.1	8	21.1	25	65.8	10	26.3
Wyoming	20	0	0.0	7	35.0	3	15.0	0	0.0	7	35.0	16	80.0	13	65.0	0	0.0	15	75.0	6	30.0
CENSUS DIVISION 9, PACIFIC	377	25	6.6	105	27.9	141	37.4	97	25.7	155	41.1	286	75.9	325	86.2	150	39.8	299	79.3	159	42.2
Alaska	12	1	8.3	4	33.3	4	33.3	2	16.7	4	33.3	9	75.0	10	83.3	3	25.0	10	83.3	2	16.7
California	229	18	7.9	66	28.8	89	38.9	68	29.7	103	45.0	175	76.4	195	85.2	103	45.0	172	75.1	118	51.5
Hawaii	11	1	9.1	3	27.3	7	63.6	4	36.4	5	45.5	10	90.9	10	90.9	5	45.5	9	81.8	3	27.3
Oregon	60	1	1.7	20	33.3	25	41.7	6	10.0	19	31.7	45	75.0	55	91.7	13	21.7	55	91.7	16	26.7
Washington	65	4	6.2	12	18.5	16	24.6	17	26.2	24	36.9	47	72.3	55	84.6	26	40.0	53	81.5	20	30.8

Table 7 (Continued)

These data include only hospital-based facilities and services as reported by responding hospitals in Section C of the 2017 AHA Annual Survey, beginning on page 217. Census divisions represent all U.S. hospitals. Community hospitals are listed separately under United States. No estimates have been made for nonresponding hospitals. Definitions of facilities and services are listed in the Glossary, page 203.

Classification	Hospitals Reporting	HIV/AIDS Services Number	HIV/AIDS Services Percent	Home Health Services Number	Home Health Services Percent	Hospice Number	Hospice Percent	Hospital-Based Outpatient Care Center Services Number	Hospital-Based Outpatient Care Center Services Percent	Immunization Program Number	Immunization Program Percent	Indigent Care Clinic Number	Indigent Care Clinic Percent	Linguistic/Translation Services Number	Linguistic/Translation Services Percent	Meals on Wheels Number	Meals on Wheels Percent	Mobile Health Services Number	Mobile Health Services Percent	Neonatal Intermediate Care Units Number	Neonatal Intermediate Care Units Percent
UNITED STATES	4,280	998	23.3	946	22.1	874	20.4	3,188	74.5	1,890	44.2	766	17.9	2,475	57.8	316	7.4	517	12.1	678	15.8
COMMUNITY HOSPITALS	3,877	931	24.0	905	23.3	827	21.3	3,082	79.5	1,790	46.2	741	19.1	2,343	60.4	307	7.9	485	12.5	677	17.5
CENSUS DIVISION 1, NEW ENGLAND	163	68	41.7	22	13.5	37	22.7	136	83.4	107	65.6	42	25.8	119	73.0	6	3.7	23	14.1	25	15.3
Connecticut	28	15	53.6	2	7.1	10	35.7	23	82.1	19	67.9	13	46.4	22	78.6	0	0.0	4	14.3	3	10.7
Maine	32	12	37.5	5	15.6	3	9.4	26	81.3	22	68.8	6	18.8	18	56.3	1	3.1	4	12.5	4	12.5
Massachusetts	56	23	41.1	9	16.1	11	19.6	48	85.7	36	64.3	13	23.2	45	80.4	3	5.4	9	16.1	14	25.0
New Hampshire	26	11	42.3	5	19.2	6	23.1	22	84.6	17	65.4	4	15.4	19	73.1	1	3.8	5	19.2	2	7.7
Rhode Island	9	5	55.6	1	11.1	3	33.3	8	88.9	6	66.7	3	33.3	8	88.9	0	0.0	0	0.0	1	11.1
Vermont	12	2	16.7	0	0.0	4	33.3	9	75.0	7	58.3	3	25.0	7	58.3	1	8.3	1	8.3	1	8.3
CENSUS DIVISION 2, MIDDLE ATLANTIC	373	172	46.1	84	22.5	117	31.4	310	83.1	217	58.2	150	40.2	259	69.4	27	7.2	81	21.7	114	30.6
New Jersey	73	44	60.3	15	20.5	28	38.4	60	82.2	43	58.9	41	56.2	54	74.0	11	15.1	25	34.2	38	52.1
New York	150	74	49.3	33	22.0	44	29.3	130	86.7	97	64.7	73	48.7	121	80.7	10	6.7	37	24.7	51	34.0
Pennsylvania	150	54	36.0	36	24.0	45	30.0	120	80.0	77	51.3	36	24.0	84	56.0	6	4.0	19	12.7	25	16.7
CENSUS DIVISION 3, SOUTH ATLANTIC	575	186	32.3	117	20.3	106	18.4	440	76.5	210	36.5	119	20.7	357	62.1	20	3.5	96	16.7	127	22.1
Delaware	10	3	33.3	1	10.0	0	0.0	5	55.6	4	44.4	2	22.2	4	44.4	0	0.0	0	0.0	2	22.2
District of Columbia	9	6	60.0	3	33.3	3	30.0	9	90.0	7	70.0	4	40.0	9	90.0	0	0.0	5	50.0	3	50.0
Florida	117	39	33.3	29	24.8	14	12.0	90	76.9	38	32.5	27	23.1	73	62.4	1	0.9	21	17.9	21	17.9
Georgia	103	30	29.1	14	13.6	18	17.5	69	67.0	26	25.2	17	16.5	66	64.1	1	1.0	12	11.7	32	31.1
Maryland	44	27	61.4	3	6.8	13	29.5	41	93.2	25	56.8	23	52.3	37	84.1	4	9.1	11	25.0	5	11.4
North Carolina	89	22	24.7	17	19.1	9	10.1	75	84.3	28	31.5	16	18.0	54	60.7	2	2.2	14	15.7	27	30.3
South Carolina	75	22	29.3	14	18.7	12	16.0	49	65.3	21	28.0	9	12.0	38	50.7	5	6.7	10	13.3	10	13.3
Virginia	76	28	36.8	24	31.6	35	46.1	61	80.3	37	48.7	16	21.1	51	67.1	4	5.3	19	25.0	11	14.5
West Virginia	52	9	17.3	12	23.1	2	3.8	41	78.8	24	46.2	5	9.6	25	48.1	3	5.8	4	7.7	2	3.8
CENSUS DIVISION 4, EAST NORTH CENTRAL	695	170	24.5	177	25.5	169	24.3	564	81.2	337	48.5	151	21.7	396	57.0	93	13.4	78	11.2	90	12.9
Illinois	162	48	29.6	39	24.1	42	25.9	133	82.1	74	45.7	34	21.0	90	55.6	23	14.2	16	9.8	34	21.0
Indiana	110	17	15.5	36	32.7	30	27.3	84	76.4	51	46.4	17	15.5	58	52.7	25	22.7	10	9.1	20	18.2
Michigan	135	49	36.3	37	27.4	39	28.9	114	84.4	90	66.7	42	31.1	85	63.0	8	5.9	20	14.8	13	9.6
Ohio	142	48	33.8	42	29.6	43	30.3	121	85.2	61	43.0	39	27.5	102	71.8	11	7.7	22	15.5	23	16.2
Wisconsin	146	8	5.5	23	15.8	15	10.3	112	76.7	61	41.8	19	13.0	61	41.8	26	17.8	10	6.8	0	0.0
CENSUS DIVISION 5, EAST SOUTH CENTRAL	308	48	15.6	47	15.3	42	13.6	189	61.4	90	29.2	28	9.1	145	47.1	6	1.9	27	8.8	52	16.9
Alabama	50	9	18.0	5	10.0	6	12.0	33	66.0	11	22.0	4	8.0	27	54.0	0	0.0	5	10.0	6	12.0
Kentucky	80	12	15.0	21	26.3	10	12.5	55	68.8	19	23.8	9	11.3	38	47.5	4	5.0	7	8.8	12	15.0
Mississippi	104	11	10.6	8	7.7	11	10.6	57	54.8	41	39.4	9	8.7	36	34.6	1	1.0	8	7.7	26	25.0
Tennessee	74	16	21.6	13	17.6	15	20.3	44	59.5	19	25.7	6	8.1	44	59.5	1	1.4	7	9.5	8	10.8
CENSUS DIVISION 6, WEST NORTH CENTRAL	614	97	15.8	216	35.2	159	25.9	490	79.8	304	49.5	59	9.6	316	51.5	96	15.6	58	9.4	75	12.2
Iowa	123	22	17.9	50	40.7	48	39.0	109	88.6	70	56.9	14	11.4	70	56.9	26	21.1	12	9.8	12	9.8
Kansas	127	11	8.7	31	24.4	14	11.0	97	76.4	41	32.3	7	5.5	54	42.5	27	21.3	6	4.7	13	10.2
Minnesota	97	16	16.5	37	38.1	37	38.1	85	87.6	59	60.8	6	6.2	49	50.5	13	13.4	11	11.3	8	8.2
Missouri	144	33	22.9	47	32.6	27	18.8	108	75.0	66	45.8	20	13.9	80	55.6	14	9.7	14	9.7	32	22.2
Nebraska	55	7	12.7	24	43.6	18	32.7	43	78.2	26	47.3	4	7.3	35	63.6	6	10.9	4	7.3	3	5.5
North Dakota	24	4	16.7	6	25.0	5	20.8	16	66.7	17	70.8	3	12.5	11	45.8	2	8.3	2	8.3	5	20.8
South Dakota	44	4	9.1	21	47.7	10	22.7	32	72.7	25	56.8	5	11.4	17	38.6	8	18.2	8	18.2	2	4.5
CENSUS DIVISION 7, WEST SOUTH CENTRAL	851	87	10.2	120	14.1	78	9.2	532	62.5	268	31.5	90	10.6	387	45.5	33	3.9	61	7.2	88	10.3
Arkansas	86	8	9.3	30	34.9	8	9.3	56	65.1	22	25.6	3	3.5	41	47.7	3	3.5	10	11.6	7	8.1
Louisiana	87	20	23.0	12	13.8	7	8.0	54	62.1	33	37.9	17	19.5	41	47.1	5	5.8	7	8.0	13	14.9
Oklahoma	113	7	6.2	17	15.0	9	8.0	77	68.1	35	31.0	9	8.0	61	54.0	11	9.7	6	5.3	10	8.8
Texas	565	52	9.2	61	10.8	51	9.0	345	61.1	178	31.5	61	10.8	244	43.2	14	2.5	38	6.7	58	10.3
CENSUS DIVISION 8, MOUNTAIN	324	63	19.4	62	19.1	64	19.8	231	71.3	151	46.6	57	17.6	201	62.0	20	6.2	43	13.3	32	9.9
Arizona	55	18	32.7	10	18.2	10	18.2	32	58.2	23	41.8	11	20.0	34	61.8	2	3.6	10	18.2	6	10.9
Colorado	69	17	24.6	14	20.3	9	13.0	57	82.6	30	43.5	14	20.3	48	69.6	6	8.7	7	10.1	7	10.1
Idaho	33	3	9.1	8	24.2	9	27.3	26	78.8	19	57.6	8	24.2	24	72.7	3	9.1	7	21.2	0	0.0
Montana	53	7	13.2	14	26.4	15	28.3	41	77.4	32	60.4	9	17.0	19	35.8	7	13.2	10	18.9	1	1.9
Nevada	27	7	25.9	6	22.2	5	18.5	14	51.9	10	37.0	4	14.8	15	55.6	0	0.0	1	3.7	4	14.8
New Mexico	29	5	17.2	7	24.1	6	20.7	23	79.3	18	62.1	5	17.2	19	65.5	2	6.9	1	3.4	4	13.8
Utah	38	3	7.9	4	10.5	5	13.2	25	65.8	9	23.7	4	10.5	30	78.9	0	0.0	6	15.8	7	18.4
Wyoming	20	3	15.0	3	15.0	5	25.0	13	65.0	10	50.0	2	10.0	12	60.0	0	0.0	1	5.0	2	10.0
CENSUS DIVISION 9, PACIFIC	377	107	28.4	101	26.8	102	27.1	296	78.5	206	54.6	70	18.6	295	78.2	15	4.0	50	13.3	75	19.9
Alaska	12	1	8.3	3	25.0	2	16.7	5	41.7	8	66.7	3	25.0	8	66.7	1	8.3	1	8.3	1	8.3
California	229	75	32.8	62	27.1	65	28.4	179	78.2	131	57.2	50	21.8	193	84.3	12	5.2	37	16.2	43	18.8
Hawaii	11	2	18.2	3	27.3	4	36.4	9	81.8	5	45.5	1	9.1	9	81.8	1	9.1	1	9.1	2	18.8
Oregon	60	13	21.7	22	36.7	20	33.3	54	90.0	29	48.3	9	15.0	41	68.3	0	0.0	7	11.7	6	10.0
Washington	65	16	24.6	11	16.9	11	16.9	49	75.4	33	50.8	7	10.8	44	67.7	1	1.5	4	6.2	23	35.4

Table 7 (Continued)

These data include only hospital-based facilities and services as reported by responding hospitals in Section C of the 2017 AHA Annual Survey, beginning on page 217. Census divisions represent all U.S. hospitals. Community hospitals are listed separately under United States. No estimates have been made for nonresponding hospitals. Definitions of facilities and services are listed in the Glossary, page 203.

CLASSIFICATION	HOSPITALS REPORTING	NEUROLOGICAL SERVICES Number	Percent	NUTRITION PROGRAMS CENTER Number	Percent	OBSTETRICS INPATIENT CARE UNITS Number	Percent	OCCUPATIONAL HEALTH SERVICES Number	Percent	ONCOLOGY SERVICES Number	Percent	ORTHOPEDIC SERVICES Number	Percent	OTHER SPECIAL CARE UNITS Number	Percent	OUTPATIENT SURGERY Number	Percent	PAIN MANAGEMENT PROGRAM Number	Percent	PALLIATIVE CARE PROGRAM Number	Percent
UNITED STATES	4,280	2,123	49.6	3,225	75.6	2,330	54.4	2,810	65.7	2,224	52.0	2,955	69.0	725	16.9	3,431	80.2	2,272	53.1	1,695	39.6
COMMUNITY HOSPITALS	3,877	2,046	52.8	3,052	78.7	2,319	59.8	2,689	69.4	2,173	56.0	2,889	74.5	705	18.2	3,366	86.9	2,192	56.5	1,632	42.1
CENSUS DIVISION 1, NEW ENGLAND	163	104	63.8	149	91.4	106	65.0	132	81.0	111	68.1	133	81.6	29	17.8	135	82.8	119	73.0	91	55.8
Connecticut	28	23	82.1	27	96.4	21	75.0	20	71.4	20	71.4	21	75.0	7	25.0	21	75.0	22	78.6	22	78.6
Maine	32	13	40.6	30	93.8	23	71.9	24	75.0	22	68.8	28	87.5	10	31.3	28	87.5	20	62.5	16	50.0
Massachusetts	56	38	67.9	50	89.3	34	60.7	50	89.3	36	64.3	45	80.4	6	10.7	45	80.4	45	80.4	25	44.6
New Hampshire	26	16	61.5	25	96.2	17	65.4	24	92.3	19	73.1	24	92.3	5	19.2	24	92.3	17	65.4	17	65.4
Rhode Island	9	7	77.8	8	88.9	4	44.4	7	77.8	7	77.8	7	77.8	1	11.1	8	88.9	6	66.7	5	55.6
Vermont	12	7	58.3	9	75.0	7	58.3	7	58.3	7	58.3	8	66.7	0	0.0	9	75.0	9	75.0	6	50.0
CENSUS DIVISION 2, MIDDLE ATLANTIC	373	271	72.7	328	87.9	221	59.2	296	79.4	268	71.8	313	83.9	87	23.3	323	86.6	260	69.7	241	64.6
New Jersey	73	56	76.7	60	82.2	43	58.9	50	68.5	56	76.7	58	79.5	15	20.5	57	78.1	55	75.3	46	63.0
New York	150	110	73.3	134	89.3	98	65.3	128	85.3	108	72.0	128	85.3	30	20.0	134	89.3	104	69.3	107	71.3
Pennsylvania	150	105	70.0	134	89.3	80	53.3	118	78.7	104	69.3	127	84.7	42	28.0	132	88.0	101	67.3	88	58.7
CENSUS DIVISION 3, SOUTH ATLANTIC	575	349	60.7	456	79.3	324	56.3	411	71.5	339	59.0	437	76.0	115	20.0	470	81.7	308	53.6	258	44.9
Delaware	9	8	66.7	6	66.7	4	44.4	5	55.6	8	55.6	6	66.7	2	22.2	5	55.6	4	44.4	5	55.6
District of Columbia	10	8	80.0	10	100.0	6	60.0	8	80.0	8	80.0	8	80.0	5	50.0	7	70.0	8	80.0	7	70.0
Florida	117	94	80.3	96	82.1	64	54.7	77	65.8	81	69.2	98	83.8	34	29.1	102	87.2	72	61.5	62	53.0
Georgia	103	51	49.5	75	72.8	55	53.4	67	65.0	50	48.5	68	66.0	15	14.6	83	80.6	46	44.7	38	36.9
Maryland	44	37	84.1	41	93.2	29	65.9	42	95.5	38	86.4	40	90.9	8	18.2	40	90.9	37	84.1	36	81.8
North Carolina	69	50	56.2	70	78.7	60	67.4	71	79.8	59	66.3	74	83.1	18	20.2	81	91.0	53	59.6	36	36.0
South Carolina	75	31	41.3	50	66.7	42	56.0	49	65.3	29	38.7	54	72.0	18	24.0	52	69.3	25	33.3	22	29.3
Virginia	76	49	64.5	68	89.5	40	52.6	65	85.5	48	63.2	59	77.6	13	17.1	61	80.3	44	57.9	39	51.3
West Virginia	52	23	44.2	40	76.9	24	46.2	27	51.9	21	40.4	30	57.7	2	3.8	39	75.0	19	36.5	17	32.7
CENSUS DIVISION 4, EAST NORTH CENTRAL	695	363	52.2	572	82.3	426	61.3	497	71.5	446	64.2	519	74.7	189	27.2	611	87.9	456	65.6	291	41.9
Illinois	162	94	58.0	120	74.1	98	60.5	107	66.0	105	64.8	123	75.9	13	8.0	144	88.9	112	69.1	75	46.3
Indiana	110	54	49.1	93	84.5	70	63.6	81	73.6	64	58.2	88	80.0	16	14.5	95	86.4	58	52.7	36	32.7
Michigan	135	77	57.0	115	85.2	77	57.0	109	80.7	90	66.7	112	83.0	29	21.5	118	87.4	84	62.2	56	41.5
Ohio	142	95	66.9	120	84.5	90	63.4	117	82.4	104	73.2	125	88.0	26	18.3	129	90.8	108	76.1	72	50.7
Wisconsin	146	43	29.5	124	84.9	91	62.3	83	56.8	83	56.8	71	48.6	105	71.9	125	85.6	94	64.4	52	35.6
CENSUS DIVISION 5, EAST SOUTH CENTRAL	308	126	40.9	175	56.8	139	45.1	146	47.4	108	35.1	158	51.3	47	15.3	218	70.8	127	41.2	84	27.3
Alabama	50	29	58.0	30	60.0	29	58.0	26	52.0	23	46.0	32	64.0	9	18.0	39	78.0	27	54.0	19	38.0
Kentucky	80	41	51.3	56	70.0	36	45.0	42	52.5	44	55.0	54	67.5	8	8.8	62	77.5	46	57.5	26	32.5
Mississippi	104	24	23.1	34	32.7	39	37.5	33	31.7	10	9.6	28	26.9	14	13.5	64	61.5	31	29.8	17	16.3
Tennessee	74	32	43.2	55	74.3	35	47.3	45	60.8	31	41.9	44	59.5	17	23.0	53	71.6	23	31.1	22	29.7
CENSUS DIVISION 6, WEST NORTH CENTRAL	614	208	33.9	460	74.9	318	51.8	414	67.4	293	47.7	387	63.0	67	10.9	533	86.8	316	51.5	200	32.6
Iowa	123	36	29.3	112	91.1	71	57.7	87	70.7	68	55.3	86	69.9	9	7.3	117	95.1	72	58.5	38	30.9
Kansas	127	27	21.3	73	57.5	59	46.5	75	59.1	38	29.9	44	46.5	10	7.9	101	79.5	58	45.7	28	22.0
Minnesota	97	36	37.1	83	85.6	67	69.1	76	78.4	53	54.6	73	75.3	12	12.4	94	96.9	54	55.7	41	42.3
Missouri	144	77	53.5	109	75.7	63	43.8	98	68.1	79	54.9	100	69.4	27	18.8	110	76.4	72	50.0	52	36.1
Nebraska	55	18	32.7	40	72.7	33	60.0	36	65.5	34	61.8	44	80.0	5	9.1	52	94.5	35	63.6	21	38.2
North Dakota	24	6	25.0	17	70.8	10	41.7	13	54.2	9	37.5	9	37.5	2	8.3	20	83.3	11	45.8	8	33.3
South Dakota	44	8	18.2	26	59.1	15	34.1	29	65.9	12	27.3	16	36.4	2	4.5	39	88.6	14	31.8	12	27.3
CENSUS DIVISION 7, WEST SOUTH CENTRAL	851	326	38.3	531	62.4	331	38.9	418	49.1	253	29.7	461	54.2	95	11.2	543	63.8	311	36.5	173	20.3
Arkansas	86	27	31.4	45	52.3	35	40.7	39	45.3	26	30.2	44	51.2	6	7.0	59	68.6	23	26.7	15	17.4
Louisiana	87	42	48.3	61	70.1	39	44.8	49	56.3	38	43.7	48	55.2	11	12.6	61	70.1	31	35.6	26	29.9
Oklahoma	113	33	29.2	57	50.4	46	40.7	54	47.8	25	22.1	63	55.8	17	15.0	78	69.0	45	39.8	20	17.7
Texas	565	224	39.6	368	65.1	211	37.3	276	48.8	164	29.0	306	54.2	61	10.8	345	61.1	212	37.5	112	19.8
CENSUS DIVISION 8, MOUNTAIN	324	128	39.5	240	74.1	200	61.7	217	67.0	149	46.0	218	67.3	35	10.8	254	78.4	151	46.6	122	37.7
Arizona	55	28	50.9	43	78.2	39	54.5	39	70.9	30	54.5	38	69.1	7	12.7	42	76.4	25	45.5	25	45.5
Colorado	69	38	55.1	52	75.4	48	69.6	56	81.2	43	62.3	53	76.8	10	14.5	59	85.5	40	58.0	33	47.8
Idaho	33	10	30.3	25	75.8	22	66.7	24	72.7	13	39.4	28	84.8	2	6.1	31	93.9	16	48.5	10	30.3
Montana	53	11	20.8	36	67.9	26	49.1	26	49.1	18	34.0	25	47.2	1	1.9	33	62.3	20	37.7	21	39.6
Nevada	27	11	40.7	17	63.0	10	37.0	14	51.9	11	40.7	16	59.3	6	22.2	18	66.7	10	37.0	8	29.6
New Mexico	27	11	41.4	20	69.0	21	72.4	18	62.1	12	41.4	18	65.5	4	13.8	25	86.2	13	44.8	7	24.1
Utah	38	10	26.3	34	89.5	27	71.1	30	78.9	14	36.8	27	71.1	5	13.2	32	84.2	17	44.7	13	34.2
Wyoming	20	8	40.0	13	65.0	16	80.0	10	50.0	8	40.0	12	60.0	0	0.0	14	70.0	10	50.0	5	25.0
CENSUS DIVISION 9, PACIFIC	377	248	65.8	324	85.9	265	70.3	279	74.0	257	68.2	329	87.3	61	16.2	344	91.2	224	59.4	235	62.3
Alaska	12	3	25.0	10	83.3	7	58.3	10	83.3	3	25.0	6	50.0	0	0.0	9	75.0	6	50.0	5	41.7
California	229	171	74.7	191	83.4	160	69.9	178	77.7	168	73.4	206	90.0	30	13.1	210	91.7	142	62.0	155	67.7
Hawaii	11	8	72.7	10	90.9	6	54.5	9	81.8	9	81.8	10	90.9	4	36.4	9	81.8	5	45.5	8	72.7
Oregon	60	25	41.7	55	91.7	49	81.7	40	66.7	38	63.3	52	86.7	5	8.3	58	96.7	32	53.3	29	48.3
Washington	65	41	63.1	58	89.2	43	66.2	42	64.6	39	60.0	55	84.6	22	33.8	58	89.2	39	60.0	38	58.5

Table 7 (Continued)

These data include only hospital-based facilities and services as reported by responding hospitals in Section C of the 2017 AHA Annual Survey, beginning on page 217. Census divisions represent all U.S. hospitals. Community hospitals are listed separately under United States. No estimates have been made for nonresponding hospitals. Definitions of facilities and services are listed in the Glossary, page 203.

CLASSIFICATION	HOSPITALS REPORTING	PALLIATIVE CARE INPATIENT UNIT Number	Percent	PATIENT CONTROLLED ANALGESIA (PCA) Number	Percent	PATIENT EDUCATION CENTER Number	Percent	PATIENT REPRESENTATIVE SERVICES Number	Percent	PHYSICAL REHABILITATION INPATIENT CARE UNITS Number	Percent	PRIMARY CARE DEPARTMENT Number	Percent	PSYCHIATRIC INPATIENT CARE UNITS Number	Percent	PSYCHIATRIC INTENSIVE OUTPATIENT SERVICES Number	Percent	RETIREMENT HOUSING Number	Percent	ROBOTIC SURGERY Number	Percent
UNITED STATES	4,280	432	10.1	3,029	70.8	2,372	55.4	3,035	70.9	1,252	29.3	1,856	43.4	1,451	33.9	590	13.8	115	2.7	1,386	32.4
COMMUNITY HOSPITALS	3,877	387	10.0	2,966	76.5	2,241	57.8	2,857	73.7	1,218	31.4	1,772	45.7	1,113	28.7	436	11.2	113	2.9	1,365	35.2
CENSUS DIVISION 1, NEW ENGLAND	163	26	16.0	129	79.1	108	66.3	130	79.8	39	23.9	105	64.4	84	51.5	42	25.8	4	2.5	60	36.8
Connecticut	28	6	21.4	22	78.6	19	67.9	23	82.1	9	32.1	20	71.4	23	82.1	17	60.7	1	3.6	19	67.9
Maine	32	5	15.6	24	75.0	16	50.0	27	84.4	10	31.3	27	84.4	10	31.3	5	15.6	2	6.3	4	12.5
Massachusetts	56	7	12.5	42	75.0	43	76.8	44	78.6	8	14.3	26	46.4	31	55.4	13	23.2	0	0.0	20	35.7
New Hampshire	26	7	26.9	23	88.5	17	65.4	20	76.9	8	30.8	20	76.9	9	34.6	3	11.5	0	0.0	10	38.5
Rhode Island	9	0	0.0	8	88.9	7	77.8	8	88.9	2	22.2	6	66.7	4	44.4	2	22.2	0	0.0	6	66.7
Vermont	12	1	8.3	10	83.3	6	50.0	8	66.7	2	16.7	6	50.0	7	58.3	2	16.7	1	8.3	1	8.3
CENSUS DIVISION 2, MIDDLE ATLANTIC	373	56	15.0	307	82.3	246	66.0	315	84.5	134	35.9	223	59.8	205	55.0	65	17.4	2	0.5	174	46.6
New Jersey	73	9	12.3	55	75.3	48	65.8	61	83.6	19	26.0	47	64.4	41	56.2	23	31.5	0	0.0	39	53.4
New York	150	34	22.7	125	83.3	96	64.0	134	89.3	56	37.3	112	74.7	87	58.0	28	18.7	2	1.3	71	47.3
Pennsylvania	150	13	8.7	127	84.7	102	68.0	120	80.0	59	39.3	64	42.7	77	51.3	14	9.3	0	0.0	64	42.7
CENSUS DIVISION 3, SOUTH ATLANTIC	575	52	9.0	440	76.5	364	63.3	431	75.0	183	31.8	233	40.5	219	38.1	81	14.1	7	1.2	233	40.5
Delaware	9	0	0.0	5	55.6	5	55.6	6	66.7	4	44.4	3	33.3	4	44.4	0	0.0	0	0.0	3	33.3
District of Columbia	10	2	20.0	7	70.0	9	90.0	8	80.0	5	50.0	6	60.0	8	80.0	2	20.0	1	10.0	5	50.0
Florida	117	11	9.4	99	84.6	73	62.4	92	78.6	36	30.8	43	36.8	41	35.0	14	12.0	4	3.4	76	65.0
Georgia	103	9	8.7	72	69.9	57	55.3	68	66.0	22	21.4	31	30.1	29	28.2	12	11.7	0	0.0	35	34.0
Maryland	44	8	18.2	39	88.6	38	86.4	44	100.0	9	20.5	22	50.0	29	65.9	19	43.2	0	0.0	22	50.0
North Carolina	89	6	6.7	74	83.1	55	61.8	69	77.5	23	25.8	42	47.2	38	42.7	12	13.5	0	0.0	35	39.3
South Carolina	75	3	4.0	52	69.3	44	58.7	46	61.3	48	64.0	22	29.3	24	32.0	8	10.7	1	1.3	18	24.0
Virginia	76	9	11.8	61	80.3	50	65.8	63	82.9	24	31.6	35	46.1	31	40.8	12	15.8	1	1.3	25	32.9
West Virginia	52	4	7.7	31	59.6	33	63.5	35	67.3	12	23.1	29	55.8	15	28.8	2	3.8	0	0.0	14	26.9
CENSUS DIVISION 4, EAST NORTH CENTRAL	695	84	12.1	519	74.7	479	68.9	554	79.7	247	35.5	352	50.6	256	36.8	109	15.7	16	2.3	237	34.1
Illinois	162	10	6.2	127	78.4	99	61.1	134	82.7	47	29.0	85	52.5	74	45.7	38	23.5	8	4.9	64	39.5
Indiana	110	14	12.7	93	84.5	68	61.8	81	73.6	39	35.5	47	42.7	32	29.1	16	14.5	3	2.7	30	27.3
Michigan	135	14	10.4	105	77.8	85	63.0	112	83.0	49	36.3	97	71.9	52	38.5	11	8.1	2	1.5	51	37.8
Ohio	142	29	20.4	118	83.1	99	69.7	117	82.4	42	29.6	73	51.4	60	42.3	28	19.7	3	2.1	61	43.0
Wisconsin	146	17	11.6	76	52.1	128	87.7	110	75.3	70	47.9	50	34.2	38	26.0	16	11.0	0	0.0	31	21.2
CENSUS DIVISION 5, EAST SOUTH CENTRAL	308	23	7.5	175	56.8	146	47.4	202	65.6	88	28.6	84	27.3	122	39.6	39	12.7	4	1.3	87	28.2
Alabama	50	5	10.0	33	66.0	31	62.0	34	68.0	17	34.0	11	22.0	20	40.0	2	4.0	2	4.0	22	44.0
Kentucky	80	7	8.8	58	72.5	43	53.8	59	73.8	16	20.0	30	37.5	38	47.5	12	15.0	0	0.0	22	27.5
Mississippi	104	5	4.8	35	33.7	41	39.4	60	57.7	40	38.5	22	21.2	41	39.4	14	13.5	0	0.0	20	19.2
Tennessee	74	6	8.1	49	66.2	31	41.9	49	66.2	15	20.3	21	28.4	23	31.1	11	14.9	2	2.7	23	31.1
CENSUS DIVISION 6, WEST NORTH CENTRAL	614	58	9.4	421	68.6	308	50.2	383	62.4	179	29.2	307	50.0	168	27.4	54	8.8	61	9.9	120	19.5
Iowa	123	5	4.1	96	78.0	64	52.0	74	60.2	28	22.8	75	61.0	22	17.9	13	10.6	15	12.2	26	21.1
Kansas	127	10	7.9	76	59.8	56	44.1	74	58.3	27	21.3	48	37.8	38	29.9	5	3.9	12	9.4	20	15.7
Minnesota	97	10	10.3	76	78.4	55	56.7	68	70.1	16	16.5	60	61.9	29	29.9	10	10.3	15	15.5	22	22.7
Missouri	144	15	10.4	104	72.2	84	58.3	104	72.2	89	61.8	55	38.2	61	42.4	18	12.5	2	1.4	34	23.6
Nebraska	55	4	7.3	35	63.6	21	38.2	30	54.5	11	20.0	27	49.1	7	12.7	2	3.6	3	5.5	9	16.4
North Dakota	24	7	29.2	12	50.0	12	50.0	15	62.5	4	16.7	16	66.7	7	29.2	3	12.5	5	20.8	5	20.8
South Dakota	44	7	15.9	22	50.0	16	36.4	18	40.9	4	9.1	26	59.1	4	9.1	3	6.8	9	20.5	4	9.1
CENSUS DIVISION 7, WEST SOUTH CENTRAL	851	37	4.3	497	58.4	342	40.2	497	58.4	217	25.5	207	24.3	219	25.7	107	12.6	10	1.2	221	26.0
Arkansas	86	3	3.5	49	57.0	30	34.9	52	60.5	22	25.6	23	26.7	31	36.0	12	14.0	1	1.2	14	16.3
Louisiana	87	6	6.9	58	66.7	45	51.7	58	66.7	37	42.5	35	40.2	38	43.7	18	20.7	4	4.6	29	33.3
Oklahoma	113	7	6.2	64	56.6	36	31.9	67	59.3	26	23.0	28	24.8	36	31.9	6	5.3	3	2.7	25	22.1
Texas	565	21	3.7	326	57.7	231	40.9	320	56.6	132	23.4	121	21.4	114	20.2	71	12.6	2	0.4	153	27.1
CENSUS DIVISION 8, MOUNTAIN	324	44	13.6	216	66.7	150	46.3	227	70.1	79	24.4	177	54.6	81	25.0	37	11.4	8	2.5	100	30.9
Arizona	55	7	12.7	36	65.5	26	47.3	39	70.9	13	23.6	15	27.3	20	36.4	9	16.4	0	0.0	26	47.3
Colorado	69	9	13.0	51	73.9	34	49.3	55	79.7	23	33.3	43	62.3	13	18.8	9	13.0	1	1.4	29	42.0
Idaho	33	6	18.2	24	72.7	19	57.6	25	75.8	10	30.3	21	63.6	7	21.2	1	3.0	0	0.0	10	30.3
Montana	53	10	18.9	27	50.9	19	35.8	31	58.5	8	15.1	35	66.0	6	11.3	2	3.8	4	7.5	10	18.9
Nevada	27	3	11.1	18	66.7	12	44.4	16	59.3	4	14.8	7	25.9	11	40.7	5	18.5	0	0.0	7	25.9
New Mexico	29	4	13.8	21	72.4	9	31.0	18	62.1	9	31.0	18	62.1	7	24.1	2	6.9	0	0.0	5	17.2
Utah	38	3	7.9	28	73.7	24	63.2	32	84.2	10	26.3	26	68.4	12	31.6	7	18.4	1	2.6	7	18.4
Wyoming	20	2	10.0	11	55.0	7	35.0	11	55.0	2	10.0	12	60.0	5	25.0	2	10.0	2	10.0	6	30.0
CENSUS DIVISION 9, PACIFIC	377	52	13.8	325	86.2	229	60.7	296	78.5	86	22.8	168	44.6	97	25.7	56	14.9	3	0.8	154	40.8
Alaska	12	1	8.3	10	83.3	9	75.0	5	41.7	1	8.3	7	58.3	2	16.7	5	41.7	0	0.0	1	8.3
California	229	32	14.0	195	85.2	140	61.1	184	80.3	58	25.3	81	35.4	59	25.8	38	16.6	0	0.0	102	44.5
Hawaii	11	1	9.1	9	81.8	9	81.8	9	81.8	1	9.1	5	45.5	3	27.3	0	0.0	0	0.0	5	45.5
Oregon	60	6	10.0	56	93.3	36	60.0	48	80.0	12	20.0	45	75.0	14	23.3	6	10.0	2	3.3	18	30.0
Washington	65	12	18.5	55	84.6	35	53.8	50	76.9	14	21.5	30	46.2	19	29.2	7	10.8	1	1.5	28	43.1

Table 7 (Continued)

These data include only hospital-based facilities and services as reported by responding hospitals in Section C of the 2017 AHA Annual Survey, beginning on page 217. Census divisions represent all U.S. hospitals. Community hospitals are listed separately under United States. No estimates have been made for nonresponding hospitals. Definitions of facilities and services are listed in the Glossary, page 203.

Classification	Hospitals Reporting	RHC No.	RHC %	Sleep Center No.	Sleep Center %	Social Work No.	Social Work %	Sports Med No.	Sports Med %	Support Groups No.	Support Groups %	Swing Bed No.	Swing Bed %	Teen Outreach No.	Teen Outreach %	Telehealth No.	Telehealth %	Tobacco No.	Tobacco %	Transport No.	Transport %
UNITED STATES	4,280	1,051	24.6	2,006	46.9	3,649	85.3	1,880	43.9	2,731	63.8	1,299	30.4	537	12.5	2,019	47.2	2,264	52.9	963	22.5
COMMUNITY HOSPITALS	3,877	1,008	26.0	1,962	50.6	3,342	86.2	1,859	47.9	2,554	65.9	1,270	32.8	511	13.2	1,850	47.7	2,097	54.1	838	21.6
CENSUS DIVISION 1, NEW ENGLAND	163	25	15.3	90	55.2	156	95.7	95	58.3	139	85.3	43	26.4	47	28.8	75	46.0	115	70.6	53	32.5
Connecticut	28	1	3.6	19	67.9	28	100.0	18	64.3	27	96.4	1	3.6	12	42.9	20	71.4	20	71.4	5	17.9
Maine	32	13	40.6	16	50.0	30	93.8	15	46.9	29	90.6	14	43.8	5	15.6	14	43.8	23	71.9	10	31.3
Massachusetts	56	2	3.6	30	53.6	52	92.9	35	62.5	48	85.7	6	10.7	19	33.9	23	41.1	36	64.3	19	33.9
New Hampshire	26	6	23.1	16	61.5	26	100.0	19	73.1	20	76.9	15	57.7	8	30.8	7	26.9	17	65.4	8	30.8
Rhode Island	9	0	0.0	4	44.4	9	100.0	3	33.3	8	88.9	1	11.1	2	22.2	3	33.3	7	77.8	6	66.7
Vermont	12	3	25.0	5	41.7	11	91.7	5	41.7	7	58.3	6	50.0	1	8.3	8	66.7	12	100.0	5	41.7
CENSUS DIVISION 2, MIDDLE ATLANTIC	373	35	9.4	215	57.6	358	96.0	203	54.4	309	82.8	53	14.2	94	25.2	206	55.2	260	69.7	123	33.0
New Jersey	73	1	1.4	44	60.3	68	93.2	42	57.5	61	83.6	5	6.8	30	41.1	41	56.2	43	58.9	41	56.2
New York	150	21	14.0	79	52.7	143	95.3	85	56.7	128	85.3	27	18.0	37	24.7	80	53.3	114	76.0	50	33.3
Pennsylvania	150	13	8.7	92	61.3	147	98.0	76	50.7	120	80.0	21	14.0	27	18.0	85	56.7	103	68.7	32	21.3
CENSUS DIVISION 3, SOUTH ATLANTIC	575	90	15.7	295	51.3	497	86.4	261	45.4	401	69.7	108	18.8	73	12.7	263	45.7	343	59.7	135	23.5
Delaware	10	1	11.1	6	60.0	7	77.8	6	60.0	5	55.6	0	0.0	3	33.3	5	55.6	3	33.3	3	33.3
District of Columbia	10	0	0.0	6	60.0	10	100.0	6	60.0	9	90.0	0	0.0	4	40.0	1	10.0	6	60.0	2	20.0
Florida	117	14	12.0	54	46.2	102	87.2	64	54.7	89	76.1	9	7.7	15	12.8	65	55.6	65	55.6	20	17.1
Georgia	103	17	16.5	55	53.4	82	79.6	38	36.9	58	56.3	29	28.2	10	9.7	42	40.8	56	54.4	20	19.4
Maryland	44	1	2.3	25	56.8	43	97.7	23	52.3	40	90.9	2	4.5	16	36.4	18	40.9	37	84.1	12	27.0
North Carolina	89	17	19.1	50	56.2	82	92.1	46	51.7	63	70.8	20	22.5	7	7.9	59	66.3	58	65.2	12	13.3
South Carolina	75	16	21.3	30	40.0	59	78.7	24	32.0	45	60.0	12	16.0	7	9.3	11	14.7	36	48.0	16	21.1
Virginia	76	9	11.8	44	57.9	68	89.5	41	53.9	58	76.3	15	19.7	9	11.8	44	57.9	51	67.1	10	13.2
West Virginia	52	15	28.8	27	51.9	44	84.6	16	30.8	34	65.4	21	40.4	2	3.8	18	34.6	30	57.7	13	25.0
CENSUS DIVISION 4, EAST NORTH CENTRAL	695	154	22.2	424	61.0	634	91.2	405	58.3	513	73.8	190	27.3	109	15.7	439	63.2	447	64.3	169	24.3
Illinois	162	45	27.8	108	66.7	145	89.5	94	58.0	130	80.2	52	32.1	26	16.0	94	58.0	93	57.4	52	32.1
Indiana	110	18	16.4	74	67.3	89	80.9	51	46.4	86	78.2	33	30.0	13	11.8	53	48.2	78	70.9	17	15.5
Michigan	135	52	38.5	91	67.4	126	93.3	86	63.7	111	82.2	28	20.7	29	21.5	75	55.6	95	70.4	34	25.2
Ohio	142	15	10.6	94	66.2	135	95.1	96	67.6	115	81.0	34	23.9	27	19.0	87	61.3	110	77.5	48	33.8
Wisconsin	146	24	16.4	57	39.0	139	95.2	78	53.4	71	48.6	43	29.5	14	9.6	130	89.0	71	48.6	18	12.3
CENSUS DIVISION 5, EAST SOUTH CENTRAL	308	86	27.9	136	44.2	254	82.5	98	31.8	159	51.3	107	34.7	27	8.8	101	32.8	133	43.2	47	15.3
Alabama	50	12	24.0	26	52.0	44	88.0	27	54.0	30	60.0	7	14.0	4	8.0	16	32.0	27	54.0	11	22.0
Kentucky	80	27	33.8	47	58.8	69	86.3	27	33.8	50	62.5	28	35.0	7	8.8	26	32.5	44	55.0	10	12.5
Mississippi	104	39	37.5	28	26.9	84	80.8	19	18.3	39	37.5	52	50.0	9	8.7	20	19.2	20	19.2	18	17.3
Tennessee	74	8	10.8	35	47.3	57	77.0	25	33.8	40	54.1	20	27.0	7	9.5	39	52.7	42	56.8	8	10.8
CENSUS DIVISION 6, WEST NORTH CENTRAL	614	292	47.6	308	50.2	507	82.6	301	49.0	385	62.7	368	59.9	49	8.0	288	46.9	301	49.0	142	23.1
Iowa	123	62	50.4	68	55.3	103	83.7	66	53.7	97	78.9	89	72.4	15	12.2	47	38.2	80	65.0	22	17.9
Kansas	127	72	56.7	39	30.7	94	74.0	46	36.2	48	37.8	87	68.5	3	2.4	52	40.9	39	30.7	26	20.5
Minnesota	97	30	30.9	54	55.7	91	93.8	53	54.6	78	80.4	51	52.6	10	10.3	57	58.8	54	55.7	17	17.5
Missouri	144	59	41.0	85	59.0	126	87.5	69	47.9	88	61.1	50	34.7	13	9.0	55	38.2	76	52.8	48	33.3
Nebraska	55	31	56.4	34	61.8	45	81.8	36	65.5	33	60.0	36	65.5	6	10.9	34	61.8	31	56.4	14	25.5
North Dakota	24	13	54.2	11	45.8	21	87.5	15	62.5	14	58.3	18	75.0	0	0.0	13	54.2	10	41.7	8	33.3
South Dakota	44	25	56.8	17	38.6	27	61.4	16	36.4	27	61.4	37	84.1	2	4.5	30	68.2	11	25.0	7	15.9
CENSUS DIVISION 7, WEST SOUTH CENTRAL	851	181	21.3	273	32.1	634	74.5	224	26.3	372	43.7	227	26.7	47	5.5	270	31.7	295	34.7	118	13.9
Arkansas	86	22	25.6	42	48.8	65	75.6	20	23.3	39	45.3	36	41.9	5	5.8	40	46.5	30	34.9	14	16.3
Louisiana	87	21	24.1	37	42.5	69	79.3	31	35.6	45	51.7	19	21.8	12	13.8	37	42.5	43	49.4	21	24.1
Oklahoma	113	26	23.0	46	40.7	78	69.0	40	35.4	44	38.9	47	41.6	4	3.5	42	37.2	48	42.5	20	17.7
Texas	565	112	19.8	148	26.2	422	74.7	133	23.5	244	43.2	125	22.1	26	4.6	151	26.7	174	30.8	63	11.2
CENSUS DIVISION 8, MOUNTAIN	324	115	35.5	146	45.1	259	79.9	134	41.4	177	54.6	135	41.7	30	9.3	150	46.3	170	52.5	75	23.1
Arizona	55	10	18.2	17	30.9	45	81.8	22	40.0	33	60.0	10	18.2	7	12.7	33	60.0	33	60.0	7	12.7
Colorado	69	22	31.9	45	65.2	52	75.4	39	56.5	44	63.8	30	43.5	8	11.6	32	46.4	40	58.0	13	18.8
Idaho	33	23	69.7	18	54.5	26	78.8	17	51.5	20	60.6	20	60.6	7	21.2	12	36.4	20	60.6	13	39.4
Montana	53	32	60.4	18	34.0	39	73.6	18	34.0	29	54.7	39	73.6	3	5.7	34	64.2	29	54.7	18	34.0
Nevada	27	4	14.8	6	22.2	21	77.8	6	22.2	13	48.1	5	18.5	0	0.0	11	40.7	11	40.7	8	29.6
New Mexico	29	7	24.1	15	51.7	27	93.1	8	27.6	15	51.7	8	27.6	1	3.4	9	31.0	16	55.2	5	17.2
Utah	38	9	23.7	17	44.7	34	89.5	15	39.5	25	65.8	11	28.9	3	7.9	12	31.6	11	28.9	4	10.5
Wyoming	20	8	40.0	10	50.0	15	75.0	9	45.0	9	45.0	12	60.0	1	5.0	7	35.0	10	50.0	7	35.0
CENSUS DIVISION 9, PACIFIC	377	73	19.4	119	31.6	350	92.8	159	42.2	277	73.5	68	18.0	61	16.2	227	60.2	200	53.1	101	26.8
Alaska	12	2	16.7	3	25.0	10	83.3	4	33.3	6	50.0	5	41.7	3	25.0	9	75.0	5	41.7	2	16.7
California	229	27	11.8	54	23.6	217	94.8	86	37.6	160	69.9	18	7.9	39	17.0	139	60.7	106	46.3	67	29.3
Hawaii	11	2	18.2	4	36.4	11	100.0	8	72.7	9	81.8	2	18.2	2	18.2	5	45.5	9	81.8	3	27.3
Oregon	60	24	40.0	29	48.3	52	86.7	31	51.7	51	85.0	29	48.3	10	16.7	34	56.7	42	70.0	19	31.7
Washington	65	18	27.7	29	44.6	60	92.3	30	46.2	51	78.5	14	21.5	7	10.8	40	61.5	38	58.5	10	15.4

AHA Hospital Statistics © 2019 Health Forum LLC, an affiliate of the American Hospital Association

Table 7 (Continued)

These data include only hospital-based facilities and services as reported by responding hospitals in Section C of the 2017 AHA Annual Survey, beginning on page 217. Census divisions represent all U.S. hospitals. Community hospitals are listed separately under United States. No estimates have been made for nonresponding hospitals. Definitions of facilities and services are listed in the Glossary, page 203.

CLASSIFICATION	HOSPITALS REPORTING	URGENT CARE CENTER Number	URGENT CARE CENTER Percent	VIOLENCE PREVENTION PROGRAM-COMMUNITY Number	VIOLENCE PREVENTION PROGRAM-COMMUNITY Percent	VIOLENCE PREVENTION PROGRAM-WORKPLACE Number	VIOLENCE PREVENTION PROGRAM-WORKPLACE Percent	VIRTUAL COLONOSCOPY Number	VIRTUAL COLONOSCOPY Percent	VOLUNTEER SERVICES DEPARTMENT Number	VOLUNTEER SERVICES DEPARTMENT Percent	WOMEN'S HEALTH SERVICES Number	WOMEN'S HEALTH SERVICES Percent	WOUND MANAGEMENT SERVICES Number	WOUND MANAGEMENT SERVICES Percent
UNITED STATES	4,280	1,052	24.6	2,267	53.0	468	10.9	752	17.6	3,176	74.2	2,225	52.0	2,910	68.0
COMMUNITY HOSPITALS	3,877	1,013	26.1	2,104	54.3	441	11.4	739	19.1	3,027	78.1	2,156	55.6	2,811	72.5
CENSUS DIVISION 1, NEW ENGLAND	163	65	39.9	116	71.2	33	20.2	44	27.0	148	90.8	118	72.4	127	77.9
Connecticut	28	14	50.0	26	92.9	6	21.4	12	42.9	25	89.3	19	67.9	23	82.1
Maine	32	13	40.6	19	59.4	2	6.3	5	15.6	28	87.5	22	68.8	26	81.3
Massachusetts	56	24	42.9	37	66.1	19	33.9	18	32.1	51	91.1	39	69.6	43	76.8
New Hampshire	26	11	42.3	19	73.1	4	15.4	5	19.2	25	96.2	24	92.3	22	84.6
Rhode Island	9	1	11.1	5	55.6	2	22.2	3	33.3	8	88.9	6	66.7	5	55.6
Vermont	12	2	16.7	10	83.3	0	0.0	1	8.3	11	91.7	8	66.7	8	66.7
CENSUS DIVISION 2, MIDDLE ATLANTIC	373	116	31.1	266	71.3	80	21.4	106	28.4	333	89.3	256	68.6	281	75.3
New Jersey	73	23	31.5	61	83.6	20	27.4	22	30.1	58	79.5	53	72.6	59	80.8
New York	150	57	38.0	107	71.3	34	22.7	47	31.3	141	94.0	111	74.0	109	72.7
Pennsylvania	150	36	24.0	98	65.3	26	17.3	37	24.7	134	89.3	92	61.3	113	75.3
CENSUS DIVISION 3, SOUTH ATLANTIC	575	120	20.9	303	52.7	54	9.4	123	21.4	481	83.7	337	58.6	414	72.0
Delaware	9	4	44.4	5	55.6	1	11.1	1	11.1	7	77.8	4	44.4	7	77.8
District of Columbia	10	0	0.0	5	50.0	3	30.0	1	10.0	10	100.0	6	60.0	10	100.0
Florida	117	25	21.4	77	65.8	17	14.5	32	27.4	98	83.8	72	61.5	87	74.4
Georgia	103	20	19.4	45	43.7	5	4.9	11	10.7	81	78.6	55	53.4	67	65.0
Maryland	44	15	34.1	33	75.0	8	18.2	12	27.3	43	97.7	26	59.1	35	79.5
North Carolina	89	26	29.2	48	53.9	9	10.1	25	28.1	81	91.0	54	60.7	68	76.4
South Carolina	75	7	9.3	22	29.3	3	4.0	12	16.0	57	76.0	43	57.3	46	61.3
Virginia	76	11	14.5	49	64.5	3	3.9	20	26.3	66	86.8	47	61.8	61	80.3
West Virginia	52	12	23.1	19	36.5	5	9.6	9	17.3	39	75.0	30	57.7	33	63.5
CENSUS DIVISION 4, EAST NORTH CENTRAL	695	298	42.9	399	57.4	102	14.7	145	20.9	557	80.1	419	60.3	477	68.6
Illinois	162	60	37.0	96	59.3	29	17.9	43	26.5	139	85.8	98	60.5	107	66.0
Indiana	110	41	37.3	50	45.5	12	10.9	16	14.5	87	79.1	60	54.5	79	71.8
Michigan	135	65	48.1	90	66.7	22	16.3	27	20.0	120	88.9	89	65.9	103	76.3
Ohio	142	60	42.3	94	66.2	20	14.1	32	22.5	130	91.5	99	69.7	113	79.6
Wisconsin	146	72	49.3	69	47.3	19	13.0	27	18.5	81	55.5	73	50.0	75	51.4
CENSUS DIVISION 5, EAST SOUTH CENTRAL	308	40	13.0	113	36.7	24	7.8	33	10.7	217	70.5	129	41.9	155	50.3
Alabama	50	6	12.0	25	50.0	1	2.0	5	10.0	40	80.0	26	52.0	31	62.0
Kentucky	80	13	16.3	35	43.8	15	18.8	12	15.0	64	80.0	44	55.0	48	60.0
Mississippi	104	10	9.6	24	23.1	1	1.0	8	7.7	64	61.5	28	26.9	33	31.7
Tennessee	74	11	14.9	29	39.2	7	9.5	8	10.8	49	66.2	31	41.9	43	58.1
CENSUS DIVISION 6, WEST NORTH CENTRAL	614	150	24.4	294	47.9	53	8.6	91	14.8	409	66.6	244	39.7	413	67.3
Iowa	123	26	21.1	55	44.7	12	9.8	15	12.2	99	80.5	59	48.0	87	70.7
Kansas	127	24	18.9	46	36.2	6	4.7	19	15.0	68	53.5	35	27.6	74	58.3
Minnesota	97	41	42.3	83	85.6	10	10.3	19	19.6	77	79.4	40	41.2	76	78.4
Missouri	144	35	24.3	74	51.4	12	8.3	20	13.9	98	68.1	68	47.2	103	71.5
Nebraska	55	6	10.9	16	29.1	5	9.1	13	23.6	31	56.4	20	36.4	31	56.4
North Dakota	24	9	37.5	8	33.3	4	16.7	2	8.3	18	75.0	11	45.8	12	50.0
South Dakota	44	9	20.5	12	27.3	4	9.1	3	6.8	18	40.9	11	25.0	30	68.2
CENSUS DIVISION 7, WEST SOUTH CENTRAL	851	86	10.1	331	38.9	48	5.6	88	10.3	459	53.9	308	36.2	518	60.9
Arkansas	86	9	10.5	26	30.2	6	7.0	9	10.5	54	62.8	31	36.0	52	60.5
Louisiana	87	17	19.5	39	44.8	4	4.6	7	8.0	53	60.9	43	49.4	52	59.8
Oklahoma	113	13	11.5	49	43.4	2	1.8	11	9.7	71	62.8	44	38.9	66	58.4
Texas	565	47	8.3	217	38.4	36	6.4	61	10.8	281	49.7	190	33.6	348	61.6
CENSUS DIVISION 8, MOUNTAIN	324	74	22.8	164	50.6	27	8.3	44	13.6	239	73.8	185	57.1	224	69.1
Arizona	55	10	18.2	34	61.8	6	10.9	16	29.1	42	76.4	34	61.8	39	70.9
Colorado	69	15	21.7	31	44.9	9	13.0	6	8.7	58	84.1	48	69.6	55	79.7
Idaho	33	11	33.3	15	45.5	2	6.1	3	9.1	26	78.8	19	57.6	21	63.6
Montana	53	14	26.4	22	41.5	1	1.9	8	15.1	34	64.2	26	49.1	34	64.2
Nevada	27	4	14.8	13	48.1	2	7.4	1	3.7	15	55.6	8	29.6	17	63.0
New Mexico	29	9	31.0	10	34.5	3	10.3	2	6.9	21	72.4	18	62.1	20	69.0
Utah	38	5	13.2	29	76.3	2	5.3	4	10.5	28	73.7	22	57.9	23	60.5
Wyoming	20	6	30.0	10	50.0	2	10.0	4	20.0	15	75.0	10	50.0	15	75.0
CENSUS DIVISION 9, PACIFIC	377	103	27.3	281	74.5	47	12.5	78	20.7	333	88.3	229	60.7	301	79.8
Alaska	12	4	33.3	9	75.0	2	16.7	2	16.7	7	58.3	5	41.7	10	83.3
California	229	55	24.0	182	79.5	38	16.6	50	21.8	209	91.3	134	58.5	180	78.6
Hawaii	11	1	9.1	7	63.6	0	0.0	2	18.2	10	90.9	9	81.8	9	81.8
Oregon	60	21	35.0	37	61.7	1	1.7	14	23.3	53	88.3	44	73.3	55	91.7
Washington	65	22	33.8	46	70.8	6	9.2	10	15.4	54	83.1	37	56.9	47	72.3

Table 7 (Continued)

These data include only hospital-based facilities and services as reported by responding hospitals in Section C of the 2017 AHA Annual Survey, beginning on page 217. Census divisions represent all U.S. hospitals. Community hospitals are listed separately under United States. No estimates have been made for nonresponding hospitals. Definitions of facilities and services are listed in the Glossary, page 203.

Classification	Hospitals Reporting	Adult Units No.	Adult Units %	Pediatric Units No.	Pediatric Units %	Cardiac Units No.	Cardiac Units %	ICU Med. Surg. No.	ICU Med. Surg. %	ICU Neonatal No.	ICU Neonatal %	ICU Other No.	ICU Other %	ICU Pediatric No.	ICU Pediatric %	Acute Long-Term No.	Acute Long-Term %	Skilled Nursing No.	Skilled Nursing %	Interm. Nursing No.	Interm. Nursing %	Other Long-Term No.	Other Long-Term %
UNITED STATES	4,280	3,604	84.2	1,670	39.0	1,066	24.9	2,616	61.1	924	21.6	459	10.7	397	9.3	259	6.1	853	19.9	337	7.9	179	4.2
COMMUNITY HOSPITALS	3,877	3,529	91.0	1,654	42.7	1,055	27.2	2,566	66.2	921	23.8	449	11.6	395	10.2	218	5.6	795	20.5	318	8.2	148	3.8
CENSUS DIVISION 1, NEW ENGLAND	163	133	81.6	79	48.5	42	25.8	115	70.6	32	19.6	14	8.6	14	8.6	9	5.5	26	16.0	20	12.3	9	5.5
Connecticut	28	22	78.6	13	46.4	11	39.3	20	71.4	12	42.9	5	17.9	2	7.1	2	7.1	2	7.1	2	7.1	0	0.0
Maine	32	28	87.5	15	46.9	5	15.6	20	62.5	3	9.4	3	9.4	3	9.4	2	6.3	12	37.5	8	25.0	5	15.6
Massachusetts	56	42	75.0	33	58.9	19	33.9	41	73.2	11	19.6	3	5.4	6	10.7	4	7.1	2	3.6	2	3.6	2	3.6
New Hampshire	26	23	88.5	13	50.0	5	19.2	19	73.1	5	19.2	2	7.7	2	7.7	0	0.0	7	26.9	5	19.2	1	3.8
Rhode Island	9	8	88.9	3	33.3	1	11.1	7	77.8	1	11.1	2	22.2	1	11.1	0	0.0	0	0.0	2	22.2	0	0.0
Vermont	12	10	83.3	2	16.7	1	8.3	8	66.7	1	8.3	0	0.0	1	8.3	1	8.3	3	25.0	1	8.3	1	8.3
CENSUS DIVISION 2, MIDDLE ATLANTIC	373	324	86.9	169	45.3	152	40.8	295	79.1	114	30.6	67	18.0	46	12.3	22	5.9	85	22.8	20	5.4	16	4.3
New Jersey	73	57	78.1	34	46.6	34	46.6	56	76.7	22	30.1	14	19.2	14	19.2	3	4.1	10	13.7	5	6.8	2	2.7
New York	150	138	92.0	80	53.3	69	46.0	125	83.3	50	33.3	28	18.7	25	16.7	12	8.0	42	28.0	11	7.3	9	6.0
Pennsylvania	150	129	86.0	55	36.7	49	32.7	114	76.0	42	28.0	25	16.7	7	4.7	7	4.7	33	22.0	4	2.7	5	3.3
CENSUS DIVISION 3, SOUTH ATLANTIC	575	480	83.5	230	40.0	174	30.3	417	72.5	143	24.9	80	13.9	61	10.6	32	5.6	114	19.8	47	8.2	29	5.0
Delaware	9	4	44.4	5	55.6	4	44.4	4	44.4	3	33.3	1	11.1	2	22.2	1	11.1	0	0.0	2	22.2	0	0.0
District of Columbia	10	6	60.0	2	20.0	5	50.0	7	70.0	6	60.0	2	20.0	2	20.0	1	10.0	4	40.0	1	10.0	3	30.0
Florida	117	100	85.5	42	35.9	56	47.9	93	79.5	42	35.9	21	17.9	24	20.5	5	4.3	13	11.1	4	3.4	4	3.4
Georgia	103	88	85.4	27	26.2	21	20.4	66	64.1	23	22.3	6	5.8	4	3.9	3	2.9	23	22.3	6	5.8	5	4.9
Maryland	44	40	90.9	29	65.9	15	34.1	38	86.4	15	34.1	6	13.6	4	9.1	4	9.1	5	11.4	1	2.3	1	2.3
North Carolina	89	80	89.9	40	44.9	24	27.0	71	79.8	20	22.5	17	19.1	11	12.4	4	4.5	17	19.1	6	6.7	2	2.2
South Carolina	75	57	76.0	40	53.3	20	26.7	49	65.3	12	16.0	15	20.0	6	8.0	9	12.0	17	22.7	12	16.0	7	9.3
Virginia	76	62	81.6	24	31.6	15	19.7	58	76.3	17	22.4	8	10.5	5	6.6	2	2.6	17	22.4	8	10.5	5	6.6
West Virginia	52	43	82.7	21	40.4	14	26.9	30	57.7	5	9.6	4	7.7	3	5.8	3	5.8	18	34.6	7	13.5	2	3.8
CENSUS DIVISION 4, EAST NORTH CENTRAL	695	605	87.1	335	48.2	185	26.6	454	65.3	122	17.6	117	16.8	72	10.4	36	5.2	108	15.5	38	5.5	29	4.2
Illinois	162	144	88.9	88	54.3	34	21.0	113	69.8	28	17.3	13	8.0	19	11.7	5	3.1	32	19.8	9	5.6	7	4.3
Indiana	110	92	83.6	54	49.1	25	22.7	72	65.5	19	17.3	7	6.4	8	7.3	8	7.3	16	14.5	10	9.1	5	4.5
Michigan	135	120	88.9	49	36.3	31	23.0	92	68.1	21	15.6	19	14.1	11	8.1	6	4.4	27	20.0	5	3.7	8	5.9
Ohio	142	127	89.4	50	35.2	46	32.4	113	79.6	25	17.6	13	9.2	11	7.7	4	2.8	19	13.4	12	8.5	4	2.8
Wisconsin	146	122	83.6	94	64.4	49	33.6	64	43.8	29	19.9	65	44.5	23	15.8	13	8.9	14	9.6	2	1.4	5	3.4
CENSUS DIVISION 5, EAST SOUTH CENTRAL	308	255	82.8	123	39.9	83	26.9	168	54.5	53	17.2	27	8.8	25	8.1	20	6.5	56	18.2	16	5.2	9	2.9
Alabama	50	41	82.0	23	46.0	18	36.0	35	70.0	14	28.0	8	16.0	5	10.0	2	4.0	8	16.0	5	10.0	0	0.0
Kentucky	80	64	80.0	22	27.5	20	25.0	50	62.5	13	16.3	5	6.3	3	3.8	7	8.8	14	17.5	4	5.0	0	0.0
Mississippi	104	92	88.5	56	53.8	29	27.9	41	39.4	14	13.5	3	2.9	9	8.7	8	7.7	23	22.1	0	0.0	6	5.8
Tennessee	74	58	78.4	22	29.7	16	21.6	42	56.8	12	16.2	11	14.9	8	10.8	3	4.1	11	14.9	7	9.5	0	0.0
CENSUS DIVISION 6, WEST NORTH CENTRAL	614	562	91.5	261	42.5	114	18.6	292	47.6	79	12.9	47	7.7	44	7.2	26	4.2	253	41.2	114	18.6	46	7.5
Iowa	123	118	95.9	58	47.2	22	17.9	62	50.4	17	13.8	8	6.5	11	8.9	6	4.9	60	48.8	34	27.6	12	9.8
Kansas	127	118	92.9	42	33.1	10	7.9	45	35.4	11	8.7	5	3.9	9	7.1	3	2.4	56	44.1	40	31.5	9	7.1
Minnesota	97	95	97.9	42	43.3	19	19.6	53	54.6	11	11.3	8	8.2	5	5.2	1	1.0	36	37.1	4	4.1	3	3.1
Missouri	144	114	79.2	77	53.5	40	27.8	80	55.6	21	14.6	15	10.4	12	8.3	11	7.6	31	21.5	12	8.3	7	4.9
Nebraska	55	51	92.7	20	36.4	11	20.0	22	40.0	10	18.2	6	10.9	3	5.5	2	3.6	29	52.7	15	27.3	6	10.9
North Dakota	24	23	95.8	9	37.5	6	25.0	11	45.8	6	25.0	3	12.5	2	8.3	2	8.3	14	58.3	2	8.3	2	8.3
South Dakota	44	43	97.7	13	29.5	6	13.6	19	43.2	3	6.8	2	4.5	2	4.5	1	2.3	27	61.4	17	38.6	7	15.9
CENSUS DIVISION 7, WEST SOUTH CENTRAL	851	612	71.9	214	25.1	142	16.7	392	46.1	173	20.3	60	7.1	56	6.6	88	10.3	79	9.3	35	4.1	14	1.6
Arkansas	86	66	76.7	23	26.7	22	25.6	39	45.3	12	14.0	4	4.7	1	1.2	8	9.3	10	11.6	3	3.5	0	0.0
Louisiana	87	65	74.7	38	43.7	24	27.6	56	64.4	28	32.2	9	10.3	15	17.2	11	12.6	18	20.7	7	8.0	6	6.9
Oklahoma	113	93	82.3	30	26.5	19	16.8	47	41.6	15	13.3	9	8.0	7	6.2	8	7.1	22	19.5	8	7.1	5	4.4
Texas	565	388	68.7	123	21.8	77	13.6	250	44.2	118	20.9	38	6.7	33	5.8	61	10.8	29	5.1	17	3.0	3	0.5
CENSUS DIVISION 8, MOUNTAIN	324	290	89.5	116	35.8	53	16.4	186	57.4	71	21.9	20	6.2	27	8.3	15	4.6	69	21.3	28	8.6	18	5.6
Arizona	55	44	80.0	12	21.8	12	21.8	35	63.6	17	30.9	7	12.7	7	12.7	4	7.3	4	7.3	4	7.3	0	0.0
Colorado	69	64	92.8	26	37.7	12	17.4	45	65.2	24	34.8	6	8.7	4	5.8	2	2.9	12	17.4	5	7.2	4	5.8
Idaho	33	32	97.0	14	42.4	5	15.2	15	45.5	8	24.2	0	0.0	2	6.1	3	9.1	7	21.2	1	3.0	1	3.0
Montana	53	51	96.2	21	39.6	7	13.2	22	41.5	6	11.3	2	3.8	5	9.4	1	1.9	21	39.6	8	15.1	6	11.3
Nevada	27	19	70.4	7	25.9	7	25.9	16	59.3	6	22.2	2	7.4	4	14.8	3	11.1	5	18.5	1	3.7	1	3.7
New Mexico	29	28	96.6	12	41.4	4	13.8	21	72.4	3	10.3	1	3.4	4	13.8	1	3.4	3	10.3	2	6.9	0	0.0
Utah	38	33	86.8	14	36.8	6	15.8	18	47.4	7	18.4	2	5.3	1	2.6	1	2.6	10	26.3	3	7.9	4	10.5
Wyoming	20	19	95.0	10	50.0	0	0.0	14	70.0	0	0.0	0	0.0	0	0.0	0	0.0	7	35.0	4	20.0	2	10.0
CENSUS DIVISION 9, PACIFIC	377	343	91.0	143	37.9	121	32.1	297	78.8	137	36.3	27	7.2	52	13.8	11	2.9	63	16.7	19	5.0	9	2.4
Alaska	12	11	91.7	4	33.3	1	8.3	5	41.7	2	16.7	1	8.3	1	8.3	2	16.7	2	16.7	5	41.7	3	25.0
California	229	206	90.0	88	38.4	85	37.1	193	84.3	104	45.4	14	6.1	37	16.2	7	3.1	47	20.5	7	3.1	4	1.7
Hawaii	11	9	81.8	2	18.2	3	27.3	9	81.8	2	18.2	2	18.2	2	18.2	0	0.0	0	0.0	2	18.2	0	0.0
Oregon	60	60	100.0	25	41.7	16	26.7	47	78.3	12	20.0	6	10.0	5	8.3	1	1.7	7	11.7	6	10.0	1	1.7
Washington	65	57	87.7	24	36.9	16	24.6	43	66.2	17	26.2	5	7.7	6	9.2	1	1.5	7	10.8	1	1.5	1	1.5

Table 7 (Continued)

These data include only hospital-based facilities and services as reported by responding hospitals in Section C of the 2017 AHA Annual Survey, beginning on page 217. Census divisions represent all U.S. hospitals. Community hospitals are listed separately under United States. No estimates have been made for nonresponding hospitals. Definitions of facilities and services are listed in the Glossary, page 203.

CARDIOLOGY AND CARDIAC SERVICES

CLASSIFICATION	HOSPITALS REPORTING	ADULT CARDIOLOGY SERVICES Number	Percent	PEDIATRIC CARDIOLOGY SERVICES Number	Percent	ADULT DIAGNOSTIC CATHETERIZATION Number	Percent	PEDIATRIC DIAGNOSTIC CATHETERIZATION Number	Percent	ADULT INTERVENTIONAL CARDIAC CATHETERIZATION Number	Percent	PEDIATRIC INTERVENTIONAL CARDIAC CATHETERIZATION Number	Percent	ADULT CARDIAC SURGERY Number	Percent	PEDIATRIC CARDIAC SURGERY Number	Percent	ADULT CARDIAC ELECTRO PHYSIOLOGY Number	Percent	PEDIATRIC CARDIAC ELECTRO PHYSIOLOGY Number	Percent	CARDIAC REHABILITATION Number	Percent
UNITED STATES	4,260	2,247	52.5	393	9.2	1,683	39.3	180	4.2	1,507	35.2	162	3.8	1,050	24.5	158	3.7	1,345	31.4	189	4.4	2,372	55.4
COMMUNITY HOSPITALS	3,877	2,196	56.6	392	10.1	1,652	42.6	180	4.6	1,481	38.2	162	4.2	1,034	26.7	158	4.1	1,322	34.1	189	4.9	2,337	60.3
CENSUS DIVISION 1, NEW ENGLAND	163	105	64.4	18	11.0	64	39.3	9	5.5	51	31.3	9	5.5	35	21.5	7	4.3	60	36.8	9	5.5	110	67.5
Connecticut	28	21	75.0	4	14.3	15	53.6	2	7.1	14	50.0	2	7.1	10	35.7	1	3.6	15	53.6	2	7.1	20	71.4
Maine	32	17	53.1	3	9.4	10	31.3	1	3.1	5	15.6	1	3.1	3	9.4	1	3.1	6	18.8	2	6.3	22	68.8
Massachusetts	56	39	69.6	7	12.5	24	42.9	3	5.4	20	35.7	3	5.4	17	30.4	3	5.4	25	44.6	4	7.1	39	69.6
New Hampshire	26	16	61.5	2	7.7	9	34.6	1	3.8	8	30.8	1	3.8	3	11.5	0	0.0	8	30.8	1	3.8	19	73.1
Rhode Island	9	7	77.8	1	11.1	5	55.6	1	11.1	1	33.3	1	11.1	1	11.1	1	11.1	5	55.6	0	0.0	3	33.3
Vermont	12	5	41.7	1	8.3	1	8.3	1	8.3	1	8.3	1	8.3	1	8.3	1	8.3	1	8.3	0	0.0	7	58.3
CENSUS DIVISION 2, MIDDLE ATLANTIC	373	278	74.5	65	17.4	200	53.6	21	5.6	174	46.6	19	5.1	108	29.0	17	4.6	153	41.0	25	6.7	226	60.6
New Jersey	73	54	74.0	16	21.9	48	65.8	2	2.7	40	54.8	2	2.7	17	23.3	2	2.7	20	27.4	3	4.1	44	60.3
New York	150	116	77.3	39	26.0	67	44.7	14	9.3	57	38.0	12	8.0	34	22.7	10	6.7	60	40.0	13	8.7	86	57.3
Pennsylvania	150	108	72.0	10	6.7	85	56.7	5	3.3	77	51.3	5	3.3	57	38.0	5	3.3	73	48.7	9	6.0	96	64.0
CENSUS DIVISION 3, SOUTH ATLANTIC	575	355	61.7	53	9.2	291	50.6	30	5.2	245	42.6	27	4.7	151	26.3	27	4.7	229	41.6	32	5.6	336	58.4
Delaware	9	6	66.7	1	11.1	5	55.6	1	11.1	5	55.6	1	11.1	4	44.4	1	11.1	3	33.3	1	11.1	4	44.4
District of Columbia	10	6	60.0	1	10.0	5	50.0	1	10.0	2	20.0	1	10.0	3	30.0	1	10.0	4	40.0	1	10.0	3	30.0
Florida	117	86	73.5	20	17.1	80	68.4	13	11.1	72	61.5	10	8.5	52	44.4	11	9.4	70	59.8	12	10.3	72	61.5
Georgia	103	54	52.4	2	1.9	48	46.6	2	1.9	40	38.8	2	1.9	17	16.5	1	1.0	36	35.0	1	1.0	44	42.7
Maryland	44	34	77.3	5	11.4	31	70.5	2	4.5	23	52.3	2	4.5	9	20.5	2	4.5	32	72.7	3	6.7	28	63.6
North Carolina	89	60	67.4	10	11.2	43	48.3	5	5.6	37	41.6	5	5.6	23	25.8	5	5.6	34	38.2	6	6.7	66	74.2
South Carolina	75	34	45.3	5	6.7	27	36.0	1	1.3	17	22.7	1	1.3	17	22.7	1	1.3	17	22.7	2	2.7	40	53.3
Virginia	76	48	63.2	6	7.9	34	44.7	4	5.3	34	44.7	4	5.3	18	23.7	4	5.3	33	43.4	4	5.3	55	72.4
West Virginia	52	27	51.9	3	5.8	18	34.6	1	1.9	15	28.8	1	1.9	8	15.4	1	1.9	10	19.2	1	1.9	24	46.2
CENSUS DIVISION 4, EAST NORTH CENTRAL	665	410	59.0	85	12.2	307	44.2	25	3.6	270	38.8	24	3.5	204	29.4	25	3.6	256	36.8	32	4.2	510	76.5
Illinois	162	110	67.9	31	19.1	85	52.5	7	4.3	80	49.4	7	4.3	61	37.7	10	6.2	72	44.4	9	5.6	124	76.5
Indiana	110	65	59.1	11	10.0	45	40.9	3	2.7	41	37.3	3	2.7	29	26.4	4	2.7	32	29.1	4	3.6	81	73.6
Michigan	135	79	58.5	18	13.3	56	41.5	4	3.0	46	34.1	3	2.2	33	24.4	4	3.0	51	37.8	4	3.0	95	70.4
Ohio	142	109	76.8	15	10.6	78	54.9	8	5.6	61	43.0	7	5.6	51	35.9	6	4.2	63	44.4	7	4.9	105	73.9
Wisconsin	146	47	32.2	10	6.8	43	29.5	3	2.1	42	28.8	3	2.1	30	20.5	2	1.4	38	26.0	5	3.4	105	71.9
CENSUS DIVISION 5, EAST SOUTH CENTRAL	308	145	47.1	17	5.5	112	36.4	12	3.9	95	30.8	8	2.6	69	22.4	12	3.9	71	23.1	11	3.6	139	45.1
Alabama	50	27	54.0	3	6.0	24	48.0	5	10.0	21	42.0	2	4.0	17	34.0	2	4.0	17	36.0	4	8.0	24	48.0
Kentucky	80	47	58.8	4	5.0	38	47.5	2	2.5	30	37.5	2	2.5	19	23.8	2	3.8	23	28.8	3	3.8	50	62.5
Mississippi	104	31	29.8	3	2.9	21	20.2	1	1.0	19	18.3	1	1.0	18	17.3	1	2.9	10	9.6	0	0.0	26	25.0
Tennessee	74	40	54.1	7	9.5	29	39.2	4	5.4	25	33.8	3	4.1	15	20.3	4	5.4	20	27.0	4	5.4	39	52.7
CENSUS DIVISION 6, WEST NORTH CENTRAL	614	236	38.4	36	5.9	147	23.9	15	2.4	144	23.5	15	2.4	95	15.5	16	2.6	121	19.7	18	2.9	454	73.9
Iowa	123	43	35.0	6	4.9	26	21.1	2	1.6	26	21.1	1	0.8	13	10.6	2	1.6	23	18.7	2	1.6	111	90.2
Kansas	127	32	25.2	6	4.7	20	15.7	0	0.0	20	16.5	0	0.0	13	10.2	1	0.8	14	11.0	5	5.2	67	52.8
Minnesota	97	46	47.4	9	9.3	21	21.6	4	4.1	20	20.6	4	4.1	16	16.5	3	3.1	21	21.6	5	5.2	87	89.7
Missouri	144	77	53.5	8	5.6	55	38.2	3	2.1	53	36.8	3	2.1	36	25.0	5	3.5	43	29.9	5	3.5	87	60.4
Nebraska	55	21	38.2	3	5.5	14	25.5	2	1.8	14	25.5	2	1.8	7	12.7	1	1.8	12	21.8	2	3.6	45	81.8
North Dakota	24	7	29.2	2	8.3	6	20.8	2	8.3	5	20.8	2	8.3	3	20.8	3	12.5	4	16.7	1	4.2	18	75.0
South Dakota	44	10	22.7	4	9.1	6	13.6	2	6.8	3	11.4	3	6.8	5	11.4	1	2.3	3	9.1	1	2.3	39	88.6
CENSUS DIVISION 7, WEST SOUTH CENTRAL	651	331	38.9	42	4.9	269	31.6	26	3.1	253	29.7	23	2.7	192	22.6	21	2.5	203	23.9	23	2.7	267	33.7
Arkansas	86	30	34.9	2	2.3	24	27.9	3	3.5	24	27.9	1	1.2	17	19.8	1	1.2	15	17.4	2	2.3	33	38.4
Louisiana	87	46	52.9	9	10.3	39	44.8	6	6.9	34	39.1	5	5.7	27	31.0	5	5.7	33	37.9	5	5.7	35	40.2
Oklahoma	113	49	43.4	4	3.5	30	26.5	2	1.8	30	26.5	2	1.8	17	15.0	2	1.8	18	15.9	2	1.8	32	28.3
Texas	565	206	36.5	27	4.8	176	31.2	15	2.7	165	29.2	15	2.7	131	23.2	13	2.3	137	24.2	14	2.5	187	33.1
CENSUS DIVISION 8, MOUNTAIN	324	146	45.1	24	7.4	108	33.3	13	4.0	106	32.7	12	3.7	62	22.6	11	3.4	81	25.0	17	5.2	148	45.7
Arizona	55	33	60.0	5	9.1	28	50.9	3	7.3	28	50.9	4	7.3	18	32.7	4	7.3	19	34.5	5	9.1	22	40.0
Colorado	69	42	60.9	4	5.8	33	47.8	3	4.3	31	44.9	3	4.3	15	21.7	2	2.9	25	36.2	5	7.2	42	60.9
Idaho	53	11	20.8	5	9.4	8	15.1	1	3.0	8	15.1	0	0.0	6	12.1	0	0.0	8	13.2	1	3.8	13	39.4
Montana	27	13	48.1	3	11.1	11	40.7	1	3.7	10	37.0	0	0.0	7	25.9	2	3.7	7	25.9	1	3.7	11	40.7
Nevada	29	17	58.6	3	10.3	9	31.0	2	6.9	9	31.0	2	6.9	4	13.8	1	6.9	6	20.7	2	6.9	12	41.4
New Mexico	29	11	28.9	1	2.6	7	18.4	1	2.6	7	18.4	1	2.6	6	15.8	1	2.6	6	15.8	1	2.6	12	21.1
Utah	11	13	30.0	3	0.0	9	15.0	1	0.0	9	15.0	1	0.0	6	10.0	1	0.0	9	15.0	1	0.0	8	65.0
Wyoming	20	6	30.0	2	10.0	3	15.0	1	0.0	3	15.0	0	0.0	0	10.0	0	0.0	3	15.0	0	0.0	13	65.0
CENSUS DIVISION 9, PACIFIC	377	241	63.9	53	14.1	185	49.1	29	7.7	169	44.8	25	6.6	134	35.5	22	5.8	161	42.7	25	6.6	162	43.0
Alaska	12	3	25.0	3	25.0	2	16.7	0	8.3	2	16.7	0	0.0	1	8.3	0	8.3	0	0.0	0	0.0	4	33.3
California	229	159	69.4	37	16.2	120	52.4	15	6.6	112	48.9	16	7.0	95	41.5	14	6.1	108	47.2	17	7.4	97	42.4
Hawaii	11	8	72.7	2	18.2	6	54.5	2	6.6	6	54.5	1	9.1	5	45.5	1	9.1	7	63.6	1	9.1	5	45.5
Oregon	60	30	50.0	6	10.0	24	40.0	6	10.0	19	31.7	3	5.0	15	25.0	3	5.0	21	35.0	4	6.7	29	48.3
Washington	65	41	63.1	7	10.8	33	50.8	5	7.7	30	46.2	5	7.7	18	27.7	3	4.6	24	36.9	3	4.6	27	41.5

Table 7 (Continued)

These data include only hospital-based facilities and services as reported by responding hospitals in Section C of the 2017 AHA Annual Survey, beginning on page 217. Census divisions represent all U.S. hospitals. Community hospitals are listed separately under United States. No estimates have been made for nonresponding hospitals. Definitions of facilities and services are listed in the Glossary, page 203.

CLASSIFICATION	HOSPITALS REPORTING	EMERGENCY SERVICES						ENDOSCOPIC SERVICES									
		EMERGENCY DEPARTMENT		PEDIATRIC EMERGENCY DEPARTMENT		TRAUMA CENTER (CERTIFIED)		ENDOSCOPIC ULTRASOUND		ABLATION OF BARRETT'S ESOPHAGUS		ESOPHAGEAL IMPEDANCE STUDY		ENDOSCOPIC RETROGRADE CHOLANGIO-PANCREATOGRAPHY		OPTICAL COLONOSCOPY	
		Number	Percent	Number	Percent	Number	Percent	Number	Percent	Number	Percent	Number	Percent	Number	Percent	Number	Percent
UNITED STATES	4,280	3,562	83.2	919	21.5	1,676	39.2	1,580	36.9	1,187	27.7	1,105	25.8	1,831	42.8	2,896	67.7
COMMUNITY HOSPITALS	3,877	3,488	90.0	909	23.4	1,664	42.9	1,544	39.8	1,161	29.9	1,083	27.9	1,801	46.5	2,839	73.2
CENSUS DIVISION 1, NEW ENGLAND	163	133	81.6	44	27.0	49	30.1	73	44.8	52	31.9	53	32.5	86	52.8	123	75.5
Connecticut	28	22	78.6	9	32.1	11	39.3	17	60.7	13	46.4	15	53.6	20	71.4	20	71.4
Maine	32	28	87.5	5	15.6	10	31.3	12	37.5	5	15.6	7	21.9	8	25.0	26	81.3
Massachusetts	56	42	75.0	18	32.1	15	26.8	28	50.0	19	33.9	19	33.9	33	58.9	38	67.9
New Hampshire	26	23	88.5	10	38.5	10	38.5	9	34.6	9	34.6	6	23.1	13	50.0	23	88.5
Rhode Island	9	8	88.9	1	11.1	1	11.1	5	55.6	4	44.4	3	33.3	7	77.8	7	77.8
Vermont	12	10	83.3	1	8.3	2	16.7	2	16.7	2	16.7	3	25.0	5	41.7	9	75.0
CENSUS DIVISION 2, MIDDLE ATLANTIC	373	315	84.5	118	31.6	112	30.0	215	57.6	165	44.2	136	36.5	258	69.2	282	75.6
New Jersey	73	57	78.1	39	53.4	13	17.8	48	65.8	40	54.8	30	41.1	51	69.9	47	64.4
New York	150	131	87.3	60	40.0	58	38.7	85	56.7	72	48.0	55	36.7	102	68.0	120	80.0
Pennsylvania	150	127	84.7	19	12.7	41	27.3	82	54.7	53	35.3	51	34.0	105	70.0	115	76.7
CENSUS DIVISION 3, SOUTH ATLANTIC	575	470	81.7	126	21.9	136	23.7	243	42.3	194	33.7	191	33.2	312	54.3	422	73.4
Delaware	9	4	44.4	4	44.4	5	55.6	2	22.2	3	33.3	3	33.3	4	44.4	5	55.6
District of Columbia	10	6	60.0	3	30.0	4	40.0	7	70.0	4	40.0	5	50.0	5	50.0	7	70.0
Florida	117	102	87.2	37	31.6	24	20.5	62	53.0	51	43.6	43	36.8	85	72.6	92	78.6
Georgia	103	84	81.6	16	15.5	18	17.5	37	35.9	30	29.1	32	31.1	52	50.5	73	70.9
Maryland	44	38	86.4	20	45.5	13	29.5	28	63.6	17	43.2	17	38.6	32	72.7	34	77.3
North Carolina	89	80	89.9	13	14.6	17	19.1	36	40.4	36	40.4	34	38.2	50	56.2	78	87.6
South Carolina	75	54	72.0	6	8.0	15	20.0	23	30.7	13	17.3	15	20.0	26	34.7	39	52.0
Virginia	76	62	81.6	22	28.9	14	18.4	33	43.4	24	31.6	27	35.5	37	48.7	57	75.0
West Virginia	52	40	76.9	5	9.6	26	50.0	15	28.8	14	26.9	15	28.8	21	40.4	37	71.2
CENSUS DIVISION 4, EAST NORTH CENTRAL	695	600	86.3	159	22.7	287	41.3	267	38.4	219	31.5	202	29.1	317	45.6	482	69.4
Illinois	162	146	90.1	52	32.1	61	37.7	79	48.8	66	40.7	52	32.1	99	61.1	128	79.0
Indiana	110	91	82.7	18	16.4	24	21.8	41	37.3	34	30.9	28	25.5	48	43.6	81	73.6
Michigan	135	115	85.2	30	22.2	58	43.0	56	41.5	37	27.4	35	25.9	61	45.2	103	76.3
Ohio	142	126	88.7	34	23.9	45	31.7	61	43.0	52	36.6	57	40.1	73	51.4	103	72.5
Wisconsin	146	122	83.6	24	16.4	99	67.8	30	20.5	21	14.4	30	20.5	36	24.7	67	45.9
CENSUS DIVISION 5, EAST SOUTH CENTRAL	308	245	79.5	47	15.3	123	39.9	84	27.3	76	24.7	71	23.1	105	34.1	163	52.9
Alabama	50	41	82.0	5	10.0	25	50.0	21	42.0	14	28.0	15	30.0	21	42.0	33	66.0
Kentucky	80	65	81.3	7	8.8	16	20.0	25	31.3	24	30.0	20	25.0	40	50.0	49	61.3
Mississippi	104	81	77.9	16	15.4	70	67.3	16	15.4	16	15.4	14	13.5	19	18.3	36	34.6
Tennessee	74	58	78.4	19	25.7	12	16.2	22	29.7	22	29.7	22	29.7	25	33.8	45	60.8
CENSUS DIVISION 6, WEST NORTH CENTRAL	614	553	90.1	109	17.8	300	48.9	145	23.6	105	17.1	105	17.1	139	22.6	442	72.0
Iowa	123	118	95.9	19	15.4	94	76.4	33	26.8	21	17.1	17	13.8	20	16.3	100	81.3
Kansas	127	113	89.0	16	12.6	33	26.0	12	9.4	16	12.6	15	11.8	20	15.7	85	66.9
Minnesota	97	93	95.9	20	20.6	75	77.3	31	32.0	20	20.6	20	20.6	25	25.8	74	76.3
Missouri	144	111	77.1	21	14.6	31	21.5	42	29.2	31	21.5	33	22.9	51	35.4	92	63.9
Nebraska	55	51	92.7	20	36.4	29	52.7	16	29.1	10	18.2	11	20.0	13	23.6	45	81.8
North Dakota	24	23	95.8	4	16.7	11	45.8	5	20.8	2	8.3	3	12.5	5	20.8	18	75.0
South Dakota	44	44	100.0	9	20.5	27	61.4	6	13.6	5	11.4	6	13.6	5	11.4	28	63.6
CENSUS DIVISION 7, WEST SOUTH CENTRAL	851	628	73.8	121	14.2	349	41.0	222	26.1	151	17.7	133	15.6	264	31.0	461	54.2
Arkansas	86	66	76.7	10	11.6	47	54.7	22	25.6	10	11.6	18	20.9	20	23.3	55	64.0
Louisiana	87	61	70.1	15	17.2	11	12.6	32	36.8	20	23.0	19	21.8	30	34.5	50	57.5
Oklahoma	113	99	87.6	13	11.5	52	46.0	21	18.6	21	18.6	15	13.3	27	23.9	71	62.8
Texas	565	402	71.2	83	14.7	239	42.3	147	26.0	100	17.7	81	14.3	187	33.1	285	50.4
CENSUS DIVISION 8, MOUNTAIN	324	283	87.3	85	26.2	163	50.3	122	37.7	83	25.6	84	25.9	112	34.6	215	66.4
Arizona	55	43	78.2	20	36.4	23	41.8	32	58.2	23	41.8	15	27.3	30	54.5	37	67.3
Colorado	69	65	94.2	15	21.7	58	84.1	26	37.7	18	26.1	22	31.9	31	44.9	52	75.4
Idaho	33	30	90.9	10	30.3	28	84.8	11	33.3	9	27.3	9	27.3	8	24.2	24	72.7
Montana	53	50	94.3	13	24.5	28	52.8	9	17.0	5	9.4	6	11.3	7	13.2	29	54.7
Nevada	27	19	70.4	6	22.2	3	11.1	11	40.7	9	33.3	7	25.9	8	29.6	16	59.3
New Mexico	29	27	93.1	6	20.7	7	24.1	12	41.4	6	20.7	7	24.1	9	31.0	21	72.4
Utah	38	31	81.6	9	23.7	19	50.0	13	34.2	10	26.3	12	31.6	15	39.5	24	63.2
Wyoming	20	18	90.0	6	30.0	15	75.0	8	40.0	3	15.0	6	30.0	4	20.0	12	60.0
CENSUS DIVISION 9, PACIFIC	377	335	88.9	111	29.4	157	41.6	209	55.4	142	37.7	130	34.5	238	63.1	306	81.2
Alaska	12	11	91.7	2	16.7	5	41.7	2	16.7	3	25.0	3	25.0	3	25.0	9	75.0
California	229	198	86.5	73	31.9	63	27.5	140	61.1	95	41.5	87	38.0	172	75.1	180	78.6
Hawaii	11	9	81.8	4	36.4	5	45.5	6	54.5	3	27.3	3	27.3	3	27.3	9	81.8
Oregon	60	59	98.3	10	16.7	40	66.7	33	55.0	20	33.3	15	25.0	21	35.0	52	86.7
Washington	65	58	89.2	22	33.8	44	67.7	28	43.1	21	32.3	22	33.8	34	52.3	56	86.2

Table 7 (Continued)

These data include only hospital-based facilities and services as reported by responding hospitals in Section C of the 2017 AHA Annual Survey, beginning on page 217. Census divisions represent all U.S. hospitals. Community hospitals are listed separately under United States. No estimates have been made for nonresponding hospitals. Definitions of facilities and services are listed in the Glossary, page 203.

CLASSIFICATION	HOSPITALS REPORTING	ASSISTIVE TECHNOLOGY CENTER Number	Percent	ELECTRODIAGNOSTIC SERVICES Number	Percent	PHYSICAL REHABILITATION OUTPATIENT SERVICES Number	Percent	PROSTHETIC ORTHOTIC SERVICES Number	Percent	ROBOT ASSISTED WALKING THERAPY Number	Percent	SIMULATED REHABILITATION ENVIRONMENT Number	Percent	PEDIATRIC CARE Number	Percent	CONSULTATION/LIAISON SERVICES Number	Percent	EDUCATION SERVICES Number	Percent	EMERGENCY SERVICES Number	Percent
UNITED STATES	4,280	1,068	25.0	1,198	28.0	3,084	72.1	856	20.0	224	5.2	1,303	30.4	531	12.4	1,527	35.7	1,120	26.2	1,516	35.4
COMMUNITY HOSPITALS	3,877	1,005	25.9	1,158	29.9	2,997	77.3	799	20.6	217	5.6	1,260	32.5	378	9.7	1,323	34.1	880	22.7	1,354	34.9
CENSUS DIVISION 1, NEW ENGLAND	163	51	31.3	60	36.8	139	85.3	41	25.2	9	5.5	59	36.2	37	22.7	100	61.3	77	47.2	83	50.9
Connecticut	28	13	46.4	12	42.9	22	78.6	9	32.1	5	17.9	13	46.4	8	28.6	22	78.6	18	64.3	19	67.9
Maine	32	9	28.1	9	28.1	26	81.3	5	15.6	1	3.1	15	46.9	7	21.9	11	34.4	8	25.0	9	28.1
Massachusetts	56	12	21.4	22	39.3	49	87.5	10	17.9	2	3.6	15	26.8	13	23.2	40	71.4	32	57.1	31	55.4
New Hampshire	26	11	42.3	8	30.8	25	96.2	9	34.6	0	0.0	10	38.5	4	15.4	15	57.7	10	38.5	14	53.8
Rhode Island	9	2	22.2	4	44.4	7	77.8	5	55.6	0	0.0	2	22.2	2	22.2	6	66.7	5	55.6	5	55.6
Vermont	12	4	33.3	5	41.7	10	83.3	3	25.0	1	8.3	4	33.3	3	25.0	6	50.0	4	33.3	5	41.7
CENSUS DIVISION 2, MIDDLE ATLANTIC	373	122	32.7	189	50.7	295	79.1	120	32.2	33	8.8	165	44.2	64	17.2	245	65.7	174	46.6	210	56.3
New Jersey	73	29	39.7	37	50.7	58	79.5	32	43.8	7	9.6	34	46.6	17	23.3	52	71.2	43	58.9	46	63.0
New York	150	48	32.0	80	53.3	133	88.7	55	36.7	15	10.0	59	39.3	35	23.3	107	71.3	78	52.0	89	59.3
Pennsylvania	150	45	30.0	72	48.0	104	69.3	33	22.0	11	7.3	72	48.0	12	8.0	86	57.3	53	35.3	75	50.0
CENSUS DIVISION 3, SOUTH ATLANTIC	575	170	29.6	183	31.8	417	72.5	173	30.1	38	6.6	203	35.3	82	14.3	230	40.0	170	29.6	242	42.1
Delaware	9	0	0.0	2	22.2	5	55.6	3	33.3	1	11.1	4	44.4	3	33.3	4	44.4	4	44.4	3	33.3
District of Columbia	10	6	60.0	5	50.0	8	80.0	4	40.0	1	10.0	5	50.0	2	20.0	6	60.0	5	50.0	7	70.0
Florida	117	45	38.5	40	34.2	96	82.1	33	28.2	10	8.5	50	42.7	19	16.2	51	43.6	31	26.5	52	44.4
Georgia	103	14	13.6	17	16.5	71	68.9	17	16.5	2	1.9	21	20.4	6	5.8	31	30.1	21	20.4	32	31.1
Maryland	44	12	27.3	23	52.3	36	81.8	16	36.4	3	6.8	18	40.9	15	34.1	33	75.0	26	59.1	32	72.7
North Carolina	89	33	37.1	33	37.1	77	86.5	20	22.5	6	6.7	41	46.1	11	12.4	37	41.6	31	34.8	39	43.8
South Carolina	75	8	10.7	8	10.7	29	38.7	49	65.3	5	6.7	17	22.7	12	16.0	22	29.3	15	20.0	31	41.3
Virginia	76	45	59.2	39	51.3	63	82.9	22	28.9	8	10.5	36	47.4	10	13.2	36	47.4	26	34.2	36	47.4
West Virginia	52	7	13.5	16	30.8	32	61.5	9	17.3	2	3.8	11	21.2	4	7.7	10	19.2	11	21.2	10	19.2
CENSUS DIVISION 4, EAST NORTH CENTRAL	695	168	24.2	257	37.0	564	81.2	163	23.5	36	5.2	273	39.3	113	16.3	296	42.6	219	31.5	265	38.1
Illinois	162	38	23.5	72	44.4	133	82.1	41	25.3	6	3.7	68	42.0	37	22.8	73	45.1	69	42.6	74	45.7
Indiana	110	30	27.3	35	31.8	87	79.1	30	27.3	6	5.5	36	32.7	10	9.1	25	22.7	23	20.9	30	27.3
Michigan	135	38	28.1	59	43.7	112	83.0	27	20.0	9	6.7	58	43.0	16	11.9	69	51.1	47	34.8	55	40.7
Ohio	142	47	33.1	63	44.4	118	83.1	32	22.5	9	6.3	65	45.8	17	12.0	69	48.6	42	29.6	62	43.7
Wisconsin	146	15	10.3	28	19.2	114	78.1	33	22.6	6	4.1	46	31.5	33	22.6	60	41.1	38	26.0	44	30.1
CENSUS DIVISION 5, EAST SOUTH CENTRAL	308	59	19.2	58	18.8	196	63.6	39	12.7	16	5.2	65	21.1	30	9.7	84	27.3	67	21.8	83	26.9
Alabama	50	8	16.0	10	20.0	36	72.0	11	22.0	4	8.0	7	14.0	6	12.0	16	32.0	13	26.0	15	30.0
Kentucky	80	20	25.0	23	28.8	59	73.8	9	11.3	6	7.5	17	21.3	7	8.8	26	32.5	19	23.8	26	32.5
Mississippi	104	11	10.6	13	12.5	54	51.9	11	10.6	4	3.8	21	20.2	9	8.7	20	19.2	19	18.3	16	15.4
Tennessee	74	20	27.0	12	16.2	47	63.5	8	10.8	2	2.7	20	27.0	8	10.8	22	29.7	16	21.6	26	35.1
CENSUS DIVISION 6, WEST NORTH CENTRAL	614	123	20.0	128	20.8	497	80.9	103	16.8	23	3.7	164	26.7	73	11.9	150	24.4	118	19.2	179	29.2
Iowa	123	33	26.8	24	19.5	103	83.7	13	10.6	3	2.4	37	30.1	18	14.6	34	27.6	31	25.2	46	37.4
Kansas	127	19	15.0	17	13.4	105	82.7	13	10.2	7	5.5	26	20.5	4	3.1	15	11.8	9	7.1	22	17.3
Minnesota	97	24	24.7	23	23.7	89	91.8	14	14.4	5	5.2	33	34.0	13	13.4	39	40.2	26	26.8	33	34.0
Missouri	144	20	13.9	34	23.6	98	68.1	33	22.9	6	4.2	45	31.3	26	18.1	40	27.8	36	25.0	54	37.5
Nebraska	55	11	20.0	13	23.6	43	78.2	17	30.9	1	1.8	13	23.6	5	9.1	11	20.0	6	10.9	9	16.4
North Dakota	24	6	25.0	6	25.0	21	87.5	5	20.8	0	0.0	4	16.7	4	16.7	5	20.8	5	20.8	6	25.0
South Dakota	44	10	22.7	11	25.0	38	86.4	7	15.9	1	2.3	6	13.6	3	6.8	6	13.6	5	11.4	9	20.5
CENSUS DIVISION 7, WEST SOUTH CENTRAL	851	191	22.4	104	12.2	480	56.4	83	9.8	35	4.1	183	21.5	68	8.0	163	19.2	133	15.6	190	22.3
Arkansas	86	19	22.1	9	10.5	51	59.3	8	9.3	4	4.7	18	20.9	8	9.3	18	20.9	12	14.0	24	27.9
Louisiana	87	26	29.9	13	14.9	54	62.1	13	14.9	2	2.3	26	29.9	6	6.9	22	25.3	17	19.5	35	40.2
Oklahoma	113	23	20.4	14	12.4	73	64.6	13	11.5	1	0.9	16	14.2	9	8.0	27	23.9	18	15.9	28	24.8
Texas	565	123	21.8	68	12.0	302	53.5	49	8.7	28	5.0	123	21.8	45	8.0	96	17.0	86	15.2	103	18.2
CENSUS DIVISION 8, MOUNTAIN	324	80	24.7	77	24.7	226	69.8	52	16.0	14	4.3	84	25.9	33	10.2	92	28.4	69	21.3	122	37.7
Arizona	55	15	27.3	17	30.9	36	65.5	13	23.6	2	3.6	20	36.4	5	9.1	23	41.8	16	29.1	22	40.0
Colorado	69	18	26.1	21	30.4	59	85.5	11	15.9	4	5.8	25	36.2	7	10.1	20	29.0	16	23.2	24	34.8
Idaho	33	11	33.3	6	18.2	24	72.7	3	9.1	1	3.0	10	30.3	3	9.1	7	21.2	7	21.2	11	33.3
Montana	53	15	28.3	11	20.8	45	84.9	7	13.2	1	1.9	8	15.1	6	11.3	12	22.6	10	18.9	16	30.2
Nevada	27	3	11.1	5	18.5	14	51.9	3	11.1	3	11.1	7	25.9	2	7.4	6	22.2	4	14.8	11	40.7
New Mexico	29	10	34.5	7	24.1	21	72.4	3	10.3	2	6.9	5	17.2	2	6.9	11	37.9	4	13.8	10	34.5
Utah	38	6	15.8	7	18.4	15	39.5	8	21.1	1	2.6	6	15.8	5	13.2	9	23.7	10	26.3	24	63.2
Wyoming	20	2	10.0	3	15.0	12	60.0	4	20.0	0	0.0	3	15.0	3	15.0	4	20.0	2	10.0	4	20.0
CENSUS DIVISION 9, PACIFIC	377	104	27.6	142	37.7	270	71.6	82	21.8	20	5.3	107	28.4	31	8.2	167	44.3	93	24.7	142	37.7
Alaska	12	1	8.3	3	25.0	10	83.3	1	8.3	0	0.0	1	8.3	1	8.3	6	50.0	5	41.7	6	50.0
California	229	55	24.0	84	36.7	152	66.4	53	23.1	11	4.8	69	30.1	20	8.7	108	47.2	60	26.2	84	36.7
Hawaii	11	3	27.3	6	54.5	8	72.7	3	27.3	0	0.0	2	18.2	2	18.2	5	45.5	3	27.3	4	36.4
Oregon	60	22	36.7	20	33.3	49	81.7	9	15.0	3	5.0	10	16.7	4	6.7	19	31.7	10	16.7	23	38.3
Washington	65	23	35.4	29	44.6	51	78.5	13	20.0	6	9.2	25	38.5	4	6.2	29	44.6	15	23.1	25	38.5

Table 7 (Continued)

These data include only hospital-based facilities and services as reported by responding hospitals in Section C of the 2017 AHA Annual Survey, beginning on page 217. Census divisions represent all U.S. hospitals. Community hospitals are listed separately under United States. No estimates have been made for nonresponding hospitals. Definitions of facilities and services are listed in the Glossary, page 203.

CLASSIFICATION	HOSPITALS REPORTING	PSYCHIATRIC SERVICES GERIATRIC SERVICES Number	Percent	OUTPATIENT SERVICES Number	Percent	PARTIAL HOSPITALIZATION PROGRAM Number	Percent	RESIDENTIAL TREATMENT Number	Percent	CT SCANNER Number	Percent	RADIOLOGY, DIAGNOSTIC DIAGNOSTIC RADIOISOTOPE FACILITY Number	Percent	ELECTRON BEAM COMPUTED TOMOGRAPHY (EBCT) Number	Percent	FULL-FIELD DIGITAL MAMMOGRAPHY (FFDM) Number	Percent	MAGNETIC RESONANCE IMAGING (MRI) Number	Percent	INTRAOPERATIVE MAGNETIC IMAGING Number	Percent
UNITED STATES	4,280	1,015	23.7	1,283	29.5	520	12.1	206	4.8	3,613	84.4	2,442	57.1	325	7.6	2,601	60.8	2,991	67.5	229	5.4
COMMUNITY HOSPITALS	3,877	802	20.7	1,057	27.3	389	10.0	102	2.6	3,529	91.0	2,297	61.8	317	8.2	2,574	66.4	2,832	73.0	221	5.7
CENSUS DIVISION 1, NEW ENGLAND	163	48	29.4	93	57.1	43	26.4	14	8.6	137	84.0	114	69.9	8	4.9	120	73.6	109	66.9	9	5.5
Connecticut	28	11	39.3	18	64.3	12	42.9	6	21.4	23	82.1	20	71.4	2	7.1	21	75.0	21	75.0	2	7.1
Maine	32	5	15.6	16	50.0	4	12.5	1	3.1	28	87.5	25	78.1	1	3.1	24	75.0	21	65.6	1	3.1
Massachusetts	56	18	32.1	34	60.7	20	35.7	5	8.9	44	78.6	39	69.6	3	5.4	39	69.6	34	60.7	5	8.9
New Hampshire	26	8	30.8	13	50.0	2	7.7	1	3.8	24	92.3	15	57.7	1	3.8	21	80.8	16	61.5	1	3.8
Rhode Island	9	2	22.2	5	55.6	3	33.3	1	11.1	8	88.9	7	77.8	0	0.0	7	77.8	8	88.9	0	0.0
Vermont	12	4	33.3	7	58.3	2	16.7	1	8.3	10	83.3	8	66.7	1	8.3	8	66.7	9	75.0	0	0.0
CENSUS DIVISION 2, MIDDLE ATLANTIC	373	130	34.9	170	45.6	66	17.7	29	7.8	327	87.7	293	78.6	51	13.7	281	75.3	295	79.1	26	7.0
New Jersey	73	26	35.6	39	53.4	22	30.1	7	9.6	57	78.1	55	75.3	14	19.2	49	67.1	55	75.3	4	5.5
New York	150	56	37.3	87	58.0	28	18.7	12	8.0	138	92.0	116	77.3	20	13.3	111	80.7	117	78.0	14	9.3
Pennsylvania	150	48	32.0	44	29.3	16	10.7	10	6.7	132	88.0	122	81.3	17	11.3	111	74.0	123	82.0	8	5.3
CENSUS DIVISION 3, SOUTH ATLANTIC	575	152	26.4	152	26.4	73	12.7	25	4.3	484	84.2	382	66.4	43	7.5	393	68.3	422	73.4	26	4.5
Delaware	9	3	33.3	6	66.7	3	33.3	1	11.1	5	55.6	4	44.4	0	0.0	3	33.3	5	55.6	0	0.0
District of Columbia	10	3	30.0	6	60.0	3	30.0	1	10.0	7	70.0	5	50.0	0	0.0	6	60.0	7	70.0	2	20.0
Florida	117	29	24.8	27	23.1	13	11.1	6	5.8	105	89.7	88	75.2	23	19.7	83	70.9	97	82.9	14	12.0
Georgia	103	21	20.4	23	22.3	13	12.6	6	5.8	87	84.5	63	61.2	2	1.9	70	68.0	76	73.8	2	1.9
Maryland	44	21	47.7	25	56.8	16	36.4	4	9.1	40	90.9	38	86.4	2	4.5	27	61.4	34	77.3	3	6.8
North Carolina	89	24	27.0	23	24.7	9	10.1	2	2.2	80	89.9	62	69.7	2	2.2	68	76.4	69	77.5	3	3.4
South Carolina	76	20	26.7	14	18.7	5	6.7	2	2.7	55	73.3	41	54.7	2	2.7	48	64.0	51	68.0	1	1.1
Virginia	76	21	27.6	23	30.3	10	13.2	5	6.6	63	82.9	51	67.1	2	2.7	54	71.1	56	73.7	4	5.3
West Virginia	52	10	19.2	8	15.4	3	5.8	2	3.8	42	80.8	30	57.7	3	5.8	34	65.4	27	51.9	0	0.0
CENSUS DIVISION 4, EAST NORTH CENTRAL	695	200	28.8	244	35.1	106	15.3	31	4.5	612	88.1	454	65.3	64	9.2	468	67.3	521	75.0	44	6.3
Illinois	162	57	35.2	75	46.3	38	23.5	5	3.1	147	90.7	108	66.7	6	3.7	123	75.9	119	73.5	9	5.6
Indiana	110	21	19.1	29	26.4	13	11.8	6	5.5	95	86.4	70	63.6	13	11.8	80	72.7	89	80.9	6	5.5
Michigan	135	34	25.2	42	31.1	18	13.3	7	5.2	119	88.1	92	68.1	10	7.4	95	70.4	94	69.6	5	3.7
Ohio	142	42	29.6	49	34.5	25	17.6	9	6.3	130	91.5	105	73.9	22	15.5	103	72.5	119	83.8	11	7.7
Wisconsin	146	46	31.5	49	33.6	12	8.2	4	2.7	121	82.9	79	54.1	13	8.9	67	45.9	100	68.5	13	8.9
CENSUS DIVISION 5, EAST SOUTH CENTRAL	308	94	30.5	70	22.7	29	9.4	19	6.2	250	81.2	168	54.5	27	8.8	161	52.3	194	63.0	17	5.5
Alabama	50	14	28.0	9	18.0	1	2.0	1	2.0	42	84.0	31	62.0	4	8.0	31	62.0	37	74.0	1	2.0
Kentucky	80	18	22.5	16	20.0	9	11.3	4	5.0	65	81.3	50	62.5	4	5.0	45	56.3	57	71.3	3	3.8
Mississippi	104	40	38.5	29	27.9	11	10.6	7	6.7	84	80.8	47	45.2	11	10.6	39	37.5	47	45.2	8	7.7
Tennessee	74	22	29.7	16	21.6	8	10.8	4	5.4	59	79.7	40	54.1	8	10.8	46	62.2	53	71.6	6	8.1
CENSUS DIVISION 6, WEST NORTH CENTRAL	614	124	20.2	176	28.7	46	7.5	24	3.9	553	90.1	246	40.1	20	3.3	377	61.4	375	61.1	23	3.7
Iowa	123	23	18.7	36	29.3	8	6.5	2	1.6	115	93.5	44	34.1	3	3.3	98	79.7	73	59.3	1	0.8
Kansas	127	17	13.4	16	12.6	6	4.7	2	1.6	112	88.2	44	34.6	5	3.9	53	41.7	58	45.7	4	3.1
Minnesota	97	19	19.6	44	45.4	13	13.4	5	5.2	96	99.0	42	43.3	2	2.1	71	73.2	75	77.3	7	7.2
Missouri	144	49	34.0	49	34.0	11	7.6	9	6.3	112	77.8	74	51.4	6	4.2	81	56.3	105	72.9	6	4.2
Nebraska	55	7	12.7	14	25.5	2	3.6	1	1.8	53	96.4	19	34.5	1	1.8	43	78.2	37	67.3	2	3.6
North Dakota	24	6	25.0	7	29.2	4	16.7	1	4.2	22	91.7	11	45.8	1	4.2	14	58.3	11	45.8	2	8.3
South Dakota	44	3	6.8	10	22.7	2	4.5	2	6.8	43	97.7	14	31.8	1	2.3	17	38.6	16	36.4	1	2.3
CENSUS DIVISION 7, WEST SOUTH CENTRAL	851	160	18.8	153	18.0	82	9.6	29	3.4	629	73.9	355	41.7	46	5.4	356	41.8	458	53.8	39	4.6
Arkansas	86	25	29.1	16	18.6	7	8.1	5	5.8	67	77.9	39	45.3	6	7.0	46	53.5	53	61.6	4	4.7
Louisiana	87	23	26.4	25	28.7	15	17.2	7	8.0	65	74.7	48	55.2	7	8.0	52	59.8	56	64.4	9	10.3
Oklahoma	113	23	20.4	20	17.7	7	6.2	7	6.2	96	85.0	44	38.9	6	5.3	54	47.8	70	61.9	2	1.8
Texas	565	89	15.8	92	16.3	53	9.4	15	2.7	401	71.0	224	39.6	27	4.8	204	36.1	279	49.4	24	4.2
CENSUS DIVISION 8, MOUNTAIN	324	51	15.7	91	28.1	31	9.6	17	5.2	280	86.4	165	50.9	27	8.3	192	59.3	225	69.4	21	6.5
Arizona	55	13	23.6	17	30.9	5	9.1	2	3.6	45	81.8	32	58.2	4	7.3	27	49.1	40	72.7	6	10.9
Colorado	69	9	13.0	19	27.5	5	7.2	2	2.9	64	92.8	45	65.2	7	10.1	48	69.6	56	81.2	6	8.7
Idaho	33	2	6.1	12	36.4	3	9.1	0	0.0	31	93.9	15	45.5	3	9.1	20	60.6	26	78.8	1	3.0
Montana	53	4	7.5	13	24.5	6	11.3	3	5.7	45	84.9	17	32.1	2	3.8	29	54.7	26	49.1	1	1.9
Nevada	27	7	25.9	11	40.7	4	14.8	3	11.1	20	74.1	14	51.9	1	3.7	12	44.4	18	66.7	1	3.7
New Mexico	29	4	13.8	8	31.0	0	0.0	0	0.0	26	89.7	13	44.8	3	10.3	19	65.5	17	58.6	4	13.8
Utah	38	9	23.7	8	21.1	6	18.4	6	15.8	32	84.2	16	42.1	3	7.9	26	68.4	29	76.3	1	2.6
Wyoming	20	3	15.0	3	15.0	1	5.0	1	5.0	17	85.0	10	50.0	4	20.0	11	55.0	13	65.0	1	5.0
CENSUS DIVISION 9, PACIFIC	377	56	14.9	114	30.2	44	11.7	18	4.8	341	90.5	265	70.3	39	10.3	253	67.1	292	77.5	24	6.4
Alaska	12	1	8.3	6	50.0	3	25.0	2	16.7	12	100.0	5	41.7	0	0.0	8	66.7	6	50.0	0	0.0
California	229	39	17.0	68	29.7	27	11.8	8	3.5	202	88.2	168	73.4	27	11.8	150	65.5	179	78.2	18	7.9
Hawaii	11	1	9.1	4	36.4	3	27.3	1	9.1	9	81.8	9	81.8	1	9.1	9	81.8	9	81.8	0	0.0
Oregon	60	4	6.7	14	23.3	5	8.3	4	6.7	59	98.3	40	66.7	4	6.7	47	78.3	49	81.8	4	6.7
Washington	65	11	16.9	22	33.8	6	9.2	3	4.6	59	90.8	43	66.2	4	12.3	39	60.0	49	75.4	2	3.1

Table 7 (Continued)

These data include only hospital-based facilities and services as reported by responding hospitals in Section C of the 2017 AHA Annual Survey, beginning on page 217. Census divisions represent all U.S. hospitals. Community hospitals are listed separately under United States. No estimates have been made for nonresponding hospitals. Definitions of facilities and services are listed in the Glossary, page 203.

Columns under **RADIOLOGY, DIAGNOSTIC**: Magneto-encephalography; Multi-slice Spiral Computed Tomography (<64 Slice CT); Multi-slice Spiral Computed Tomography (64+ Slice CT); Positron Emission Tomography (PET); Positron Emission Tomography/CT (PET/CT); Single Photon Emission Computerized Tomography (SPECT); Ultrasound. Columns under **RADIOLOGY, THERAPEUTIC**: Image-Guided Radiation Therapy (IGRT); Intensity-Modulated Radiation Therapy (IMRT); Proton Beam Therapy.

CLASSIFICATION	HOSPITALS REPORTING	MAGNETO-ENCEPHALOGRAPHY No.	Pct.	MULTI-SLICE SPIRAL CT (<64 SLICE) No.	Pct.	MULTI-SLICE SPIRAL CT (64+ SLICE) No.	Pct.	PET No.	Pct.	PET/CT No.	Pct.	SPECT No.	Pct.	ULTRASOUND No.	Pct.	IGRT No.	Pct.	IMRT No.	Pct.	PROTON BEAM No.	Pct.
UNITED STATES	4,280	119	2.8	2,317	54.1	2,428	56.7	753	17.6	996	23.0	1,649	38.5	3,512	82.1	1,078	25.2	1,120	26.2	131	3.1
COMMUNITY HOSPITALS	3,877	114	2.9	2,274	58.7	2,382	61.4	732	18.9	963	24.8	1,610	41.5	3,427	88.4	1,058	27.3	1,101	28.4	124	3.2
CENSUS DIVISION 1, NEW ENGLAND	163	5	3.1	95	58.3	105	64.4	32	19.6	47	28.8	87	53.4	143	87.7	57	35.0	55	33.7	7	4.3
Connecticut	28	0	0.0	15	53.6	22	78.6	10	35.7	18	64.3	18	64.3	25	89.3	19	67.9	17	60.7	1	3.6
Maine	32	0	0.0	18	56.3	15	46.9	3	9.4	5	15.6	12	37.5	28	87.5	5	15.6	6	18.8	0	0.0
Massachusetts	56	4	7.1	33	58.9	42	75.0	13	23.2	17	30.4	29	51.8	48	85.7	23	41.1	22	39.3	5	8.9
New Hampshire	26	1	3.8	15	57.7	16	61.5	3	11.5	4	15.4	15	57.7	24	92.3	6	23.1	6	23.1	0	0.0
Rhode Island	9	0	0.0	7	77.8	5	55.6	2	22.2	1	11.1	6	66.7	8	88.9	1	11.1	1	11.1	1	11.1
Vermont	12	0	0.0	7	58.3	5	41.7	1	8.3	2	16.7	7	58.3	10	83.3	3	25.0	3	25.0	0	0.0
CENSUS DIVISION 2, MIDDLE ATLANTIC	373	12	3.2	239	64.1	262	70.2	92	24.7	131	35.1	216	57.9	329	88.2	157	42.1	170	45.6	18	4.8
New Jersey	73	4	5.5	49	67.1	47	64.4	25	34.2	32	43.8	45	61.6	58	79.5	35	47.9	39	53.4	2	2.7
New York	150	3	2.0	103	68.7	109	72.7	35	23.3	45	30.0	84	56.0	137	91.3	61	40.7	65	43.3	11	7.3
Pennsylvania	150	5	3.3	87	58.0	106	70.7	32	21.3	54	36.0	87	58.0	134	89.3	61	40.7	66	44.0	5	3.3
CENSUS DIVISION 3, SOUTH ATLANTIC	575	17	3.0	373	64.9	359	62.4	115	20.0	152	26.4	279	48.5	487	84.7	195	33.9	196	34.1	14	2.4
Delaware	10	1	10.0	5	55.6	7	70.0	1	11.1	4	44.4	4	44.4	5	55.6	4	44.4	4	44.4	0	0.0
District of Columbia	10	1	10.0	5	50.0	7	70.0	6	60.0	6	60.0	8	80.0	8	80.0	4	40.0	4	40.0	0	0.0
Florida	117	6	5.1	91	77.8	90	76.9	37	31.6	47	40.2	61	52.1	104	88.9	44	37.6	40	34.2	2	1.7
Georgia	103	2	1.9	57	55.3	58	56.3	19	18.4	28	27.2	35	34.0	87	84.5	32	31.1	30	29.1	1	1.0
Maryland	44	1	2.3	32	72.7	35	79.5	11	25.0	12	27.3	31	70.5	39	88.6	24	54.5	23	52.3	3	6.8
North Carolina	89	2	2.2	66	74.2	55	61.8	12	13.5	23	25.8	52	58.4	83	93.3	37	41.6	40	44.9	5	5.6
South Carolina	75	2	2.7	42	56.0	37	49.3	5	6.7	10	13.3	22	29.3	57	76.0	11	14.7	14	18.7	0	0.0
Virginia	76	2	2.6	42	55.3	49	64.5	13	17.1	13	17.1	47	61.8	63	82.9	28	36.8	30	39.5	3	3.9
West Virginia	52	0	0.0	33	63.5	23	44.2	11	21.2	9	17.3	20	38.5	41	78.8	11	21.2	11	21.2	0	0.0
CENSUS DIVISION 4, EAST NORTH CENTRAL	695	26	3.7	369	53.1	455	65.5	159	22.9	202	29.1	340	48.9	601	86.5	206	29.6	221	31.8	24	3.5
Illinois	162	3	1.9	99	61.1	118	72.8	32	19.8	52	32.1	80	49.4	141	87.0	54	33.3	60	37.0	5	3.1
Indiana	110	6	5.5	61	55.5	73	66.4	23	20.9	28	25.5	44	40.0	93	84.5	38	34.5	40	36.4	5	4.5
Michigan	135	4	3.0	71	52.6	96	71.1	23	17.0	34	25.2	68	50.4	123	91.1	37	27.4	43	31.9	4	3.0
Ohio	142	8	5.6	98	69.0	99	69.7	48	33.8	57	40.1	83	58.5	130	91.5	49	34.5	47	33.1	7	4.9
Wisconsin	146	5	3.4	40	27.4	69	47.3	33	22.6	31	21.2	65	44.5	114	78.1	28	19.2	31	21.2	3	2.1
CENSUS DIVISION 5, EAST SOUTH CENTRAL	308	6	1.9	156	50.6	158	51.3	50	16.2	53	17.2	111	36.0	248	80.5	66	21.4	68	22.1	7	2.3
Alabama	50	1	2.0	32	64.0	25	50.0	8	16.0	13	26.0	18	36.0	41	82.0	12	24.0	12	24.0	0	0.0
Kentucky	80	2	2.5	42	52.5	49	61.3	13	16.3	15	18.8	35	43.8	66	82.5	16	20.0	18	22.5	2	2.5
Mississippi	104	1	1.0	42	40.4	40	38.5	15	14.4	10	9.6	30	28.8	83	79.8	14	13.5	13	12.5	2	1.9
Tennessee	74	2	2.7	40	54.1	44	59.5	14	18.9	15	20.3	28	37.8	58	78.4	24	32.4	25	33.8	3	4.1
CENSUS DIVISION 6, WEST NORTH CENTRAL	614	13	2.1	311	50.7	296	48.2	70	11.4	114	18.6	174	28.3	503	81.9	104	16.9	109	17.8	15	2.4
Iowa	123	1	0.8	67	54.5	61	49.6	12	9.8	22	17.9	21	17.1	116	94.3	17	13.8	16	13.0	2	1.6
Kansas	127	2	1.6	67	52.8	36	28.3	8	6.3	12	9.4	21	16.5	91	71.7	15	11.8	15	11.8	3	2.4
Minnesota	97	3	3.1	47	48.5	64	66.0	12	12.4	20	20.6	35	36.1	86	88.7	18	18.6	21	21.6	1	1.0
Missouri	144	4	2.8	61	42.4	82	56.9	20	13.9	42	29.2	55	38.2	108	75.0	35	24.3	36	25.0	5	3.5
Nebraska	55	2	3.6	32	58.2	27	49.1	10	18.2	11	20.0	12	21.8	50	90.9	11	20.0	12	21.8	2	3.6
North Dakota	24	1	4.2	15	62.5	10	41.7	4	16.7	4	16.7	6	25.0	17	70.8	3	12.5	3	12.5	1	4.2
South Dakota	44	0	0.0	22	50.0	16	36.4	4	9.1	3	6.8	10	22.7	35	79.5	5	11.4	6	13.6	1	2.3
CENSUS DIVISION 7, WEST SOUTH CENTRAL	851	16	1.9	391	45.9	342	40.2	84	9.9	105	12.3	186	21.9	588	69.1	96	11.3	105	12.3	14	1.6
Arkansas	86	2	2.3	36	41.9	39	45.3	10	11.6	11	12.8	19	22.1	65	75.6	8	9.3	8	9.3	1	1.2
Louisiana	87	1	1.1	42	48.3	43	49.4	15	17.2	23	26.4	24	27.6	64	73.6	19	21.8	21	24.1	3	3.4
Oklahoma	113	0	0.0	58	51.3	48	42.5	14	12.4	19	16.8	24	21.2	86	76.1	19	16.8	20	17.7	1	0.9
Texas	565	13	2.3	255	45.1	212	37.5	45	8.0	52	9.2	119	21.1	373	66.0	49	8.7	56	9.9	9	1.6
CENSUS DIVISION 8, MOUNTAIN	324	7	2.2	151	46.6	194	59.9	58	17.9	67	20.7	94	29.0	270	83.3	76	23.5	76	23.5	16	4.9
Arizona	55	2	3.6	33	60.0	30	54.5	13	23.6	17	30.9	25	45.5	43	78.2	13	23.6	13	23.6	4	7.3
Colorado	69	2	2.9	39	56.5	53	76.8	17	24.6	18	26.1	20	29.0	64	92.8	22	31.9	22	31.9	4	5.8
Idaho	33	0	0.0	15	45.5	17	51.5	3	9.1	4	12.1	7	21.2	30	90.9	5	15.2	7	21.2	2	6.1
Montana	53	1	1.9	26	49.1	21	39.6	5	9.4	7	13.2	11	20.8	40	75.5	11	20.8	10	18.9	1	1.9
Nevada	27	0	0.0	10	37.0	13	48.1	5	18.5	6	22.2	4	14.8	19	70.4	3	11.1	3	11.1	1	3.7
New Mexico	29	1	3.4	13	44.8	20	69.0	3	10.3	4	13.8	5	17.2	26	89.7	6	20.7	7	24.1	2	6.9
Utah	38	1	2.6	8	21.1	27	71.1	9	23.7	9	23.7	17	44.7	32	84.2	11	28.9	10	26.3	1	2.6
Wyoming	20	0	0.0	7	35.0	13	65.0	3	15.0	2	10.0	5	25.0	16	80.0	5	25.0	4	20.0	1	5.0
CENSUS DIVISION 9, PACIFIC	377	17	4.5	232	61.5	257	68.2	93	24.7	115	30.5	162	43.0	343	91.0	121	32.1	120	31.8	16	4.2
Alaska	12	0	0.0	7	58.3	5	41.7	0	0.0	0	0.0	1	8.3	11	91.7	2	16.7	1	8.3	0	0.0
California	229	15	6.6	140	61.1	161	70.3	64	27.9	82	35.8	108	47.2	208	90.8	82	35.8	81	35.4	11	4.8
Hawaii	11	0	0.0	4	36.4	8	72.7	0	0.0	2	18.2	3	27.3	9	81.8	2	18.2	2	18.2	0	0.0
Oregon	60	1	1.7	38	63.3	40	66.7	13	21.7	12	20.0	31	51.7	58	96.7	15	25.0	15	25.0	3	5.0
Washington	65	1	1.5	43	66.2	43	66.2	16	24.6	19	29.2	19	29.2	57	87.7	20	30.8	21	32.3	2	3.1

Table 7 (Continued)

These data include only hospital-based facilities and services as reported by responding hospitals in Section C of the 2017 AHA Annual Survey, beginning on page 217. Census divisions represent all U.S. hospitals. Community hospitals are listed separately under United States. No estimates have been made for nonresponding hospitals. Definitions of facilities and services are listed in the Glossary, page 203.

Column groups: RADIOLOGY, THERAPEUTIC (Shaped Beam Radiation System; Stereotactic Radiosurgery); TRANSPLANT (Kidney; Liver; Lung).

CLASSIFICATION	HOSPITALS REPORTING	Shaped Beam No.	Shaped Beam %	Stereotactic No.	Stereotactic %	Bone Marrow No.	Bone Marrow %	Heart No.	Heart %	Kidney No.	Kidney %	Liver No.	Liver %	Lung No.	Lung %	Tissue No.	Tissue %	Other No.	Other %
UNITED STATES	4,280	924	21.6	895	20.9	204	4.8	141	3.3	224	5.2	139	3.2	85	2.0	461	10.8	228	5.3
COMMUNITY HOSPITALS	3,877	909	23.4	887	22.9	199	5.1	136	3.5	218	5.6	135	3.5	81	2.1	452	11.7	222	5.7
CENSUS DIVISION 1, NEW ENGLAND	163	51	31.3	49	30.1	12	7.4	6	3.7	15	9.2	6	3.7	4	2.5	20	12.3	10	6.1
Connecticut	28	16	57.1	16	57.1	1	3.6	2	7.1	2	7.1	2	7.1	0	0.0	2	7.1	1	3.6
Maine	32	5	15.6	4	12.5	0	0.0	0	0.0	1	3.1	0	0.0	0	0.0	1	3.1	0	0.0
Massachusetts	56	20	35.7	20	35.7	9	16.1	4	7.1	9	16.1	4	7.1	4	7.1	11	19.6	6	10.7
New Hampshire	26	6	23.1	6	23.1	1	3.8	0	0.0	1	3.8	0	0.0	0	0.0	1	3.8	1	3.8
Rhode Island	9	1	11.1	1	11.1	0	0.0	0	0.0	1	11.1	0	0.0	0	0.0	2	22.2	1	11.1
Vermont	12	3	25.0	2	16.7	1	8.3	0	0.0	1	8.3	0	0.0	0	0.0	3	25.0	1	8.3
CENSUS DIVISION 2, MIDDLE ATLANTIC	373	143	38.3	118	31.6	32	8.6	16	4.3	33	8.8	19	5.1	9	2.4	90	24.1	41	11.0
New Jersey	73	37	50.7	30	41.1	2	2.7	2	2.7	4	5.5	2	2.7	2	2.7	24	32.9	5	6.8
New York	150	56	37.3	40	26.7	16	10.7	6	4.0	13	8.7	6	4.0	2	1.3	36	24.0	17	11.3
Pennsylvania	150	50	33.3	48	32.0	14	9.3	8	5.3	16	10.7	11	7.3	5	3.3	30	20.0	19	12.7
CENSUS DIVISION 3, SOUTH ATLANTIC	575	168	29.2	153	26.6	39	6.8	25	4.3	32	5.6	20	3.5	14	2.4	73	12.7	39	6.8
Delaware	9	4	44.4	3	33.3	2	22.2	1	11.1	2	22.2	1	11.1	0	0.0	0	0.0	0	0.0
District of Columbia	10	5	50.0	4	40.0	3	30.0	2	20.0	3	30.0	1	10.0	0	0.0	3	30.0	2	20.0
Florida	117	36	30.8	44	37.6	10	8.5	9	7.7	10	8.5	7	6.0	6	5.1	20	17.1	7	6.0
Georgia	103	29	28.2	30	29.1	4	3.9	2	1.9	3	2.9	2	1.9	1	1.0	10	9.7	3	2.9
Maryland	44	19	43.2	17	38.6	4	9.1	2	4.5	2	4.5	2	4.5	2	4.5	8	18.2	6	13.6
North Carolina	89	34	38.2	18	20.2	4	4.5	4	4.5	5	5.6	4	4.5	2	2.2	7	7.9	9	10.1
South Carolina	75	11	14.7	10	13.3	4	5.3	1	1.3	1	1.3	1	1.3	1	1.3	4	5.3	3	4.0
Virginia	76	21	27.6	17	22.4	6	7.9	4	5.3	5	6.6	2	2.6	2	2.6	16	21.1	7	9.2
West Virginia	52	9	17.3	10	19.2	2	3.8	0	0.0	1	1.9	0	0.0	0	0.0	5	9.6	2	3.8
CENSUS DIVISION 4, EAST NORTH CENTRAL	695	181	26.0	163	23.5	30	4.3	25	3.6	35	5.0	22	3.2	19	2.7	76	10.9	26	3.7
Illinois	162	49	30.2	46	28.4	10	6.2	6	3.7	9	5.6	6	3.7	4	2.5	17	10.5	7	4.3
Indiana	110	29	26.4	25	22.7	1	0.9	3	2.7	3	2.7	1	0.9	1	0.9	7	6.4	3	2.7
Michigan	135	38	28.1	35	25.9	7	5.2	6	4.4	10	7.4	6	4.4	5	3.7	22	16.3	7	5.2
Ohio	142	42	29.6	39	27.5	7	4.9	6	4.2	9	6.3	6	4.2	5	3.5	24	16.9	6	4.2
Wisconsin	146	23	15.8	18	12.3	5	3.4	4	2.7	4	2.7	3	2.1	4	2.7	6	4.1	3	2.1
CENSUS DIVISION 5, EAST SOUTH CENTRAL	308	50	16.2	61	19.8	13	4.2	11	3.6	11	3.6	9	2.9	5	1.6	22	7.1	15	4.9
Alabama	50	8	16.0	12	24.0	2	4.0	2	4.0	2	4.0	2	4.0	1	2.0	3	6.0	3	6.0
Kentucky	80	13	16.3	15	18.8	4	5.0	3	3.8	3	3.8	2	2.5	2	2.5	10	12.5	3	3.8
Mississippi	104	11	10.6	13	12.5	2	1.9	2	1.9	1	1.0	1	1.0	0	0.0	3	2.9	2	1.9
Tennessee	74	18	24.3	21	28.4	5	6.8	4	5.4	5	6.8	3	4.1	2	2.7	6	8.1	7	9.5
CENSUS DIVISION 6, WEST NORTH CENTRAL	614	84	13.7	75	12.2	16	2.6	14	2.3	24	3.9	15	2.4	9	1.5	37	6.0	26	4.2
Iowa	123	16	13.0	13	10.6	2	1.6	2	1.6	5	4.1	2	1.6	2	1.6	4	3.3	2	1.6
Kansas	127	13	10.2	10	7.9	1	0.8	1	0.8	1	0.8	1	0.8	0	0.0	4	3.1	4	3.1
Minnesota	97	12	12.4	15	15.5	2	2.1	3	3.1	4	4.1	3	3.1	3	3.1	8	8.2	3	3.1
Missouri	144	27	18.8	22	15.3	5	3.5	5	3.5	8	5.6	6	4.2	2	1.4	13	9.0	10	6.9
Nebraska	55	10	18.2	9	16.4	2	3.6	2	3.6	1	1.8	1	1.8	1	1.8	5	9.1	3	5.5
North Dakota	24	2	8.3	3	12.5	1	4.2	1	4.2	3	12.5	1	4.2	1	4.2	2	8.3	2	8.3
South Dakota	44	4	9.1	3	6.8	1	2.3	0	0.0	2	4.5	1	2.3	0	0.0	2	4.5	2	4.5
CENSUS DIVISION 7, WEST SOUTH CENTRAL	851	79	9.3	108	12.7	21	2.5	17	2.0	34	4.0	21	2.5	11	1.3	43	5.1	30	3.5
Arkansas	86	6	7.0	12	14.0	2	2.3	2	2.3	2	2.3	1	1.2	0	0.0	4	4.7	1	1.2
Louisiana	87	15	17.2	21	24.1	4	4.6	1	1.1	4	4.6	3	3.4	1	1.1	6	6.9	5	5.7
Oklahoma	113	15	13.3	15	13.3	3	2.7	1	0.9	4	3.5	2	1.8	1	0.9	6	5.3	3	2.7
Texas	565	43	7.6	60	10.6	12	2.1	13	2.3	24	4.2	15	2.7	9	1.6	27	4.8	21	3.7
CENSUS DIVISION 8, MOUNTAIN	324	65	20.1	62	19.1	15	4.6	9	2.8	15	4.6	12	3.7	6	1.9	43	13.3	11	3.4
Arizona	55	11	20.0	14	25.5	5	9.1	3	5.5	5	9.1	5	9.1	3	5.5	10	18.2	5	9.1
Colorado	69	20	29.0	12	17.4	3	4.3	2	2.9	4	5.8	4	5.8	1	1.4	9	13.0	4	5.8
Idaho	33	4	12.1	7	21.2	1	3.0	0	0.0	0	0.0	0	0.0	0	0.0	2	6.1	0	0.0
Montana	53	9	17.0	11	20.8	1	1.9	0	0.0	0	0.0	0	0.0	0	0.0	3	5.7	0	0.0
Nevada	27	3	11.1	4	14.8	1	3.7	0	0.0	1	3.7	0	0.0	0	0.0	1	3.7	0	0.0
New Mexico	29	5	17.2	2	6.9	1	3.4	0	0.0	2	6.9	0	0.0	0	0.0	0	0.0	0	0.0
Utah	38	10	26.3	9	23.7	3	7.9	4	10.5	3	7.9	3	7.9	2	5.3	17	44.7	2	5.3
Wyoming	20	3	15.0	3	15.0	0	0.0	0	0.0	0	0.0	0	0.0	0	0.0	1	5.0	0	0.0
CENSUS DIVISION 9, PACIFIC	377	103	27.3	106	28.1	26	6.9	18	4.8	25	6.6	15	4.0	8	2.1	57	15.1	30	8.0
Alaska	12	1	8.3	1	8.3	0	0.0	0	0.0	0	0.0	0	0.0	0	0.0	0	0.0	0	0.0
California	229	70	30.6	74	32.3	18	7.9	15	6.6	18	7.9	11	4.8	7	3.1	45	19.7	21	9.2
Hawaii	11	0	0.0	1	9.1	1	9.1	0	0.0	1	9.1	1	9.1	0	0.0	0	0.0	0	0.0
Oregon	60	13	21.7	10	16.7	2	3.3	1	1.7	2	3.3	1	1.7	0	0.0	5	8.3	3	5.0
Washington	65	19	29.2	20	30.8	5	7.7	2	3.1	4	6.2	2	3.1	1	1.5	6	9.2	4	6.2

Table 8

MSAs

Metropolitan Statistical Areas

Metropolitan Statistical Areas (MSAs) definitions announced by the U.S. Office of Management and Budget (OMB) effective June 6, 2003 were added with the 2006 edition.

According to the OMB, an MSA is a geographical designation that represents an integrated social and economic unit with a large population nucleus. Under these standards, an area qualifies for recognition as an MSA if there is a city within the area of at least 50,000 with a total metropolitan population of at least 100,000. MSAs are defined as entire counties. In addition to the county containing the main city, an MSA also includes additional counties having strong economic and social ties to the central county. Such counties must have a specified level of commuting to the central counties and must meet certain standards regarding metropolitan character, such as population density.

When an MSA encompasses two or more central cities, up to three cities may be specified in the MSA title. They will be listed in order of population size. When a single central city exists, the MSA is named for that particular city. A MSA may extend beyond a single state.

An MSA containing a single core with a population of 2.5 million or more may be subdivided to form smaller groupings of counties referred to as Metropolitan Divisions. Where they exist the Metropolitan Divisions are shown in this table rather than the entire MSA.

TABLE 8

U.S. CENSUS DIVISION 1, NEW ENGLAND

U.S. Community Hospitals
(Nonfederal, short-term general and other special hospitals)

2017 Utilization, Personnel and Finances

CLASSIFICATION	Hospitals	Beds	Admissions	Inpatient Days	Adjusted Inpatient Days	Average Daily Census	Adjusted Average Daily Census	Average Stay (days)	Surgical Operations	NEWBORNS Bassinets	NEWBORNS Births	OUTPATIENT VISITS Emergency	OUTPATIENT VISITS Total
UNITED STATES	5,262	798,921	34,305,620	186,198,977	398,570,958	510,123	1,092,133	5.4	28,221,774	55,181	3,656,809	144,814,804	766,076,124
Nonmetropolitan	1,875	112,806	3,115,229	20,415,212	70,105,531	55,939	192,099	6.6	3,649,248	9,005	358,113	22,487,032	131,567,025
Metropolitan	3,387	686,115	31,190,391	165,783,765	328,465,427	454,184	900,034	5.3	24,572,526	46,176	3,298,696	122,327,772	634,509,099
CENSUS DIVISION 1, NEW ENGLAND.	194	32,381	1,575,699	8,500,057	20,915,514	23,289	57,301	5.4	1,355,096	2,199	142,432	7,169,939	49,105,875
Nonmetropolitan	55	3,373	133,712	807,012	2,823,700	2,211	7,732	6.0	154,772	328	12,102	885,682	8,279,131
Metropolitan	139	29,008	1,441,987	7,693,045	18,091,814	21,078	49,569	5.3	1,200,324	1,871	130,330	6,284,257	40,826,744
Connecticut	32	7,086	371,009	1,993,586	4,361,176	5,461	11,948	5.4	321,535	438	35,626	1,698,661	9,333,607
Nonmetropolitan	2	123	7,171	31,633	91,028	87	249	4.4	4,245	9	640	44,683	338,466
Metropolitan	30	6,963	363,838	1,961,953	4,270,148	5,374	11,699	5.4	317,290	429	34,986	1,653,978	8,995,141
Bridgeport-Stamford-Norwalk	6	1,595	87,892	446,511	1,018,139	1,223	2,791	5.1	73,880	113	11,445	390,081	1,994,236
Hartford-West Hartford-East Hartford	11	2,547	125,595	701,606	1,404,982	1,922	3,849	5.6	117,733	133	11,589	616,050	3,078,217
New Haven-Milford	9	2,225	121,316	684,589	1,441,137	1,875	3,948	5.6	99,130	109	9,048	433,543	2,352,184
Norwich-New London	2	435	22,720	104,403	312,358	286	855	4.6	21,178	42	2,335	157,615	819,500
Worcester	2	161	6,315	24,844	93,532	68	256	3.9	5,369	32	569	56,689	751,004
Maine	34	3,410	132,963	860,280	2,333,472	2,357	6,390	6.5	148,416	246	12,260	682,348	6,330,586
Nonmetropolitan	21	1,151	38,279	281,503	1,002,738	772	2,744	7.4	46,017	122	3,832	292,873	2,686,229
Metropolitan	13	2,259	94,684	578,777	1,330,734	1,585	3,646	6.1	102,399	124	8,428	389,475	3,644,357
Bangor	4	519	25,868	134,686	303,805	369	834	5.2	29,297	22	1,982	76,871	823,309
Lewiston-Auburn	2	540	16,610	145,261	406,170	398	1,112	8.7	12,623	35	1,235	70,606	1,050,438
Portland-South Portland	7	1,200	52,206	298,830	620,759	818	1,700	5.7	60,479	67	5,211	241,998	1,770,610
Massachusetts	75	15,650	780,695	4,139,660	9,920,640	11,344	27,181	5.3	616,564	1,025	65,673	3,323,247	22,875,366
Nonmetropolitan	3	133	6,872	26,913	102,390	74	281	3.9	6,503	28	685	57,143	308,719
Metropolitan	72	15,517	773,823	4,112,747	9,818,250	11,270	26,900	5.3	610,061	997	64,988	3,266,104	22,566,647
Barnstable Town	3	414	22,384	104,517	296,326	286	812	4.7	14,015	18	1,206	113,169	892,267
Boston	26	6,467	325,384	1,855,978	4,069,336	5,087	11,149	5.7	273,023	316	25,243	1,022,568	9,026,883
Cambridge-Newton-Framingham	19	4,045	198,631	1,008,971	2,681,590	2,764	7,346	5.1	141,647	321	19,862	870,477	5,875,177
Pittsfield	2	300	15,091	68,690	221,855	188	608	4.6	13,707	24	813	79,089	431,914
Providence-Warwick	4	1,090	55,090	255,256	590,746	699	1,618	4.6	36,075	69	4,328	373,510	1,513,258
Springfield	8	1,557	73,078	379,370	906,002	1,042	2,484	5.2	56,763	94	5,342	386,110	2,260,329
Worcester	10	1,644	84,165	439,965	1,052,395	1,204	2,883	5.2	74,831	155	8,194	421,181	2,566,819
New Hampshire	28	2,784	125,925	650,448	1,991,627	1,781	5,456	5.2	123,977	260	12,671	653,750	5,387,438
Nonmetropolitan	17	1,221	54,571	293,248	1,025,174	802	2,807	5.4	64,055	94	4,184	258,341	3,050,646
Metropolitan	11	1,563	71,354	357,200	966,453	979	2,649	5.0	59,922	166	8,487	395,409	2,336,792
Manchester-Nashua	5	838	40,397	195,063	541,091	535	1,483	4.8	29,065	102	5,013	173,638	1,183,023
Rockingham County-Strafford County	6	725	30,957	162,137	425,362	444	1,166	5.2	30,857	64	3,474	221,771	1,153,769
Rhode Island	11	2,156	115,669	554,246	1,285,811	1,519	3,523	4.8	90,390	114	10,853	500,399	2,089,570
Metropolitan	11	2,156	115,669	554,246	1,285,811	1,519	3,523	4.8	90,390	114	10,853	500,399	2,089,570
Providence-Warwick	11	2,156	115,669	554,246	1,285,811	1,519	3,523	4.8	90,390	114	10,853	500,399	2,089,570
Vermont	14	1,295	49,438	301,837	1,022,788	827	2,803	6.1	54,214	116	5,349	311,534	3,089,308
Nonmetropolitan	12	745	26,819	173,715	602,370	476	1,651	6.5	33,952	75	2,761	232,642	1,895,071
Metropolitan	2	550	22,619	128,122	420,418	351	1,152	5.7	20,262	41	2,588	78,892	1,194,237
Burlington-South Burlington	2	550	22,619	128,122	420,418	351	1,152	5.7	20,262	41	2,588	78,892	1,194,237

MSAs

TABLE 8

U.S. CENSUS DIVISION 1, NEW ENGLAND

U.S. Community Hospitals
(Nonfederal, short-term general and other special hospitals)

2017 Utilization, Personnel and Finances

FULL-TIME EQUIVALENT PERSONNEL					FULL-TIME EQUIV. TRAINEES			EXPENSES						
								LABOR				TOTAL		
Physicians and Dentists	Registered Nurses	Licensed Practical Nurses	Other Salaried Personnel	Total Personnel	Medical and Dental Residents	Other Trainees	Total Trainees	Payroll (in thousands)	Employee Benefits (in thousands)	Total (in thousands)	Percent of Total	Amount (in thousands)	Adjusted per Admission	Adjusted per Inpatient Day
146,381	1,558,038	76,534	2,704,453	5,216,348	118,075	9,440	127,515	$363,806,143	$96,687,285	$460,493,398	47.7	$966,204,239	$13,126.02	$2,424.17
16,529	156,072	20,966	348,592	631,393	1,972	334	2,306	37,559,678	9,847,876	47,407,559	50.0	94,728,753	8,855.26	1,351.23
129,852	1,401,966	55,568	2,355,861	4,584,955	116,103	9,106	125,209	326,246,465	86,839,408	413,085,839	47.4	871,475,486	13,852.21	2,653.17
14,752	74,267	2,312	176,624	299,513	10,165	1,293	11,458	22,295,233	5,794,859	28,090,091	48.2	58,229,116	14,681.10	2,784.02
1,808	8,171	556	21,738	36,337	489	33	522	2,744,627	681,469	3,426,099	55.5	6,174,918	12,881.72	2,186.82
12,944	66,096	1,756	154,886	263,176	9,676	1,260	10,936	19,550,606	5,113,390	24,663,992	47.4	52,054,198	14,928.47	2,877.22
1,371	15,789	316	31,432	55,985	2,066	66	2,132	4,211,431	1,015,375	5,226,806	44.9	11,649,294	13,842.50	2,671.14
18	247	9	729	1,095	0	0	0	64,359	15,033	79,393	54.4	146,049	7,078.43	1,604.44
1,353	15,542	307	30,703	54,890	2,066	66	2,132	4,147,071	1,000,342	5,147,413	44.7	11,503,245	14,012.51	2,693.88
381	3,513	64	7,236	13,014	458	10	468	1,026,778	232,302	1,259,079	43.9	2,869,009	14,269.35	2,817.90
693	5,190	107	12,565	20,687	202	49	251	1,477,263	397,631	1,874,893	47.0	3,992,477	15,195.66	2,841.66
201	6,071	121	8,300	17,429	1,406	5	1,411	1,328,674	283,501	1,612,175	42.0	3,842,936	14,476.84	2,666.60
41	621	0	1,727	2,628	0	2	2	238,857	75,263	314,121	51.3	612,702	9,023.06	1,961.54
37	147	15	875	1,132	0	0	0	75,500	11,646	87,145	46.8	186,121	7,830.09	1,989.92
1,805	7,738	332	20,890	34,102	343	24	367	2,320,735	621,346	2,942,081	52.9	5,561,475	15,353.05	2,383.35
547	2,590	159	7,735	12,392	11	7	18	765,949	195,232	961,181	53.6	1,793,013	12,376.96	1,788.12
1,258	5,148	173	13,155	21,710	332	17	349	1,554,786	426,114	1,980,900	52.6	3,768,462	17,336.47	2,831.87
369	1,396	33	2,896	5,157	28	16	44	420,349	111,826	532,175	51.6	1,031,946	17,278.00	3,396.74
243	794	60	1,813	3,191	20	0	20	245,857	46,975	292,832	50.4	580,505	13,989.41	1,429.22
646	2,958	80	8,446	13,362	284	1	285	888,581	267,312	1,155,893	53.6	2,156,012	18,562.30	3,473.19
8,624	36,315	1,006	89,384	149,555	6,193	1,097	7,290	10,936,478	2,900,085	13,836,560	46.2	29,941,210	15,541.49	3,018.07
17	268	10	644	1,036	1	2	3	86,855	19,349	106,205	45.8	232,142	8,721.55	2,267.23
8,607	36,047	996	88,740	148,519	6,192	1,095	7,287	10,849,623	2,880,735	13,730,355	46.2	29,709,069	15,637.03	3,025.90
83	505	8	1,744	2,472	0	0	0	281,831	77,054	358,885	52.0	689,793	10,539.56	2,327.82
5,281	19,224	410	47,475	79,498	4,622	962	5,584	5,707,415	1,561,697	7,269,110	43.0	16,919,180	23,619.58	4,157.73
1,519	7,714	249	19,466	32,225	496	71	567	2,309,656	577,533	2,887,188	52.5	5,501,044	9,894.05	2,051.41
82	593	75	1,695	2,640	75	7	82	230,201	59,262	289,462	58.1	515,982	10,498.54	2,325.76
38	1,889	33	4,291	6,891	12	1	13	546,326	145,207	691,533	54.0	1,279,496	9,990.36	2,165.90
600	2,701	45	5,525	10,556	355	33	388	749,699	164,369	914,070	46.9	1,949,491	11,068.04	2,151.75
1,004	3,421	176	8,544	14,237	632	21	653	1,024,495	295,612	1,320,107	46.3	2,854,082	13,669.24	2,711.99
1,455	6,885	345	17,538	29,410	487	19	506	2,244,299	573,848	2,818,149	55.0	5,127,353	12,939.07	2,574.45
880	3,590	216	8,416	14,838	472	19	491	1,314,690	325,201	1,639,893	57.6	2,848,583	14,802.52	2,778.63
575	3,295	129	9,122	14,572	15	0	15	929,610	248,647	1,178,256	51.7	2,278,771	11,179.76	2,357.87
393	1,888	66	5,066	8,175	0	0	0	510,066	135,496	645,562	51.7	1,248,323	10,810.33	2,307.05
182	1,407	63	4,056	6,397	15	0	15	419,544	113,151	532,694	51.7	1,030,448	11,662.58	2,422.52
477	4,353	75	9,480	16,135	730	47	777	1,454,182	388,087	1,842,269	52.5	3,510,874	12,961.09	2,730.47
477	4,353	75	9,480	16,135	730	47	777	1,454,182	388,087	1,842,269	52.5	3,510,874	12,961.09	2,730.47
477	4,353	75	9,480	16,135	730	47	777	1,454,182	388,087	1,842,269	52.5	3,510,874	12,961.09	2,730.47
1,020	3,187	238	7,900	14,326	346	40	386	1,128,107	296,119	1,424,226	58.4	2,438,910	14,449.97	2,384.57
346	1,476	162	4,214	6,976	5	5	10	512,774	126,654	639,427	55.4	1,155,132	12,185.06	1,917.64
674	1,711	76	3,686	7,350	341	35	376	615,334	169,465	784,799	61.1	1,283,778	17,352.10	3,053.58
674	1,711	76	3,686	7,350	341	35	376	615,334	169,465	784,799	61.1	1,283,778	17,352.10	3,053.58

MSAs

MSAs

CLASSIFICATION	Hospitals	Beds	Admissions	Inpatient Days	Adjusted Inpatient Days	Average Daily Census	Adjusted Average Daily Census	Average Stay (days)	Surgical Operations	NEWBORNS Bassinets	NEWBORNS Births	OUTPATIENT VISITS Emergency	OUTPATIENT VISITS Total
UNITED STATES	5,262	798,921	34,305,620	186,198,977	398,570,958	510,123	1,092,133	5.4	28,221,774	55,181	3,656,809	144,814,804	766,076,124
Nonmetropolitan	1,875	112,806	3,115,229	20,415,212	70,105,531	55,939	192,099	6.6	3,649,248	9,005	358,113	22,487,032	131,567,025
Metropolitan	3,387	686,115	31,190,391	165,783,765	328,465,427	454,184	900,034	5.3	24,572,526	46,176	3,298,696	122,327,772	634,509,099
CENSUS DIVISION 2, MIDDLE ATLANTIC	451	110,228	4,952,686	28,747,702	56,683,759	78,752	155,310	5.8	4,016,103	6,063	453,226	19,015,614	114,508,470
Nonmetropolitan	73	7,471	210,581	1,693,544	5,703,263	4,638	15,623	8.0	296,309	450	18,445	1,590,621	10,547,342
Metropolitan	378	102,757	4,742,105	27,054,158	50,980,496	74,114	139,687	5.7	3,719,794	5,613	434,781	17,424,993	103,961,128
New Jersey	82	21,201	1,076,863	5,085,634	8,849,847	13,930	24,243	4.7	573,477	1,315	97,326	3,785,951	15,427,252
Metropolitan	82	21,201	1,076,863	5,085,634	8,849,847	13,930	24,243	4.7	573,477	1,315	97,326	3,785,951	15,427,252
Allentown-Bethlehem-Easton	2	183	7,227	32,492	76,032	89	208	4.5	6,691	0	0	49,984	151,823
Atlantic City-Hammonton	4	841	41,193	190,094	367,300	521	1,007	4.6	17,200	58	1,800	125,422	437,481
Camden	12	3,214	138,867	749,514	1,260,354	2,052	3,451	5.4	86,999	115	11,829	567,650	1,732,396
New York-Jersey City-White Plains	35	9,790	570,263	2,315,007	4,020,935	6,340	11,014	4.1	268,657	691	52,287	1,723,483	7,876,943
Newark	19	5,638	251,034	1,444,848	2,446,124	3,958	6,703	5.8	145,069	359	25,567	975,531	4,022,621
Ocean City	1	178	6,735	28,120	78,908	77	216	4.2	3,734	16	364	43,863	203,245
Trenton	5	759	35,654	196,171	388,145	538	1,063	5.5	24,256	36	3,360	186,018	568,756
Vineland-Bridgeton	2	376	18,911	100,692	156,481	276	429	5.3	14,173	32	1,838	75,683	312,055
Wilmington	2	222	6,979	28,696	55,568	79	152	4.1	6,698	8	281	38,317	121,932
New York	168	51,808	2,272,583	14,972,556	28,923,081	41,019	79,235	6.6	2,040,855	3,006	221,466	8,632,643	57,600,133
Nonmetropolitan	35	3,874	98,781	954,233	3,150,951	2,613	8,632	9.7	149,920	244	9,979	800,378	5,697,837
Metropolitan	133	47,934	2,173,802	14,018,323	25,772,130	38,406	70,603	6.4	1,890,935	2,762	211,487	7,832,265	51,902,296
Albany-Schenectady-Troy	9	2,265	111,762	642,617	1,282,524	1,761	3,514	5.7	99,610	110	7,759	388,279	2,931,407
Binghamton	2	618	26,774	143,583	473,552	393	1,297	5.4	39,729	38	2,394	99,061	2,705,105
Buffalo-Cheektowaga-Niagara Falls	10	4,141	140,663	1,171,590	2,065,924	3,210	5,660	8.3	160,954	240	12,847	480,205	2,648,901
Dutchess County-Putnam County	3	597	33,244	145,805	287,193	399	787	4.4	34,641	39	3,471	124,392	554,061
Elmira	2	407	14,597	85,383	183,675	234	504	5.8	11,068	20	1,085	85,433	428,652
Glens Falls	1	314	13,058	64,850	167,926	178	460	5.0	11,011	16	1,046	50,914	739,474
Ithaca	1	193	6,596	29,282	110,981	80	304	4.4	7,176	21	857	30,135	272,753
Kingston	3	280	10,062	55,128	95,278	151	261	5.5	3,768	20	286	54,170	131,099
Nassau County-Suffolk County	21	7,511	418,972	2,494,507	4,407,052	6,835	12,074	6.0	340,357	472	39,333	1,213,603	6,292,525
New York-Jersey City-White Plains	58	25,684	1,147,347	7,555,163	12,832,702	20,699	35,152	6.6	966,748	1,389	119,080	4,349,352	25,967,846
Rochester	10	3,071	126,592	901,044	2,336,213	2,469	6,401	7.1	114,223	178	11,088	489,124	5,289,045
Syracuse	6	1,905	87,001	511,212	969,651	1,400	2,657	5.9	71,073	133	7,835	270,327	2,435,848
Utica-Rome	4	687	27,700	162,429	394,660	444	1,081	5.9	19,317	48	2,425	119,255	1,043,874
Watertown-Fort Drum	3	261	9,434	55,730	164,799	153	451	5.9	11,260	38	1,981	78,015	461,706
Pennsylvania	201	37,219	1,603,240	8,689,512	18,910,831	23,803	51,832	5.4	1,401,771	1,742	134,434	6,597,020	41,481,085
Nonmetropolitan	38	3,597	111,800	739,311	2,552,312	2,025	6,991	6.6	146,389	206	8,466	790,243	4,849,505
Metropolitan	163	33,622	1,491,440	7,950,201	16,358,519	21,778	44,841	5.3	1,255,382	1,536	125,968	5,806,777	36,631,580
Allentown-Bethlehem-Easton	11	2,433	108,917	636,388	1,343,056	1,743	3,681	5.8	91,635	80	9,627	448,802	2,318,224
Altoona	4	496	23,226	120,568	283,504	330	776	5.2	21,274	20	1,138	89,144	475,680
Bloomsburg-Berwick	5	789	36,869	204,970	517,597	562	1,418	5.6	30,899	34	2,617	129,293	1,572,560
Chambersburg-Waynesboro	2	327	15,992	64,786	168,352	178	461	4.1	12,521	31	1,773	78,024	481,494
East Stroudsburg	2	311	15,203	63,221	125,638	174	367	4.2	6,954	20	1,100	64,537	220,278
Erie	6	1,041	41,748	216,584	419,835	594	1,152	5.2	36,180	63	3,806	152,386	484,452
Gettysburg	1	76	3,944	15,463	55,884	42	153	3.9	4,022	16	497	30,662	197,941
Harrisburg-Carlisle	9	1,915	83,515	465,255	942,655	1,274	2,583	5.6	72,350	74	7,496	271,807	2,314,393
Johnstown	3	608	20,728	114,757	244,020	314	668	5.5	15,886	14	1,885	67,234	516,257
Lancaster	5	984	45,860	203,403	437,242	557	1,199	4.4	47,124	77	6,213	181,059	2,089,701
Lebanon	1	162	7,392	35,526	101,994	97	279	4.8	6,934	19	691	54,050	251,121
Montgomery County-Bucks County-Chester County	23	4,027	187,774	843,738	1,671,307	2,312	4,578	4.5	143,431	277	22,936	643,739	3,770,070
Philadelphia	27	7,873	350,230	1,969,728	3,663,553	5,395	10,033	5.6	296,277	280	23,893	1,245,176	7,458,176
Pittsburgh	35	7,891	343,526	1,943,157	3,954,791	5,325	10,837	5.7	300,814	302	24,605	1,356,495	7,872,403
Reading	5	1,063	47,708	217,166	466,043	595	1,278	4.6	24,959	56	4,279	179,193	1,560,426
Scranton-Wilkes-Barre-Hazleton	10	1,611	69,806	359,193	853,960	983	2,340	5.1	58,351	55	5,809	284,176	2,338,610
State College	2	333	15,525	67,633	156,988	185	430	4.4	12,504	5	1,368	58,120	330,832
Williamsport	3	401	12,849	101,555	258,632	278	708	7.9	12,196	15	1,015	68,328	305,738
York-Hanover	5	877	43,225	221,439	474,997	606	1,301	5.1	41,809	71	4,144	187,691	1,332,131
Youngstown-Warren-Boardman	4	404	17,403	85,671	218,471	234	599	4.9	19,262	27	1,076	216,861	741,093

TABLE 8

U.S. CENSUS DIVISION 2, MIDDLE ATLANTIC

U.S. Community Hospitals
(Nonfederal, short-term general and other special hospitals)

2017 Utilization, Personnel and Finances

MSAs

FULL-TIME EQUIVALENT PERSONNEL					FULL-TIME EQUIV. TRAINEES			EXPENSES LABOR				EXPENSES TOTAL		
Physicians and Dentists	Registered Nurses	Licensed Practical Nurses	Other Salaried Personnel	Total Personnel	Medical and Dental Residents	Other Trainees	Total Trainees	Payroll (in thousands)	Employee Benefits (in thousands)	Total (in thousands)	Percent of Total	Amount (in thousands)	Adjusted per Admission	Adjusted per Inpatient Day
146,381	1,558,038	76,534	2,704,453	5,216,348	118,075	9,440	127,515	$363,806,143	$96,687,285	$460,493,398	47.7	$968,204,239	$13,126.02	$2,424.17
16,529	156,072	20,966	348,592	631,393	1,972	334	2,306	37,559,678	9,847,876	47,407,559	50.0	94,728,753	8,855.26	1,351.23
129,852	1,401,966	55,568	2,355,861	4,584,955	116,103	9,106	125,209	326,246,465	86,839,408	413,085,839	47.4	871,475,486	13,852.21	2,653.17
29,476	218,603	9,219	417,706	780,327	31,407	1,091	32,498	58,518,345	16,300,363	74,818,710	50.7	147,584,661	15,182.22	2,603.65
1,000	9,608	1,498	23,352	41,251	202	10	212	2,400,795	646,504	3,047,296	51.8	5,886,922	8,464.08	1,032.20
28,476	208,995	7,721	394,354	739,076	31,205	1,081	32,286	56,117,550	15,653,860	71,771,414	50.7	141,697,739	15,699.94	2,779.45
3,140	38,228	766	69,538	128,667	2,727	85	2,812	9,513,058	2,104,153	11,617,214	49.1	23,641,357	12,445.92	2,671.39
3,140	38,228	766	69,538	128,667	2,727	85	2,812	9,513,058	2,104,153	11,617,214	49.1	23,641,357	12,445.92	2,671.39
9	326	3	571	1,082	24	1	25	77,975	17,537	95,513	53.2	179,415	10,721.61	2,359.73
53	1,456	40	2,567	4,828	64	0	64	423,623	94,827	518,451	52.3	991,534	12,571.43	2,699.52
801	5,078	164	10,432	18,807	346	5	351	1,173,371	279,913	1,453,286	44.0	3,301,940	13,905.54	2,619.85
1,231	18,493	298	31,737	59,477	1,146	55	1,201	4,367,247	949,337	5,316,586	48.4	10,981,016	10,975.48	2,730.96
922	10,335	157	20,030	36,110	929	17	946	2,849,446	591,474	3,440,919	51.9	6,631,546	15,458.73	2,711.04
0	215	0	527	890	0	7	7	55,008	17,076	72,084	57.1	126,166	6,675.82	1,598.91
114	1,549	48	2,625	5,180	65	0	65	353,256	87,049	440,305	47.2	932,737	12,565.84	2,403.06
5	540	39	730	1,616	149	0	149	159,724	51,861	211,586	58.2	363,786	11,978.87	2,324.80
5	236	17	319	677	4	0	4	53,406	15,078	68,484	51.4	133,215	9,880.93	2,397.33
16,972	105,632	5,666	223,112	403,170	19,866	496	20,362	33,137,778	10,072,595	43,210,371	55.0	78,608,242	18,198.03	2,717.77
560	4,933	843	12,916	22,245	59	4	63	1,373,443	365,430	1,738,874	54.3	3,205,036	9,989.67	1,017.16
16,412	100,699	4,823	210,196	380,925	19,807	492	20,299	31,764,334	9,707,164	41,471,497	55.0	75,401,206	18,856.63	2,925.69
344	4,823	166	8,539	16,710	569	9	578	1,014,428	206,154	1,220,582	44.2	2,760,306	12,420.83	2,152.24
307	1,277	186	3,835	6,175	99	0	99	369,074	102,589	471,663	48.9	964,400	10,564.71	2,036.52
418	7,233	539	11,790	22,925	65	95	160	1,589,083	599,592	2,188,674	55.1	3,969,676	15,912.12	1,921.50
0	1,242	1	1,437	3,135	0	1	1	254,666	90,544	345,210	41.8	825,129	12,548.54	2,873.08
140	511	125	2,473	3,565	110	1	111	161,243	42,007	203,250	47.5	427,961	13,968.31	2,329.99
67	512	50	1,214	2,187	0	0	0	162,876	28,454	191,330	54.9	348,210	10,298.11	2,073.59
11	396	9	797	1,392	2	5	7	73,765	27,095	100,860	50.2	200,782	8,031.59	1,809.15
0	454	9	729	1,439	4	0	4	84,388	25,645	110,032	56.5	194,802	11,511.10	2,044.57
4,466	18,234	423	37,878	68,711	4,040	12	4,052	6,230,363	1,693,967	7,924,330	59.0	13,424,945	18,141.50	3,046.24
9,020	53,425	1,937	115,975	207,951	13,312	315	13,627	18,895,474	6,024,336	24,719,809	54.9	45,057,894	22,926.99	3,511.18
1,249	7,556	790	14,280	27,362	913	52	965	1,785,415	458,980	2,244,395	56.8	3,948,955	12,636.53	1,690.32
197	3,307	400	7,502	12,661	642	0	642	901,806	313,352	1,215,159	52.2	2,327,205	15,052.49	2,400.04
111	1,242	109	2,720	4,764	39	2	41	310,980	60,837	371,817	56.6	656,664	10,284.81	1,663.87
82	487	79	1,027	1,948	12	0	12	130,774	33,613	164,386	55.9	294,279	10,782.99	1,785.68
9,364	74,743	2,787	125,056	248,490	8,814	510	9,324	15,867,510	4,123,615	19,991,125	44.1	45,337,062	12,946.54	2,397.41
440	4,675	655	10,436	19,006	143	6	149	1,027,351	281,073	1,308,422	48.8	2,681,886	7,157.75	1,050.77
8,924	70,068	2,132	114,620	229,484	8,671	504	9,175	14,840,159	3,842,542	18,682,703	43.8	42,655,176	13,640.13	2,607.52
798	5,177	95	9,812	18,797	487	0	487	1,071,996	228,177	1,300,173	44.2	2,938,997	12,780.97	2,188.29
59	909	48	1,387	2,680	11	2	13	170,996	43,487	214,484	42.8	500,920	8,960.36	1,766.89
550	1,850	175	4,092	7,944	441	1	442	376,796	106,470	483,265	38.7	1,249,250	12,925.91	2,413.56
3	520	10	1,287	2,087	0	38	38	149,431	58,773	208,204	58.0	358,765	8,484.66	2,131.04
43	575	18	914	1,850	19	2	21	114,510	28,247	142,757	47.4	300,873	9,963.34	2,394.76
59	1,900	51	2,229	5,071	44	1	45	247,335	58,313	305,647	37.9	806,236	9,987.81	1,920.36
0	179	2	295	633	0	0	0	41,513	14,471	55,984	35.0	159,812	11,211.70	2,859.70
1,294	4,191	388	9,687	17,475	887	7	894	968,152	271,280	1,239,433	43.6	2,840,971	16,316.54	3,013.80
16	674	47	1,814	2,871	108	0	108	165,217	43,242	208,459	49.4	422,404	9,273.40	1,731.02
134	1,729	66	3,659	6,683	52	0	52	458,434	142,664	601,099	46.4	1,296,521	13,070.29	2,965.22
0	263	3	453	920	18	0	18	62,583	18,113	80,696	40.0	201,969	9,516.97	1,980.21
691	7,784	135	11,691	23,564	325	6	331	1,636,485	401,326	2,037,813	47.8	4,263,304	11,166.77	2,550.88
3,431	20,398	317	31,726	64,728	4,536	242	4,778	5,068,450	1,307,929	6,376,378	47.7	13,377,179	20,687.95	3,651.42
1,448	15,770	319	20,036	45,157	1,340	188	1,528	2,513,714	611,458	3,125,172	36.0	8,693,010	11,895.08	2,198.10
31	1,989	73	4,301	7,530	125	4	129	485,590	137,153	622,743	50.1	1,242,333	12,096.71	2,665.70
313	2,456	198	5,008	9,266	73	12	85	484,583	126,503	611,088	38.8	1,576,298	9,432.30	1,845.87
14	425	8	1,104	1,802	1	0	1	181,630	54,438	236,069	57.4	411,356	11,347.76	2,620.30
1	595	100	971	2,003	19	0	19	130,025	35,143	165,168	45.8	360,865	12,074.72	1,395.28
15	1,842	54	3,056	6,034	163	1	164	383,207	123,762	506,968	40.4	1,253,491	13,121.30	2,638.94
24	842	25	1,098	2,389	22	0	22	129,511	31,591	161,103	40.2	400,623	8,625.56	1,833.76

TABLE **8**

U.S. CENSUS DIVISION 3, SOUTH ATLANTIC

U.S. Community Hospitals
(Nonfederal, short-term general and other special hospitals)

2017 Utilization, Personnel and Finances

CLASSIFICATION	Hospitals	Beds	Admissions	Inpatient Days	Adjusted Inpatient Days	Average Daily Census	Adjusted Average Daily Census	Average Stay (days)	Surgical Operations	NEWBORNS Bassinets	Births	OUTPATIENT VISITS Emergency	Total
UNITED STATES	5,262	798,921	34,305,620	186,198,977	398,570,958	510,123	1,092,133	5.4	28,221,774	55,181	3,656,809	144,814,804	766,076,124
Nonmetropolitan	1,875	112,806	3,115,229	20,415,212	70,105,531	55,939	192,099	6.6	3,649,248	9,005	358,113	22,487,032	131,587,025
Metropolitan	3,387	686,115	31,190,391	165,783,765	328,465,427	454,184	900,034	5.3	24,572,526	46,176	3,298,696	122,327,772	634,509,099
CENSUS DIVISION 3, SOUTH ATLANTIC	772	156,661	6,984,783	38,275,242	77,983,992	104,856	213,647	5.5	5,402,768	10,050	692,369	29,427,572	118,914,570
Nonmetropolitan	195	17,438	519,758	3,565,723	10,433,611	9,766	28,591	6.9	510,419	1,259	51,041	4,007,731	15,115,604
Metropolitan	577	139,223	6,465,025	34,709,519	67,550,381	95,090	185,056	5.4	4,892,349	8,791	641,328	25,419,841	103,798,966
Delaware	8	2,111	103,162	555,629	1,100,176	1,521	3,014	5.4	91,987	118	10,972	470,429	2,088,914
Metropolitan	8	2,111	103,162	555,629	1,100,176	1,521	3,014	5.4	91,987	118	10,972	470,429	2,088,914
Dover	1	351	18,909	96,008	218,482	263	599	5.1	15,664	12	2,212	94,223	565,654
Salisbury	2	254	16,453	67,904	161,019	186	441	4.1	20,176	25	1,698	86,431	519,547
Wilmington	5	1,506	67,800	391,717	720,675	1,072	1,974	5.8	56,147	81	7,062	289,775	1,003,713
District of Columbia	11	3,542	127,666	938,804	1,622,083	2,571	4,445	7.4	109,516	190	14,592	474,464	2,562,089
Metropolitan	11	3,542	127,666	938,804	1,622,083	2,571	4,445	7.4	109,516	190	14,592	474,464	2,562,089
Washington-Arlington-Alexandria	11	3,542	127,666	938,804	1,622,083	2,571	4,445	7.4	109,516	190	14,592	474,464	2,562,089
Florida	220	55,111	2,569,757	13,018,789	23,383,010	35,666	64,059	5.1	1,500,038	2,690	203,121	9,198,458	26,306,272
Nonmetropolitan	20	920	36,253	155,469	454,400	426	1,242	4.3	34,290	52	1,816	284,094	832,040
Metropolitan	200	54,191	2,533,504	12,863,320	22,928,610	35,240	62,817	5.1	1,465,748	2,638	201,305	8,914,364	25,474,232
Cape Coral-Fort Myers	4	1,540	81,043	368,231	586,176	1,009	1,606	4.5	42,361	100	6,119	285,443	535,121
Crestview-Fort Walton Beach-Destin	5	540	25,742	105,896	212,756	289	582	4.1	20,583	49	2,612	131,787	384,399
Deltona-Daytona Beach-Ormond Beach	6	1,527	68,483	356,925	770,809	978	2,112	5.2	38,597	66	3,867	310,886	1,057,813
Fort Lauderdale-Pompano Beach-Deerfield Beach	17	4,987	224,185	1,166,990	2,063,651	3,198	5,652	5.2	117,034	256	21,431	863,391	2,007,368
Gainesville	3	1,462	74,682	407,971	662,312	1,118	1,815	5.5	55,071	40	4,659	177,080	1,211,622
Homosassa Springs	2	332	17,256	70,387	141,597	193	388	4.1	11,923	20	1,367	54,435	213,846
Jacksonville	14	4,125	207,997	1,028,571	1,853,364	2,817	5,078	4.9	144,504	263	17,090	854,339	2,072,303
Lakeland-Winter Haven	5	1,606	77,250	344,081	634,755	943	1,739	4.5	43,130	62	5,447	389,139	599,390
Miami-Miami Beach-Kendall	25	7,886	313,165	1,901,875	3,249,882	5,209	8,901	6.1	170,439	317	25,856	1,065,787	3,756,750
Naples-Immokalee-Marco Island	3	964	31,334	177,596	313,970	486	860	5.7	15,820	36	3,341	139,491	397,900
North Port-Sarasota-Bradenton	10	2,258	95,444	477,792	791,686	1,308	2,171	5.0	58,279	63	5,327	302,055	1,025,943
Ocala	4	661	37,874	180,094	323,181	493	885	4.8	17,293	34	1,236	65,937	220,887
Orlando-Kissimmee-Sanford	14	6,468	331,502	1,684,058	2,881,325	4,614	7,895	5.1	187,259	362	31,741	1,279,332	2,995,195
Palm Bay-Melbourne-Titusville	9	1,574	73,764	357,492	648,599	980	1,777	4.8	40,709	73	5,292	275,132	746,072
Panama City	5	586	28,232	154,928	293,601	425	804	5.5	20,868	37	1,903	77,290	267,895
Pensacola-Ferry Pass-Brent	7	1,348	66,681	330,016	649,297	904	1,779	4.9	48,894	65	6,432	310,074	1,019,183
Port St. Lucie	4	937	57,392	258,453	477,968	708	1,310	4.5	27,582	64	4,515	177,451	291,327
Punta Gorda	3	681	27,272	142,174	246,477	390	676	5.2	17,800	22	969	79,279	180,126
Sebastian-Vero Beach	3	454	20,713	104,675	233,578	287	640	5.1	14,631	22	1,007	73,625	137,611
Sebring	2	277	14,990	65,910	139,688	180	382	4.4	12,192	29	1,114	72,500	211,484
Tallahassee	4	798	44,257	211,993	419,320	581	1,149	4.8	23,965	62	4,692	146,075	880,337
Tampa-St. Petersburg-Clearwater	35	9,204	425,669	2,096,351	3,770,067	5,744	10,328	4.9	230,388	404	32,290	1,270,395	3,746,297
The Villages	1	40	485	11,242	11,564	31	32	23.2	945	0	0	8	90
West Palm Beach-Boca Raton-Delray Beach	15	3,936	188,092	859,619	1,552,987	2,355	4,256	4.6	105,481	192	12,998	513,433	1,515,273
Georgia	147	25,244	1,003,595	6,348,851	13,902,530	17,396	38,091	6.3	761,869	1,890	123,813	4,740,490	19,418,640
Nonmetropolitan	56	5,504	128,624	1,243,387	3,614,283	3,405	9,907	9.7	133,901	328	15,210	940,858	3,535,354
Metropolitan	91	19,740	874,971	5,105,464	10,288,247	13,991	28,184	5.8	627,968	1,562	108,603	3,799,632	15,883,286
Albany	2	467	18,585	107,059	266,022	294	728	5.8	13,741	42	2,249	86,208	1,069,128
Athens-Clarke County	3	559	30,132	147,568	276,430	404	758	4.9	23,838	54	3,976	134,934	520,603
Atlanta-Sandy Springs-Roswell	45	10,290	492,110	2,815,483	5,539,148	7,717	15,175	5.7	337,822	839	67,652	2,163,148	8,945,126
Augusta-Richmond County	8	1,665	70,120	397,531	748,915	1,088	2,052	5.7	61,158	114	6,325	307,424	1,344,857
Brunswick	1	532	12,124	144,872	333,221	397	913	11.9	9,846	8	1,268	52,239	235,054
Chattanooga	1	179	6,309	55,658	153,808	152	421	8.8	4,845	15	723	26,913	123,644
Columbus	5	1,156	37,431	201,184	399,819	553	1,095	5.4	26,880	76	4,758	173,366	533,031
Dalton	2	239	10,462	44,156	97,987	121	268	4.2	4,554	40	1,752	76,895	297,272
Gainesville	1	906	38,599	255,217	457,301	699	1,253	6.6	23,063	77	4,505	147,769	548,455
Hinesville	1	25	1,600	5,227	23,076	14	63	3.3	1,844	6	309	5,717	37,577
Macon-Bibb County	5	1,040	45,720	267,966	469,047	735	1,286	5.9	34,298	106	3,289	131,380	566,035
Rome	3	602	27,938	143,496	293,704	392	804	5.1	17,134	30	2,294	120,440	397,103
Savannah	7	1,308	52,514	347,530	816,940	953	2,237	6.6	42,762	71	5,649	217,480	628,620
Valdosta	3	414	14,684	96,973	207,855	266	569	6.6	8,024	40	1,546	60,241	289,941
Warner Robins	4	358	16,643	75,544	204,974	206	562	4.5	18,159	44	2,308	95,478	366,840

TABLE 8

U.S. CENSUS DIVISION 3, SOUTH ATLANTIC

U.S. Community Hospitals
(Nonfederal, short-term general and other special hospitals)

2017 Utilization, Personnel and Finances

FULL-TIME EQUIVALENT PERSONNEL					FULL-TIME EQUIV. TRAINEES			EXPENSES						
								LABOR				TOTAL		
Physicians and Dentists	Registered Nurses	Licensed Practical Nurses	Other Salaried Personnel	Total Personnel	Medical and Dental Residents	Other Trainees	Total Trainees	Payroll (in thousands)	Employee Benefits (in thousands)	Total (in thousands)	Percent of Total	Amount (in thousands)	Adjusted per Admission	Adjusted per Inpatient Day
146,381	1,558,038	76,534	2,704,453	5,216,346	118,075	9,440	127,515	$363,806,143	$96,687,285	$460,493,398	47.7	$966,204,239	$13,126.02	$2,424.17
16,529	156,072	20,966	348,592	631,393	1,972	334	2,306	37,559,678	9,847,876	47,407,559	50.0	94,728,753	8,855.26	1,351.23
129,852	1,401,966	55,568	2,355,861	4,584,955	116,103	9,106	125,209	326,246,465	86,839,408	413,085,839	47.4	871,475,486	13,852.21	2,653.17
19,782	296,560	12,863	467,496	944,484	18,744	926	19,670	60,645,871	15,098,523	75,744,384	46.2	163,845,482	11,470.73	2,101.01
1,678	22,454	2,877	44,611	85,449	359	19	378	4,605,073	1,180,691	5,785,759	48.2	11,998,358	7,747.40	1,149.97
18,104	274,106	9,986	422,885	859,035	18,385	907	19,292	56,040,798	13,917,833	69,958,625	46.1	151,847,123	11,923.52	2,247.91
651	5,562	186	11,578	19,872	370	12	382	1,471,307	449,445	1,920,753	57.3	3,350,001	16,003.75	3,044.97
651	5,562	186	11,578	19,872	370	12	382	1,471,307	449,445	1,920,753	57.3	3,350,001	16,003.75	3,044.97
66	866	34	1,898	3,209	0	0	0	249,664	70,408	320,072	58.7	545,265	12,671.44	2,495.70
119	876	60	1,757	3,148	0	0	0	168,274	58,298	226,573	48.7	465,094	11,776.03	2,888.44
466	3,820	92	7,923	13,515	370	12	382	1,053,369	320,739	1,374,108	58.7	2,339,642	18,451.44	3,246.46
1,534	7,481	198	13,532	25,973	1,769	26	1,795	2,007,753	414,948	2,422,699	51.6	4,692,277	21,181.22	2,892.75
1,534	7,481	198	13,532	25,973	1,769	26	1,795	2,007,753	414,948	2,422,699	51.6	4,692,277	21,181.22	2,892.75
1,534	7,481	198	13,532	25,973	1,769	26	1,795	2,007,753	414,948	2,422,699	51.6	4,692,277	21,181.22	2,892.75
4,769	95,867	3,113	138,940	286,511	5,489	146	5,635	18,247,431	4,398,025	22,645,453	46.1	49,114,874	10,485.45	2,100.45
77	1,446	180	2,611	5,101	14	1	15	258,493	58,182	316,674	47.7	664,439	6,165.00	1,462.23
4,892	94,421	2,933	136,329	281,410	5,475	145	5,620	17,988,939	4,339,843	22,328,779	46.1	48,450,434	10,587.20	2,113.10
202	2,025	107	3,625	7,119	313	20	333	536,785	93,653	630,438	52.1	1,210,905	9,348.23	2,065.77
26	714	42	1,031	2,148	22	0	22	137,657	31,869	169,525	46.0	368,286	6,897.01	1,731.03
161	2,084	100	4,773	7,830	40	0	40	546,717	133,650	680,367	50.3	1,353,270	8,918.46	1,755.65
704	8,358	287	10,692	23,964	356	14	370	1,546,313	320,269	1,866,584	47.3	3,950,051	9,807.73	1,914.11
19	3,389	70	4,673	9,582	644	5	649	607,306	174,236	781,542	46.8	1,670,927	13,705.11	2,522.87
37	515	22	846	1,659	19	2	21	83,418	20,890	104,309	46.6	223,938	6,456.15	1,581.52
571	7,952	114	8,601	21,202	625	23	648	1,312,583	370,133	1,682,715	42.1	3,994,944	10,488.61	2,155.51
6	2,662	26	3,495	7,582	0	0	0	448,392	107,951	556,343	47.4	1,173,714	8,237.05	1,849.08
642	14,405	475	20,655	42,202	1,681	19	1,700	2,920,505	678,825	3,599,329	45.3	7,942,687	14,511.70	2,443.99
3	1,388	40	1,475	3,535	20	2	22	207,376	34,669	242,044	45.8	528,427	9,291.83	1,683.05
152	3,393	243	4,527	9,846	94	0	94	589,163	122,483	711,644	46.5	1,531,668	9,422.17	1,934.69
79	1,591	64	2,246	4,712	60	3	63	213,592	50,513	264,104	45.6	579,140	8,652.40	1,792.00
668	13,656	312	21,914	41,851	536	7	543	2,454,193	752,767	3,206,961	47.9	6,701,181	11,785.16	2,325.73
43	2,104	52	2,464	5,931	19	2	21	476,939	106,831	583,770	47.9	1,218,203	9,002.26	1,878.21
45	740	62	1,405	2,657	27	2	29	177,819	47,818	225,637	50.2	449,353	7,833.49	1,530.49
80	2,221	85	2,926	6,407	79	6	85	363,525	74,114	437,640	38.6	1,134,713	8,457.60	1,747.60
148	1,786	90	3,205	6,178	29	0	29	342,360	85,692	428,051	49.6	863,526	8,127.53	1,806.66
14	840	22	973	2,253	19	0	19	128,222	29,285	157,507	43.5	361,940	7,729.80	1,468.45
107	701	20	1,289	2,557	7	0	7	180,305	28,184	208,489	53.0	393,503	8,450.44	1,684.68
32	555	35	902	1,875	3	0	3	110,360	29,832	140,192	53.3	262,920	8,254.18	1,882.20
146	1,603	98	2,432	4,955	73	3	76	341,947	67,565	409,512	48.7	840,202	9,639.32	2,003.72
679	16,258	393	24,285	49,114	686	33	719	3,121,443	724,329	3,845,771	44.9	8,572,211	11,182.93	2,273.76
0	44	10	60	148	0	0	0	6,574	1,166	7,740	49.6	15,599	31,260.43	1,348.92
128	5,437	164	7,835	16,103	123	4	127	1,135,444	253,120	1,388,565	44.7	3,109,126	9,036.32	2,002.03
2,440	42,456	2,730	70,403	141,235	1,461	327	1,788	9,000,462	2,210,801	11,211,262	45.4	24,699,064	11,603.19	1,776.59
455	5,511	1,041	12,239	22,932	49	8	57	1,275,893	331,894	1,607,787	49.4	3,257,303	8,505.00	901.23
1,985	36,945	1,689	58,164	118,303	1,412	319	1,731	7,724,568	1,878,907	9,603,475	44.8	21,441,761	12,282.91	2,084.10
4	749	61	1,545	2,721	19	0	19	151,991	38,137	190,128	35.5	535,498	11,899.68	2,012.98
55	1,213	50	1,958	3,751	26	4	30	234,599	57,745	292,343	46.5	628,548	10,889.41	2,273.80
1,071	21,705	846	32,077	67,721	861	182	1,043	4,556,457	1,120,069	5,676,527	44.7	12,696,469	13,002.51	2,292.13
21	3,122	162	4,034	8,850	30	3	33	628,557	140,811	769,368	44.0	1,748,441	13,240.55	2,334.63
92	330	14	683	1,397	0	0	0	155,112	31,100	186,212	54.9	339,075	12,159.32	1,017.57
29	259	28	568	1,043	7	1	8	60,454	19,275	79,730	50.8	157,074	9,009.11	1,021.23
156	1,358	72	2,366	4,653	89	5	94	244,600	53,978	298,578	40.0	746,909	9,904.77	1,868.12
24	385	25	825	1,374	0	0	0	112,333	29,571	141,904	47.4	299,096	12,599.37	3,052.41
62	1,427	40	2,880	4,784	0	105	105	312,313	82,786	395,100	47.3	834,590	12,067.18	1,825.03
7	57	13	154	270	0	0	0	20,438	5,660	26,098	52.8	49,465	7,002.35	2,143.55
114	1,782	59	2,713	5,733	127	3	130	314,000	83,384	397,384	42.9	927,231	11,892.76	1,976.84
57	1,021	95	2,107	3,787	43	0	43	256,130	71,101	327,231	52.0	629,105	10,846.26	2,141.97
221	2,052	93	3,683	7,006	161	14	175	410,338	74,754	485,092	41.9	1,156,699	11,069.31	1,415.89
58	849	34	1,316	2,674	31	2	33	144,820	36,926	181,747	46.7	389,355	14,043.47	1,873.21
14	636	97	1,255	2,539	18	0	18	122,424	33,609	156,033	51.3	304,207	6,680.43	1,484.12

Table continues

MSAs

TABLE 8

U.S. CENSUS DIVISION 3, SOUTH ATLANTIC CONTINUED

U.S. Community Hospitals
(Nonfederal, short-term general and other special hospitals)

2017 Utilization, Personnel and Finances

CLASSIFICATION	Hospitals	Beds	Admissions	Inpatient Days	Adjusted Inpatient Days	Average Daily Census	Adjusted Average Daily Census	Average Stay (days)	Surgical Operations	NEWBORNS Bassinets	NEWBORNS Births	OUTPATIENT VISITS Emergency	OUTPATIENT VISITS Total
Maryland	51	11,607	581,640	2,991,695	5,790,149	8,197	15,862	5.1	513,765	963	64,273	2,403,879	9,304,872
Nonmetropolitan	4	362	15,513	84,429	221,317	232	607	5.4	16,718	30	1,042	93,243	465,198
Metropolitan	47	11,245	566,127	2,907,266	5,568,832	7,965	15,255	5.1	497,047	933	63,231	2,310,636	8,839,674
Baltimore-Columbia-Towson	24	7,286	350,537	1,893,046	3,548,676	5,186	9,721	5.4	343,017	471	34,571	1,285,962	5,474,178
California-Lexington Park	1	103	7,423	29,833	71,064	82	195	4.0	8,572	16	1,188	50,278	181,111
Cumberland	1	321	11,673	85,518	190,666	234	522	7.3	7,398	20	915	46,820	584,172
Hagerstown-Martinsburg	1	278	15,794	66,664	135,661	183	372	4.2	8,366	41	1,757	72,868	198,530
Salisbury	4	479	24,396	118,385	301,114	324	825	4.9	24,092	28	1,873	116,749	718,340
Silver Spring-Frederick-Rockville	8	1,774	101,288	451,597	823,477	1,238	2,257	4.5	57,086	255	18,247	349,549	941,589
Washington-Arlington-Alexandria	7	895	49,574	241,689	444,855	662	1,217	4.9	43,105	90	4,103	349,535	601,549
Wilmington	1	109	5,442	20,534	53,319	56	146	3.8	5,411	12	577	38,875	140,205
North Carolina	114	21,841	1,018,888	5,545,924	12,720,448	15,196	34,851	5.4	880,857	1,566	113,203	4,960,946	23,573,949
Nonmetropolitan	47	4,219	169,604	871,000	2,490,938	2,385	6,826	5.1	151,020	416	18,654	1,347,795	4,761,512
Metropolitan	67	17,622	849,284	4,674,924	10,229,510	12,811	28,025	5.5	729,837	1,150	94,549	3,613,151	18,812,437
Asheville	6	1,270	61,177	310,563	730,837	851	2,002	5.1	61,488	58	5,306	227,524	1,653,245
Burlington	1	200	10,126	40,718	128,850	112	353	4.0	9,993	21	1,305	67,103	294,926
Charlotte-Concord-Gastonia	18	4,293	216,867	1,132,402	2,430,761	3,101	6,660	5.2	177,522	341	26,885	1,009,894	3,851,742
Durham-Chapel Hill	7	2,276	103,028	679,218	1,493,826	1,861	4,093	6.6	102,267	62	9,520	255,561	2,776,450
Fayetteville	2	649	33,751	166,762	326,167	457	893	4.9	13,422	48	4,614	160,978	296,563
Goldsboro	1	274	10,866	50,621	122,702	139	336	4.7	12,783	36	1,213	68,902	148,150
Greensboro-High Point	6	1,622	76,220	400,427	874,101	1,098	2,394	5.3	43,644	108	8,768	365,386	2,232,942
Greenville	1	974	37,446	246,237	365,162	675	1,000	6.6	20,662	42	3,581	121,313	404,193
Hickory-Lenoir-Morganton	4	759	33,308	160,704	377,418	441	1,033	4.8	32,150	59	3,646	159,529	839,612
Jacksonville	1	149	6,629	27,963	87,118	77	239	4.2	5,481	23	1,464	60,672	136,270
Myrtle Beach-Conway-North Myrtle Beach	2	79	5,258	18,019	63,807	49	174	3.4	6,727	5	473	37,620	200,537
New Bern	1	201	12,702	64,102	139,281	176	382	5.0	14,854	7	1,099	67,786	174,509
Raleigh	5	1,841	89,907	502,461	1,195,037	1,376	3,274	5.6	98,056	165	14,303	478,098	3,090,488
Rocky Mount	3	410	15,951	96,050	206,378	264	566	6.0	10,717	34	1,506	96,766	255,189
Wilmington	2	779	42,340	225,171	486,882	617	1,334	5.3	39,397	43	4,182	163,730	487,808
Winston-Salem	7	1,846	93,708	553,506	1,201,183	1,517	3,292	5.9	80,674	98	6,684	272,289	1,969,813
South Carolina	70	12,357	525,641	2,822,503	5,780,300	7,731	15,835	5.4	508,011	842	52,509	2,471,755	9,429,926
Nonmetropolitan	15	1,849	51,969	315,377	844,377	863	2,314	6.1	46,055	160	4,945	413,144	1,363,758
Metropolitan	55	10,508	473,672	2,507,126	4,935,923	6,868	13,521	5.3	461,956	682	47,564	2,058,611	8,066,168
Augusta-Richmond County	2	310	12,587	62,007	115,029	170	315	4.9	8,271	18	1,023	62,474	158,696
Charleston-North Charleston	7	1,914	92,150	500,762	938,662	1,373	2,571	5.4	100,232	116	9,816	404,927	1,912,182
Charlotte-Concord-Gastonia	4	538	22,439	121,729	235,667	333	646	5.4	14,121	8	2,153	114,829	265,985
Columbia	9	2,127	101,402	538,909	950,729	1,475	2,604	5.3	74,338	149	9,542	321,581	1,473,373
Florence	7	1,181	44,807	243,055	442,598	665	1,213	5.4	51,425	60	3,334	174,049	495,424
Greenville-Anderson-Mauldin	14	2,120	98,620	490,774	1,091,738	1,346	2,990	5.0	109,841	145	11,078	471,188	2,185,670
Hilton Head Island-Bluffton-Beaufort	3	331	17,677	75,098	158,084	206	433	4.2	18,684	52	2,155	95,984	286,715
Myrtle Beach-Conway-North Myrtle Beach	4	893	41,414	209,205	424,669	572	1,163	5.1	38,633	66	3,205	215,723	587,258
Spartanburg	4	856	34,227	200,066	401,841	548	1,101	5.8	36,704	44	3,952	137,808	554,451
Sumter	1	238	8,349	65,521	176,906	180	485	7.8	9,707	24	1,306	60,248	146,414
Virginia	95	17,840	797,032	4,513,293	9,964,095	12,361	27,294	5.7	724,709	1,383	90,720	3,522,286	18,158,886
Nonmetropolitan	26	2,317	63,479	492,505	1,394,434	1,351	3,820	7.8	59,560	132	4,910	497,130	1,698,748
Metropolitan	69	15,523	733,553	4,020,788	8,569,661	11,010	23,474	5.5	665,149	1,251	85,810	3,025,156	16,460,138
Blacksburg-Christiansburg-Radford	4	241	15,704	64,092	167,093	175	457	4.1	18,947	26	1,763	88,148	276,762
Charlottesville	3	790	39,752	220,678	499,303	604	1,367	5.6	94,098	42	3,294	115,282	2,689,699
Harrisonburg	1	244	13,820	52,764	163,289	145	447	3.8	20,778	16	1,742	71,138	636,979
Kingsport-Bristol-Bristol	2	141	9,187	36,679	92,820	101	255	4.0	6,659	16	624	40,014	159,778
Lynchburg	2	1,174	31,730	317,016	733,649	868	2,010	10.0	16,723	39	2,708	127,680	804,150
Richmond	16	3,624	160,253	912,284	1,653,285	2,498	4,528	5.7	108,759	253	14,440	436,186	1,985,514
Roanoke	3	1,155	64,660	372,296	649,180	1,019	1,778	5.8	49,785	67	4,642	288,408	788,052
Staunton-Waynesboro	1	215	10,749	40,967	130,778	112	358	3.8	15,642	21	1,153	57,578	768,166
Virginia Beach-Norfolk-Newport News	17	3,491	166,402	892,919	2,127,238	2,445	5,828	5.4	174,051	299	18,165	873,122	5,184,774
Washington-Arlington-Alexandria	19	3,963	198,624	990,174	2,105,660	2,712	5,768	5.0	142,651	465	35,129	853,017	2,773,627
Winchester	1	485	22,672	120,919	247,366	331	678	5.3	17,056	7	2,150	74,583	392,837

MSAs

TABLE 8

U.S. CENSUS DIVISION 3, SOUTH ATLANTIC CONTINUED

U.S. Community Hospitals
(Nonfederal, short-term general and other special hospitals)

2017 Utilization, Personnel and Finances

FULL-TIME EQUIVALENT PERSONNEL					FULL-TIME EQUIV. TRAINEES			EXPENSES						
								LABOR				TOTAL		
Physicians and Dentists	Registered Nurses	Licensed Practical Nurses	Other Salaried Personnel	Total Personnel	Medical and Dental Residents	Other Trainees	Total Trainees	Payroll (in thousands)	Employee Benefits (in thousands)	Total (in thousands)	Percent of Total	Amount (in thousands)	Adjusted per Admission	Adjusted per Inpatient Day
1,998	26,868	417	46,332	88,425	1,744	159	1,903	6,126,830	1,405,974	7,532,801	47.3	15,928,893	13,811.20	2,751.03
56	647	36	1,246	2,293	10	2	12	135,425	36,382	171,806	49.0	350,656	8,332.29	1,584.41
1,942	26,221	381	45,086	86,132	1,734	157	1,891	5,991,405	1,369,592	7,360,995	47.3	15,578,237	14,018.69	2,797.40
1,621	18,135	218	31,186	60,102	1,621	147	1,768	4,160,100	947,298	5,107,399	46.8	10,922,342	15,977.54	3,077.86
10	299	2	501	994	0	0	0	68,634	12,217	80,851	47.8	169,121	9,564.61	2,379.85
35	494	23	849	1,548	0	0	0	109,581	40,227	149,808	46.4	322,864	12,405.93	1,693.35
5	646	11	903	1,812	0	0	0	105,644	29,209	134,854	43.6	309,164	9,618.99	2,278.94
77	984	48	2,201	3,820	3	3	6	246,786	57,576	304,362	48.7	624,865	10,006.49	2,075.18
87	3,436	51	5,344	10,223	32	4	36	763,307	168,993	932,299	47.7	1,956,260	10,758.55	2,375.61
78	1,996	26	3,540	6,640	78	3	81	467,581	100,371	567,951	50.9	1,116,361	11,954.52	2,509.49
29	231	2	562	993	0	0	0	69,771	13,700	83,471	53.1	157,260	11,128.75	2,949.42
2,741	48,221	1,774	78,884	157,437	3,315	52	3,367	9,802,004	2,568,270	12,370,271	45.7	27,043,563	11,254.84	2,125.99
444	7,601	574	13,987	26,736	98	5	103	1,403,735	347,685	1,751,417	48.3	3,623,258	7,191.37	1,454.58
2,297	40,620	1,200	64,897	130,701	3,217	47	3,264	8,398,269	2,220,585	10,618,854	45.3	23,420,304	12,332.94	2,289.48
148	2,647	60	4,255	8,810	6	3	9	512,526	120,216	632,743	38.4	1,648,571	11,134.10	2,255.73
26	552	2	566	1,579	0	0	0	74,691	27,483	102,174	44.8	228,062	7,117.38	1,769.98
256	9,149	247	13,285	27,063	126	8	134	1,793,497	473,588	2,267,085	42.4	5,346,151	11,099.20	2,199.37
79	6,850	75	9,749	20,524	1,512	9	1,521	1,455,872	401,324	1,857,196	43.0	4,322,794	19,332.97	2,893.77
170	1,115	152	3,186	5,281	33	1	34	320,059	83,518	403,578	55.7	724,587	10,611.53	2,221.52
0	451	12	696	1,488	0	0	0	86,812	36,449	123,261	52.1	236,393	8,975.36	1,926.56
501	3,721	204	5,974	12,555	57	0	57	680,022	215,742	895,764	48.7	1,838,513	10,967.88	2,103.32
259	1,800	70	3,866	6,904	397	2	399	349,220	113,430	462,650	45.7	1,012,959	18,241.32	2,774.00
168	1,425	39	2,568	5,023	8	0	8	348,184	91,183	439,365	50.0	878,566	11,040.18	2,327.83
0	292	16	476	960	0	0	0	52,543	16,239	68,782	47.8	143,873	6,966.55	1,651.47
22	173	16	372	683	1	0	1	51,913	12,425	64,338	47.4	135,750	7,082.85	2,127.51
1	614	4	832	1,874	0	0	0	97,705	27,550	125,255	46.2	271,047	9,820.91	1,946.05
482	5,486	59	7,591	16,324	7	0	7	1,182,941	241,252	1,424,193	52.0	2,739,189	12,560.13	2,292.14
2	724	38	1,171	2,284	0	0	0	133,147	35,098	168,244	51.0	329,774	8,926.09	1,597.91
0	1,404	30	2,737	5,285	11	0	11	339,179	102,073	441,252	47.9	920,770	10,712.61	1,891.16
183	4,217	176	7,573	14,064	1,059	24	1,083	919,959	223,015	1,142,974	43.2	2,643,304	12,716.08	2,200.58
1,919	23,559	772	33,168	72,409	1,480	4	1,484	4,172,978	1,213,740	5,386,720	44.5	12,103,968	11,002.52	2,094.00
158	2,046	128	3,945	7,883	35	0	35	452,185	120,997	573,182	46.1	1,242,548	8,894.92	1,471.56
1,761	21,513	644	29,223	64,526	1,445	4	1,449	3,720,793	1,092,743	4,813,538	44.3	10,861,420	11,309.07	2,200.48
14	373	11	372	1,008	0	0	0	63,678	15,360	79,038	44.4	178,186	7,952.59	1,549.05
24	4,396	94	4,908	11,915	712	0	712	819,505	264,837	1,084,343	43.2	2,509,444	13,977.54	2,673.43
7	758	32	1,013	2,443	6	0	6	134,250	33,254	167,503	44.1	380,234	8,837.10	1,613.44
146	4,666	141	7,314	13,949	289	2	291	879,656	302,221	1,181,878	51.0	2,316,337	12,537.61	2,436.38
82	1,878	60	2,348	5,440	50	0	50	335,233	78,679	413,912	44.6	928,817	11,015.65	2,098.56
1,314	5,052	90	6,000	15,362	284	0	284	795,943	205,520	1,001,465	39.8	2,514,669	10,836.99	2,303.36
29	629	26	985	2,060	16	2	18	117,308	37,513	154,821	46.2	334,830	8,967.54	2,118.05
15	1,278	66	1,371	3,440	29	0	29	215,127	56,076	271,203	40.9	663,142	7,920.48	1,561.55
115	2,023	120	4,187	7,461	59	0	59	289,711	81,671	371,382	43.1	862,107	12,188.53	2,145.39
15	460	4	725	1,448	0	0	0	70,381	17,612	87,993	50.7	173,654	7,703.56	981.62
2,780	34,972	2,362	52,581	110,109	2,460	159	2,619	7,441,495	1,732,985	9,174,479	45.2	20,280,705	11,445.58	2,035.38
175	2,721	394	4,808	9,713	85	2	87	537,569	137,167	674,734	46.5	1,451,404	7,743.05	1,040.86
2,605	32,251	1,968	47,773	100,396	2,375	157	2,532	6,903,926	1,595,818	8,499,745	45.1	18,829,301	11,883.60	2,197.20
14	656	44	970	2,034	5	0	5	135,437	30,191	165,627	46.1	359,256	8,834.32	2,150.04
127	2,737	160	3,674	8,780	811	0	811	651,841	177,073	828,915	45.7	1,815,569	19,082.53	3,636.21
167	661	103	1,065	2,312	0	10	10	149,460	34,759	184,219	47.0	391,653	9,157.40	2,398.53
2	315	36	353	838	33	0	33	43,082	10,514	53,596	37.7	141,986	6,111.39	1,529.69
199	1,059	285	4,103	6,101	21	14	35	406,894	90,676	497,570	53.7	925,715	12,743.00	1,261.80
231	7,413	337	10,754	21,567	910	82	992	1,488,846	351,934	1,840,779	44.8	4,113,352	14,017.60	2,487.99
588	2,924	135	3,751	9,016	319	4	323	705,690	148,807	854,498	50.2	1,701,458	14,828.17	2,620.93
85	442	80	1,039	1,865	0	0	0	130,335	34,052	164,386	51.8	317,600	9,255.71	2,428.55
659	7,390	565	11,300	23,691	5	40	45	1,485,390	365,272	1,850,662	44.6	4,147,041	10,439.79	1,949.50
514	7,795	202	9,368	21,554	271	7	278	1,524,119	315,624	1,839,745	41.4	4,438,503	10,470.49	2,107.89
19	859	21	1,396	2,638	0	0	0	182,834	36,915	219,748	46.1	477,167	10,287.98	1,928.99

Table continues

TABLE 8

U.S. CENSUS DIVISION 3, SOUTH ATLANTIC CONTINUED

U.S. Community Hospitals
(Nonfederal, short-term general and other special hospitals)

2017 Utilization, Personnel and Finances

CLASSIFICATION	Hospitals	Beds	Admissions	Inpatient Days	Adjusted Inpatient Days	Average Daily Census	Adjusted Average Daily Census	Average Stay (days)	Surgical Operations	NEWBORNS Bassinets	NEWBORNS Births	OUTPATIENT VISITS Emergency	OUTPATIENT VISITS Total
West Virginia	56	7,008	257,402	1,539,754	3,721,201	4,217	10,196	6.0	312,016	408	19,166	1,184,865	8,071,022
Nonmetropolitan	27	2,267	54,316	403,556	1,413,862	1,104	3,875	7.4	68,875	141	4,464	431,467	2,458,994
Metropolitan	29	4,741	203,086	1,136,198	2,307,339	3,113	6,321	5.6	243,141	267	14,702	753,398	5,612,028
Beckley	4	483	18,437	104,411	254,727	286	697	5.7	17,240	29	1,004	83,320	280,448
Charleston	6	1,185	47,365	259,942	538,704	712	1,476	5.5	81,833	68	3,763	163,132	1,075,525
Cumberland	1	25	964	2,914	13,126	8	36	3.0	641	0	0	7,350	44,334
Hagerstown-Martinsburg	1	195	8,642	37,260	93,291	102	256	4.3	11,011	21	1,057	60,505	263,510
Huntington-Ashland	4	786	45,495	220,028	412,582	603	1,130	4.8	42,632	55	3,009	107,508	983,556
Morgantown	4	937	42,440	254,330	427,687	697	1,172	6.0	43,438	10	2,549	87,908	1,246,068
Parkersburg-Vienna	2	280	12,789	67,840	121,612	186	333	5.3	10,098	22	1,315	49,331	269,880
Washington-Arlington-Alexandria	1	25	1,341	3,719	18,135	10	50	2.8	2,820	4	198	24,782	68,327
Weirton-Steubenville	1	167	6,309	32,117	108,035	88	296	5.1	6,937	21	428	38,740	473,697
Wheeling	4	614	18,916	140,912	235,470	386	645	7.4	25,957	37	1,379	120,623	853,354
Winchester	1	44	388	12,725	83,970	35	230	32.8	534	0	0	10,199	53,329

MSAs

TABLE 8

U.S. CENSUS DIVISION 3, SOUTH ATLANTIC CONTINUED

U.S. Community Hospitals
(Nonfederal, short-term general and other special hospitals)

2017 Utilization, Personnel and Finances

FULL-TIME EQUIVALENT PERSONNEL					FULL-TIME EQUIV. TRAINEES			EXPENSES						
								LABOR				TOTAL		
Physicians and Dentists	Registered Nurses	Licensed Practical Nurses	Other Salaried Personnel	Total Personnel	Medical and Dental Residents	Other Trainees	Total Trainees	Payroll (in thousands)	Employee Benefits (in thousands)	Total (in thousands)	Percent of Total	Amount (in thousands)	Adjusted per Admission	Adjusted per Inpatient Day
950	11,574	1,311	22,078	42,513	656	41	697	2,375,611	704,336	3,079,946	46.4	6,632,137	10,837.11	1,782.26
313	2,482	524	5,775	10,791	68	1	69	541,773	148,384	690,159	49.0	1,408,750	7,619.97	996.38
637	9,092	787	16,303	31,722	588	40	628	1,833,838	555,951	2,389,787	45.8	5,223,387	12,229.66	2,263.81
44	474	126	938	1,855	0	2	2	89,836	24,565	114,401	40.8	280,403	6,647.46	1,100.80
214	2,345	269	4,038	8,165	169	1	170	522,138	142,355	664,493	46.9	1,416,360	14,345.79	2,629.20
6	44	5	111	195	0	1	1	8,386	2,262	10,648	48.4	21,980	5,062.17	1,674.53
3	416	12	574	1,220	0	0	0	61,125	15,905	77,030	39.6	194,450	8,986.52	2,084.34
83	1,596	107	2,733	5,332	0	7	7	308,816	125,251	434,066	47.6	912,479	10,141.69	2,211.63
73	2,256	131	4,115	7,779	362	25	387	457,827	142,769	600,596	42.9	1,398,438	18,274.02	3,269.77
82	491	31	1,030	1,893	18	0	18	76,802	24,932	101,734	41.3	246,471	10,172.57	2,026.70
0	97	2	147	298	0	2	2	15,934	3,928	19,862	44.0	45,189	6,910.62	2,491.79
48	290	19	675	1,187	0	0	0	78,341	19,488	97,829	54.5	179,654	8,465.45	1,662.92
79	1,060	75	1,861	3,636	39	2	41	204,603	52,335	256,939	50.9	504,815	12,888.78	2,143.86
5	23	10	81	162	0	0	0	10,028	2,161	12,189	52.7	23,149	9,042.56	275.68

TABLE 8

U.S. CENSUS DIVISION 4, EAST NORTH CENTRAL

U.S. Community Hospitals
(Nonfederal, short-term general and other special hospitals)

2017 Utilization, Personnel and Finances

CLASSIFICATION	Hospitals	Beds	Admissions	Inpatient Days	Adjusted Inpatient Days	Average Daily Census	Adjusted Average Daily Census	Average Stay (days)	Surgical Operations	NEWBORNS Bassinets	NEWBORNS Births	OUTPATIENT VISITS Emergency	OUTPATIENT VISITS Total
UNITED STATES	5,262	798,921	34,305,820	186,198,977	398,570,958	510,123	1,092,133	5.4	28,221,774	55,181	3,656,809	144,814,804	766,076,124
Nonmetropolitan	1,875	112,806	3,115,229	20,415,212	70,105,531	55,939	192,099	6.6	3,649,248	9,005	358,113	22,487,032	131,567,025
Metropolitan	3,387	686,115	31,190,391	165,783,765	328,465,427	454,184	900,034	5.3	24,572,526	46,176	3,298,696	122,327,772	634,509,099
CENSUS DIVISION 4, EAST NORTH CENTRAL	798	120,736	5,214,548	26,260,795	62,145,974	71,943	170,269	5.0	4,695,893	9,305	516,804	23,897,233	160,604,227
Nonmetropolitan	271	16,391	545,078	2,828,182	11,658,450	7,750	31,943	5.2	729,405	1,602	58,011	4,157,893	29,367,431
Metropolitan	527	104,345	4,669,470	23,432,613	50,487,524	64,193	138,326	5.0	3,966,488	7,703	458,793	19,739,340	131,236,796
Illinois	189	31,996	1,364,376	6,882,225	15,603,539	18,851	42,745	5.0	1,047,991	2,510	141,539	5,630,049	37,575,437
Nonmetropolitan	58	3,221	106,251	510,968	1,976,916	1,400	5,415	4.8	131,948	263	9,322	723,268	5,568,870
Metropolitan	131	28,775	1,258,125	6,371,257	13,626,623	17,451	37,330	5.1	916,043	2,247	132,217	4,906,781	32,006,567
Bloomington	3	372	15,533	62,388	127,233	171	349	4.0	12,367	52	2,359	62,945	308,550
Carbondale-Marion	4	398	23,518	85,079	275,764	233	755	3.6	16,293	43	2,286	122,300	528,491
Champaign-Urbana	4	655	31,558	156,955	417,596	430	1,144	5.0	22,913	49	3,650	148,426	1,762,190
Chicago-Naperville-Arlington Heights	69	19,025	843,273	4,402,410	8,900,819	12,059	24,384	5.2	579,195	1,391	88,347	3,043,251	20,529,324
Danville	2	130	5,402	18,300	58,788	50	161	3.4	3,699	26	587	47,073	199,770
Davenport-Moline-Rock Island	5	586	19,938	89,690	272,320	246	747	4.5	17,534	68	1,910	114,654	627,210
Decatur	2	534	16,197	70,456	195,232	193	535	4.3	12,235	40	1,416	78,492	417,450
Elgin	7	1,027	44,292	200,107	446,844	549	1,224	4.5	34,392	97	4,873	206,594	1,436,538
Kankakee	2	474	16,493	77,977	224,271	214	614	4.7	13,516	35	1,338	74,830	615,695
Lake County-Kenosha County	5	844	45,400	190,075	460,405	520	1,261	4.2	37,828	114	5,886	203,225	1,148,179
Peoria	7	1,261	53,371	289,608	609,897	793	1,671	5.4	55,022	67	4,789	184,253	1,459,149
Rockford	4	875	40,893	196,609	396,673	538	1,087	4.8	32,231	92	4,919	174,690	825,477
Springfield	3	927	44,580	220,450	425,290	604	1,165	4.9	36,174	44	3,594	125,104	749,873
St. Louis	14	1,667	57,677	311,153	815,491	851	2,233	5.4	42,644	129	6,263	320,944	1,398,671
Indiana	132	17,821	715,442	3,686,520	8,884,237	10,099	24,339	5.2	645,822	1,618	77,809	3,526,829	20,912,820
Nonmetropolitan	41	2,638	77,709	446,423	1,979,871	1,223	5,426	5.7	102,371	268	9,983	656,913	4,249,478
Metropolitan	91	15,183	637,733	3,240,097	6,904,366	8,876	18,913	5.1	543,451	1,350	67,826	2,869,916	16,663,342
Bloomington	3	331	13,796	61,101	152,309	168	417	4.4	9,476	50	2,037	72,911	983,431
Cincinnati	1	62	3,873	13,262	36,667	36	100	3.4	5,359	11	381	22,253	145,326
Columbus	1	197	9,221	34,649	89,784	95	246	3.8	12,011	20	1,247	45,024	254,268
Elkhart-Goshen	2	352	15,874	61,755	151,873	170	416	3.9	15,932	54	2,681	93,417	442,109
Evansville	7	1,206	53,127	281,633	563,755	770	1,544	5.3	40,712	62	4,418	173,748	1,129,253
Fort Wayne	10	1,676	76,371	373,767	740,453	1,024	2,030	4.9	96,301	146	7,886	264,798	1,430,418
Gary	13	2,637	93,136	546,243	1,166,235	1,496	3,195	5.9	65,622	224	6,653	485,131	2,109,160
Indianapolis-Carmel-Anderson	28	5,464	226,356	1,203,432	2,497,378	3,298	6,840	5.3	171,774	497	25,134	1,097,884	7,152,653
Kokomo	3	318	11,126	43,323	113,602	119	311	3.9	8,006	28	1,215	60,564	382,991
Lafayette-West Lafayette	3	414	20,169	92,431	226,343	253	620	4.6	17,392	50	3,589	97,167	457,681
Louisville-Jefferson County	8	595	28,237	119,898	323,006	328	884	4.2	31,002	52	3,108	119,885	607,093
Michigan City-La Porte	2	300	11,351	46,586	109,757	128	300	4.1	11,784	35	1,222	59,521	296,347
Muncie	2	378	16,488	96,747	174,049	265	477	5.9	5,618	20	1,352	57,251	291,058
South Bend-Mishawaka	3	760	34,022	165,287	296,614	453	813	4.9	25,288	58	4,279	118,208	366,150
Terre Haute	5	493	24,586	99,983	262,541	273	720	4.1	27,174	43	2,624	102,154	615,404
Michigan	145	24,987	1,148,126	5,774,074	13,695,125	15,819	37,524	5.0	977,739	1,635	106,026	5,088,160	38,218,914
Nonmetropolitan	54	3,541	115,286	670,987	3,037,982	1,838	8,326	5.8	164,910	288	11,611	815,222	6,499,955
Metropolitan	91	21,446	1,032,840	5,103,087	10,657,143	13,981	29,198	4.9	812,829	1,347	94,415	4,272,938	31,718,959
Ann Arbor	5	1,621	88,237	474,507	1,043,793	1,300	2,860	5.4	88,145	69	8,458	211,970	4,510,732
Battle Creek	3	301	12,158	56,924	151,601	156	415	4.7	10,244	26	965	88,124	711,475
Bay City	2	348	15,540	78,430	148,160	215	406	5.0	10,546	14	821	45,737	333,103
Detroit-Dearborn-Livonia	20	5,170	252,240	1,257,364	2,493,772	3,445	6,831	5.0	174,054	288	20,758	1,099,436	7,031,391
Flint	4	1,229	59,108	303,996	538,945	833	1,477	5.1	37,814	89	5,069	221,833	1,348,265
Grand Rapids-Wyoming	11	2,335	112,069	551,300	1,195,558	1,511	3,277	4.9	106,862	205	13,429	565,879	4,744,382
Jackson	2	445	19,018	91,331	197,573	250	541	4.8	9,914	19	1,619	81,451	493,628
Kalamazoo-Portage	4	921	42,893	198,125	429,835	543	1,178	4.6	39,790	73	4,800	186,645	1,577,958
Lansing-East Lansing	6	1,052	47,051	236,873	512,231	649	1,403	5.0	37,071	42	4,711	265,312	1,717,895
Midland	1	304	13,546	50,961	124,958	140	342	3.8	14,373	23	1,382	39,176	265,992
Monroe	1	100	6,450	28,022	75,593	77	207	4.3	4,752	7	672	41,268	154,590
Muskegon	2	432	19,458	82,886	209,253	227	573	4.3	18,984	26	1,903	110,559	1,077,978
Niles-Benton Harbor	2	344	12,591	53,887	111,555	147	306	4.3	5,497	35	1,726	96,714	536,029
Saginaw	3	848	39,209	214,688	435,795	588	1,195	5.5	20,000	31	2,984	150,964	686,912
South Bend-Mishawaka	1	25	343	1,099	10,752	3	29	3.2	533	0	0	10,550	100,864
Warren-Troy-Farmington Hills	24	5,971	292,929	1,422,694	2,977,769	3,897	8,158	4.9	234,250	400	25,118	1,057,320	6,429,765

TABLE 8

U.S. CENSUS DIVISION 4, EAST NORTH CENTRAL

U.S. Community Hospitals
(Nonfederal, short-term general and other special hospitals)

2017 Utilization, Personnel and Finances

FULL-TIME EQUIVALENT PERSONNEL					FULL-TIME EQUIV. TRAINEES			EXPENSES						
								LABOR				TOTAL		
Physicians and Dentists	Registered Nurses	Licensed Practical Nurses	Other Salaried Personnel	Total Personnel	Medical and Dental Residents	Other Trainees	Total Trainees	Payroll (in thousands)	Employee Benefits (in thousands)	Total (in thousands)	Percent of Total	Amount (in thousands)	Adjusted per Admission	Adjusted per Inpatient Day
146,381	1,558,038	76,534	2,704,453	5,216,348	118,075	9,440	127,515	$363,806,143	$96,687,285	$460,493,398	47.7	$966,204,239	$13,126.02	$2,424.17
16,529	156,072	20,966	348,592	631,393	1,972	334	2,306	37,559,678	9,847,876	47,407,559	50.0	94,728,753	8,855.26	1,351.23
129,852	1,401,966	55,568	2,355,861	4,584,955	116,103	9,106	125,209	326,246,465	86,839,408	413,085,839	47.4	871,475,486	13,852.21	2,653.17
26,903	254,041	9,277	457,825	863,244	24,054	2,139	26,193	58,839,732	15,178,856	74,018,581	47.1	157,010,030	12,685.23	2,526.47
3,122	28,043	3,071	68,098	116,525	241	78	319	7,246,152	2,053,247	9,299,394	50.2	18,516,031	8,709.22	1,588.21
23,781	225,998	6,206	389,727	746,719	23,813	2,061	25,874	51,593,580	13,125,610	64,719,187	46.7	138,493,999	13,509.81	2,743.13
7,433	63,926	1,765	111,021	214,430	7,464	597	8,061	14,175,692	3,671,352	17,847,039	45.5	39,236,138	12,483.42	2,514.57
546	5,666	695	13,201	23,218	30	4	34	1,361,772	405,790	1,767,559	51.5	3,428,850	8,562.66	1,734.44
6,887	58,260	1,070	97,820	191,212	7,434	593	8,027	12,813,919	3,265,563	16,079,480	44.9	35,807,288	13,055.88	2,627.74
7	707	14	915	1,954	21	3	24	111,402	30,802	142,204	43.7	325,491	10,353.10	2,558.23
7	932	43	1,535	2,848	22	0	22	168,115	47,702	215,817	37.2	580,147	8,536.46	2,103.78
26	1,672	69	1,977	4,612	33	0	33	277,150	72,514	349,664	36.1	968,383	12,117.51	2,318.95
5,691	39,289	526	63,685	127,994	6,692	415	7,107	9,069,581	2,269,910	11,339,491	45.3	25,028,740	14,352.89	2,811.96
2	195	8	247	594	0	0	0	34,681	8,275	42,957	36.6	117,394	6,740.60	1,996.91
58	906	25	1,620	2,909	0	0	0	165,945	41,748	207,692	41.9	496,185	8,261.90	1,822.06
81	665	89	1,445	2,633	15	0	15	166,717	40,854	207,571	50.1	414,447	9,145.31	2,122.85
134	2,144	20	4,460	7,729	0	4	4	407,300	94,111	501,410	40.3	1,244,256	11,905.39	2,784.54
71	723	26	1,468	2,529	21	0	21	174,348	37,876	212,224	47.5	448,365	9,494.51	1,990.29
206	2,167	16	4,548	8,047	24	5	29	446,754	98,200	544,953	44.6	1,220,645	11,285.86	2,651.24
277	3,022	51	4,357	8,733	295	9	304	586,495	146,298	732,793	47.3	1,548,715	14,127.38	2,539.31
241	1,922	50	3,257	6,343	6	152	158	354,955	162,609	517,563	51.1	1,013,727	12,318.81	2,555.57
4	1,609	43	3,601	6,071	286	3	289	364,620	96,637	461,258	40.2	1,147,478	13,367.33	2,698.11
82	2,307	90	4,705	8,216	19	2	21	485,856	118,027	603,883	48.1	1,255,315	7,882.28	1,539.34
2,288	32,935	1,553	61,658	113,948	1,269	161	1,430	7,883,952	1,972,290	9,856,242	44.4	22,215,113	12,694.79	2,500.51
617	4,236	568	11,013	18,546	9	45	54	1,172,938	302,861	1,475,798	50.2	2,940,323	8,614.03	1,485.11
1,671	28,699	985	50,645	95,402	1,260	116	1,376	6,711,015	1,669,429	8,380,444	43.5	19,274,790	13,683.67	2,791.68
22	707	23	1,009	2,247	2	5	7	131,225	32,559	163,784	42.1	389,029	11,003.49	2,554.21
0	124	10	371	599	0	0	0	34,447	11,567	46,014	57.9	79,502	7,424.52	2,168.21
4	310	19	1,019	1,577	0	0	0	80,218	25,445	105,664	41.6	254,004	10,630.44	2,829.05
36	898	22	1,630	2,885	10	1	11	152,928	50,672	203,600	41.4	491,728	12,527.15	3,237.76
207	2,219	68	3,945	7,592	87	26	113	525,746	148,538	674,284	47.4	1,422,244	12,809.55	2,522.81
8	3,107	67	4,394	8,487	5	0	5	507,196	140,967	648,164	36.1	1,797,792	11,531.70	2,427.96
178	4,085	145	6,572	12,412	89	8	97	833,505	216,955	1,050,459	44.9	2,341,626	11,936.35	2,007.85
768	11,078	396	20,914	39,219	896	52	948	3,202,961	732,083	3,935,046	44.6	8,824,495	17,838.36	3,533.50
30	455	19	781	1,481	4	0	4	95,243	24,746	119,989	44.2	271,170	9,307.99	2,387.02
183	1,041	41	1,816	3,526	2	2	4	272,547	69,999	342,545	46.8	731,491	14,501.92	3,231.78
114	1,125	93	2,769	4,686	0	1	1	210,105	46,646	256,751	42.9	598,179	7,877.20	1,851.91
55	434	19	1,118	1,811	5	0	5	126,012	31,552	157,563	44.7	352,656	13,160.28	3,213.06
0	594	23	845	1,859	66	14	80	117,607	30,545	148,153	40.0	370,383	12,109.18	2,128.04
33	1,558	15	2,070	4,206	62	7	69	237,946	59,667	297,613	39.4	754,662	12,262.96	2,544.26
33	964	25	1,392	2,815	32	0	32	183,328	47,488	230,815	38.7	595,829	8,872.58	2,269.47
5,478	54,001	1,561	93,608	180,873	7,147	334	7,481	12,469,788	2,902,701	15,372,489	48.4	31,762,863	12,039.66	2,319.28
688	5,542	628	14,303	24,138	81	20	101	1,504,983	409,745	1,914,728	48.6	3,942,666	8,445.40	1,297.79
4,790	48,459	933	79,305	156,735	7,066	314	7,380	10,964,805	2,492,956	13,457,761	48.4	27,820,197	12,812.44	2,610.47
72	6,903	127	11,649	21,060	1,494	0	1,494	1,505,400	454,832	1,960,230	49.1	3,991,238	20,254.85	3,823.78
69	698	35	1,314	2,533	2	4	6	186,486	40,045	226,532	57.6	393,446	11,683.28	2,595.27
9	527	12	1,141	1,888	9	0	9	132,998	24,829	157,827	51.9	304,125	10,215.13	2,052.68
1,696	11,859	82	15,609	35,180	2,500	134	2,634	2,733,157	528,522	3,261,678	49.1	6,637,954	13,303.21	2,661.81
49	2,609	39	3,541	7,035	378	15	393	543,934	143,419	687,353	54.1	1,270,158	12,066.17	2,356.75
727	5,068	289	10,873	19,892	115	74	189	1,121,473	287,997	1,409,470	40.1	3,515,779	14,528.55	2,940.70
102	914	43	2,157	3,844	110	3	113	263,883	40,775	304,657	56.3	540,954	12,460.07	2,738.00
327	2,046	36	3,216	6,960	210	11	221	547,939	138,138	686,077	54.6	1,256,427	13,329.66	2,923.05
251	2,197	27	4,038	7,845	272	5	277	606,715	157,361	764,075	55.2	1,383,302	12,726.81	2,700.54
9	662	9	1,116	2,130	32	21	53	114,944	32,967	147,911	38.5	384,351	11,571.61	3,075.84
4	217	3	414	738	58	0	58	50,087	10,697	60,784	46.3	131,306	7,546.30	1,737.01
129	907	14	2,018	3,444	78	12	90	242,421	52,093	294,514	52.4	562,217	11,217.65	2,686.78
64	943	32	1,490	2,964	32	3	35	153,057	38,487	191,543	47.3	404,707	16,436.80	3,627.87
206	1,363	58	3,801	6,100	0	0	0	388,001	92,100	480,101	53.1	904,768	12,778.16	2,076.13
6	31	0	103	155	0	0	0	11,922	3,669	15,591	60.1	25,922	7,724.08	2,410.90
1,070	11,515	127	16,825	34,967	1,776	32	1,808	2,362,390	447,026	2,809,418	46.0	6,113,544	10,033.50	2,053.06

Table continues

MSAs

TABLE 8

U.S. CENSUS DIVISION 4, EAST NORTH CENTRAL CONTINUED

U.S. Community Hospitals
(Nonfederal, short-term general and other special hospitals)

2017 Utilization, Personnel and Finances

MSAs

CLASSIFICATION	Hospitals	Beds	Admissions	Inpatient Days	Adjusted Inpatient Days	Average Daily Census	Adjusted Average Daily Census	Average Stay (days)	Surgical Operations	NEWBORNS Bassinets	Births	OUTPATIENT VISITS Emergency	Total
Ohio..................................	198	33,621	1,452,329	7,266,478	16,110,992	19,912	44,147	5.0	1,335,037	2,437	128,419	7,152,080	44,213,731
Nonmetropolitan..................	59	4,543	165,222	712,770	2,268,762	1,954	6,215	4.3	229,437	532	16,717	1,416,713	8,586,754
Metropolitan	139	29,078	1,287,107	6,553,708	13,842,230	17,958	37,932	5.1	1,105,600	1,905	111,702	5,735,367	35,626,977
Akron................................	8	1,888	81,021	422,786	967,595	1,158	2,656	5.2	65,633	111	7,422	436,345	2,652,740
Canton-Massillon................	5	1,084	41,967	240,138	528,422	658	1,448	5.7	30,498	97	4,196	188,382	1,313,477
Cincinnati.........................	20	4,738	207,522	1,055,931	2,027,561	2,895	5,557	5.1	191,211	360	19,624	827,186	4,903,833
Cleveland-Elyria................	31	7,608	326,229	1,784,922	4,072,760	4,891	11,159	5.5	338,985	333	23,036	1,304,406	12,301,442
Columbus.........................	23	5,655	256,527	1,295,075	2,531,965	3,548	6,936	5.0	206,554	416	28,679	1,111,862	6,133,922
Dayton.............................	13	2,386	114,483	510,212	1,098,771	1,395	3,009	4.5	90,266	111	11,454	593,154	2,386,995
Huntington-Ashland............	1	8	215	446	1,490	1	4	2.1	1,622	0	0	897	4,850
Lima................................	5	525	27,530	112,533	238,622	308	654	4.1	22,169	78	2,377	110,113	712,533
Mansfield..........................	2	278	12,323	52,412	134,041	143	368	4.3	8,154	33	1,057	57,664	386,622
Springfield.........................	2	283	14,591	67,048	139,850	183	383	4.6	8,938	25	463	69,876	350,644
Toledo..............................	13	2,399	107,371	522,324	1,137,287	1,434	3,117	4.9	92,002	164	8,119	406,006	2,432,929
Weirton-Steubenville...........	3	402	10,438	72,754	174,451	199	478	7.0	6,125	18	484	46,937	387,573
Wheeling...........................	3	211	4,533	34,746	87,149	96	239	7.7	7,641	0	0	72,130	244,660
Youngstown-Warren-Boardman	10	1,613	82,357	382,381	702,266	1,049	1,924	4.6	35,802	159	4,791	510,409	1,414,757
Wisconsin	134	12,311	534,275	2,651,498	7,852,081	7,262	21,514	5.0	689,304	1,105	63,011	2,500,115	19,683,325
Nonmetropolitan..................	59	2,448	80,610	487,034	2,394,919	1,335	6,561	6.0	100,739	251	10,378	545,777	4,462,374
Metropolitan	75	9,863	453,665	2,164,464	5,457,162	5,927	14,953	4.8	588,565	854	52,633	1,954,338	15,220,951
Appleton...........................	3	352	15,281	65,725	172,540	180	473	4.3	35,543	43	2,264	70,434	462,392
Duluth..............................	1	25	542	2,860	49,199	8	135	5.3	1,834	0	0	13,700	52,762
Eau Claire........................	6	565	23,648	107,148	271,006	292	742	4.5	29,389	32	2,307	69,451	623,661
Fond du Lac.......................	2	158	7,343	28,774	119,640	79	328	3.9	15,360	23	849	39,228	773,508
Green Bay.........................	6	702	33,567	134,091	422,077	368	1,156	4.0	47,090	95	4,438	140,320	1,705,852
Janesville-Beloit................	4	306	15,352	63,009	201,016	173	551	4.1	16,132	15	1,729	88,516	1,462,572
La Crosse-Onalaska...........	2	360	20,719	91,285	352,515	251	965	4.4	26,729	20	2,407	80,956	739,756
Lake County-Kenosha County........	3	513	21,620	88,212	240,888	242	660	4.1	21,550	51	2,982	197,336	1,027,280
Madison	10	1,600	76,859	422,007	1,056,639	1,155	2,894	5.5	176,369	86	8,130	205,320	1,864,925
Milwaukee-Waukesha-West Allis	24	3,908	176,550	901,993	1,872,698	2,470	5,132	5.1	147,823	333	19,440	802,309	4,893,608
Minneapolis-St. Paul-Bloomington...	4	78	3,485	9,831	58,822	27	162	2.8	5,822	19	949	28,879	211,939
Oshkosh-Neenah................	4	359	15,861	63,475	160,965	173	441	4.0	26,846	59	2,622	60,799	399,529
Racine..............................	2	393	15,506	81,021	235,204	222	645	5.2	12,650	31	1,604	73,338	685,624
Sheboygan........................	2	182	7,905	26,721	84,312	73	231	3.4	11,571	17	1,064	36,235	175,637
Wausau............................	2	362	19,427	78,312	159,641	214	438	4.0	13,857	30	1,848	47,517	141,906

TABLE 8

U.S. Community Hospitals
(Nonfederal, short-term general and other special hospitals)

2017 Utilization, Personnel and Finances

FULL-TIME EQUIVALENT PERSONNEL					FULL-TIME EQUIV. TRAINEES			EXPENSES						
								LABOR				TOTAL		
Physicians and Dentists	Registered Nurses	Licensed Practical Nurses	Other Salaried Personnel	Total Personnel	Medical and Dental Residents	Other Trainees	Total Trainees	Payroll (in thousands)	Employee Benefits (in thousands)	Total (in thousands)	Percent of Total	Amount (in thousands)	Adjusted per Admission	Adjusted per Inpatient Day
9,759	75,335	3,407	131,674	253,707	7,238	727	7,965	17,322,181	4,618,253	21,940,431	49.7	44,155,244	13,268.76	2,740.69
853	8,706	953	18,349	33,269	120	9	129	1,878,743	568,281	2,447,023	49.8	4,917,053	8,821.85	2,167.28
8,906	66,629	2,454	113,325	220,438	7,118	718	7,836	15,443,438	4,049,973	19,493,408	49.7	39,238,191	14,163.43	2,834.67
620	4,540	227	9,578	16,136	521	70	591	1,000,889	251,217	1,252,106	49.7	2,519,948	13,317.28	2,604.34
186	1,982	196	4,692	7,868	80	10	90	360,955	98,115	459,070	50.7	906,211	10,168.78	1,714.94
1,397	10,302	252	20,417	36,745	1,373	181	1,554	2,706,732	688,409	3,395,139	49.9	6,800,064	16,134.92	3,353.81
3,383	19,084	862	32,291	64,804	2,864	374	3,238	5,214,767	1,420,120	6,634,886	56.1	11,821,013	15,856.79	2,902.46
2,870	13,275	324	22,113	44,655	1,415	42	1,457	2,780,161	764,369	3,544,530	45.3	7,826,692	14,823.11	3,091.15
104	6,401	72	8,169	17,617	432	10	442	1,242,106	269,766	1,511,871	46.2	3,274,303	12,886.49	2,979.97
0	28	2	41	81	0	0	0	4,079	840	4,919	32.2	15,258	21,250.18	10,240.02
62	1,044	67	1,832	3,493	22	26	48	186,872	59,083	245,955	43.1	570,877	9,486.00	2,392.39
3	554	35	928	1,724	0	0	0	101,433	32,094	133,527	51.0	262,034	8,235.41	1,954.88
39	477	20	843	1,594	16	2	18	98,906	25,191	124,096	44.9	276,636	8,969.16	1,978.09
87	4,708	160	6,989	13,817	179	0	179	1,045,684	262,033	1,307,717	44.7	2,925,580	13,143.24	2,572.42
50	567	36	1,023	2,044	0	0	0	105,587	31,558	137,145	48.9	280,205	9,522.05	1,606.21
18	285	19	497	956	6	1	7	46,472	11,406	57,878	46.8	123,785	9,911.55	1,420.39
87	3,382	182	3,912	8,904	210	2	212	548,795	135,773	684,569	41.9	1,635,584	10,555.63	2,329.01
1,945	27,844	991	59,864	100,286	936	320	1,256	6,988,118	2,014,260	9,002,380	45.8	19,640,672	12,934.68	2,501.33
418	3,893	227	11,232	17,354	1	0	1	1,327,715	366,571	1,694,286	51.5	3,287,140	9,130.21	1,372.55
1,527	23,951	764	48,632	82,932	935	320	1,255	5,660,403	1,647,690	7,308,094	44.7	16,353,532	14,117.09	2,996.71
0	661	38	1,142	2,069	0	0	0	143,597	37,115	180,712	43.8	412,825	10,178.87	2,392.63
0	40	36	178	265	0	0	0	23,765	6,059	29,824	65.3	45,639	4,894.76	927.64
217	1,258	66	2,208	4,033	5	0	5	367,799	106,902	474,701	55.5	855,952	14,566.92	3,158.42
47	408	102	1,487	2,118	0	0	0	147,121	42,068	189,190	48.4	390,684	12,783.33	3,265.50
128	1,735	154	4,035	6,548	0	0	0	465,723	120,047	585,770	46.8	1,252,799	11,377.81	2,968.18
240	716	21	2,140	3,335	20	0	20	267,147	84,297	351,443	47.9	733,451	14,893.93	3,648.72
173	1,384	106	2,886	4,876	16	15	31	529,751	149,385	679,137	58.3	1,165,133	14,580.02	3,305.20
47	1,308	32	2,935	4,813	20	2	22	281,203	82,038	363,242	50.5	719,285	11,998.87	2,985.97
213	4,343	53	9,846	16,176	671	134	805	1,051,123	367,538	1,418,661	48.8	2,905,622	17,302.27	2,749.87
441	9,504	89	16,646	30,062	187	169	356	1,809,141	497,315	2,306,455	37.7	6,124,325	16,164.84	3,270.32
21	202	6	646	940	0	0	0	70,233	17,195	87,428	46.8	186,875	9,146.63	3,176.95
0	724	18	1,367	2,334	0	0	0	134,036	36,877	170,913	42.8	399,080	9,449.71	2,479.30
0	687	29	1,393	2,362	0	0	0	129,623	38,275	167,899	40.5	414,118	8,930.93	1,760.68
0	322	1	553	962	0	0	0	61,381	18,437	79,818	39.1	204,196	8,187.47	2,421.90
0	659	13	1,170	2,039	16	0	16	178,760	44,141	222,901	41.0	543,548	13,854.36	3,404.81

MSAs

TABLE 8   U.S. CENSUS DIVISION 5, EAST SOUTH CENTRAL

U.S. Community Hospitals
(Nonfederal, short-term general and other special hospitals)

2017 Utilization, Personnel and Finances

CLASSIFICATION	Hospitals	Beds	Admissions	Inpatient Days	Adjusted Inpatient Days	Average Daily Census	Adjusted Average Daily Census	Average Stay (days)	Surgical Operations	NEWBORNS Bassinets	NEWBORNS Births	OUTPATIENT VISITS Emergency	OUTPATIENT VISITS Total
UNITED STATES	5,262	798,921	34,305,620	186,198,977	398,570,958	510,123	1,092,133	5.4	28,221,774	55,181	3,656,809	144,814,804	766,076,124
Nonmetropolitan	1,875	112,806	3,115,229	20,415,212	70,105,531	55,939	192,099	6.6	3,649,248	9,005	358,113	22,487,032	131,567,025
Metropolitan	3,387	686,115	31,190,391	165,783,765	328,465,427	454,184	900,034	5.3	24,572,526	46,176	3,298,696	122,327,772	634,509,099
CENSUS DIVISION 5, EAST SOUTH CENTRAL	433	61,933	2,408,935	13,763,525	29,894,267	37,711	81,941	5.7	2,072,330	3,938	205,116	10,175,145	44,085,711
Nonmetropolitan	223	18,964	512,134	3,350,777	9,133,073	9,181	25,033	6.5	535,560	1,265	49,658	3,121,941	12,972,884
Metropolitan	210	42,969	1,896,801	10,412,748	20,761,194	28,530	56,908	5.5	1,536,770	2,673	155,458	7,053,204	31,112,827
Alabama	102	15,216	628,563	3,596,377	7,487,275	9,853	20,530	5.7	598,205	1,097	55,178	2,327,525	9,259,809
Nonmetropolitan	40	2,586	73,822	406,058	1,209,949	1,112	3,315	5.5	100,633	186	6,087	431,224	1,804,574
Metropolitan	62	12,630	554,741	3,190,319	6,277,326	8,741	17,215	5.8	497,572	911	49,091	1,896,301	7,455,235
Anniston-Oxford-Jacksonville	3	402	16,101	84,078	170,795	230	468	5.2	10,853	15	1,299	37,362	159,705
Auburn-Opelika	1	560	15,067	142,373	371,488	390	1,018	9.4	17,570	38	2,108	56,083	175,793
Birmingham-Hoover	18	4,738	193,732	1,209,796	2,222,814	3,314	6,106	6.2	190,383	379	15,718	609,751	2,788,583
Columbus	2	83	3,788	21,324	48,150	58	132	5.6	5,017	0	0	14,275	21,028
Daphne-Fairhope-Foley	3	298	17,249	69,624	158,371	191	434	4.0	16,530	37	1,402	86,291	304,662
Decatur	2	153	6,798	34,560	100,207	95	274	5.1	6,566	20	518	41,510	208,665
Dothan	5	770	34,474	216,939	468,612	595	1,284	6.3	34,019	57	3,131	86,562	374,675
Florence-Muscle Shoals	3	560	25,122	109,038	273,463	299	750	4.3	15,272	48	2,127	71,559	230,318
Gadsden	3	603	22,558	116,356	187,883	319	515	5.2	21,972	26	901	66,265	153,886
Huntsville	4	1,245	64,484	317,421	666,910	870	1,828	4.9	65,228	93	6,463	252,098	1,060,822
Mobile	6	1,430	70,394	406,748	706,893	1,114	1,936	5.8	47,363	92	6,408	206,140	686,621
Montgomery	8	1,101	50,731	273,815	523,706	750	1,434	5.4	43,703	64	5,596	228,830	666,393
Tuscaloosa	4	687	34,243	188,247	378,034	516	1,036	5.5	23,096	42	3,420	139,575	624,084
Kentucky	109	14,115	560,311	3,109,708	6,965,017	8,522	19,085	5.5	533,098	856	51,034	2,551,891	14,413,737
Nonmetropolitan	66	5,629	183,395	979,939	2,662,215	2,687	7,297	5.3	205,269	426	16,966	1,128,384	5,277,799
Metropolitan	43	8,486	376,916	2,129,769	4,302,802	5,835	11,788	5.7	327,829	430	34,068	1,423,507	9,135,938
Bowling Green	4	680	23,205	162,005	326,395	444	894	7.0	18,547	19	2,469	80,343	231,156
Cincinnati	7	977	49,913	237,485	479,358	650	1,312	4.8	34,099	38	4,490	200,251	1,661,796
Clarksville	2	158	6,097	32,371	76,255	89	209	5.3	3,732	18	584	35,716	185,538
Elizabethtown-Fort Knox	2	308	13,909	67,766	227,204	185	623	4.9	14,884	26	1,712	70,124	451,642
Evansville	1	124	4,003	18,229	63,626	50	174	4.6	3,724	15	655	28,332	332,799
Huntington-Ashland	2	588	23,053	184,948	399,173	506	1,094	8.0	25,532	18	1,881	182,186	1,237,773
Lexington-Fayette	11	2,244	93,694	559,648	1,060,604	1,534	2,905	6.0	78,395	125	6,711	279,223	2,400,101
Louisville-Jefferson County	13	3,047	145,923	783,000	1,468,709	2,146	4,025	5.4	129,860	141	13,507	474,203	1,670,102
Owensboro	1	360	17,119	84,317	201,478	231	552	4.9	19,056	30	2,059	73,129	965,031
Mississippi	100	12,328	378,375	2,481,030	5,773,183	6,795	15,829	6.6	276,248	709	35,445	1,805,514	6,747,529
Nonmetropolitan	71	7,052	163,904	1,370,070	3,556,557	3,751	9,745	8.4	134,083	407	17,288	907,593	3,543,824
Metropolitan	29	5,276	214,471	1,110,960	2,216,626	3,044	6,084	5.2	142,165	302	18,157	897,921	3,203,705
Gulfport-Biloxi-Pascagoula	7	1,297	47,039	226,115	431,878	620	1,194	4.8	38,947	84	4,112	282,640	1,165,736
Hattiesburg	4	778	36,930	177,105	303,435	485	831	4.8	18,690	28	3,677	121,091	243,450
Jackson	14	2,712	111,109	619,146	1,282,406	1,697	3,514	5.6	78,557	148	8,355	397,308	1,552,592
Memphis	4	489	19,393	88,594	198,907	242	545	4.6	5,971	42	2,013	96,882	241,927
Tennessee	122	20,274	841,686	4,576,410	9,668,792	12,541	26,497	5.4	664,779	1,276	63,459	3,490,215	13,664,636
Nonmetropolitan	46	3,697	91,013	594,710	1,704,352	1,631	4,676	6.5	95,575	246	9,317	654,740	2,346,687
Metropolitan	76	16,577	750,673	3,981,700	7,964,440	10,910	21,821	5.3	569,204	1,030	54,142	2,835,475	11,317,949
Chattanooga	5	1,821	87,029	483,153	923,236	1,324	2,529	5.6	71,791	109	6,734	286,609	1,184,143
Clarksville	1	247	13,364	52,843	87,404	145	239	4.0	7,587	30	447	75,057	195,660
Cleveland	1	187	8,886	38,552	83,441	106	229	4.3	6,223	19	1,068	47,143	91,543
Jackson	1	690	29,961	173,930	355,221	477	973	5.8	18,983	33	3,041	101,345	215,041
Johnson City	5	864	40,615	222,674	472,455	611	1,295	5.5	18,365	42	2,617	117,780	404,769
Kingsport-Bristol-Bristol	6	924	38,914	181,214	367,050	496	1,006	4.7	24,592	73	2,434	139,490	473,220
Knoxville	12	2,645	120,719	644,387	1,290,295	1,765	3,536	5.3	106,223	149	9,187	493,299	1,905,582
Memphis	13	3,390	145,030	819,733	1,521,570	2,247	4,167	5.7	88,185	219	13,764	637,889	1,871,608
Morristown	3	320	12,090	51,962	117,773	142	322	4.3	13,308	25	1,134	74,080	216,228
Nashville-Davidson-Murfreesboro-Franklin	29	5,489	254,065	1,313,252	2,745,995	3,597	7,525	5.2	213,947	331	13,716	862,783	4,760,155

2017 Utilization, Personnel and Finances

	FULL-TIME EQUIVALENT PERSONNEL				FULL-TIME EQUIV. TRAINEES			EXPENSES						
								LABOR				TOTAL		
Physicians and Dentists	Registered Nurses	Licensed Practical Nurses	Other Salaried Personnel	Total Personnel	Medical and Dental Residents	Other Trainees	Total Trainees	Payroll (in thousands)	Employee Benefits (in thousands)	Total (in thousands)	Percent of Total	Amount (in thousands)	Adjusted per Admission	Adjusted per Inpatient Day
146,381	1,558,038	76,534	2,704,453	5,216,348	118,075	9,440	127,515	$363,806,143	$96,687,285	$460,493,398	47.7	$966,204,239	$13,126.02	$2,424.17
16,529	156,072	20,966	348,592	631,393	1,972	334	2,306	37,559,678	9,847,876	47,407,559	50.0	94,728,753	8,855.26	1,351.23
129,852	1,401,966	55,568	2,355,861	4,584,955	116,103	9,106	125,209	326,246,465	86,839,408	413,085,839	47.4	871,475,486	13,852.21	2,653.17
7,264	103,348	5,853	158,525	326,962	5,644	431	6,075	19,107,314	4,709,635	23,816,940	45.7	52,142,988	9,856.27	1,744.25
1,582	22,845	2,353	42,058	82,397	320	78	398	4,195,402	1,066,625	5,262,027	47.8	11,007,707	7,608.58	1,205.26
5,682	80,503	3,500	116,467	244,565	5,324	353	5,677	14,911,912	3,643,010	18,554,913	45.1	41,135,281	10,702.32	1,981.35
1,456	27,985	1,224	37,705	80,496	1,728	47	1,775	4,269,032	1,062,418	5,331,452	46.0	11,596,935	8,712.05	1,548.89
193	3,076	295	6,110	11,368	32	3	35	480,454	123,950	604,405	48.2	1,254,421	5,483.06	1,036.75
1,263	24,909	929	31,595	69,128	1,696	44	1,740	3,788,579	938,467	4,727,047	45.7	10,342,514	9,382.19	1,647.60
34	452	37	926	1,694	17	2	19	95,719	27,276	122,994	51.9	237,207	6,960.30	1,388.84
44	733	51	1,743	3,021	0	5	5	143,297	39,622	182,920	51.9	352,139	8,957.10	947.92
225	9,516	202	10,391	24,712	909	0	909	1,530,458	350,105	1,880,563	42.8	4,391,885	12,128.09	1,975.82
2	142	9	219	443	13	0	13	20,895	4,031	24,926	37.1	67,187	9,416.50	1,395.36
38	583	34	975	1,931	16	0	16	95,157	23,488	118,645	47.2	251,620	6,467.72	1,588.80
33	292	37	668	1,213	7	0	7	52,573	16,394	68,967	51.1	135,030	6,802.16	1,347.51
145	1,380	136	2,117	4,449	75	3	78	214,007	61,195	275,202	46.2	596,260	8,377.62	1,272.40
56	665	40	1,360	2,424	17	3	20	109,829	33,216	143,045	52.1	274,545	4,360.08	1,003.96
6	754	44	664	1,875	13	0	13	103,147	21,331	124,478	40.9	304,100	8,108.48	1,618.56
261	4,382	130	3,727	9,356	24	1	25	466,195	157,260	623,455	51.5	1,211,253	8,878.59	1,816.22
240	2,761	72	4,022	8,279	406	8	414	414,649	102,654	517,302	45.8	1,130,397	9,139.92	1,599.11
84	1,992	58	2,591	5,501	1	1	2	313,214	49,945	363,160	42.3	858,751	8,627.11	1,639.76
95	1,257	79	2,192	4,230	198	21	219	229,438	51,951	281,390	52.9	532,139	7,639.09	1,407.65
996	25,214	1,054	36,954	77,111	1,239	27	1,266	4,762,069	1,250,481	6,012,547	44.5	13,526,306	10,336.49	1,942.03
642	8,240	613	15,047	29,203	161	15	176	1,591,169	440,202	2,031,371	47.4	4,281,255	8,260.78	1,608.16
354	16,974	441	21,907	47,908	1,078	12	1,090	3,170,900	810,279	3,981,176	43.1	9,245,051	11,697.64	2,148.61
46	768	20	1,185	2,605	19	0	19	239,727	59,059	298,786	46.4	643,943	14,505.83	1,972.89
38	2,160	47	2,518	5,279	30	0	30	424,918	110,136	535,054	49.0	1,091,786	10,786.80	2,277.60
28	285	24	555	1,057	7	0	7	57,093	14,665	71,757	48.1	149,316	10,199.87	1,958.11
78	539	21	1,694	2,536	0	0	0	146,921	36,492	183,413	55.8	328,544	6,912.51	1,446.03
27	219	13	549	942	8	8	16	39,631	14,881	54,512	49.5	110,153	7,883.87	1,731.26
103	1,118	33	1,962	3,870	88	4	92	248,470	68,081	316,550	45.9	690,245	12,808.05	1,729.19
30	4,673	88	5,947	13,591	901	0	901	849,874	218,267	1,068,140	41.8	2,553,862	13,447.04	2,407.93
4	6,563	183	6,032	15,575	25	0	25	1,012,206	236,576	1,248,782	39.8	3,139,362	11,046.12	2,137.50
0	649	12	1,465	2,453	0	0	0	152,061	52,121	204,182	38.0	537,839	13,148.17	2,669.47
915	15,688	1,382	24,352	52,092	746	67	813	3,064,933	723,828	3,788,763	48.5	7,806,530	9,035.07	1,352.21
510	7,354	946	12,892	26,391	60	47	107	1,422,160	343,858	1,766,020	48.4	3,645,808	8,541.87	1,025.09
405	8,334	436	11,460	25,701	686	20	706	1,642,773	379,970	2,022,743	48.6	4,160,721	9,516.55	1,877.05
231	2,407	115	2,620	6,615	7	0	7	460,395	102,033	562,428	51.2	1,098,770	11,839.55	2,544.17
46	1,124	50	2,052	4,104	64	5	69	228,893	55,910	284,803	51.2	614,289	9,624.14	2,024.45
128	4,124	245	6,025	13,184	615	0	615	835,215	195,771	1,030,986	48.6	2,122,195	8,985.76	1,654.85
0	679	26	763	1,798	0	15	15	118,269	26,256	144,526	44.4	325,468	7,329.86	1,636.28
3,897	34,461	2,193	59,514	117,263	1,931	290	2,221	7,011,279	1,672,909	8,684,178	45.2	19,213,218	10,754.21	1,987.14
237	4,175	499	8,009	15,435	67	13	80	701,619	158,615	860,231	47.1	1,826,222	6,692.16	1,071.51
3,660	30,286	1,694	51,505	101,828	1,864	277	2,141	6,309,660	1,514,293	7,823,947	45.0	17,386,995	11,486.52	2,183.08
386	2,978	155	4,909	9,737	222	187	409	619,990	162,149	782,139	44.0	1,698,808	10,391.28	1,840.06
10	487	16	546	1,262	22	0	22	69,323	15,632	84,955	44.0	192,921	8,727.86	2,207.23
0	330	16	299	867	0	0	0	45,463	8,436	53,899	42.3	127,472	6,627.75	1,527.69
3	999	127	2,644	4,385	0	0	0	235,323	61,829	297,152	47.2	629,608	10,289.40	1,772.44
0	1,060	63	1,268	2,919	0	1	1	177,660	45,927	223,587	42.2	529,564	6,942.19	1,120.88
46	1,539	76	2,282	4,623	25	2	27	266,485	65,261	331,747	41.8	793,915	9,764.77	2,162.96
287	4,762	274	6,767	14,441	39	60	99	922,597	207,452	1,130,048	45.5	2,483,145	10,248.44	1,924.48
296	5,735	123	7,988	16,882	78	12	90	1,230,305	298,374	1,528,678	41.5	3,684,727	12,993.19	2,421.66
7	428	23	537	1,203	5	1	6	68,118	13,820	81,938	45.6	179,767	6,517.53	1,526.38
2,625	11,968	821	24,265	45,509	1,473	14	1,487	2,674,397	635,412	3,309,804	46.8	7,067,070	13,169.50	2,573.59

MSAs

TABLE 8

U.S. CENSUS DIVISION 6, WEST NORTH CENTRAL

U.S. Community Hospitals
(Nonfederal, short-term general and other special hospitals)

2017 Utilization, Personnel and Finances

CLASSIFICATION	Hospitals	Beds	Admissions	Inpatient Days	Adjusted Inpatient Days	Average Daily Census	Adjusted Average Daily Census	Average Stay (days)	Surgical Operations	NEWBORNS Bassinets	Births	OUTPATIENT VISITS Emergency	Total
UNITED STATES	5,262	798,921	34,305,620	186,198,977	398,570,958	510,123	1,092,133	5.4	28,221,774	55,181	3,656,809	144,814,804	766,076,124
Nonmetropolitan	1,875	112,806	3,115,229	20,415,212	70,105,531	55,939	192,099	6.6	3,649,248	9,005	358,113	22,487,032	131,567,025
Metropolitan	3,387	686,115	31,190,391	165,783,765	328,465,427	454,184	900,034	5.3	24,572,526	46,176	3,298,696	122,327,772	634,509,099
CENSUS DIVISION 6, WEST NORTH CENTRAL	707	66,538	2,364,074	14,368,825	37,309,608	39,375	102,220	6.1	2,153,923	4,670	263,309	9,279,951	69,229,781
Nonmetropolitan	452	21,567	441,222	4,041,989	14,801,473	11,085	40,553	9.2	564,148	1,606	56,729	2,797,592	24,265,216
Metropolitan	255	44,971	1,922,852	10,326,836	22,508,135	28,290	61,667	5.4	1,589,775	3,064	206,580	6,482,359	44,964,565
Iowa	117	9,365	315,667	1,937,198	6,133,329	5,310	16,803	6.1	334,728	721	38,237	1,346,809	11,571,214
Nonmetropolitan	83	3,786	79,217	698,576	3,109,345	1,917	8,518	8.8	129,610	302	9,914	533,721	5,394,130
Metropolitan	34	5,579	236,450	1,238,622	3,023,984	3,393	8,285	5.2	205,118	419	28,323	815,088	6,177,084
Ames	2	254	8,718	59,625	157,843	164	433	6.8	10,720	17	1,177	31,896	211,648
Cedar Rapids	4	737	28,159	152,558	525,182	418	1,439	5.4	25,044	54	3,250	118,839	999,689
Davenport-Moline-Rock Island	3	504	24,440	95,899	186,054	262	509	3.9	12,922	33	2,755	100,805	284,143
Des Moines-West Des Moines	7	1,448	67,667	352,635	727,047	966	1,992	5.2	45,427	118	10,182	208,435	969,296
Dubuque	3	360	14,127	72,898	148,988	200	409	5.2	13,523	34	1,520	50,958	145,305
Iowa City	3	1,036	42,137	269,333	588,494	737	1,613	6.4	37,076	67	3,556	94,661	1,894,984
Omaha-Council Bluffs	3	278	13,704	53,955	124,946	148	342	3.9	11,625	22	986	55,592	168,608
Sioux City	3	361	17,707	81,000	154,276	222	422	4.6	11,281	35	2,273	67,094	341,448
Waterloo-Cedar Falls	6	601	19,791	100,719	411,154	276	1,126	5.1	37,500	39	2,624	86,808	1,161,963
Kansas	144	9,899	316,472	1,910,634	4,917,563	5,233	13,473	6.0	269,617	664	36,477	1,195,636	8,284,595
Nonmetropolitan	99	4,106	76,222	698,760	2,402,576	1,915	6,584	9.2	91,211	283	9,198	395,012	3,426,244
Metropolitan	45	5,793	240,250	1,211,874	2,514,987	3,318	6,889	5.0	178,406	381	27,279	800,624	4,858,351
Kansas City	19	2,667	116,566	588,810	1,265,641	1,610	3,469	5.1	90,563	189	13,195	354,133	3,058,247
Lawrence	1	142	6,919	24,373	102,124	67	280	3.5	5,360	20	1,052	39,337	207,349
Manhattan	4	277	6,354	46,427	151,469	127	415	7.3	6,396	26	1,208	32,504	260,626
Topeka	5	791	33,074	164,539	338,520	451	927	5.0	22,315	39	2,704	102,864	419,398
Wichita	16	1,916	77,337	387,725	657,233	1,063	1,798	5.0	53,772	107	9,120	271,786	912,731
Minnesota	129	13,992	557,820	3,310,521	8,311,813	9,068	22,772	5.9	559,453	1,256	66,404	2,092,544	13,844,212
Nonmetropolitan	76	3,835	81,917	811,087	3,102,466	2,223	8,501	9.9	127,578	327	12,527	571,669	5,362,048
Metropolitan	53	10,157	475,903	2,499,434	5,209,347	6,845	14,271	5.3	431,875	929	53,877	1,520,875	8,482,164
Duluth	10	1,163	39,729	253,496	723,781	694	1,983	6.4	40,760	74	2,985	128,330	1,830,319
Grand Forks	2	123	1,428	27,047	114,462	74	314	18.9	3,586	11	236	10,420	103,319
Mankato-North Mankato	2	162	10,102	39,281	87,773	107	240	3.9	8,610	16	1,359	38,472	268,691
Minneapolis-St. Paul-Bloomington	31	6,390	334,686	1,584,488	3,012,783	4,340	8,253	4.7	249,487	687	42,744	1,166,635	4,972,894
Rochester	4	1,587	60,448	405,514	798,478	1,111	2,188	6.7	110,243	109	3,446	104,772	717,004
St. Cloud	4	732	29,510	189,608	472,070	519	1,293	6.4	19,189	32	3,107	72,246	589,937
Missouri	126	18,930	773,308	4,141,096	9,856,095	11,349	27,002	5.4	587,266	1,195	71,671	3,090,141	24,850,074
Nonmetropolitan	53	2,919	90,101	442,477	1,763,330	1,214	4,830	4.9	83,637	267	10,428	655,133	5,327,623
Metropolitan	73	16,011	683,207	3,698,619	8,092,765	10,135	22,172	5.4	503,629	928	61,243	2,435,008	19,522,451
Cape Girardeau	3	547	21,720	107,695	231,973	295	636	5.0	16,864	40	1,991	78,871	1,222,069
Columbia	4	1,008	42,324	226,442	392,333	620	1,075	5.4	36,191	55	3,946	106,050	1,153,447
Jefferson City	3	246	12,352	49,129	152,592	135	418	4.0	9,886	28	1,476	81,633	718,206
Joplin	5	678	29,081	156,536	380,159	429	1,041	5.4	17,189	59	3,059	152,147	1,172,436
Kansas City	23	3,802	164,757	909,201	2,032,544	2,490	5,568	5.5	102,878	176	14,021	683,444	3,847,001
Springfield	5	1,560	72,871	378,041	951,744	1,036	2,607	5.2	69,536	84	6,986	218,326	2,508,143
St. Joseph	1	352	16,201	67,790	179,358	186	491	4.2	12,141	28	1,584	61,421	1,171,561
St. Louis	29	7,818	323,901	1,803,785	3,772,062	4,944	10,336	5.6	238,944	458	28,180	1,053,116	7,729,588
Nebraska	94	6,975	204,819	1,427,631	3,486,921	3,910	9,555	7.0	206,511	497	24,334	816,532	5,620,876
Nonmetropolitan	66	2,881	60,167	540,594	1,695,702	1,481	4,645	9.0	66,845	248	5,634	343,249	2,498,600
Metropolitan	28	4,094	144,652	887,037	1,791,219	2,429	4,910	6.1	139,666	249	18,700	473,283	3,122,276
Grand Island	4	312	7,270	65,330	193,890	179	531	9.0	5,317	34	973	30,814	144,127
Lincoln	8	1,526	44,515	340,452	559,109	932	1,532	7.6	26,085	49	4,928	136,003	457,969
Omaha-Council Bluffs	16	2,256	92,867	481,255	1,038,220	1,318	2,847	5.2	108,264	166	12,799	306,466	2,520,180
North Dakota	40	3,210	88,600	683,497	2,066,051	1,877	5,660	7.7	100,565	158	13,254	408,172	2,274,792
Nonmetropolitan	32	1,704	21,863	330,672	1,184,978	909	3,246	15.1	25,746	54	3,552	129,664	748,407
Metropolitan	8	1,506	66,737	352,825	881,073	968	2,414	5.3	74,819	104	9,702	278,508	1,526,385
Bismarck	3	486	22,758	103,683	273,462	284	749	4.6	19,934	36	2,622	52,184	360,991
Fargo	3	658	31,688	166,758	436,523	458	1,196	5.3	44,435	43	4,193	95,558	548,729
Grand Forks	2	362	12,291	82,384	171,088	226	469	6.7	10,450	25	2,887	130,766	616,665
South Dakota	57	4,167	107,388	958,248	2,537,836	2,628	6,955	8.9	95,783	179	12,932	328,117	2,784,018
Nonmetropolitan	43	2,336	31,735	519,823	1,543,076	1,426	4,229	16.4	39,521	125	5,476	169,144	1,508,164
Metropolitan	14	1,831	75,653	438,425	994,760	1,202	2,726	5.8	56,262	54	7,456	158,973	1,275,854
Rapid City	5	596	22,845	160,955	334,510	442	917	7.0	10,675	24	2,108	70,751	280,137
Sioux City	1	40	1,190	4,459	11,379	12	31	3.7	1,551	0	0	6,024	19,306
Sioux Falls	8	1,195	51,618	273,011	648,871	748	1,778	5.3	44,036	30	5,348	82,198	976,411

MSAs

TABLE 8

U.S. CENSUS DIVISION 6, WEST NORTH CENTRAL

U.S. Community Hospitals
(Nonfederal, short-term general and other special hospitals)

2017 Utilization, Personnel and Finances

FULL-TIME EQUIVALENT PERSONNEL					FULL-TIME EQUIV. TRAINEES			EXPENSES						
								LABOR				TOTAL		
Physicians and Dentists	Registered Nurses	Licensed Practical Nurses	Other Salaried Personnel	Total Personnel	Medical and Dental Residents	Other Trainees	Total Trainees	Payroll (in thousands)	Employee Benefits (in thousands)	Total (in thousands)	Percent of Total	Amount (in thousands)	Adjusted per Admission	Adjusted per Inpatient Day
146,381	1,558,038	76,534	2,704,453	5,216,348	118,075	9,440	127,515	$363,806,143	$96,687,285	$460,493,398	47.7	$966,204,239	$13,126.02	$2,424.17
16,529	156,072	20,966	348,592	631,393	1,972	334	2,306	37,559,678	9,847,876	47,407,559	50.0	94,728,753	8,855.26	1,351.23
129,852	1,401,966	55,568	2,355,861	4,584,955	116,103	9,106	125,209	326,246,465	86,839,408	413,085,839	47.4	871,475,486	13,852.21	2,653.17
16,276	121,671	9,773	249,397	449,505	5,101	575	5,676	29,431,276	7,323,303	36,754,583	49.4	74,332,888	12,680.15	1,992.33
3,388	26,489	4,560	63,356	111,758	121	23	144	6,588,746	1,683,722	8,272,475	50.5	16,366,016	9,646.85	1,105.70
12,888	95,182	5,213	186,041	337,747	4,980	552	5,532	22,842,529	5,639,581	28,482,108	49.1	57,966,872	13,915.50	2,575.37
1,211	16,163	1,013	33,315	58,965	827	156	983	3,595,307	976,093	4,571,398	48.8	9,376,783	10,328.48	1,528.82
562	5,716	592	12,623	22,251	33	0	33	1,245,549	339,241	1,584,791	50.2	3,149,609	8,919.78	1,012.95
649	10,447	421	20,692	36,714	794	156	950	2,349,758	636,852	2,986,607	48.0	6,227,174	11,225.13	2,059.26
3	370	11	751	1,285	0	0	0	75,408	25,682	101,090	48.4	208,695	10,530.07	1,322.17
44	1,120	54	2,808	4,503	0	0	0	263,406	68,316	331,722	46.6	711,488	8,014.42	1,354.75
2	753	16	982	1,935	0	0	0	126,227	22,585	148,811	34.2	435,505	8,786.19	2,340.74
224	2,894	49	5,170	9,580	228	15	243	661,891	157,719	819,610	51.1	1,602,380	11,747.39	2,203.96
13	593	18	1,120	1,891	0	0	0	108,320	23,646	131,966	44.0	300,238	10,137.00	2,015.18
120	2,562	25	5,156	9,225	558	139	697	588,296	221,266	809,561	48.1	1,684,193	19,282.30	2,861.87
11	344	10	578	1,088	0	0	0	78,366	21,248	99,614	47.0	211,892	6,483.25	1,695.87
75	845	26	1,571	2,851	2	0	2	161,319	36,819	198,139	50.4	393,501	11,403.17	2,550.63
157	966	212	2,556	4,356	6	2	8	286,525	59,570	346,094	50.9	679,283	8,933.82	1,652.14
1,847	16,020	1,427	27,718	55,401	44	213	257	3,618,231	819,956	4,438,187	50.9	8,717,687	11,056.99	1,772.77
492	4,574	698	10,163	19,078	0	2	2	1,033,804	241,402	1,275,270	52.6	2,423,587	9,097.62	1,008.75
1,355	11,446	729	17,555	36,323	44	211	255	2,584,427	578,493	3,162,917	50.3	6,294,100	12,056.88	2,502.64
898	6,341	222	9,117	19,387	1	209	210	1,522,926	339,276	1,862,200	51.0	3,650,087	13,668.89	2,883.98
64	335	45	1,001	1,588	0	0	0	98,616	19,123	117,739	49.1	239,773	8,270.61	2,347.86
23	277	22	406	842	0	0	0	58,901	12,306	71,207	48.0	148,475	7,930.52	980.23
279	1,394	339	2,850	5,685	0	0	0	404,164	96,651	500,815	58.8	851,874	12,008.38	2,516.47
91	3,099	101	4,181	8,821	43	2	45	499,819	111,138	610,956	43.5	1,403,891	10,296.61	2,136.06
6,855	27,736	2,279	70,939	119,762	2,171	89	2,260	8,196,155	2,182,514	10,378,671	53.5	19,400,142	15,220.20	2,334.04
881	5,003	1,220	13,193	22,688	10	6	16	1,440,793	391,876	1,832,668	50.7	3,617,533	10,851.11	1,166.02
5,974	22,733	1,059	57,746	97,074	2,161	83	2,244	6,755,362	1,790,638	8,546,003	54.1	15,782,609	16,767.68	3,029.67
583	1,913	268	5,286	8,687	7	0	7	759,929	185,440	945,369	59.7	1,584,164	16,619.60	2,188.73
15	120	38	333	573	1	2	3	28,388	6,185	34,573	58.6	59,008	9,538.98	515.53
146	506	62	724	1,658	0	0	0	144,423	37,798	182,221	47.1	386,858	17,290.54	4,407.49
2,854	14,463	378	26,665	49,579	862	81	943	4,605,900	1,234,299	5,840,201	54.4	10,728,577	16,870.18	3,561.02
2,351	4,316	127	22,191	31,729	1,276	0	1,276	840,687	224,624	1,065,312	49.0	2,174,455	17,736.32	2,723.25
25	1,415	186	2,547	4,848	15	0	15	376,036	102,292	478,327	56.3	849,547	14,441.94	1,799.62
3,405	37,312	2,639	71,304	128,005	1,906	90	1,996	8,199,093	2,059,303	10,258,396	45.4	22,608,624	12,126.61	2,293.87
629	4,165	964	10,707	18,223	42	4	46	1,082,418	283,588	1,366,005	48.6	2,811,310	7,843.27	1,594.32
2,776	33,147	1,675	60,597	109,782	1,864	86	1,950	7,116,675	1,775,716	8,892,391	44.9	19,797,314	13,146.11	2,446.30
186	1,102	157	2,521	4,369	0	0	0	306,807	66,051	372,857	46.9	794,693	16,513.11	3,425.80
43	1,600	253	3,857	6,195	404	31	435	375,639	115,297	490,936	39.4	1,244,741	16,443.08	3,172.67
103	557	130	1,314	2,295	3	0	3	137,288	35,738	173,025	47.4	365,230	9,383.64	2,393.51
243	1,349	81	2,520	4,919	22	0	22	340,944	72,177	413,121	52.8	782,915	10,727.94	2,059.44
565	7,620	214	14,727	25,836	182	49	231	1,807,024	439,964	2,246,986	46.2	4,860,236	14,525.16	2,391.21
865	3,827	424	10,767	17,391	26	0	26	773,904	187,497	961,402	44.6	2,157,695	11,317.34	2,267.10
193	749	206	2,350	3,697	0	0	0	274,027	70,649	344,676	54.2	635,581	14,827.84	3,543.64
578	16,343	210	22,541	45,080	1,227	6	1,233	3,101,042	788,344	3,889,388	43.4	8,956,223	12,756.46	2,374.36
877	11,655	923	21,612	40,287	43	7	50	2,613,935	628,725	3,242,665	48.7	6,656,755	13,430.84	1,909.06
352	3,448	640	8,073	14,504	16	2	18	850,492	219,714	1,070,210	48.9	2,188,501	11,455.48	1,290.62
525	8,207	283	13,539	25,783	27	5	32	1,763,442	409,012	2,172,455	48.6	4,468,254	14,669.83	2,494.53
13	314	38	608	1,161	0	0	0	62,335	17,797	80,132	40.3	199,028	11,487.89	1,026.50
36	2,252	87	3,342	6,673	13	4	17	392,633	108,227	500,861	45.8	1,094,273	13,896.41	1,957.17
476	5,641	158	9,589	17,949	14	1	15	1,308,474	282,988	1,591,462	50.1	3,174,954	15,226.28	3,058.07
1,117	6,047	812	11,020	21,891	39	9	48	1,621,699	323,566	1,945,266	51.9	3,747,439	14,484.03	1,813.82
223	1,356	229	4,075	6,676	1	3	4	428,357	86,497	514,854	52.8	974,452	10,846.41	822.34
894	4,691	583	6,945	15,215	38	6	44	1,193,343	237,069	1,430,412	51.6	2,772,987	16,419.09	3,147.28
255	1,324	151	1,999	4,463	1	0	1	385,698	68,638	454,337	54.8	829,680	13,572.39	3,033.99
559	2,157	394	3,027	7,053	1	0	1	600,145	115,567	715,712	51.8	1,382,125	16,380.35	3,166.21
80	1,210	38	1,919	3,699	36	6	42	207,499	52,864	260,363	46.4	561,182	23,936.09	3,280.00
964	6,738	680	13,489	25,194	71	11	82	1,586,856	333,146	1,920,000	50.2	3,825,457	14,039.20	1,507.37
249	2,227	217	4,522	8,338	19	6	25	507,333	121,345	628,677	52.3	1,201,025	11,513.77	778.33
715	4,511	463	8,967	16,856	52	5	57	1,079,523	211,801	1,291,323	49.2	2,624,433	15,605.65	2,638.26
110	714	80	2,451	3,799	18	5	23	243,187	25,723	268,909	42.2	637,375	14,304.07	1,905.40
1	57	6	102	197	0	0	0	17,452	3,837	21,289	40.6	52,500	17,286.65	4,613.72
604	3,740	377	6,414	12,860	34	0	34	818,884	182,241	1,001,125	51.7	1,934,558	16,044.31	2,981.42

MSAs

TABLE 8

U.S. CENSUS DIVISION 7, WEST SOUTH CENTRAL

U.S. Community Hospitals
(Nonfederal, short-term general and other special hospitals)

2017 Utilization, Personnel and Finances

CLASSIFICATION	Hospitals	Beds	Admissions	Inpatient Days	Adjusted Inpatient Days	Average Daily Census	Adjusted Average Daily Census	Average Stay (days)	Surgical Operations	NEWBORNS Bassinets	NEWBORNS Births	OUTPATIENT VISITS Emergency	OUTPATIENT VISITS Total
UNITED STATES	5,262	798,921	34,305,620	186,198,977	398,570,958	510,123	1,092,133	5.4	28,221,774	55,181	3,656,809	144,814,804	766,076,124
Nonmetropolitan	1,875	112,806	3,115,229	20,415,212	70,105,531	55,939	192,099	6.6	3,649,248	9,005	358,113	22,487,032	131,567,025
Metropolitan	3,387	686,115	31,190,391	165,783,765	328,465,427	454,184	900,034	5.3	24,572,526	46,176	3,298,696	122,327,772	634,509,099
CENSUS DIVISION 7, WEST SOUTH CENTRAL	908	103,632	4,140,484	22,004,809	44,603,227	60,294	122,248	5.3	3,399,120	7,500	526,266	18,272,095	72,217,938
Nonmetropolitan	296	14,517	390,904	1,823,474	6,295,587	4,999	17,249	4.7	343,322	1,204	49,642	2,914,077	12,502,109
Metropolitan	612	89,115	3,749,580	20,181,335	38,307,640	55,295	104,999	5.4	3,055,798	6,296	476,624	15,358,018	59,715,829
Arkansas	88	9,664	363,070	1,861,122	4,125,703	5,097	11,301	5.1	298,118	754	35,517	1,519,156	6,148,539
Nonmetropolitan	49	3,139	86,853	443,472	1,395,726	1,213	3,824	5.1	68,057	221	9,362	543,518	2,368,152
Metropolitan	39	6,525	276,217	1,417,650	2,729,977	3,884	7,477	5.1	230,061	533	26,155	975,638	3,780,387
Fayetteville-Springdale-Rogers	8	1,071	47,044	195,881	378,038	536	1,035	4.2	46,038	91	7,346	214,784	727,632
Fort Smith	6	807	34,517	180,062	331,978	494	910	5.2	34,968	45	3,467	138,965	465,149
Hot Springs	3	475	19,927	99,450	185,818	273	511	5.0	16,238	27	1,360	68,771	230,584
Jonesboro	3	681	29,643	147,456	325,781	404	892	5.0	17,768	46	2,120	102,808	392,134
Little Rock-North Little Rock-Conway	17	3,180	135,730	741,078	1,391,674	2,030	3,810	5.5	110,598	296	11,113	398,676	1,726,562
Pine Bluff	1	286	9,207	53,227	111,459	146	305	5.8	4,451	28	749	46,815	224,674
Texarkana	1	25	149	496	5,229	1	14	3.3	0	0	0	4,819	13,652
Louisiana	163	15,649	582,708	3,269,781	7,315,504	8,954	20,042	5.6	490,088	961	61,233	2,884,237	13,032,029
Nonmetropolitan	45	2,077	58,583	297,695	891,153	815	2,444	5.1	55,437	122	5,680	352,959	1,429,461
Metropolitan	118	13,572	524,125	2,972,086	6,424,351	8,139	17,598	5.7	434,651	839	55,553	2,531,278	11,602,568
Alexandria	6	761	30,425	175,855	318,031	482	872	5.8	19,585	55	2,902	147,780	474,022
Baton Rouge	20	2,804	88,603	605,930	1,498,653	1,658	4,106	6.8	67,156	155	11,131	430,982	2,917,601
Hammond	8	405	14,936	90,739	182,593	247	499	6.1	20,025	26	1,260	110,164	622,649
Houma-Thibodaux	7	566	23,259	115,044	324,826	315	890	4.9	20,161	44	3,122	162,840	683,573
Lafayette	19	1,505	60,139	333,733	694,690	914	1,903	5.5	41,556	133	7,727	309,130	1,174,149
Lake Charles	8	759	28,329	149,765	337,798	410	925	5.3	25,409	54	3,053	144,596	576,914
Monroe	11	926	33,770	188,554	360,572	517	988	5.6	21,217	49	3,403	141,559	497,326
New Orleans-Metairie	28	4,108	160,735	913,273	1,916,361	2,503	5,248	5.7	150,797	212	16,369	757,848	3,156,516
Shreveport-Bossier City	11	1,738	83,929	399,193	790,827	1,093	2,167	4.8	68,745	111	6,586	326,379	1,499,818
Oklahoma	129	11,475	420,377	2,278,209	5,032,340	6,245	13,788	5.4	409,360	787	48,385	1,915,881	7,847,667
Nonmetropolitan	64	3,203	82,917	408,399	1,343,989	1,120	3,683	4.9	88,777	269	10,214	630,642	2,639,733
Metropolitan	65	8,272	337,460	1,869,810	3,688,351	5,125	10,105	5.5	320,583	518	38,171	1,285,239	5,207,934
Enid	3	345	9,270	54,306	108,969	149	298	5.9	8,338	16	1,293	37,554	158,718
Fort Smith	2	69	1,545	5,547	24,109	15	66	3.6	1,142	9	253	14,538	34,902
Lawton	2	548	14,564	125,731	303,631	344	832	8.6	13,118	43	2,040	73,476	239,357
Oklahoma City	32	4,266	171,536	980,965	1,896,411	2,688	5,196	5.7	197,546	278	19,348	743,613	3,222,808
Tulsa	26	3,044	140,545	703,261	1,355,231	1,929	3,713	5.0	100,439	172	15,237	416,058	1,552,149
Texas	528	66,844	2,774,329	14,595,697	28,129,680	39,998	77,117	5.3	2,201,554	4,998	381,131	11,952,821	45,189,703
Nonmetropolitan	138	6,098	162,551	673,908	2,664,719	1,851	7,298	4.1	131,051	592	24,386	1,386,958	6,064,763
Metropolitan	390	60,746	2,611,778	13,921,789	25,464,961	38,147	69,819	5.3	2,070,503	4,406	356,745	10,565,863	39,124,940
Abilene	6	731	24,538	131,206	252,092	359	691	5.3	20,796	27	2,669	95,034	400,657
Amarillo	5	936	41,647	199,767	333,628	547	914	4.8	29,422	54	4,309	122,635	396,065
Austin-Round Rock	29	3,542	163,246	830,428	1,423,566	2,275	3,900	5.1	124,945	341	26,563	747,223	2,872,494
Beaumont-Port Arthur	9	1,075	43,481	217,845	439,191	596	1,203	5.0	37,458	76	4,847	201,618	538,857
Brownsville-Harlingen	6	1,114	42,678	224,315	348,612	615	955	5.3	25,866	88	6,809	163,659	328,050
College Station-Bryan	5	529	24,146	91,786	216,336	252	592	3.8	24,057	73	3,839	113,001	549,705
Corpus Christi	6	1,266	53,908	296,181	489,843	812	1,342	5.5	48,316	73	6,498	246,223	594,404
Dallas-Plano-Irving	82	10,894	486,671	2,575,739	4,608,589	7,061	12,628	5.3	348,494	765	64,336	2,210,258	6,400,576
El Paso	13	2,052	88,984	437,654	743,308	1,200	2,039	4.9	61,349	205	13,939	377,005	1,431,374
Fort Worth-Arlington	41	5,651	253,907	1,355,243	2,310,187	3,712	6,330	5.3	207,571	414	35,097	1,164,506	3,279,583
Houston-The Woodlands-Sugar Land	90	15,839	675,509	3,806,420	7,399,859	10,430	20,321	5.6	528,212	1,164	97,228	2,510,423	11,152,263
Killeen-Temple	6	1,015	47,370	216,725	541,731	594	1,485	4.6	41,780	66	4,674	212,646	2,034,635
Laredo	4	569	22,200	123,426	225,788	339	619	5.6	19,633	66	5,440	95,417	260,019
Longview	3	297	11,947	57,481	118,351	157	323	4.8	16,107	47	2,071	48,620	149,072
Lubbock	9	1,373	59,725	309,234	562,929	848	1,542	5.2	46,850	94	5,361	163,284	740,579
McAllen-Edinburg-Mission	8	2,197	90,917	442,401	812,469	1,212	2,225	4.9	105,185	185	15,328	323,564	857,864
Midland	4	372	12,996	75,348	147,540	206	404	5.8	8,339	27	2,380	64,779	159,104
Odessa	4	620	19,322	105,931	193,430	289	529	5.5	18,276	60	4,010	76,021	371,925
San Angelo	2	441	17,616	84,654	188,031	232	515	4.8	20,307	36	2,013	65,907	186,014
San Antonio-New Braunfels	26	6,247	262,671	1,439,204	2,437,688	3,944	6,680	5.5	199,613	348	32,955	897,849	3,709,859
Sherman-Denison	5	486	25,063	127,292	212,705	348	583	5.1	34,851	45	1,573	85,219	196,339
Texarkana	5	692	23,232	128,810	236,297	352	647	5.5	11,441	31	2,635	109,964	250,625
Tyler	8	1,245	53,054	290,857	521,271	799	1,429	5.5	44,704	30	3,456	143,358	1,156,064
Victoria	5	565	17,978	98,580	190,912	270	524	5.5	13,022	30	1,986	76,758	249,440
Waco	3	542	30,636	159,413	344,265	437	944	5.2	18,940	41	4,785	158,982	664,807
Wichita Falls	6	456	18,336	95,849	166,343	261	455	5.2	14,969	20	1,944	91,910	194,566

MSAs

TABLE 8

U.S. CENSUS DIVISION 7, WEST SOUTH CENTRAL

U.S. Community Hospitals
(Nonfederal, short-term general and other special hospitals)

2017 Utilization, Personnel and Finances

FULL-TIME EQUIVALENT PERSONNEL					FULL-TIME EQUIV. TRAINEES			EXPENSES						
								LABOR				TOTAL		
Physicians and Dentists	Registered Nurses	Licensed Practical Nurses	Other Salaried Personnel	Total Personnel	Medical and Dental Residents	Other Trainees	Total Trainees	Payroll (in thousands)	Employee Benefits (in thousands)	Total (in thousands)	Percent of Total	Amount (in thousands)	Adjusted per Admission	Adjusted per Inpatient Day
146,381	1,558,038	76,534	2,704,453	5,216,348	118,075	9,440	127,515	$363,806,143	$96,687,285	$460,493,398	47.7	$966,204,239	$13,126.02	$2,424.17
16,529	156,072	20,966	348,592	631,393	1,972	334	2,306	37,559,678	9,847,876	47,407,559	50.0	94,728,753	8,855.26	1,351.23
129,852	1,401,966	55,568	2,355,861	4,584,955	116,103	9,106	125,209	326,246,465	86,839,408	413,085,839	47.4	871,475,486	13,852.21	2,653.17
7,481	179,798	14,381	263,755	555,677	5,640	1,379	7,019	36,664,850	8,701,159	45,366,001	44.4	102,290,621	11,485.77	2,293.35
951	16,929	4,109	33,713	66,755	146	29	175	3,609,843	867,501	4,477,347	47.2	9,476,308	6,655.26	1,505.23
6,530	162,869	10,272	230,042	488,922	5,494	1,350	6,844	33,055,007	7,833,659	40,888,654	44.1	92,814,313	12,405.06	2,422.87
1,225	15,177	1,631	24,597	49,832	130	33	163	2,833,267	607,866	3,441,131	46.7	7,372,516	8,870.02	1,786.97
328	3,529	885	7,330	14,178	58	13	71	735,762	165,324	901,085	52.5	1,716,521	6,109.03	1,229.84
897	11,648	746	17,267	35,654	72	20	92	2,097,505	442,542	2,540,046	44.9	5,655,995	10,280.06	2,071.81
172	2,022	172	2,917	6,276	25	1	26	295,228	60,799	356,026	44.2	805,654	8,379.40	2,131.15
95	969	114	1,838	3,589	1	0	1	192,359	38,133	230,491	39.9	578,375	8,434.07	1,742.21
26	638	34	662	1,617	0	1	1	97,269	24,820	122,088	43.0	283,748	7,532.47	1,527.02
49	1,141	38	1,601	3,350	25	3	28	172,295	43,269	215,563	43.7	492,856	7,531.99	1,512.84
539	6,417	309	9,545	19,336	21	10	31	1,257,746	261,477	1,519,223	46.0	3,299,872	12,618.43	2,371.15
15	429	71	631	1,358	0	5	5	76,984	13,351	90,335	48.6	186,046	9,649.69	1,669.19
1	32	8	73	128	0	0	0	5,626	694	6,320	66.9	9,445	6,012.24	1,806.32
1,973	25,823	3,461	41,477	85,752	429	56	485	4,969,828	1,068,552	6,038,380	42.3	14,288,867	10,591.03	1,953.23
170	2,516	402	5,182	9,803	17	4	21	531,390	129,763	661,157	48.7	1,358,538	7,242.48	1,524.47
1,803	23,307	2,999	36,295	75,949	412	52	464	4,438,437	938,789	5,377,223	41.6	12,930,329	11,131.78	2,012.71
8	1,191	110	1,334	3,265	0	0	0	187,281	42,412	229,692	41.7	551,104	9,713.81	1,732.86
463	4,234	480	7,463	14,832	97	0	97	935,056	200,821	1,135,876	43.1	2,633,812	11,867.17	1,757.45
114	778	148	1,235	2,765	1	1	2	212,324	40,196	252,519	55.0	459,160	14,136.71	2,514.67
63	966	148	2,412	4,138	0	4	4	215,453	47,305	262,758	45.4	578,243	8,236.14	1,780.16
93	2,335	282	3,248	7,094	9	2	11	419,001	96,218	515,220	41.0	1,257,870	9,905.50	1,810.69
105	1,294	241	2,510	4,769	5	9	14	215,990	53,705	269,695	42.0	641,948	9,601.52	1,900.39
40	1,198	201	1,706	3,772	0	2	2	236,552	54,145	290,698	43.4	669,093	10,009.17	1,855.64
572	8,042	894	11,325	24,573	300	20	320	1,588,144	307,030	1,895,173	39.1	4,846,037	13,831.59	2,528.77
345	3,269	495	5,062	10,741	0	14	14	428,636	96,956	525,592	40.6	1,293,062	7,644.38	1,635.08
825	16,756	1,589	26,972	54,870	190	67	257	3,347,645	774,082	4,121,730	42.6	9,667,546	9,832.59	1,921.08
263	3,530	702	6,988	13,955	59	5	64	766,802	178,576	945,380	47.0	2,013,331	7,041.88	1,498.03
562	13,226	887	19,984	40,915	131	62	193	2,580,843	595,507	3,176,350	41.5	7,654,215	10,976.82	2,075.24
5	321	26	567	1,036	0	1	1	65,318	14,554	79,872	41.9	190,800	10,115.05	1,750.96
6	48	26	191	322	0	0	0	15,899	4,653	20,552	58.0	35,442	5,450.11	1,470.08
105	386	173	1,146	2,023	25	0	25	144,716	24,461	169,177	49.3	343,429	9,814.77	1,131.07
355	7,434	418	10,627	22,394	94	60	154	1,454,537	343,333	1,797,868	41.0	4,382,974	12,296.11	2,311.19
91	5,037	244	7,453	15,140	12	1	13	900,373	208,506	1,108,881	41.0	2,701,570	9,631.33	1,993.44
3,458	122,042	7,700	170,709	365,223	4,891	1,223	6,114	25,514,110	6,250,659	31,764,760	44.8	70,961,692	12,357.67	2,522.66
190	7,354	2,060	14,213	28,819	12	7	19	1,575,889	393,838	1,969,725	44.9	4,387,918	6,554.86	1,646.67
3,268	114,688	5,640	156,496	336,404	4,879	1,216	6,095	23,938,221	5,856,821	29,795,035	44.8	66,573,774	13,123.40	2,614.33
1	1,110	170	1,665	3,607	0	56	56	177,998	39,312	217,311	43.2	502,669	10,303.76	1,993.99
0	1,443	91	2,154	4,259	0	6	6	251,243	56,555	307,798	44.6	690,674	9,414.09	2,070.19
304	7,075	227	8,374	18,911	355	36	391	1,242,934	274,909	1,517,842	38.0	3,989,152	13,407.43	2,802.22
3	1,751	221	1,951	4,604	0	0	0	286,028	60,170	346,197	43.6	794,009	8,341.74	1,807.89
0	1,193	136	1,238	3,342	2	0	2	242,193	52,187	294,378	46.4	634,244	9,019.02	1,819.34
0	960	71	1,579	2,875	0	0	0	167,824	42,990	210,814	41.7	505,408	9,014.51	2,336.22
64	2,082	103	3,181	6,461	190	3	193	391,841	103,393	495,234	40.2	1,232,204	13,550.38	2,515.51
413	23,446	591	29,799	64,204	1,679	31	1,710	5,072,676	1,176,820	6,249,496	45.3	13,803,345	14,641.09	2,995.13
64	3,428	94	4,116	9,462	0	0	0	596,460	139,603	736,064	37.8	1,947,368	12,520.61	2,619.87
19	11,711	522	14,305	31,485	308	3	311	2,241,652	565,886	2,807,538	44.3	6,333,527	13,855.37	2,741.56
1,783	33,938	1,049	47,509	103,102	1,148	1,026	2,174	8,203,340	2,160,396	10,363,731	47.1	22,017,031	15,769.83	2,975.33
0	1,917	307	4,381	7,315	456	4	460	415,641	98,531	514,173	40.9	1,257,108	10,191.22	2,320.54
0	620	38	990	2,011	0	0	0	112,717	24,647	137,364	43.8	313,741	7,299.37	1,389.54
0	475	12	447	1,137	0	0	0	72,218	14,019	86,237	40.7	211,954	7,787.58	1,790.89
0	2,673	218	3,441	7,643	0	0	0	439,562	129,833	569,395	40.2	1,415,396	12,283.55	2,514.34
108	2,977	173	4,324	9,220	5	1	6	485,748	108,256	594,004	48.4	1,227,886	7,205.77	1,511.30
2	452	47	1,228	2,068	7	1	8	129,183	33,459	162,641	52.9	307,715	10,546.13	2,085.64
1	751	70	1,258	2,406	0	14	14	153,615	40,691	194,306	44.5	436,609	12,285.35	2,257.20
0	634	67	1,102	2,247	0	0	0	131,579	26,776	158,355	42.2	375,212	9,564.91	1,995.48
261	9,384	698	12,444	27,942	610	20	630	1,867,430	409,468	2,276,896	44.2	5,154,893	10,939.07	2,114.66
67	1,034	40	1,556	2,954	17	0	17	148,772	39,766	188,537	50.2	375,426	8,502.26	1,765.01
1	953	125	1,081	2,549	0	0	0	144,931	31,104	176,035	43.7	403,044	8,567.38	1,705.67
83	2,152	331	3,717	7,930	75	6	81	457,684	112,577	570,262	43.4	1,310,100	12,622.00	2,513.28
34	725	94	1,207	2,378	0	0	0	144,033	36,306	180,340	49.6	363,869	9,805.66	1,905.95
60	1,110	58	1,953	3,596	27	9	36	208,036	51,250	259,287	43.4	596,936	8,854.25	1,733.94
0	694	87	1,496	2,696	0	0	0	152,884	27,916	180,800	48.3	374,253	10,617.41	2,249.89

TABLE 8 — U.S. CENSUS DIVISION 8, MOUNTAIN

U.S. Community Hospitals
(Nonfederal, short-term general and other special hospitals)

2017 Utilization, Personnel and Finances

CLASSIFICATION	Hospitals	Beds	Admissions	Inpatient Days	Adjusted Inpatient Days	Average Daily Census	Adjusted Average Daily Census	Average Stay (days)	Surgical Operations	NEWBORNS Bassinets	NEWBORNS Births	OUTPATIENT VISITS Emergency	OUTPATIENT VISITS Total
UNITED STATES	5,262	798,921	34,305,620	186,198,977	398,570,958	510,123	1,092,133	5.4	28,221,774	55,181	3,656,809	144,814,804	766,076,124
Nonmetropolitan	1,875	112,806	3,115,229	20,415,212	70,105,531	55,939	192,099	6.6	3,649,248	9,005	358,113	22,487,032	131,567,025
Metropolitan	3,387	686,115	31,190,391	165,783,765	328,465,427	454,184	900,034	5.3	24,572,526	46,176	3,298,696	122,327,772	634,509,099
CENSUS DIVISION 8, MOUNTAIN	440	49,910	2,088,118	10,849,687	24,507,049	29,722	67,147	5.2	1,760,103	4,253	256,103	8,741,450	48,133,773
Nonmetropolitan	201	8,592	209,046	1,504,197	6,446,335	4,118	17,668	7.2	315,384	850	36,640	1,794,750	10,647,670
Metropolitan	239	41,318	1,879,072	9,345,490	18,060,714	25,604	49,479	5.0	1,444,719	3,403	219,463	6,946,700	37,486,103
Arizona	83	13,918	651,064	3,079,118	5,873,444	8,440	16,094	4.7	489,271	1,037	73,229	2,173,898	8,559,792
Nonmetropolitan	9	307	12,889	37,679	155,440	104	427	2.9	20,248	48	2,804	110,992	351,983
Metropolitan	74	13,611	638,175	3,041,439	5,718,004	8,336	15,667	4.8	469,023	989	70,425	2,062,906	8,207,809
Flagstaff	3	342	15,036	70,190	123,559	193	338	4.7	17,127	33	1,710	70,234	196,678
Lake Havasu City-Kingman	4	585	25,220	120,785	247,892	331	679	4.8	21,664	33	1,952	142,923	560,231
Phoenix-Mesa-Scottsdale	46	9,044	437,184	2,104,638	3,889,339	5,768	10,657	4.8	313,846	682	50,130	1,145,266	5,194,161
Prescott	3	320	16,044	56,526	133,442	155	366	3.5	10,137	64	1,810	93,947	268,944
Sierra Vista-Douglas	4	160	6,407	23,799	98,285	66	269	3.7	5,048	10	831	65,149	194,215
Tucson	12	2,713	119,975	592,208	1,049,158	1,622	2,875	4.9	89,085	133	10,714	470,720	1,494,799
Yuma	2	447	18,309	73,293	176,329	201	483	4.0	12,116	34	3,278	74,667	298,781
Colorado	89	10,793	445,190	2,225,569	4,903,255	6,094	13,434	5.0	394,051	963	59,221	2,000,092	9,398,669
Nonmetropolitan	40	1,459	35,509	249,644	1,029,978	681	2,822	7.0	63,714	145	6,156	299,393	1,888,041
Metropolitan	49	9,334	409,681	1,975,925	3,873,277	5,413	10,612	4.8	330,337	818	53,065	1,700,699	7,510,628
Boulder	4	617	31,913	126,126	266,644	346	730	4.0	25,856	106	5,905	126,476	656,130
Colorado Springs	5	1,050	54,226	226,165	439,194	620	1,204	4.2	34,698	84	7,100	227,866	986,105
Denver-Aurora-Lakewood	27	5,787	241,713	1,241,815	2,334,730	3,402	6,398	5.1	201,967	481	30,290	962,212	4,429,781
Fort Collins	5	660	32,546	131,754	317,503	361	870	4.0	25,018	60	4,673	153,996	582,431
Grand Junction	3	409	15,543	77,392	157,474	212	431	5.0	11,176	38	1,473	72,353	354,952
Greeley	3	316	11,919	61,880	125,698	169	344	5.2	8,454	15	1,590	34,353	177,346
Pueblo	2	495	21,821	110,793	232,034	303	635	5.1	23,168	34	2,034	123,443	323,883
Idaho	46	3,531	142,843	722,719	1,730,860	1,982	4,744	5.1	137,221	312	19,347	697,045	5,835,422
Nonmetropolitan	27	1,019	30,605	172,624	580,265	473	1,591	5.6	44,993	105	6,026	194,435	1,762,452
Metropolitan	19	2,512	112,238	550,095	1,150,595	1,509	3,153	4.9	92,228	207	13,321	502,610	4,072,970
Boise City	10	1,437	65,931	309,493	623,589	848	1,708	4.7	60,765	113	8,493	276,017	3,019,301
Coeur d'Alene	3	364	16,237	81,708	181,302	225	497	5.0	13,238	18	1,830	54,347	359,622
Idaho Falls	3	358	16,010	97,035	189,556	267	520	6.1	6,271	35	867	105,641	304,256
Lewiston	1	123	5,071	15,023	34,264	41	94	3.0	3,273	22	740	26,333	135,758
Logan	1	55	612	12,792	48,275	35	132	20.9	1,020	4	87	1,156	6,853
Pocatello	1	175	8,377	34,044	73,809	93	202	4.1	7,661	15	1,304	39,116	247,180
Montana	55	3,622	98,752	772,654	3,353,597	2,115	9,192	7.8	105,872	238	11,091	496,531	4,383,962
Nonmetropolitan	47	2,114	42,484	399,474	2,503,050	1,093	6,861	9.4	49,281	133	5,380	314,918	2,238,309
Metropolitan	8	1,508	56,268	373,180	850,547	1,022	2,331	6.6	56,591	105	5,711	181,613	2,145,653
Billings	4	671	28,814	164,425	347,225	450	951	5.7	23,677	57	2,733	89,743	1,065,146
Great Falls	2	522	12,248	138,926	348,682	381	956	11.3	11,803	24	1,396	38,777	608,852
Missoula	2	315	15,206	69,829	154,640	191	424	4.6	21,111	24	1,582	53,093	471,655
Nevada	44	6,475	287,029	1,622,253	2,959,372	4,442	8,106	5.7	157,328	330	22,228	987,106	3,273,924
Nonmetropolitan	11	378	7,533	62,880	247,489	171	679	8.3	14,983	31	1,372	94,023	381,299
Metropolitan	33	6,097	279,496	1,559,373	2,711,883	4,271	7,427	5.6	142,345	299	20,856	893,083	2,892,625
Carson City	2	240	13,062	63,816	120,825	175	331	4.9	9,156	12	980	40,279	312,713
Las Vegas-Henderson-Paradise	24	4,603	212,237	1,196,614	2,078,843	3,277	5,694	5.6	92,218	212	14,622	653,630	1,762,614
Reno	7	1,254	54,197	298,943	512,215	819	1,402	5.5	40,971	75	5,254	199,174	817,298
New Mexico	41	3,876	179,750	903,657	2,194,284	2,473	6,012	5.0	172,476	510	18,730	1,035,170	6,368,199
Nonmetropolitan	25	1,206	43,507	187,009	639,785	511	1,753	4.3	61,033	161	6,804	484,196	2,062,002
Metropolitan	16	2,670	136,243	716,648	1,554,499	1,962	4,259	5.3	111,443	349	11,926	550,974	4,306,197
Albuquerque	10	1,858	95,297	532,233	1,113,796	1,458	3,051	5.6	69,801	267	7,851	357,046	3,096,714
Farmington	1	198	9,894	45,098	102,668	124	281	4.6	5,916	22	1,003	64,446	785,301
Las Cruces	4	395	18,921	87,316	188,076	238	516	4.6	25,060	36	1,769	80,610	279,576
Santa Fe	1	219	12,131	52,001	149,959	142	411	4.3	10,666	24	1,303	48,872	144,606

FULL-TIME EQUIVALENT PERSONNEL					FULL-TIME EQUIV. TRAINEES			EXPENSES						
								LABOR				TOTAL		
Physicians and Dentists	Registered Nurses	Licensed Practical Nurses	Other Salaried Personnel	Total Personnel	Medical and Dental Residents	Other Trainees	Total Trainees	Payroll (in thousands)	Employee Benefits (in thousands)	Total (in thousands)	Percent of Total	Amount (in thousands)	Adjusted per Admission	Adjusted per Inpatient Day
146,381	1,558,038	76,534	2,704,453	5,216,348	118,075	9,440	127,515	$363,806,143	$96,687,285	$460,493,398	47.7	$966,204,239	$13,126.02	$2,424.17
16,529	156,072	20,966	348,592	631,393	1,972	334	2,306	37,559,678	9,847,876	47,407,559	50.0	94,728,753	8,855.26	1,351.23
129,852	1,401,966	55,568	2,355,861	4,584,955	116,103	9,106	125,209	326,246,465	86,839,408	413,085,839	47.4	871,475,486	13,852.21	2,653.17
8,357	96,985	3,612	165,711	320,064	3,493	322	3,815	21,853,690	5,399,307	27,252,992	46.0	59,207,230	13,345.71	2,415.93
1,956	12,932	1,269	30,920	55,132	56	22	78	3,417,265	854,648	4,271,915	50.4	8,470,019	11,356.26	1,313.93
6,401	84,053	2,343	134,791	264,932	3,437	300	3,737	18,436,425	4,544,659	22,981,077	45.3	50,737,212	13,747.77	2,809.26
2,084	28,206	589	39,671	81,472	1,000	87	1,087	5,662,953	1,317,716	6,980,665	45.1	15,492,617	12,226.17	2,637.74
64	677	51	1,394	2,617	2	2	4	194,480	45,157	239,638	54.0	443,366	8,428.36	2,852.33
2,020	27,529	538	38,277	78,855	998	85	1,083	5,468,473	1,272,559	6,741,027	44.8	15,049,251	12,390.66	2,631.91
64	794	15	1,685	2,838	2	5	7	173,636	49,203	222,839	45.0	494,855	18,362.66	4,005.01
59	1,103	69	1,878	3,689	42	3	45	239,858	64,130	303,988	49.1	618,551	11,986.96	2,495.24
1,713	19,483	306	24,948	53,503	888	67	955	3,771,238	900,339	4,671,572	45.2	10,343,358	12,623.87	2,659.41
54	581	1	1,476	2,363	0	1	1	171,535	48,051	219,587	48.9	449,055	11,824.39	3,365.17
15	284	11	629	1,118	7	0	7	70,165	15,293	85,457	49.2	173,714	6,996.13	1,767.45
70	4,615	126	6,485	13,079	41	4	45	859,907	155,770	1,015,678	40.6	2,504,716	11,929.32	2,387.36
45	669	10	1,176	2,265	18	5	23	182,134	39,772	221,906	47.7	465,003	10,593.76	2,637.13
2,085	21,895	689	39,819	73,281	639	73	712	5,150,553	1,258,831	6,409,384	44.9	14,271,275	15,048.98	2,910.57
456	2,589	278	6,736	11,582	5	9	14	737,356	190,810	928,167	50.2	1,847,289	13,338.31	1,793.52
1,629	19,306	411	33,083	61,699	634	64	698	4,413,196	1,068,021	5,481,217	44.1	12,423,986	15,341.53	3,207.62
109	1,377	20	2,761	4,896	0	2	2	345,854	78,616	424,470	47.4	896,020	13,196.95	3,360.36
144	1,653	19	3,409	5,864	14	0	14	414,564	105,553	520,117	43.9	1,185,775	11,342.68	2,699.89
970	12,597	268	20,375	38,831	497	20	517	2,847,848	679,862	3,527,710	44.6	7,902,755	17,127.40	3,384.87
136	1,174	50	2,064	3,989	30	2	32	343,405	95,939	439,344	41.3	1,062,915	14,337.94	3,347.73
83	781	21	1,468	2,730	26	1	27	161,847	41,765	203,611	39.2	518,884	16,503.43	3,295.05
93	701	16	1,132	2,176	37	2	39	114,520	25,687	140,207	36.8	380,987	15,595.67	3,030.97
94	1,023	17	1,874	3,413	30	37	67	185,158	40,600	225,758	47.4	476,650	10,367.14	2,054.22
1,081	7,340	593	16,154	30,055	74	55	129	2,139,264	485,733	2,624,996	49.2	5,339,961	16,118.20	3,085.15
258	1,705	283	4,230	7,772	13	5	18	467,314	116,772	584,087	49.7	1,175,988	11,984.96	2,026.64
823	5,635	310	11,924	22,283	61	50	111	1,671,950	368,960	2,040,909	49.0	4,163,972	17,857.48	3,618.97
632	3,658	175	8,133	15,221	12	50	62	1,157,257	252,027	1,409,283	49.3	2,855,949	21,329.29	4,579.86
113	629	28	1,878	2,969	18	0	18	241,297	57,190	298,487	54.8	544,401	14,921.22	3,002.73
19	670	36	860	1,883	24	0	24	125,815	28,701	154,516	42.8	361,123	11,722.12	1,905.10
19	214	12	390	758	6	0	6	59,461	15,120	74,581	48.0	155,227	13,421.01	4,530.34
9	78	13	208	363	1	0	1	11,893	3,316	15,209	52.9	28,731	12,437.61	595.15
31	386	46	455	1,089	0	0	0	76,227	12,606	88,833	40.6	218,540	12,066.05	2,968.93
1,225	5,495	424	14,003	23,968	58	17	75	1,512,345	329,303	1,841,650	51.5	3,574,680	13,184.67	1,065.92
568	2,947	213	7,632	12,900	12	1	13	706,990	168,932	875,923	52.9	1,657,025	11,507.92	662.00
657	2,548	211	6,371	11,068	46	16	62	805,355	160,371	965,727	50.4	1,917,654	15,083.73	2,254.61
379	1,223	60	3,330	5,700	28	14	42	451,654	94,786	546,441	52.3	1,044,877	17,078.73	3,009.22
154	691	72	1,595	2,834	0	0	0	215,186	43,994	259,179	55.0	471,474	14,578.67	1,352.16
124	634	79	1,446	2,534	18	2	20	138,515	21,591	160,107	39.9	401,304	11,938.59	2,595.08
259	10,320	393	15,468	31,411	199	2	201	2,155,889	587,200	2,743,091	47.0	5,832,396	11,078.35	1,970.82
37	455	42	1,256	2,103	0	0	0	120,110	28,989	149,099	50.4	295,890	10,168.04	1,195.57
222	9,865	351	14,212	29,308	199	2	201	2,035,780	558,211	2,593,992	46.9	5,536,506	11,131.61	2,041.57
0	449	5	733	1,351	0	0	0	93,399	22,116	115,515	43.3	266,837	10,308.56	2,208.46
213	7,321	325	10,074	21,254	195	2	197	1,570,628	444,783	2,015,412	48.0	4,200,937	11,174.52	2,020.81
9	2,095	21	3,405	6,703	4	0	4	371,752	91,312	463,065	43.3	1,068,732	11,185.76	2,086.49
1,045	8,219	439	14,527	28,630	418	36	454	2,134,943	513,634	2,648,575	46.1	5,744,622	12,545.42	2,617.99
247	1,962	186	4,020	7,685	20	3	23	539,880	125,033	664,912	47.7	1,393,140	9,119.85	2,177.51
798	6,257	253	10,507	20,945	398	33	431	1,595,063	388,601	1,983,663	45.6	4,351,482	14,260.28	2,799.28
565	4,805	208	7,203	15,019	372	33	405	1,133,455	275,287	1,408,720	43.7	3,223,066	15,595.76	2,893.77
75	377	7	947	1,747	0	0	0	148,894	45,278	194,172	63.7	304,848	13,534.35	2,969.26
70	784	35	1,089	2,373	26	0	26	159,136	31,250	190,386	44.6	427,032	10,421.26	2,270.53
88	291	3	1,268	1,806	0	0	0	153,579	36,807	190,385	48.0	396,536	11,335.10	2,644.30

Table continues

MSAs

TABLE 8

U.S. CENSUS DIVISION 8, MOUNTAIN CONTINUED

U.S. Community Hospitals
(Nonfederal, short-term general and other special hospitals)

2017 Utilization, Personnel and Finances

CLASSIFICATION	Hospitals	Beds	Admissions	Inpatient Days	Adjusted Inpatient Days	Average Daily Census	Adjusted Average Daily Census	Average Stay (days)	Surgical Operations	NEWBORNS Bassinets	Births	OUTPATIENT VISITS Emergency	Total
Utah	53	5,712	240,934	1,139,575	2,388,994	3,123	6,542	4.7	257,150	692	46,271	1,112,859	8,983,922
Nonmetropolitan	18	661	14,874	105,615	382,644	291	1,048	7.1	29,330	96	4,367	136,798	933,370
Metropolitan	35	5,051	226,060	1,033,960	2,006,350	2,832	5,494	4.6	227,820	596	41,904	976,061	8,050,552
Logan	2	150	7,095	19,369	52,192	53	143	2.7	9,995	36	2,536	71,263	369,473
Ogden-Clearfield	8	1,068	38,895	194,871	346,919	534	950	5.0	35,285	114	7,547	183,941	694,505
Provo-Orem	7	752	35,547	147,584	288,438	403	791	4.2	40,801	123	9,814	135,490	1,167,586
Salt Lake City	17	2,836	127,222	608,733	1,192,770	1,668	3,265	4.8	126,082	307	19,621	531,453	5,238,332
St. George	1	245	17,301	63,403	126,031	174	345	3.7	15,857	16	2,386	53,914	580,656
Wyoming	29	1,983	42,556	384,142	1,103,243	1,053	3,023	9.0	46,734	171	5,986	238,749	1,329,883
Nonmetropolitan	24	1,448	21,645	289,272	907,684	794	2,487	13.4	31,802	131	3,731	159,995	1,030,214
Metropolitan	5	535	20,911	94,870	195,559	259	536	4.5	14,932	40	2,255	78,754	299,669
Casper	4	297	10,867	46,948	94,560	128	259	4.3	10,013	24	1,023	37,987	117,109
Cheyenne	1	238	10,044	47,922	100,999	131	277	4.8	4,919	16	1,232	40,767	182,560

MSAs

TABLE **8**

U.S. CENSUS DIVISION 8, MOUNTAIN
CONTINUED

U.S. Community Hospitals
(Nonfederal, short-term general and other special hospitals)

2017 Utilization, Personnel and Finances

| | FULL-TIME EQUIVALENT PERSONNEL | | | | FULL-TIME EQUIV. TRAINEES | | | EXPENSES | | | | | | |
| | | | | | | | | LABOR | | | | TOTAL | | |
Physicians and Dentists	Registered Nurses	Licensed Practical Nurses	Other Salaried Personnel	Total Personnel	Medical and Dental Residents	Other Trainees	Total Trainees	Payroll (in thousands)	Employee Benefits (in thousands)	Total (in thousands)	Percent of Total	Amount (in thousands)	Adjusted per Admission	Adjusted per Inpatient Day
272	12,994	334	20,776	41,227	1,101	52	1,153	2,414,131	728,049	3,142,179	43.3	7,255,420	14,002.82	3,037.02
75	934	96	1,923	3,602	0	2	2	188,436	56,820	245,257	44.0	557,443	9,744.14	1,456.82
197	12,060	238	18,853	37,625	1,101	50	1,151	2,225,696	671,229	2,896,922	43.3	6,697,977	14,531.38	3,338.39
4	386	9	537	1,090	0	2	2	62,511	19,536	82,047	38.6	212,438	11,112.51	4,070.32
30	1,840	72	2,600	5,410	33	5	38	326,069	88,912	414,981	43.5	953,459	12,686.90	2,748.36
26	1,776	38	2,219	4,820	38	19	57	288,314	89,334	377,648	43.7	864,832	11,629.87	2,998.33
132	7,327	119	12,363	23,998	1,030	23	1,053	1,405,760	426,383	1,832,142	43.8	4,179,744	16,206.27	3,504.23
5	731	0	1,134	2,307	0	1	1	143,040	47,063	190,104	39.0	487,504	14,175.76	3,868.13
306	2,516	151	5,293	10,020	4	0	4	683,611	178,842	862,452	50.8	1,696,260	14,623.44	1,537.52
251	1,663	120	3,729	6,871	4	0	4	462,699	122,135	584,832	53.2	1,099,878	14,950.49	1,211.74
55	853	31	1,584	3,149	0	0	0	220,912	56,707	277,620	46.6	596,382	14,056.34	3,049.63
29	454	20	814	1,605	0	0	0	103,261	29,632	132,894	43.2	307,971	14,485.96	3,256.89
26	399	11	750	1,544	0	0	0	117,651	27,074	144,726	50.2	288,411	13,624.86	2,855.58

MSAs

TABLE 8

U.S. CENSUS DIVISION 9, PACIFIC

U.S. Community Hospitals
(Nonfederal, short-term general and other special hospitals)

2017 Utilization, Personnel and Finances

CLASSIFICATION	Hospitals	Beds	Admissions	Inpatient Days	Adjusted Inpatient Days	Average Daily Census	Adjusted Average Daily Census	Average Stay (days)	Surgical Operations	NEWBORNS Bassinets	Births	OUTPATIENT VISITS Emergency	Total
UNITED STATES	5,262	798,921	34,305,620	186,198,977	398,570,958	510,123	1,092,133	5.4	28,221,774	55,181	3,656,809	144,814,804	766,076,124
Nonmetropolitan	1,875	112,806	3,115,229	20,415,212	70,105,531	55,939	192,099	6.6	3,649,248	9,005	358,113	22,487,032	131,567,025
Metropolitan	3,387	686,115	31,190,391	165,783,765	328,465,427	454,184	900,034	5.3	24,572,526	46,176	3,298,696	122,327,772	634,509,099
CENSUS DIVISION 9, PACIFIC	559	96,902	4,576,293	23,428,335	44,527,568	64,181	122,050	5.1	3,366,438	7,203	601,184	18,835,805	89,275,779
Nonmetropolitan	109	4,493	152,794	800,314	2,810,039	2,191	7,707	5.2	199,929	441	25,845	1,216,745	7,869,638
Metropolitan	450	92,409	4,423,499	22,628,021	41,717,529	61,990	114,343	5.1	3,166,509	6,762	575,339	17,619,060	81,406,141
Alaska	21	1,630	52,418	381,239	938,064	1,047	2,571	7.3	64,808	184	8,465	381,678	2,221,433
Nonmetropolitan	15	576	11,535	113,064	437,456	311	1,200	9.8	18,219	50	2,319	116,726	853,697
Metropolitan	6	1,054	40,883	268,175	500,608	736	1,371	6.6	46,589	134	6,146	264,952	1,367,736
Anchorage	5	838	36,085	219,699	402,056	603	1,101	6.1	42,116	118	5,196	191,645	1,002,214
Fairbanks	1	216	4,798	48,476	98,552	133	270	10.1	4,473	16	950	73,307	365,522
California	362	73,195	3,452,477	17,744,125	32,262,599	48,605	88,448	5.1	2,336,888	5,090	446,852	13,460,106	57,157,019
Nonmetropolitan	30	1,343	50,892	266,305	833,201	728	2,285	5.2	67,111	111	6,710	436,462	2,314,423
Metropolitan	332	71,852	3,401,585	17,477,820	31,429,398	47,877	86,163	5.1	2,269,777	4,979	440,142	13,023,644	54,842,596
Anaheim-Santa Ana-Irvine	27	5,840	277,898	1,280,036	2,308,974	3,508	6,325	4.6	194,410	422	40,650	920,509	4,168,520
Bakersfield	11	1,644	69,994	351,948	803,768	964	2,203	5.0	47,730	103	12,436	332,397	940,784
Chico	4	530	34,490	146,008	303,278	400	830	4.2	22,389	37	2,945	129,580	999,832
El Centro	2	268	11,788	42,418	116,838	116	320	3.6	9,371	33	3,237	97,955	367,287
Fresno	8	1,753	93,241	457,184	857,289	1,253	2,347	4.9	44,849	127	11,251	251,865	1,197,785
Hanford-Corcoran	2	248	19,201	48,370	111,838	132	306	2.5	12,872	20	795	117,028	528,675
Los Angeles-Long Beach-Glendale	89	21,310	992,772	5,190,781	8,686,549	14,219	23,796	5.2	598,388	1,532	118,946	3,289,056	11,614,879
Madera	2	464	16,157	90,231	147,912	247	405	5.6	15,409	10	1,016	155,814	429,200
Merced	2	230	14,617	52,703	97,815	144	268	3.6	6,197	28	3,528	104,810	245,454
Modesto	6	1,113	57,028	287,242	487,312	786	1,335	5.0	35,374	70	7,723	262,458	553,399
Napa	2	289	11,237	51,209	120,302	140	329	4.6	11,563	10	862	38,111	188,262
Oakland-Hayward-Berkeley	20	4,471	218,031	1,152,180	2,025,855	3,157	5,549	5.3	133,522	291	26,801	1,052,581	4,286,515
Oxnard-Thousand Oaks-Ventura	7	1,275	67,830	323,052	687,207	886	1,882	4.8	41,878	101	8,903	247,560	1,327,795
Redding	5	574	22,431	149,708	297,537	409	815	6.7	14,111	10	1,713	58,132	236,942
Riverside-San Bernardino-Ontario	38	7,737	355,481	1,733,430	3,093,237	4,750	8,542	4.9	235,847	556	50,073	1,511,027	4,549,088
Sacramento-Roseville-Arden-Arcade	17	3,865	210,008	1,002,332	1,754,188	2,747	4,807	4.8	151,870	265	21,836	666,536	3,485,492
Salinas	4	738	33,022	157,607	306,437	432	839	4.8	20,600	79	5,709	152,376	648,223
San Diego-Carlsbad	20	5,860	294,085	1,623,938	2,674,808	4,449	7,327	5.5	235,068	363	39,478	1,001,924	3,661,531
San Francisco-Redwood City-South San Francisco	17	4,942	177,120	1,267,146	2,339,254	3,470	6,408	7.2	136,301	172	17,833	630,862	4,658,100
San Jose-Sunnyvale-Santa Clara	11	3,265	161,266	839,550	1,605,808	2,299	4,400	5.2	124,914	312	25,439	593,438	4,184,503
San Luis Obispo-Paso Robles-Arroyo Grande	4	392	16,662	68,101	165,307	186	453	4.1	13,569	39	2,344	86,832	296,803
San Rafael	3	391	15,950	63,513	138,431	174	379	4.0	13,462	15	1,272	81,839	321,960
Santa Cruz-Watsonville	3	359	16,586	70,582	150,167	193	411	4.3	15,228	50	3,024	76,856	304,035
Santa Maria-Santa Barbara	5	858	38,372	224,244	432,928	614	1,185	5.8	23,687	48	5,297	143,132	506,765
Santa Rosa	8	821	36,277	178,969	404,364	490	1,108	4.9	28,610	54	4,933	191,812	618,268
Stockton-Lodi	7	1,115	60,670	253,191	559,624	694	1,533	4.2	37,316	101	9,536	342,499	1,490,780
Vallejo-Fairfield	4	672	35,755	138,047	277,522	377	761	3.9	23,769	61	4,625	217,342	1,833,591
Visalia-Porterville	2	595	32,166	179,601	363,625	492	996	5.6	13,276	40	6,119	218,434	939,280
Yuba City	2	233	11,450	54,499	111,224	149	304	4.8	8,197	30	1,818	50,879	258,848
Hawaii	23	2,594	111,293	706,540	1,554,195	1,935	4,256	6.3	85,417	161	19,322	452,405	2,668,237
Nonmetropolitan	8	564	20,049	120,420	398,590	329	1,091	6.0	16,981	45	5,681	81,504	393,382
Metropolitan	15	2,030	91,244	586,120	1,155,605	1,606	3,165	6.4	68,436	116	13,641	370,901	2,274,855
Kahului-Wailuku-Lahaina	4	258	11,387	60,435	144,482	166	396	5.3	3,531	26	3,177	25,448	131,127
Urban Honolulu	11	1,772	79,857	525,685	1,011,123	1,440	2,769	6.6	64,905	90	10,464	345,453	2,143,728
Oregon	61	6,906	348,059	1,572,311	3,378,583	4,309	9,253	4.5	334,751	674	43,286	1,584,195	12,031,591
Nonmetropolitan	26	979	41,398	155,512	562,374	426	1,542	3.8	45,418	134	5,798	322,826	2,637,220
Metropolitan	35	5,927	306,661	1,416,799	2,816,209	3,883	7,711	4.6	289,333	540	37,488	1,261,369	9,394,371
Albany	2	95	4,097	13,981	62,922	38	172	3.4	8,556	14	831	50,533	526,087
Bend-Redmond	2	307	19,145	72,881	129,507	200	355	3.8	20,269	40	2,242	64,441	190,357
Corvallis	1	182	8,990	44,423	90,236	122	247	4.9	9,853	20	1,004	28,539	443,536
Eugene	5	631	37,073	170,421	294,357	467	807	4.6	24,291	53	3,991	164,231	460,646
Grants Pass	1	111	7,562	27,538	59,225	75	162	3.6	5,140	12	789	39,741	260,452
Medford	3	494	24,243	116,659	213,149	320	584	4.8	18,098	34	2,310	92,176	943,011
Portland-Vancouver-Hillsboro	17	3,589	175,649	845,081	1,710,730	2,316	4,684	4.8	183,959	318	21,270	654,748	5,859,759
Salem	4	518	29,902	125,815	256,083	345	700	4.2	19,167	49	5,051	166,960	710,523

MSAs

TABLE 8

U.S. Community Hospitals
(Nonfederal, short-term general and other special hospitals)

2017 Utilization, Personnel and Finances

FULL-TIME EQUIVALENT PERSONNEL					FULL-TIME EQUIV. TRAINEES			EXPENSES						
								LABOR				TOTAL		
Physicians and Dentists	Registered Nurses	Licensed Practical Nurses	Other Salaried Personnel	Total Personnel	Medical and Dental Residents	Other Trainees	Total Trainees	Payroll (in thousands)	Employee Benefits (in thousands)	Total (in thousands)	Percent of Total	Amount (in thousands)	Adjusted per Admission	Adjusted per Inpatient Day
146,381	1,558,038	76,534	2,704,453	5,216,348	118,075	9,440	127,515	$363,806,143	$96,687,285	$460,493,398	47.7	$966,204,239	$13,126.02	$2,424.17
16,529	156,072	20,966	348,592	631,393	1,972	334	2,306	37,559,678	9,847,876	47,407,559	50.0	94,728,753	8,855.26	1,351.23
129,852	1,401,966	55,568	2,355,861	4,584,955	116,103	9,106	125,209	326,246,465	86,839,408	413,085,839	47.4	871,475,486	13,852.21	2,653.17
16,090	212,765	9,244	347,414	676,572	13,827	1,284	15,111	56,449,833	18,181,278	74,631,116	49.2	151,561,222	17,288.19	3,403.76
1,044	8,601	673	20,746	35,789	38	42	80	2,751,776	813,471	3,565,247	52.2	6,832,474	12,774.18	2,431.45
15,046	204,164	8,571	326,668	640,783	13,789	1,242	15,031	53,698,057	17,367,807	71,065,869	49.1	144,728,749	17,581.49	3,469.26
442	3,365	151	5,746	11,717	81	20	101	1,104,963	237,472	1,342,437	50.8	2,642,629	19,994.92	2,817.11
195	817	87	2,276	4,064	13	10	23	431,953	117,171	549,125	55.1	996,455	18,507.01	2,277.84
247	2,548	64	3,470	7,653	68	10	78	673,011	120,301	793,312	48.2	1,646,174	21,017.76	3,288.35
206	2,105	47	2,672	6,147	50	8	58	562,138	91,288	653,426	48.4	1,351,008	19,702.89	3,360.25
41	443	17	798	1,506	18	2	20	110,873	29,013	139,886	47.4	295,166	30,261.07	2,995.03
9,859	159,857	7,603	252,341	496,563	11,017	1,068	12,085	40,812,363	14,291,387	55,103,751	49.7	110,902,411	17,531.03	3,437.49
154	2,941	269	5,836	10,593	9	7	16	767,351	271,083	1,038,436	48.9	2,124,179	13,757.46	2,549.42
9,705	156,916	7,334	246,505	485,970	11,008	1,061	12,069	40,045,013	14,020,303	54,065,315	49.7	108,778,231	17,625.44	3,461.03
236	11,918	346	19,072	36,346	198	14	212	2,549,320	905,531	3,454,851	45.8	7,549,077	14,906.05	3,269.45
147	2,869	210	4,986	9,579	23	2	25	670,115	214,631	884,747	47.8	1,849,877	13,198.98	2,301.51
26	1,665	84	2,953	5,425	2	1	3	384,994	135,684	520,678	50.7	1,026,364	14,787.62	3,384.23
26	482	43	964	1,740	7	1	8	100,704	29,891	130,594	51.7	252,609	7,781.20	2,162.04
288	3,004	136	5,612	10,577	226	14	240	762,579	204,726	967,304	47.1	2,055,127	11,320.33	2,307.24
52	670	50	1,208	2,394	14	1	15	135,570	33,173	168,744	45.7	368,949	8,290.61	3,298.95
3,212	46,643	2,445	72,096	145,056	3,479	465	3,944	11,117,820	3,619,466	14,737,284	50.2	29,375,421	17,451.26	3,381.71
4	929	32	1,386	2,975	13	5	18	234,206	98,617	332,823	52.2	637,397	23,282.21	4,309.30
0	510	37	664	1,381	30	0	30	129,022	48,873	177,895	49.8	357,217	12,421.92	3,651.97
29	2,750	52	2,637	6,308	22	5	27	517,392	186,553	703,944	49.0	1,437,272	15,746.79	2,949.39
21	615	19	1,193	2,049	2	0	2	176,867	65,974	242,840	46.9	518,142	19,151.42	4,307.01
544	8,206	458	14,485	26,755	307	21	328	2,726,891	1,058,389	3,785,279	50.6	7,473,526	18,576.54	3,689.07
111	2,504	134	4,258	8,118	107	2	109	751,330	231,901	983,233	48.4	2,029,772	13,991.96	2,953.65
59	942	62	1,569	3,083	29	2	31	266,376	66,953	333,329	46.9	710,295	15,903.07	2,387.25
313	17,045	1,041	21,180	47,733	627	63	690	3,097,182	945,060	4,042,245	47.3	8,540,960	13,395.04	2,761.17
380	9,791	276	14,860	28,408	984	14	998	2,836,254	1,120,852	3,957,106	51.2	7,734,923	20,845.14	4,409.40
45	1,544	58	2,729	5,098	11	1	12	543,502	219,983	763,486	61.3	1,245,577	19,272.13	4,064.71
112	14,867	536	18,945	39,756	1,182	382	1,564	3,124,947	1,009,020	4,133,967	49.2	8,404,239	17,372.31	3,142.00
2,326	10,234	432	18,138	35,708	1,990	24	2,014	3,494,412	1,473,058	4,967,471	50.3	9,884,132	29,972.35	4,225.34
658	8,739	375	16,844	29,607	1,304	14	1,318	3,371,123	1,464,212	4,835,335	51.6	9,368,894	30,736.23	5,834.38
28	684	28	958	1,996	8	0	8	178,008	46,289	224,297	49.7	450,891	11,244.73	2,727.60
62	763	42	1,533	2,709	21	3	24	247,431	81,265	328,696	53.7	612,415	17,503.08	4,423.98
29	698	13	1,010	1,928	12	2	14	230,294	72,052	302,346	50.8	595,709	16,497.53	3,966.98
63	1,332	46	2,793	4,788	80	3	83	483,529	126,052	609,581	48.8	1,250,262	18,040.78	2,887.92
102	1,567	83	2,738	5,125	64	3	67	437,980	138,989	576,970	46.6	1,237,082	15,560.58	3,059.33
226	2,745	122	4,914	9,294	85	10	95	582,240	167,535	749,775	49.0	1,528,650	11,386.25	2,731.57
70	1,500	41	2,835	4,923	25	5	30	438,406	121,630	560,036	51.7	1,082,400	14,817.45	3,900.23
490	1,167	113	3,016	5,351	136	2	138	297,503	92,699	390,202	50.6	770,611	11,873.08	2,119.25
46	524	20	929	1,760	20	2	22	159,014	41,242	200,257	46.5	430,441	18,338.49	3,870.04
526	4,558	197	8,756	16,454	55	19	74	1,451,443	394,457	1,845,900	49.4	3,738,397	15,355.09	2,405.36
55	675	63	1,505	2,683	8	5	13	220,686	63,165	283,849	47.9	592,005	9,372.21	1,485.25
471	3,883	134	7,251	13,771	47	14	61	1,230,757	331,293	1,562,051	49.6	3,146,392	17,451.16	2,722.72
41	423	21	785	1,485	16	1	17	121,615	31,640	153,255	47.3	323,713	11,808.31	2,240.51
430	3,460	113	6,466	12,286	31	13	44	1,109,142	299,653	1,408,796	49.9	2,822,679	18,463.00	2,791.63
1,785	17,459	195	28,682	55,579	1,328	63	1,391	4,654,254	1,394,600	6,048,856	50.0	12,089,477	15,572.76	3,578.27
382	2,312	58	5,993	9,999	4	3	7	744,898	211,289	956,187	53.5	1,788,167	11,836.52	3,179.68
1,403	15,147	137	22,689	45,580	1,324	60	1,384	3,909,355	1,183,311	5,092,669	49.4	10,301,310	16,475.51	3,657.86
94	298	6	808	1,432	0	15	15	132,286	43,303	175,589	56.5	310,943	16,953.42	4,941.72
104	849	7	2,111	3,280	5	0	5	191,213	50,827	242,040	53.8	449,638	13,054.55	3,471.92
109	444	7	801	1,637	107	10	117	168,858	55,710	224,567	52.5	428,068	23,441.67	4,743.88
108	1,309	14	1,775	3,634	0	11	11	381,909	95,672	477,582	47.7	1,001,719	15,579.80	3,403.07
22	288	13	481	966	0	0	0	65,207	23,357	88,564	53.4	165,888	10,200.35	2,800.98
43	1,276	23	1,837	3,781	0	2	2	244,095	86,778	330,873	44.4	745,924	16,448.16	3,499.54
776	9,209	58	12,391	26,097	1,209	22	1,231	2,338,565	721,888	3,060,455	48.4	6,324,161	17,363.72	3,696.76
147	1,474	9	2,485	4,753	3	0	3	387,222	105,777	492,999	56.3	874,969	13,654.54	3,416.74

Table continues

MSAs

TABLE 8   **U.S. CENSUS DIVISION 9, PACIFIC CONTINUED**

U.S. Community Hospitals
(Nonfederal, short-term general and other special hospitals)

2017 Utilization, Personnel and Finances

CLASSIFICATION	Hospitals	Beds	Admissions	Inpatient Days	Adjusted Inpatient Days	Average Daily Census	Adjusted Average Daily Census	Average Stay (days)	Surgical Operations	NEWBORNS Bassinets	Births	OUTPATIENT VISITS Emergency	Total
Washington	92	12,577	612,046	3,024,120	6,394,127	8,285	17,522	4.9	544,574	1,094	83,259	2,957,421	15,197,499
Nonmetropolitan	30	1,031	28,920	145,013	578,418	397	1,589	5.0	52,200	101	5,337	259,227	1,670,916
Metropolitan	62	11,546	583,126	2,879,107	5,815,709	7,888	15,933	4.9	492,374	993	77,922	2,698,194	13,526,583
Bellingham	1	225	14,999	68,561	131,731	188	361	4.6	7,724	10	1,437	64,464	95,148
Bremerton-Silverdale	1	260	12,972	55,962	123,753	153	339	4.3	10,456	22	2,050	80,049	309,051
Kennewick-Richland	4	449	25,374	104,244	265,393	285	727	4.1	24,217	43	4,668	255,587	900,515
Lewiston	1	25	1,217	3,904	17,586	11	48	3.2	2,238	0	0	16,310	98,379
Longview	1	180	7,455	32,208	73,459	88	201	4.3	4,319	14	826	44,668	230,277
Mount Vernon-Anacortes	3	241	11,557	48,097	147,188	131	402	4.2	12,181	35	1,525	162,853	810,668
Olympia-Tumwater	2	402	23,767	110,362	175,989	302	482	4.6	25,262	49	2,631	80,978	408,608
Portland-Vancouver-Hillsboro	2	623	34,462	149,064	262,916	408	720	4.3	17,986	82	5,415	146,675	559,461
Seattle-Bellevue-Everett	22	5,131	270,483	1,366,867	2,703,422	3,745	7,407	5.1	203,368	393	35,866	979,365	6,800,460
Spokane-Spokane Valley	9	1,616	58,723	347,257	635,948	952	1,743	5.9	83,689	124	6,870	258,911	1,097,052
Tacoma-Lakewood	6	1,368	73,731	378,941	727,611	1,039	1,994	5.1	54,330	105	9,626	337,843	932,653
Walla Walla	2	136	5,937	32,121	105,171	88	288	5.4	5,870	14	683	29,964	219,511
Wenatchee	4	430	23,891	107,986	232,438	296	637	4.5	16,321	47	2,781	79,489	347,581
Yakima	4	460	18,558	73,533	213,104	202	584	4.0	24,413	55	3,544	161,038	717,219

MSAs

TABLE 8

U.S. CENSUS DIVISION 9, PACIFIC CONTINUED

U.S. Community Hospitals
(Nonfederal, short-term general and other special hospitals)

2017 Utilization, Personnel and Finances

FULL-TIME EQUIVALENT PERSONNEL					FULL-TIME EQUIV. TRAINEES			EXPENSES						
								LABOR				TOTAL		
Physicians and Dentists	Registered Nurses	Licensed Practical Nurses	Other Salaried Personnel	Total Personnel	Medical and Dental Residents	Other Trainees	Total Trainees	Payroll (in thousands)	Employee Benefits (in thousands)	Total (in thousands)	Percent of Total	Amount (in thousands)	Adjusted per Admission	Adjusted per Inpatient Day
3,478	27,526	1,098	51,889	96,259	1,346	114	1,460	8,426,810	1,863,361	10,290,172	46.4	22,188,310	17,217.11	3,470.11
258	1,856	196	5,136	8,450	4	17	21	586,888	150,763	737,650	55.4	1,331,668	11,849.27	2,302.26
3,220	25,670	902	46,753	87,809	1,342	97	1,439	7,839,922	1,712,599	9,552,522	45.8	20,856,642	17,729.93	3,586.26
103	634	45	1,019	2,007	0	4	4	195,860	52,899	248,759	49.3	504,655	17,511.18	3,830.95
58	589	25	1,066	2,070	26	2	28	119,392	28,442	147,834	36.7	402,454	14,029.63	3,252.07
206	1,125	51	2,368	4,550	23	25	48	394,357	61,322	455,679	53.4	853,604	13,113.60	3,216.38
12	92	10	222	386	1	2	3	27,950	7,539	35,489	48.4	73,257	13,363.26	4,165.66
32	360	20	669	1,260	8	1	9	106,429	27,063	133,491	48.0	277,841	16,340.68	3,782.25
80	634	68	1,462	2,686	14	1	15	202,066	60,291	262,357	51.0	514,204	14,552.25	3,493.52
14	1,121	34	1,298	2,860	4	0	4	224,925	27,247	252,173	56.6	445,625	11,429.50	2,532.12
177	1,531	23	2,189	4,456	45	1	46	329,625	83,291	412,917	50.8	813,525	13,387.39	3,094.24
1,767	12,284	311	23,032	42,659	1,100	55	1,155	4,156,700	931,920	5,088,619	45.5	11,190,777	21,105.91	4,139.49
83	2,408	38	4,364	7,671	33	1	34	610,022	95,732	705,756	39.1	1,806,920	17,708.83	2,841.30
410	2,640	199	4,670	8,944	80	2	82	823,273	196,574	1,019,847	44.4	2,297,747	16,067.49	3,157.93
68	373	17	681	1,359	0	0	0	107,099	10,219	117,319	47.6	246,345	15,483.67	2,342.33
51	936	25	1,432	2,940	8	2	10	251,874	64,880	316,754	44.6	710,126	14,206.50	3,055.12
159	943	36	2,281	3,961	0	1	1	290,349	65,179	355,528	49.4	719,563	13,078.20	3,376.58

MSAs

Statistics for Health Care Systems and their Hospitals

The following tables describing health care systems refers to information in section B of the 2019 *AHA Guide*. Table 1 shows the number of health care systems by type of control. Table 2 provides a breakdown of the number of systems that own, lease, sponsor or contract manage hospitals within each control category. Table 3 gives the number of hospitals and beds in each control category as well as total hospitals and beds. Finally, Table 4 shows the percentage of hospitals and beds in each control category.

For more information on health care systems, please write to the Section for Health Care Systems, 155 N. Wacker Drive, Chicago, Illinois 60606 or call 312/422–3000.

Table 1. Multihospital Health Care Systems, by Type of Organizaton Control

Type of Control	Code	Number of Systems
Catholic (Roman) church–related	CC	27
Other church–related	CO	7
Subtotal, church–related		34
Other not–for–profit	NP	309
Subtotal, not–for–profit		343
Investor Owned	IO	77
Federal Government	FG	5
Total		425

Table 2. Multihospital Health Care Systems, by Type of Ownership and Control

Type of Ownership	Catholic Church–Related (CC)	Other Church–Related (CO)	Total Church–Related (CC + CO)	Other Not–for–Profit (NP)	Total Not–for–Profit (CC, CO, + NP)	Investor–Owned (IO)	Federal Government (FG)	All Systems
Systems that only own, lease or sponsor	21	6	27	188	215	17	4	236
Systems that only contract–manage	0	0	0	12	12	4	0	16
Systems that manage, own, lease, or sponsor	6	1	7	109	116	56	1	173
Total	27	7	34	309	343	77	5	425

Table 3. Hospitals and Beds in Multihospital Health Care Systems, by Type of Ownership and Control

Type of Ownership	Catholic Church–Related (CC) H	B	Other Church–Related (CO) H	B	Total Church–Related (CC + CO) H	B	Other Not–for–Profit (NP) H	B	Total Not–for–Profit (CC, CO, + NP) H	B	Investor–Owned (IO) H	B	Federal Government (FG) H	B	All Systems H	B
Owned, leased or sponsored	580	105,725	76	17,639	656	123,364	1,659	350,107	2,315	473,471	1,374	164,789	204	40,232	3,893	678,492
Contract–managed	44	2,494	3	485	47	2,979	120	9,233	167	12,212	88	4,623	0	0	255	16,835
Total	624	108,219	79	18,124	703	126,343	3,318	359,340	4,021	485,683	1,462	169,412	204	40,232	5,687	695,327

H = hospitals; B = beds.

Table 4. Hospitals and Beds in Multihospital Health Care Systems, by Type of Ownership and Control as a Percentage of All Systems

Type of Ownership	Catholic Church–Related (CC) H	B	Other Church–Related (CO) H	B	Total Church–Related (CC + CO) H	B	Other Not–for–Profit (NP) H	B	Total Not–for–Profit (CC, CO, + NP) H	B	Investor–Owned (IO) H	B	Federal Government (FG) H	B	All Systems H	B
Owned, leased or sponsored	14.9	15.6	1.9	2.6	16.9	18.2	42.6	51.6	59.5	69.8	35.3	24.3	5.2	5.9	99.9	100
Contract managed	17.3	14.8	1.2	2.9	18.4	17.7	47.1	51.6	65.5	72.5	34.5	24.3	0	5.9	100.1	99.5
Total	10.9	15.6	1.4	2.6	12.4	18.2	58.3	51.6	70.7	69.9	25.7	24.3	3.6	5.9	99.9	100

H = hospitals; B = beds.
*Please note that figures may not always equal the provided subtotal or total percentages due to rounding.

Glossary

This glossary explains specific terms as they are used in the tables and text of AHA Hospital Statistics

Ablation of Barrett's esophagus: Premalignant condition that can lead to adenocarcinoma of the esophagus. The non surgical ablation of the premalignant tissue in Barrett's esophagus by the application of thermal energy or light through an endoscope passed from the mouth into the esophagus.

Acute long term care: Provider specialized acute hospital care to medically complex patients who are critically ill, have multisystem complications and/or failure, and require hospitalization averaging 25 days, in a facility offering specialized treatment programs and therapeutic intervention on a 24 hour/7day a week basis.

Adjusted admission: An aggregate measure of workload reflecting the sum of admissions and equivalent admissions attributed to outpatient services. The number of equivalent admissions attributed to outpatient services is derived by multiplying admissions by the ratio of outpatient revenue to inpatient revenue.

$$\text{Adjusted admissions} = \text{admissions} + \left[\text{admissions} * \left(\frac{\text{outpatient revenue}}{\text{inpatient revenue}}\right)\right]$$

Adjusted average daily census: An estimate of the average number of patients (both inpatients and outpatients) receiving care each day during the reporting period, which is usually 12 months. The figure is derived by dividing the number of inpatient day equivalents (also called adjusted inpatient days) by the number of days in the reporting period.

Adjusted inpatient days: An aggregate measure of workload reflecting the sum of inpatient days and equivalent patient days attributed to outpatient services. The number of equivalent patient days attributed to outpatient services is derived by multiplying inpatient days by the ratio of outpatient revenue to inpatient revenue.

$$\text{Adjusted inpatient days} = \text{inpatient days} + \left[\text{inpatient days} * \left(\frac{\text{outpatient revenue}}{\text{inpatient revenue}}\right)\right]$$

Admissions: The number of patients, excluding newborns, accepted for inpatient service during the reporting period; the number includes patients who visit the emergency room and are later admitted for inpatient service.

Adult Cardiac Surgery: Includes minimally invasive procedures that include surgery done with only a small incision or no incision at all, such as through a laparoscope or an endoscope and more invasive major surgical procedures that include open chest and open heart surgery.

Adult Cardiology Services: An organized clinical service offering diagnostic and interventional procedures to manage the full range of adult heart conditions.

Adult day care program: Program providing supervision, medical and psychological care, and social activities for older adults who live at home or in another family setting, but cannot be alone or prefer to be with others during the day. May include intake assessment, health monitoring, occupational therapy, personal care, noon meal, and transportation services.

Adult Diagnostic/invasive catheterization: (also called coronary angiography or coronary arteriography) is used to assist in diagnosing complex heart conditions. Cardiac angiography involves the insertion of a tiny catheter into the artery in the groin then carefully threading the catheter up into the aorta where the coronary arteries originate. Once the catheter is in place, a dye is injected which allows the cardiologist to see the size, shape, and distribution of the coronary arteries. These images are used to diagnose heart disease and to determine, among other things, whether or not surgery is indicated.

Adult Interventional cardiac catheterization: Non surgical procedure that utilizes the same basic principles as diagnostic catheterization and then uses advanced techniques to improve the heart's function. It can be a less-invasive alternative to heart surgery.

Airborne infection isolation room: A single-occupancy room for patient care where environmental factors are controlled in an effort to minimize the transmission of those infectious agents, usually spread person to person by droplet nuclei associated with coughing and inhalation. Such rooms typically have specific ventilation requirements for controlled ventilation, air pressure and filtration.

Alcoholism-chemical dependency partial hospitalization services: Organized hospital services providing intensive day/evening outpatient services of three hour or more duration, distinguished from other outpatient visits of one hour.

Alcoholism-chemical dependency pediatric services: Provides diagnosis and therapeutic services to pediatric patients with alcoholism or other drug dependencies. Includes care for inpatient/residential treatment for patients whose course of treatment involves more intensive care than provided in an outpatient setting or where patient requires supervised withdrawal.

Alcoholism-drug abuse or dependency inpatient care: Provides diagnosis and therapeutic services to patients with alcoholism or other drug dependencies. Includes care for inpatient/residential treatment for patients whose course of treatment involves more intensive care than provided in an outpatient setting or where patient requires supervised withdrawal.

Alcoholism-drug abuse or dependency outpatient services: Organized hospital services that provide medical care and/or rehabilitative treatment services to outpatients for whom the primary diagnosis is alcoholism or other chemical dependency.

Alzheimer Center: Facility that offers care to persons with Alzheimer's disease and their families through an integrated program of clinical services, research, and education.

Ambulance services: Provision of ambulance services to the ill and injured who require medical attention on a scheduled or unscheduled basis.

Ambulatory Surgery Center: Facility that provides care to patients requiring surgery who are admitted and discharged on the same day. Ambulatory surgery centers are distinct from same day surgical units within the hospital outpatient departments for purposes of Medicare payments.

Arthritis treatment center: Specifically equipped and staffed center for the diagnosis and treatment of arthritis and other joint disorders.

Assisted living: A special combination of housing, supportive services, personalized assistance and health care designed to respond to the individual needs of those who need help in activities of daily living and instrumental activities of daily living. Supportive services are available, 24 hours a day, to meet scheduled and unscheduled needs, in a way that promotes maximum independence and dignity for each resident and encourages the involvement of a resident's family, neighbor and friends.

Assistive Technology Center: A program providing access to specialized hardware and software with adaptations allowing individuals greater independence with mobility, dexterity, or increased communication options.

Auxiliary: A volunteer community organization formed to assist the hospital in carrying out its purpose and to serve as a link between the institution and the community.

Average daily census: The average number of people served on an inpatient basis on a single day during the reporting period; the figure is calculated by dividing the number of inpatient days by the number of days in the reporting period.

Bariatric/weight control services: Bariatrics is the medical practice of weight reduction.

Beds: Number of beds regularly maintained (set up and staffed for use) for inpatients as of the close of the reporting period. Excludes newborn bassinets.

Bed-size category: Hospitals are categorized by the number of beds set up and staffed for use at the end of the reporting period. The eight categories in Hospital Statistics are: 6 to 24 beds; 25 to 49; 50 to 99; 100 to 199; 200 to 299; 300 to 399; 400 to 499; and 500 or more.

Birthing room-LDR room-LDRP room: A single-room type of maternity care with a more homelike setting for families than the traditional three-room unit (labor/delivery/recovery) with a separate postpartum area. A birthing room combines labor and delivery in one room. An LDR room accommodates three stages in the birthing process—labor, delivery, and recovery. An LDRP room accommodates all four stages of the birth process—labor, delivery, recovery, and postpartum.

Births: Total number of infants born in the hospital during the reporting period. Births do not include infants transferred from other institutions, and are excluded from admission and discharge figures.

Blood Donor Center: A facility that performs, or is responsible for the collection, processing, testing or distribution of blood and components.

Bone marrow transplant: See definition for Transplant services on page 213.

Breast cancer screening/mammograms: Mammography screening – The use of breast x-ray to detect unsuspected breast cancer in asymptomatic women. Diagnostic mammography – The x-ray imaging of breast tissue in symptomatic women who are considered to have a substantial likelihood of having breast cancer already.

Burn care: Provides care to severely burned patients. Severely burned patients are those with any of the following: (1) second-degree burns of more than 25% total body surface area for adults or 20% total body surface area for children: (2) third-degree burns of more than 10% total body surface area; (3) any severe burns of the hands, face, eyes, ears, or feet; or (4) all inhalation injuries, electrical burns, complicated burn injuries involving fractures and other major traumas, and all other poor risk factors.

Cardiac electrophysiology: Evaluation and management of patients with complex rhythm or conduction abnormalities, including diagnostic testing, treatment of arrhythmias by catheter ablation or drug therapy, and pacemaker/defibrillator implantation and follow-up.

Cardiac intensive care: Provides patient care of a more specialized nature than the usual medical and surgical care, on the basis of physicians' orders and approved nursing care plans. The unit is staffed with specially trained nursing personnel and contains monitoring and specialized support or treatment equipment for patients who, because of heart seizure, open-heart surgery, or other life-threatening conditions, require intensified, comprehensive observation and care. May include myocardial infarction, pulmonary care, and heart transplant units.

Cardiac Rehabilitation: A medically supervised program to help heart patients recover quickly and improve their overall physical and mental functioning. The goal is to reduce risk of another cardiac event or to keep an already present heart condition from getting worse. Cardiac rehabilitation programs include: counseling to patients, an exercise program, helping patients modify risk factors such as smoking and high blood pressure, providing vocational guidance to enable the patient to return to work, supplying information on physical limitations and lending emotional support.

Case management: A system of assessment, treatment planning, referral and follow-up that ensures the provision of comprehensive and continuous services and the coordination of payment and reimbursement for care.

Chaplaincy/pastoral care services: A service ministering religious activities and providing pastoral counseling to patients, their families, and staff of a health care organization.

Chemotherapy: An organized program for the treatment of cancer by the use of drugs or chemicals.

Children's wellness program: A program that encourages improved health status and a healthful lifestyle of children through health education, exercise, nutrition and health promotion.

Chiropractic services: An organized clinical service including spinal manipulation or adjustment and related diagnostic and therapeutic services.

Closed physician-hospital organization (Closed PHO): A joint venture between the hospital and physicians who have been selected on the basis of cost-effectiveness and/or high quality. The PHO can act as a unified agent in managed care contracting, own a managed care plan, own and operate ambulatory care centers or ancillary services projects, or provide administrative services to physician members.

Community health education: Education that provides health information to individuals and populations, as well as support for personal, family and community health decisions with the objective of improving health status.

Community hospitals: All nonfederal, short-term general, and special hospitals whose facilities and services are available to the public. (Special hospitals include obstetrics and gynecology; eye, ear, nose, and throat; rehabilitation; orthopedic; and other individually described specialty services.) Short-term general and special childrens hospitals are also considered to be community hospitals.

A hospital may include a nursing-home-type unit and still be classified as short-term, provided that the majority of its patients are admitted to units where the average length of stay is less than 30 days. Therefore, statistics for community hospitals often include some data about such nursing-home-type units. An example is furnished by Montana, where in 1995 63.6 percent of all hospitals classified as community hospitals include nursing-home-type units. Expense, revenue, utilization, and personnel data for these hospitals include data about their nursing-home-type units. Thus, total admissions to Montana community hospitals in 1995 were 96,154; total inpatient days, 997,759; total expenses, $791,806,393; and total payroll expenses, $352,583,331. If nursing-home-type unit data were excluded, these same items would be 94,034; 457,340; 752,567,865; and $328,911841, respectively.

Note that before 1972, hospital units of institutions such as prison and college infirmaries were included in the category of community hospitals. Including these units made this category equivalent to the short- term general and other special hospitals category. Although these hospital units are few in number and small in size, this change in definition should be taken into consideration when comparing data.

Community outreach: A program that systematically interacts with the community to identify those in need of services, alerting persons and their families to the availability of services, locating needed services, and enabling persons to enter the service delivery system.

Complementary and alternative medicine services: Organized hospital services or formal arrangements to providers that provide care or treatment not based solely on traditional western allopathic medical teachings as instructed in most U.S. medical schools. Includes any of the following: acupuncture, chiropractic, homeopathy, osteopathy, diet and lifestyle changes, herbal medicine, message therapy, etc.

Computer assisted orthopedic surgery (CAOS): Orthopedic surgery using computer technology, enabling three-dimensional graphic models to visualize a patient's anatomy.

Control: The type of organization responsible for establishing policy concerning the overall operation of hospitals. The three major categories are government (including federal, state, and local); nongovernment (nonprofit); and investor-owned (for-profit).

Crisis prevention: Services provided in order to promote physical and mental well being and the early identification of disease and ill health prior to the onset and recognition of symptoms so as to permit early treatment.

CT scanner: Computed tomographic scanner for head or whole body scans.

Deduction from revenue: The difference between revenue at full established rates (gross) and the payment actually received from payers (net).

Dental Services: An organized dental service or dentists on staff, not necessarily involving special facilities, providing dental or oral services to inpatients or outpatients.

Diagnostic radioisotope facility: The use of radioactive isotopes (Radiopharmaceuticals) as tracers or indicators to detect an abnormal condition or disease.

Electrodiagnostic Services: Diagnostic testing services for nerve and muscle function including services such as nerve conduction studies and needle electromyography.

Electron beam computed tomography (EBCT): A high tech computed tomography scan used to detect coronary artery disease by measuring coronary calcifications. This imaging procedure uses electron beams which are magnetically steered to produce a visual of the coronary artery and the images are produced faster than conventional CT scans.

Emergency department: Hospital facilities for the provision of unscheduled outpatient services to patients whose conditions require immediate care.

Emergency room visits: The number of visits to the emergency unit. When emergency outpatients are admitted to the inpatient areas of the hospital, they are counted as emergency room visits and subsequently, as inpatient admissions.

Emergency services: Health services that are provided after the onset of a medical condition that manifests itself by symptoms of sufficient severity, including severe pain, that the absence of immediate medical attention could reasonably be expected by a prudent layperson, who possesses an average knowledge of health and medicine, to result in placing the patient's health in serious jeopardy.

Enabling services: A program that is designed to help the patient access health care services by offering any of the following: transportation services and/or referrals to local social services agencies.

Endoscopic retrograde cholangiopancreatography (ERCP): A procedure in which a catheter is introduced through an endoscope into the bile ducts and pancreatic ducts. Injection of contrast materials permits detailed x-ray of these structures. The procedure is used diagnostically as well as therapeutically to relieve obstruction or remove stones.

Endoscopic ultrasound: Specially designed endoscope that incorporates an ultrasound transductor used to obtain detailed images of organs in the chest and abdomen. The endoscope can be passed through the mouth or the anus. When combined with needle biopsy the procedure can assist in diagnosis and staging of cancer.

Enrollment (insurance) assistance services: A program that provides enrollment assistance for patients who are potentially eligible for public health insurance programs such as Medicaid, State Children's Health Insurance, or local/state indigent care programs. The specific services offered could include explanation of benefits, assist applicants in completing the application and locating all relevant documents, conduct eligibility interviews, and/or forward applications and documentation to state/local social service or health agency.

Equity model: An arrangement that allows established practitioners to become shareholders in a professional corporation in exchange for tangible and intangible assets of their existing practices.

Esophageal impedance study: A test in which a catheter is placed through the nose into the esophagus to measure whether gas or liquids are passing from the stomach into the esophagus and causing symptoms.

Expenses: Includes all expenses for the reporting period including payroll, non-payroll, and all operating expenses. *Payroll expenses* include all salaries and wages. *Non-payroll expenses* are all professional fees and those salary expenditures excluded from payroll. *Labor related expenses* are defined as payroll expenses plus employee benefits. *Non-labor related expenses* are all other non-payroll expenses. Bad debt has been reclassified from an expense to a deduction from revenue in accordance with the revised AICPA Audit Guide. Note: Financial data may not add due to rounding.

Expenses per adjusted admission stay: Total expenses divided by adjusted admissions (see *adjusted admission*).

Expenses per adjusted inpatient days: Expenses divided by adjusted inpatient days (see *adjusted inpatient days*).

Extracorporeal shock wave lithotripter (ESWL): A medical device used for treating stones in the kidney or urethra. The device disintegrates kidney stones noninvasively through the transmission of acoustic shock waves directed at the stones.

Fertility Clinic: A specialized program set in an infertility center that provides counseling and education as well as advanced reproductive techniques such as: injectable therapy, reproductive surgeries, treatment for endometriosis, male factor infertility, tubal reversals, in vitro fertilization (IVF), donor eggs, and other such services to help patients achieve successful pregnancies.

Fitness center: Provides exercise, testing, or evaluation programs and fitness activities to the community and hospital employees.

Foundation: A corporation, organized as a hospital affiliate or subsidiary, that purchases both tangible and intangible assets of one or more medical group practices. Physicians remain in a separate corporate entity but sign a professional services agreement with the foundation.

Freestanding outpatient care center: A facility owned and operated by the hospital, that is physically separate from the hospital and provides various medical treatments and diagnostic services on an outpatient basis only. Laboratory and radiology services are usually available.

Full-field digital mammography (FFDM): Combines the x-ray generators and tubes used in analog screen-film mammography (SFM) with a detector plate that converts the x-rays into a digital signal.

Full time equivalent employees (FTE): Full time personnel on payroll plus one half of the part time personnel on payroll. For purposes of *AHA Hospital Statistics*, full time and part time medical and dental residents/interns and other trainees are excluded from the calculation.

General medical-surgical care: Provides acute care to patients in medical and surgical units on the basis of physicians' orders and approved nursing care plans.

Genetic testing/counseling: A service equipped with adequate laboratory facilities and directed by a qualified physician to advise parents and prospective parents on potential problems in cases of genetic defects. A genetic test is the analysis of human DNA, RNA, chromosomes, proteins, and certain metabolites in order to detect heritable disease-related genotypes, mutations, phenotypes, or karyotypes for clinical purposes. Genetic tests can have diverse purposes, including the diagnosis of genetic diseases in newborns, children, and adults; the identification of future health risks; the prediction of drug responses; and the assessment of risks to future children.

Geriatric services: The branch of medicine dealing with the physiology of aging and the diagnosis and treatment of disease affecting the aged. Services could include: Adult day care; Alzheimer's diagnostic-assessment services; Comprehensive geriatric assessment; Emergency response system; Geriatric acute care unit; and/or Geriatric clinics.

Government, nonfederal, state, local: Controlled by an agency of state, county, or city government.

Gross inpatient revenue: Revenue from services rendered to inpatients at full established rates (also known as "charges").

Gross outpatient revenue: Revenue from services rendered to outpatients at full established rates.

Group practice without walls: In this organization, the hospital sponsors the formation of a physician group or provides capital to physicians to establish one. The group shares administrative expenses, although the physicians remain independent practitioners.

Group Purchasing Organization: An organization whose primary function is to negotiate contracts for the purpose of purchasing for members of the group or has a central supply site for its members.

Health fair: Community health education events that focus on the prevention of disease and promotion of health through such activities as audiovisual exhibits and free diagnostic services.

Health Research: Organized hospital research program in any of the following areas: basic research, clinical research, community health research, and/or research on innovative health care delivery.

Health screening: A preliminary procedure such as a test or examination to detect the most characteristic sign or signs of a disorder that may require further investigation.

Heart transplant: See definition for Transplant services on page 213.

Hemodialysis: Provision of equipment and personnel for the treatment of renal insufficiency on an inpatient or outpatient basis.

HIV-AIDS services: (could include). *HIV-AIDS* unit – Special unit or team designated and equipped specifically for diagnosis, treatment, continuing care planning, and counseling services for HIV-AIDS patients and their families. *General inpatient care for HIV-AIDS* – Inpatient diagnosis and treatment for human immunodeficiency virus and acquired immunodeficiency syndrome patients, but dedicated unit is not available. *Specialized outpatient program for HIV-AIDS* – Special outpatient program providing diagnostic, treatment, continuing care planning, and counseling for HIV-AIDS patients and their families.

Home health services: Service providing nursing, therapy, and health-related homemaker or social services in the patient's home.

Hospice: A program providing palliative care, chiefly medical relief of pain and supportive services, addressing the emotional, social, financial, and legal needs of terminally ill patients and their families. Care can be provided in a variety of settings, both inpatient and at home.

Hospital unit: The hospital operation, excluding activity pertaining to nursing-home-type unit (as described below), for the following items: Admissions, Beds, FTEs (full-time, part-time, and total), Inpatient Days, Length of Stay, Net Revenue, and Total Expense.

Hospital unit of institutions: A hospital unit that is not open to the public and is contained within a nonhospital unit. An example is an infirmary that is contained within a college.

Hospitals in a network: Hospitals participating in a group that may include other hospitals, physicians, other providers, insurers, and/or community agencies that work together to coordinate and deliver a broad spectrum of services to the community.

Hospitals in a system: Hospitals belonging to a corporate body that owns and/or manages health provider facilities or health-related subsidiaries; the system may also own non-health-related facilities.

Image-guided radiation therapy (IGRT): Automated system for image-guided radiation therapy that enables clinicians to obtain high-resolution x-ray images to pinpoint tumor sites, adjust patient positioning when necessary, and complete a treatment, all within the standard treatment time slot, allowing for more effective cancer treatments.

Immunization program: Program that plans, coordinates and conducts immunization services in the community.

Indemnity fee for service: The traditional type of health insurance, in which the insured is reimbursed for covered expenses without regard to choice of provider. Payment up to a stated limit may be made either to the individual incurring and claiming the expense, or directly to providers.

Independent practice association (IPA): An IPA is a legal entity that holds managed care contracts and contracts with physicians, usually in solo practice, to provide care either on a fee-for-services or capitated basis. The purpose of an IPA is to assist solo physicians in obtaining managed care contracts.

Indigent care clinic: Health care services for uninsured and underinsured persons where care is free of charge or charged on a sliding scale. This would include "free clinics" staffed by volunteer practitioners, but could also be staffed by employees with sponsoring health care organizations subsidizing the cost of service.

Inpatient days: The number of adult and pediatric days of care, excluding newborn days of care, rendered during the entire reporting period.

Inpatient palliative care unit: An inpatient palliative care ward is a physically discreet, inpatient nursing unit where the focus is palliative care. The patient care focus is on symptom relief for complex patients who may be continuing to undergo primary treatment. Care is delivered by palliative medicine specialists.

Inpatient surgeries: Surgical services provided to patients who remain in the hospital overnight.

Integrated salary model: In this arrangement, physicians are salaried by the hospital or other entity of a health system to provide medical services for primary care and specialty care.

Intensity-Modulated Radiation Therapy (IMRT): A type of three-dimensional radiation therapy, which improves the targeting of treatment delivery in a way that is likely to decrease damage to normal tissues and allows varying intensities.

Intermediate nursing care: Provides health-related services (skilled nursing care and social services) to residents with a variety of physical conditions or functional disabilities. These residents do not require the care provided by a hospital or skilled nursing facility, but do need supervision and support services.

Intraoperative magnetic resonance imaging: An integrated surgery system which provides an MRI system in an operating room. The system allows for immediate evaluation of the degree to tumor resection while the patient is undergoing a surgical resection. Intraoperative MRI exists when a MRI (low-field or high-field) is placed in the operating theater and is used during surgical resection without moving the patient from the operating room to the diagnostic imaging suite.

Investor-owned, for-profit: Investor-owned, for-profit hospitals are those controlled on a for-profit basis by an individual, partnership, or profit-making corporation.

Kidney transplant: See definition for Transplant services on page 213.

Labor-related expenses: Payroll expenses plus employee benefits. *Non-labor-related expenses refers to* all other nonpayroll expenses, such as interest depreciation, supplies, purchased services, professional fees, and others.

Length of stay (LOS): LOS refers to the average number of days a patient stays at the facility. Short-term hospitals are those where the average LOS is less than 30 days. Long-term hospitals are those where the average LOS is 30 days or more. The figure is derived by dividing the number of inpatient days by the number of admissions.

Note that this publication carries two LOS variables: *total facility length of stay and hospital unit length of stay. Total facility* includes admissions and inpatient days from nursing-home-type units under control of the hospital. In *hospital unit length of stay*, nursing home utilization is subtracted.

Licensed practical nurse (LPN): A nurse who has graduated from an approved school of practical (vocational) nursing and works under the supervision of registered nurses and/or physicians.

Linguistic/Translation services: Services provided by the hospital designed to make health care more accessible to non-English speaking patients and their physicians.

Liver transplant: See definition for Transplant services on page 213.

Long-term: Hospitals are classified either short-term or long-term according to the average length of stay (LOS). A long-term hospital is one in which the average LOS is 30 days or more.

Lung transplant: See definition for Transplant services on page 213.

Magnetic resonance imaging (MRI): The use of a uniform magnetic field and radio frequencies to study tissue and structure of the body. This procedure enables the visualization of biochemical activity of the cell in vivo without the use of ionizing radiation, radio-isotopic substances, or high-frequency sound.

Magnetoencephalography: a noninvasive neurophysiological measurement tool used to study magnetic fields generated by neuronal activity of the brain. The primary uses of MEG include assisting surgeons in localizing the source of epilepsy, sensory mapping, and the study of brain function. When it is combined with structural imaging, it is known as magnetic source imaging (MSI).

Management services organization (MSO): A corporation owned by the hospital or a physician/hospital joint venture that provides management services to one or more medical group practices. As part of a full-service management agreement, the MSO purchases the tangible assets of the practices and leases them back, employs all non-physician staff, and provides all supplies/administrative systems for a fee.

Meals on wheels: A hospital sponsored program which delivers meals to people, usually the elderly, who are unable to prepare their own meals. Low cost, nutritional meals are delivered to individuals' homes on a regular basis.

Medical surgical intensive care: Provides patient care of a more intensive nature than the usual medical and surgical care, on the basis of physicians' orders and approved nursing care plans. These units are staffed with specially trained nursing personnel and contain monitoring and specialized support equipment for patients who, because of shock, trauma, or other life-threatening conditions, require intensified, comprehensive observation and care. Includes mixed intensive care units.

Mobile health services: Vans and other vehicles used to deliver primary care services.

Multi-slice spiral computed tomography (<64 slice CT): A specialized computed tomography procedure that provides three-dimensional processing and allows narrower and multiple slices with increased spatial resolution and faster scanning times as compared to a regular computed tomography scan.

Multi-slice spiral computed tomography (64+ slice CT): Involves the acquisition of volumetric tomographic x-ray absorption data expressed in Hounsfield units using multiple rows of detectors. 64+ systems reconstruct the equivalent of 64 or greater slices to cover the imaged volume.

Neonatal intensive care: A unit that must be separate from the newborn nursery providing intensive care to all sick infants including those with the very lowest birth weights (less than 1500 grams). NICU has potential for providing mechanical ventilation, neonatal surgery, and special care for the sickest infants born in the hospital or transferred from another institution. A full-time neonatologist serves as director of the NICU.

Neonatal intermediate care: A unit that must be separate from the normal newborn nursery and that provides intermediate and/or recovery care and some specialized services, including immediate resuscitation, intravenous therapy, and capacity for prolonged oxygen therapy and monitoring.

Net patient revenue: The estimated net realizable amounts from patients, third-party payers, and others for services rendered. The number includes estimated retroactive adjustments called for by agreements with third-party payers; retroactive adjustments are accrued on an estimated basis in the period the related services are rendered and then adjusted later as final settlements are determined.

Net total revenue: Net patient revenue plus all other revenue, including contributions, endowment revenue, governmental grants, and all other payments not made on behalf of individual patients.

Neurological services: Services provided by the hospital dealing with the operative and nonoperative management of disorders of the central, peripheral, and autonomic nervous system.

Nongovernment, nonprofit: Hospitals that are nongovernment, nonprofit are controlled by not-for-profit organizations, including religious organizations (Catholic hospitals, for example), fraternal societies, and others.

Nursing-home-type unit/facility: A unit/ facility that primarily offers the following type of services to a majority of all admissions:

- *Skilled nursing:* The provision of medical and nursing care services, health-related services, and social services under the supervision of a registered nurse on a 24-hour basis.

- *Intermediate care:* The provision, on a regular basis, of health-related care and services to individuals who do not require the degree of care or treatment that a skilled nursing unit is designed to provide.

- *Personal care:* The provision of general supervision and direct personal care services for residents who require assistance in activities of daily living but who do not need nursing services or inpatient care. Medical and nursing services are available as needed.

- *Sheltered/residential care:* The provision of general supervision and protective services for residents who do not need nursing services or continuous personal care services in the conduct of daily life. Medical and nursing services are available as needed.

Nutrition programs: Those services within a health care facility which are designed to provide inexpensive, nutritionally sound meals to patients.

Obstetrics: Levels should be designated: (1) unit provides services for uncomplicated maternity and newborn cases; (2) unit provides services for uncomplicated cases, the majority of complicated problems, and special neonatal services; and (3) unit provides services for all serious illnesses and abnormalities and is supervised by a full-time maternal/fetal specialist.

Occupational health services: Includes services designed to protect the safety of employees from hazards in the work environment.

Oncology services: Inpatient and outpatient services for patients with cancer, including comprehensive care, support and guidance in addition to patient education and prevention, chemotherapy, counseling and other treatment methods.

Open physician hospital organization (Open PHO): A joint venture between the hospital and all members of the medical staff who wish to participate. The open PHO can act as a unified agent in managed care contracting, own a managed care plan, own and operate ambulatory care centers or ancillary services projects, or provide administrative services to physician members.

Optical colonoscopy: An examination of the interior of the colon using a long, flexible, lighted tube with a small built-in camera.

Orthopedic services: Services provided for the prevention or correction of injuries or disorders of the skeletal system and associated muscles, joints and ligaments.

Osteopathic hospitals: Osteopathic medicine is a medical practice based on a theory that diseases are due chiefly to a loss of structural integrity, which can be restored by manipulation of the neuro-muscular and skeletal systems, supplemented by therapeutic measures (such as medicine or surgery).

Other Intensive Care: A specially staffed, specialty equipped, separate section of a hospital dedicated to the observation, care, and treatment of patients with life threatening illnesses, injuries, or complications from which recovery is possible. It provides special expertise and facilities for the support of vital function and utilizes the skill of medical nursing and other staff experienced in the management of these problems.

Other long-term care: Provision of long-term care other than skilled nursing care or intermediate care for those who do not require daily medical or nursing services, but may require some assistance in the activities of daily living. This can include residential care, elderly care, or sheltered care facilities for developmentally disabled.

Other special care: Provides care to patients requiring care more intensive than that provided in the acute area, yet not sufficiently intensive to require admission to an intensive care unit. Patients admitted to this area are usually transferred here from an intensive care unit once their condition has improved. These units are sometimes referred to as definitive observation, step-down, or progressive care units.

Other transplant: See definition for Transplant services on page 213.

Outpatient care: Treatment provided to patients who do not remain in the hospital for overnight care. Hospitals may deliver outpatient care on site or through a facility owned and operated by the hospital, but physically separate from the hospital. In addition to treating minor illnesses or injuries, a free-standing center will stabilize seriously ill or injured patients before transporting them to a hospital. Laboratory and radiology services are usually available.

Outpatient care center (Freestanding): A facility owned and operated by the hospital, but physically separate from the hospital, that provides various medical treatments on an outpatient basis only. In addition to treating minor illnesses or injuries, the center will stabilize seriously ill or injured patients before transporting them to a hospital. Laboratory and radiology services are usually available.

Outpatient care center-services (Hospital-based): Organized hospital health care services offered by appointment on an ambulatory basis. Services may include outpatient surgery, examination, diagnosis, and treatment of a variety of medical conditions on a nonemergency basis, and laboratory and other diagnostic testing as ordered by staff or outside physician referral.

Outpatient surgery: Scheduled surgical services provided to patients who do not remain in the hospital overnight. The surgery may be performed in operating suites also used for inpatient surgery, specially designated surgical suites for outpatient surgery, or procedure rooms within an outpatient care facility.

Outpatient visit: A visit by a patient who is not lodged in the hospital while receiving medical, dental, or other services. Each visit an outpatient makes to a discrete unit constitutes one visit regardless of the number of diagnostic and/or therapeutic treatments that the patient receives. Total outpatient visits should include all clinic visits, referred visits, observation services, outpatient surgeries, and emergency room visits.

Pain Management Program: A recognized clinical service or program providing specialized medical care, drugs or therapies for the management of acute or chronic pain or other distressing symptom, administered by specially trained physicians and other clinicians, to patients suffering from acute illness of diverse causes.

Palliative Care Inpatient Unit: An inpatient palliative care ward is a physically discreet, inpatient nursing unit where the focus is palliative care. The patient care focus is on symptom relief for complex patients who may be continuing to undergo primary treatment. Care is delivered by palliative medicine specialists.

Palliative care program: An organized program providing specialized medical care, drugs or therapies for the management of acute or chronic pain and/or the control of symptoms administered by specially trained physicians and other clinicians; and supportive care services, such as counseling on advanced directives, spiritual care, and social services, to patients with advanced disease and their families.

Patient Controlled Analgesia (PCA): Patient-controlled Analgesia (PCA) is intravenously administered pain medicine under the patient's control. The patient has a button on the end of a cord than can be pushed at will, whenever more pain medicine is desired. This button will only deliver more pain medicine at pre-determined intervals, as programmed by the doctor's order.

Patient education center: Written goals and objectives for the patient and/or family related to therapeutic regimens, medical procedures, and self care.

Patient representative services: Organized hospital services providing personnel through whom patients and staff can seek solutions to institutional problems affecting the delivery of high-quality care and services.

Payroll expenses: Includes all salaries and wages. All professional fees and salary expenditures excluded from payroll, such as employee benefits, are defined as nonpayroll expenses and are included in total expenses.

Pediatric Cardiac Surgery: Includes minimally invasive procedures that include surgery done with only a small incision or no incision at all, such as through a laparoscope or an endoscope and more invasive major surgical procedures that include open chest and open heart surgery.

Pediatric Cardiology Services: An organized clinical service offering diagnostic and interventional procedures to manage the full range of pediatric heart conditions.

Pediatric Diagnostic/invasive catheterization: (also called coronary angiography or coronary arteriography) is used to assist in diagnosing complex heart conditions. Cardiac angiography involves the insertion of a tiny catheter into the artery in the groin then carefully threading the catheter up into the aorta where the coronary arteries originate. Once the catheter is in place, a dye is injected which allows the cardiologist to see the size, shape, and distribution of the coronary arteries. These images are used to diagnose heart disease and to determine, among other things, whether or not surgery is indicated.

Pediatric intensive care: Provides care to pediatric patients that is of a more intensive nature than that usually provided to pediatric patients. The unit is staffed with specially trained personnel and contains monitoring and specialized support equipment for treatment of patients who, because of shock, trauma, or other life-threatening conditions, require intensified, comprehensive observation and care.

Pediatric Interventional cardiac catheterization: Non surgical procedure that utilizes the same basic principles as diagnostic catheterization and then uses advanced techniques to improve the heart's function. It can be a less-invasive alternative to heart surgery.

Pediatric medical-surgical care: Provides acute care to pediatric patients on the basis of physicians' orders and approved nursing care plans.

Personnel: Number of persons on the hospital payroll at the end of the reporting period. Personnel are recorded in *Hospital Statistics* as full-time equivalents (FTEs), which are calculated by adding the number of full-time personnel to one-half the number of part-time personnel, excluding medical and dental residents, interns, and other trainees. *Per 100 adjusted census* indicates the ratio of personnel to adjusted average daily census, calculated on a per-100 basis.

Physical rehabilitation inpatient care: Provides care encompassing a comprehensive array of restoration services for the disabled and all support services necessary to help patients attain their maximum functional capacity.

Physical rehabilitation outpatient services: Outpatient program providing medical, health-related, therapy, social, and/or vocational services to help disabled persons attain or retain their maximum functional capacity.

Population: Population refers to the residential population of the United States. This includes both civilian and military personnel. Note that population is being used to calculate the values *for community health indicators per 1000 population.*

Positron emission tomography/CT (PET/CT): Provides metabolic functional information for the monitoring of chemotherapy, radiotherapy and surgical planning.

Positron emission tomography scanner (PET): A nuclear medicine imaging technology which uses radioactive (positron emitting) isotopes created in a cyclotron or generator and computers to produce composite pictures of the brain and heart at work. PET scanning produces sectional images depicting metabolic activity or blood flow rather than anatomy.

Primary care department: A unit or clinic within the hospital that provides primary care services (e.g. general pediatric care, general internal medicine, family practice, gynecology) through hospital-salaried medical and/or nursing staff, focusing on evaluating and diagnosing medical problems and providing medical treatment on an outpatient basis.

Prosthetic and Orthotic Services: Services providing comprehensive prosthetic and orthotic evaluation, fitting, and training.

Proton beam therapy: A form of radiation therapy which administers proton beams. While producing the same biologic effects as x-ray beams, the energy distribution of protons differs from conventional x-ray beams in that they can be more precisely focused in tissue volumes in a three-dimensional pattern resulting in less surrounding tissue damage than conventional radiation therapy permitting administration of higher doses.

Psychiatric pediatric care: The branch of medicine focused on the diagnosis, treatment and prevention of mental, emotional and behavioral disorders in pediatric patients.

Psychiatric consultation-liaison services: Provides organized psychiatric consultation/liaison services to nonpsychiatric hospital staff and/or departments on psychological aspects of medical care that may be generic or specific to individual patients.

Psychiatric education services: Provides psychiatric educational services to community agencies and workers such as schools, police, courts, public health nurses, welfare agencies, clergy, and so forth. The purpose is to expand the mental health knowledge and competence of personnel not working in the mental health field and to promote good mental health through improved understanding, attitudes, and behavioral patterns.

Psychiatric emergency services: Services of facilities available on a 24-hour basis to provide immediate unscheduled out-patient care, diagnosis, evaluation, crisis intervention, and assistance to persons suffering acute emotional or mental distress.

Psychiatric geriatric services: Provides care to emotionally disturbed elderly patients, including those admitted for diagnosis and those admitted for treatment.

Psychiatric inpatient care: Provides acute or long-term care to emotionally disturbed patients, including patients admitted for diagnosis and those admitted for treatment

of psychiatric problems, on the basis of physicians' orders and approved nursing care plans. Long-term care may include intensive supervision to the chronically mentally ill, mentally disordered, or other mentally incompetent persons.

Psychiatric intensive outpatient services: A prescribed course of treatment in which the patient receives outpatient care no less than three times a week (which might include more than one service/day)

Psychiatric outpatient services: Provides medical care, including diagnosis and treatment, of psychiatric outpatients.

Psychiatric partial hospitalization program: Organized hospital services of intensive day/evening outpatient services of three hours of more duration, distinguished from other outpatient visits of one hour.

Psychiatric residential treatment: Overnight psychiatric care in conjunction with an intensive treatment program in a setting other than a hospital.

Radiology, diagnostic: The branch of radiology that deals with the utilization of all modalities of radiant energy in medical diagnoses and therapeutic procedures using radiologic guidance. This includes, but is not restricted to, imaging techniques and methodologies utilizing radiation emitted by x-ray tubes, radionnuclides, and ultrasonographic devices and the radiofrequency electromagnetic radiation emitted by atoms.

Radiology, therapeutic: The branch of medicine concerned with radioactive substances and using various techniques of visualization, with the diagnosis and treatment of disease using any of the various sources of radiant energy. Services could include: megavoltage radiation therapy; radioactive implants; stereotactic radiosurgery; therapeutic radioisotop facility; X-ray radiation therapy.

Registered nurse (RN): A nurse who has graduated from an approved school of nursing and who is currently registered by the state. RNs are responsible for the nature and quality of all nursing care that patients receive. In these tables, the number of RNs does not include those registered nurses more appropriately reported in other occupational categories, such as facility administrators, which are listed under *all other personnel* (Tables 1 and 2).

Rehabilitation services: A wide array of restoration services for disabled and recuperating patients, including all support services necessary to help them attain their maximum functional capacity.

Retirement housing: A facility which provides social activities to senior citizens, usually retired persons, who do not require health care but some short-term skilled nursing care may be provided. A retirement center may furnish housing and may also have acute hospital and long-term care facilities, or it may arrange for acute and long term care through affiliated institutions.

Robot-assisted walking therapy: A form of physical therapy that uses a robotic device to assist patients who are relearning how to walk.

Robotic surgery: The use of mechanical guidance devices to remotely manipulate surgical instrumentation.

Rural: A rural hospital is located outside a Metropolitan Statistical Area (MSA), as designated by the U.S. Office of Management and Budget (OMB) effective June 6, 2003. An urban area is a geographically defined, integrated social and economic unit with a large population nucleus. Micropolitan areas, which are new to the OMB June 6, 2003 definitions, continue to be classified as rural for purposes of this publication.

Rural Health Clinic: A clinic located in a rural, medically under-served area in the United States that has a separate reimbursement structure from the standard medical office under the Medicare and Medicaid programs.

Shaped beam radiation system: A precise, non-invasive treatment that involves targeting beams of radiation that mirrors the exact size and shape of a tumor at a specific area of a tumor to shrink or destroy cancerous cells. This procedure delivers a therapeutic dose of radiation that conforms precisely to the shape of the tumor, thus minimizing the risk to nearby tissues.

Simulated rehabilitation environment: Rehabilitation focused on retraining functional skills in a contextually appropriate environment (simulated home and community settings) or in a traditional setting (gymnasium) using motor learning principles.

Single photon emission computerized tomography (SPECT): A nuclear medicine imaging technology that combines existing technology of gamma camera imaging with computed tomographic imaging technology to provide a more precise and clear image.

Skilled nursing care: Provides non-acute medical and skilled nursing care services, therapy, and social services under the supervision of a licensed registered nurse on a 24-hour basis.

Sleep Center: Specially equipped and staffed center for the diagnosis and treatment of sleep disorders.

Social work services (could include): Organized services that are properly directed and sufficiently staffed by qualified individuals who provide assistance and counseling to patients and their families in dealing with social, emotional, and environmental problems associated with illness or disability, often in the context of financial or discharge planning coordination.

Sports medicine: Provision of diagnostic screening and assessment and clinical and rehabilitation services for the prevention and treatment of sports-related injuries.

Stereotactic radiosurgery: Stereotactic radiosurgery (SRS) is a radiotherapy modality that delivers a high dosage of radiation to a discrete treatment area in as few as one treatment session. Includes gamma knife, cyberknife, etc.

Support groups: A hospital sponsored program that allows a group of individuals with the same or similar problems who meet periodically to share experiences, problems, and solutions in order to support each other.

Surgical operations: Those surgical operations, whether major or minor, performed in the operating room(s). A surgical operation involving more than one surgical procedure is still considered only one surgical operation.

Swing bed services: A hospital bed that can be used to provide either acute or long-term care depending on community or patient needs. To be eligible a hospital must have a Medicare provider agreement in place, have fewer than 100 beds, be located in a rural area, do not have a 24 hour nursing service waiver in effect, have not been terminated from the program in the prior two years, and meet various service conditions.

Teen outreach services: A program focusing on the teenager which encourages an improved health status and a healthful lifestyle including physical, emotional, mental, social, spiritual and economic health through education, exercise, nutrition and health promotion.

Telehealth: A broad variety of technologies and tactics to deliver virtual medical, public health, health education delivery and support services using telecommunications technologies. Telehealth is used more commonly as it describes the wide range of diagnosis and management, education, and other related fields of health care. This includes, but are not limited to: dentistry, counseling, physical and occupational therapy, home health, chronic disease monitoring and management, disaster management and consumer and professional education.

Tissue transplant: See definition for Transplant services below.

Tobacco treatment/cessation program: Organized hospital services with the purpose of ending tobacco-use habits of patients addicted to tobacco/nicotine.

Transplant services: The branch of medicine that transfers an organ or tissue from one person to another or from one body part to another to replace a diseased structure or to restore function or to change appearance. Services could include: bone marrow transplant program; heart, lung, kidney, intestine, or tissue transplant. The other transplant services include transplant services other than bone marrow, heart, kidney, liver, lung, tissue and heart/lung or other multi-transplant surgeries.

Transportation to health facilities: A long-term care support service designed to assist the mobility of the elderly. Some programs offer improved financial access by offering reduced rates and barrier-free buses or vans with ramps and lifts to assist the elderly or handicapped; others offer subsidies for public transport systems or operate mini-bus services exclusively for use by senior citizens.

Trauma center (certified): A facility to provide emergency and specialized intensive care to critically ill and injured patients. **Level 1:** A regional resource trauma center, which is capable of providing total care for every aspect of injury and plays a leadership role in trauma research and education. **Level 2:** A community trauma center, which is capable of providing trauma care to all but the most severely injured patients who require highly specialized care. **Level 3:** A rural trauma hospital, which is capable of providing care to a large number of injury victims and can resuscitate and stabilize more severely injured patients so that they can be transported to Level 1 or 2 facilities.

Ultrasound: The use of acoustic waves above the range of 20,000 cycles per second to visualize internal body structures.

Urban: An urban hospital is located inside a Metropolitan Statistical Area (MSA), designated by the U.S. Office of Management and Budget effective June 6, 2003. An urban areas is a geographically defined, integrated social and economic unit with a large population base. Micropolitan areas, which are new to the OMB June 6, 2003 definitions, are not considered to be urban for purposes of this publication.

Urgent care center: A facility that provides care and treatment for problems that are not life-threatening but require attention over the short term.

Violence prevention programs for the workplace: A violence prevention program with goals and objectives for preventing workplace violence against staff and patients.

Violence prevention programs for the community: An organized program that attempts to make a positive impact on the type(s) of violence a community is experiencing. For example, it can assist victims of violent crimes, e.g., rape, or incidents, e.g., bullying, to hospital or to community services to prevent further victimization or retaliation. A program that targets the underlying circumstances that contribute to violence such as poor housing, insufficient job training, and/or substance abuse through means such as direct involvement and support, education, mentoring, anger management, crisis intervention and training programs would also qualify.

Virtual colonoscopy: Noninvasive screening procedure used to visualize, analyze and detect cancerous or potentially cancerous polyps in the colon.

Volunteer services department: An organized hospital department responsible for coordinating the services of volunteers working within the institution.

Women's health center/services: An area set aside for coordinated education and treatment services specifically for and promoted to women as provided by this special unit. Services may or may not include obstetrics but include a range of services other than OB.

Wound Management Services: Services for patients with chronic wounds and nonhealing wounds often resulting from diabetes, poor circulation, improper seating and immunocompromising conditions. The goals are to progress chronic wounds through stages of healing, reduce and eliminate infections, increase physical function to minimize complications from current wounds and prevent future chronic wounds. Wound management services are provided on an inpatient or outpatient basis, depending on the intensity of service needed.

2017 AHA Annual Survey
American Hospital Association

Please return to:
AHA Annual Survey
155 N Wacker Drive
Suite 400
Chicago IL 60606

A. REPORTING PERIOD (please refer to the instructions and definitions at the end of this questionnaire)

Report data for a full 12-month period, preferably your last completed fiscal year (365 days). Be consistent in using the same reporting period for responses throughout various sections of this survey.

1. Reporting Period used (beginning and ending date) ...... __ __ / __ __ / __ __ __ __   to __ __ / __ __ / __ __ __ __
            Month Day   Year   Month Day   Year

2. a. Were you in operation 12 full months
      at the end of your reporting period? .... YES ☐ NO ☐

   b. Number of days open
      during reporting period .... _____

3. Indicate the beginning of your current fiscal year .... __ __ / __ __ / __ __ __ __
            Month Day Year

B. ORGANIZATIONAL STRUCTURE

1. CONTROL

Indicate the type of organization that is responsible for establishing policy for overall operation of your hospital. CHECK ONLY ONE:

Government, nonfederal
- ☐ 12 State
- ☐ 13 County
- ☐ 14 City
- ☐ 15 City-County
- ☐ 16 Hospital district or authority

Nongovernment, not-for-profit (NFP)
- ☐ 21 Church-operated
- ☐ 23 Other not-for-profit (including NFP Corporation)

Investor-owned, for-profit
- ☐ 31 Individual
- ☐ 32 Partnership
- ☐ 33 Corporation

Government, federal
- ☐ 41 Air Force
- ☐ 42 Army
- ☐ 43 Navy
- ☐ 44 Public Health Service
- ☐ 45 Veterans' Affairs
- ☐ 46 Federal other than 41-45 or 47-48
- ☐ 47 PHS Indian Service
- ☐ 48 Department of Justice

2. SERVICE

Indicate the ONE category that BEST describes your hospital or the type of service it provides to the MAJORITY of patients:

- ☐ 10 General medical and surgical
- ☐ 11 Hospital unit of an institution (prison hospital, college infirmary)
- ☐ 12 Hospital unit within a facility for persons with intellectual disabilities
- ☐ 13 Surgical
- ☐ 22 Psychiatric
- ☐ 33 Tuberculosis and other respiratory diseases
- ☐ 41 Cancer
- ☐ 42 Heart
- ☐ 44 Obstetrics and gynecology
- ☐ 45 Eye, ear, nose, and throat

- ☐ 46 Rehabilitation
- ☐ 47 Orthopedic
- ☐ 48 Chronic disease
- ☐ 62 Intellectual disabilities
- ☐ 80 Acute long-term care hospital
- ☐ 82 Alcoholism and other chemical dependency
- ☐ 49 Other - specify treatment area: _____

B. ORGANIZATIONAL STRUCTURE (continued)

3. OTHER

a. Does your hospital restrict admissions primarily to children? .... YES ☐   NO ☐

b. Does the hospital itself operate subsidiary corporations? .... YES ☐   NO ☐

c. Is the hospital contract managed? If yes, please provide the name, city, and state of the organization.... YES ☐   NO ☐

Name: _____   City: _____   State: _____

d. Is the hospital a participant in a network? ....YES ☐   NO ☐

If yes, please provide the name, city, state and telephone number of the network(s).

Name: _____   City: _____   State: _____ Telephone_____

Name: _____   City: _____   State: _____ Telephone_____

Name: _____   City: _____   State: _____ Telephone_____

e. Is your hospital owned in whole or in part by physicians or a physician group?............................... YES ☐   NO ☐

f. If you checked 80 Acute long-term care hospital (LTCH) in Section B2 (Service), please indicate if you are a freestanding LTCH or a LTCH arranged within a general acute care hospital.

☐ Free standing LTCH   ☐ LTCH arranged in a general acute care hospital

If you are arranged in a general acute care hospital, what is your host hospital's name?

Name_____ City_____ State_____

C. FACILITIES AND SERVICES

For each service or facility listed below, please check all the categories that describe how each item is provided **as of the last day of the reporting period**. Check all categories that apply for an item. If you check column (1) C1-19, please include the number of **staffed beds**.
The sum of the beds reported in 1-19 should equal Section E(1b), beds set up and staffed on page 11.

	(1) Owned or provided by my hospital or its subsidiary	(2) Provided by my Health System (in my local community)	(3) Provided through a formal contractual arrangement or joint venture with another provider that is not in my system (in my local community)	(4) Do Not Provide
1. General medical-surgical care ....(#Beds_____)	☐	☐	☐	☐
2. Pediatric medical-surgical care ....(#Beds_____)	☐	☐	☐	☐
3. Obstetrics..............[Hospital level of unit (1-3):(_____)] (#Beds_____)	☐	☐	☐	☐
4. Medical-surgical intensive care.....................(#Beds_____)	☐	☐	☐	☐
5. Cardiac intensive care ....(#Beds_____)	☐	☐	☐	☐
6. Neonatal intensive care ....(#Beds_____)	☐	☐	☐	☐
7. Neonatal intermediate care...........................(#Beds_____)	☐	☐	☐	☐
8. Pediatric intensive care................................(#Beds_____)	☐	☐	☐	☐
9. Burn care..(#Beds_____)	☐	☐	☐	☐
10. Other special care _____.............(#Beds_____)	☐	☐	☐	☐
11. Other intensive care_____ ....(#Beds_____)	☐	☐	☐	☐
12. Physical rehabilitation.................................(#Beds_____)	☐	☐	☐	☐
13. Alcoholism-chemical dependency care ....(#Beds_____)	☐	☐	☐	☐
14. Psychiatric care ....(#Beds_____)	☐	☐	☐	☐
15. Skilled nursing care ....(#Beds_____)	☐	☐	☐	☐
16. Intermediate nursing care ....(#Beds_____)	☐	☐	☐	☐
17. Acute long-term care ....(#Beds_____)	☐	☐	☐	☐
18. Other long-term care ....(#Beds_____)	☐	☐	☐	☐
19. Other care _____ ....(#Beds_____)	☐	☐	☐	☐
20. Adult day care program	☐	☐	☐	☐
21. Airborne infection isolation room....................(#rooms_____)	☐	☐	☐	☐
22. Alcoholism-chemical dependency care services				
a. Alcoholism-chemical dependency pediatric services ..(#Beds_____)	☐	☐	☐	☐
b. Alcoholism-chemical dependency outpatient services....................	☐	☐	☐	☐
c. Alcoholism-chemical dependency partial hospitalization services	☐	☐	☐	☐
23. Alzheimer center..	☐	☐	☐	☐
24. Ambulance services	☐	☐	☐	☐
25. Ambulatory surgery center...	☐	☐	☐	☐
26. Arthritis treatment center	☐	☐	☐	☐
27. Assisted living...	☐	☐	☐	☐
28. Auxiliary..	☐	☐	☐	☐
29. Bariatric/weight control services...............................	☐	☐	☐	☐
30. Birthing room/LDR room/LDRP room	☐	☐	☐	☐
31. Blood donor center	☐	☐	☐	☐
32. Breast cancer screening/mammograms.......................	☐	☐	☐	☐

C. FACILITIES AND SERVICES (continued)

	(1) Owned or provided by my hospital or its subsidiary	(2) Provided by my Health System (in my local community)	(3) Provided through a formal contractual arrangement or joint venture with another provider that is not in my system (in my local community)	(4) Do Not Provide
33. Cardiology and cardiac surgery services				
a. Adult cardiology services	☐	☐	☐	☐
b. Pediatric cardiology services	☐	☐	☐	☐
c. Adult diagnostic catheterization	☐	☐	☐	☐
d. Pediatric diagnostic catheterization	☐	☐	☐	☐
e. Adult interventional cardiac catheterization	☐	☐	☐	☐
f. Pediatric interventional cardiac catheterization	☐	☐	☐	☐
g. Adult cardiac surgery	☐	☐	☐	☐
h. Pediatric cardiac surgery	☐	☐	☐	☐
i. Adult cardiac electrophysiology	☐	☐	☐	☐
j. Pediatric cardiac electrophysiology	☐	☐	☐	☐
k. Cardiac rehabilitation	☐	☐	☐	☐
34. Case management	☐	☐	☐	☐
35. Chaplaincy/pastoral care services	☐	☐	☐	☐
36. Chemotherapy	☐	☐	☐	☐
37. Children's wellness program	☐	☐	☐	☐
38. Chiropractic services	☐	☐	☐	☐
39. Community outreach	☐	☐	☐	☐
40. Complementary and alternative medicine services	☐	☐	☐	☐
41. Computer assisted orthopedic surgery (CAOS)	☐	☐	☐	☐
42. Crisis prevention	☐	☐	☐	☐
43. Dental services	☐	☐	☐	☐
44. Emergency services				
a. Emergency department	☐	☐	☐	☐
b. Pediatric emergency department	☐	☐	☐	☐
c. Trauma center (certified)........ [Hospital level of unit (1-3) _____]	☐	☐	☐	☐
45. Enabling services	☐	☐	☐	☐
46. Endoscopic services				
a. Optical colonoscopy	☐	☐	☐	☐
b. Endoscopic ultrasound	☐	☐	☐	☐
c. Ablation of Barrett's esophagus	☐	☐	☐	☐
d. Esophageal impedance study	☐	☐	☐	☐
e. Endoscopic retrograde cholangiopancreatography (ERCP)	☐	☐	☐	☐
47. Enrollment (insurance) assistance services	☐	☐	☐	☐
48. Extracorporeal shock wave lithotripter (ESWL)	☐	☐	☐	☐
49. Fertility clinic	☐	☐	☐	☐
50. Fitness center	☐	☐	☐	☐
51. Freestanding outpatient care center	☐	☐	☐	☐
52. Geriatric services	☐	☐	☐	☐
53. Health fair	☐	☐	☐	☐
54. Community health education	☐	☐	☐	☐

C. FACILITIES AND SERVICES (continued)

	(1) Owned or provided by my hospital or its subsidiary	(2) Provided by my Health System (in my local community)	(3) Provided through a formal contractual arrangement or joint venture with another provider that is not in my system (in my local community)	(4) Do Not Provide
55. Genetic testing/counseling	☐	☐	☐	☐
56. Health screenings	☐	☐	☐	☐
57. Health research	☐	☐	☐	☐
58. Hemodialysis	☐	☐	☐	☐
59. HIV/AIDS services	☐	☐	☐	☐
60. Home health services	☐	☐	☐	☐
61. Hospice program	☐	☐	☐	☐
62. Hospital-based outpatient care center services	☐	☐	☐	☐
63. Immunization program	☐	☐	☐	☐
64. Indigent care clinic	☐	☐	☐	☐
65. Linguistic/translation services	☐	☐	☐	☐
66. Meals on wheels	☐	☐	☐	☐
67. Mobile health services	☐	☐	☐	☐
68. Neurological services	☐	☐	☐	☐
69. Nutrition program	☐	☐	☐	☐
70. Occupational health services	☐	☐	☐	☐
71. Oncology services	☐	☐	☐	☐
72. Orthopedic services	☐	☐	☐	☐
73. Outpatient surgery	☐	☐	☐	☐
74. Pain management program	☐	☐	☐	☐
75. Palliative care program	☐	☐	☐	☐
76. Palliative care inpatient unit	☐	☐	☐	☐
77. Patient controlled analgesia (PCA)	☐	☐	☐	☐
78. Patient education center	☐	☐	☐	☐
79. Patient representative services	☐	☐	☐	☐
80. Physical rehabilitation services				
a. Assistive technology center	☐	☐	☐	☐
b. Electrodiagnostic services	☐	☐	☐	☐
c. Physical rehabilitation outpatient services	☐	☐	☐	☐
d. Prosthetic and orthotic services	☐	☐	☐	☐
e. Robot-assisted walking therapy	☐	☐	☐	☐
f. Simulated rehabilitation environment	☐	☐	☐	☐
81. Primary care department	☐	☐	☐	☐
82. Psychiatric services				
a. Psychiatric consultation-liaison services	☐	☐	☐	☐
b. Psychiatric pediatric care (#Beds____)	☐	☐	☐	☐
c. Psychiatric geriatric care (#Beds____)	☐	☐	☐	☐
d. Psychiatric education services	☐	☐	☐	☐
e. Psychiatric emergency services	☐	☐	☐	☐
f. Psychiatric outpatient services	☐	☐	☐	☐
g. Psychiatric intensive outpatient services	☐	☐	☐	☐
h. Psychiatric partial hospitalization services – adult	☐	☐	☐	☐
i. Psychiatric partial hospitalization services – pediatric	☐	☐	☐	☐
j. Psychiatric residential treatment – adult	☐	☐	☐	☐
k. Psychiatric residential treatment – pediatric	☐	☐	☐	☐

C. FACILITIES AND SERVICES (continued)

	(1) Owned or provided by my hospital or its subsidiary	(2) Provided by my Health System (in my local community)	(3) Provided through a formal contractual arrangement or joint venture with another provider that is not in my system (in my local community)	(4) Do Not Provide
83. Radiology, diagnostic				
a. CT Scanner	☐	☐	☐	☐
b. Diagnostic radioisotope facility	☐	☐	☐	☐
c. Electron beam computed tomography (EBCT)	☐	☐	☐	☐
d. Full-field digital mammography (FFDM)	☐	☐	☐	☐
e. Magnetic resonance imaging (MRI)	☐	☐	☐	☐
f. Intraoperative magnetic resonance imaging	☐	☐	☐	☐
g. Magnetoencephalography (MEG)	☐	☐	☐	☐
h. Multi-slice spiral computed tomography (<64+ slice CT)	☐	☐	☐	☐
i. Multi-slice spiral computed tomography (64+ slice CT)	☐	☐	☐	☐
j. Positron emission tomography (PET)	☐	☐	☐	☐
k. Positron emission tomography/CT (PET/CT)	☐	☐	☐	☐
l. Single photon emission computerized tomography (SPECT)	☐	☐	☐	☐
m. Ultrasound	☐	☐	☐	☐
84. Radiology, therapeutic				
a. Image-guided radiation therapy (IGRT)	☐	☐	☐	☐
b. Intensity-modulated radiation therapy (IMRT)	☐	☐	☐	☐
c. Proton beam therapy	☐	☐	☐	☐
d. Shaped beam radiation system	☐	☐	☐	☐
e. Stereotactic radiosurgery	☐	☐	☐	☐
85. Retirement housing	☐	☐	☐	☐
86. Robotic surgery	☐	☐	☐	☐
87. Rural health clinic	☐	☐	☐	☐
88. Sleep center	☐	☐	☐	☐
89. Social work services	☐	☐	☐	☐
90. Sports medicine	☐	☐	☐	☐
91. Support groups	☐	☐	☐	☐
92. Swing bed services	☐	☐	☐	☐
93. Teen outreach services	☐	☐	☐	☐
94. Tobacco treatment/cessation program	☐	☐	☐	☐
95. Telehealth				
a. Consultation and office visits	☐	☐	☐	☐
b. eICU	☐	☐	☐	☐
c. Stroke care	☐	☐	☐	☐
d. Psychiatric and addiction treatment	☐	☐	☐	☐
e. Remote patient monitoring				
1. Post-discharge	☐	☐	☐	☐
2. Ongoing chronic care management	☐	☐	☐	☐

C. FACILITIES AND SERVICES (continued)

	(1) Owned or provided by my hospital or its subsidiary	(2) Provided by my Health System (in my local community)	(3) Provided through a formal contractual arrangement or joint venture with another provider that is not in my system (in my local community)	(4) Do Not Provide
96. Transplant services				
a. Bone marrow	☐	☐	☐	☐
b. Heart	☐	☐	☐	☐
c. Kidney	☐	☐	☐	☐
d. Liver	☐	☐	☐	☐
e. Lung	☐	☐	☐	☐
f. Tissue	☐	☐	☐	☐
g. Other	☐	☐	☐	☐
97. Transportation to health services	☐	☐	☐	☐
98. Urgent care center	☐	☐	☐	☐
99. Violence prevention programs				
a. For the workplace	☐	☐	☐	☐
b. For the community	☐	☐	☐	☐
100. Virtual colonoscopy	☐	☐	☐	☐
101. Volunteer services department	☐	☐	☐	☐
102. Women's health center/services	☐	☐	☐	☐
103. Wound management services	☐	☐	☐	☐

104. Does your organization routinely integrate behavioral health services in the following care areas?
Integration ranges from co-located physical and behavioral health providers, with some screening and treatment planning, to fully integrated care where behavioral and physical health providers function as a true team in a shared practice.

	Yes	No
a. Emergency services	☐	☐
b. Primary care services	☐	☐
c. Acute inpatient care	☐	☐
d. Extended care	☐	☐

105. In which of the following physician arrangements does your hospital or system/network participate? Column 3 refers to the networks that were identified in section B, question 3d. For hospital level physician arrangements that are reported in column 1, please report the number of physicians involved.

		(1) My Hospital	(2) My Health System	(3) My Health Network	(4) Do Not Provide
a. Independent Practice Association (IPA)	(# of physicians _____)	☐	☐	☐	☐
b. Group practice without walls	(# of physicians _____)	☐	☐	☐	☐
c. Open Physician-Hospital Organization (PHO)	(# of physicians _____)	☐	☐	☐	☐
d. Closed Physician-Hospital Organization (PHO)	(# of physicians _____)	☐	☐	☐	☐
e. Management Service Organization (MSO)	(# of physicians _____)	☐	☐	☐	☐
f. Integrated Salary Model	(# of physicians _____)	☐	☐	☐	☐
g. Equity Model	(# of physicians _____)	☐	☐	☐	☐
h. Foundation	(# of physicians _____)	☐	☐	☐	☐
i. Other, please specify _____	(# of physicians _____)	☐	☐	☐	☐

106. Looking across all the relationships identified in question 105, what is the total number of physicians (count each physician only once) that are engaged in an arrangement with your hospital that allows for joint contracting with payors or shared responsibility for financial risk or clinical performance between the hospital and physician? (arrangement may be at the hospital, system or network level)

_____ number of physicians

C. FACILITIES AND SERVICES (continued)

107a. Does your hospital participate in any joint venture arrangements with physicians or physician groups? YES ☐ NO ☐

107b. If your hospital participates in any joint ventures with physicians or physician groups, please indicate which types of services are involved in those joint ventures. (Check all that apply)

   1. ☐ Limited service hospital
   2. ☐ Ambulatory surgical centers
   3. ☐ Imaging centers
   4. ☐ Other _____

107c. If you selected 'a. Limited service hospital', please tell us what type(s) of services are provided. (Check all that apply)

   1. ☐ Cardiac
   2. ☐ Orthopedic
   3. ☐ Surgical
   4. ☐ Other _____

107d. Does your hospital participate in joint venture arrangements with organizations other than physician groups? YES ☐ NO ☐

D. INSURANCE AND ALTERNATIVE PAYMENT MODELS

INSURANCE

1. Does your hospital/system have a health plan license? Yes ☐ No ☐

    a. If yes, in what states? States: _____

    b. Does your hospital/system partner with an insurer to offer insurance products? Yes ☐ No ☐

    c. Does your hospital/system offer insurance products (either via ownership or joint ventures)? Yes ☐ No ☐

    d. If yes, please indicate the insurance products and the total medical enrollment (check all that apply)

Insurance Products	Hospital	System	JV	Medical Enrollment	No	Do not know
1. Medicare Advantage	☐	☐	☐	_____	☐	☐
2. Medicaid Managed Care	☐	☐	☐	_____	☐	☐
3. Health Insurance Marketplace ("exchange")	☐	☐	☐	_____	☐	☐
4. Other Individual Market	☐	☐	☐	_____	☐	☐
5. Small Group	☐	☐	☐	_____	☐	☐
6. Large Group	☐	☐	☐	_____	☐	☐

If you have answered 'no' to all parts of question 1, please skip to question 5.

2. Does your **health plan** make capitated payments to physicians either within or outside of your network for specific groups or enrollees?

    a. Physicians within your network Yes ☐ No ☐ Do not know ☐

    b. Physicians outside your network Yes ☐ No ☐ Do not know ☐

3. Does your **health plan** make bundled payments to providers in your network or to outside providers?

    a. Providers within your network Yes ☐ No ☐ Do not know ☐

    b. Providers outside your network Yes ☐ No ☐ Do not know ☐

4. Does your **health plan** offer shared risk contracts to either providers in your network or to outside providers? (i.e., other than capitation or bundled payment.)

    a. Providers within your network Yes ☐ No ☐ Do not know ☐

    b. Providers outside your network Yes ☐ No ☐ Do not know ☐

D. INSURANCE AND ALTERNATIVE PAYMENT MODELS (continued)

ALTERNATIVE PAYMENT MODELS

5. What percentage of your **hospital's** patient revenue is paid on a capitated basis? _____ %

    a. In total, how many enrollees do you serve under capitated contracts?   Total enrollees: _____

6. Does your **hospital** participate in a bundled payment program involving care settings outside of the hospital (e.g., physician, outpatient, post-acute)?   Yes ☐   No ☐

    a. If yes, does your **hospital** share upside or downside risk for any of those outside providers?   Yes ☐   No ☐

    b. If yes, what percentage of the **hospital's** patient revenue is paid through bundled payment arrangements?   _____ %

7. What percentage of your **hospital's** patient revenue is paid on a shared risk basis (other than capitated or bundled payments)?   _____ %

8. Does your **hospital** contract directly with employers or a coalition of employers to provide care on a capitated, predetermined, or shared risk basis?   Yes ☐   No ☐

9. Does your **hospital** have contracts with commercial payors where payment is tied to performance on quality/safety metrics?   Yes ☐   No ☐

10. Has your **hospital** or **health care system** established an accountable care organization (ACO)?   Yes ☐   No ☐

    a. If yes, please indicate the patient populations that are served in the ACO. (check all that apply)

        1. ☐ Medicaid
        2. ☐ Medicare
        3. ☐ Privately insured
        4. ☐ Direct-to-Employer
        5. ☐ Other, please specify: _____

11. Do any hospitals and/or physician groups with your system, or the system itself, plan to participate in any of the following risk arrangements in the next three years? (check all that apply)

        a. ☐ Shared savings/losses
        b. ☐ Bundled payment
        c. ☐ Capitation
        d. ☐ ACO (ownership)
        e. ☐ ACO (joint venture)
        f. ☐ Health plan (ownership)
        g. ☐ Health plan (joint venture)
        h. ☐ Other, please specify: _____
        i. ☐ None

12. Does your hospital/system have an established medical home program?

        a. Hospital   Yes ☐   No ☐
        b. System   Yes ☐   No ☐

13. Has your hospital/system established a clinically integrated network?

        a. Hospital   Yes ☐   No ☐
        b. System   Yes ☐   No ☐

E. TOTAL FACILITY BEDS, UTILIZATION, FINANCES, AND STAFFING

Please report beds, utilization, financial, and staffing data for the 12-month period that is consistent with the period reported on page 1. Report financial data for reporting period only. Include within your operations all activities that are wholly owned by the hospital, including subsidiary corporations regardless of where the activity is physically located. Please do not include within your operations distinct and separate divisions that may be owned by your hospital's parent corporation. If final figures are not available, please estimate. Round to the nearest dollar. Report all personnel who were on the payroll and whose payroll expenses are reported in E3f. (Please refer to specific definitions on pages 25-27.)

> **Fill out column (2) if hospital owns and operates a nursing home type unit/facility.**
> **Column (1) should be the combined total of hospital plus nursing home unit/facility.**

1. BEDS AND UTILIZATION

	(1) Total Facility	(2) Nursing Home Unit/Facility
a. Total licensed beds		
b. Beds set up and staffed for use at the end of the reporting period		
c. Bassinets set up and staffed for use at the end of the reporting period		
d. Births (exclude fetal deaths)		
e. Admissions (exclude newborns; include neonatal & swing admissions)		
f. Inpatient days (exclude newborns; include neonatal & swing days)		
g. Emergency department visits		
h. Total outpatient visits (include emergency department visits & outpatient surgeries)		
i. Inpatient surgical operations		
j. Number of operating rooms		
k. Outpatient surgical operations		

2. MEDICARE/MEDICAID UTILIZATION

	(1) Total Facility	(2) Nursing Home Unit/Facility
a1. Total Medicare (Title XVIII) inpatient discharges (including Medicare Managed Care)		
a2. How many Medicare inpatient discharges were Medicare Managed Care?		
b1. Total Medicare (Title XVIII) inpatient days (including Medicare Managed Care)		
b2. How many Medicare inpatient days were Medicare Managed Care?		
c1. Total Medicaid (Title XIX) inpatient discharges (including Medicaid Managed Care)		
c2. How many Medicaid inpatient discharges were Medicaid Managed Care?		
d1. Total Medicaid (Title XIX) inpatient days (including Medicaid Managed Care)		
d2. How many Medicaid inpatient days were Medicaid Managed Care?		

3. FINANCIAL

	(1) Total Facility	(2) Nursing Home Unit/Facility
*a. Net patient revenue (treat bad debt as a deduction from gross revenue)	.00	.00
*b. Tax appropriations	.00	
*c. Other operating revenue	.00	
*d. Nonoperating revenue	.00	
*e. TOTAL REVENUE (add 3a thru 3d)	.00	.00
f. Payroll expense (only)	.00	.00
g. Employee benefits	.00	.00
h. Depreciation expense (for reporting period only)	.00	
i. Interest expense	.00	
j. Pharmacy expense	.00	
k. Supply expense (other than pharmacy)	.00	
l. All other expenses	.00	
m. TOTAL EXPENSES (add 3f thru 3l. Exclude bad debt)	.00	.00

E. TOTAL FACILITY BEDS, UTILIZATION, FINANCES, AND STAFFING (continued)

4. REVENUE BY TYPE

*a. Total gross inpatient revenue .... _____ .00

*b. Total gross outpatient revenue .... _____ .00

*c. Total gross patient revenue .... _____ .00

5. UNCOMPENSATED CARE & PROVIDER TAXES

*a. Bad debt (Revenue forgone at full established rates. Include in gross revenue.) .... _____ .00

*b. Financial assistance (Includes charity care) (Revenue forgone at full-established rates. Include in gross
revenue.) .... _____ .00

*c. Is your bad debt (5a) reported on the basis of full charges?   Yes ☐   No ☐

*d. Does your state have a provider Medicaid tax/assessment program?   Yes ☐   No ☐

*e. If yes, please report the total gross amount paid into the program. .... _____ .00

*f. Due to differing accounting standards, please indicate whether the provider tax/assessment amount is included in:

    1. Total expenses   Yes ☐   No ☐

    2. Deductions from net patient revenue   Yes ☐   No ☐

6. REVENUE BY PAYOR (report total facility gross & net figures)

	(1) Gross	(2) Net
*a. GOVERNMENT		
(1) Medicare:		
a) Fee for service patient revenue	.00	.00
b) Managed care revenue	.00	.00
c) Total (a + b)	.00	.00
(2) Medicaid:		
a) Fee for service patient revenue	.00	.00
b) Managed care revenue	.00	.00
c) Medicaid Graduate Medical Education (GME) payments		.00
d) Medicaid Disproportionate Share Hospital Payments (DSH)		.00
e) Medicaid Supplemental Payments (not including Medicaid Disproportionate Share Hospital (DSH) Payments		.00
f) Other Medicaid		.00
g) Total (a thru f)	.00	.00
(3) Other government	.00	.00
*b. NONGOVERNMENT		
(1) Self-pay	.00	.00
(2) Third-party payors:		
a) Managed care (includes HMO and PPO)	.00	.00
b) Other third-party payors	.00	.00
c) Total third-party payors (a + b)	.00	.00
(3) All other nongovernment	.00	.00
*c. TOTAL	.00	.00

(Total gross should equal 4c on page 12. Total net should equal 3a on page 11.)

	(1) Inpatient	(2) Outpatient
*d. If you report Medicaid Supplemental Payments on line 6.a(2)e, please break the payment total into inpatient and outpatient care.	.00	.00

*e. If you are a government owned facility (control codes 12-16), does your facility
participate in the Medicaid intergovernmental transfer or certified public expenditures
program?   Yes ☐   No ☐

	(1) Gross	(2) Net
*f. If yes, please report gross and net revenue.	.00	.00

Are the financial data on pages 11-13 from your audited financial statement?   Yes ☐   No ☐

E. TOTAL FACILITY BEDS, UTILIZATION, FINANCES, AND STAFFING (continued)

7. FIXED ASSETS

a. Property, plant and equipment at <u>cost</u>.. _____.00

b. Accumulated <u>depreciation</u>.. _____.00

c. Net property, plant and equipment (a–b)... _____.00

d. Total gross square feet of your physical plant used for or in support of your healthcare activities...................... _____

8. TOTAL CAPITAL EXPENSES

Include all expenses used to acquire assets, including buildings, remodeling projects, equipment, or property .... _____.00

9. INFORMATION TECHNOLOGY AND CYBERSECURITY

a. IT operating expense .... _____.00

b. IT capital expense.. _____.00

c. Number of employed IT staff (in FTEs) .... _____

d. Number of outsourced IT staff (in FTEs) .... _____

*e. What percentage of your IT budget is spent on security?... _____%

*f. Which of the following cybersecurity measures does your hospital or health system currently deploy?
(check all that apply)

    1. Annual risk assessment.. ☐
    2. Incident response plan .... ☐
    3. Intrusion detection systems .... ☐
    4. Mobile device encryption .... ☐
    5. Mobile device data wiping... ☐
    6. Penetration testing to identify security vulnerabilities .... ☐
    7. Strong password requirements .... ☐
    8. Two-factor authentication .... ☐

*g. Does your hospital or health system board oversight of risk
management and reduction specifically include consideration of   Yes ☐   No ☐   Unsure ☐
cybersecurity risk?

*h. Does your hospital or health system have cybersecurity insurance?   Yes ☐   No ☐   Unsure ☐

*i. Is your hospital or health system participating in cybersecurity
information-sharing activities with an outside information sharing and   Yes ☐   No ☐   Unsure ☐
analysis organization to identify threats and vulnerabilities?

---

* These data will be treated as confidential and not released without written permission. AHA will however, share these data with your respective state hospital association and, if requested, with your appropriate metropolitan/regional association.

For members of the Catholic Health Association of the United States (CHA), AHA will also share these data with CHA unless there are objections expressed by checking this box ☐

E. TOTAL FACILITY BEDS, UTILIZATION, FINANCES, AND STAFFING (continued)

10. STAFFING

Report full-time (35 hours or more) and part-time (less than 35 hours) personnel who were on the hospital/facility **payroll at the end of your reporting period.** Include members of religious orders for whom dollar equivalents were reported. Exclude private-duty nurses, volunteers, and all personnel whose salary is financed entirely by outside research grants. Exclude physicians and dentists who are paid on a fee basis. FTE is the total number of hours worked by all employees over the full (12 month) reporting period divided by the normal number of hours worked by a full-time employee for that same time period. For example, if your hospital considers a normal workweek for a full-time employee to be 40 hours, a total of 2,080 would be worked over a full year (52 weeks). If the total number of hours worked by all employees on the payroll is 208,000, then the number of Full-Time Equivalents (FTE) is 100 (employees). The FTE calculation for a specific occupational category such as registered nurses is exactly the same. The calculation for each occupational category should be based on the number of hours worked by staff employed in that specific category.

For each occupational category, please report the number of staff vacancies as of the last day of your reporting period. A vacancy is defined as a budgeted staff position which is unfilled as of the last day of the reporting period and for which the hospital is actively seeking either a full-time or part-time permanent replacement. Personnel who work in more than one area should be included only in the category of their primary responsibility and should be counted only once.

		(1) Full-Time (35 hr/wk or more) On Payroll	(2) Part-Time (Less than 35hr/wk) On Payroll	(3) FTE	(4) Vacancies
a.	Physicians				
b.	Dentists				
c.	Medical and dental residents/interns				
d.	Other trainees				
e.	Registered nurses				
f.	Licensed practical (vocational) nurses				
g.	Nursing assistive personnel				
h.	Radiology technicians				
i.	Laboratory technicians				
j.	Pharmacists licensed				
k.	Pharmacy technicians				
l.	Respiratory therapists				
m.	All other personnel				
n.	Total facility personnel (add 10a through 10m)				

(Total facility personnel (a-n) should include hospital and nursing home type unit/facility, if applicable.

Nursing home type unit/facility personnel should also be reported separately in 10o and 10p.)

o. Nursing home type unit/facility registered nurses				
p. Total nursing home type unit/facility personnel				

q. For your employed RN FTEs reported above (E.10.e, column 3) please report the number of full-time equivalents who are involved in direct patient care.

Number of direct
_____ patient care FTEs

E. TOTAL FACILITY BEDS, UTILIZATION, FINANCES, AND STAFFING (continued)

11. PRIVILEGED PHYSICIANS

Report the total number of physicians with privileges at your hospital by type of relationship with the hospital. <u>The sum of the physicians reported in 11a-11f should equal the total number of privileged physicians (11g) in the hospital.</u>

	(1) Total Employed	(2) Total Individual Contract	(3) Total Group Contract	(4) Not Employed or Under Contract	(5) Total Privileged (add columns 1-4)
a. Primary care (general practitioner, general internal medicine, family practice, general pediatrics, obstetrics/gynecology, geriatrics)	_____	_____	_____	_____	_____
b. Emergency medicine	_____	_____	_____	_____	_____
c. Hospitalist	_____	_____	_____	_____	_____
d. Intensivist	_____	_____	_____	_____	_____
e. Radiologist/pathologist/anesthesiologist	_____	_____	_____	_____	_____
f. Other specialist	_____	_____	_____	_____	_____
g. Total (add 11a-11f)	_____	_____	_____	_____	_____

12. HOSPITALISTS

a. Do hospitalists provide care for patients in your hospital? (if no, please skip to 13) .... Yes ☐ No ☐ (If yes, please report in E.11.c)

b. If yes, please report the total number of full-time equivalent (FTE) hospitalists .... _____ FTE

13. INTENSIVISTS

a. Do intensivists provide care for patients in your hospital? (if no, please skip to 14) .... Yes ☐ No ☐ (If yes, please report in E.11.d)

b. If yes, please report the total number of FTE intensivists and assign them to the following areas. Please indicate whether the intensive care area is closed to intensivists. (Meaning that only intensivists are authorized to care for ICU patients.)

		FTE	Closed to Intensivists
1.	Medical-surgical intensive care	_____	☐
2.	Cardiac intensive care	_____	☐
3.	Neonatal intensive care	_____	☐
4.	Pediatric intensive care	_____	☐
5.	Other intensive care	_____	☐
6.	Total	_____	

14. ADVANCED PRACTICE REGISTERED NURSES/PHYSICIAN ASSISTANTS

a. Do advanced practice nurses/physician assistants provide care for patients in your hospital? (if no, please skip to 15) YES ☐ NO ☐

b. If yes, please report the number of full time, part time and FTE advanced practice nurses and physician assistants who provide care for patients in your hospital.

Advanced Practice Registered Nurses _____ Full-time _____ Part-time _____ FTE

Physician Assistants _____ Full-time _____ Part-time _____ FTE

c. If yes, please indicate the type of service provided. (check all that apply)

☐ Primary care ☐ Anesthesia services (Certified registered nurse anesthetist) ☐ Emergency department care

☐ Other specialty care ☐ Patient education ☐ Case management ☐ Other

15. FOREIGN EDUCATED NURSES

a. Did your facility hire more foreign-educated nurses (including contract or agency nurses) to help fill RN vacancies in 2017 vs. 2016?

More ☐ Less ☐ Same ☐ Did not hire foreign nurses ☐

b. From which countries/continents are you recruiting foreign-educated nurses? (check all that apply)

Africa ☐ South Korea ☐ Canada ☐ Philippines ☐ China ☐ India ☐ Other ☐

F. SUPPLEMENTAL INFORMATION

1. Does your hospital provide services through one or more satellite facilities?   YES ☐   NO ☐

1a. If yes, please indicate the type of service offered along with the number of satellite facilities providing that service.

Number of facilities

- **a.** Primary care clinic ☐ _____
- **b.** Specialty clinic ☐ _____
- **c.** Urgent care ☐ _____
- **d.** Ambulatory surgery ☐ _____
- **e.** Rehabilitation ☐ _____
- **f.** Psychiatric care ☐ _____
- **g.** Substance abuse/chemical dependency ☐ _____
- **h.** Skilled nursing ☐ _____
- **i.** Residential care ☐ _____
- **j.** Other extended care ☐ _____
- **k.** Laboratory ☐ _____
- **l.** Diagnostic imaging center ☐ _____
- **m.** Other, please specify:_____ ☐ _____

2. Does the hospital participate in a group purchasing arrangement?   YES ☐   NO ☐

If yes, please provide the name, city, and state of the group purchasing organization(s).

Name: _____ City: _____ State: _____

Name: _____ City: _____ State: _____

Name: _____ City: _____ State: _____

3. Does the hospital purchase medical/surgical supplies directly through a distributor?   YES ☐   NO ☐
   If yes, please provide the name of the distributor(s).

Name: _____

Name: _____

Name: _____

4. If your hospital hired RNs during the reporting period, how many were new graduates from nursing schools? _____

5. Describe the extent of your hospital's current partnerships with the following types of organizations for community or population health improvement initiatives

	Not Involved	Collaboration	Formal Alliance
a. Health care providers outside your system	☐	☐	☐
b. Local or state public health organizations	☐	☐	☐
c. Local or state human/social service organizations	☐	☐	☐
d. Other local or state government	☐	☐	☐
e. Non-profit organizations	☐	☐	☐
f. Faith-based organizations	☐	☐	☐
g. Health insurance companies	☐	☐	☐
h. Schools	☐	☐	☐
i. Local businesses or chambers of commerce	☐	☐	☐
j. Other (list)_____	☐	☐	☐

6. Does your hospital have an established patient and family advisory council that meets regularly to actively engage the perspectives of patients and families?   YES ☐   NO ☐

F. SUPPLEMENTAL INFORMATION (continued)

7. Does your hospital have a policy or guidelines that facilitate unrestricted access, 24 hours a day, to hospitalized patients by family and other partners in care according to patient preference?

    a. ☐ Exists across all units

    b. ☐ Exists across some units

    c. ☐ Does not exist in any hospital unit

Use this space for comments or to elaborate on any information supplied on this survey. Refer to the response by page, section and item name.

_____

_____

_____

_____

_____

_____

As declared previously, hospital specific revenue data are treated as confidential. AHA's policy is not to release these data without written permission from your institution. The AHA will however, share these data with your respective state hospital association and if requested with your appropriate metropolitan/regional association.

On occasion, the AHA is asked to provide these data to external organizations, both public and private, for their use in analyzing crucial health care policy or research issues. The AHA is requesting your permission to allow us to release your confidential data to those requests that we consider legitimate and worthwhile. In every instance of disclosure, the receiving organization will be prohibited from releasing hospital specific information.

Please indicate below whether or not you agree to these types of disclosure:

[   ] I hereby grant AHA permission to release my hospital's revenue data to external users that the AHA determines have a legitimate and worthwhile need to gain access to these data subject to the user's agreement with the AHA not to release hospital specific information.

_____   _____

Chief Executive Officer   Date

[   ] I do not grant AHA permission to release my confidential data.

_____   _____

Chief Executive Officer   Date

Does your hospital or health system have an Internet or Homepage address?   Yes ☐   No ☐

If yes, please provide the address: http:// _____

Thank you for your cooperation in completing this survey. If there are any questions about your responses to this survey, who should be contacted?

_____ _____ (   )_____

Name (please print)   Title   (Area Code) Telephone Number

___/___/___   _____ (   )_____

Date of Completion   Chief Executive Officer   Hospital's Main Fax Number

Contact Email address: _____

NOTE: PLEASE PHOTOCOPY THE INFORMATION FOR YOUR HOSPITAL FILE BEFORE RETURNING THE ORIGINAL FORM TO THE AMERICAN HOSPITAL ASSOCIATION. ALSO, PLEASE FORWARD A PHOTOCOPY OF THE COMPLETED QUESTIONNAIRE TO YOUR STATE HOSPITAL ASSOCIATION.

THANK YOU

SECTION A
REPORTING PERIOD
Instructions

INSTRUCTIONS AND DEFINITIONS FOR THE 2017 ANNUAL SURVEY OF HOSPITALS.
For purposes of this survey, a hospital is defined as the organization or corporate entity licensed or registered as a hospital by a state to provide diagnostic and therapeutic patient services for a variety of medical conditions, both surgical and nonsurgical.

1. **Reporting period used (beginning and ending date):** Record the beginning and ending dates of the reporting period in an eight-digit number: for example, January 1, 2017 should be shown as 01/01/2017. Number of days should equal the time span between the two dates that the hospital was open. If you are reporting for less than 365 days, utilization and finances should be presented for days reported only.
2. **Were you in operation 12 full months at the end of your reporting period?** If you are reporting for less than 365 days, utilization and finances should be presented for days reported only.
3. **Number of days open during reporting period:** Number of days should equal the time span between the two dates that the hospital was open.

SECTION B
ORGANIZATIONAL STRUCTURE
Instructions and Definitions

1. **CONTROL**
   Check the box to the left of the type of organization that is responsible for establishing policy for overall operation of the hospital.
   Government, nonfederal.
      State. Controlled by an agency of state government.
      County. Controlled by an agency of county government.
      City. Controlled by an agency of municipal government.
      City-County. Controlled jointly by agencies of municipal and county governments.
      Hospital district or authority. Controlled by a political subdivision of a state, county, or city created solely for the purpose of establishing and maintaining medical care or health-related care institutions.
   Nongovernment, not for profit. Controlled by not-for-profit organizations, including religious organizations (Catholic hospitals, for example), community hospitals, cooperative hospitals, hospitals operated by fraternal societies, and so forth.
   Investor owned, for profit. Controlled on a for profit basis by an individual, partnership, or a profit making corporation.
   Government, federal. Controlled by an agency or department of the federal government.
2. **SERVICE**
   Indicate the ONE category that best describes the type of service that your hospital provides to the majority of patients.
   General medical and surgical. Provides diagnostic and therapeutic services to patients for a variety of medical conditions, both surgical and nonsurgical.
   Hospital unit of an institution. Provides diagnostic and therapeutic services to patients in an institution.
   Hospital unit within a facility for persons with intellectual disabilities. Provides diagnostic and therapeutic services to persons with intellectual disabilities.
   Surgical. An acute care specialty hospital where 2/3 or more of its inpatient claims are for surgical/diagnosis related groups.
   Psychiatric. Provides diagnostic and therapeutic services to patients with mental or emotional disorders.
   Tuberculosis and other respiratory diseases. Provides medical care and rehabilitative services to patients for whom the primary diagnosis is tuberculosis or other respiratory diseases.
   Cancer. Provides medical care to patients for whom the primary diagnosis is cancer.
   Heart. Provides diagnosis and treatment of heart disease.
   Obstetrics and gynecology. Provides medical and surgical treatment to pregnant women and to mothers following delivery. Also provides diagnostic and therapeutic services to women with diseases or disorders of the reproductive organs.
   Eye, ear, nose, and throat. Provides diagnosis and treatment of diseases and injuries of the eyes, ears, nose, and throat.
   Rehabilitation. Provides a comprehensive array of restoration services for people with disabilities and all support services necessary to help them attain their maximum functional capacity.
   Orthopedic. Provides corrective treatment of deformities, diseases, and ailments of the locomotive apparatus, especially affecting the limbs, bones, muscles, and joints.
   Chronic disease. Provides medical and skilled nursing services to patients with long-term illnesses who are not in an acute phase, but who require an intensity of services not available in nursing homes.
   Intellectual disabilities. Provides health-related care on a regular basis to patients with developmental or intellectual disabilities who cannot be treated in a skilled nursing unit.
   Acute long-term care hospital. Provides high acuity interdisciplinary services to medically complex patients that require more intensive recuperation and care than can be provided in a typical nursing facility.
   Alcoholism and other chemical dependency. Provides diagnostic and therapeutic services to patients with alcoholism or other drug dependencies.
3. **OTHER**
   a. **Children admissions.** A hospital whose primary focus is the health and treatment of children and adolescents.
   b. **Subsidiary.** A company that is wholly controlled by another or one that is more than 50% owned by another organization.
   c. **Contract managed.** General day-to-day management of an entire organization by another organization under a formal contract. Managing organization reports directly to the board of trustees or owners of the managed organization; managed organization retains total legal responsibility and ownership of the facility's assets and liabilities.
   d. **Network.** A group of hospitals, physicians, other providers, insurers and/or community agencies that voluntarily work together to coordinate and deliver health services.

Owned/provided by the hospital or its subsidiary. All patient revenues, expenses and utilization related to the provision of the service are reflected in the hospital's statistics reported elsewhere in this survey.

Provided by my health system (in my local community). Another health care provider in the same system as your hospital provides the service and patient revenue, expenses, and utilization related to the provision of the service are recorded at the point where the service was provided and would not be reflected in your hospital's statistics reported elsewhere in this survey. (A system is a corporate body that owns, leases, religiously sponsors and/or manages health providers)

Provided through a partnership or joint venture with another provider that is not in my system. All patient revenues and utilization related to the provision of the service are recorded at the site where the service was provided and would not be reflected in your hospital statistics reported elsewhere in this survey. (A joint venture is a contractual arrangement between two or more parties forming an unincorporated business. The participants in the arrangement remain independent and separate outside of the venture's purpose.)

1. **General medical-surgical care.** Provides acute care to patients in medical and surgical units on the basis of physicians' orders and approved nursing care plans.
2. **Pediatric medical-surgical care.** Provides acute care to pediatric patients on the basis of physicians' orders and approved nursing care plans.
3. **Obstetrics.** For service owned or provided by the hospital, level should be designated: (1) unit provides services for uncomplicated maternity and newborn cases; (2) unit provides services for uncomplicated cases, the majority of complicated problems, and special neonatal services; and (3) unit provides services for all serious illnesses and abnormalities and is supervised by a full-time maternal/fetal specialist.
4. **Medical-surgical intensive care.** Provides patient care of a more intensive nature than the usual medical and surgical care, on the basis of physicians' orders and approved nursing care plans. These units are staffed with specially trained nursing personnel and contain monitoring and specialized support equipment for patients who because of shock, trauma or other life-threatening conditions require intensified comprehensive observation and care. Includes mixed intensive care units.
5. **Cardiac intensive care.** Provides patient care of a more specialized nature than the usual medical and surgical care, on the basis of physicians' orders and approved nursing care plans. The unit is staffed with specially trained nursing personnel and contains monitoring and specialized support or treatment equipment for patients who, because of heart seizure, open-heart surgery, or other life-threatening conditions, require intensified, comprehensive observation and care. May include myocardial infarction, pulmonary care, and heart transplant units.
6. **Neonatal intensive care.** A unit that must be separate from the newborn nursery providing intensive care to all sick infants including those with the very lowest birth weights (less than 1500 grams). NICU has potential for providing mechanical ventilation, neonatal surgery, and special care for the sickest infants born in the hospital or transferred from another institution. A full-time neonatologist serves as director of the NICU.
7. **Neonatal intermediate care.** A unit that must be separate from the normal newborn nursery and that provides intermediate and/or recovery care and some specialized services, including immediate resuscitation, intravenous therapy, and capacity for prolonged oxygen therapy and monitoring.
8. **Pediatric intensive care.** Provides care to pediatric patients that is of a more intensive nature than that usually provided to pediatric patients. The unit is staffed with specially trained personnel and contains monitoring and specialized support equipment for treatment of patients who, because of shock, trauma, or other life-threatening conditions, require intensified, comprehensive observation and care.
9. **Burn care.** Provides care to severely burned patients. Severely burned patients are those with any of the following: (1) second-degree burns of more than 25% total body surface area for adults or 20% total body surface area for children: (2) third-degree burns of more than 10% total body surface area; (3) any severe burns of the hands, face, eyes, ears, or feet; or (4) all inhalation injuries, electrical burns, complicated burn injuries involving fractures and other major traumas, and all other poor risk factors.
10. **Other special care.** Provides care to patients requiring care more intensive than that provided in the acute area, yet not sufficiently intensive to require admission to an intensive care unit. Patients admitted to this area are usually transferred here from an intensive care unit once their condition has improved. These units are sometimes referred to as definitive observation, step-down or progressive care units.
11. **Other intensive care.** A specially staffed, specialty equipped, separate section of a hospital dedicated to the observation, care, and treatment of patients with life-threatening illnesses, injuries, or complications from which recovery is possible. It provides special expertise and facilities for the support of vital function and utilizes the skill of medical nursing and other staff experienced in the management of these problems.
12. **Physical rehabilitation.** Provides care encompassing a comprehensive array of restoration services for people with disabilities and all support services necessary to help patients attain their maximum functional capacity.
13. **Alcoholism-chemical dependency care.** Provides diagnosis and therapeutic services to patients with alcoholism or other drug dependencies. Includes care for inpatient/residential treatment for patients whose course of treatment involves more intensive care than provided in an outpatient setting or where patient requires supervised withdrawal.
14. **Psychiatric care.** Provides acute or long-term care to patients with mental or emotional disorders, including patients admitted for diagnosis and those admitted for treatment of psychiatric disorders, on the basis of physicians' orders and approved nursing care plans. Long-term care may include intensive supervision to persons with chronic/severe mental illness.
15. **Skilled nursing care.** Provides non-acute medical and skilled nursing care services, therapy, and social services under the supervision of a licensed registered nurse on a 24-hour basis.
16. **Intermediate nursing care.** Provides health-related services (skilled nursing care and social services) to residents with a variety of physical conditions or functional disabilities. These residents do not require the care provided by a hospital or skilled nursing facility, but do need supervision and support services.
17. **Acute long-term care.** Provides specialized acute hospital care to medically complex patients who are critically ill, have multisystem complications and/or failure, and require hospitalization averaging 25 days, in a facility offering specialized treatment programs and therapeutic intervention on a 24-hour/7 days a week basis.
18. **Other long-term care.** Provision of long-term care other than skilled nursing care or intermediate care for those who do not require daily medical or nursing services, but may requires some assistance in the activities of daily living. This can include residential care, elderly care, or care facilities for those with developmental or intellectual disabilities.
19. **Other care.** (specify) Any type of care other than those listed above.
    The sum of the beds reported in Section C 1-19 should equal what you have reported in Section E(1b) for beds set up and staffed.
20. **Adult day care program.** Program providing supervision, medical and psychological care, and social activities for older adults who live at home or in another family setting, but cannot be alone or prefer to be with others during the day. May include intake assessment, health monitoring, occupational therapy, personal care, noon meal, and transportation services.
21. **Airborne infection isolation room.** A single-occupancy room for patient care where environmental factors are controlled in an effort to minimize the transmission of those infectious agents, usually spread person to person by droplet nuclei associated with coughing and inhalation. Such rooms typically have specific ventilation requirements for controlled ventilation, air pressure and filtration.

22. **Alcoholism-chemical dependency care services.**
  a. **Alcoholism-chemical dependency pediatric care services.** Provides diagnosis and therapeutic services to pediatric patients with alcoholism or other drug dependencies. Includes care for inpatient/residential treatment for patients whose course of treatment involves more intensive care than provided in an outpatient setting or where patient requires supervised withdrawal. Please report staffed beds. <u>The beds reported here should also be reported under 13, alcoholism-chemical dependency care. This line item should be a breakout of the pediatric beds only.</u>
  b. **Alcoholism-chemical dependency outpatient services.** Organized hospital services that provide medical care and/or rehabilitative treatment services to outpatients for whom the primary diagnosis is alcoholism or other chemical dependency.
  c. **Alcoholism-chemical dependency partial hospitalization services.** Organized hospital services providing intensive day/evening outpatient services of three hour or more duration, distinguished from other outpatient visits of one hour.
23. **Alzheimer center.** Facility that offers care to persons with Alzheimer's disease and their families through an integrated program of clinical services, research, and education.
24. **Ambulance services.** Provision of ambulance service to the ill and injured who require medical attention on a scheduled and unscheduled basis.
25. **Ambulatory surgery center.** Facility that provides care to patients requiring surgery that are admitted and discharged on the same day. Ambulatory surgery centers are distinct from same day surgical units within the hospital outpatient departments for purposes of Medicare payment.
26. **Arthritis treatment center.** Specifically equipped and staffed center for the diagnosis and treatment of arthritis and other joint disorders.
27. **Assisted living.** A special combination of housing, supportive services, personalized assistance and health care designed to respond to the individual needs of those who need help in activities of daily living and instrumental activities of daily living. Supportive services are available, 24 hours a day, to meet scheduled and unscheduled needs, in a way that promotes maximum independence and dignity for each resident and encourages the involvement of a resident's family, neighbor and friends.
28. **Auxiliary.** A volunteer community organization formed to assist the hospital in carrying out its purpose and to serve as a link between the institution and the community.
29. **Bariatric/weight control services.** The medical practice of weight reduction.
30. **Birthing room/LDR room/LDRP room.** A single-room type of maternity care with a more homelike setting for families than the traditional three-room unit (labor/delivery/recovery) with a separate postpartum area. A birthing room combines labor and delivery in one room. An LDR room accommodates three stages in the birthing process--labor, delivery, and recovery. An LDRP room accommodates all four stages of the birth process--labor, delivery, recovery, and postpartum.
31. **Blood donor center.** A facility that performs, or is responsible for the collection, processing, testing or distribution of blood and components.
32. **Breast cancer screening/mammograms.** Mammography screening - The use of breast x-ray to detect unsuspected breast cancer in asymptomatic women. Diagnostic mammography - The x-ray imaging of breast tissue in symptomatic women who are considered to have a substantial likelihood of having breast cancer already.
33. **Cardiology and cardiac surgery services.** Services which include the diagnosis and treatment of diseases and disorders involving the heart and circulatory system.
  a-b. Cardiology services. An organized clinical service offering diagnostic and interventional procedures to manage the full range of heart conditions.
  c-d. Diagnostic catheterization. (also called coronary angiography or coronary arteriography) is used to assist in diagnosing complex heart conditions. Cardiac angiography involves the insertion of a tiny catheter into the artery in the groin then carefully threading the catheter up into the aorta where the coronary arteries originate. Once the catheter is in place, a dye is injected which allows the cardiologist to see the size, shape, and distribution of the coronary arteries. These images are used to diagnose heart disease and to determine, among other things, whether or not surgery is indicated.
  e-f. Interventional cardiac catheterization. Nonsurgical procedure that utilizes the same basic principles as diagnostic catheterization and then uses advanced techniques to improve the heart's function. It can be a less invasive alternative to heart surgery.
  g-h. Cardiac surgery. Includes minimally invasive procedures that include surgery done with only a small incision or no incision at all, such as through a laparoscope or an endoscope and more invasive major surgical procedures that include open chest and open heart surgery.
  i-j. Cardiac electrophysiology. Evaluation and management of patients with complex rhythm or conduction abnormalities, including diagnostic testing, treatment of arrhythmias by catheter ablation or drug therapy, and pacemaker/defibrillator implantation and follow-up.
  k. Cardiac rehabilitation. A medically supervised program to help heart patients recover quickly and improve their overall physical and mental functioning. The goal is to reduce risk of another cardiac event or to keep an already present heart condition from getting worse. Cardiac rehabilitation programs include: counseling to patients, an exercise program, helping patients modify risk factors such as smoking and high blood pressure, providing vocational guidance to enable the patient to return to work, supplying information on physical limitations and lending emotional support.
34. **Case management.** A system of assessment, treatment planning, referral and follow-up that ensures the provision of comprehensive and continuous services and the coordination of payment and reimbursement for care.
35. **Chaplaincy/pastoral care services.** A service ministering religious activities and providing pastoral counseling to patients, their families, and staff of a health care organization.
36. **Chemotherapy.** An organized program for the treatment of cancer by the use of drugs or chemicals.
37. **Children's wellness program.** A program that encourages improved health status and a healthful lifestyle of children through health education, exercise, nutrition and health promotion.
38. **Chiropractic services.** An organized clinical service including spinal manipulation or adjustment and related diagnostic and therapeutic services.
39. **Community outreach.** A program that systematically interacts with the community to identify those in need of services, alerting persons and their families to the availability of services, locating needed services, and enabling persons to enter the service delivery system.
40. **Complementary and alternative medicine services.** Organized hospital services or formal arrangements to providers that provide care or treatment not based solely on traditional western allopathic medical teachings as instructed in most U.S. medical schools. Includes any of the following: acupuncture, chiropractic, homeopathy, osteopathy, diet and lifestyle changes, herbal medicine, massage therapy, etc.
41. **Computer assisted orthopedic surgery (CAOS).** Orthopedic surgery using computer technology, enabling three-dimensional graphic models to visualize a patient's anatomy.
42. **Crisis prevention.** Services provided in order to promote physical and mental wellbeing and the early identification of disease and ill health prior to the onset and recognition of symptoms so as to permit early treatment.
43. **Dental services.** An organized dental service or dentists on staff, not necessarily involving special facilities, providing dental or oral services to inpatients or outpatients.
44. **Emergency services.** Health services that are provided after the onset of a medical condition that manifests itself by symptoms of sufficient severity, including severe pain, that the absence of immediate medical attention could reasonably be expected by a prudent layperson, who possesses an average knowledge of health and medicine, to result in placing the patient's health in serious jeopardy.
  a-b. Emergency department. Hospital facilities for the provision of unscheduled outpatient services to patients whose conditions require immediate care.
  c. Trauma center (certified). A facility to provide emergency and specialized intensive care to critically ill and injured patients. For service owned or provided by the hospital, please specify trauma level. Level 1: A regional resource trauma center, which is capable of providing total care for every aspect of injury and plays a leadership role in trauma research and education. Level 2: A community trauma center, which is capable of

providing trauma care to all but the most severely injured patients who require highly specialized care. Level 3: A rural trauma hospital, which is capable of providing care to a large number of injury victims and can resuscitate and stabilize more severely injured patients so that they can be transported to level 1 or 2 facilities.

45. **Enabling services.** A program that is designed to help the patient access health care services by offering any of the following: transportation services and/or referrals to local social services agencies.

46. **Endoscopic services.**
   a. **Optical colonoscopy.** An examination of the interior of the colon using a long, flexible, lighted tube with a small built-in camera.
   b. **Endoscopic ultrasound.** Specially designed endoscope that incorporates an ultrasound transducer used to obtain detailed images of organs in the chest and abdomen. The endoscope can be passed through the mouth or the anus. When combined with needle biopsy the procedure can assist in diagnosis of disease and staging of cancer.
   c. **Ablation of Barrett's esophagus.** Premalignant condition that can lead to adenocarcinoma of the esophagus. The nonsurgical ablation of premalignant tissue in Barrett's esophagus by the application of thermal energy or light through an endoscope passed from the mouth into the esophagus.
   d. **Esophageal impedance study.** A test in which a catheter is placed through the nose into the esophagus to measure whether gas or liquids are passing from the stomach into the esophagus and causing symptoms.
   e. **Endoscopic retrograde cholangiopancreatography (ERCP).** A procedure in which a catheter is introduced through an endoscope into the bile ducts and pancreatic ducts. Injection of contrast material permits detailed x-ray of these structures. The procedure is used diagnostically as well as therapeutically to relieve obstruction or remove stones.

47. **Enrollment (insurance) assistance services.** A program that provides enrollment assistance for patients who are potentially eligible for public health insurance programs such as Medicaid, State Children's Health Insurance, or local/state indigent care programs. The specific services offered could include explanation of benefits, assist applicants in completing the application and locating all relevant documents, conduct eligibility interviews, and/or forward applications and documentation to state/local social service or health agency.

48. **Extracorporeal shock wave lithotripter (ESWL).** A medical device used for treating stones in the kidney or urethra. The device disintegrates kidney stones noninvasively through the transmission of acoustic shock waves directed at the stones.

49. **Fertility clinic.** A specialized program set in an infertility center that provides counseling and education as well as advanced reproductive techniques such as: injectable therapy, reproductive surgeries, treatment for endometriosis, male factor infertility, tubal reversals, in vitro fertilization (IVF), donor eggs, and other such services to help patients achieve successful pregnancies.

50. **Fitness center.** Provides exercise, testing, or evaluation programs and fitness activities to the community and hospital employees.

51. **Freestanding outpatient care center.** A facility owned and operated by the hospital, that is physically separate from the hospital and provides various medical treatments and diagnostic services on an outpatient basis only. Laboratory and radiology services are usually available.

52. **Geriatric services.** The branch of medicine dealing with the physiology of aging and the diagnosis and treatment of disease affecting the aged. Services could include: Adult day care; Alzheimer's diagnostic-assessment services; Comprehensive geriatric assessment; Emergency response system; Geriatric acute care unit; and/or Geriatric clinics.

53. **Health fair.** Community health education events that focus on the prevention of disease and promotion of health through such activities as audiovisual exhibits and free diagnostic services.

54. **Community health education.** Education that provides health information to individuals and populations as well as support for personal, family and community health decisions with the objective of improving health status.

55. **Genetic testing/counseling.** A service equipped with adequate laboratory facilities and directed by a qualified physician to advise patients on potential genetic diagnosis of vulnerabilities to inherited diseases. A genetic test is the analysis of human DNA, RNA, chromosomes, proteins, and certain metabolites in order to detect heritable disease-related genotypes, mutations, phenotypes, or karyotypes for clinical purposes. Genetic tests can have diverse purposes, including the diagnosis of genetic diseases in newborns, children, and adults; the identification of future health risks; the prediction of drug responses; and the assessment of risks to future children.

56. **Health screening.** A preliminary procedure such as a test or examination to detect the most characteristic sign or signs of a disorder that may require further investigation.

57. **Health research.** Organized hospital research program in any of the following areas: basic research, clinical research, community health research, and/or research on innovative health care delivery.

58. **Hemodialysis.** Provision of equipment and personnel for the treatment of renal insufficiency on an inpatient or outpatient basis.

59. **HIV/AIDS services.** Diagnosis, treatment, continuing care planning, and counseling services for HIV/AIDS patients and their families. Could include: HIV/AIDS unit, special unit or designated team, general inpatient care, or specialized outpatient program.

60. **Home health services.** Service providing nursing, therapy, and health-related homemaker or social services in the patient's home.

61. **Hospice.** A program providing palliative care, chiefly medical relief of pain and supportive services, addressing the emotional, social, financial, and legal needs of terminally ill patients and their families. Care can be provided in a variety of settings, both inpatient and at home.

62. **Hospital-based outpatient care center-services.** Organized hospital health care services offered by appointment on an ambulatory basis. Services may include outpatient surgery, examination, diagnosis, and treatment of a variety of medical conditions on a nonemergency basis, and laboratory and other diagnostic testing as ordered by staff or outside physician referral.

63. **Immunization program.** Program that plans, coordinates and conducts immunization services in the community.

64. **Indigent care clinic.** Health care services for uninsured and underinsured persons where care is free of charge or charged on a sliding scale. This would include "free clinics" staffed by volunteer practitioners, but could also be staffed by employees with the sponsoring health care organization subsidizing the cost of service.

65. **Linguistic/translation services.** Services provided by the hospital designed to make health care more accessible to non-English speaking patients and their physicians.

66. **Meals on wheels.** A hospital sponsored program which delivers meals to people, usually the elderly, who are unable to prepare their own meals. Low cost, nutritional meals are delivered to individuals' homes on a regular basis.

67. **Mobile health services.** Vans and other vehicles used for delivery to primary care services.

68. **Neurological services.** Services provided by the hospital dealing with the operative and nonoperative management of disorders of the central, peripheral, and autonomic nervous systems.

69. **Nutrition programs.** Services within a health care facility which are designed to provide inexpensive, nutritionally sound meals to patients.

70. **Occupational health services.** Includes services designed to protect the safety of employees from hazards in the work environment.

71. **Oncology services.** Inpatient and outpatient services for patients with cancer, including comprehensive care, support and guidance in addition to patient education and prevention, chemotherapy, counseling and other treatment methods.

72. **Orthopedic services.** Services provided for the prevention or correction of injuries or disorders of the skeletal system and associated muscles, joints and ligaments.

73. **Outpatient surgery.** Scheduled surgical services provided to patients who do not remain in the hospital overnight. The surgery may be performed in operating suites also used for inpatient surgery, specially designated surgical suites for outpatient surgery, or procedure rooms within an outpatient care facility.

74. **Pain management program.** A recognized clinical service or program providing specialized medical care, drugs or therapies for the management of acute or chronic pain and other distressing symptoms, administered by specially trained physicians and other clinicians, to patients suffering from acute illnesses of diverse causes.

75. **Palliative care program.** An organized program providing specialized medical care, drugs or therapies for the management of acute or chronic pain and/or the control of symptoms administered by specially trained physicians and other clinicians; and supportive care services, such as counseling on advanced directives, spiritual care, and social services, to patients with advanced diseases and their families.

76. **Palliative care inpatient unit.** An inpatient palliative care ward is a physically discreet, inpatient nursing unit where the focus is palliative care. The patient care focus is on symptom relief for complex patients who may be continuing to undergo primary treatment. Care is delivered by palliative medicine specialists.

77. **Patient controlled analgesia (PCA).** Intravenously administered pain medicine under the patient's control. The patient has a button on the end of a cord than can be pushed at will, whenever more pain medicine is desired. This button will only deliver more pain medicine at predetermined intervals, as programmed by the doctor's order.

78. **Patient education center.** Written goals and objectives for the patient and/or family related to therapeutic regimens, medical procedures, and self-care.

79. **Patient representative services.** Organized hospital services providing personnel through whom patients and staff can seek solutions to institutional problems affecting the delivery of high quality care and services.

80. **Physical rehabilitation services.** Program providing medical, health-related, therapy, social, and/or vocational services to help people with disabilities attain or retain their maximum functional capacity.
    a. **Assistive technology center.** A program providing access to specialized hardware and software with adaptations allowing individuals greater independence with mobility, dexterity, or increased communication options.
    b. **Electrodiagnostic services.** Diagnostic testing services for nerve and muscle function such as nerve conduction studies and needle electromyography.
    c. **Physical rehabilitation outpatient services.** Outpatient program providing medical, health-related, therapy, social, and/or vocational services to help people with disabilities attain or retain their maximum functional capacity.
    d. **Prosthetic and orthotic services.** Services providing comprehensive prosthetic and orthotic evaluation, fitting, and training.
    e. **Robot-assisted walking therapy.** A form of physical therapy that uses a robotic device to assist patients who are relearning how to walk.
    f. **Simulated rehabilitation environment.** Rehabilitation focused on retraining functional skills in a contextually appropriate environment (simulated home and community settings) or in a traditional setting (gymnasium) using motor learning principles.

81. **Primary care department.** A unit or clinic within the hospital that provides primary care services (e.g., general pediatric care, general internal medicine, family practice, gynecology) through hospital-salaried medical and/or nursing staff, focusing on evaluating and diagnosing medical problems and providing medical treatment on an outpatient basis.

82. **Psychiatric services.** Services provided by the hospital that offer immediate initial evaluation and treatment to patients with mental or emotional disorders.
    a. **Psychiatric consultation-liaison services.** Provides organized psychiatric consultation/liaison services to nonpsychiatric hospital staff and/or departments on psychological aspects of medical care that may be generic or specific to individual patients.
    b. **Psychiatric pediatric services.** The branch of medicine focused on the diagnosis, treatment and prevention of mental, emotional and behavioral disorders in pediatric patients. Please report the number of staffed beds. The beds reported here should be included in the staffed bed count for 14 psychiatric care.
    c. **Psychiatric geriatric services.** Provides care to elderly patients with mental or emotional disorders, including those admitted for diagnosis and those admitted for treatment. Please report the number of staffed beds. The beds reported here should be included in the staffed bed count for 14 psychiatric care.
    d. **Psychiatric education services.** Provides psychiatric educational services to community agencies and workers such as schools, police, courts, public health nurses, welfare agencies, clergy, and so forth. The purpose is to expand the mental health knowledge and competence of personnel not working in the mental health field and to promote good mental health through improved understanding, attitudes, and behavioral patterns.
    e. **Psychiatric emergency services.** Services of facilities available on a 24-hour basis to provide immediate unscheduled outpatient care, diagnosis, evaluation, crisis intervention, and assistance to persons suffering acute emotional or mental distress.
    f. **Psychiatric outpatient services.** Provides medical care, including diagnosis and treatment, of psychiatric outpatients.
    g. **Psychiatric intensive outpatient services.** A prescribed course of treatment in which the patient receives outpatient care no less than three times a week (which might include more than one service/day)
    h-i. **Psychiatric partial hospitalization program – adult/pediatric.** Organized hospital services providing intensive day/evening outpatient services of three hours or more duration, distinguished from other outpatient visits of one hour.
    j-k. **Psychiatric residential treatment – adult/pediatric.** Overnight psychiatric care in conjunction with an intensive treatment program in a setting other than a hospital.

83. **Radiology, diagnostic.** The branch of radiology that deals with the utilization of all modalities of radiant energy in medical diagnoses and therapeutic procedures using radiologic guidance. This includes, but is not restricted to, imaging techniques and methodologies utilizing radiation emitted by x-ray tubes, radionuclides, and ultrasonographic devices and the radiofrequency electromagnetic radiation emitted by atoms.
    a. **CT Scanner.** Computed tomographic scanner for head or whole body scans.
    b. **Diagnostic radioisotope facility.** The use of radioactive isotopes (Radiopharmaceuticals) as tracers or indicators to detect an abnormal condition or disease.
    c. **Electron beam computed tomography (EBCT).** A high tech computed tomography scan used to detect coronary artery disease by measuring coronary calcifications. This imaging procedure uses electron beams which are magnetically steered to produce a visual of the coronary artery and the images are produced faster than conventional CT scans.
    d. **Full-field digital mammography (FFDM).** Combines the x-ray generators and tubes used in analog screen-film mammography (SFM) with a detector plate that converts the x-rays into a digital signal.
    e. **Magnetic resonance imaging (MRI).** The use of a uniform magnetic field and radio frequencies to study tissue and structure of the body. This procedure enables the visualization of biochemical activity of the cell in vivo without the use of ionizing radiation, radioisotopic substances or high-frequency sound.
    f. **Intraoperative magnetic resonance imaging.** An integrated surgery system which provides an MRI system in an operating room. The system allows for immediate evaluation of the degree to tumor resection while the patient is undergoing a surgical resection. Intraoperative MRI exists when a MRI (low-field or high-field) is placed in the operating theater and is used during surgical resection without moving the patient from the operating room to the diagnostic imaging suite.
    g. **Magnetoencephalography (MEG).** A noninvasive neurophysiological measurement tool used to study magnetic fields generated by neuronal activity of the brain. MEG provides direct information about the dynamics of evoked and spontaneous neural activity and its location in the brain. The primary uses of MEG include assisting surgeons in localizing the source of epilepsy, sensory mapping, and the study of brain function. When it is combined with structural imaging, it is known as *magnetic source imaging* (MSI).

h. **Multi-slice spiral computed tomography (<64+slice CT).** A specialized computed tomography procedure that provides three-dimensional processing and allows narrower and multiple slices with increased spatial resolution and faster scanning times as compared to a regular computed tomography scan.

i. **Multi-slice spiral computed tomography (64+ slice CT).** Involves the acquisition of volumetric tomographic x-ray absorption data expressed in Hounsfield units using multiple rows of detectors. 64+ systems reconstruct the equivalent of 64 or more slices to cover the imaged volume.

j. **Positron emission tomography (PET).** A nuclear medicine imaging technology which uses radioactive (positron emitting) isotopes created in a cyclotron or generator and computers to produce composite pictures of the brain and heart at work. PET scanning produces sectional images depicting metabolic activity or blood flow rather than anatomy.

k. **Positron emission tomography/CT (PET/CT).** Provides metabolic functional information for the monitoring of chemotherapy, radiotherapy and surgical planning.

l. **Single photon emission computerized tomography (SPECT).** A nuclear medicine imaging technology that combines existing technology of gamma camera imaging with computed tomographic imaging technology to provide a clearer and more precise image.

m. **Ultrasound.** The use of acoustic waves above the range of 20,000 cycles per second to visualize internal body structures.

84. **Radiology, therapeutic.** The branch of medicine concerned with radioactive substances and using various techniques of visualization, with the diagnosis and treatment of disease using any of the various sources of radiant energy. Services could include: megavoltage radiation therapy; radioactive implants; stereotactic radiosurgery; therapeutic radioisotope facility; X-ray radiation therapy.

a. **Image-guided radiation therapy (IGRT).** Automated system for image-guided radiation therapy that enables clinicians to obtain high-resolution x-ray images to pinpoint tumor sites, adjust patient positioning when necessary, and complete a treatment, all within the standard treatment time slot, allowing for more effective cancer treatments.

b. **Intensity-Modulated Radiation Therapy (IMRT).** A type of three-dimensional radiation therapy which improves treatment delivery by targeting a tumor in a way that is likely to decrease damage to normal tissues and allows for varying intensities.

c. **Proton beam therapy.** A form of radiation therapy which administers proton beams. While producing the same biologic effects as x-ray beams, the energy distribution of protons differs from conventional x-ray beams: proton beams can be more precisely focused in tissue volumes in a three-dimensional pattern, resulting in less surrounding tissue damage than conventional radiation therapy, permitting administration of higher doses.

d. **Shaped beam radiation system.** A precise, noninvasive treatment that involves targeted beams of radiation that mirror the exact size and shape of a tumor at a specific area to shrink or destroy cancerous cells. This procedure delivers a therapeutic dose of radiation that conforms precisely to the shape of the tumor, thus minimizing the risk to nearby tissues.

e. **Stereotactic radiosurgery.** A radiotherapy modality that delivers a high dosage of radiation to a discrete treatment area in as few as one treatment session. Includes Gamma Knife, Cyberknife, etc.

85. **Retirement housing.** A facility that provides social activities to senior citizens, usually retired persons, who do not require health care but some short-term skilled nursing care may be provided. A retirement center may furnish housing and may also have acute hospital and long-term care facilities, or it may arrange for acute and long-term care through affiliated institutions.

86. **Robotic surgery.** The use of mechanical guidance devices to remotely manipulate surgical instrumentation.

87. **Rural health clinic.** A clinic located in a rural, medically under-served area in the United States that has a separate reimbursement structure from the standard medical office under the Medicare and Medicaid programs.

88. **Sleep center.** Specially equipped and staffed center for the diagnosis and treatment of sleep disorders.

89. **Social work services.** Could include: organized services that are properly directed and sufficiently staffed by qualified individuals who provide assistance and counseling to patients and their families in dealing with social, emotional, and environmental problems associated with illness or disability, often in the context of financial or discharge planning coordination.

90. **Sports medicine.** Provision of diagnostic screening, assessment, clinical and rehabilitation services for the prevention and treatment of sports-related injuries.

91. **Support groups.** A hospital sponsored program that allows a group of individuals with common experiences or issues who meet periodically to share experiences, problems, and solutions in order to support each other.

92. **Swing bed services.** A hospital bed that can be used to provide either acute or long-term care depending on community or patient needs. To be eligible a hospital must have a Medicare provider agreement in place, have fewer than 100 beds, be located in a rural area, not have a 24-hour nursing service waiver in effect, have not been terminated from the program in the prior two years, and meet various service conditions.

93. **Teen outreach services.** A program focusing on the teenager which encourages an improved health status and a healthful lifestyle including physical, emotional, mental, social, spiritual and economic health through education, exercise, nutrition and health promotion.

94. **Tobacco treatment/cessation program.** Organized hospital services with the purpose of ending tobacco-use habits of patients addicted to tobacco/nicotine.

95. **Telehealth.** A broad variety of technologies and tactics to deliver virtual medical, public health, health education delivery and support services using telecommunications technologies. Telehealth is used more commonly as it describes the wide range of diagnosis and management, education, and other related fields of health care. This includes, but are not limited to: dentistry, counseling, physical and occupational therapy, home health, chronic disease monitoring and management, disaster management and consumer and professional education.

b. **eICU.** An electronic intensive care unit (eICU), also referred to as a tele-ICU, is a form of telemedicine that uses state of the art technology to provide an additional layer of critical care service. The goal of an eICU is to optimize clinical experience and facilitate 24-hour a day care by ICU caregivers.

c. **Stroke care.** Stroke telemedicine is a consultative modality that facilitates the care of patients with acute stroke by specialists at stroke centers.

d. **Psychiatric and addiction treatment.** Telepsychiatry can involve a range of services including psychiatric evaluations, therapy, patient education, and medication management.

e. **Remote patient monitoring.** The use of digital technologies to collect medical and other forms of health data from individuals in one location and electronically transmit the information securely to health care providers in a different location for assessment and recommendation.

96. **Transplant services.** The branch of medicine that transfers an organ or tissue from one person to another or from one body part to another, to replace a diseased structure or to restore function or to change appearance. Services could include: Bone marrow, heart, lung, kidney, intestine, or tissue transplant. Please include heart/lung or other multi-transplant surgeries in 'other'.

97. **Transportation to health facilities.** A long-term care support service designed to assist the mobility of the elderly. Some programs offer improved financial access by offering reduced rates and barrier-free buses or vans with ramps and lifts to assist the elderly or people with disabilities; others offer subsidies for public transport systems or operate mini-bus services exclusively for use by senior citizens.

98. **Urgent care center.** A facility that provides care and treatment for problems that are not life threatening but require attention over the short term.

99. **Violence Prevention**

a. **Workplace.** A violence prevention program with goals and objectives for preventing workplace violence against staff and patients.

b. **Community.** An organized program that attempts to make a positive impact on the type(s) of violence a community is experiencing. For example, it can assist victims of violent crimes, e.g., rape, or incidents, e.g., bullying, to hospital or to community services to prevent further victimization or retaliation. A program that targets the underlying circumstances that contribute to violence such as poor housing, insufficient job training, and/or substance abuse through means such direct involvement and support, education, mentoring, anger management, crisis intervention and training programs would also qualify.

---

100. **Virtual colonoscopy.** Noninvasive screening procedure used to visualize, analyze and detect cancerous or potentially cancerous polyps in the colon.

101. **Volunteer services department.** An organized hospital department responsible for coordinating the services of volunteers working within the institution.

102. **Women's health center/services.** An area set aside for coordinated education and treatment services specifically for and promoted to women as provided by this special unit. Services may or may not include obstetrics but include a range of services other than OB.

103. **Wound management services.** Services for patients with chronic wounds and nonhealing wounds often resulting from diabetes, poor circulation, improper seating and immunocompromising conditions. The goals are to progress chronic wounds through stages of healing, reduce and eliminate infections, increase physical function to minimize complications from current wounds and prevent future chronic wounds. Wound management services are provided on an inpatient or outpatient basis, depending on the intensity of service needed.

104. Integration ranges from co-located physical and behavioral health providers, with some screening and treatment planning, to fully integrated care where behavioral and physical health providers function as a true team in a shared practice.

105. **Physician arrangements.** An integrated healthcare delivery program implementing physician compensation and incentive systems for managed care services.
   a. **Independent practice association (IPA).** A legal entity that holds managed care contracts. The IPA then contracts with physicians, usually in solo practice, to provide care either on a fee-for-service or capitated basis. The purpose of an IPA is to assist solo physicians in obtaining managed care contracts.
   b. **Group practice without walls.** Hospital sponsors the formation of, or provides capital to physicians to establish, a "quasi" group to share administrative expenses while remaining independent practitioners.
   c. **Open physician-hospital organization (PHO).** A joint venture between the hospital and all members of the medical staff who wish to participate. The PHO can act as a unified agent in managed care contracting, own a managed care plan, own and operate ambulatory care centers or ancillary services projects, or provide administrative services to physician members.
   d. **Closed physician-hospital organization (PHO).** A PHO that restricts physician membership to those practitioners who meet criteria for cost effectiveness and/or high quality.
   e. **Management services organization (MSO).** A corporation, owned by the hospital or a physician/hospital joint venture, that provides management services to one or more medical group practices. The MSO purchases the tangible assets of the practices and leases them back as part of a full-service management agreement, under which the MSO employs all non-physician staff and provides all supplies/administrative systems for a fee.
   f. **Integrated salary model.** Physicians are salaried by the hospital or another entity of a health system to provide medical services for primary care and specialty care.
   g. **Equity model.** Allows established practitioners to become shareholders in a professional corporation in exchange for tangible and intangible assets of their existing practices.
   h. **Foundation.** A corporation, organized either as a hospital affiliate or subsidiary, which purchases both the tangible and intangible assets of one or more medical group practices. Physicians remain in a separate corporate entity but sign a professional services agreement with the foundation.

106. Of all physician arrangements listed in question 105 (a-i), indicate the total number of physicians (count each physician only once) that are engaged in an arrangement with your hospital that allows for joint contracting with payers or shared responsibility for financial risk or clinical performance between the hospital and physician (arrangement may be at the hospital, system or network level). *Joint contracting* does not include contracting between physicians participating in an independent practice.

107. **Joint venture.** A contractual arrangement between two or more parties forming an unincorporated business. The participants in the arrangement remain independent and separate outside of the venture's purpose.

SECTION D
INSURANCE AND ALTERNATIVE PAYMENT MODELS
Definitions

5. **Capitation.** An at-risk payment arrangement in which an organization receives a fixed prearranged payment and in turn guarantees to deliver or arrange all medically necessary care required by enrollees in the capitated plan. The fixed amount is specified within contractual agreements between the payer and the involved organization. The fixed payment amount is based on an actuarial assessment of the services required by enrollees and the costs of providing these services, recognizing enrollees' adjustment factors such as age, sex, and family size.

6. **Bundling.** Bundling is a payment mechanism whereby a provider entity receives a single payment for services provided across one or parts of the care continuum. For example, an entity might receive a single payment for the hospital and physician services provided as part of an inpatient stay or might receive a single payment for the post-acute care services involved in a single episode of care. The entity then has responsibility for compensating each of the individual providers involved in the episode of care.

7. **Shared risk payments.** A payment arrangement in which a hospital and a managed care organization share the risk of adverse claims experience. Methods for sharing risk could include: capitation with partial refunds or supplements if billed hospital charges or costs differ from capitated payments, and service or discharge-based payments with withholds and bonus payouts that depend on expenditure targets

10. **Accountable Care Organization (ACO) Contract.** An ACO contract has two essential elements: (1) accountability for the total costs of care for the population of patients attributed to the primary care physicians in the organization; (2) financial incentives that link the magnitude of bonus payments to performance on quality measures (which could include technical quality, patient experience and/or health outcome measures) This will generally involve a contract where the payer establishes a target budget for one or more years for the total costs of care for the agreed-upon patient population, the payer tracks actual spending and performance on quality; and the provider receives bonus payments that could include a share of savings that are (or are not) contingent on meeting quality targets, with (or without) additional bonuses related to performance on those quality measures.

12. **Patient-Centered Medical Home.** The medical home concept refers to the provision of comprehensive primary care services that facilitates communication and shared decision-making between the patient, his/her primary care providers, other providers, and the patient's family.

13. **Clinically integrated network.** A clinically integrated network is a collection of healthcare providers, such as physicians, hospitals, and post-acute care treatment providers, that come together to improve patient care and reduce overall healthcare costs. Clinically integrated networks rely on evidence-based care guidelines to provide high-quality care across participating providers.

For the purposes of this survey, a nursing home type unit/facility provides **long-term care for the elderly or other patients requiring chronic care** in a non-acute setting in any of the following categories: *Skilled nursing care *Intermediate care *Other long-term care (see page 19) The nursing home type unit/facility is to be owned and operated by the hospital. Only one legal entity may be vested with title to the physical property or operate under the authority of a duly executed lease of the physical property.

1. a. **Total licensed beds.** Report the total number of beds authorized by the state licensing (certifying) agency.
   b. **Beds set up and staffed.** Report the number of beds regularly available (those set up and staffed for use) at the end of the reporting period. Report only operating beds, not constructed bed capacity. Include all bed facilities that are set up and staffed for use by inpatients that have no other bed facilities, such as pediatric bassinets, isolation units and quiet rooms. Exclude newborn bassinets and bed facilities for patients receiving special procedures for a portion of their stay and who have other bed facilities assigned to or reserved for them. Exclude, for example, labor room, post anesthesia, or postoperative recovery room beds, psychiatric holding beds, observation beds, and beds that are used only as holding facilities for patients prior to their transfer to another hospital.
   c. **Bassinets set up and staffed.** Report the number of normal newborn bassinets. Do not include neonatal intensive care or intermediate care bassinets. These should be reported on page 3, C6 and C7.
   d. **Births.** Total births should exclude fetal deaths.
   e. **Admissions.** Include the number of adult and pediatric admissions (exclude births). This figure should include all patients admitted during the reporting period, including neonatal and swing admissions.
   f. **Inpatient days.** Report the number of adult and pediatric days of care rendered during the entire reporting period. Do not include days of care rendered for normal infants born in the hospital, but do include those for their mothers. Include days of care for infants born in the hospital and transferred into a neonatal care unit. Also include swing bed inpatient days. An inpatient day of care (also commonly referred to as a <u>patient day</u> or a <u>census day</u>, or by some federal hospitals as an <u>occupied bed day</u>) is a period of service between the census-taking hours on two successive calendar days, the day of discharge being counted only when the patient was admitted the same day.
   g. **Emergency department visits.** Should reflect the number of visits to the emergency unit. Emergency outpatients can be admitted to the inpatient areas of the hospital, but they are still counted as emergency visits and subsequently as inpatient admissions.
   h. **Total outpatient visits.** A visit by a patient who is not lodged in the hospital while receiving medical, dental, or other services. Each appearance of an outpatient in each unit constitutes one visit regardless of the number of diagnostic and/or therapeutic treatments that the patient receives. Total outpatient visits should include all clinic visits, referred visits, observation services, outpatient surgeries (also reported on line E1k), home health service visits, and emergency department visits (also reported on line E1g).
   Clinic visits should reflect total number of visits to each specialized medical unit that is responsible for the diagnosis and treatment of patients on an outpatient, nonemergency basis. (e.g., alcoholism, dental, gynecology.) Visits to the satellite clinics and primary group practices should be included if revenue is received by the hospital.
   Referred visits should reflect total number of outpatient ancillary visits to each specialty unit of the hospital established for providing technical aid used in the diagnosis and treatment of patients. Examples of such units are diagnostic radiology, EKG, and pharmacy.
   Observation services are those services furnished on a hospital's premises, including use of a bed and periodic monitoring by a hospital's nursing or other staff, which are reasonable and necessary to evaluate an outpatient's condition or determine the need for a possible admission to the hospital as an inpatient. Observation services usually do not exceed 24 hours; however, there is no hourly limit on the extent to which they may be used.
   Home health service visits are visits by home health personnel to a patient's residence.
   i. **Inpatient surgical operations.** Count each patient undergoing surgery as one surgical operation regardless of the number of surgical procedures that were performed while the patient was in the operating or procedure room.
   j. **Operating room.** A unit/room of a hospital or other health care facility in which surgical procedures requiring anesthesia are performed.
   k. **Outpatient surgical operations.** For outpatient surgical operations, please record operations performed on patients who do not remain in the hospital overnight. Include all operations whether performed in the inpatient operating rooms or in procedure rooms located in an outpatient facility. Include an endoscopy only when used as an operative tool and not when used for diagnosis alone. Count each patient undergoing surgery as one surgical operation regardless of the number of surgical procedures that were performed while the patient was in the operating or procedure room.

2a2. **Managed Care Medicare Discharges.** A discharge day where a Medicare Managed Care Plan is the source of payment.
2b2. **Managed Care Medicare Inpatient Days.** An inpatient day where a Medicare Managed Care Plan is the source of payment.
2c2. **Managed Care Medicaid Discharges.** A discharge day where a Medicaid Managed Care Plan is the source of payment.
2d2. **Managed Care Medicaid Inpatient Days.** An inpatient day where a Medicaid Managed Care Plan is the source of payment.
3a. **Net patient revenue.** Reported at the estimated net realizable amounts from patients, third-party payers, and others for services rendered, including estimated retroactive adjustments under reimbursement agreements with third-party payers. Retroactive adjustments are accrued on an estimated basis in the period the related services are rendered and adjusted in future periods, as final settlements are determined.
3b. **Tax appropriations.** A predetermined amount set aside by the government from its taxing authority to support the operation of the hospital.
3c. **Other operating revenue.** Revenue that arises from the normal day-to-day operations from services other than health care provided to patients. Includes sales and services to nonpatients, and revenue from miscellaneous sources (rental of hospital space, sale of cafeteria meals, gift shop sales). Also include operating gains in this category.
3d. **Nonoperating revenue.** Includes investment income, extraordinary gains and other nonoperating gains.
3e. **Total revenue.** Add net patient revenue, tax appropriations, other operating revenue and nonoperating revenue.
3f. **Payroll expenses.** Include payroll for all personnel including medical and dental residents/interns and trainees.
3g. **Employee benefits.** Includes social security, group insurance, retirement benefits, workman's compensation, unemployment insurance, etc.
3h. **Depreciation expense (for reporting period only).** Report only the depreciation expense applicable to the reporting period. The amount should also be included in accumulated depreciation (E7b).
3i. **Interest expense.** Report interest expense for the reporting period only.
3j. **Pharmacy Expense.** Includes the cost of drugs and pharmacy supplies requested to patient care departments and drugs charged to patients.
3k. **Supply expense.** The net cost of all tangible items that are expensed including freight, standard distribution cost, and sales and use tax minus rebates. This would exclude labor, labor-related expenses and services as well as some tangible items that are frequently provided as part of labor costs.
3l. **All other expenses.** Any total facility expenses not included in 3f-3k.
3m. **Total expenses.** Add 3f-3l. Includes all payroll and non-payroll expenses as well as any nonoperating losses (including extraordinary losses). **Treat bad debt as a deduction from gross patient revenue and not as an expense.**
4a. **Total gross inpatient revenue.** The hospital's full-established rates (charges) for all services rendered to inpatients.
4b. **Total gross outpatient revenue.** The hospital's full-established rates (charges) for all services rendered to outpatients.
4c. **Total gross patient revenue.** Add total gross inpatient revenue and total gross outpatient revenue.

5. **Uncompensated care.** Care for which no payment is expected or no charge is made. It is the sum of bad debt and charity care absorbed by a hospital or other health care organization in providing medical care for patients who are uninsured or are unable to pay.

5a. **Bad debt.** The provision for actual or expected uncollectibles resulting from the extension of credit. Report as a deduction from gross revenue. **For Question 6 (Revenue by payor), if you cannot break out your bad debt by payer, deduct the amount from self-pay.**

5b. **Financial Assistance (Includes charity care).** Financial assistance and charity care refer to health services provided free of charge or at reduced rates to individuals who meet certain financial criteria. For purposes of this survey, charity care is measured on the basis of revenue forgone, at full-established rates.

5d. **Medicaid Provider Tax, Fee or Assessment.** Dollars paid as a result of a state law that authorizes collecting revenue from specified categories of providers. Federal matching funds may be received for the revenue collected from providers and some or all of the revenues may be returned directly or indirectly back to providers in the form of a Medicaid payment.

6. **REVENUE BY PAYER**

   6a1. Medicare. Should agree with the Medicare utilization reported in questions E2a1-E2b2.

   6a1a. Fee for service patient revenue. Include traditional Medicare fee-for-service.

   6a1c. Total. Medicare revenue (add Medicare fee for service patient revenue and Medicare managed care revenue).

   6a2. Medicaid. Should agree with Medicaid utilization reported in questions E2c1-E2d2.

   6a2a. Fee for service patient revenue. Do not include Medicaid disproportionate share payments (DSH) or other Medicaid supplemental payments. Report in 'net' column only.

   6a2c. Medicaid Graduate Medical Education (GME) payments. Payments for the cost of approved graduate medical education (GME) programs. Report in 'net' column only.

   6a2d. Medicaid disproportionate share payment (DSH). DSH minus associated provider taxes or assessments. Report in 'Net' column only.

   6a2e. Medicaid supplemental payments. Supplemental payments the Medicaid program pays the hospital that are NOT Medicaid DSH, minus associated provider taxes or assessments. Report in 'Net' column only.

   6a2f. Other Medicaid. Any Medicaid payments such as delivery system reform incentive program (DSRIP) payments that are not included in lines 6a2a-e. Report in 'net' column only.

   6e. Medicaid Intergovernmental Transfers (IGT) or certified public expenditure program. Exchange of public funds between different levels of government (e.g., county, city, or another state agency) to the state Medicaid agency.

7a-c. **Fixed Assets.** Represent land and physical properties that are consumed or used in the creation of economic activity by the health care entity. The historical or acquisition costs are used in recording fixed assets. Net plant, property, and equipment represent the original costs of these items less accumulated depreciation and amortization.

7d. **Gross Square Footage.** Include all inpatient, outpatient, office, and support space used for or in support of your health care activities. Exclude exterior, roof, and garage space in the figure.

8. **Capital Expenses.** Expenses used to acquire assets, including buildings, remodeling projects, equipment, or property.

9. **Information Technology and Cybersecurity.**

   a. **IT Operating expense.** Exclude department depreciation and operating dollars paid against capital leases.

   b. **IT Capital expense.** Include IT capital expense for the current year only. Any capital expense that is carried forward from the previous year should be excluded from this figure. Include IT related capital included in the budget of other departments. (e.g., lab, radiology) if known or can be reasonably estimated. Include the total value of capital leases to be signed in the current year.

   c. **Number of Employed IT staff (in FTEs).** Number of full-time equivalent (FTE) staff employed in the IT department/organization and on the hospital payroll.

   d. **Total number of outsourced IT staff (in FTEs).** i.e., contracted staff.

   e. **Cybersecurity.** Measures taken to protect against the criminal or unauthorized use of electronic data.

STAFFING

10. **Full-Time Equivalent (FTE)** is the total number of hours worked by all employees over the full 12-month reporting period, divided by the normal number of hours worked by a full-time employee for that same time period. For example, if your hospital considers a normal workweek for a full-time employee to be 40 hours, a total of 2,080 would be worked over a full year (52 weeks). If the total number of hours worked by all employees on the payroll is 208,000, then the number of full-time equivalents (FTE) is 100 (employees). The FTE calculation for a specific occupational category such as registered nurses is exactly the same. The calculation for each occupational category should be based on the number of hours worked by staff employed in that specific category.

   a-b. **Physicians and dentists.** Include only those physicians and dentists engaged in clinical practice and on the payroll. Those who hold administrative positions should be reported in all other personnel. (10m)

   d. **Other trainees.** A trainee is a person who has not completed the necessary requirements for certification or met the qualifications required for full salary under a related occupational category. Exclude medical and dental residents/interns who should be reported on line 10c.

   e. **Registered nurses.** Nurses who have graduated from approved schools of nursing and who are currently registered by the state. They are responsible for the nature and quality of all nursing care that patients receive. Do not include any registered nurses more appropriately reported in other occupational categories, such as facility administrators, and therefore listed under all other personnel. (10m)

   f. **Licensed practical (vocational) nurses.** Nurses who have graduated from an approved school of practical (vocational) nursing who work under the supervision of registered nurses and/or physicians.

   g. **Nursing assistive personnel.** Certified nursing assistant or equivalent unlicensed staff who assist registered nurses in providing patient care related services as assigned by and under the supervision of a registered nurse.

   h. **Radiology technicians.** Technical positions in imaging fields, including, but not limited to, radiology, sonography, nuclear medicine, radiation therapy, CT, MRI.

   i. **Laboratory technicians.** Professional and technical positions in all areas of the laboratory, including, but not limited to, histology, phlebotomy, microbiology, pathology, chemistry, etc.

   j. **Pharmacists, licensed.** Persons licensed within the state who are concerned with the preparation and distribution of medicinal products.

   k. **Pharmacy technicians.** Persons who assist the pharmacist with selected activities, including medication profile reviews for drug incompatibilities, typing labels and prescription packaging, handling of purchase records and inventory control.

   l. **Respiratory Therapists.** An allied health professional who specializes in scientific knowledge and theory of clinical problems of respiratory care. Duties include the collection and evaluation of patient data to determine an appropriate care plan, selection and assembly of equipment, conduction of therapeutic procedures, and modification of prescribed plans to achieve one or more specific objectives.

   m. **All other personnel.** This should include all other personnel not already accounted for in other categories.

   n. **Total facility personnel.** Add 10a-10m. Includes the total facility personnel - hospital plus nursing home type unit/facility personnel (for those hospitals that own and operate a nursing home type unit/facility.)

   o-p. **Nursing home type unit/facility personnel.** These lines should be filled out only by hospitals that own and operate a nursing home type unit/facility, where only one legal entity is vested with title to the physical property or operates under the authority of a duly executed lease of the physical property. If nursing home type unit/facility personnel are reported on the total facility personnel lines (10a-m), but cannot be broken out, please leave blank.

q. **Direct patient care RN.** Registered nurses providing care directly to patients. Direct patient care responsibilities are patient-centered nursing activities carried out in the presence of the patient (such as admission, transfer/discharge, patient teaching, patient communication, treatments, counseling, and administration of medication.)

11. **Privileged Physicians.** Report the total number of physicians (by type) on the medical staff with privileges except those with courtesy, honorary and provisional privileges. Do not include residents or interns. Physicians that provide only non-clinical services (administrative services, medical director services, etc.) should be excluded.

    Employed by your hospital. Physicians that are either direct hospital employees or employees of a hospital subsidiary corporation.

    Individual contract. An independent physician under a formal contract to provide services at your hospital including at outpatient facilities, clinics and offices

    Group contract. A physician that is part of a group (group practice, faculty practice plan or medical foundation) under a formal contract to provide services at your hospital including at inpatient and outpatient facilities, clinics and offices.

    Not employed or under contract. Other physicians with privileges that have no employment or contractual relationship with the hospital to provide services.

    The sum of the physicians reported in 11a-11f should equal the total number of privileged physicians in the hospital.

    a. **Primary care.** A physician that provides primary care services including general practice, general internal medicine, family practice, general pediatrics, obstetrics/gynecology and geriatrics.

    b. **Emergency medicine.** Physicians who provide care in the emergency department.

    c. **Hospitalist.** Physicians whose primary professional focus is the care of hospitalized medical patients (through clinical, education, administrative and research activity).

    d. **Intensivist.** A physician with special training to work with critically ill patients. Intensivists generally provided medical-surgical, cardiac, neonatal, pediatric and other types of intensive care.

    e. **Radiologist/pathologist/anesthesiologist. Radiologist.** A physician who has specialized training in imaging, including but not limited to radiology, sonography, nuclear medicine, radiation therapy, CT, MRI. **Pathologist.** A physician who examines samples of body tissues for diagnostic purposes. **Anesthesiologist.** A physician who specializes in administering medications or other agents that prevent or relieve pain, especially during surgery.

    f. **Other specialist.** Other physicians not included in the above categories that specialize in a specific type of equithom.

14. **Advanced Practice Registered Nurses.** Registered nurses with advanced didactic and clinical education, knowledge, skills, and scope of practice. Includes: **Physician assistant.** A healthcare professional licensed to practice medicine with supervision of a licensed physician. **Nurse practitioner.** A registered nurse with at least a master's degree in nursing and advanced education in primary care, capable of independent practice in a variety of settings. **Clinical nurse specialist (CNS).** A registered nurse who, through a formal graduate degree (masters or doctorate) CNS education program, has expertise in a specialty area of nursing practice. CNSs are clinical experts in the diagnosis and treatment of illness, and the delivery of evidence-based nursing interventions.

14c. **Primary care.** Medical services including general practice, general internal medicine, family practice, general pediatrics, obstetrics/gynecology.

    Emergency department care. The provision of unscheduled outpatient services to patients whose conditions require immediate care in the emergency department setting.

    Other specialty care. A clinic that provides specialized medical care beyond the scope of primary care.

    Patient education. Goals and objectives for the patient and/or family related to therapeutic regimens, medical procedures and self-care.

    Case management. A system of assessment, treatment planning, referral and follow-up that ensures the provision of comprehensive and continuous services and the coordination of payment and reimbursement for care.

    Other. Any type of care other than those listed above.

15. **Foreign-educated nurses.** Individuals who are foreign born and received basic nursing education in a foreign country. In general many of these nurses come to the US on employment-based visas which allow them to obtain a green card.

SECTION F. SUPPLEMENTAL INFORMATION
DEFINITIONS

1. **Satellite facility.** Services are available at a facility geographically remote from the hospital campus.
2. **Group Purchasing Organization.** An organization whose primary function is to negotiate contracts for the purpose of purchasing for members of the group or has a central supply site for its members.
3. **Distributor.** An entity that typically does not manufacture most of its own products but purchases and re-sells these products. Such a business usually maintains an inventory of products for sales to hospitals and physician offices and others.
5. **Types of Partnerships:**
   a. Health care providers outside your system (Include other hospitals health care systems, FQHCs, community clinics)
   b. Local or state public health organizations (Include public health departments, institutes, etc.)
   c. Local or state human/social service organizations (Include food, housing/rental assistance, energy assistance, transportation assistance)
   d. Local or state government (Include municipal, city or county government, including public safety and policy/legislative initiatives at a local level)
   e. Non-profit organizations (Include National health associations, United Way, YMCA, Service leagues, healthy communities coalitions)
   f. Faith-based organizations
   g. Health insurance companies
   h. Schools (Include childhood, primary and secondary schools and colleges/universities)
   i. Local businesses or chambers of commerce
   j. Other (list)

   Scale of partnerships:
   Not involved. No current partnerships with this type of organization
   Collaboration. Exchange information and share resources for a similar mission to enhance the capacity of the other partner
   Formal Alliance. Formalized partnership (binding agreement) among multiple organizations with merged initiatives, common goals and metrics

6. **Patient and family advisory council.** Advisory council dedicated to the improvement of quality in patient and family care. The advisory council is comprised of past/present patients, family members, and hospital staff.

DATE DUE